The Curious Reader

The Curious Reader

Exploring Personal and Academic Inquiry

SECOND EDITION

Bruce Ballenger
Boise State University

Michelle Payne
Boise State University

New York   San Francisco   Boston
London   Toronto   Sydney   Tokyo   Singapore   Madrid
Mexico City   Munich   Paris   Cape Town   Hong Kong   Montreal

Publisher: Joseph Opiela
Development Editor: Katharine Glynn
Marketing Manager: Alexandra Smith
Senior Supplements Editor: Donna Campion
Production Manager: Donna DeBenedictis
Project Coordination, Text Design, and Electronic Page Makeup:
    Elm Street Publishing Services, Inc.
Cover Designer/Manager: John Callahan
Cover Art: The Stock Illustration Source
Photo Researcher: Vivette Porges
Senior Manufacturing Buyer: Dennis J. Para
Printer and Binder/Cover Printer: Courier Corporation/Stoughton

For permission to use copyrighted material, grateful acknowledgement is made to the
copyright holders on pp. 511–515, which are hereby made part of this copyright page.

Library of Congress Cataloging-in-Publication Data
The curious reader: exploring personal and academic inquiry / [edited by]
    Bruce Ballenger, Michelle Payne.—2nd ed.
        p. cm.
Includes bibliographical references and index.
    ISBN 0-321-36522-4
1. College readers. 2. English language—Rhetoric—Problems, exercises, etc.
    3. Academic writing—Problems, exercises, etc.
    I. Ballenger, Bruce P. II. Payne, Michelle.
    PE1417.C787   2006
    808'.0427—dc22

                                                                2005013386

Please visit us at http://www.ablongman.com

ISBN 0-321-36522-4

1 2 3 4 5 6 7 8 9 10—CRS—08 07 06 05

To Bruce's daughter Julia, who gets curiouser
and curiouser, and to Michelle's grandparents,
Irv and Ann Kreynhagen Rumph.

Contents

Chapter 3

How Do You Know? 37

PART II: FORMS FOR DISCOVERY

Chapter 4

The Researched Essay: "Essaying" as a Mode of Inquiry 49

C h a p t e r 6

The Ethnographic Essay:
Ethnography as a Mode of Inquiry 240

Chapter 7

Fields of Writing: Making Sense of Formal Research 321

Preface for Instructors

Does the world really need another composition textbook? This was among the first questions we asked ourselves when we considered collaborating on the book you're reading now. Every year, dozens of new titles and new editions of old titles appear on the writing textbook market. Did we have something more to add? Obviously we decided that we did. Whether we're right is your call.

Since we're beginning with confessions, here's another one: Neither of us has used readers with much success in our composition courses. For one thing, our goal is to keep writing at the center of the course, and an overemphasis on having students read and respond to assigned readings can undermine that aim. Some of our talented colleagues seem to have worked out the right balance but we have often struggled with it. But there's another reason for our difficulty using readers—we were never satisfied that they actually succeeded in generating enough writing that went beyond analytical responses to the individual readings themselves. While such responses are important—and we certainly encourage them here—we've always wanted a reader that inspired students to take off with the topics in their own ways, perhaps using the readings as a starting point for larger investigations, writing projects motivated by the students' own questions.

The Curious Reader: Exploring Personal and Academic Inquiry is the book we always wanted to have. We believe it has some new things to say about reading and writing; it also emphasizes the many ways that reading can inspire a writer's own questions about the world. This is a book that is as much about writing as it is about reading, maybe more. We never stop prompting, prodding, and provoking student writing in this text. We don't want them to put their pens down.

What else justifies our belief that *The Curious Reader: Exploring Personal and Academic Inquiry* makes a fresh contribution to the glutted textbook market? We believe this text is one of the first composition readers that bridges the gap between "creative" and academic writing, while introducing students to the unique reading strategies of writers who research. *The Curious Reader* begins with essays and creative nonfiction articles that most students will be surprised to discover are research-based, and chapter by chapter the book leads students to see the many connections between all fact-based writing, whether it's a personal essay or an article from a scholarly journal. *The Curious Reader* invites students to discover that many of their assumptions about fact-based writing are wrong: academic writing can be personal, creative writing can involve research, "facts" do not necessarily mean truth, and serious academic research can even take place in a grocery store or in a local church.

But *The Curious Reader: Exploring Personal and Academic Inquiry* also focuses an entire chapter on researching across disciplines, something we've always wanted our students to do but have often struggled to teach. The chapter on disturbing photographs immerses students in the ethical, social, and historical ambiguities of photographing disturbing events. It shows them how perspectives from different disciplines can lead to questions they hadn't considered before. Just as importantly, this chapter focuses on the role that our own beliefs and feelings play in academic inquiry. Instead of encouraging students to put those beliefs and feelings aside, this chapter shows students how to put them in dialogue with research material. In fact, the third chapter of *The Curious Reader* uniquely focuses students' attention on their own learning styles and epistemological stances, and how the reading and researching process can change their views on how knowledge is made. Few readers invite students into this kind of metacognitive work, but we believe it is crucial for students to reflect on their literacy histories, their beliefs about knowledge, and their beliefs about learning as they negotiate various discourse communities, both within and outside the academy. In short, this chapter asks them to reflect on their roles as readers and researchers.

This book also highlights some of the unique reading strategies students should practice when they read as researchers. Few composition readers explicitly explore methods of reading outside of brief treatments of the topic in a preface or introduction, and even fewer address the specialized reading practices used by writers who research. *The Curious Reader* makes reading strategies a main topic throughout the text, and devotes an entire chapter to how students might adjust their reading habits when tackling a scholarly article for a research paper. Students will learn that the habits of mind they need when pursuing any line of inquiry are parallel to the habits of mind they need when reading. Reading and inquiry are similar processes. The text also features an entirely new way of looking at reading—how to read ethnographically—that draws on the basic idea that academic writing is a kind of culture that students must first observe as outsiders, much the way a sociologist studies an urban neighborhood or an anthropologist studies a Central American village. Reading ethnographically invites students into various writing communities by asking them to be observers as well as participants. Throughout the text we encourage students to read in this way, reading rhetorically across genres and disciplines.

We hope that instructors like the logical sequence of the book, moving students in early chapters from more creative research essays and articles to more difficult scholarship, all the while reminding students of the connections between these seemingly unlike genres. All of the chapters feature projects and assignments students can pursue inspired by the readings, and most chapters include assignments the entire class can pursue for a week or more.

New to the Second Edition

Based on the feedback and ideas we've received from reviewers of the first edition and from instructors who currently use the book, we have made several changes in the second edition of *The Curious Reader*. If you have used the book in the past, you'll find many of the same readings, as well as the same focus on reading strategies, personal and academic inquiry, learning strategies, and reading across genres and disciplines. You'll find the same core philosophy about research and reading that was in the first edition, and you'll see familiar questions at the end of each essay. In fact, if you've already developed a syllabus around the first edition, you won't have to make too many substantial changes with this one. A few readings have been replaced with more engaging ones, a few more academic researched essays have been included, and what used to be the last chapter in the first edition, "Coming to Know: Readings on Inquiry," has become Chapter 3, "How Do You Know?" without those individual readings. Several people told us they struggled with using that last chapter, so we've come up with another approach that we think is more effective. In the end, we hope you find this edition clearer in purpose, more engaging for students, more flexible for your courses, and more beneficial for students.

So what, specifically, has changed? Here's what's different:

Structure and Organization. The book is divided into two sections, more clearly indicating how chapters are designed to work together. Part I, "The Process of Inquiry," helps students understand inquiry-based learning and research, and includes revised versions of Chapters 1 and 2, as well as a new Chapter 3.

- Chapter 1, now titled "Acquiring the Inquiry Habit," is revised and streamlined. Its central question is, "What are the ways of seeing and thinking that encourage curious research?" Students are given four key inquiry categories—exploring, explaining, evaluating, and reflecting—that show them how to explore their ideas and measure them against the ideas of others in the book.

- Chapter 2, newly titled "The Inquiring Reader," offers reading strategies and perspectives that guide students to become critical readers. Its central question is, "How can students read as curious researchers?" It includes new coverage on reading visual images, including tables and graphs.

- The new Chapter 3, "How Do You Know?" includes exercises that help students see the value of not only beginning their assignments with questions rather than answers, but encourages them to really explore their thinking critically. Its central question is, "How do students sort through conflicting claims, self-doubts, and ambiguity to discover the truth of what they think?" Readers of the first edition will recognize here the concepts from Chapter 8 in the first edition.

The second part of the book, Part II, "Forms for Discovery," collects chapters that focus on specific genres and forms that writers use in the process of inquiry, forms that students will most likely be writing and reading.

Chapter titles more tightly reflect the focus of the chapter, specifically referring to the *kind* of writing being featured and the *mode of inquiry* it emphasizes.

- Chapter 4 is now "The Researched Essay: 'Essaying' as a Mode of Inquiry."
- Chapter 5 is now "The Personal Academic Essay: Boundary Crossing as a Mode of Inquiry."
- Chapter 6 is now "The Ethnographic Essay: Ethnography as a Mode of Inquiry."

The last two chapters emphasize reading *across* genres and disciplines as a mode of inquiry.

- Chapter 7 is now "Fields of Writing: Making Sense of Formal Research."
- Chapter 8 is now "Reading and Writing Across Genres and Disciplines: The Ethics of Publishing Disturbing Pictures."

Each chapter is more clearly connected to the ones before and after, and:

- Academic and personal inquiry are addressed in every chapter.
- Visual rhetoric is integrated throughout.
- Four kinds of inquiry questions from Chapter 1 are used to organize the reading questions.
- Each chapter challenges students to reflect on how they make meaning, what learning styles they use, how they approach reading, and how they are situated as readers/writers/learners.
- Each chapter prompts students to reflect on their reading strategies.

Kinds of Readings. We've replaced less popular essays with new ones on surprising subjects, written in an engaging style, demonstrating a wider range of research and academic inquiry. For example, in Chapters 5 through 8 we've added more research essays written for an academic audience.

Chapter 4, "The Researched Essay: Essaying as a Mode of Inquiry," focuses on research-based, creative nonfiction essays where the author's point of view is central to the subject. We have included an array of new readings on such topics as why we need flies, the love of knitting, and whether the NASA moon landing was faked.

Chapter 5, "The Personal Academic Essay: Boundary Crossing as a Mode of Inquiry," invites students to compare personal academic essays and formal academic essays from the fields of business, anthropology, and literary studies and written by the same writers. Students identify the modes of academic inquiry that both types of essays share—the conventions that shape how knowledge is made in that field—as well as evaluate the conventions that are "broken" in the personal academic essays.

Chapter 6, "The Ethnographic Essay: Ethnography as a Mode of Inquiry," invites students to read both academic articles and creative nonfiction essays that draw on ethnographic research methods like field observations and interviews. We've included two new articles in this chapter, an academic piece on Nazi rock and a selection from a memoir that describes snake-handling in religious services.

Chapter 7, "Fields of Writing: Making Sense of Formal Research," includes new readings, excerpts on cross-gender friendships from the disciplines of psychology, business, communication studies, sociology, and English studies. Students read like ethnographers for the academic conventions used, and also as researchers in dialogue with the ideas in the texts.

Chapter 8, "Reading and Writing Across Genres and Disciplines: The Ethics of Publishing Disturbing Pictures," includes new readings on publishing war photos, academic analyses of the effects of disturbing images, as well as a transcript of journalists discussing the ethics and personal consequences of viewing, editing, and discussing traumatic images. Also, a new student essay has been added for Chapter 8.

Additional Features. The second edition of *The Curious Reader* offers new photographs and visuals that give ample opportunity to practice critical analysis of images. More strategies for reading and researching are given in Part I, including using and evaluating evidence, choosing reading strategies appropriate to the purpose and the rhetorical context of the text itself, sorting through competing claims, and understanding how individuals' own backgrounds and identities shape how they read and research. In addition, a new appendix, "Documentating Sources: MLA and APA Citation," provides concise guidelines for citing sources, including electronic sources, in both MLA and APA style.

How to Use This Book

While *The Curious Reader: Exploring Personal and Academic Inquiry* is particularly well suited to the composition course that emphasizes research, it can be successful in nearly any course where instructors want to demonstrate the connections between personal and academic writing. Users of Bruce Ballenger's *The Curious Researcher: A Guide to Writing Research Papers* will find that this book naturally complements that text, demonstrating the many ways that the exploratory research essay is connected to more formal research. However, *The Curious Reader* also shows how "subjective" writing is not an anomaly in scholarship but an approach that is used across the disciplines.

Instructors who don't use *The Curious Researcher,* or who want to use this text in a course that focuses on more than research writing, will find that *The Curious Reader* has a sufficient variety of essays and assignments to qualify it as the major text for nearly any kind of writing course. At the same time, this book reinforces the fundamental idea that *any* kind of writing can be informed by many sources of information, not just the so-called research paper. Beginning with the inquiry-based notion that writing is inspired by questions, not answers, *The Curious Reader* shows how any piece of writing—a personal essay, a description, a term paper, a reading response—can grow from its opening question in many different directions. A personal essay can become a research paper, a description an ethnography, and a reading response a piece of autobiographical criticism. If a goal of the writing course is to encourage students to see how a brief draft or short assignment can develop into a more extensive examination of a topic, then *The Curious Reader* is an ideal text.

In general, we suggest that you assign all of the chapters in Part I, "Acquiring the Inquiry Habit," before those in Part II, "Forms for Discovery." Students will read more effectively and approach their writing assignments with more motivation and interest if they've been introduced to the ideas behind inquiry-based learning in Part I. It might also be useful to require students to respond to the readings using one of the dialogue forms we discuss in Chapter 2. If students know they have to use the dialogue approach (or whatever structure you prefer), they'll approach each reading with a stronger sense of purpose and they will get in the habit of reading dialectically and critically.

We hope you find the exercises in the book helpful, but you don't necessarily have to assign all of them. The activities in Chapters 1 through 3 can be assigned while students are in the process of reading the chapter, or they can be assigned separately—during class time, for example. The same is true for the end-of-essay questions. You choose the questions that best fit your goals for the day. For example, if you don't want students focusing on how a reading is structured in terms of craft because you don't want them focused on that in their own essays yet, then you can choose questions that help them start a new project or develop their own responses to the ideas in the reading. We developed the questions to be flexible while also reflective of the core philosophy on inquiry that is central to the book. The questions and activities in the book help you teach inquiry implicitly and explicitly, but they can also be assigned in a way that emphasizes a particular genre, set of academic conventions, or research method.

Instructor's Manual. In addition to the writing activities in the textbook itself, we've developed an instructor's manual to help in course planning. In it instructors will find not only summaries of each of the readings but chapter highlights, additional in-class and out-of-class activities, discussion questions, assignments, and additional resources. They'll also find at least two syllabi to consult when designing the course and an overview of the main principles that inform the text.

ACKNOWLEDGMENTS

Our collaboration on this book made it much better than it would have been if one of us had been the sole author. As you'll discover in Chapter 7, we are close friends, best friends, even. That made the work a source of joy, something you may sense as you read it. We also bring different sensibilities, ideas, and interests to *The Curious Reader*. Michelle is an expert, for example, at teaching reading and academic writing; Bruce is an established scholar in essay writing and inquiry-based teaching. The result is a book that is more than the sum of its authors.

We had lots of help, however.

Bruce is particularly grateful to his mentors Thomas Newkirk, the late Robert Connors, and of course, Donald Murray, all faculty he worked with at the University of New Hampshire years ago. Each contributed in his own way to Bruce's work on research-based writing and his habit of writing textbooks. Brock Dethier and Barry Lane are among Bruce's best friends and intellectual confidants on the teaching of writing. Most of all, Bruce's wife Karen has seen him through multiple editions of textbooks, careers, and dreams. He loves her more than he can say.

Michelle is especially grateful to several faculty whom she worked with at the University of New Hampshire: Thomas Newkirk, Patricia Sullivan, Cindy Gannett, and Melody Graulich (now at Utah State University). All of their influences are visible in this text. In addition, she can't forget the work of Donna Qualley of Western Washington State University, work that has informed her thinking about reading. She is also thankful for the feedback her faculty writing group offered on this project: Marcy Newman, Tara Penry,

Jacky O'Connor, and Leslie Durham. And lastly, Michelle thanks her husband Steve for talking through ideas with her, helping her search for good material, supporting her when she needed time to write, and having faith in it all. She loves him deeply.

Many other colleagues and friends have influenced our thinking on this project. Among them are Lad Tobin, Karen Uehling, Devan Cook, Brock Dethier, Elizabeth Chiseri-Strater, Bonnie Sunstein, Whitney Douglas, Susan Hudson, Carol Scheiss, Jill Heney, Julie Ewing, Sarah Bosarge, Sherry Gropp, Nancy DeJoy, Marlys Hersey, Steve Barrett, Chad Gibbs, Deborah Coxwell-Teague, and Stephen Doran. Most of all, we are grateful to our students. Every year and every semester we find that they have more to teach us and we have more to learn.

Like any textbook, many people have been involved with the genesis, revision, and production of the book. Joe Opiela, English editor at Allyn & Bacon and Longman, liked the idea of *The Curious Reader* from the beginning, and was always generous with his wisdom. Our agent, Michael Rosenberg, represented us so well we could concentrate on the writing. Debbie Bergeson handled permissions, an arduous task for a reader, with tenacity and persistence. The copyeditors at Elm Street Publishing Services, Inc., led on this project by Heather Johnson, did a great job doing what good copyeditors do: saving authors from embarrassment. We are also grateful to the reviewers of early drafts of this edition and reviewers of the first edition, including: Pat Bizzaro, East Carolina University; Susan Leigh Brooks, Bethel University; Corla Dawson, Missouri Western State College; Nancy DeJoy, Milikin University; Eric Freeze, Ohio University; Bill Lalicker, West Chester University; Christine Leichiter, The College of New Jersey; Richard Marback, Wayne State University; Lisa McClure, Southern Illinois University; James McDonald, University of Louisiana at Lafayette; David G. Miller, Mississippi College; Joe Moxley, University of South Florida; Michael Robertson, The College of New Jersey; Shirley K. Rose, Purdue University; Maurice Scharton, Illinois State University; Diana Simon, Raritan Valley Community College; Deborah Coxwell Teague, Florida State University; Stephen Wilhoit, University of Dayton; and Bronwyn T. Williams, University of Louisville.

We hope you enjoy working with this text as much as we've enjoyed writing and revising it. Yet books often also give back to their authors; that's why they write them. What we didn't expect is that *The Curious Reader* would enrich the friendship between its authors, a relationship we thought was pretty special before we started the book. Our appreciation for each other has deepened, and that may be the thing about which we are most grateful. That alone made the effort worthwhile.

BRUCE BALLENGER
MICHELLE PAYNE

Preface for Students

How do we hope you will use the material in *The Curious Reader: Exploring Personal and Academic Inquiry?* First, we hope it will change forever the way you see writing in general and researched-based writing in particular. As teachers of writing we have found very few textbooks that feature the variety of ways writers use research, whether those writers are university professors, professional writers, journalists, or students, and so our students have a difficult time imagining what we mean when we ask them to begin with what makes them curious and compose a research essay that is engaging.

We also hope that *The Curious Reader* will acquaint you with a new self, a reader who is rarely content to be an intellectual coach potato, one who isn't satisfied with pastel islands of highlighter and who revels in writing in books (if they don't belong to the library). Learn to like this reader within. You'll need him or her.

This book is also intended to help you with your writing. To help you learn more about how to shape your essays, we have questions at the end of each reading that are organized around the inquiry strategies we talk about in Chapter 1 and Chapter 2: exploring, explaining, evaluating, and reflecting. The exploring questions focus on helping you figure out what you think about the reading. The explaining and evaluating questions invite you to look more closely at how a writer composed her text, the choices she made about whether to include herself in the writing, what kind of evidence she needed to explore her subject, and how she organized the material to make it interesting for readers. The reflecting questions invite you to reflect on what you've learned and what you might do more effectively next time as a reader and writer. Those questions, in short, ask you to read as writers, looking closely at the craft and conventions that writers use depending on their subject, their audience, their purpose. You can read these essays as models, then, and ask yourself what you can learn about writing from the choices the writers make about how they compose their essays and how they pursue their subjects.

But we will also be asking you to read these pieces to get ideas for your own inquiry projects. Jillian Sim's essay on researching her grandmother's family history might inspire you to follow up on all those stories your own grandfather used to tell. Or Ann Hodgman's piece on eating dog food might propel you to experiment with different kinds of wrinkle cream or fat substitutes. We hope at least some of these readings will make you wonder about something you hadn't considered before, such as yarn or flies or cross-gender friendships. At the end of each article we'll have writing prompts that you can use to generate your own ideas for research projects based on the readings for that section ("Personal Investigations: Inquiry Projects"). You will also find questions about the features of the text that make it engaging or that show the writer having a dialogue with his/her research ("Craft and Conventions: Explaining and Evaluating").

Last, we'll have questions on inquiry ("Inquiries on Inquiry: Exploring and Reflecting"). Those will ask you to think about (1) the research and writing process the writers may have gone through as they were exploring their questions; (2) the inquiry strategies or stances we mentioned earlier and how they are illustrated in the essays; (3) the different kinds of writing in each chapter and how that writing is shaped by different contexts (we will often ask, for example, how the piece you've read compares to "academic" writing you may have done in other classes); (4) what your personal responses were to the essay; and (5) what reading strategies you used. We believe it's important for students to use readings not just as models for the writing they'll be doing, but to have readings invite them back into their own writing and thinking.

The Curious Reader is organized to show you the fundamental *connections* among all kinds of research-based writing, from a treatise on Gravy Train to an academic article on cross-gender friendship. Part I begins with three brief chapters about academic inquiry that inform the rest of the chapters. Chapter 1, "Acquiring the Inquiry Habit," introduces you to the importance of asking questions—as a writer as well as a *reader*. Chapter 2, "The Inquiring Reader," builds on that chapter to show you inquiry-based strategies for reading. You'll return to this chapter throughout the book, and we hope the strategies you learn will help you no matter what kinds of reading you do. Chapter 3, "How Do We Know?" challenges you to think about your own learning styles, your beliefs about how knowledge is made, and your approach to making sense of conflicting claims.

In Part II, you'll read examples of three distinct genres in which research is commonly used, in both the public and the academic domains. Chapter 4 introduces you to the researched essay, an often-exploratory piece on a topic intended for a more general audience. Chapters 4 through 6 demonstrate how some of the conventions of the essay have actually shaped academic writing, from ethnographies to literary analyses. Some of these articles will surprise you. You may have never expected to read serious scholarship that tells stories, uses the first person, or involves scene and character as well a citation and argument. Some of these chapters will challenge you to understand academic forms of writing from a perspective you may not be used to, that of comparing formal academic research to informal, personal academic research.

Chapter 7 may be the heart of the book. We return once again to a challenging academic article on a pretty interesting topic—cross-gender friendship—and invite you to look over Michelle's shoulder as she works to makes sense of it for a writing project of her own. As the chapter progresses, you'll take over, practicing some of the reading methods Michelle models. You'll read excerpts from studies in different disciplines and how each approaches the subject (from business and psychology to communication studies, English studies, and sociology). It will give you experience reading as you prepare for writing a researched essay, challenging you to read as an ethnographer of other disciplines while you also read critically. For that reason, the questions at the end of the readings are different from those in the other chapters. We call them "Reader Reflections" because you are being asked to use reflection as a mode of inquiry in this chapter. This chapter will also reveal how the methods and habits of mind from more creative approaches can be used in almost any kind of fact-based writing, including the formal research paper.

Chapter 8, "Readings Across Genres and Disciplines: The Ethics of Publishing Disturbing Photos," introduces a fascinating topic—the ethics of publishing photographs of tragedy and death in American newspapers—and features a range of essays and articles from across the disciplines that focus explicitly or implicitly on that topic. The suggested assignment in this chapter invites you to use all of the reading and writing strategies you've experienced in earlier chapters to explore your own response to the complex issues involved with disturbing photographs.

If you walk away from using textbook with several new strategies for reading (particularly for academic texts, especially those that are challenging or somewhat uninteresting to you), with a renewed sense of curiosity and wonder about the world that motivates you to do research, and with a fuller repertoire of writing strategies for different genres, then this book will have helped accomplish what we'd hoped. But you—as much if not more so than your instructor or this book—are the key to making sure these are the results. This book demands that you be an active learner, and that isn't always comfortable or easy. Nor does it need to be. What makes such challenges worthwhile and motivating, though, is the experience of solving a problem or being surprised or gratified when you suddenly see something in a new way. That's often what is happening when our students say, "This course was fun, but I learned a lot, too." We hope that's your experience, too.

BRUCE BALLENGER
MICHELLE PAYNE

1

Acquiring the Inquiry Habit

A s children, we're wired for inquiry. This week, Julia, Bruce's daughter, decided she was interested in wild birds. She parked herself on the living room couch, surrounded by field guides to birds, and began to ask questions.

"How can you tell the difference between birds besides comparing their colors?"

"Why do sparrows seem to have larger beaks than woodpeckers?"

"What's the fastest bird?"

It's commonplace that children ask questions. Lots of them. But isn't it interesting how rarely adults seem driven by a similar kind of curiosity? Sure, we ask questions, but frequently the motive is to get some necessary information, not to nourish our sense of wonder.

"How can I get an A in this course?"

"What's the fastest way to get to the soccer game?"

"Do you know where I can find something for my backache?"

These kinds of questions are surely useful, but we ask them with a singular purpose—to solve an immediate problem—and the information we gather isn't necessarily that interesting beyond its application to the problem at hand. Usually, we're most interested in quickly resolving the problem of getting an A, or making it to the soccer game, or relieving the backache. We certainly don't ask questions like these to raise more questions. What we want is answers.

START WITH QUESTIONS BEFORE ANSWERS

Inquiry implies a quite different way of seeing the world. And it's not a way of seeing that comes naturally to most adults. First of all, inquirers *often begin with questions rather than answers.* Rather than seeing a rock on the sidewalk and dismissing it as "just a rock," a geologist will wonder what kind it is, and how it got there. Rather than quickly concluding that believing in "family values" is an obvious virtue, a philosopher will ask "what do we mean by family values," or "what might be the opposite of a family value?"

To engage in inquiry is, in a sense, to become a child again, with a sense of wonder about nearly everything, including what is most familiar and even what seems commonsensical.

Exercise 1.1   *Twenty Ways to See a Blackbird*

Here are three pictures of things you probably see every day: an apple, a water bottle, and a common crow. Familiarity may not breed contempt, but it certainly makes things seem uninteresting. Seeing as an active inquirer promises that even the most commonplace things can pique your curiosity.

STEP 1: Choose one of the three objects pictured here. In small groups or individually in your journal, spend a full ten minutes generating questions about that object. Generate questions both about the particular crow, apple, or water bottle you see in the photograph as well as questions about crows, apples, or water bottles generally. This is a brainstorm so don't censor yourself.

STEP 2: Look at the list of questions you generated. Some of them will be silly, some will be uninteresting, but a few might cause a small spark of curiosity. Imagine that you are an editor for a general interest magazine such as *Discover* or *Natural History,* charged with assigning a freelance writer to research and write an article on crows, apples, and bottled water. Which of the questions on your list would be appropriate *opening questions* for such an assignment? Circle them.

Inquiring into the Exercise

1. What are the qualities of a "researchable" question?
2. How does an inquiry-based approach influence the way you see familiar things?

Elements of Inquiry

1. Begin with questions, not answers.
2. Extend the process by openly exploring the subject.
3. Choose a strategy of inquiry.
4. Share discoveries with rhetorical context in mind.

USE AN OPEN-ENDED PROCESS

Children aren't particularly patient. Bruce's daughter Julia is interested in why sparrows have larger beaks than woodpeckers but she's not inclined to spend a whole lot of time exploring the evolution of bird beaks.

"Can't you just tell me, Dad?"

Approaching the world with questions may be a childlike quality, but discovering good questions that may take time to answer is not. Another quality of inquiry is *a willingness to prolong the process of discovery by exploring a range of answers, hoping to find the truest ones.* It's true, for example, that a strong research paper usually has a main point, a thesis, a controlling idea. Frequently, the approach to deciding on a thesis is to decide on one pretty early in the process.

> The U.S. should do more to address the AIDS problem in southern Africa.

> Downloading music from peer-to-peer networks on the Internet is unethical because it undermines intellectual property rights.

> Ken Kesey's character Nurse Ratched in *One Flew Over the Cuckoo's Nest* represents the author's misogynistic themes in the novel.

You might arrive at theses like these because you think you already know the answer before you ask a question. Or you might decide to commit to a thesis early because it is more "efficient" to know your point before you begin to do much research. Neither of these motives is bad. But they work against genuine inquiry because they short-circuit the process of asking questions, collecting evidence, measuring your discoveries against your prior beliefs, or even changing your mind. Deciding on an answer at the beginning of the process of inquiry often eliminates one of its most important elements: *exploration.*

We sometimes do an exercise in our writing courses with four small, ordinary rocks. We ask four or five groups of students to generate a list of observations of a rock, passing it from hand to hand, and record those observations on a large piece of newsprint on the wall. The exercise inspires laughter, particularly in the beginning, as the students offer fairly obvious observations: it's a rock, it's hard, it's got sharp edges, it's black and white, and so on. But the groups get quieter as the minutes tick by and the list grows longer and the observations more difficult to conjure. Incredibly, nearly every group can fill a piece of newsprint. The next step is for each group to circle the most "interesting" observation on its list. Typically it's found toward the middle or the end of each list.

The success of this exercise depends on something most of us are unaccustomed to doing: suspending judgment. After all, everyone can tell it's just an ordinary rock, not something worth a second look. But if you're willing to keep the process of inquiry open, resisting the temptation to rush to the easiest conclusion, then you might see something you don't expect, even in something you've seen before. This willingness to suspend judgment, and to see ambiguity and uncertainty as a natural part of the process of inquiry, is a perspective shared by most of the writers in this book.

In fact, in a telling piece of research a few years ago comparing the views of college instructors with those of their students toward the research process, one of the sharpest contrasts was this: *The instructors saw research as an open process and their students saw it as a closed one.* In other words, while students seemed to think that writing a research paper involved rushing to judgment as quickly as possible about a thesis or quickly forming an opinion, their instructors saw the process as more exploratory and uncertain. Doubt, and even confusion, was simply part of the deal.

CHOOSE AN INQUIRY STRATEGY

You already know that scientists rely on methods of exploration that, among other things, help ensure that the experiment can be repeated by someone else and achieve the same results. The scientific method helps get at the truth of the way things are in the natural and physical world. Getting at the truth of the way things are is the main goal of academic inquiry, not just in the sciences but in the arts, humanities, and social sciences as well. These other disciplines have methods, too, and when you're asked to write papers for your political science or philosophy or English classes you'll learn some of the methods that are unique to each discipline. But there are certain ways of thinking that they all share, and that you can apply in a range of college writing and reading situations.

A strategy for inquiry—a relatively systematic way of posing questions, collecting, and analyzing evidence, introducing creativity, and coming to conclusions—is the key to getting to the truth of things. In *The Curious*

FIGURE 1–1

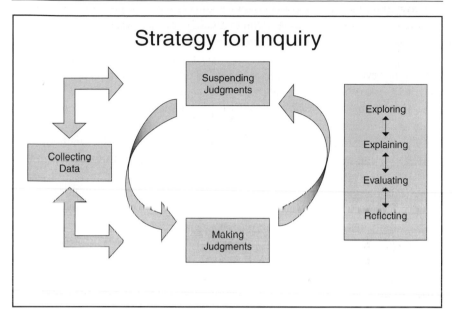

This is the strategy for inquiry you'll be using throughout *The Curious Reader*

Reader, you'll be asked to discover what you think about topics ranging from how to write a good research essay to the ethics of publishing pictures of the dead and dying in the local newspaper. We'll be encouraging you to use a strategy for inquiry (see Figure 1.1) to help you explore your ideas and meas ure them against the ideas of others that you'll read in this book.

In some ways, this strategy is a lot like the one that scientists use in its reliance on collecting and analyzing data, but in this case the "data" comes from the readings and pictures, as well as your own experiences and observa tions. The process also involves postponing judgment until you have had a chance to explore your thinking. And, lastly, it challenges you to harness two fairly contrary modes of thought—the creative and the critical—and use them both strategically to come up with your best ideas.

In this model, thinking "creatively" means allowing yourself to think openly, withholding quick judgments. This is amazingly hard to do sometimes, particularly when we're thinking about things that we may already believe we know a lot about. On the other hand, thinking "critically" here means moving toward judgment, rather than away from it. You evaluate the evidence you've explored and try to make some sense of it. Notice how the strategy of inquiry suggests there is back and forth between these two ways of thinking. (In the next chapter, we'll show you how you can encourage this back and forth through something called the double-entry or dialogue journal.) Also notice how important it is to collect data throughout the process, both to help you explore your subject and to help you evaluate your discoveries.

When we talk about a strategy for inquiry, we're really talking about a method for changing not just the way you think about something, but how you see it. Imagine, for example, that you're taking photographs of the house you grew up in. This is a place you may know intimately, and that you've seen every day for years. How can you see it freshly? By looking closely, looking again and again, and finding angles for seeing you aren't used to. Shoot some pictures lying on your back looking up through the tangle of honeysuckle vines on the shingled south wall at sunset. Shoot through a broken window in the attic. It's likely you'll see your house in ways you've never quite seen it before.

In an inquiry project, the questions you ask yourself about your subject are like angle and distance in photography. They shift your field of vision and line of sight. Inquiry questions can be grouped in four broad categories: those that explore, explain, evaluate, and reflect. Part of the inquiry strategy is to use these kinds of questions to help you shift what you see in the readings as an aid to discovery. In follow-up questions included at the end of each reading, we'll encourage you to ask questions like these:

- **Exploring:** What do I notice first? And then what? And then? What interests me about this? What additional questions does it raise? How do my own personal knowledge and experiences affect the way I feel and what I see?

- **Explaining:** How does this work? Why does it work? What do I understand it to be saying? How does it compare to something else?

- **Evaluating:** What's most convincing here? What's least convincing? What do I see that supports what I believe? What do I see that complicates or contradicts what I believe? What is the most important argument? What do I think about it?

- **Reflecting:** What do I notice about how I think about or do this? How do I compare how I approach this task with how I approach another one? How well did I do this? How might I do it better next time?

Typically, experienced writers and readers ask these kinds of questions without thinking about it. Some of our students do, too. But more often we encounter students who are uncomfortable with how disruptive questions can be in the steady march toward coming to quick conclusions about what they think. Questions *are* disruptive. They are meant to be. But they are disruptive in ways that will encourage you to discover more and think more deeply, and this is ultimately the goal of inquiry. In fact, it's discovery—learning things you didn't expect, and finding out what you didn't know you knew—that is the big payoff for daring to ask questions that make you pause and wonder.

FIGURE 1–2

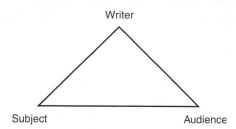

The rhetorical triangle illustrates the dynamic relationships among writers, subjects, and audiences.

INVESTIGATE IN A RHETORICAL CONTEXT

Reading and writing rarely take place in a vacuum. They are activities we do for particular purposes and audiences. For instance, consider the following situations in which inquiry might occur:

1. You're given a research assignment in political science to write a paper on the electoral college system for choosing the president of the United States.

2. You're a research scientist writing a paper on an investigation of the relationship between global warming and the shrinking of glaciers in the past four decades in a national park in Montana.

3. You're writing an essay for your composition class that explores the growth in demand for bottled water in the United States in the past ten years.

Each of these situations suggests a different rhetorical situation. This means simply that when you're investigating the electoral college, the melting of glaciers, or the growing market for bottled water, you must consider how to address your audience, what to say about your subject, and how to present yourself in each of these situations. Each situation will be different, of course, but Figure 1.2 shows the fundamental rhetorical triangle writers and researchers apply to their work.

Exercise 1.2   *Practice with the Strategy of Inquiry*

Probably the best way to understand the strategy of inquiry we encourage you to use in this book is to try it out. Though you'll be applying the method mostly to reading essays and articles, it can work in any situation in which you want to find out what you think.

Consider the picture shown on the next page. You recognize the place. But what does looking at this picture make you think about? At first, maybe

not much. But let's extend the process of inquiry a bit and use writing to discover what this image might inspire you to think or feel.

STEP 1: **Suspend Judgment and Collect Data.** Look closely at the picture. Write fast in your notebook *for five minutes* about what it makes you think about or feel. And then what? And then? And then? Follow this narrative of thought, stopping only to take another close look at the image. Don't worry about being eloquent or grammatically correct. You are writing to yourself.

STEP 2: **Make Judgments and Evaluate the Data.** Reread your raw writing from Step 1. Pay attention to what, if anything, surprised you about what you said, or what seems most interesting or significant. Then, in your notebook, compose an answer to the following question: *What is the most significant thing that you came to understand about the photograph of the planet that probably wouldn't have occurred to you if you hadn't written about it?*

Don't worry if your answer to this question isn't really deep or profound. After all, you've only given the photograph a few minutes of open-ended thinking-through-writing.

STEP 3: **Collect More Data to Evaluate Your Idea.** Read what you wrote in Step 2 to a partner, a small group, or the class. Discuss how your insight arose from the picture.

- What exactly did you see in the photograph that made you think the things you thought?
- What other information might you look for elsewhere that would help you think more about the insight you discovered?
- What further questions do your new understandings raise—about you, about the photograph, about the planet, or about photography?

Invite your partner, your group, or your class to contribute to your thinking about this.

STEP 4: **Reflect on the Process.** How did your experience with this exercise help you to understand the strategy of inquiry described in Figure 1.1? How might you apply it to responding to the readings in this book?

As an example of different rhetorical situations, consider a scientist writing a research article on global warming who will address an audience of other experts. What might this mean? For one thing, she will write the article in a format that is accepted by that audience and in a language that scientific experts expect. As author of the article, the scientist will present herself as a peer who is knowledgeable about the subject and has used accepted methods of investigation. Contrast that rhetorical situation with your research essay for your composition class on the growth of the bottled water market. Your audience will be classmates rather than marketing experts. How might this influence what you say and how you say it? What does it imply about the method of investigation you might choose?

Most inquiry-based investigations are done in some rhetorical context—for some purpose, with some audience in mind. This fundamentally influences the process of inquiry—how long it takes, the methods used, and how to share what has been learned.

INQUIRY AND RESEARCH

A great deal of the research and writing you'll do in college is research-based. This book will help get you ready for this, but we also hope that it will fundamentally shift your understanding of the why and how of research, not just in school, but in life. Here's how:

- We will show you the range of ways in which research is reported, including in nonacademic settings. You may be relieved to discover that not all research is the formal, author-evacuated writing you may have experienced reading and writing in school.
- Understanding how to "read" the rhetorical situation in which you're writing will give you a lot of help in determining how to present your work so that it's most convincing.
- Though each chapter in *The Curious Reader* will introduce you to a different way of presenting the results of the writer's investigations, we will emphasize that behind the scenes, the *kind of thinking* that produced these results is often similar and includes some of the elements of inquiry introduced to you to in this chapter.
- We'll also show you that reading is an act of inquiry, too, and that some of the same methods that you use to write an essay on the sneaky marketing of bottled water or the drawbacks of the electoral college can also be used to come to conclusions about what you read in this—or any—book.

2

The Inquiring Reader

No doubt the title to this chapter makes you think about standing in line at the grocery store looking at *The National Enquirer,* wondering where in the world they get the stories that fill its pages. "Enquiring minds want to know." The publication describes itself as "Celebrity News, Investigative Reporting, and Gossip," and if you're like us, you can't help reading the front-page headlines splashed across full-color photos of Prince or Kelly Ripa or Anna Nicole Smith: "Prince of Chutzpah: Singer's Posse Turns Low-Key Meal into High Drama"; "Kelly Ripa's Husband Caught with This Beauty!"; "Anna Nicole Drug Meltdown." While we may not want to admit it, we want to know the story, what happened and why. We're curious. We want to know.

But you probably don't associate your response to stories and photos like those in *The National Enquirer* with your response to the reading you are *assigned* to do for classes. You read your biology textbook because you have to pass the test, and maybe because you also find the subject interesting. Or you read a Victorian novel for your English literature class, only to find out later that the plot actually did keep you reading. You might *become* curious after reading something for class, but you probably don't stand in front of your dorm room bookshelf and feel compelled by curiosity to choose your textbook over your favorite magazine.

Exercise 2.1   *Autobiography of a Reader*

Explore in a fastwrite (see box on page 12), your own history as a reader. In telling this story, you may discover the origins of some of your feelings and beliefs about the process.

STEP 1: Think back to moments, scenes, situations, or people that you associate with reading. Perhaps you recall a day in the local public library, surrounded by stacks of note cards, reading the *Encyclopaedia Britannica* for a paper on China. Or maybe you remember sitting on the couch with your

---

Fastwriting

You'll see the term *fastwriting* a lot in the exercises throughout the book. Sometimes called "freewriting," fastwriting is a way to generate ideas quickly without judging them or worrying about periods and spelling. You simply:

- Turn off your internal critic and start writing anything that comes to mind.
- You can use a pen and paper or the computer.
- Don't correct anything, and don't worry if you seem to end up somewhere you didn't expect. That's part of the point! It's a great method to encourage surprise and explore ideas.

---

father, your head resting on his chest, feeling the vibrations of his voice as he read *Lassie Come Home*. Tell this story in a fastwrite with as much detail as you can. Write for five minutes.

STEP 2: Describe how you usually read for your other classes. How do you read books or magazines that aren't required for school, but that you read for pleasure? Finish this sentence, *"Reading is like. . . ."* Then, in your journal, draw that process, using whatever metaphors seem to capture your approach.

STEP 3: Now spend two or three minutes fastwriting or composing an answer to the following questions: *Do you think you're a good reader? Why or why not? How would you describe your own reading habits and methods?*

It's not surprising, then, that you might struggle to read something for your college classes, but find the stuff you read outside of class much easier and more pleasurable to read. After all, *The National Enquirer* and *The Curious Reader* seemingly don't have anything in common, right? Well, that's a question we'll ask you to consider throughout this book. What might the two kinds of texts have in common? What makes you want to read something— or to read more *about* something? Why do some people find popular magazines more pleasurable to read than academic essays or textbooks? What might we learn from reading *The National Enquirer* that we can apply to the essays in *The Curious Reader?*

Exercise 2.2   *What Makes a "Good Reader"?*

We often learn best when we've had time to think about the beliefs we already have about the new material, discovering which beliefs and strategies are helpful and which are not. Our beliefs about what makes an effective reader strongly influence how well we read.

STEP 1: To begin thinking about what you believe, choose *two* qualities from the list below that you believe best characterize a "good" reader.

- Only has to read things once to understand what an author is saying
- Can find the hidden meanings in the text
- Takes notes while reading
- Reads slowly and carefully, and doesn't proceed unless she understands what she has read
- Pays attention to his feelings about what he is reading
- Tries to find support for what she already believes
- Understands that all sources and all authors are biased
- Tries to find the author's theme or thesis
- Focuses mostly on the important parts of the text, things like the beginning, ending, and titles
- Pays most attention to details, facts, statistics
- Avoids reading things that don't interest him
- Reads with certain questions or goals in mind

STEP 2: Next, fastwrite in your journal for seven minutes.

- *Why* do you believe those two qualities are what make someone a good reader?
- Which of the qualities above describe *you* as a reader? Do you consider yourself a "good reader"? Why or why not?

Then, in small groups or as a whole class, discuss the most common qualities everyone chose. What differences do you notice? What does everyone seem to agree on?

INQUIRING MINDS AND INTELLECTUAL COUCH POTATOES

In spite of all the different kinds of things our students read, they often tell us they consider themselves to be "poor readers" or "not very well-read." Some admit they have never finished a novel. Some were told by reading tests that they had trouble with comprehension. Some believe they are slow readers because they don't know enough vocabulary. And yet we see our students, outside of class, reading with very little trouble the university newspaper, or a mystery novel, or their e-mail, or even complex technical material they need for something else. In fact, despite the myth that people read less than they did before the electronic age, studies show that we are indeed reading as much if not more. Book sales are high, especially among certain age groups. And online reading has skyrocketed. So why do you think students still consider themselves such mediocre readers—or tell us they hate to read?

We've found that many of these attitudes are based on beliefs about what it means to be a "good" reader, beliefs that are often contrary to reading effectively in college. Here are a few of them:

- If you're a good reader, then reading is a matter of decoding words quickly.
- Good readers read without difficulty and find the main idea and any hidden meanings with little effort.
- Good readers only need to read a piece once to get the main idea.
- The key is to find the main point in a piece of writing; there is usually only one.
- A "good" piece of writing is one that keeps the reader interested by focusing on an interesting subject; its subject is something readers can "relate to."

You might find some of these beliefs familiar, and they may apply to certain kinds of reading. You'll find an article in *Time* or *People* may not, in fact, demand a second reading for you to understand the writer's overall point. But when you encounter a text that you find difficult and confusing—or even one that challenges your beliefs and values—these beliefs may create some problems. You might end up feeling like a slow reader, lacking the intelligence to make sense of the words in front of you. And yet you probably aren't either of

---

Strategies for Inquiring Readers

- Understand the rhetorical context.
- Choose an inquiry strategy.
- Begin with questions, not answers.
- Be willing to suspend judgment and tolerate ambiguity.
- Search for surprise.
- Engage in dialectical thinking, moving from doubt to belief, creative to critical thinking, details to reflection.

FIGURE 2–1

Meaning

these things. Unfortunately, these beliefs construct a reader as an intellectual couch potato, passively hunting for hidden meanings or collecting information to fit some preconceived idea that usually belongs to someone else. Reading then becomes a matter of simply receiving the meaning that is already in the text, as if that meaning is the same for everyone, regardless of context. Figure 2.1 illustrates this linear model of the reading process.

The model shown in Figure 2.1 may reflect how you *feel* as a reader, especially when your purpose for reading is to memorize information or find relevant research for a paper. But it doesn't account for the role a reader plays in creating meaning out of a text, moving back and forth between the reader's knowledge and the text's information, between the reader's questions and the text's gaps or ambiguity. We read more effectively when we understand reading as a process of inquiry, a recursive model like the one shown in Figure 2.2, where a reader has a conversation with the text, poses questions, collects new information, connects that information with other knowledge, assesses what the writer says, and then believes or discounts it, all in the process of critically examining what the writer says. The reader is not an intellectual couch potato here, but an "enquiring mind who wants to know."

START WITH QUESTIONS BEFORE ANSWERS

As young children we learn to read not simply by learning letters and words, but in part because we ask questions. In fact, children learn to read by asking questions about what they see on the page and pretending to read books themselves before they can actually read the words. Michelle's two-year-old

FIGURE 2–2

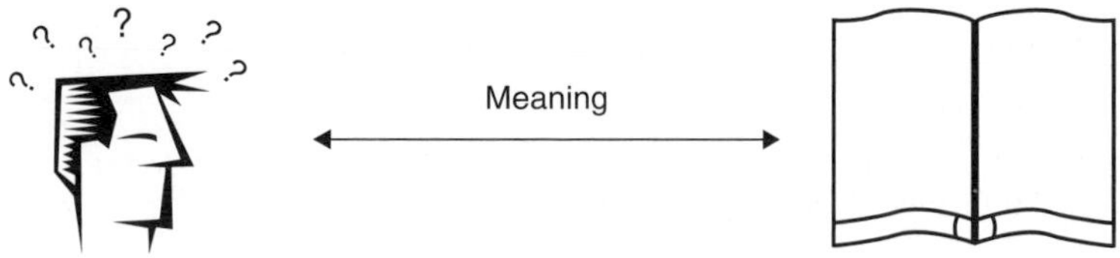

Meaning

daughter, Nicole, constantly asks about the images she sees in her books, particularly when they confuse her.

"Why is she doing that, Mommy?" she asked the other day as they were reading *One Morning in Maine.* She was pointing to Sal, the little girl in the story, who had her hand in her mouth, searching for her loose tooth, not realizing she had lost it in the sand. Not having lost a tooth herself, Nicole couldn't understand what Sal was doing. She didn't have a framework for what those words meant. The next day, as they were reading *The Cat in the Hat,* Nicole pointed to Thing One and Thing Two and asked, "Who's that?" Even Michelle repeating the characters' names didn't answer her question. She didn't have a context for understanding what the words meant, so she kept asking who they were. Eventually Michelle described them as friends of the Cat in the Hat. That seemed to assuage her curiosity enough that they could read on. Each page raised a new question, and while Nicole still doesn't know who Thing One and Thing Two are, she did learn what was happening in the story. She didn't simply "receive" that information, she actively created it by asking questions.

It's easier to see reading as a process of inquiry for children because children are learning for the first time what a narrative is, what characters do, why certain things happen. They are engaged in constant dialogue with the book and the adult reading to them. And that dialogue helps them construct a meaning about the story. They don't understand the words on the page right away, and in fact may not fully understand the story until it's been read to them several times.

Although it may sound surprising, the very habits that encourage learning for a two-year-old do the same for adults. When we encounter something

---

Types of Reading Behaviors

What do you actually *do,* if anything, when you read for school?

- Underline
- Highlight
- Make marginal notes
- Write in your journal
- Converse with someone about the text
- Reread
- Skim
- Take lots of breaks
- Copy down important passages or facts

unfamiliar—a word we don't know, an essay that doesn't follow the pattern we expect, an argument that we can't quite understand—we are in the same position as Nicole is, even though we're older and can read the words on the page. What will help us make meaning of the difficult and unfamiliar is asking questions, questions that are part of a conversation with someone else (like the author or someone who knows more than we do). Unfortunately, many of us give up before we ask questions, believing we just aren't good readers, or that the material is not interesting to us and therefore not worth reading. But what if we didn't give up and decided to keep reading? What might help us understand a challenging or uninteresting text better?

READING BEHAVIORS AND PERSPECTIVES

Think about what you usually do when you read. Physically. Do you have a pen in your hand? Are you listening to music or half-watching television? Do you underline or write comments and questions in the margins? Do you talk to other people about it?

The answers probably depend on the kind of reading you're doing and why. You might not highlight and underline *People* because you find most of the material relatively easy to understand and you don't need to return to the articles for a research paper. But for school reading, you might highlight or skim the text or write in your journal, depending on how difficult the material is and why you need to learn it. If you are uncertain about what to do, whether or not to underline, or even what kinds of questions to write in the margins, you might not mark the text at all.

How do you decide what to do? First, you need to understand your purpose for reading. Are you reading for pleasure? Are you reading to learn more about something you find interesting and yet confusing? Are you going to write an essay about what you discover, or mainly report what others have said? Most often, your purpose for reading in college will fall in these last two categories, and that means you'll need to have a pen in hand to mark the confusing parts, note the questions you have and connections you find, summarize what you've read, and reflect critically on it. The box, "Using Reading Perspectives," on page 18, lists several different approaches you might take to a text, perspectives that you can use like you change camera lenses to give you different angles on what you read. These angles help you understand a text more effectively. As you look at the sidebar, which reading perspectives seem most familiar? Which do you seem to use the most? Why?

Once you understand what your purposes are in reading a text, you can become more conscious about *how* you read it—the questions you ask of the text, the comments you put in the margins, and the strategies you use for that particular purpose.

Using Reading Perspectives

When we read, we always adopt certain perspectives toward a text. Most of the time we do this unconsciously, but one of the best ways to read strategically is to consciously *shift* our perspective while we read. Like changing lenses on a camera, or shifting the angle, distance, or time of day we take a photograph of something, this shift in reading perspective illuminates different aspects of a text. Here are some of the perspectives you might take:

- **Believing:** What the author says is probably true. Which ideas can I relate to? What information should I use? What seems especially sound about the argument?

- **Doubting:** What are the text's weaknesses? What ideas don't jibe with my own experience? What are the gaps in the information or the argument? What isn't believable about it?

- **Updating:** What does this add to what I already know about the subject?

- **Hunting and gathering:** What can I collect from the text that I might be able to use?

- **Interpreting:** What might be the meaning of this?

- **Pleasure-seeking:** I just want to enjoy the text and be entertained by it.

- **Connecting:** How does this information relate to my own experiences? What is its relationship to other things I've read? Does it verify, extend, or contradict what other authors have said?

- **Reflecting:** How was this written? What makes it particularly effective or ineffective?

- **Resisting:** This doesn't interest me. Why do I have to read it? Isn't *Survivor* on television right now?

TECHNIQUES FOR STRATEGIC READING

So you've been assigned something to read for your course—maybe from this textbook, maybe from one of your other classes. You're in a hurry, most likely, because you have a lot of homework to do in between classes and work. You're tempted to quickly scan the material and then in class wait to hear what your professor has to say about it. So you do that, but it turns out during class that your professor wants you to discuss your responses to the reading and write an analysis of how it was written. Unfortunately, you found the material boring and difficult to understand, and you didn't read it closely, so you don't have much to say. As a result, you lose participation points for that day. You also can't complete the written in-class reading response, and that hurts your daily homework points. What other choice do you have? What might you have done differently?

In this section we'll describe several techniques you can use—consciously—for effective reading, whether or not you're interested in the text you've been assigned. Just as a golfer learns strategies for improving his swing or a basketball player learns techniques for improving her left-handed dribble, a reader needs to have several different strategies to draw from that fit the reading purpose. At first it might feel too time-consuming to be so conscious about what you're doing as you read, but with practice these strategies will become almost instinctual and you will read more effectively *and* efficiently.

Choose an Inquiry Strategy

In Chapter 1 we talked about writing as a form of inquiry, and we suggested that writers choose different strategies of inquiry—different kinds of questions—depending on the rhetorical situation, that is, depending on the audience, purpose, and subject of the essay. These questions help writers explore their subject from many angles, and encourage dialectical thinking, moving from suspending judgment to coming to conclusions.

This same idea applies when you read. Let's look again at the inquiry questions we talked about in Chapter 1 and Figure 1.1 on page 5. When might you use these questions as you read? For which reading situations do each of them seem most useful?

- **Exploring:** What do I notice first? And then what? And then? What interests me about this? What additional questions does it raise? How do my own personal knowledge and experiences affect the way I feel and what I see?

- **Explaining:** How does this work? Why does it work? What do I understand it to be saying? How does it compare to something else?

- **Evaluating:** What's most convincing here? What's least convincing? What do I see that supports what I believe? What do I see that complicates or contradicts what I believe? What is the most important argument? What do I think about it?

- **Reflecting:** What do I notice about how I think about or do this? How do I compare how I approach this task with how I approach another one? How well did I do this? How might I do it better next time?

Depending on your purpose for reading a text, you'll choose particular questions to help you think critically and creatively about it. For example, suppose you are taking a literature class. Your instructor may want you to focus on the imagery used in a poem and how that imagery contributes to the ideas in the poem. In that case, you would use *exploring* questions:

- What do I notice first about the images in the poem? And then what? And then?
- What interests me about these images?
- What additional questions do these images raise?
- How do my own personal knowledge and experiences affect the way I feel and what I see in the poem?

If you are assigned to read an essay and write a paper about the author's main argument, you'll identify and list the individual points made and how they are supported. But you won't stop there because your purpose is to explain how persuasive the argument is. You would use the *explaining* questions:

- How do the specific points in the essay support the essay's main idea?
- Why does it work—is the argument effective?
- What do I understand it to be saying?
- How does it compare to other perspectives I have read or heard on this topic?

In your dialogue journal or the margins of the story, you'll ask these questions and others, engaging in dialectical thinking—believing and doubting—as you explore possible answers. If your biology instructor assigns a chapter in your textbook so you can learn a particular concept, you might use explaining questions, as well, to help you understand and remember the material.

Another time, your instructor may want you to examine how effectively the writer uses outside research. In that case, you might rely more on *evaluating* questions:

- What is the most convincing research given here? Least?
- What sources do I see that support what I believe? Contradict it?
- What is the most or least convincing argument?

But sometimes your instructor will ask you to reflect on your reading process or what an essay has taught you about researching. Either of those assignments will require *reflecting* questions:

- What do I notice about my reading process?
- How does that process compare to how I do other similar tasks?
- What was effective about my process? How might I do it better next time?

How does all this apply to the essays you'll read in this textbook? We hope that the questions we pose at the end of the essays will help you figure out which inquiry approach to use when you read for a particular purpose. We also hope they will help you read like a research writer. The questions at the end of the essays are organized around the four methods of inquiry detailed above, and are designed to give you multiple ways of reading a text and figuring out what the text means. But no matter what you read, you'll want to begin by figuring out your purpose for reading, and then choose an inquiry strategy that is best suited to that purpose.

Understand the Rhetorical Context

No matter what you read, it's important to keep in mind who wrote it, who the intended audience seems to be, what the subject or focus is, and how those elements all work together to create meaning. Sometimes a text is challenging to read because we are not the intended audience. For instance, the writer may use language for the specialists in the field rather than readers outside that community. Sometimes a writer's choice for organizing his essay may seem odd or confusing, but if that structure is what his intended audience expects, it's not such an odd choice.

When you read, then, make some notes in the margins about who the writer is, who the intended or implied audience is, what the writer's purpose seems to be, and how he approaches his subject relative to these features.

Avoid Making Pastel Islands

When you read, use both your eyes and your hand, but be sure you're gripping a pen, not a highlighter. We tell our students that they need to leave their highlighters in their drawers when they read so they can avoid making "pastel islands"* on the pages of their books. While it may be nice to have pages and pages that look like watercolor paintings, you'll get more out of reading when you use a pen and do the following:

- Make notes in the margins.
- Draw circles around ideas.
- Underline important concepts.
- Mark the things that are confusing, that strike you as important, that you have questions about.
- Mark the words and ideas that are unfamiliar and later try to look them up.
- Jot in the margins of each paragraph or section the main idea and purpose of the information within the context of the essay when you need to get a clearer sense of how the writer is constructing his or her argument.

You can even use Post-it® notes if you want. Instead of making watercolor paintings of your reading, then, the goal is to make the page look like a comic

---

*From Ann Berthoff, *Forming/Thinking/Writing: The Composing Imagination.* Rochelle Park, NJ: Hayden Book Co., 1978.

strip—covered with bubbles of your conversation with the writer, doodles of what you think and feel as you write. You can even be so creative as to draw a picture of the author so you have a sense of a real person talking to you as you read.

Reading a text without a pen in hand is not much different from sitting in a lecture class and not taking notes or not asking the professor questions when you don't understand what he's said. You may trust that the information will just find a slot somewhere in your mind, but you risk the unreliability of short-term memory. Writing things down, such as putting comments in the margins of your books, moves information into long-term memory where it can easily be remembered and used again. Most importantly, writing things down is the first crucial step in composing a research essay that will be a carefully considered exploration of a question you care about instead of just a simple report of information.

Read Twice

Once you have a pen in hand, you've moved from being a passive to an active reader. Effective readers not only read actively, though, they also read material a couple of times because they know that no one can fully understand and question a text until it is reread. That may sound rather strange, the whole idea that readers don't "get it" the first time they read, but it's true. Even readers as practiced as professors read the material they use in their writing, research, and teaching several times. Every time we read we revise our initial understanding of the text, coming to new ideas and new questions. The "main idea" in a piece is not something to be found like a word in the dictionary—readers figure out what that main idea is after several readings, marking what seems significant, following the writer's clues, and discussing what they see with other people. That's why we suggest that on a first read of an article you don't stop much to look up words or mark the text. While we do advise you to mark the words and ideas you don't know and to note anything that comes to mind as you read, it's helpful to wait until you've finished the piece once before you read it again carefully, taking notes, and turning the page into a comic strip full of your comments and ideas.

Be a Conversationalist

So you have your pen, you've read the article at least twice and have decorated it with your insights, questions, and underlinings based on the inquiry strategies that seem best. Now what? Are you prepared to dive into writing your research paper or to talk about an assigned reading from this book? You would certainly be in good shape if you stopped here, but it would be really difficult to flip through pages and pages of marked text when you're trying to write or to participate in class discussion. We've found that a good way to

What Is a Dialogue Journal?

The basic principle of keeping a dialogue journal is that you have a dialogue with the text, asking questions, making connections, noting memories and association. Here's how it works:

You can either draw a line down the middle of a page to make two columns, or you can use the spine of your notebook for the line and have two facing pages be the columns.

What the text says:	**What I think:**
In the left column, write out the passages from the reading that confuse you, surprise you, make you think of other ideas, and so on.	In the right column, write out your response to the passages in the left column. Sometimes you'll do a fastwrite, other times you may jot quick thoughts down.
Use direct quotes, paraphrases, summaries, facts, arguments.	Play the believing game. Play the doubting game, question the source.
Note page numbers next to each passage or summary/paraphrase.	List questions you have about the idea; your emotional response; other ideas this connects to.

Continue this process for the entire reading, moving back and forth across the columns. Remember that you want to explore your response to a piece, make connections to other works and your own writing, and analyze the writer's choices in terms of language, style, detail, and so forth. Be sure to note all the bibliographic information from the source at the top of the page.

take notes on your reading, notes that reflect the habits of mind we've been talking about in this chapter, is to actually have a conversation with the writer and his or her ideas in a reading journal, a place where you can do some fastwriting and extend your marginal comments.

Remember how Michelle's daughter Nicole asks endless questions while they are reading stories together? Even though you don't have a real person to talk to when you read, you can still have that kind of conversation.

"What's that?"

"Why is he doing that?"

"A turtle, Mommy—look! Like that big one at the zoo!"

"Mommy, do you like green eggs and ham?"

All the associations you make while you read, all the questions you have, can be recorded literally like a dialogue in what we call a double-entry or dialogue journal. It reflects the way we constantly move from details to reflection, from understanding to questioning, from critical to creating thinking when we read and write. On one side of the page you write what the author says, and on the other you record your side of the conversation with the author (see sidebar, "What Is a Dialogue Journal?").

Exercise 2.3   *Practicing Dialectical Thinking*

STEP 1: Read one of the essays in Chapters 4 to 8 of *The Curious Reader,* either one you choose or one that your instructor assigns.

STEP 2: On a blank page on the left side of your notebook or journal, carefully copy lines or passages from the essay that you found interesting, puzzling, provocative, or central to its argument, as you understand it.

STEP 3: **Play the Believing Game.** To start with, assume the truth of the author's claims. *What evidence from your own experience or knowledge, or from the text itself, might lead you to believe some of the things said in the essay?* Explore this in a fastwrite on the right side of your journal, opposite the side on which you copied the passage. If the writing stalls, look left and find something to respond to in one of the quoted passages you collected.

STEP 4: **Play the Doubting Game.** Skip a few lines, and shift your stance to one that is critical of the essay's claims. What do you suspect might be the weakness of the argument? What do you know from your own experience and knowledge that contradicts these claims? What does the essay fail to consider? Do this in a fastwrite just below the one you completed in Step 1. Again, if your pen slows, look on the left-facing side for quotations from the excerpt that will get you going again.

STEP 5: **Make a Claim of Your Own.** Based on what you've learned from the two contrary perspectives—believing and doubting—compose a paragraph that states what you believe about the main idea in the essay.

STEP 6: **Reflect on the Process.** Reflect on your experience with this exercise. Make an entry in your journal that explores some of the following questions:

• What, if anything, do you understand about your reading habits now that you didn't fully understand before this exercise?

• Which came more easily—doubting or believing? What perspectives on the topic might not have emerged if you hadn't been forced to shift stances?

• Can you see any similarities between your writing and reading processes? Differences?

Sample Dialogue Journal

Here's an example of the dialogue journal one of our students generated after reading the essay "Celibate Passion" by Kathleen Norris. Notice that the student chose to collect quoted passages from the Norris essay in the left column rather than summaries or paraphrases. The student nicely addresses what she notices in the passages she chose, and turns them inward, as an opportunity to examine her own experiences. Choose passages that you want to work out in writing because you find them confusing, or to unravel an author's claims with questions. The right column or page is for your thinking, pondering, speculating, believing, and doubting.

READING JOURNAL

Text	Response
"With someone who is practicing celibacy well, we sense we're being listened to in a refreshingly deep way. And this is the purpose of celibacy, not to attain some impossibly cerebral goal mistakenly conceived as 'holiness' but to make oneself available to others, body and soul." (Norris 133)	*Norris has approached this topic in a novel way. By focusing on relationships that are formed for reasons other than physical, Norris gives a picture of how celibacy allows for stronger relationships to be formed between people rather than men and women. She made a comment earlier in her piece about how she had misinterpreted the attentions of a man who was not celibate and her disappointment that the interest he was showing her was not for interest's sake but rather the means to an end. I also think that Norris brings up a good point that the celibacy allows us to concentrate body and soul on someone else without looking at them as objects, particularly when it is a man and a woman. Sadly, Norris is too right about this situation. Luckily for me though I've been able to find friends who make themselves available to me, both male and female.*

Text	**Response**
"One of the reasons I enjoy celibates is that they tend to value friendship very highly. And my friendships . . . give me some hope that men and women don't live in alternate universes." (Norris 132)	*My friendships have grown more important to me as I continue to go through life and try to survive all the changes and circumstances that seem to come along. I do find that the friendship that brings me the most comfort at times of crisis is my friend Christian. There is just something about having a strong and supportive male friend to help me through the rough spots. As Norris says, it gives me hope.*
"The younger celibates of my acquaintance are more edgy . . . more obviously struggling to contain their desires for intimacy . . . loneliness intensified by the incomprehension of others. In a culture that denies the value of their striving, they are made to feel like fools, or worse." (Norris 131)	*I think this passage relates to pretty much every time someone has to make a decision that goes against the main flow. Norris describes in detail the difficulty of fighting not only yourself and learning control but also having to fight everyone else. I know in my life that I've often felt like the outsider simply because I wasn't doing what the majority was. Sometimes I simply chose not to participate and that was enough to set me apart as being different. I didn't even have to do something else to fill that space. By virtue of abstaining I left myself open to ridicule.*

Exercise 2.4   *Responding to Difficult Texts*

If you haven't already, you'll soon encounter readings in your college courses that are especially challenging to read. It won't matter if you find them boring or difficult—you'll still be expected to read them. So how might you apply what you've learned in this chapter to a challenging essay? You'll get more practice with this kind of reading as it relates to writing a research essay in Chapter 7, but for now we'd like you to read a challenging essay from *The Curious Reader.* If the choice is yours, we suggest you consider "Looking at Women" (page 93), "Grief and a Headhunter's Rage" (page 178), "Subcultures, Pop Music, and Politics: Skinheads and 'Nazi Rock' in England and Germany" (page 301), or any of the academic articles in Chapter 7.

STEP 1: **Collect.** As you read the essay, use the double-entry journal technique to collect lines or passages from the text that you find significant, interesting, or puzzling. Carefully copy these on the left side of your journal. Consider reading the essay through once *without* taking notes and begin collecting in your journal during the second or third reading.

STEP 2: **Explore.** When you feel satisfied you've collected enough, use the lines or passages you've gathered on the left side as prompts for fastwriting on the right. When the writing stalls, skip a line, look to the left, and find something else to jumpstart your writing. *When you can, write about your own observations and experiences with the essay's subject to help you think about what the author is trying to say. Tell stories.* Remember, questions, not answers, should direct your fastwriting. Keep writing until you feel you have a grip on some of what the author seems to be saying about the subject and your own response to those ideas.

STEP 3: **Focus.** Adopt a critical mode of thinking for a moment. Use the writing and information you've collected so far, and compose a paragraph response that summarizes, in your own words, the author's argument and offers your own response to it. This response should complete the following sentence: *Based on your understanding, the most significant thing this author has to say is. . . .*

STEP 4: **Reflect.** Finally, make an entry in your journal in which you reflect on your experience with this exercise. Some questions that might prompt this thinking include the following:

- Did your reading process in this exercise differ significantly from the process you used in Exercise 2.3?
- What did you find most helpful about the double-entry journal method? What was least helpful?
- Can you connect any moments of insight or discovery in your journal with particular moves you made, perhaps asking a certain question or shifting the focus of your writing?
- How did you struggle with this reading? How did it come easily? What might you do differently when you encounter texts like these?

   If you've believed for a while that reading is about "finding" the "right" meaning quickly, you may be a little confused by all this talk about dialectical thinking and critical reading. That's okay. Whenever we learn something new, we are often confused—after all, learning means our old ways of doing things are being challenged, like trying to ride a bicycle after being on a tricycle or dribbling a basketball left-handed after always doing it right-handed before. It feels frustrating at times. You wobble unsteadily as you learn the new skill. Learning how to read actively and critically is a similar process: The way you've read material in high school may not work anymore in college, and that older way of reading can collide with the newer one you're learning; you may feel pretty wobbly and self-conscious for a while. It will take some time to feel comfortable reading in a way that challenges some of your beliefs about reading.

READING IMAGES

One thing you're probably well practiced reading is images—photographs, advertisements, paintings, billboards, and so on. We've found that our students have sometimes "read" more visual images than they've read written texts, and that they are quite skilled at describing how the image works, what it conveys, and how it connects to other similar images. We'll be asking you in this book to read some visual images, and you'll encounter them in your textbooks as well as in the research sources you find for the essays you write. How might you apply what you've learned about reading written texts to reading visual or graphic texts? What reading strategies might be best suited?

Once again you'll need to consider your purpose for analyzing the image: Are you going to explain something about it, such as how all the visual elements work together? Evaluate its effectiveness or its key themes? Explore your personal responses to it? Reflect on your own analysis? Once you've determined that purpose, you can focus the questions you'll ask on particular categories of inquiry. Then, just as we said about written texts, you'll want to consider the rhetorical situation within which the image has meaning: Who is the intended or implied audience? What purpose does the image seem to serve? What is the central subject or theme and how is it treated or represented? What are the key ideas and how are they being conveyed? This analysis might involve learning more about how color and light function in photography or about layout principles in graphic design, especially if you don't have much background in art, photography, or graphic arts.

Exercise 2.5   *Reading Images*

If an image is a kind of text that can be read like writing can, then the recursive reading model and dialectical thinking should help you analyze pictures, paintings, and ads, too. Try to apply those methods to the images that follow.

STEP 1: Closely examine each of the images shown on pages 29 to 32. Choose one you want to work with.

STEP 2: Begin your reading of the images as you would a printed text, using the dialectical approach. Open your journal to two blank opposing pages.

Thor Flying with Hammer (© 2005 Marvel/Corbis)

Doctors Tugging at Pill

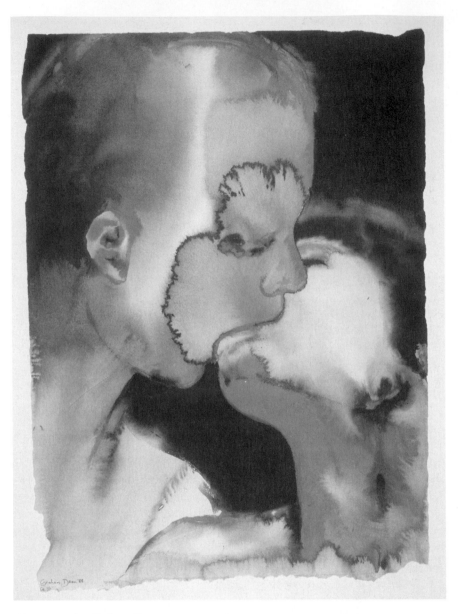

The Kiss II by Graham Dean

Begin on the left side and explore your reaction. Fastwrite about the image, letting the writing wander wherever it leads you. But begin with the following prompt: *When I first look at this picture, I think or feel _____. And then I think _____. And then. . . . And then. . . .* Whenever the writing stalls, repeat the phrase "And then." Write for five minutes without stopping.

STEP 3: Now work on the right side, using your more critical mind. Reread your fastwrite, and then try to focus your thinking about the picture by an-

The Wedding by Graham Dean

swering the question: *What story or stories does the image seem to be telling?* Remember that what makes a picture powerful is that it tells stories that transcend the moment the image captures, trying to say something larger about its subject, about our lives, or about a product.

STEP 4: Now return to the image, looking at it again closely. On the left side of your journal, collect information—specific details—from the picture or

Compartment C, Car 293 by Edward Hopper

advertisement that seems to provide support for the story or stories you believe the image inspires. Here's where it helps to know a little about the
grammar of images or the particular ways images are organized to communicate to viewers.

- What is the main visual subject? Where do you find your eyes are drawn,
  and how is that accomplished?

- Are there clues about context, things such as *when* or *where* the image
  was created?

- Are there rhetorical clues? What do you see in the image (or text) that
  suggests it targeted a particular audience? Does it include text or visual
  details that suggest a certain story, theme, or message?

- If you have access to the Web, view these images in color. How does the use of color contribute to the mood of each image?

STEP 5: On the right side page of your notebook, compose a 250-word response that explains, using supporting evidence from the picture you chose, your interpretation of its meaning.

The most common kinds of images you may encounter when you research a subject will be graphic representations of information, such as tables and charts and graphs. Sometimes it takes an insider in the discipline to understand them, but these graphics have a particular rhetoric to them that can help you read them better. It's quite challenging to cram a lot of facts into a small space and make that information not simply engaging, but easy to navigate and understand. Consider the table on pages 34–35 we found in *Discover*. What is the first thing you notice about the table? The small images of a brain scattered throughout? The definitions to the side? How is this image drawing your eye, where is it asking you to focus? The largest images are those within the death table itself, so that's where our eyes tend to go. But why use these images of a heart, a brain, a set of lungs, a stick figure in a fallen position? What do those images suggest about the audience for this table? What strategy does the designer use to distill a great deal of information into a short space?

These are the kinds of questions you'll want to ask yourself when you encounter such graphics, and you can use the dialogue journal to do so. Graphic representations of information use some of the same principles of design that photographs and advertisements do—ways of using color and space to draw the eye's attention; using images to represent something larger and more complex; creating drama and tension through the placement of images, color, and shading. The inquiry questions we've been using throughout this chapter will help you identify the ways this table works, and we give you an opportunity to practice that in the next exercise.

Exercise 2.6   Reading Graphics

Spend some time looking closely at the table, "Top 10 Causes of Death in the U.S. by Age," on page 34.

STEP 1: On the left side of your journal or notebook, begin noting the details in this image that stand out to you without thinking too much about why.

STEP 2: On the right side, fastwrite about your impressions, ideas, analysis of each of those details on the left side. Use the four categories of inquiry questions to help you focus:

Top 10 causes of death in the US, by age

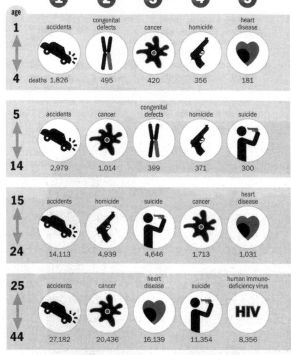

DEFINITIONS

Accidents are unintentional injuries, including motor vehicle accidents and medical errors. (See below.)

Benign neoplasms are tumors that do not spread throughout the body.

Cancer includes all forms of malignant neoplasms (tumors that grow and spread throughout the body).

Cerebrovascular diseases include stroke (damage to the brain by an interruption of its blood supply), atherosclerosis (narrowing of the arteries) and ruptured brain aneurysm.

Diabetes mellitus is the more common form of diabetes (the other is diabetes insipidus) and has two types. Insulin-dependent Type I is the more severe, and usually first appears in people under 35. Non-insulin-dependent Type II occurs mainly in people over 40.

Lower respiratory diseases include emphysema and asthma.

Nephritis is inflammation of the kidneys.

Septicemia is blood poisoning.

Influenza has surpassed AIDS as a lethal killer and contributes to an average 36,000 annual deaths in the US

Source: Centers for Disease Control and Prevention, 2003.

More people die as a result of **medical errors** than from motor vehicle accidents, breast cancer or AIDS. Reports of the numbers vary widely, but some are as high as **180,000 deaths a year.** It is also possible that some deaths due to hospital errors are never reported as such. **Medication errors** alone, occurring either in or out of the hospital, are estimated to account for over **7,000 deaths** in the US annually.

Source: *To Err is Human: Building a Safer Health System,* National Academy Press, 1999.

Source: "Top 10 Causes of Death in the U.S. by Age," from *Understanding Health Care,* by Richard Saul Wurman, in *Discover,* July 2003, pp. 42–43.

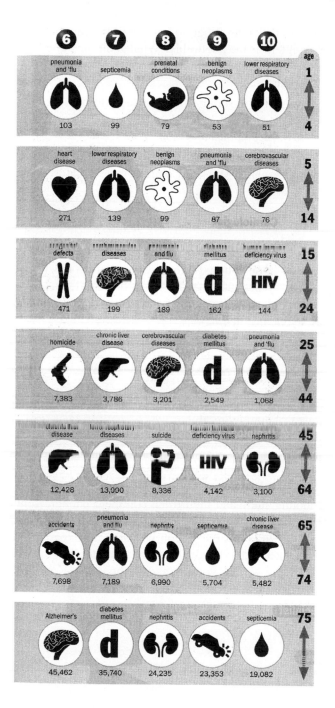

- *Explore* your responses to the table: What do I notice first? And then what? And then? What interests me about this? What additional questions does that raise? How do my own personal knowledge and experiences affect the way I feel and what I see?

- *Explain* how you think it works to summarize complex information: How does this work? Why does it work? What do I understand it to be saying? How does it compare to other graphics and tables I've seen?

- *Evaluate* how effective the table is: What is most convincing here? Least? What do I see that supports what I believe? Contradicts it? What is the most or least convincing argument?

STEP 3: Compose a 250-word paragraph about the conclusions you've come to about the table, what you learned from reading it critically.

STEP 4: In your journal, *reflect* on your experience trying to read this image. What was most challenging? What came easily? What did you learn? What might you do differently next time you encounter a table like this? How does reading a table compare to reading an essay?

READERS ARE CURIOUS

If you like some of the essays you read in this book and have a few things you're genuinely curious to know more about, you're well on your way to learning more than just how to put a research paper together. It's easy to throw a bunch of facts together, choose an attractive font, use subtitles, and have a clear thesis. It's much more challenging to begin with a desire to know more about something—like a five-year-old looking at an ant hill or a ten-year-old watching a shooting star—and then to be confident enough to not only gather all the information you can, but to ask even more questions and make additional connections with other things you've learned or experienced. Curiosity, conversation, connections. Discovering what you don't know. All of these are at the heart of any writing you do, and we hope the essays you find in this book will stretch your sense of what is possible when a writer sits down to write.

3

How Do You Know?

A few years ago, Bruce's family was sitting in a restaurant in Lucca, Italy, a small city in Italy's Tuscany region, and on the wall was a reproduction of Botticelli's famous painting, *The Birth of Venus.* Julia, then 9, kept staring at the work, ignoring a plate full of pasta, her forehead wrinkled quizzically. "Is that supposed to be good art?" she said, loudly enough to raise the eyebrows of nearby couples. We all laughed, of course. Botticelli was a famous Renaissance artist, and this painting of the Greek goddess is among his most renowned works. We had seen it a week earlier at the Ufitzi Gallery in Florence.

"Uh, yea, it's supposed to be good art," Bruce said. "You don't think so?"

"Not really," Julia said.

Had Bruce known more about the painting or the painter he might have tried to explain why critics would call this painting one of the best representations of the spirit of the Italian Renaissance. He would have said something about the anomaly of a painting like this, one that focuses on classical myth rather than Biblical events. He might have pointed out the grace of the image, achieved in part by subtle exaggeration of certain features, like the length of her neck or the odd position of her arm. Had he known all of that, he might have put on a convincing display of artistic knowledge that would have returned Julia to her pasta piatti, satisfied that *The Birth of Venus* was, indeed, a magnificent work of art. But Bruce had just *heard* it was famous, and thought it looked pretty cool.

We mention this anecdote because it raises several questions that are always central to academic inquiry:

1. Why do *we* believe that something might be true?
2. What evidence might convince *someone else* to believe that it is true?
3. What *kinds* of truths are subject to debate?

Exercise 3.1   *Your Ways of Knowing*

Each of us operates from a certain set of beliefs about how we know something is true in certain situations, yet we rarely talk about these beliefs. But such discussion can be very useful because sometimes the assumptions at the core of our beliefs limit how we read and how we research in an academic setting.

Consider the following statements. In most cases, which of the following assertions do you agree with?

- Everyone is entitled to his or her own opinion. You can't say that one person's opinion is better than another's.
- There is a big difference between a fact and an opinion.
- When two experts disagree, one of them has to be wrong.
- There is usually a right answer to every question.
- When I have an opinion, I'm usually not very confident about it.

STEP 1: Choose one or more of these assertions as a starting point for fast-writing. Begin by telling yourself whether you agree or disagree with the statement, and then write, adding questions about what you're thinking whenever you can. Use these questions to keep you writing for seven minutes. Don't worry if you find yourself changing your mind, or failing to come to definite conclusions. Don't hesitate to pull another statement from the list into your fastwrite if it will help keep you thinking-through-writing.

STEP 2: In class, discuss what you wrote about in your journal. What did you end up focusing on? Did your thinking change? What further questions did your writing and thinking raise about the statement you started with?

Discussion Questions

1. Is a fact simply a different kind of opinion?
2. How does truth depend on context?
3. How do you know what to think when two experts disagree?
4. In which cases is there always a "right" answer? In which cases isn't there a "right" answer?
5. How does it make you feel to consider that much of what we know may be constantly changing rather than static?

Bruce's daughter is inclined to believe uncritically that everything he says is true, even about art, in which he is hardly an expert. Most of us as children simply accept the authority of adults, just as most of us as students accept the authority of teachers. This is natural. But in college, suddenly instructors are inviting you to offer your own opinions about subjects, including those in which the instructor is clearly an expert.

Many students welcome this opportunity. And why not? It means that someone else cares about what you think, and occasionally you feel pretty strongly about something. In *The Curious Reader* we'll often invite you to offer your own analysis or interpretation of an essay in the book. But you may find that when you try to do so, your instructor or other students may challenge your ideas: "I don't see it quite that way . . . " or "What makes you think that, exactly?" or "Do you have any evidence to support that interpretation?"

ENTITLED TO YOUR OWN OPINION

We've both been teaching for many years, and every semester there is always at least one moment, often during a lively debate in class about a reading or a public issue, when someone says, usually with exasperation, "Well, that's your opinion." This is often a gracious gesture, a way of defusing the conflict. But there's an assumption behind it that is really worth talking about, particularly in a class that encourages inquiry through research and writing. It's an assumption that might be stated this way: "You're entitled to your opinion, but you can't say yours is better than mine." But is this true? Is it really impossible to make judgments about the worth of someone's opinion simply because they're entitled to have one in the first place? And if it is true, how would we get to the truth of anything? We could simply halt the process of inquiry, throw up our hands, and celebrate the right to have differing opinions. In conversation this sometimes is the polite thing to do, but in an academic setting it would bring a halt to new discoveries.

It actually *is* possible to judge the quality of someone's opinion. But the methods you will use to evaluate someone else's ideas—and, in turn, the approaches you might take to make your ideas *persuasive* to someone else—depend on the situation. Writers often talk about this as a *rhetorical situation.* Put simply, that means that you have to consider several things simultaneously, especially who you're writing for and why. This will influence what you say and how you say it, especially what information you might offer that will make your opinion convincing.

An obvious example is in a court, where there are explicit "rules of evidence." For instance, evidence that is hearsay, or a statement that is made outside the courtroom, is allowed in a trial under only certain conditions. The kind of evidence that can be offered about the character of someone who gives testimony is strictly defined as well.

Exercise 3.2   *Knowing What Is Appropriate Evidence*

We always use evidence when we're writing. Generally speaking, evidence helps clarify, support, or extend some kind of assertion we're making about ourselves or the world. Strong evidence is particularly important when you're trying to *persuade* someone else to see things the way you see them. But what exactly is "strong" evidence, and how do you know when you have it? Strong evidence is the most convincing evidence, and that depends on the situation—what you're writing about, why you're writing about it, and for whom.

Legal rules of evidence are much stricter than, say, acceptable evidence for making a case in a paper for your marketing class. But if you want your opinion to count, you'll spend some time thinking about types of evidence you might offer that are most persuasive in a particular situation.

Consider the rhetorical situations in the left column below. Can you match each situation with the *strongest* type of evidence among those listed in the right column? What would be the *weakest* source of evidence in each situation? Why?

Situation	Types of Evidence
A. You're writing a paper for your political science class arguing that the electoral college should be abolished. *Audience:* Your professor	1. Data from experiment conducted by writer
B. You're writing an editorial essay for the student newspaper that is critical of favoritism toward student athletes. *Audience:* Students and administrators who read the student paper	2. Example from writer's personal experience

Situation	Types of Evidence
C. You're writing a letter to a friend at another school who disagrees with you about your position on favoritism toward student athletes. *Audience:* Your friend Willis who plays basketball for another college	3. Quotation from published primary source[*]
D. You're writing a personal essay for your composition class on what it was like to grow up with an alcoholic parent. *Audience:* Other students in your class, and the instructor	4. Quotation from published secondary source[†]
E. You're a student member of a grade appeals board, and you're writing a ruling that denies a student's request for a higher grade in his nursing class. *Audience:* The student who filed the appeal, other board members, the instructor of the course	5. Writer's personal observation
F. You're writing a response paper about an essay in *The Curious Reader. Audience:* Your instructor and students in your workshop group in class	6. Information from a book written by an expert
	7. Information from interview with an expert
	8. Systematically collected field observations
	9. Something a friend said
	10. Information by a general interest magazine such as *Newsweek*
	11. Statistics from a survey conducted by *CBS News*
	12. Information from clinical observations

[*]A primary published source is information from direct evidence. In literature, it might be the novel or poem you're writing about; in history, the diary, letter, or newspaper account describing the event or person; in science, the results of an original experiement.

[†]A secondary published source describes, often secondhand, the direct evidence. In literature, that might be someone else's article on the novel; in history, a book that tells a story based on diaries, letters, or newspaper accounts; in science, an article that describes findings from other people's work.

Discussion Questions

1. What makes evidence persuasive in one situation and not another?

2. What else would it be helpful to know to make a judgment about what evidence would be most persuasive in each situation?

3. What type of evidence isn't listed in the right column that you would propose adding?

NOT ENTITLED TO AN OPINION

A 1986 study revealed some interesting things about how some women feel about expressing their opinions. In a book called *Women's Ways of Knowing*, the authors describe some women as "received knowers."* These are people who are likely to believe that knowledge resides outside of themselves—in a teacher, a friend, a husband, a physician—and therefore they are often very, very good listeners. "Received knowers" may be surprised—and relieved— to hear that someone thinks exactly as they do about something, and therefore they feel as if it's unnecessary to state their opinions. In our classes, we often hear this from mostly silent students who, when asked why they didn't con- tribute to a discussion, might say, "I was thinking the same thing as Aaron, and he said it better than I could anyway."

Imagine how someone who believes that whatever knowledge he or she possesses probably came from someone else might feel when suddenly asked to write a paper making an original argument. "You mean I'm supposed to come up with my own opinion? I'm no expert on this! What kind of teaching is this, anyway! Why don't you just tell me what you want me to do and I'll do it!" For people who think this way, the idea that they might be capable of actually contributing, even in a small way, to knowledge about a subject is preposterous.

The authors of *Women's Ways of Knowing* also argue that "received know- ers" don't tolerate uncertainty at all well. They really would prefer to get the "right" answer rather than muck about exploring ideas or raising questions that get in the way of coming to a quick conclusion. These are students who may hate interpreting poetry or analyzing the meaning of an essay. They are cer- tainly students who would not be keen on the process of inquiry that is at the heart of this book. Why spend so much time asking questions when you can simply find someone who already has the answer? A similar study that was published before *Women's Ways of Knowing* called such thinkers "dualists."

It isn't a character flaw to be a received knower or a dualist. And, in fact, most people aren't *simply* received knowers or dualists. People are much more complicated than that. They may feel a great deal of authority over what they know in one part of their lives and lack confidence that they're en- titled to know anything in another. For instance, a parent of a five-year-old might have strong opinions about how to best get toddlers to sleep—ideas that may even differ from sleep experts—and then attend a biology class and feel it would be wrong to contradict the teacher's opinions about global warming.

---

*Belenky et. al. *Women's Ways of Knowing*. New York: Basic Books, 1986. The authors are quick to point out that this is a perspective that men can certainly have as well.

OPINIONS IN AN UNCERTAIN WORLD

Actually, most first-year college students are probably not dualists but relativists. They're pretty sure that most academic knowledge is debatable rather than certain, though they might concede the sciences come closest to establishing indisputable "facts." They do have opinions about things. They're pretty sure that just because they read it in a book doesn't make it true, and that some so-called experts don't know what they're talking about. While they are inclined to believe that everyone is entitled to his or her own opinion, they also don't believe there is always a right or wrong answer, particularly in fields other than science.

"One of the things that bugs me about English," a student who is a relativist would say, "is that the professor is always trying to push his own interpretation of the story. There are lots of interpretations. Why is his the only right one?"

Of course, it may be that an instructor really is peddling a particular interpretation, but more often professors really want students to come up with their own ideas, but those ideas need to be developed and supported by *evidence*. And it's in this hunt for evidence, especially if it takes students to the library or online, that an interesting thing happens. Students often discover that where they expected agreement, they find argument. They find that one author will make an assertion supported by evidence and another will make an opposing assertion that is just as strongly backed up with evidence. Suddenly, the world can seem a much more uncertain place, and that isn't always a very comfortable realization.

Bruce once had a student who came to this realization in the middle of writing a research paper. Michael, 18, had learned to succeed at school by pleasing the teacher and giving only so much of himself in his papers. Writing a research paper was a familiar routine to him. Dream up a thesis, gather up a bunch of facts that support it, dump them in the paper, and get out. But Bruce's class was inquiry-based, and Michael was confronted with the opportunity to explore something that actually interested him: the impact of sex and violence in television programming on young viewers.

The more Michael read about the subject, the harder it was for him to come to any clear conclusion. It started to make him crazy. Studies seemed to be contradictory, experts made conflicting claims, and basic "facts" about television viewing were contested. Michael began to realize that academic knowledge may not be a stable thing, and it was unsettling.

"Not having any clue about what's right or wrong is very, very odd," he said one day.

The thinking about thinking that Michael was experiencing is one of the aims of a college education, and because composition classes focus on both process and language as a method of thought, there's often an emphasis on this special kind of self-awareness. You'll find this focus in *The Curious Reader*, too, when we ask you to reflect on what you think about what you've read and how you might think about it differently. The set of questions, "Inquiries on Inquiry: Exploring and Reflecting," at the end of each reading also will challenge you to reconsider both your beliefs about the ideas in the essays as well as your assumptions about the *kind* of research and writing you encounter in each reading.

Exercise 3.3   *Practice with Believing and Doubting*

The digital revolution, like most revolutions, is a blessing and a curse. We are stunned at the availability of information online these days for student researchers, and the incredible efficiency of searches that yield in seconds what used to take hours of paging through bound indexes. We love the Internet. But we hate it, too. Not only does it demand keen hunting skills because so much information out there is suspect, but the ease of gathering and transferring electronic text makes plagiarism ever more tempting.

According to a recent study, about 40 percent of college students admit that they committed plagiarism. What's to be done? The two opposing viewpoints that follow suggest two very different alternatives. John Barrie, president of a company called Turnitin.com, argues that universities should use software similar to that his company provides to detect plagiarism. These are programs that build massive databases of student papers culled from the Internet or submitted by instructors who subscribe to the service. Rebecca Moore Howard, a professor at Syracuse, argues that "teaching, not software, is the key to preventing plagiarism." She believes that the explosion of electronic texts is a "revolution in literacy," and requires teachers to develop new approaches to help students deal with it.

STEP 1: Read each essay. Choose the one *with which you disagree*, at least after an initial reading.

STEP 2: In your notebook, begin by playing "the believing game" with the essay you chose. Ask yourself the following questions, and fastwrite your responses, letting your quick writing tell you what you think.

- What part of this can I agree with?
- What does this say that I hadn't considered?
- What seems the strongest point?
- In which ways am I sympathetic to the writer's thoughts or feelings about this?

STEP 3: Skip a few lines in your notebook. Now play the "doubting game," exploring your answers to the following questions by writing fast.

* What part of this do I disagree with?
* What questions does this raise for me?
* What seems the weakest point, the flimsiest evidence?
* What are the gaps in the argument? What has the writer failed to consider?

AT ISSUE: *SHOULD EDUCATORS USE COMMERCIAL SERVICES TO COMBAT PLAGIARISM?*

John Barrie, *President, Turnitin.com*: Written for the CQ Researcher, September 2003

I spent more than 10 years researching how our brains create a conscious representation of the world, and the takehome message is that we draw from the past to create the present. Academic endeavors work in a similar manner. Students from elementary school to postgraduate are constantly learning from and building upon the corpus of prior work from their peers, authors of books or journal articles, lectures from faculty or from information found on the Internet. One of the best methods for learning involves collaboration or peer review among groups of students in order to share ideas and criticism regarding course material.

Subsequent intellectual accomplishments of students—or academics—are sometimes measured by their ability to distill weeks, months or years of hard work into a manuscript of original thought. For example, a high-school student might compose a book report about Othello while a college undergrad might write a manuscript regarding the sublime philosophy of Nietzsche. In either case, the faculty is attempting to ascertain whether that student has understood the course material. The problem begins when faculty cannot determine whether a student wrote a term paper or plagiarized it from other sources. But is that a problem?

Turnitin receives about 15,000 papers *per day* from students in 51 countries writing across the curriculum, and about 30 percent of those papers are less than original. This is supported by the largest-ever study of plagiarism involving more than 18,000 students on 23 campuses. The study (released this month by Rutgers University Professor Donald McCabe) concluded that nearly 40 percent of college undergraduates admitted to plagiarizing term papers using information cut-and-pasted from the Internet.

This raises the obvious question: "Why is Internet plagiarism growing exponentially in the face of honor codes, vigilant faculty and severe punishments ranging all the way to expulsion?" The answer: The status quo doesn't work, and our society's future leaders are rapidly building a foundation of shaky ethics while cheating their way to a degree.

The real shame is that while some administrators shirk their responsibility to face the problem or are in complete dereliction of their duty as educators by not demanding original work from all students, ethical, hard-working students are being out-competed by their cheating peers—and it's an outrage.

Digital plagiarism is a digital problem and demands a digital solution, whether it's Turnitin or otherwise. No one wants to live in a society populated by Enron executives.

Rebecca Moore Howard, *Associate Professor of Writing and Rhetoric, Syracuse University*: Written for the CQ Researcher, September 2003

Teaching, not software, is the key to preventing plagiarism. Today's students can access an array of electronic texts and images unimaginable just 20 years ago, and students' relationship to the practice of information-sharing has changed along with the technology.

But today's students lack extensive training and experience in working carefully from print sources, and they may not understand that they need to learn this skill. They may also find it difficult to differentiate between kinds of sources on the Internet. With information arriving as a cacophony of electronic voices, even well-intentioned students have difficulty keeping track of—much less citing—who said what.

Moreover, the sheer volume of available information frequently leaves student writers feeling that they have nothing new to say about an issue. Hence too many students—one in three, according to a recent survey conducted by Rutgers University Professor Donald McCabe—may fulfill assignments by submitting work they have not written.

Were we in the throes of widespread moral decay, capture-and-punishment might provide an appropriate deterrent. We are, however, in the midst of a revolution in literacy, and teachers' responses must be more complex. They must address the underlying issues, students' ability to conduct research, comprehend extended written arguments, evaluate sources and produce their own persuasive written texts, in explicit dialogue with their sources.

Classrooms must engage students in text and in learning—communicating a value to these activities that extends beyond grades earned and credentials accrued. McCabe, who is a founder of the renowned Center for Academic Integrity at Duke University, recommends pedagogy and policies that speak to the causes of plagiarism, rather than buying software for detection and punishment. In a 2003 position statement, the Council of Writing Program Administrators urges, "Students should understand research assignments as opportunities for genuine and rigorous inquiry and learning." The statement offers extensive classroom suggestions for teachers and cautions that using plagiarism-catching software may "justify the avoidance of responsible teaching methods."

Buying software instead of revitalizing one's teaching means that teachers, like students, have allowed the electronic environment to encourage a reductive, automated vision of the educational experience. As one of my colleagues recently remarked, "The 'world's leading plagiarism-prevention system' is not Turnitin.com—it's careful pedagogy."

Questions for Discussion

1. How difficult was it to play the believing game with the article with which you initially disagreed?
2. Did you change your mind about anything?
3. What effect did the requirement that you adopt *both* perspectives have on your thinking about the plagiarism issue? What did you consider that you would have probably ignored? What did you learn that you didn't expect to learn?

BELIEVING AND DOUBTING

Do you remember the time when you had no trouble believing that wondrous and mysterious things were true? Carpets could fly. Dogs could talk. World peace was within reach. The girl next door really could be president. This inclination to believe the improbable made you an easy target for the cynical—say, an older brother or sister—who couldn't resist sharing that Santa Claus did not live at the North Pole or that wolves liked to dine on people.

After enough of these broadsides on our willingness to believe, it often became harder to be open. If we were lucky, we simply became more skeptical rather than more cynical, but once we passed through that door it seemed there was no turning back: We came to see the act of believing the unlikely as dangerously naive.

School seems to reinforce such skepticism. Bruce's student Michael, who came to believe that it's difficult to trust that anything is certain, therefore concluded that everything should be doubted. This is understandable—and skepticism *is* a useful perspective when you're involved in inquiry—but to allow doubt to bully believing into submission will deny you new ways of seeing.

Writing teacher Peter Elbow observes that "doubt caters too comfortably to your natural impulse to protect and retain views we already hold," while

---

Believing

- What part of this can I agree with?
- What does this say that I hadn't considered?
- What seems the strongest point?
- In what ways am I sympathetic to how the writer thinks or feels about this?

Doubting

- What part of this do I disagree with?
- What questions does this raise for me?

---

believing allows us to "feel the force" of others' points of view. To try, at least for awhile, to see things from the other person's perspective, to see the merit in some of their assertions and the relevance of some of their ideas, is a good idea not just in college but in life. This is how you learn. How you change. And also how you think more deeply about your own convictions, finding new ways to understand how you feel.

But it's also a genuine challenge to play the believing game when your first impulse is to disagree. To "try on" the perspective of someone else, even if you don't disagree, is hard enough. But to try to see the merit of an argument you don't particularly like can seem darn near impossible. But there's another reason some people resist breaking with their skepticism: It risks messing up their thinking, and prolonging the process.

Our natural impulse, particularly in school, is to limit most writing projects to duck-hunting expeditions. Decide quickly on a thesis and then go find all the information you can to support it. This is certainly more efficient. You can write your papers better at the last minute. But it also produces writing that is predictable and lacking in insight. This brings us back to where this chapter began—the importance not just of beginning with questions rather than answers, but having the patience to really *explore* what you think, to prolong the process of inquiry so you're more likely to discover what you didn't know you felt. That's the real payoff for inquiry-based projects. That's what makes the "inefficiencies" of the process worthwhile: the pleasures of discovery. And discovery is the main enterprise of the university you've decided to join.

4

The Researched Essay: "Essaying" as a Mode of Inquiry

In this era of prepackaged thought, the essay is the closest thing we have, on paper, to a record of the individual mind at work and play. It is an amateur's raid in a world of specialists. Feeling overwhelmed by data, random information, the flotsam and jetsam of mass culture, we relish the spectacle of a single consciousness making sense of a portion of the chaos.

—Scott Russell Sanders

Pick up almost any general interest magazine such as *Smithsonian, Audubon, Outside, Harper's,* or *Esquire,* or log on to an online magazine such as *Slate* or *Salon,* and you'll find articles similar to those you're about to read in this chapter: lively and topical pieces with strong voices and often lively, personal styles. While you may not be a regular reader of such articles, you're undoubtedly familiar with the genre. That, among other things, is what the waiting rooms in doctors' offices are for. What you probably didn't consider is that these magazine articles are essentially research papers. *Huh? But aren't research papers supposed to be pretty formal?* Okay. There *are* some differences between these essays and the traditional academic paper. But consider what research papers and these magazine articles have in common: They are all based on fairly extensive research that included a whole range of sources, including interview field observation, and library research. All of them have some kind of thesis or central idea or question that provides a focus for the investigation and the essay. All of them involve discoveries of some kind. Some make claims that are supported by evidence, and some test claims against the evidence.

The articles in this chapter *are* forms of research writing that are relevant to academic writing because they represent some of the finest examples of inquiry at work, and best of all, they transform facts into something worth reading. How do they do that? Are the techniques and methods that these writers use to bring fact-based writing to life things that you can call on in your own work? We think so, of course, which is why we encourage you to keep a running list in your research notebook of the devices and techniques these writers use to keep their work lively and engaging even though they are full of information. For example, one thing you should notice is the many ways that narrative structure is used in these pieces, and how many different kinds of narratives there are here. Here are some other things to watch for:

- What is the balance between narrative and exposition, showing and telling in each of these essays? How do they compare in that regard?
- Where do you typically find a thesis, or controlling idea?
- Do the leads, or introductions, of these essays have anything in common? How are they different?
- What kinds of sources of information do these writers seem to rely on most?
- What are the many ways, beyond simply talking about themselves, that these writers register their presence in these researched essays?

As important as it is to recognize that a piece like "No Wonder They Call Me a Bitch" has some academic features is also noticing what it *doesn't* share with the typical term paper. For example, the essays aren't documented and don't include bibliographies. They tend not to rely as heavily on academic sources. In addition, several of the essays here also make *the process of the search* the backbone of the piece. One important discussion to have in class is what accounts for these differences. Why, for instance, is it typically unnecessary for a magazine writer to include a bibliography? As you do these things, you may begin to understand how—like all writing—the approach in a research-based piece is closely tied to context: why something is written, for whom, and under what circumstances. The research paper is simply not a monolithic thing.

A research paper, for example, is not necessarily a research *essay*. When Scott Russell Sanders writes in the opening epigraph that the essayist is a "single consciousness" attempting to make "sense of a portion of the chaos," he could be describing any research scientist. But the essay is a bit more peculiar in its methods than a conventional research paper. Generally speaking, the essayist is not out *to prove* something but to *find something out*. This may lead the writer to indulge in useful digressions, or to propose some tentative truth about the way things are, only to undo it five paragraphs later. The *process* of coming to know something, for the essayist, is as important as *what* she comes to know.

As you read the essays in this chapter, hold these contraries in your mind: these are and are not research papers. Some of the questions at the end of each essay might help you sort this out. We think, however, that the research *essay* is an outstanding introduction to methods of inquiry in college writing because it powerfully demonstrates those habits of mind so central to academic thinking: suspending judgment, tolerating ambiguity, dialectical thinking, question-asking, suspending judgment, and taking responsibility for one's ideas about things. It also is one of the few types of research-based writing that draws on all four methods of inquiry: exploring, explaining, evaluating, and reflecting. Unlike most academic articles, which conceal this thinking process, the essayist often makes it an explicit part of the story she tells. See if you notice when that happens as you read the chapter. As you read these pieces, then, look for these qualities of the researched essay:

- An engaging writing style that registers the writer's presence, sometimes using "I"
- As essay that begins with questions—the purpose is to *find something out*
- A structure that is often is a narrative of the writer's thinking as it evolves
- The writer uses multiple sources of information (interview, observation, experience, and library research)

We hope you'll also look for ways that each essay reflects qualities of more formal academic writing, including creating an argument, using credible evidence, applying methods of academic inquiry, acknowledging what has already been said about the subject, and so on. What might you learn about research writing for *any* genre based on reading these essays?

And even if your instructor doesn't ask you to write essays like these, we hope you will at least borrow some of the techniques these writers use to powerfully communicate their own sense of wonder about dog food, flies, the moon landing, women, genealogy, and obesity.

No Wonder They Call Me a Bitch
Ann Hodgman

Ever wonder what dog food tastes like? Ann Hodgman always wanted to try a Gaines-burger, so she decided to spend a week eating dog food, everything from canned food to dog treats. In this humorous essay, Hodgman takes us through the sensuous tastes of dog food and shows us the power of observation, experimentation, and curiosity in writing a researched essay. First published in Spy *magazine (1989), this essay was chosen as one of* The Best American Essays of 1990. *We think you'll agree that such plaudits are well deserved.*

As you read, note the way Hodgman follows her questions, no matter how unconventional, to learn more about dog food, and how she positions herself as a writer and researcher in the essay. How would the essay be different if she didn't use "I" in this piece? Besides the topic itself, what makes the essay so funny? How does Hodgman register her "voice" on the page? Where does her research seem to surprise her and propel new questions for her inquiry?

I've always wondered about dog food. Is a Gaines-burger really like a hamburger? Can you fry it? Does dog food "cheese" taste like real cheese? Does Gravy Train actually make gravy in the dog's bowl, or is that brown liquid just dissolved crumbs? And exactly what *are* by-products?

Having spent the better part of a week eating dog food, I'm sorry to say that I now know the answers to these questions. While my dachshund, Shortie, watched in agonies of yearning, I gagged my way through can after can of stinky, white-flecked mush and bag after bag of stinky, fat-drenched nuggets. And now I understand exactly why Shortie's breath is so bad.

Of course, Gaines-burgers are neither mush nor nuggets. They are, rather, a miracle of beauty and packaging—or at least that's what I thought when I was little. I used to beg my mother to get them for our dogs, but she always said they were too expensive. When I finally bought a box of cheese-flavored Gaines-burgers—after 20 years of longing—I felt deliciously wicked.

"Dogs love real beef," the back of the box proclaimed proudly. "That's why Gaines-burgers is the only beef burger for dogs with real beef and no meat by-products!" The copy was accurate: meat by-products did not appear in the list of ingredients. Poultry by-products did, though—right there next to preserved animal fat.

One Purina spokesman told me that poultry by-products consist of necks, intestines, undeveloped eggs and other "carcass remnants," but not feathers, heads or feet. When I told him I'd been eating dog food, he said, "Oh, you're kidding! Oh no!" (I came to share his alarm when, weeks later, a second Purina spokesman said that Gaines-burgers *do* contain poultry heads and feet—but *not* undeveloped eggs.)

Up close my Gaines-burger didn't much resemble chopped beef. Rather, it looked—and felt—like a single long, extruded piece of redness that had been chopped into segments and formed into a patty. You could make one at home if you had a Play-Doh Fun Factory.

I turned on the skillet. While I waited for it to heat up I pulled out a shred of cheese-colored material and palpated it. Again, like Play-Doh, it was quite malleable. I made a little cheese bird out of it; then I counted to three and ate the bird.

There was a horrifying rush of cheddar taste, followed immediately by the dull tang of soybean flour—the main ingredient in Gaines-burgers. Next I tried a piece of red extrusion. The main difference between the meat-flavored and cheese-flavored extrusions is one of texture. The "cheese" chews like fresh Play-Doh, whereas the "meat" chews like Play-Doh that's been sitting out on a rug for a couple of hours.

Frying only turned the Gaines-burger black. There was no melting, no sizzling, no warm meat smells. A cherished childhood illusion was gone. I flipped the patty into the sink, where it immediately began leaking rivulets of red dye.

As alarming as the Gaines-burgers were, their soy meal began to seem like an old friend when the time came to try some *canned* dog foods. I decided to try the Cycle foods first. When I opened them, I thought about how rarely I use can openers these days, and I was suddenly visited by a long-forgotten sensation of can-opener distaste. *This* is the kind of unsavory place can openers spend their time when you're not watching! Every time you open a can of, say, Italian plum tomatoes, you infect them with invisible particles of by-product.

I had been expecting to see the usual homogeneous scrapple inside, but each can of Cycle was packed with smooth, round, oily nuggets. As if someone at Gaines had been tipped off that a human would be tasting the stuff, the four Cycles really were different from one another. Cycle-1, for puppies, is wet and soyish. Cycle-2, for adults, glistens nastily with fat, but it's passably edible—a lot like some canned Swedish meatballs I once got in a care package at college. Cycle-3, the "lite" one, for fatties, had no specific flavor; it just tasted like dog food. But at least it didn't make me fat.

Cycle-4, for senior dogs, had the smallest nuggets. Maybe old dogs can't open their mouths as wide. This kind was far sweeter than the other three Cycles—almost like baked beans. It was also the only one to contain "dried beef digest," a mysterious substance that the Purina spokesman defined as "enzymes" and my dictionary defined as "the products of digestion."

Next on the menu was a can of Kal-Kan Pedigree with Chunky Chicken. Chunky chicken? There were chunks in the can, certainly—big, purplish-brown chunks. I forked one chunk out (by now I was becoming more callous) and found that while it had no discernible chicken flavor, it wasn't bad except for its texture—like meat loaf with ground-up chicken bones.

In the world of canned dog food, a smooth consistency is a sign of low quality—lots of cereal. A lumpy, frightening, bloody, stringy horror is a sign of high quality—lots of meat. Nowhere in the world of wet dog foods was this demonstrated better than in the fanciest I tried—Kal Kan's Pedigree Select Dinners. These came not in a can but in a tiny foil packet with a picture of an imperious Yorkie. When I pulled open the container, juice spurted all over my hand, and the first chunk I speared was trailing a long gray vein. I shrieked and went instead for a plain chunk, which I was able to swallow only after taking a break to read some suddenly fascinating office equipment catalogs. Once again, though, it tasted no more alarming than, say, canned hash.

Still, how pleasant it was to turn to *dry* dog food! Gravy Train was the first I tried, and I'm happy to report that it really does make a "thick, rich, real beef gravy" when you mix it with water. Thick and rich, anyway. Except for a lingering rancid-fat flavor, the gravy wasn't beefy, but since it tasted primarily like tap water, it wasn't nauseating either.

My poor dachshund just gets plain old Purina Dog Chow, but Purina also makes a dry food called Butcher's Blend that comes in Beef, Bacon, and Chicken flavor. Here we see dog food's arcane semiotics at its best: a red triangle with a *T* stamped into it is supposed to suggest beef; a tan curl, chicken; and a brown *S,* a piece of bacon. Only dogs understand these messages. But Butcher's Blend does have an endearing slogan: "Great Meaty Tastes—without bothering the Butcher!" *You know, I wanted to buy some meat, but I just couldn't bring myself to bother the butcher. . . .*

Purina O.N.E. ("Optimum Nutritional Effectiveness") is targeted at people who are unlikely ever to worry about bothering a tradesperson. "We chose chicken as a primary ingredient in Purina O.N.E. for several reasonings," the long, long essay on the back of the bag announces. Chief among these reasonings, I'd guess, is the fact that chicken appeals to people who are—you know—*like us.* Although our dogs do nothing but spend 18-hour days alone in the apartment, we still want them to be *premium* dogs. We want them to cut down on red meat, too. We also want dog food that comes in a bag with an attractive design, a subtle typeface and no kitschy pictures of slobbering golden retrievers.

Besides that, we want a list of the Nutritional Benefits of our dog food—and we get it on O.N.E. One thing I especially like about this list is its constant references to a dog's "hair coat," as in "Beef tallow is good for the dog's skin and hair coat." (On the other hand, beef tallow merely provides palatability, while the dried beef digest in Cycle provides palatability *enhancement.*)

I hate to say it, but O.N.E. was pretty palatable. Maybe that's because it has about 100 percent more fat than, say, Butcher's Blend. Or maybe I'd been duped by the packaging; that's been known to happen before.

As with people food, dog snacks taste much better than dog meals. They're better-looking too. Take Milk-Bone Flavor Snacks. The loving-hands-at-home prose describing each flavor is colorful; the writers practically choke on their own exuberance. Of bacon they say, "It's so good, your dog will think it's hot off the frying pan." Of liver: "The only taste your dog wants more than liver—is even more liver!" Of poultry: "All those farm fresh flavors deliciously mixed in one biscuit. Your dog will bark with delight!" And of vegetable: "Gardens of taste! Specially blended to give your dog that vegetable flavor he wants—but can rarely get!"

Well, I may be a sucker, but advertising *this* emphatic just doesn't convince me. I lined up all seven flavors of Milk-Bone Flavor Snacks on the floor. Unless my dog's palate is a lot more sensitive than mine—and considering that she steals dirty diapers out of the trash and eats them, I'm loath to think it is—she doesn't detect any more difference in the seven flavors than I did when I tried them.

I much preferred Bonz, the hard-baked, bone-shaped snack stuffed with simulated marrow. I liked the bone part, that is; it tasted almost exactly like the cornmeal it was made of. The mock-marrow inside was a bit more problematic: in addition to looking like the sludge that collects in the treads of my running shoes, it was bursting with tiny hairs.

I'm sure you have a few dog food questions of your own. To save us time, I've answered them in advance.

Q. Are those little cans of Mighty Dog actually branded with the sizzling word BEEF, *the way they show in the commercials?*

A. You should know by now that that kind of thing never happens.

Q. Does chicken-flavored dog food taste like chicken-flavored cat food?

A. To my surprise, chicken cat food was actually a little better—more chickeny. It tasted like inferior canned pâté.

Q. Was there any dog food that you just couldn't bring yourself to try?

A. Alas, it was a can of Mighty Dog called Prime Entree with Bone Marrow. The meat was dark, dark brown, and it was surrounded by gelatin that was almost black. I knew I would die if I tasted it, so I put it outside for the raccoons.

Personal Investigations: Inquiry Projects

1. One of the interesting features of "No Wonder They Call Me a Bitch" is its method. Of course, it's downright disgusting to actually eat dog food, but you have to admire Hodgman's willingness to experiment. The one-week time frame for such an experiment is something to consider. What question could you pose that could be explored with a week's worth of experimentation? Or what hypothesis could you test? How about spending a week living on the typical diet of an American five-year-old, for example, and then research its dietary implications?

2. Hodgman just scratched the surface of the pet food topic. Can you think of other questions about pet food you might explore in a research essay?

Craft and Conventions: Explaining and Evaluating

3. Humor and research seem like unlikely companions. Is that because levity tends to undermine the serious purposes of research? If so, how does Hodgman manage to maintain the humor without undercutting her purpose of making a serious point about dog food? Or does she?

4. Hodgman tells us the story of her research, and this forms the backbone of the essay. Why might she decide to use this structure? Why do we see it so little in academic research? How effective is this structure? Why or why not?

5. Where exactly in the essay do you *first* realize that Hodgman has a serious purpose here? If she has a thesis, how would you put it in your own words?

Inquiries on Inquiry: Exploring and Reflecting

6. What inquiry habits—suspending judgment and tolerating ambiguity, question asking, dialectical thinking, and taking responsibility for her own ideas—does Hodgman bring to her dog food experiment? Which passages or moments in the essay offer explicit evidence for these academic stances?

7. If you were to write a more academic version of "No Wonder They Call Me a Bitch," how would you revise this essay? What things would you change? In what other directions might you push the research? What might you leave the same?

8. In what ways does this essay fit your expectations of a research essay? In what ways does it not? What in your own experience has influenced those expectations and therefore how you read this essay?

9. Which reading strategies did you use for this piece? Review Chapter 2 for our suggestions about how to read: What was your purpose? Which inquiry strategies did you use? How did you mark up the essay? Why?

Why Did God Make Flies?

Richard Conniff

This essay opens with a scene many of us are familiar with, the writer gazing at a fly sitting on his beer glass, preening itself with its legs. And, as the title suggests, Conniff begins wondering about the purpose of flies. This research essay narrates what he discovers, but in a way that makes even the ordinary housefly a fascinating read. Conniff does more than answer the basic questions about how flies land upside down on ceilings, how they eat, and how they reproduce. He also tells the story of our hatred for flies, taking us back to periods where we sprayed towns with the insecticide DDT in order to kill them, only to end up poisoning ourselves. His ultimate answer to his question is that God created flies to punish human arrogance.

As you read, pay attention to the way Conniff presents his information: When does he use narrative? Why? When does he move into exposition? Why? How often does he use "I," and what effect does this have on your engagement with the essay? What does Conniff do as a writer to make what many of us would consider a rather disgusting creature fascinating?

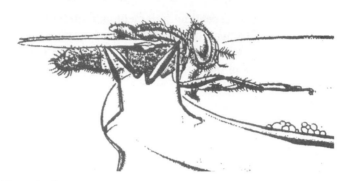

Fly on beaker.

Richard Conniff, who won the 1997 National Magazine Award for his writing in Smithsonian, *often writes about the world's more repulsive creatures. "Nature gives me the creeps," says Conniff, "and the more I learn the creepier and more wonderful it gets."*

Though I have been killing them for years now, I have never tested the notion, recorded in one collection of country sayings, that with a little cream and sugar, a fly "tastes very much like a black raspberry." So it's possible I'm speaking too hastily when I say there is nothing to like about flies. Unlike the poet who welcomed a "busy, curious fly" to his drinking cup, I don't cherish them for reminding me that life is short. Nor do I much admire them for their function in clearing away carrion and waste. It is, after all, possible to believe in the grand scheme of recycling without necessarily liking undertakers.

Among poets, I tend to side with Ogden Nash, who once wrote: "God in His wisdom / Made the fly / And then forgot / To tell us why."

A fly is standing on the rim of my beer glass as I write these words. Its vast, mosaic eyes look simultaneously lifeless and mocking. It grooms itself methodically, its forelegs twining together like the arms of a Sybarite luxuriating in bath oil. Its hind legs twitch across the upper surface of its wings. It pauses, well-fed and at rest, to contemplate the sweetness of life.

We are lucky enough to live in an era when scientists quantify such things, and so as I type and wait my turn to drink, I know that the fly is neither busy nor curious; the female spends 40.6 percent of her time doing nothing but contemplating the sweetness of life. I know that she not only eats unspeakable things, but that she spends an additional 29.7 percent of her time spitting them back up again and blowing bubbles with her vomit. The male is slightly less assiduous at this deplorable pastime, but one diligent researcher has reported that a well-fed fly may also defecate every four and a half minutes. Flies seldom trouble us as a health threat anymore, at least in the developed world, but they are capable of killing. And when we are dead (or sooner, in some cases), they dine on our corrupted flesh.

It is of course mainly this relentless intimacy with mankind that makes flies and particularly houseflies so contemptible. Leeches or dung beetles may appall us, but by and large they satisfy their depraved appetites out of our sight. Flies, on the other hand, routinely flit from diaper pail to dinner table, from carrion to picnic basket. They are constantly among us, tramping across our food with God knows what trapped in the sticky hairs of their half-dozen legs.

Twice in this century, Americans have waged war against flies, once in a futile nationwide "swat the fly" campaign, and again, disastrously, with DDT foggings after World War II. The intensity of these efforts, bordering at times on the fanatic, may bewilder modern readers. "Flies or Babies? Choose!" cried a headline in the *Ladies' Home Journal*, in 1920. But our bewilderment is not entirely due to greater tolerance or environmental enlightenment. If we have the leisure to examine the fly more rationally now, it is mainly because we don't suffer its onslaughts as our predecessors did. Urban living has separated us from livestock, and indoor plumbing has helped us control our own wastes, thus controlling flies. But if that changed tomorrow, we would come face-to-face with the enlightened, modern truth: With the possible exception of *Homo sapiens,* it is hard to imagine an animal as disgusting or improbable as the housefly. No bestiary concocted out of the nightmares of the medieval mind could have come up with such a fantastic animal. If we want to study nature in its most exotic permutations, the best place to begin is here, at home, on the rim of my beer glass.

In North America, more than a dozen fly species visit or live in the house. It is possible to distinguish among some of them only by such microscopic criteria as the pattern of veins in the wings, and so all of them end up being cursed as houseflies. Among the more prominent are the blue and the green bottleflies, with their iridescent abdomens, and the biting stable flies, which have served this country as patriots, or at least as provocateurs. On July 4, 1776, their biting encouraged decisiveness among delegates considering the Declaration of Independence: "Treason," Thomas Jefferson wrote, "was preferable to discomfort."

The true housefly, *Musca domestica,* of course does not bite. (You may think this is something to like about flies, until you find out what they do instead.) *M. domestica,* a drab fellow of salt-and-pepper complexion, is the world's most widely distributed insect species and probably also the most familiar, a status achieved through its pronounced fondness for breeding in pig, horse, or human excrement. In choosing at some point in the immemorial past to concentrate on the wastes around human habitations, *M. domestica* made a brilliant career move. The earliest known human representation of what appears to be a housefly is on a Mesopotamian cylinder seal from 3000 B.C.* But houseflies were probably with us even before we had houses, and they spread with human culture.

Like us, the housefly is prolific, opportunistic, and inclined toward exploration. It can adapt to either vegetable or meat diets, preferably somewhat ripe. It will lay its eggs not just in excrement, but in a rotting mass of lime peels, in bird nests, in carrion, or even in flesh wounds that have become infected and malodorous. Other flies aren't so flexible. For instance, *M. autumnalis,* a close relative, prefers cattle dung, and winds up sleeping in the pasture more than in houses or yards.

But while the housefly's adaptability and evolutionary generalization may be admirable, it raises one of the first great questions about flies: Why this dismaying appetite for abomination?

Houseflies not only defecate constantly, but do so in liquid form, which means they are in constant danger of dehydration. The male can slake his thirst and also get most of the energy he needs from nectar. But fresh manure is a good source of water, and it contains the dissolved protein the female needs to make eggs. She also lays her eggs in excrement or amid decay so that when they hatch, the maggots will have a smorgasbord of nutritious microorganisms on which to graze.

Houseflies bashing around the kitchen or the garbage shed thus have their sensors attuned to things that smell sweet, like flowers or bananas, and to foul-smelling stuff like ammonium carbonate, hydrogen sulfide, and trimethylamines, the products of fermentation and putrefaction. (Ecstasy for the fly is the stinkhorn fungus, a source of sugar that smells like rotting meat.) The fly's jerky, erratic flight amounts to a way of covering large territories in search of these scents, not just for food, but for romance and breeding sites. Like dung beetles and other flying insects, the fly will zigzag upwind when it gets a whiff of something good (or, as often happens, something bad) and follow the scent plume to its source.

Hence the second diabolical question about the housefly: How does it manage to fly so well? Why is it so adept at evading us when we swat it?

---

*Somewhat later, the ancient Romans used a poultice of mashed houseflies as a treatment for baldness. Flies are hairy, and the theory was that it might rub off on bald men.

How come it always seems to land on its feet, usually upside down on the ceiling, having induced us to plant a fist on the spot where it used to be, in the middle of the strawberry trifle, which is now spattered across table-cloth, walls, loved ones, and honored guests?

When we launch an ambush as the oblivious fly preens and pukes, its pressure sensors alert it to the speed and direction of the descending hand. Its wraparound eyes are also acutely sensitive to peripheral movement, and they register changes in light about ten times faster than we do. (A movie fools the gullible human eye into seeing continuous motion by showing it a sequence of twenty-four still pictures a second. To fool a fly would take more than two hundred frames a second.) The alarm flashes directly from the brain to the middle set of legs via the largest, and therefore the fastest, nerve fiber in the body. This causes so-called starter muscles to contract, simultaneously revving up the wing muscles and pressing down the middle legs, which catapult the fly into the air.

The fly's wings beat 165 to 200 times a second, and while this isn't all that fast for an insect, it's more than double the wingbeat of the fastest hummingbird, and about 20 times faster than any repetitious movement the human nervous system can manage. The trick brought off by house-flies and many other insects is to remove the wingbeat from direct nerv-ous system control, once it's switched on. Instead, two systems of mus-cles, for upstroke and downstroke, are attached to the hull of the fly's midsection, and trigger each other to work in alternation. When one set contracts, it deforms the hull, stretching the other set of muscles and mak-ing them contract automatically a fraction of a second later. To keep this seesaw rhythm going, openings in the midsection stoke the muscles with oxygen directly from the outside (the fly has no lungs). Its blood (which lacks hemoglobin and is therefore colorless) meanwhile pumps fuel for the cells to burn at a rate 14 times faster than when the fly is at rest. Flies can turn a sugar meal into usable energy so fast that an exhausted fly will resume flight almost instantly after eating. In humans . . . but you don't want to know how ploddingly inadequate humans are by comparison.

Once airborne, the fly's antennae, between its eyes, help regulate flight, vibrating in response to airflow. The fly also uses a set of stubby wings in back, called halteres, as a gyroscopic device. Flies are skillful at veering and dodging; it sometimes seems that they are doing barrel rolls and Immelmann turns to amuse themselves while we flail and curse. But one thing they cannot do is fly upside down to land on a ceiling. This phe-nomenon puzzled generations of upward-glaring, strawberry-trifle-drenched human beings, until high-speed photography supplied the expla-nation. The fly approaches the ceiling rightside up, at a steep angle. Just before impact, it reaches up with its front limbs, in the manner of Super-man exiting a telephone booth for takeoff. As these forelegs get a grip with claws and with the sticky, glandular hairs of the footpads, the fly swings its other legs up into position. Then it shuts down its flight motor, out of swatting range and at ease.

While landing on the ceiling must be great fun, humans tend to be more interested in what flies do when they land on food, and so I trapped the fly on the rim of my beer glass. (Actually, I waited till it found a less coveted perch, then slowly lowered a mayonnaise jar over it.) I'd been reading a book called *To Know a Fly* by Vincent Dethier, in which he describes a simple way of seeing how the fly's proboscis works. First, I refrigerated the fly to slow it down and anesthetize it. Then I attempted to attach a thin stick to its wing surface with the help of hot wax. It got away. I brought it back and tried again. My son Jamie, who was then four years old, winced and turned aside when I applied the wax. "I'm glad I'm not a fly," he said, "or you might do that to me." I regarded him balefully but refrained from mentioning the ant colony he had annihilated on our front walk.

Having finally secured the fly, I lowered its feet into a saucer of water. Flies have taste buds in their feet, and when they walk into something good (bad), the proboscis, which is normally folded up neatly inside the head, automatically flicks down. No response. I added sugar to the water, an irresistible combination. Nothing. More sugar. Still nothing. My son wandered off, bored. I apologized to the fly, killed it, and decided to look up the man who had put me in the awkward position of sympathizing with a fly, incidentally classing me in my son's eyes as a potential war criminal.

Dethier, a biologist at the University of Massachusetts, turned out to be a gentle, deferential fellow in his mid-seventies, with weathered, finely wrinkled skin and a pair of gold-rimmed oval eyeglasses on a beak nose. He suggested mildly that my fly might not have responded because it was outraged at the treatment it received. It may also have eaten recently, or it may have been groggy from hibernation. (Some flies sit out the winter in diapause, in which hormones induce inactivity in response to shortened day length. But cold, not day length, is what slows down hibernating species like the housefly, and the sudden return of warmth can start them up again. This is why a fly may miraculously take wing on a warm December afternoon in the space between my closed office window and the closed storm window outside, a phenomenon I had formerly regarded as new evidence for spontaneous generation.) Dethier has spent a lifetime studying the fly's sense of taste, "finding out where their tongues and noses are, as it were." He explained the workings of the proboscis for me.

Fly taste buds are vastly more sensitive than ours, another reason to dislike them. Dethier figured this out by taking saucers of water containing steadily decreasing concentrations of sugar. He found the smallest concentration a human tongue could taste. Then he found the smallest concentration that caused a hungry fly to flick out its proboscis. The fly, with fifteen hundred taste hairs arrayed on its feet and in and around its mouth, was ten million times more sensitive.

When the fly hits paydirt, the proboscis telescopes downward and the fleshy lobes at the tip puff out. These lips can press down tight to feed on a thin film of liquid, or they can cup themselves around a droplet. They are grooved crosswise with a series of parallel gutters, and when the fly starts pumping, the liquid gets drawn up through these gutters. The narrow zigzag openings of the gutters filter the food, so that even when it dines on excrement, the fly can "choose" some microorganisms and reject others. A drop of vomit may help dissolve the food, making it easier to lap up. Scientists have also suggested that the fly's prodigious vomiting may be a way of mixing enzymes with the food to aid digestion.

If necessary, the fly can peel its lips back out of the way and apply its mouth directly to the object of its desire. While it does not have true teeth, the mouth of the housefly is lined with a jagged, bladelike edge, which is useful for scraping. In his book *Flies and Disease,* Bernard Greenberg, a forensic entomologist at the University of Illinois in Chicago, writes that some blowflies (like the one on the rim of my beer glass, which turned out to be an olive green blowfly, *Phormia regina*) "can bring one hundred fifty teeth into action, a rather effective scarifier for the superficial inoculation of the skin, conjunctiva, or mucous membranes."

Hence the final great question about flies: What awful things are they inoculating us with when they flit across our food or land on our sleeping lips to drink our saliva? Over the years, authorities have suspected flies of spreading more than sixty diseases, from diarrhea to plague and leprosy. As recently as 1951, the leading expert on flies repeated without demurring the idea that the fly was "the most dangerous insect known," a remarkable assertion in a world that also includes mosquitoes. One entomologist tried to have the housefly renamed the "typhoid fly."

The hysteria against flies early in this century arose, with considerable help from scientists and the press, out of the combined ideas that germs cause disease and that flies carry germs. In the Spanish-American War, easily ten times as many soldiers died of disease, mostly typhoid fever, as died in battle. Flies were widely blamed, especially after a doctor observed particles of lime picked up in the latrines still clinging to the legs of flies crawling over army food. Flies were not "dipterous angels," but "winged sponges speeding hither and thither to carry out the foul behests of Contagion." North American schools started organizing "junior sanitary police" to point the finger at fly-breeding sites. Cities sponsored highly publicized "swat the fly" campaigns. In Toronto in 1912, a girl named Beatrice White killed 543,360 flies, altogether weighing 212.25 pounds, and won a $50 first prize. This is a mess of flies, 108.7 swatted for every penny in prize money, testimony to the slowness of summers then and to the remarkable agility of children—or perhaps to the overzealous imagination of contest sponsors. The figure does not include the 2.8 million dead flies submitted by losing entrants. (The "swat the fly" spirit still lives in China. In 1992, Beijing issued 200,000 flyswatters and launched a major sanitation campaign under the slogan, "Mobilize the Masses to Build a City of No Flies.")

But it took the pesticide DDT, developed in World War II and touted afterward as "the killer of killers," to raise the glorious prospect of "a fly-less millennium." The fly had by then been enshrined in the common lore as a diabolical killer. In one of the "archy and mehitabel" poems by Don Marquis, a fly visits garbage cans and sewers to "gather up the germs of typhoid influenza and pneumonia on my feet and wings" and spread them to humanity, declaring "it is my mission to help rid the world of these wicked persons / i am a vessel of righteousness."

Public health officials were deadly serious about conquering this arch-fiend, and for them DDT was "a veritable godsend." They recommended that parents use wallpaper impregnated with DDT in nurseries and play-rooms to protect children. Cities suffering polio epidemics frequently used airplanes to fog vast areas "in the belief that the fly factor in the spread of infantile paralysis might thus be largely eliminated." Use of DDT actually provided some damning evidence against flies, though not in connection with polio. Hidalgo County in Texas, on the Mexican border, divided its towns into two groups, and sprayed one with DDT to eliminate flies. The number of children suffering and dying from acute diarrheal infection caused by *Shigella* bacteria declined in the sprayed areas but remained the same in the unsprayed areas. When DDT spraying was stopped in the first group and switched to the second, the dysentery rates began to reverse. Then the flies developed resistance to DDT, a small hitch in the godsend. In state parks and vacation spots, where DDT had provided relief from the fly nuisance, people began to notice that songbirds were also disappearing.

In the end, the damning evidence was that we were contaminating our water, ourselves, and our affiliated population of flies with our own filth (not to mention DDT). Given access to human waste through inadequate plumbing or sewage treatment, flies can indeed pick up an astonishing va-riety of pathogens. They can also reproduce at a god-awful rate; in one study, 4,042 flies hatched from a scant shovelful, one-sixth of a cubic foot, of buried night soil. But whether all those winged sponges can trans-mit the contaminants they pick up turns out to be a tricky question, the Hi-dalgo County study being one of the few clear-cut exceptions. Of polio, for instance, Bernard Greenberg writes, "there is ample evidence that hu-man populations readily infect flies. . . . But we are woefully ignorant whether and to what extent flies return the favor."

Flies thus probably are not, as one writer declared in the throes of the hysteria, "monstrous" beings "armed with horrid mandibles . . . and dripping poison." A fly's bristling unlovely body is not, after all, a playground for microbes. Indeed, bacterial populations on the fly's exterior tend to decline quickly under the triple threat of compulsive cleaning, desiccation, and ultraviolet radiation. (Maggots actually produce a substance in their gut that kills off whole populations of bacteria, which is one reason doctors have sometimes used them to clean out infected wounds.) The fly's "microbial cargo," to use Greenberg's phrase, tends to reflect human uncleanliness. In one study, flies from a city neighborhood with poor facilities carried up to 500 million bacteria, while flies from a prim little suburb not far away yielded a maximum count of only 100,000.

But wait. While I am perfectly happy to suggest that humans are viler than we like to think, and flies less so, I do not mean to rehabilitate the fly. Any animal that kisses offal one minute and dinner the next is at the very least a social abomination. What I am coming around to is St. Augustine's idea that God created flies to punish human arrogance, and not just the calamitous technological arrogance of DDT. Flies are, as one biologist has remarked, the resurrection and the reincarnation of our own dirt, and this is surely one reason we smite them down with such ferocity. They mock our notions of personal grooming with visions of lime particles, night soil, and dog leavings. They toy with our delusions of immortality, buzzing in the ear as a memento mori. (Dr. Greenberg assures me that fly maggots can strip a human corpse roughly halfway to the bone in several weeks, if the weather is fine. Then they hand the job over to other insects.) Flies are our fate, and one way or another they will have us.

It is a pretty crummy joke on God's part, of course, but there's no point in getting pouty about it and slipping into unhealthy thoughts about nature. What I intend to do, by way of evening the score, is hang a strip of flypaper and also cultivate the local frogs and snakes, which have a voracious appetite for flies (flycatchers don't, by the way; they prefer wasps and bees). Perhaps I will get the cat interested, as a sporting proposition. Meanwhile I plan to get a fresh beer and sit back with my feet up and a tightly rolled newspaper nearby. Such are the consolations of the ecological frame of mind.

Personal Investigations: Inquiry Projects

1. Richard Conniff has made something of a specialty of writing about things that normally turn people off. His book, *Spineless Wonders,* takes up the cause of small invertebrates of all sorts, and "Why Did God Make Flies?" comes from that collection. As a research project, look

around your world and find something that is either little appreciated, or perhaps downright despised. Title the draft "Why Did God Make _____?" and then go on to discover some redeeming or impressive quality of your poorly regarded subject. For example, "Why Did God Make Garden Slugs?"

2. Conniff's essay begins with an everyday scene, a fly on the edge of a glass preening itself. Ordinarily we wouldn't pay much attention to that fly because it's so common, and yet that is part of what makes this essay so interesting. Make a list in your journal of other everyday things that are usually unnoticed, such as drivers who don't use turn signals, flowers that wilt once they are cut, or the ritual of setting the table a certain way. Then choose one of the items on your list to research and develop an essay around what you discover.

Craft and Conventions: Explaining and Evaluating

3. Reread the first few paragraphs of the essay until you've reached what seems to be the end of the lead. In other words, which paragraphs set up what the essay will be about—the central questions it will pursue, the writer's tone of voice and angle on the subject, the expectations that will be fulfilled for the reader? How can you tell when the essay shifts from this introductory section to the main body? In small groups, discuss what you've found and then present to the class the specific ways the lead sets up the essay.

4. One way that research writers register their presence in their writing, even work that includes the voices and ideas of others, is to find their own way of saying things. Conniff is a master at this. Find a passage in "Why Did God Make Flies?" that stands out in this respect.

5. Conniff uses comparisons and analogies throughout this essay as he presents the research he's found. Choose a paragraph where he uses analogies and comparisons and underline all the places you find them. Then, fastwrite in your journal (or discuss in small groups) what difference, if any, those comparisons make in the effectiveness of the essay and/or its overall purpose and theme.

6. Like the other essays in this chapter, Conniff does not use citations to indicate where his information comes from. Read the essay a second time with an eye to discovering the kinds of sources he used. Although you probably won't be able to identify the titles of many of the books or articles he consulted, you can probably tell whether the information is from observation, interview, common knowledge, published research studies, or other print sources. How varied are Conniff's sources? How persuasive are they and why?

Inquiries on Inquiry: Exploring and Reflecting

7. Describe your experience reading this essay. What engaged you and made you want to keep reading? What did you struggle with? At what point, if any, were you tempted to stop reading and why? What reading strategies did you find yourself using as you read?

8. Which of the five habits of mind of intellectual inquiry are most evident in this essay: suspending judgment, tolerating ambiguity, asking questions, dialectical thinking, and taking responsibility for one's ideas?

9. What have you learned about writing a research essay from reading Conniff's piece? What might you do in your own writing that Conniff does in his?

10. In your journal, fastwrite about your initial response to this essay. What interested you the most? The least? What stood out to you? What questions did it raise? Explore how your response to the essay changed as you read it.

11. Summarize your personal response to this essay in a sentence or two. Then, skip a line and fastwrite about why you feel this way. What in your background and/or experiences influence how you respond to this essay? Think not just about your literal experiences with flies, but also about Conniff's thesis that God created flies to punish human arrogance—or anything else in the essay that got your attention for some reason.

Yarn

Kyoko Mori

Like Richard Conniff's essay on flies, Kyoko Mori's essay on yarn turns a seemingly boring subject into a fascinating story about the literal and metaphoric meanings of knitting and what it tells us about ourselves. Originally published in The Harvard Review *in 2003, this essay was selected for* The Best American Essays 2004, *which is an honor for an essayist. As you read we hope you'll see why it was considered such an excellent piece. In it Mori weaves together several scenes of her own knitting experiences with historical information you'll find surprising. Did you know that sweaters were not worn as a common piece of clothing until the nineteenth century? Or that brides in Latvia used to knit more than 200 pairs of mittens before they got married? While many of us have read about the recent resurgence of knitting, from celebrities to college students to a growing number of men, we probably don't know what makes it so appealing or what its history can tell us about knitting now.*

Mori skillfully gives us this information using a collage or segmented essay structure, and you'll notice several threads woven through those segments. Mittens, in particular, change meanings as the essay progresses. What do you notice about how each segment is crafted as an independent unit? How does Mori connect her own experience with knitting over the years to the historical and cultural information she uncovers? In what ways does she make the subject of yarn interesting?

1

THE YELLOW MITTENS I made in seventh-grade home economics proved that I dreamed in color. For the unit on knitting, we were supposed to turn in a pair of mittens. The two hands had to be precisely the same size so that when we held them together, palm to palm, no extra stitches would stick out from the thumb, the tips of the fingers, or the cuff. Somewhere between making the fourth and the fifth mitten to fulfill this requirement, I dreamed that the ball of yellow yarn in my bag had turned green. Chartreuse, leaf, Granny Smith, lime, neon, acid green. The brightness was electric. I woke up knowing that I was, once again, doomed for a D in home ec.

I don't remember what possessed me to choose yellow yarn for that assignment. Yellow was a color I never liked; perhaps I was conceding defeat before I started. Mittens, as it turns out, are just about the worst project possible for a beginner. Each hand has to be knitted as a very small tube, with the stitches divided among four pointed needles that twist and slip unless you are holding them with practiced confidence. The pair won't be the same size if you drop or pick up extra stitches along the way, skip a couple of decreases in shaping the top, or knit too tightly in your nervousness and then let up in relief as you approach the end. You might inadvertently make two right mittens or two lefts because you forgot that the thumb has to be started in a different position for each hand. I ended up with two right hands of roughly the same size and three left hands that could have been illustrations for a fairy tale. *Once upon a time there lived three brothers, each with only one hand—large, medium, and very small—and, even though the villagers laughed at them and called them unkind names, the brothers could do anything when they put their three left hands together. . . .*

I didn't knit again until graduate school when I met a woman from Germany with a closetful of beautiful sweaters. Sabina came to our seminar wearing a soft angora cardigan one week, a sturdy fisherman's pullover the next.

"I make all my sweaters," she said. "I can teach you."

I told her about my mitten fiasco.

"Knitting is easy," Sabina insisted. "A sweater's bigger than a mitten but much simpler."

"The patterns will confuse me."

"You don't need patterns. You can make things up as you go."

Sabina took me to a local yarn store, where I bought skeins of red cotton yarn. Following her instructions, I first knit the body of the sweater: two flat pieces, front and back, with a few simple decreases to shape the shoulders and the neck. The pieces were surprisingly easy to sew together. Sabina showed me how to pick up the stitches along the arm opening, connect the new yarn, and knit the sleeves, going from the shoulder to the wrist. I finished the sweater in a month. The result was slightly lop-sided—one sleeve was half an inch wider than the other around the elbow—but the arms looked more or less even once I put the sweater on. The small mistakes in a knitted garment disappear when the garment is on the body, where it belongs. That might have been the most important thing I learned from my first sweater.

In the twenty years since then, I've made sweaters, vests, hats, bed-spreads, lap blankets, shawls, scarves, socks, and mittens. Like most people who knit, I have bags of yarn stashed in my closet for future projects. The bags are a record of the cities where I've wandered into yarn stores: Madison, Portland, Cambridge, New Orleans, Evanston, Washington, D.C. Like hair salons, yarn stores have slightly witty names: Woolgathering, Woolworks, Woolcotts, the Knitting Tree, the Quarter Stitch (New Orleans), Fiber Space. Inside each store, the walls are lined with plastic crates bursting with color. My friend Yenkuei took up knitting because she fell in love with the fuchsia sleeveless sweater in the window of Woolcotts in Harvard Square, floating, she thought, and beckoning to her. Another friend, who doesn't knit, comes along just to touch. She goes from shelf to shelf fingering the rayon chenilles, angoras, alpacas, and silk-cotton blends while I'm trying to figure out how much yarn I need. When I was five, in kindergarten, I was horrified to see other kids stick their fingers in the library paste, scoop up the pale glop, and put it in their mouths, but I tried to eat the raspberry-colored crayon on my teacher's desk because it looked so delicious. Knitting is about that same hunger for color. I never again picked up yellow yarn.

2

Knitting is a young craft. The oldest surviving examples—blue and white cotton socks and fabric fragments discovered in an Egyptian tomb—are dated around A.D. 1200. Knitting probably originated in Egypt or another Arabic country around that time and reached Europe through Spain. Two knitted cushions, found in the tomb of a thirteenth-century Castilian prince and princess, are the oldest known European artifacts of knitting. Once it reached Europe, the craft spread quickly. By the fourteenth century, Italian and German artists were painting the Virgin Mary knitting in a domestic setting.

Most of the early knitting in Europe was for socks and stockings. Elizabeth I preferred the knitted silk stockings from France to the woven-and-sewn foot coverings made in England. Mary, Queen of Scots, wore two pairs of French stockings—one plain white and the other patterned with gold stitches—on the day of her execution; the stockings were held up with green garters. By the end of the sixteenth century, cheap metal needles became widely available, enabling the rural families throughout England to knit socks and stockings during the winter months to supplement their income.

In the cities, guilds controlled the licensing of knitting workshops. An apprentice would spend three years working under one master and three more traveling as a "journeyman," to learn new techniques from various masters, before he could submit samples of his work for the guild's approval. In Vienna at the beginning of the seventeenth century, the samples had to include a six-colored tablecloth, a beret, a pair of silk stockings, and a pair of gloves.

Sweaters are not on this list because in Vienna at that time, as in most of Europe, upper-body garments such as shirts, tunics, vests, and jackets were cut and sewn from woven fabrics only. The first knitted upper-body garments were made in the fifteenth century, in the Channel Islands of Guernsey and Jersey, where fishermen and sailors needed thick tunics made of wool to repel water and protect against the cold. Although these garments spread slowly across the rest of Europe among laborers, they did not become popular as "sweaters" until the 1890s when American athletes wore heavy, dark blue pullovers before and after contests to ward off the chills.

Knitting is an activity that can be performed anywhere, while weaving requires a loom, a complicated piece of equipment that takes up space and is difficult to move. Still, the earliest proof of woven cloth predates knitting by more than eight thousand years. Clay balls found in Iraq and dated around 7000 B.C. have clear impressions of woven textiles on them. Numerous images of weavers are preserved on papyruses and tomb paintings from ancient Egypt. In the *Odyssey,* Penelope weaves and unweaves a funeral cloth to ward off the suitors; in Greek mythology, Aracne is turned into a spider when she challenges Athena to a weaving contest and loses. The knitting Madonnas of the fourteenth century represent some of the earliest depictions of women knitting, and no Greek hero's wife or foolish mortal ever won praise or punishment for this simple activity.

3

As with people, so with garments: the strengths and the weaknesses are often one and the same. A knitted garment, whose loose construction traps air next to the body, is warmer but more fragile than a woven one, and the stretching property of yarn makes knitting a less precise but more forgiving craft than sewing. On a knitted fabric, one broken loop can release all the loops, causing the fabric to "run." This same quality allows a knitter to unravel the yarn on purpose, undo a few inches of work, and correct a mistake she has discovered. Even after the garment is finished, a knitter can snip one of the stitches, carefully unravel one round of knitting, put the loops back on a needle, and redo the bottom of the sweater or the sleeve to make it smaller, larger, or a different shape. Sewing doesn't allow the same flexibility.

My first home ec sewing project was no better than the mittens: an Oxford shirt with cuffs, buttonholes, darts along the bust line, and square collars; a pleated skirt with a zipper closure. I'm sure there are much easier things to sew. Still, in sewing, you can't get away from cutting, assembling, and fitting. If you cut the pieces wrong, you'll have to buy more cloth and lay out the pattern again. If the finished shirt is half an inch too small, it's not going to stretch the way a sweater will.

Even the words "thread" (the stringlike material we sew with) and "yarn" (the stringlike material we knit with) convey different degrees of flexibility. Thread holds together and restricts, while yarn stretches and gives. Thread is the overall theme that gives meaning to our words and thoughts—to lose the thread is to be incoherent or inattentive. A yarn is a long, pointless, but usually amusing story whose facts have been exaggerated. It is infinitely more relaxing to listen to a yarn than to a lecture whose thread we must follow.

In my first ten years of knitting, I took full advantage of the forgiving quality of yarn and made hats and scarves from patterns that had only five- to ten-sentence directions. For sweaters, I made three tubes (one big tube for the body, two smaller tubes for the sleeves) and then knitted them together at the yoke and shoulders so I didn't have to sew the pieces together at the end. If, halfway through the body or the sleeve, I noticed the piece getting wider faster than I'd expected, I simply stopped increasing stitches; if the piece looked too small, I increased more. It was just as Sabina had told me: I could make things up as I went along.

My favorite project was a hat from a pattern I found in a yarn store on a visit to Portland, Oregon. I bought the thick mohair yarn and extra needles so I could start knitting the first one in my hotel room. The hat, which I finished on the flight home the next day, looked more like a lampshade; the brim came down to my shoulders. At home, I threw this enormous hat in the washer, set it on hot wash and cold rinse, and ran the cycle twice. Just as the pattern promised, the hat came out shrunk and "felted": the stitches had contracted till they were invisible, leaving a dense, fuzzy nap. I reshaped the hat on a mixing bowl about the size of my head, and by the time it dried, it looked like a professionally made bowler.

The washing-machine hat became a staple of my gift-giving. A few years later, I visited an antiques mall with a couple who had fallen in love with an oak dresser they thought was too expensive. Every weekend for two months, they brought a different friend to look at the dresser, to ooh and aah over it, and help them work up the nerve to spend the money. The antiques mall was a huge place out in the country, and we had to walk what felt like three city blocks crammed with furniture and knickknacks. When we finally got to the right section, I failed my friends completely by not noticing the dresser because to the right of it, on a small table, was a wooden hat form. To an untrained eye, the hat form looks like a wooden head, but I knew what it was. Tired of reshaping hats over a bowl, I had been trying to order one (except all the modern hat forms were made of Styrofoam and I didn't think I could stand the squeaky noise they would make). I grabbed the wooden head and walked around with it tightly clutched under my arm while my friends showed me all the other oak dressers, every one of them inferior to the one they wanted. At the counter, I paid $12 for my find.

This fall, I brought the wooden head with me to Wisconsin because I still make those hats for gifts. But in the past five years, I've graduated to more complicated patterns. I had gotten tired of the rugged look of the make-it-as-you-go kind of sweater, but more than that, my reasons for knitting have changed. In my twenties and thirties, I wanted everything I did to express what I considered my essential nature: casual, relaxed, and intuitively creative, rather than formal, precise, and meticulous. That's why I chose knitting over sewing, running and cycling over tennis or golf. Now, in my mid-forties, I look instead for balance. If following step-by-step instructions doesn't come naturally to me, that is all the more reason for me to try it. I would rather knit from a complicated pattern and make a few mistakes than execute an easier one flawlessly.

The folklore among knitters is that everything handmade should have at least one mistake so an evil spirit will not become trapped in the maze of perfect stitches. A missed increase or decrease, a crooked seam, a place where the tension is uneven—the mistake is a crack left open to let in the light. The evil spirit I want to usher out of my knitting and my life is at once a spirit of laziness and of overachieving. It's that little voice in my head that says, I won't even try this because it doesn't come naturally to me and I won't be very good at it.

4

A friend of mine fell in love with a young man at college because he was knitting a sweater between classes the first time she saw him. She concluded that he must be an extraordinarily sensitive and creative man, though eventually she found out he was neither. This man, whom I never met, is the only contemporary male knitter I know of, besides Kaffe Fasset, the British sweater designer.

Knitting wasn't always a feminine craft. The knitting masters and apprentices of the medieval guilds were all men, since women were not admitted into guilds. Before the Industrial Revolution, both men and women, of all ages, knitted socks in the countryside. The fishermen and the sailors from the English Channel Islands made their own sweaters during their long sea voyages. In the late nineteenth century, the Japanese samurai whose clans were faltering tried to supplement their income by knitting *tabi,* split-toed Japanese socks (essentially, mittens for feet). Even so, knitting—like sewing, spinning, weaving, and embroidery—has been historically associated with women's household skills and marriageability. One of the most remarkable examples involves the mitten.

In Latvia, until the early twentieth century, every girl learned to knit by the age of six so she could get an early start on her dowry chest. A full dowry chest would decrease the number of cattle her family would have to pay the groom's family when it came time for her to marry. The main contents of the dowry chest were mittens with multicolored, geometrical designs. On the day of the wedding, these mittens were distributed to all the participants from the carriage driver to the minister, as well as to the numerous relatives, in-laws, and neighbors. At the feast after the ceremony, the bride and the groom ate with mittened hands to invite good luck. At the end of the day, the bride walked around the inside and outside of her new home, laying mittens (to be collected later by her mother-in-law) on all the important locations: the hearth, the doors, the windows, the cow barn, the sheep shed, the beehives, and the garden. To properly complete these marriage rites, a bride needed one to two hundred pairs of mittens. The mittens were treasured as heirlooms, and the complicated knitting patterns were meant to show off a young woman's patience—her ability to perform meticulous and repetitive work—as well as her skill.

When my Japanese home ec teacher decided to teach us how to knit mittens, the assignment was, in a sense, grimly appropriate, since the not-so-hidden purpose of home ec was also to give us skills that showed off our patience and meticulousness. After the semester of knitting and sewing, we were required to take several semesters of cooking, in which we made elaborate casseroles and soufflés and desserts, food to impress people, food for parties, not the kind of food I would cook for myself when I moved out to live on my own.

In most schools in the United States and Japan now, home ec is an elective, open to both girls and boys. Young women in Latvia no longer make two hundred pairs of mittens in order to get married. Of course I'm happy for these changes, though a part of me worries whether anyone will preserve these centuries-old crafts. I have not met one man who has ever knitted, sewn, or embroidered clothes for his partner or children—or a woman knitter, quilter, garment maker, or embroiderer who has not made something for the men and the children among her family and friends. I don't know what to do with the weight of history and the way it affects our daily lives.

At least on a purely personal level, I've reconciled myself to the mitten. Last year in Cambridge, I tackled the ultimate mitten. The pattern, marked for "experienced knitters," called them "flip-flop mittens" because the top half could be made to flip back like a hinged lid, exposing the fingers in a fingerless glove. I thought of them as cat mittens: at the necessary moment, the sheath pulled back and out came the claws. It was a slow and complicated project. To achieve the gauge for the pattern, I had to use number zero needles, which were thinner than satay sticks. The fuzzy mohair yarn made the stitches difficult to see, and each finger had to be knitted separately. It took me two months to make myself a pair. Then I started another pair for my friend Junko, whose hands are smaller than the smallest measurement in the directions. I was proud of having managed to follow the directions and, at the same time, make a few adjustments on my own, until I finished the second mitten and realized that—only on that hand—I had made the top flip forward instead of back. After thirty years, I was back where I'd started: I had been blown back into the mitten purgatory of mismatched hands.

The next morning, I sat down and thought of the various tricks I'd learned. I looked at knitting books, went over the notes I'd made in the margins of some patterns. Finally I figured out how to unravel just a few rows of stitches and detach the flip at the front make a new edging for it, and graft the stitches to the back of the hand so that the flip now faced the right way. The procedure left a small scar, hardly noticeable in the fuzzy mohair. When I gave the mittens to Junko, I showed her my mistake. Across the back of her left hand stretched a faint broken line, like a rural road on a map of the desert, a path across unknown terrain.

Personal Investigations: Inquiry Projects

1. Mori mentions the renewed interest in knitting in the last few years, but she doesn't explore why it has happened or what it means. Given what you've learned from Mori's essay, speculate on why more people are

knitting now than even fifteen years ago. Fastwrite in your journal for seven minutes about possible reasons for this resurgence. Then research this question and compose an essay based on what you've found.

2. In your journal, make a list of the hobbies, crafts, and other artistic activities you or a family member or friend do on a regular basis. Once you've made a list, circle the two items that are the most important to you or your family member or friend.

   - Fastwrite about why they are important.
   - Then compose at least two significant scenes of you or your family member or friend doing this activity.
   - Next, in writing explain to an audience who knows little about this activity what it is, how it is done, what materials are used, how other people might perceive it, and why it is so enjoyable or important to those who choose it.
   - Then, make a list of all the questions you have about the activity.
   - Last, reflect on the writing you've done and consider developing a research essay on this activity.

Craft and Conventions: Explaining and Evaluating

3. In your journal, briefly summarize each section of the essay (each section is numbered). What does each focus on? What purpose does it seem to serve in the essay? How does it relate (or not) to the segments around it? What "threads" hold the segments together?

4. Compare this essay to Richard Conniff's essay, "Why Did God Make Flies?" Given the qualities of the research essay described in the introduction to this chapter, what do these two essays have in common? In what ways are they different? Answer this question in terms of how the essays are organized, how each writer uses research, how the writer establishes his/her presence in the essay and stance toward the subject, and how the essays demonstrate inquiry.

5. The author's experience knitting mittens opens and closes this essay. Why? What do we understand about mittens at the end of the essay that we didn't when we read the first page? What realization has the author come to?

6. If you had to choose one or two paragraphs that are the most central to this essay—that capture the essay's overall purpose and point—what would they be? Why?

7. What do you find most convincing about this essay? Why?

8. Given the associations you had with knitting before you read this essay, how has this essay reinforced or changed those beliefs? What effect, if any, has this essay had on how you perceive knitting?

Inquiries on Inquiry: Exploring and Reflecting

9. Segmented essays can be more challenging to read than more traditionally organized essays such as "My Secret History" or "Let Them Eat Fat," which appear later in this chapter. Describe your reading experience with this essay. What was challenging for you and why? What was easiest and why? What reading strategies (see Chapter 2) did you have to use?

10. Which habits of mind of academic inquiry does Mori demonstrate in this essay? Use specific passages in your answer.

11. In your journal or notebook, use this seed sentence to start a five-minute fastwrite: *When I started reading this essay, I thought/felt . . . and then . . . and then . . .*

12. What in your own experience affected how you read this essay? What experiences have you had with knitting or other domestic arts? What role, if any, have they played in your family history? What associations do you have with them and why?

13. If you've had little experience with knitting, you might feel like an outsider to this essay. What other ways did you find to relate to this essay? What did it remind you of or make you think differently about? Why?

Did NASA Fake the Moon Landing?

Ray Villard

Published in July 2004, this article reviews the claims made by those who believe NASA never went to the moon but instead created an elaborate hoax and filmed the landing on a movie set. Why would a reputable magazine such as Astronomy *draw attention to theories that only 5 percent of the population believes, let alone a series of claims most people would find laughable? Maybe in part because FOX-TV showed a documentary on these conspiracy theories in 2003 and millions of people watched it. Twice. Clearly the images of* Apollo *landing on the moon, for many people, do not prove the event occurred, suggest-*

ing how limited such visual evidence can be, no matter how "true" it may be.

If you aren't familiar with the conspiracy theories about a moon-landing hoax, don't worry. Ray Villard writes this article in such a way that we learn what this group believes as the piece progresses. Instead of using a narrative to organize his essay, Villard borrows from a classical form of argument where the writer examines and refutes one claim at a time. There's no mistaking Ray Villard's attitude toward these theories, even though he rarely uses "I." And yet, although he seems to find them literally unbelievable, he still researches their claims seriously and analyzes their arguments. As you read, consider the evidence he uses to disprove the claims. What kind of research did he need to do in order to write this article? What makes Villard's argument more or less persuasive than those of the conspiracy theorists?

To quash any lingering doubts as to whether or not we went to the Moon, Astronomy is setting the record straight, once and for all.

The seven Project Apollo manned expeditions to the Moon will long be remembered as expressions of America's pioneering spirit and sheer technological prowess. That is, if the landings really happened.

For the past several decades, a small group of NASA-watching sleuths has repeatedly tried to pawn off the incredulous idea that the Apollo Moon program really was an elaborate, $30 billion hoax filmed in a movie studio. This group believes the United States needed to cement its world leadership during the Cold War by pretending to pull off what really was a technologically impossible stunt. Moon hoax proponents think they've come up with suspicious evidence that scientists, investigative reporters, and everyone else on Earth apparently has overlooked for more than thirty years. The far-out idea drew 15 million viewers when FOX-TV twice ran a documentary on this subject in 2003.

Seeds of doubt

In the October 30, 1938, theatrical radio adaptation of H. G. Wells's *War of the Worlds,* actor Orson Welles managed inadvertently to convince 1.2 million Americans that martians were invading Earth. So, for conspiracy theorists, it's easy to imagine that with $30 billion and the awesome power of the United States government, the world could be made to believe almost anything. If Hollywood can fake perfectly believable dinosaurs, space aliens, and fantasy planets, why not a visit to the Moon?

A former aerospace technical writer, Bill Kaysing kicked off the Moon conspiracy idea in 1975 in a self-published book with the blunt title *We Never Went to the Moon.* Several copycats have followed him— *Moongate: Suppressed Findings of the U.S. Space Program* by William L.

Is this the moon or Nevada? The facts clearly show the manned landings on the
Moon could not have been faked. Here, lunar module pilot Buzz Aldrin walks on the
surface of the Moon near the leg of the lunar module Eagle during the Apollo 11
extravehicular activity. Astronaut Neil Armstrong, commander, took this photograph
with a 70mm lunar-surface camera.

Brian [1984], Ralph Rene's *NASA Mooned America* [1994], and *Dark
Moon-Apollo And the Whistle Blowers* by Mary Bennet and others [1999].

But don't expect to find these books on The New York Times best-
seller list. According to a 1999 Gallup poll, an inconsequential 5 percent
of the population in the United States actually believes we never went to
the Moon. (Coincidentally, this is the same percentage of the population
estimated to be intoxicated at any given time.) However, 42 percent of the
American population believes the government routinely hides information from us. This generalized suspicion keeps the Moon hoax idea pop-
ping up like a zombie in some cult-classic horror film: You blow its
brains out, but the monster just keeps lumbering along.

Fuzzy logic

It doesn't help Moon conspiracy theorists that not one person from the Apollo era's 35,000 NASA employees or 200,000 contractors has ever stepped forward with "whistle-blowing" insider testimony or "smoking-gun" memos about a staged event. Conspiracy theorists also need to explain how the Hollywood special-effects wizards who presumably pulled off Academy-Award-winning moonwalk scenes have managed to remain stone silent for decades (despite the fact it would look great on their resumes!). This lack of proof forces conspiracy theorists to counter that the government scared and murdered potential tattletales, including its own astronaut-heroes in a reprehensible assertion that the tragic 1967 Apollo 1 fire was rigged. A casual browse through Moon conspiracy Internet sites is a mind-numbing journey into the dark side of common sense. The conspiracy theorists are their own worst enemies. They serve up a witch's brew of paranoia, lamebrain science, goofy amateur photo-analysis, and gaping contradictions in logic you could sail the Titanic through. *Dark Moon* author Mary Bennet purportedly uncovered "secret" documents that show Apollo was a hoax. Bill Brian [*Moongate*] agrees Apollo was a scam but, suspects we reached the Moon with the aid of a secret, anti-gravity device that NASA reverse-engineered by copying parts of a captured, alien flying saucer.

Mission implausible

Under cold scrutiny, everyday logic, and low-level science, Apollo conspiracy theories implode faster than a black hole. NASA's own actions are inconsistent with how anyone would attempt to pull off a Moon hoax. If what actually happened during the Apollo program was scripted, the government showed a penchant for gambling and brinkmanship. For example, the government "pretended" to almost kill one of the crews (Apollo 13) to boost television ratings. NASA also had an astronaut "pretend" to break a camera (Apollo 12) after squandering billions of dollars on Hollywood special effects.

The scientific samples, photographic evidence, and telemetry from the Moon are incontrovertible. For this to be otherwise, the world's foremost planetary scientists would have to be dead wrong [imagine the book: *Moon Rock Analysis for Dummies*]. Or even more fantastic, scientists have their own international conspiracy to pawn off phony data—an idea even more impossible than a government conspiracy.

The hours of astronaut moonwalk video are far too complex to have been faked with 1960s motion-picture special-effects technology (unless the Apollo billions were really spent building a time machine to bring

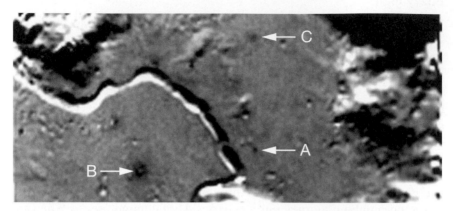

Lunar orbiters have gathered recent evidence that we've been to the Moon. This image, taken by the Clementine spacecraft, shows a diffuse dark spot at the exact location of Apollo 15's lunar module, Falcon. Lunar geologists believe the discoloration was caused by the craft's engine blast at takeoff. The other designated areas B and C are related to fresh impact craters.

back from the future an image-rendering computer and powerful animation software).

Seeing is believing

One Moon conspiracy theorist claim is that you can't simply look at the Moon and directly see evidence of human visitation. The six lunar-lander descent stages left on the Moon are small compared to our satellite as a whole—only about 15 feet across. Even the eagle-eyed Hubble Space Telescope can see an object no smaller than 265 feet across at the Moon's distance. However, two researchers, Misha Kreslavsky of Brown University and Yuri Shkuratov of the Kharkov Astronomical Observatory in the Ukraine, recently uncovered the first direct visual evidence of human visitation to the Moon. They had been comparing the 1994 Clementine lunar orbiter images with Apollo images taken more than thirty years ago for evidence of fresh cratering activity. In doing so, they discovered a disturbed regolith [but no impact crater] around the exact location of the Apollo 15 landing site.

Five small, nuclear-powered stations left behind by the astronauts transmitted telemetry information from twenty-five separate experiments, yielding information about the Moon's seismic activity, subsurface temperature, rate of micrometeorite impacts, and other surface

A plume of flame signaled the liftoff of the Apollo 11 Saturn V space vehicle at 9:32 A.M. EDT on July 16, 1969, as astronauts Neil Armstrong, Michael Collins, and Buzz Aldrin headed from Kennedy Space Center Launch Complex 39A to the Moon.

properties. In 1977, the experiments were turned off for budgetary reasons. However, the central station transmitters continue to send signals that have been used for spacecraft navigation checks, gravitational experiments, mapping planetary positions, and precisely measuring Earth's shape. The stations also include a small mirror array called a retroreflector that astronomers have used to bounce laser beams off the Moon for more than thirty years to precisely measure distances to an accuracy of three-quarters of an inch.

Some 842 pounds of Moon rocks—ancient anthracites, lava basalts, and breccias (agglomerations of fractured pieces from meteorite impacts)—have been shared with the worldwide geology community. Radioisotope dating of these samples indicates ages significantly older (4.4 billion years) than the oldest Earth rocks (3.8 billion years), meaning the rocks are very well preserved, partly because they are bone-dry. You simply don't walk down to the beach and pick up a 4.4 billion-year-old rock. Trying to fool the entire geology community is like trying to fool Mother Nature. Where did these rocks come from if not from the Moon's surface?

Fantastic voyage

Fundamental to the conspiracy theory is our supposed inability to go to the Moon. Some scientists were saying the very same thing at the time American pioneer Robert Goddard was launching rockets in a Massachusetts farm field. The thought of humans traveling to the Moon was so fantastic even early science-fiction writers didn't predict it happening for centuries to come.

Going to the Moon certainly was rocket science. But you don't need breakthrough physics or warp-drive to make the trip. The modern rocket engine is based on science principles formulated by Isaac Newton centuries ago. The hardest part of going to the Moon is climbing out of Earth's gravitational field. The immense launch complex at NASA's Kennedy Space Center in Florida and the extraordinary Saturn V rockets that hurled our astronaut pioneers to the Moon were what accomplished this task, and nothing was phony about them. Ask any one of the thousands of media or VIP guests who witnessed the mighty rockets climb majestically on Promethean flames into the topaz Florida skies.

Besides, NASA didn't need such a brawny rocket for a hoax. It could have launched a few small rockets (Saturn 1-B class) and explained it was assembling the Moon ship in low Earth orbit (a strategy considered in the 1960s). Also, hoaxers could have gotten away with a single vehicle. The actual lunar orbit rendezvous approach—requiring a separate orbiter and lander vehicle—was so complex it automatically invited scrutiny by doubters.

To the danger zone

To be sure, space travel is hazardous. One obstacle cited by detractors is the Van Allen radiation belts, which are caused by Earth's magnetic field. Electrons and protons zipping along magnetic field lines can degrade elec-

Solar flares are a danger to astronauts in space. This hydrogen-alpha image of the Sun (the bright area to the upper right of the image is a large flare) was taken on June 7, 2003, from Portal, Arizona.

tronics on spacecraft. But rushing toward the Moon at 7 miles (11 km) a second, the Apollo astronauts spent just a few hours within the belts.

The biggest potential threat for space travelers is from solar flares. The radiation from a giant flare is equal to 40 billion atomic bombs exploding at once. Fortunately, this amount of radiation is dispersed widely through space.

Also, the Sun was at a minimum in its 11-year cycle of activity during the Apollo years, so deadly flares were rare. A radiation sensor outside the Apollo 12 spacecraft registered one small solar flare, but no increase in radiation dose to the crewmen in the spacecraft was detected.

Another popular Moon conspiracy idea is that micrometeoroids would have sandblasted the spacecraft either in space or on the Moon's

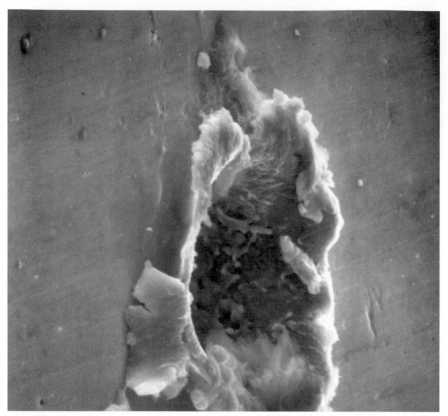

Micrometeorites are not a threat to astronauts because impacts from them are rare and the holes they leave are tiny. This micrometeorite impact occurred on one of the metal test-collectors of Skylab, which orbited Earth from 1973 to 1979.

surface. This far-out claim has no basis in reality. It's well documented that even when Earth passes through a particularly intense meteoroid shower, nothing happens to spacecraft. The November 1999 Leonid meteor storm, the most intense since the dawn of the space age, dramatized this point. Not one of 700 operational satellites was damaged during the Leonid meteoroid onslaught.

Is it real or computer graphics?

The crux of the conspiracy theory is the allegation that the moonwalks were filmed on a huge movie set. The argument for synthetic images seems very believable when you look at a film like *Red Planet* (2000), which offers convincing panoramas of astronauts trudging across Mars.

Today we take all these fantasy scenes for granted thanks to the revolution in computer graphics and digital-image processing made possible by microcomputers. Now, images can be completely fabricated with precise control of all scene elements: lighting, texture, motion, and choreography.

Cinema special-effects technology of the 1960s was an emerging art and was truly primitive by today's awesome capabilities. No microcomputers, digital-image processing, or 3-D animation software existed. The decade's landmark space film, *2001: A Space Odyssey,* illustrates the pinnacle of special-effects capability in the 1960s. *2001*'s special effects took more than two years to complete, employed an army of technicians and some of the movie industry's top effects-experts, and swallowed a big chunk of the film's $10.5 million budget.

Even by 1977, all the fantastic *Star Wars* scenes were classic studio effects. Making the final film involved the laborious process of optical printing, where separated elements of a scene had to be assembled directly onto motion-picture film by repeated passes of the film through gigantic optical printers. The film pioneered the computer motion-controlled camera—critical for crafting space scenes as good as the Apollo footage.

Quiet on the Moon set

The first images from the 1969 Apollo 11 landing are so fuzzy it seems like almost anything could have been pulled off—except the effects of the Moon's 1/6 gravity on astronaut motion. A cinematically naive assertion by Moon hoax advocates is that all scenes were filmed in the Nevada desert. To do this, technicians would have needed to block out the sky—an inconceivable task to pull off without the use of a matte box in front of the lens to block some of the camera's view. This would have required that the camera remain stationary.

A key problem with a matte box is that shadows would have noticeably changed direction, shifting from west to east as the Sun moved across the sky during the hours of filming. (The Sun moves 15° per hour across Earth's sky, but 13° per day across the Moon's.)

Lunar photography 101

A boringly long and trivial list of conspiracy "proofs" exists that argues the moonwalks were artificially lit with classic Hollywood studio lighting. These claims prove only one thing—the conspiracy theorists know less about photography than a high school freshman joining the camera club. Despite truly boneheaded assertions to the contrary, all Apollo images are absolutely accurate and consistent with the reality of a single, re-

Apollo is blasted off the lunar surface on its way to rendezvous with the orbiting command module and then back to Earth. Everything about the launch, which was documented on film by a camera aboard the lunar roving vehicle, appeared exactly as it should in 1/6 gravity.

ally bright light source—the Sun. The only "fill" lighting is from sunlight reflecting off the lunar surface.

Allegations of multiple shadows from multiple lights are red herrings. You can duplicate the Apollo shadows by taking pictures of select fore-ground and background objects on a sunny day with a $10 camera. The shadows are always parallel but converge toward a point on the horizon as seen in wide-angle lenses.

Topping it off is the highly publicized "gotcha" that there are no stars in the lunar sky. Perhaps the accusers forgot it was daytime on the Moon when pictures were shot. Try photographing stars at midnight with a sim-ple camera pre-set for a sunny day and see what develops. The film used in the primitive Apollo cameras—and even that in the cameras on the space

Astronaut Alan Shepard, Apollo 14 commander, stands by the U.S. flag on the Moon's Fra Mauro Highlands. The fact that no stars appear in the sky is a result of the brilliant lunar landscape contrasting with the dark sky. The photographic film used in 1971 did not have sufficient dynamic range to record such differences in brightness.

shuttle today—does not approach the dynamic range needed to capture faint starlight in a sunlit scene. As in *2001* and other space movies, Hollywood special-effects wizards could have inserted stars for artistic effect, but this would have been a dead giveaway the Apollo images were fake.

Mirror on reality

NASA's choice of reflective coatings on helmet visors for the Apollo astronauts also challenges the concept of a fraud. Any catalog photographer will tell you he or she spends hours setting up the lighting to photograph a shiny

Shadows in Apollo images are consistent with what would be expected on the surface of an airless body at the Moon's distance from the Sun. This Apollo 14 image shows a front view of the lunar module Antares reflecting a circular flare caused by the brilliant Sun.

object like a toaster. The mirrored surface reflects the camera and studio, so a photographer must build a "tent" around the object to reflect the light.

The astronaut helmets were not only reflective gold (for protection against ultraviolet radiation) but also curved, so they acted like wide-angle rear-view mirrors (caution: cinematographer may be closer than he appears). The helmets would have reflected the entire hoax setup: lighting, cameras, and the soundstage technicians. Today, digital trickery allows for realistic reflections to be inserted onto visors. If the Apollo footage really was faked, NASA never would have selected such helmets. In all space movies—including *2001*—astronauts have clear, see-through

Astronaut Alan Bean, lunar module pilot for Apollo 12, holds a container filled with lunar soil collected during extravehicular activity. The visor reflects no technicians or sound stage equipment, a tough feat to pull off if this picture had been taken in a studio on Earth.

helmets. NASA could have done the same, and no one would have been any wiser.

Peter Pan on the Moon

I find it amazing that Moon conspiracy theorists obsess over nerdy details about lighting but blithely ignore the precise motion of all objects in the Moon's 1/6-gravity environment. This is the real nail in the coffin against faked Moon videos. Using real actors, it is absolutely impossible to duplicate motion in the absence of gravity or reduced gravity convincingly unless the shot is heavily reprocessed or synthesized digitally.

Dust captured on film behaved exactly as expected in the Moon's reduced gravity. In this photograph, astronaut Eugene Cernan, Apollo 17 mission commander, kicks up a bit of dust while driving the lunar roving vehicle during the early part of the first Apollo 17 extravehicular activity at the Taurus-Littrow landing site.

Conspiracy theorists can't dismiss hours and hours of Apollo footage showing all lunar objects following simple ballistic paths that appeared completely different than they would under the tug of Earth's gravity. This can't be done with slow motion or other conventional film effects. Endless subtleties exist in the Apollo scenes showing the precise, gentle pull of gravity on a true extraterrestrial world: the way dust flew along long, shallow parabolic trajectories when it was kicked up; the trajectories of myriad foil pieces blasted off the lander when the Apollo 16 ascent module lifted off. A final tour de force is footage of the entire Moon rover bouncing along on big arcs.

Curtain call

Thanks to FOX-TV's gambit for ratings, the Moon hoax got some time back in the spotlight, but the effect was minimal. This way-out idea will always hover on the dim periphery of basic common sense, alongside the outrageous collection of other equally absurd "it-never-happened" conspiracy theories.

But the Moon conspiracy folks discredit American heroes, anger a lot of space engineers and scientists, and exasperate NASA spokespersons. The "we-never-went-to-the-Moon" authors come off to the vast majority of the thinking public as nothing more than fools.

For as long as there is a civilization on Earth, the intelligence, boldness, and bravery of the men and women behind the Apollo missions will be remembered. That will never be said for their detractors. All they have managed to do is try and put our national heritage up for sale—and for nothing more than TV ratings.

Personal Investigations: Inquiry Projects

1 Make a quick list in your notebook about all the cultural or historical "truths" that have been called into question in the last several years. For example, some have argued that the Holocaust never happened, and some believe that President John F. Kennedy was not, in fact, killed by Lee Harvey Oswald. Or, search www.google.com using the word "hoax" and see what you find. Choose one thing from your list and fastwrite about it, exploring what you believe about it and why, as well as what questions you have about it.

   Then find at least two articles or credible Web sites that explain the claims made by the groups who argue something didn't happen or was a hoax. Go back to your journal and fastwrite about what you've read, first playing the believing game, summarizing what you've read and assuming you believe it; then playing the doubting game, being skeptical of the claims. Finally, review what you've written and underline possible subjects for a research essay.

Craft and Conventions: Explaining and Evaluating

2. This essay contains a lot of photos that are central to its arguments. In your journal, fastwrite about each of the photos and how they relate to the essay overall. What purposes do they serve? How would the essay be different if there were no photos and captions?

3. Compose a 250-word summary of this article's main points—what are the main counterarguments to the hoax theories? What are the key critiques and proofs?

4. Reread this essay and carefully note in your journal each of the conspiracy theorists' claims that Villard is examining, leaving room between each of them. Then, underneath each claim, note the reasons and evidence Villard uses to refute or disprove it. How convincing do you find Villard's own analysis of the conspiracy theories?

5. Villard uses subheadings for each section of his essay. How effective are they? Why not simply rely on the internal organization of the essay, allowing the reader to move smoothly from one paragraph to another, rather than make the organization so explicit?

6. Given the subtitle of the essay ("To quash lingering doubts as to whether or not we went to the Moon, *Astronomy* is setting the record straight, once and for all"), it would seem that Villard didn't really approach his research question by first suspending judgment. Do you see evidence that he did more than set out to prove NASA right?

7. Do some research on the moon-landing hoax, using a search engine such as Google or Yahoo! and compare what you find to Villard's article. How well does he represent the claims of the conspiracy theorists as they are represented on the Internet Web sites you've found? How well does he refute their claims, especially compared to the information available on these questions?

Inquiries on Inquiry: Exploring and Reflecting

8. Beliefs that the moon landing was faked come in part from skepticism about the "truth" that photographic images can convey. As you reread Villard's essay, focus on the criteria he uses to establish that the images are true and accurate. Summarize those criteria in a paragraph or two and share with your small group. If you have time, do some research in the Internet about the credibility of visual images and revise your criteria to reflect what you've found. Then together agree on (1) the questions or criteria you might use to determine the credibility of images, and (2) the guidelines writers might follow when deciding whether and how to use images as a part of their written arguments.

9. Describe your experience of reading this essay. What did you think at first? And then? What did you struggle with and/or find easy? By the end of the essay, what did you understand differently?

10. What have you learned about writing a researched essay from reading this one?

11. When you first read the title of this essay, what did you think? Had you heard about these hoax theories before? What did you think about a magazine like *Astronomy* publishing a critique of these theories? Fastwrite about your initial responses to this essay, before you read it and then afterward.

12. Using a dialogue journal approach, record on the left side of your notebook all the quotes/passages/facts/theories that immediately got your attention. Then on the right side fastwrite about each one and what you think about it. What questions does it raise for you? What does it make you think about? What surprised you?

Looking at Women
Scott Russell Sanders

Inquiry is driven by questions, not answers, and so, too, is the essay form, at least as it was originally conceived by Michelle de Montaigne, the sixteenth-century Frenchman who first called his meditations on travel, sex, the education of children, cannibals, and lying essais. The essay in French means "to attempt," or "to try." This is a far cry from the school essays most of us have written, compositions that often say what they're going to say, say it, and then say what they said. Discovery is not part of the deal.

Scott Russell Sanders's essay, "Looking at Women," is written in that earlier essay tradition. Sanders begins with an anecdote from his youth, the memory of seeing an attractive 14-year-old girl cross at a stoplight while Sanders sat with a friend in the back of his mother's car. "Check out that chassis," said the friend. This becomes an occasion for Sanders, many years later, to wonder "How should a man look at women?"

It is a question that he explores in the essay you are about to read, and part of the pleasure in reading it is following Sanders's "narrative of thought" as he turns the question this way and that, trying to arrive at some comfortable understanding. "Looking at Women" was first published in the Georgia Review, *and later in Scott Russell Sanders's essay collection,* Secrets of the Universe *(1991). Sanders, who teaches creative writing at Indiana University, is among the finest contemporary American essayists, sharing that distinction with several other writers in this chapter.*

Sanders did not set out to write a research essay. He simply started with a memory that raised a question that, it turned out, reading the works of others might help answer. His resort to research was simply a natural move, one that all kinds of writers make all the time. Understood this way, research is simply another source of information—no better or worse than memory or observation—but another handhold a writer can seize as he gropes his way toward understanding.

As you read "Looking at Women," notice how effectively Sanders probes his personal experiences for meaning, using the work of others, such as Simone De Beauvoir, to help clarify but also to complicate. The essay, because it is often driven by a question rather than a thesis, invites such complications. You will also be impressed to see the range of sources that Sanders uses, from early feminist theorists like De Beauvoir, to the English novelist D. H. Lawrence, to Joan Didion, to his wife Ruth. Sanders writes that the essay is "an amateur's raid in a world of specialists," and such an amateur never hesitates to cover a lot of territory rather than settle in one spot, as most academic specialists do.

Sanders's insights here are likely to provoke a lively class discussion. In some ways, the essay raises more questions than answers, and that's something good research—and good writing—will often do.

On that sizzling July afternoon, the girl who crossed at the stoplight in front of our car looked, as my mother would say, as though she had been poured into her pink shorts. The girl's matching pink halter bared her stomach and clung to her nubbin breasts, leaving little to the imagination, as my mother would also say. Until that moment, it had never made any difference to me how much or little a girl's clothing revealed, for my imagination had been entirely devoted to other mysteries. I was 11. The girl was about 14, the age of my buddy Norman who lounged in the back seat with me. Staring after her, Norman elbowed me in the ribs and murmured, "Check out that chassis."

His mother glared around from the driver's seat. "Hush your mouth."

"I was talking about that sweet Chevy," said Norman, pointing out a souped-up jalopy at the curb.

"I know what you were talking about," his mother snapped.

No doubt she did know, since mothers could read minds, but at first I myself did not have a clue. Chassis? I knew what it meant for a car, an airplane, a radio, or even a cannon to have a chassis. But could a girl have one as well? I glanced after the retreating figure, and suddenly noticed with a sympathetic twitching in my belly the way her long raven ponytail swayed in rhythm to her walk and the way her fanny jostled in those pink shorts. In July's dazzle of sun, her swinging legs and arms flashed at me a code I could almost read.

As the light turned green and our car pulled away, Norman's mother cast one more scowl at her son in the rearview mirror, saying, "Just think how it makes her feel to have you two boys gawking at her."

How? I wondered.

"Makes her feel like hot stuff," said Norman, owner of a bold mouth.

"If you don't get your mind out of the gutter, you're going to wind up in the state reformatory," said his mother.

Norman gave a snort. I sank into the seat, and tried to figure out what power had sprung from that sashaying girl to zap me in the belly.

Only after much puzzling did it dawn on me that I must finally have drifted into the force field of sex, as a space traveler who has lived all his years in free-fall might rocket for the first time within gravitational reach of a star. Even as a bashful 11-year-old I knew the word *sex*, of course, and I could paste that name across my image of the tantalizing girl. But a label for a mystery no more explains a mystery than the word *gravity* explains gravity. As I grew a beard and my taste shifted from girls to women, I acquired a more cagey language for speaking of desire. I picked up disarming theories. First by hearsay and then by experiment, I learned the delicious details of making babies. I came to appreciate the urgency for propagation that litters the road with maple seeds and drives salmon up waterfalls and yokes the newest crop of boys to the newest crop of girls. Books in their killjoy wisdom taught me that all the valentines and violins, the waltzes and glances, the long fever and ache of romance were merely embellishments on biology's instructions that we multiply our kind. And yet, the fraction of desire that actually leads to procreation is so vanishingly small as to seem irrelevant. In his lifetime a man sways to a million longings, only a few of which, or perhaps none at all, ever lead to the fathering of children.

Now, 30 years away from that July afternoon, firmly married, twice a father, I am still humming from the power unleashed by the girl in pink shorts, still wondering how it made her feel to have two boys gawk at her, still puzzling over how to dwell in the force field of desire.

How should a man look at women? It is a peculiarly and perhaps neurotically human question. Billy goats do not fret over how they should look at nanny goats. They look or don't look, as seasons and hormones dictate, and feel what they feel without benefit of theory. There is more billy goat in most men than we care to admit. None of us, however, is pure goat. To live utterly as an animal would make the business of sex far tidier but also drearier. If we tried, like Rousseau, to peel off the layers of civilization and imagine our way back to some pristine man and woman who have not yet been corrupted by hand-me-down notions of sexuality, my hunch is that we would find, in our speculative state of nature, that men regarded women with appalling simplicity. In any case, unlike goats, we dwell in history. What attracts our eyes and rouses our blood is only partly instinctual. Other forces contend in us as well, the voices of books and religions, the images of art and film and advertising, the entire chorus of culture. Norman's telling me to relish the sight of females and his mother's telling me to keep my eyes to myself are only two of the many voices quarreling in my head.

If there were a rule book for sex, it would be longer than the one for baseball (that byzantine sport), more intricate and obscure than tax instructions from the Internal Revenue Service. What I present here are a few images and reflections that cling, for me, to this one item in such a compendium of rules: How should a man look at women?

Well before I was to see any women naked in the flesh, I saw a bevy of them naked in photographs, hung in a gallery around the bed of my freshman roommate at college. A *Playboy* subscriber, he would pluck the centerfold from its staples each month and tape another airbrushed lovely to the wall. The gallery was in place when I moved in, and for an instant before I realized what I was looking at, all that expanse of skin reminded me of a meat locker back in Newton Falls, Ohio. I never quite shook that first impression, even after I had inspected the pinups at my leisure on subsequent days. Every curve of buttock and breast was news to me, an innocent kid from the Puritan back roads. Today you would be hard pressed to find a college freshman as ignorant as I was of female anatomy, if only because teenagers now routinely watch movies at home that would have been shown, during my teen years, exclusively on the fly-speckled screens of honky-tonk cinemas or in the basement of the Kinsey Institute. I studied those alien shapes on the wall with a curiosity that was not wholly sexual, a curiosity tinged with the wonder that astronomers must have felt when they pored over the early photographs of the far side of the moon.

The paper women seemed to gaze back at me, enticing or mocking, yet even in my adolescent dither I was troubled by the phony stare, for I knew this was no true exchange of looks. Those mascaraed eyes were not fixed on me but on a camera. What the models felt as they posed I could only guess—perhaps the boredom of any numbskull job, perhaps the weight of dollar bills, perhaps the sweltering lights of fame, perhaps a tingle of the power that launched a thousand ships.

Whatever their motives, these women had chosen to put themselves on display. For the instant of the photograph, they had become their bodies, as a prizefighter does in the moment of landing a punch, as a weight lifter does in the moment of hoisting a barbell, as a ballerina does in the whirl of a pirouette, as we all do in the crisis of making love or dying. Men, ogling such photographs, are supposed to feel that where so much surface is revealed there can be no depths. Yet I never doubted that behind the makeup and the plump curves and the two dimensions of the image there was an inwardness, a feeling self as mysterious as my own. In fact, during moments when I should have been studying French or thermodynamics, I would glance at my roommate's wall and invent mythical lives for those goddesses. The lives I made up were adolescent ones, to be sure; but so was mine. Without that saving aura of inwardness, these women in the glossy photographs would have become merely another category of objects for sale, alongside the sports cars and stereo systems and liquors advertised in the same pages. If not extinguished, however, their humanity was severely reduced. And if by simplifying themselves they had lost some human essence, then by gaping at them I had shared in the theft.

What did that gaping take from me? How did it affect my way of seeing other women, those who would never dream of lying nude on a fake tiger rug before the million-faceted eye of a camera? The bodies in the photographs were implausibly smooth and slick and inflated, like balloon caricatures that might be floated overhead in a parade. Free of sweat and scars and imperfections, sensual without being fertile, tempting yet impregnable, they were Platonic ideals of the female form, divorced from time and the dither of living, excused from the perplexities of mind. No actual woman could rival their insipid perfection.

The swains who gathered to admire my roommate's gallery discussed the pinups in the same tones and in much the same language as the farmers back home in Ohio used for assessing cows. The relevant parts of male or female bodies are quickly named—and, the *Kamasutra* and Marquis de Sade notwithstanding, the number of ways in which those parts can be stimulated or conjoined is touchingly small—so these studly conversations were more tedious than chitchat about the weather. I would lie on my bunk pondering calculus or Aeschylus and unwillingly hear the same few nouns and fewer verbs issuing from one mouth after another, and I would feel smugly superior. Here I was, improving my mind, while theirs wallowed in the notorious gutter. Eventually the swains would depart, leaving me in peace, and from the intellectual heights of my bunk I would glance across at those photographs . . . and yield to the gravity of lust. Idiot flesh! How stupid that a counterfeit stare and artful curves, printed in millions of copies on glossy paper, could arouse me. But there it was, not the first proof of my body's automatism and not the last.

Nothing in men is more machinelike than the flipping of sexual switches. I have never been able to read with a straight face the claims made by D. H. Lawrence and lesser pundits that the penis is a god, a lurking dragon. It more nearly resembles a railroad crossing signal, which stirs into life at intervals to announce, "Here comes a train." Or, if the penis must be likened to an animal, let it be an ill-trained circus dog, sitting up and playing dead and heeling whenever it takes a notion, oblivious of the trainer's commands. Meanwhile, heart, lungs, blood vessels, pupils, and eyelids all assert their independence like the members of a rebellious troupe. Reason stands helpless at the center of the ring, cracking its whip.

While he was president, Jimmy Carter raised a brouhaha by confessing in a *Playboy* interview, of all shady places, that he occasionally felt lust in his heart for women. What man hasn't, aside from those who feel lust in their hearts for other men? The commentators flung their stones anyway. Naughty, naughty, they chirped. Wicked Jimmy. Perhaps Mr. Carter could derive some consolation from psychologist Allen Wheelis, who, in *The Doctor of Desire,* blames male appetite on biology: "We have been selected for desiring. Nothing could have convinced us by argument that it would be worthwhile to chase endlessly and insatiably after women, but something has transformed us from within, a plasmid has invaded our DNA, has twisted our nature so that now this is exactly what we *want* to do." Certainly, by Darwinian logic, those males who were most avid in their pursuit of females were also the most likely to pass on their genes. Consoling it may be, yet it is finally no solution to blame biology. "I am extremely sexual in my desires: I carry them everywhere and at all times," William Carlos Williams tells us on the opening page of his *Autobiography.* "I think that from that arises the drive which empowers us all. Given that drive, a man does with it what his mind directs. In the manner in which he directs that power lies his secret." I agree with the honest doctor. Whatever the contents of my DNA, however potent the influence of my ancestors, I still must direct that rebellious power. I still must live with the consequences of my looking and my longing.

Aloof on their blankets like goddesses on clouds, the pinups did not belong to my funky world. I was invisible to them, and they were immune to my gaze. Not so the women who passed me on the street, sat near me in classes, shared a table with me in the cafeteria: it was risky to stare at them. They could gaze back, and sometimes did, with looks both puzzling and exciting. It only complicated matters for me to realize that so many of these strangers had taken precautions that men should notice them. The girl in matching pink halter and shorts who set me humming in my eleventh year might only have wanted to keep cool in the sizzle of July. But these alluring college femmes had deeper designs. Perfume, eye shadow, uplift bras (about which I learned in the Sears catalog), curled hair, stockings, jewelry, lipstick, lace—what were these if not hooks tossed into male waters?

I recall being mystified in particular by spike heels. They looked painful to me, and dangerous. Danger may have been the point, since the spikes would have made good weapons—they were affectionately known, after all, as stilettos. Or danger may have been the point in another sense, because a woman teetering along on such heels is tipsy, vulnerable, broadcasting her need for support. And who better than a man to prop her up, some guy who clomps around in brogans wide enough for the cornerstones of flying buttresses? (For years after college, I felt certain that spike heels had been forever banned, like bustles and foot binding, but lately they have come back in fashion, and once more one encounters women teetering along on knife points.)

Back in those days of my awakening to women, I was also baffled by lingerie. I do not mean underwear, the proletariat of clothing, and I do not mean foundation garments, pale and sensible. I mean what the woman who lives in the house behind ours—owner of a shop called "Bare Essentials" refers to as "intimate apparel." Those two words announce that her merchandise is both sexy and expensive. These flimsy items cost more per ounce than truffles, more than frankincense and myrrh. They are put-ons whose only purpose is in being taken off. I have a friend who used to attend the men's-only nights at "Bare Essentials," during which he would invariably buy a slinky outfit or two, by way of proving his serious purpose, outfits that wound up in the attic because his wife would not be caught dead in them. Most of the customers at the shop are women, however, as the models are women, and the owner is a woman. What should one make of that? During my college days I knew about intimate apparel only by rumor, not being that intimate with anyone who would have tricked herself out in such finery, but I could see the spike heels and other female trappings everywhere I turned. Why, I wondered then and wonder still, do so many women decorate themselves like dolls?

On this question as on many others, Simone De Beauvoir has clarified matters for me, writing in *The Second Sex:* "The 'feminine' woman in making herself prey tries to reduce man, also, to her carnal passivity; she occupies herself in catching him in her trap, in enchaining him by means of the desires she arouses in him in submissively making herself a thing." Those women who transform themselves into dolls, in other words, do so because that is the most potent identity available to them. "It must be admitted," De Beauvoir concedes, "that the males find in woman more complicity than the oppressor usually finds in the oppressed. And in bad faith they take authorization from this to declare that she has *desired* the destiny they have imposed on her."

Complicity, oppressor, bad faith: such terms yank us into a moral realm unknown to goats. While I am saddled with enough male guilt to believe three-quarters of De Beauvoir's claim, I still doubt that men are so entirely to blame for the turning of women into sexual dolls. I believe human history is more collaborative than her argument would suggest. It seems unlikely to me that one half the species could have "imposed" a destiny on the other half, unless that other half were far more craven than the females I have known. Some women have expressed their own skepticism on this point. Thus Joan Didion in her essay "The Women's Movement": "That many women are victims of condescension and exploitation and sex-role stereotyping was scarcely news, but neither was it news that other women are not: nobody forces women to buy the package." De Beauvoir herself recognized that many members of her sex refuse to buy the "feminine" package: "The emancipated woman, on the contrary, wants to be active, a taker, and refuses the passivity man means to impose on her."

Since my college years, back in the murky 1960s, emancipated women have been discouraging their unemancipated sisters from making spectacles of themselves. Don't paint your face like a clown's or drape your body like a mannequin's, they say. Don't bounce on the sidelines in skimpy outfits, screaming your fool head off, while men compete in the limelight for victories. Don't present yourself to the world as a fluff pastry, delicate and edible. Don't waddle across the stage in a bathing suit in hopes of being named Miss This or That.

A great many women still ignore the exhortations. Wherever a crown for beauty is to be handed out, many still line up to stake their claims. Recently, Miss Indiana Persimmon Festival was quoted in our newspaper about the burdens of possessing the sort of looks that snag men's eyes. "Most of the time I enjoy having guys stare at me," she said, "but every once in a while it makes me feel like a piece of meat." The news photograph showed a cheerleader's perky face, heavily made-up, with starched hair teased into a blond cumulus. She put me in mind not of meat but of a plastic figurine, something you might buy from a booth outside a shrine. Nobody should ever be seen as meat, mere juicy stuff to satisfy an appetite. Better to appear as a plastic figurine, which is not meant for eating, and which is a gesture, however crude, toward art. James Joyce described the aesthetic response as a contemplation of form without the impulse to action. Perhaps that is what Miss Indiana Persimmon Festival wishes to inspire in those who look at her, perhaps that is what many women who paint and primp themselves desire: to withdraw from the touch of hands and dwell in the eye alone, to achieve the status of art.

By turning herself (or allowing herself to be turned) into a work of art, does a woman truly escape men's proprietary stare? Not often, says the British critic John Berger in *Ways of Seeing*. Summarizing the treatment of women in Western painting, he concludes that—with a few notable exceptions, such as works by Rubens and Rembrandt—the woman on canvas is a passive object displayed for the pleasure of the male viewer, especially for the owner of the painting, who is, by extension, owner of the woman herself. Berger concludes: "Men look at women. Women watch themselves being looked at. This determines not only most relations between men and women but also the relation of women to themselves. The surveyor of woman in herself is male: the surveyed female. Thus she turns herself into an object—and most particularly an object of vision: a sight."

That sweeping claim, like the one quoted earlier from De Beauvoir, also seems to me about three-quarters truth and one-quarter exaggeration. I know men who outdo the peacock for show, and I know women who are so fully possessed of themselves that they do not give a hang whether anybody notices them or not. The flamboyant gentlemen portrayed by Van Dyck are no less aware of being *seen* than are the languid ladies portrayed by Ingres. With or without clothes, both gentlemen and ladies may conceive of themselves as objects of vision, targets of envy or admiration or desire. Where they differ is in their potential for action: the men are caught in the midst of a decisive gesture or on the verge of making one; the women wait like fuel for someone else to strike a match.

I am not sure the abstract nudes favored in modern art are much of an advance over the inert and voluptuous ones of the old school. Think of two famous examples: Duchamp's *Nude Descending a Staircase* (1912), where the faceless woman has blurred into a waterfall of jagged shards, or Picasso's *Les Demoiselles d'Avignon* (1907), where the five angular damsels have been hammered as flat as cookie sheets and fitted with African masks. Neither painting invites us to behold a woman, but instead to behold what Picasso or Duchamp can make of one.

The naked women in Rubens, far from being passive, are gleefully active, exuberant, their sumptuous pink bodies like rain clouds or plump nebulae. "His nudes are the first ones that ever made me feel happy about my own body," a woman friend told me in one of the Rubens galleries of

the Prado Museum. I do not imagine any pinup or store-window mannequin or bathing-suited Miss Whatsit could have made her feel that way.
The naked women in Rembrandt, emerging from the bath or rising from
bed, are so private, so cherished in the painter's gaze, that we as viewers
see them not as sexual playthings but as loved persons. A man would do
well to emulate that gaze.

I have never thought of myself as a sight. How much that has to do with
being male and how much with having grown up on back roads where
money was scarce and eyes were few, I cannot say. As a boy, apart from
combing my hair when I was compelled to and regretting the patches on
my jeans (only the poor wore patches), I took no trouble over my appearance. It never occurred to me that anybody outside my family, least of all
a girl, would look at me twice. As a young man, when young women did
occasionally glance my way, without any prospect of appearing handsome I tried at least to avoid appearing odd. A standard haircut and the
cheapest versions of the standard clothes were camouflage enough. Now
over the frontier of 40, I have achieved once more that boyhood condition
of invisibility, with less hair to comb and fewer patches to humble me.
    Many women clearly pass through the world aspiring to invisibility.
Many others just as clearly aspire to be conspicuous. Women need not
make spectacles of themselves in order to draw the attention of men. Indeed, for my taste, the less paint and fewer bangles the better. I am as
helpless in the presence of subtle lures as a male moth catching a whiff of
pheromones. I am a sucker for hair ribbons, a scarf at the throat, toes leaking from sandals, teeth bared in a smile. By contrast, I have always been
more amused than attracted by the enameled exhibitionists whom our biblical mothers would identify as brazen hussies or painted Jezebels or, in
the extreme cases, as whores of Babylon.
    To encounter female exhibitionists in their full glory and variety, you
need to go to a city. I never encountered ogling as a full-blown sport until I
visited Rome, where bands of Italian men joined with gusto in appraising
the charms of every passing female, and the passing females vied with one
another in demonstrating their charms. In our own cities the most notorious
bands of oglers tend to be construction gangs or street crews, men who
spend much of their day leaning on the handles of shovels or pausing between bursts of riveting guns, their eyes tracing the curves of passersby.
The first time my wife and kids and I drove into Boston we followed the
signs to Chinatown, only to discover that Chinatown's miserably congested
main street was undergoing repairs. That street also proved to be the city's
home for X-rated cinemas and girlie shows and skin shops. LIVE SEX ACTS
ON STAGE, PEEP SHOWS, PRIVATE BOOTHS. Caught in a traffic jam, we spent

an hour listening to jackhammers and wolf whistles as we crept through the few blocks of pleasure palaces, my son and daughter with their noses out the windows, my wife and I steaming. Lighted marquees peppered by burnt-out bulbs announced the titles of sleazy flicks; life-size posters of naked women flanked the doorways of clubs; leggy strippers in miniskirts, the originals for some of the posters, smoked on the curb between numbers.

After we had finally emerged from the zone of eros, 8-year-old Jesse inquired, "What was *that* place all about?"

"Sex for sale," my wife Ruth explained.

That might carry us some way toward a definition of pornography: making flesh into a commodity, flaunting it like any other merchandise, divorcing bodies from selves. By this reckoning, there is a pornographic dimension to much advertising, where a charge of sex is added to products ranging from cars to shaving cream. In fact, the calculated imagery of advertising may be more harmful than the blatant imagery of the pleasure palaces, that frank raunchiness which Kate Millett refers to, in *Sexual Politics,* as the "truthful explicitness of pornography." One can leave the X-rated zone of the city, but one cannot escape the sticky reach of commerce, which summons girls to the high calling of cosmetic glamour, fashion, and sexual display, while it summons boys to the panting chase.

You can recognize pornography, according to D. H. Lawrence, "by the insult it offers, invariably, to sex, and to the human spirit" (from *Pornography and Obscenity,* a pamphlet he wrote amid the controversy surrounding *Lady Chatterley's Lover*). He should know, Millett argues in *Sexual Politics,* for in her view Lawrence himself was a purveyor of patriarchal and often sadistic pornography. I think she is correct about the worst of Lawrence, and that she identifies a misogynist streak in his work; but she ignores his career-long struggle to achieve a more public, tolerant vision of sexuality as an exchange between equals. Besides, his novels and stories all bear within themselves their own critiques. In *Language and Silence,* George Steiner reminds us that "the list of writers who have had the genius to enlarge our actual compass of sexual awareness, who have given the erotic play of the mind a novel focus, an area of recognition previously unknown or fallow, is very small." Lawrence belongs on that brief list. The chief insult to the human spirit is to deny it, to pretend that we are merely conglomerations of molecules, to pretend that we exist purely as bundles of appetites or as food for the appetites of others.

Men commit that insult toward women out of ignorance, but also out of dread. Allen Wheelis again, in *The Doctor of Desire:* "Men gather in pornographic shows, not to stimulate desire, as they may think, but to diminish fear. It is the nature of the show to reduce the woman, discard her individuality, her soul, make her into an object, thereby enabling the man to handle her with greater safety, to use her as a toy. . . . As women move increasingly toward equality, the felt danger to men increases, leading to an increase in pornography and, since there are some men whose fears cannot even so be stilled, to an increase also in violence against women."

Make her into an object: all the hurtful ways for men to look at women are variations on this betrayal. "Thus she turns herself into an object," writes Berger. A woman's ultimate degradation is in "submissively making herself a thing," writes De Beauvoir. To be turned into an object—whether by the brush of a painter or the lens of a photographer or the eye of a voyeur, whether by hunger or poverty or enslavement, by mugging or rape, bullets or bombs, by hatred, racism, car crashes, fires, or falls—is for each of us the deepest dread; and to reduce another person to an object is the primal wrong.

Caught in the vortex of desire, we have to struggle to recall the wholeness of persons, including ourselves. In *The Second Sex,* De Beauvoir speaks of the temptation we all occasionally feel to give up the struggle for a self and lapse into the inertia of matter: "Along with the ethical urge of each individual to affirm his subjective existence, there is also the temptation to forgo liberty and become a thing." A woman in particular, given so much encouragement to lapse into thinghood, "is often very well pleased with her role as the *Other.*"

Yet one need not forgo liberty and become a thing, without a center or a self, in order to become the Other. In our mutual strangeness, men and women can be doorways one for another, openings into the creative mystery that we share by virtue of our existence in the flesh. "To be sensual," James Baldwin writes in *The Fire Next Time,* "is to respect and rejoice in the force of life, of life itself, and to be *present* in all that one does, from the effort of loving to the breaking of bread." The effort of loving is reciprocal, not only in act but in desire, an *I* addressing a *Thou,* a meeting in that vivid presence. The distance a man stares across at a woman, or a woman at a man, is a gulf in the soul, out of which a voice cries, *Leap, leap.* One day all men may cease to look on themselves as prototypically human and on women as lesser miracles; women may cease to feel themselves the targets for desire; men and women both may come to realize that we are all mere flickerings in the universal fire; and then none of us, male or female, need give up humanity in order to become the Other.

Ever since I gawked at the girl in pink shorts, I have dwelt knowingly in the force field of sex. Knowingly or not, it is where we all dwell. Like the masses of planets and stars, our bodies curve the space around us. We transmit signals constantly, radio sources that never go off the air. We cannot help being centers of attraction and repulsion for one another. That is not all we are by a long shot, nor all we are capable of feeling, and yet, even after our much-needed revolution in sexual consciousness, the power of eros will still turn our heads and hearts. In a world without beauty pageants, there will still be beauty, however its definition may have changed. As long as men have eyes, they will gaze with yearning and confusion at women.

When I return to the street with the ancient legacy of longing coiled in my DNA, and the residues from a thousand generations of patriarchs silting my brain, I encounter women whose presence strikes me like a slap of wind in the face. I must prepare a gaze that is worthy of their splendor.

Personal Investigations: Inquiry Projects

1. We are all implicated in "the force field of sex," writes Scott Russell Sanders. This is something that may be evident, if you look closely enough, on your own campus. In Chapter 6, we introduce you to some of the methods of ethnography, including how to conduct field observations that might produce evidence of the many "webs of culture" in which we are all entangled. Sexual attraction and sexual attention are one of its threads. As a mini-ethnography project, conduct a series of field observations on your campus focusing on the interaction between men and women (or students of the same sex if you're interested in gay culture). Go to places on campus where this interaction is likely, and describe in some detail in a notebook what you see (for tips on how to develop field notes, see page 245). After a series of such field observations, begin to develop theories about "the force field of sex" and how it seems to operate on your campus. For example, what are women's roles and rituals in these interactions? What are the men's?

2. Begin as Sanders did—writing a scene in which you describe looking at women or looking at men. Analyze your own gaze. Are you comfortable with it? Troubled by it? What questions does it raise that research might help answer?

Craft and Conventions: Explaining and Evaluating

3. Examine closely how Sanders brings outside sources into his essay. In particular, examine the four paragraphs on pages 103 and 104 where Sanders cites writer D. H. Lawrence, feminist Kate Millett, language

theorist George Steiner, and psychologist Allen Wheelis. How and where does Sanders orchestrate these voices to speak not just to him but also to each other? What do you notice about how he prepares the reader for a quotation and follows it up? In what ways would you say that Sanders "controls" quotations?

4. Like many of the essays in this chapter, Sanders begins with an anecdote rather than the conventional introduction that simply introduces the topic and possibly a thesis. In what ways is this anecdotal lead more effective? Do you have a strong enough sense—soon enough—what Sanders's purpose is in the essay?

5. The final line of the essay where Sanders concludes that he "must prepare a gaze" at women "that is worthy of their splendor" seems to sum up what he is trying to say. But is it really as simple as that? What questions does that idea raise? For example, what makes a gaze "worthy"? And what is the nature of this "splendor" Sanders seems to see in women? Do you agree with Sanders's perspectives?

Inquiries on Inquiry: Exploring and Reflecting

6. "Looking at Women" uses a wide variety of sources, including a novelist, a psychologist, several feminists, a politician, a poet, and an essayist. Most of us probably wouldn't think to explore answers to the question we pose by looking in so many different places? But why not?

7. Inquiry is driven by questions, not answers, and this is clearly the case in "Looking at Women." But do you sense that Sanders employs the other habits of mind that are often a part of the process of inquiry? Does he seem to suspend judgment and tolerate ambiguity? Does he play both the believing game and the doubting game with his sources and with his own tentative conclusions? Do you sense a *genuine* passion to know the answers to the questions Sanders is raising here, or is it just a pose?

8. This essay may have surprised you because it focuses more on philosophical questions and sources than essays such as "Why Did God Make Flies?" or "Did NASA Fake the Moon Landing?" It explores questions rather than seeks to prove a particular answer. As you read this piece, how did you respond to the structure and to the ideas Sanders is exploring? What frustrated you? What surprised you? What in your own experience seems to influence your response to this essay? As you answer these questions, see what you discover about yourself as a reader.

Dinosaur Dreams: Reading the Bones of America's Psychic Mascot

Jack Hitt

Ever wonder why Americans are so fascinated with dinosaurs? We see them everywhere, from museums and children's books to movies such as Jurassic Park *and documentaries on PBS. In this research essay, Jack Hitt wonders about "the causes of America's periodic obsession with dinosaurs" and discovers that "the popular dinosaur is a wholly owned projection of the nationalist psyche of the United States." Originally published by* Harper's Magazine *in October 2001, this essay examines the history of dinosaur discoveries within the context of what was happening in America at the time. Hitt draws from multiple sources of information, from popular culture images of dinosaurs, observations of dinosaur exhibits in museums, and profiles of dinosaur experts to records of the earliest discoveries of fossils in the U.S. and books published over the years.*

Like the other research essays in this chapter, "Dinosaur Dreams" has a distinctive and engaging writing style: The voice is witty and funny, the analogies current and insightful, and the profiles of dinosaurs and their discoverers dramatic and memorable. Hitt uses small narrative scenes throughout the essay, as well as short informational paragraphs, and together they form an interesting argument about what our obsession with dinosaurs tells us about our national psyche. As you read, mark the places where you see Hitt commenting on or analyzing his research sources, doing more than simply reporting information and connecting it to other claims he's made.

Sixty-five million years ago, conservatively speaking, the last dinosaurs lay down and died—on the ground, beside rivers, in tar pits. Then, about a hundred years ago, they got back up and have been pretty busy ever since. Hardly a week goes by that they don't make the news because of a new theory about either how they lived or how they died. There might be word of a new prime-time TV deal, another revelry (Dinofest V is planned for next year), a new exhibit, the goings-on of paleontological hunk Paul Sereno, a Spielberg script, a hot toy, a legal dispute about some bones, an egg.

In America, where dinosaurs do most of their work (and always have), they periodically disappear from view and then resurface, like John Travolta or Democrats, capturing and losing our cycling interest. Dinosaurs are distinctly American, not only because our scholars have so often been at the forefront of fossil discoveries and paleontological theory but because the popular dinosaur is a wholly owned projection of the nationalist psyche of the United States. Their periodic rebirth in pop culture neatly signals deep tectonic shifts in our sense of ourself as a country. Even glancing appearances can be telling. After Newt Gingrich rampaged through the House of Representatives and seized power in 1994, he placed a skull of T. rex in his office. When the current resident of the White House got a new dog, he called him, strangely, "Barney"—a name most closely associated with a phony dinosaur who masks his cheerful dimness with sticky compassion.

It's been almost exactly a century since the first one stood up in New York City amid a Miramaxian media circus, and, bookending nicely, we seem to be in the clutches of another rage. One recent estimate asserts that there are probably more dinosaurs on the earth now than there were in the Mesozoic Era. The current rate of finding new species is one every seven weeks. Half of all the known dinosaurs have been discovered in the last few decades. What really marks our era are the new tools—amino-acid mapping, the CAT scan, treadmill-energetics studies—that permit us once again to read meaning in the bones and to imagine the world that was when they held up flesh.

Determining the causes of America's periodic obsession with dinosaurs is tricky. They have done a lot of heavy lifting, culturewise. Besides in children's narratives (where dinosaurs still rule the world), they have served as political totems, deranged kitsch, icons of domesticated terror, cultural mules for Darwin's (still) troubling theory, and environmental Cassandras resurrected to act out her famous final words, "I will endure to die."

In the pop-culture chaos that is uniquely our own and that swirls around paleontology's quiet drudgery, certain dinosaurs burble up to the top of our celebrity-oriented mass-media-marketplace mosh pit to float about in plain view, gazed upon by everyone. And we the people elevate them out of that frenzy as surely and by the same circuitously collective route as we do Ricky Martin, Stone Phillips, Cameron Diaz, or Tom Wolfe. Going in and out of fashion, these giants are creations of our own making as much as the paleontologists', perhaps more so. In demanding to see them, we sculpt their meaning; like outsized Schrödinger's cats, their existence depends on whether or not we have decided to look at them.

None of these gargantuans has been more gawked at than *Tyrannosaurus rex,* the Mick Jagger of dinosaurs. And yet he's been absent on the national stage lately (as if he were off in rehab plotting his comeback tour), and there's a reason. Controversial scholarship has turned up a new interpretation of how the great meat-eater lived, and it is so at odds with T. rex's public persona that even scholars hate to talk

The head of a brontosaurus

about him anymore. In a sense, the scientific reality of the King of the Tyrant Lizards has laid bare our symbolic uses of him. So T. is in hiding.

Developed by the self-credentialed iconoclast Jack Horner, the theory holds that T. was not the great predator who marauded through primordial landscapes but rather a slow, putzy scavenger that poked around the Cretaceous countryside in search of maggoty carrion.

Horner can mount a great deal of technical evidence to prove that T. was no hunter, and I have seen him turn an audience completely around in an hour. T. had densely muscled legs with calves the length of his thighs, which are good for walking but lousy for pouncing. T. had poor eyesight, not a great trait, since hunters typically track prey at twilight. CAT scans of T.'s skulls have revealed massively dominant olfactories; he could smell from as far away as fifty to seventy miles, a handy adaptation if the meat you're looking for is malodorously ripe.

Famous predators, like lions or velociraptors, have powerful forearms to catch their lunch or to hold their prey while they rip fresh muscle from the bone with their backlegs. T.'s arms were thalidomidal, about as helpful as having two fussy little hands growing out of your nipples. "T. rex couldn't even clap," Horner points out.

T. didn't walk the way every comic book and *National Geographic* magazine used to show—upright, head raised, front claws poised—rampant, as heraldic buffs say. None of the preserved trackways showing the footprints of theropods (T.'s family) have an impression of a dragging tail between them. Rather T. probably waddled, like the ten-ton vulture he was, tail straight out, body parallel to the ground like a . . . I believe the heraldic term is wuss.

Horner has nothing but critics, and they resist his logic with the willful stubbornness of biblical creationists weighing the merits of evolutionary theory. They will admit that T. ambulated like a monstrous sandpiper, but they insist he was still a predator, dammit. Even though many museums have reset T. in his new posture, they typically turn the head and open the jaws, as if he were just glancing at you while racing by en route to some old-fashioned predatory mayhem.* Unlike Cretaceous Era dinosaurs, twentieth-century ones do not die easily.

If you ask Horner why early curators first set T. in a predator's stance, he'll tell you it was because the "ceilings in museums were too high and they had to fill the space." To prove his point, he'll betray an embarrassing secret: the early curators had to smash and whittle T. rex's bones and then remove vertebrae to assemble him into that fighting posture. "There was more Barnum than science in those earliest displays," Horner says. "The curators realized it was a spectacle for the nation, and that's why T. rex looked the way he did. It was what the country wanted to see."

Dinosaurs had been discovered long before modern America took up the cause, but they were easily incorporated into nearby myth. Native Americans assumed the large bones belonged to the "father of buffaloes." In England a 1677 discovery was identified as a "human thigh bone of one of the giants mentioned in the Bible." A fossilized trackway in Connecticut of a giant three-toed creature had long been thought by locals to be that of the avian god Thunderbird until more advanced colonials corrected them to understand that it was the footprint of the "raven of Noah."

It was an English scientist who first announced in 1841 that these giant bone discoveries belonged to some new order of creature he decided to call "dinosauria." And the first full dinosaur, the iguanodon, was an entirely British discovery. But those early dinosaurs say more about the Old

---

*In Tim Haines's best-selling book, *Walking with Dinosaurs,* the author tries his hand at sustaining T.'s ebbing machismo by using a tactic of contemporary memoir publishing, the sexually explicit detail. In Haines's imagination, here are two T.s doing the nasty: "She raises her tail and he approaches quickly from behind. When he attempts to mount her, he uses his tiny forelimbs to steady himself by hooking into the thick hide of her back. The coupling is brief, but it is the first of many. . . . By staying close, he . . . increases his chances of fertilizing her by mating repeatedly. . . . " That's our boy.

World's pinched imagination than about its paleontology. Iguanodon refers to a reptile's tooth, and the image the English conjured from those bones was nothing more than an obese crocodile on four piano legs. Such are the rhinocerine quadrupeds that populate the first dino narrative, Sir Arthur Conan Doyle's *The Lost World.* Until Darwin, one wasn't able, intellectually, to describe a world that didn't already exist. The geological *Weltanschauung* was biblical and stagnant, yet almost immediately it was clear that we had discovered a potent new metaphor.

The first big show of dinosaurs opened in England in 1854. To inaugurate the spectacle, the officials visibly set the dinner table inside the reconstructed body of an iguanodon. Later a famous French feast to celebrate the arrival of an American dinosaur included *"hors d'oeuvres paléontologiques"* and *"potage bisque aux Eryon jurassiques."* We eat dinosaurs and they eat us. We partake of their dinosaurness, they partake of our humanness. From the beginning there was a commingling, something vaguely divine. As with Christian communion, we acknowledged our desire to become them by dining on them while being consumed by them. Theophagy is not a notion that casually erupts in a culture, even kitschily.

Yet the full promise of those early dinosaurs would require New World vision. In 1858 a professor of anatomy at the University of Pennsylvania named Joseph Leidy examined an early hadrosaurus discovered in New Jersey and came to the revolutionary insight that this monster didn't tread the ground like some brute from the bestiary but stood up. Leidy was an early pioneer of the new American field "natural history"—the very phrase overturning the biblical view of the earth as static with a rather New World ideal of looking at nature as an unfolding story, a "history." . . .

The first dinosaur bone ever identified was a huge double ball joint discovered in England in 1677. When it was illustrated in 1763, the artist Richard Brookes noted its resemblance to a monstrous pair of testicles. Brookes may have thought it belonged to a well-endowed biblical giant, but he may just have been goofing around when he named it. Marshites don't like to tell this story. But, as W.J.T. Mitchell argues in *The Last Dinosaur Book,* since it is the first bone ever identified, "by the strictest rules of biological nomenclature, *Scrotum humanum* is the true name of the dinosaur."

Scrotum humanum. Dinosaurology has never been able to quite shake its Jim Carreyness, which may explain why the field attracts so many kids and amateurs. Dinosaur theorists don't need advanced degrees in organic chemistry or technical prowess with superaccelerators—just a willingness to master the quite knowable bank of dinosaur findings, a chore that often begins just before first grade. The professional work can begin shortly thereafter. Three years ago, a dinosaur expert in New Mexico discovered a new creature in the Moreno hills and wrote an award-winning book about it—*Zuniceratops christopheri,* named for Christopher Wolfe, who was eight years old at the time.

Because just what is the intellectual task of paleontologists young and old? To take a few toylike objects—really big, really cool bones—and to imagine an entire world. It's a kind of intellectual play that is never troubled by comparison with any rigorous empirical reality. The only competition is some other imagined world that seems that much more neato.

In the first decade of the twentieth century, people everywhere were hungry to see the first inhabitants of this world as they emerged from the mythic frontier of the American West. Unlike England's, America's dinosaurs were easy to find. The nonacidic prairie soils of the West coupled with constant wind erosions and mild rains meant that at those early dinosaur digs, like Como Bluff and Bone Cabin Quarry, skeletons were often just lying exposed on the ground. The first dinosaur to go on tour was a plaster cast of a diplodocus, one of the long-necked sauropods that would eventually become world famous by the name of brontosaurus. For those willing to look closely, the connection between emerging American power and the vigor extant in the skeleton was apparent. That traveling dinosaur and a subsequent discovery were known, scientifically, as *Diplodocus carnegii* and *Apatosaurus louisae,* after their patrons, Andrew and Louise Carnegie.

New York's American Museum of Natural History unveiled the first permanent display: a brontosaurus in 1905, paired in 1910 with a T. rex. Figuring out how to hold up, say, T. rex's 2,000-pound pelvis was a chore. But as luck would have it, the industrial revolution was outfitting every American home with the new fangled marvel of indoor plumbing. And that's what the curators chose—the same L joints, sink traps, U brackets, and threaded pipes that forged the infrastructure of America's emerging empire also cantilevered the spines, jaws, breastplates, and hipbones of those two great beasts.[†] It was certainly as much a celebration of our new power as it was of the dinosaurs, and right away they assumed oddly familiar personalities. The brontosaurus was a long-necked galoot—a cud-chewing, vegetarian, gentle giant. Then just across the aisle, the psychic opposite: T. rex, frenzied carnivorous killer. An interesting

---

[†]Those two dinosaurs continue to reside at the American Museum of Natural History. In a 1995 redesign of the museum's expanded collection, the original duo were set aside in a separate room—the dinosaur of dinosaur exhibits. The original armature still holds up those bones, and that old blackened plumbing is easily as beautiful as the fossils themselves. The great dinosaurs had lain down 65 million years ago, and what put them once again on their feet? The tensile strength of Pittsburgh steel.

Tyrannosaurus rex statue

pair those two, and it is no coincidence that their erection occurred just before we entered World War I, revealing to the world the character of a new global species—the American: A big, dumb rube, until provoked—then berserker rage.

It is difficult to imagine the effect those first displays must have had on the minds of our great-grandparents. But consider: You had to make a big trip to New York to see them. Newspaper descriptions and the occasional picture only stoked the desire to go. Meanwhile, all around you, a greatness was coming together—electrical wiring, indoor plumbing, the plane, the car, the movie—and it was being assembled around, over, and through you into a colossus larger than anything since Rome. The emotion that surged when you tilted back your head to look at those early dinosaurs was awe, for sure, but it was also a suffused patriotism. The skeletons gave substance and turgor to a novel feeling of giantness that citizens must have

Brontosaurus sculpture

felt as they sensed their own inexorable participation in a new American project of pure immensity, an awareness that something dinosaurian in scope was rising up in the world: The first modern superpower. . . .

Like everybody else, dinosaurs turned off and dropped out in the sixties and seventies. There were some minor shifts. It was in this era that Horner developed his other controversial theory: that dinosaurs parented. Horner is almost single-handedly responsible for getting dinosaurs in touch with their feminine side. He had discovered some dinosaur eggs and hatchlings surrounded by fossilized "regurgitated food" and adult dung—the detritus of a mother animal caring for its helpless nest-bound offspring. Dinosaurs had come a long way from the macho "terrible lizards" that erupted *ab ovo,* ready to begin their rampages. One of Horner's discoveries was *Maiasaura* (the first use of the feminine "a" ending versus the masculine "us"), meaning "good mother lizard." Around this time, in case you don't recall, the hottest talk-show host was Phil Donahue and the president was Jimmy Carter.

Dinosaurs' next epic pop-cultural leap in the national consciousness was the movie *Jurassic Park*. Like every curator before him, Spielberg sensed it was once again time to rearrange the Rorschachian bones. The star of that movie was the velociraptor. The brontosaurus and the T. rex make almost cameo appearances, like Robert Mitchum in the *Cape Fear* remake—an insider's nod to the grizzled original. The brontosaurus has only one significant scene, sneezing a few gallons of dino snot all over the kids. Still the goofball, after all these aeons. T. rex assumes his familiar role as enraged killer, but he's still a patriot, arriving at the end to save the day, like the cavalry.

And just who was the velociraptor in this 1993 movie? For a dinosaur, he was small, human-sized, and warm-blooded. The scientist in the film noted its jugular instincts ("lethal at eight months"), cunning ("problem-solving intelligence"), and strategic adaptability ("they remember"). At a time when the Japanese seemed to be taking over the world, we gazed upon a new beast—the global-business warrior, physically downsized, entrepreneurially fleet, rapaciously alert, ready for the dissolution of the nation-state. If the Pacific Rim was poised to take over the world, then this dinosaur was our response; an image that reflected how we conceived of our enemy as much as how we conceived of our new selves. The old-economy capitalist (T. rex) is there but sidelined, yielding to the distinctive features of the new-economy capitalist—lean, mean, smart, fast, and fatal. Many of the incidental descriptions of *Jurassic Park*'s velociraptor could easily be dropped into a *Fortune* magazine profile of Henry Kravis, "Chainsaw" Al Dunlop, or Larry Ellison, without any editing. Even its Latinate name eerily foreshadowed its future metaphorical role. "Velociraptor" means fast-footed thief.

After *Jurassic Park*'s success, the American Museum of Natural History shook up the bones once again and then, in 1995, tossed them out into a new display that received widespread praise. What the visitor sees is very much a new world, fully reimagined as a time of environmental balance. These dinos are shown in familial clusters, in mini-dioramas under glass. Many are small and seem as approachable in their outsized terrariums as gerbils in a suburban den. They are poised not to kill but to mate and to remind us, as the Disney movies do, of the Great Circle of Life. One display comes across like an intact family brimming with centrist heterosexual values—a mom and pop psittacosauri, plus three little hatchling psitts, gathered together, possibly on their way to church. A rare dinosaur fetus is also on display. The sum total points toward a very Al Gore–like dinosaur—the ecosaur.

At least, I think that's what it means. In these tenuous epistemological days, the museum adopts an unnerving tone. Each display states a bit of current dino theory and then mercilessly undercuts itself. One glass case explains the latest nasal theory regarding duckbills, but then beside the text a yellow warning label reads: "These are all intriguing hypotheses, but the fossils do not give us enough evidence to test whether any of them are correct. The mystery remains unresolved." That's a bit too much post-modern uncertainty to hang at the eye level of a ten-year-old, don't you think?

When I asked a museum official what he thought the entirety of such an exhibit added up to, he said, "Dinosaurs were the most successful life form that ever lived on this planet, and they became extinct. Extinction is a real part of life, and it's not so bad. When the dinosaur died out, the world went on and other species were created. One of those species was the human form. I think that, in all likelihood, our species will become extinct, and when that happens, that's probably not a bad thing."

So let me get this straight. We don't know anything and we're doomed. What a distance we've traveled since we looked at that first *Scrotum humanum* and saw our own lusty selves. Ecosaur doesn't begin to capture the sagging confidence and fear of empire-wide failure embodied here. Let's upgrade. Apocalyptosaurus.

Fortunately, it wasn't long before the osteo-reply to apocalyptosaurus arrived. In the winter of 1999, the National Geographic Society announced a "feathered dinosaur" exhibit with fresh specimens from China. The entire display represented a Tony Bennett–like revival for Yale paleontologist John Ostrom, whose brilliant hypothesis about the fate of dinosaurs had gotten obscured in the last two decades of fervent debate about extinction.

Among dozens of theories about the dinosaurs' fate—including global warming, subterranean-gas leaks, magnetic fields, trans-species miscegenation, and, of course, the meteor from outer space—Ostrom's idea suggests that some dinosaurs may have just evolved. Their stream-lined progeny got leaner, faster, and feathered before taking to the air. Right now they are pecking seed from the feeder dangling outside my window. Simple, elegant—parsimonious, as paleontologists like to say—and yet from a nationalist view you can understand why it was ignored. Dinosaurs evolving into the larger family of life instead of going down in a blaze of intergalactic holocaust? No way.

But there was another side to this revival. At the time, America's status as superpower, as well as keeper of dinosaurs, was beginning to be challenged by China. Amid reports about China's theft of nuclear secrets, clandestine arms sales, and independent space exploration, word came that China was building the world's largest dinosaur park in Chuanjie province.

Authorities there had discovered two skeletons of dinosaurs fossilized in mid-battle—an extremely rare find of obvious commercial appeal.

"Chuanjie has now passed Utah in the United States," Chinese papers continually boast (quoting an American expert) "to become the largest burial ground of dinosaurs in the world." A staggering announcement, given China's previous clumsy attempts to enter the paleontological major league. A 1983 China find, for instance, was named *Gongbusaurus*, literally, "Ministry of Public Works-osaurus."

And now a truly brilliant Chinese breakthrough—the discovery of a feathered dinosaur, and possible proof of Ostrom's theory—was visiting America. In the exhibit, these specimens were not mere bones but taxidermically dressed up, as if stuffed after a recent hunt, feathered from head to toe in harvest colors of sedge brown, crimson red, and dark yellow, all posed in the most aggressive postures possible: raised claws, open teeth, wings volant. They looked like enraged fanged turkeys. And hidden right there in the taxonomic name was their true significance: *Sinornithosaurus millenii*—"Chinese bird-reptile of the new millennium." Freshly discovered, freshly minted—a brand-new, slimmed-down dinosaur metaphor had sprouted wings and flown off to Asia. Maybe, it seemed, America was bowing out of the game.

But then maybe not. A few weeks after the exhibit arrived in Washington (Chinese dinosaurs in the bosom of our capital—the horror, the horror!), paleo-patriots could breathe easier. Scandal erupted when it was charged that one of the exhibits was a fake. Under headlines "Piltdown Bird" and "Buyer Beware," articles wallowed in new information that Chinese peasants were cobbling together different fossils, often with glue and paint, to feed the international market. The implication was clear. Like videocassettes in a free-trade dispute, Chinese fossils were just more cheap pirated fakes being dumped in the lucrative American marketplace.

Scarcely a few weeks later came an announcement from Hollywood, Florida. A philanthropist named Michael Feinberg had purchased a fossil for a museum there, and it had been closely reexamined. In the words of a breathless AP reporter, it was "a 75-million-year-old creature with a roadrunner's body, arms that resembled clawed wings and hair-like feathers." You want feathers? America's got your feathers right here. "A dinosaur Rosetta stone," said a museum associate, just in case anyone underestimated its significance. The Linnaean name of America's new proof of birdness was as rich in meaning as *Sinornithosaurus millenii*. In its own moist and Disneyesque way, the new find reincarnated that old blend of the bront's amiability with T. rex's dormant ferocity: *Bambiraptor*.

Our Mona Lisa, as Ostrom described it. A sentimentalized dinosaur for a sentimentalized time. In the tradition begun with *Diplodocus*

Tyrannosaurus rex sculpture

carnegii a century ago, the full name of the latest celebrity dinosaur is *Bambiraptor feinbergi.*

Driving a stake through the heart of the Chinese bird-dinosaur has since become a seasonal blood sport. Last year, China announced a true birdlike dinosaur discovery. They called it *Protopteryx* (meaning "first feather"). As if. Professor Alan Feduccia of the University of North Carolina at Chapel Hill looked at the evidence and immediately laughed it off as "dino-fuzz."

But feathers hardly matter anymore because paleontologists are still cooing over the latest proof of dinosaur warm-bloodedness. This confirmation, found last year, derives from the discovery of the first intact dinosaur organ—a heart—that had miraculously survived fossilization. Described as a grapefruit-sized, reddish-brown stone, it was found in the heart of the heart of the country: South Dakota. True dino-land. America—where modern dinosaurs first stirred and where they still thrive. Reddish brown, the description reads, as if the blood were still in it, almost beating. That's how it goes with dinosaurs. We're always getting closer to the true dinosaur, the next dinosaur, the best dinosaur. It's America's task. There is always another one on the way. With only a fourth of the dinosaur fossils estimated to have been found, the empire has a ways to go.

Each subsequent discovery will conceal new messages in its bones, hints of our superpower's new place in this world and our hearts. The new bones will stand up and the old ones will lie down. The theories will wax and wane. But no matter what we may think the newest dinosaur means for that month, or that decade, it will really be about what every dinosaur has always been about—not extinction but the other, deeper dream of this nation: the big comeback, the perpetual *novus ordo* of America, the unexpected feat of resurrection.

Personal Investigations: Inquiry Projects

1. In your journal, fastwrite for ten minutes about your own memories of dinosaurs—trips to museums, school projects, movies and TV programs, roadside replicas, and so on. Which particular kinds of dinosaurs do you remember seeing the most? How interested were you in learning more about them? Why? As you look back now, what was going on in American culture at the time most of your memories take place?

   Reread your fastwrite and underline the places where your own experience seems to parallel Jack Hitt's argument about what dinosaurs have meant during various historical periods in American culture. Then, fastwrite about the ways your own experience is similar to and different from what Hitt describes.

2. Hitt's research question seems to come from his random observations that dinosaurs seem to pop up and then fade away in popular culture. What else in American culture seems to reappear and disappear like dinosaurs? What do American's seem to be fascinated with right now and why?

Craft and Conventions: Explaining and Evaluating

3. Look closely at the lead paragraphs of this essay. In what ways do they set up the rest of the essay in terms of the tone, the writer's attitude toward the subject, the questions the writer will address, and the stance the writer will take on the answers to those questions?

4. Choose two different colored highlighters or pens. Reread half of the essay, using one color to mark the places where the writer is speaking, and another color to mark the places where research/facts/outside sources are used. What do you notice about the ways Hitt integrates his own voice with the sources he is using?

5. Choose your favorite paragraph in this essay and type it up. Then, in the margins, point out to your instructor or classmates what you love about

it—what does Hitt do in this paragraph that you find effective and admirable, that you would like to emulate as a writer yourself?

6. Which of Hitt's arguments seems the most or least convincing to you? Why?

7. How effectively does Hitt demonstrate the features of inquiry we've discussed in this chapter?

Inquiries on Inquiry: Reflecting and Exploring

8. Hitt's sentences, though lively and full of analogies, are not to be read quickly. He packs a lot of information in a few words and complex sentence structures, and that quality may have affected your experience in reading the essay. What did you struggle with when you read this piece? What seemed easy? Why? What strategies did you have to use to read this essay and why? Compare your reading experience here with that of another essay in this chapter.

9. Choose two other essays from this chapter, in addition to this one, and fastwrite about what each has taught you about writing a research essay. What do you understand now as a researcher and writer that you did not understand before you read these pieces?

10. Using your dialogue journal, record on the left side all the passages, details, and ideas that struck you as you read this essay. Then on the right side fastwrite about why they struck you and what you think about them. What questions do they raise? What in your own experience do these details or ideas remind you of? What surprised you the most?

11. Fastwrite for seven minutes about whether you found this essay interesting or not. Were you engaged? Did you keep reading because you wanted to? What about this essay seemed to affect that? What in your own experience seemed to affect that?

My Secret History

Jillian A. Sim

More than the other essays in this chapter, this piece is organized by the story of the author's research: the questions that begin her search into her grandmother's and great-grandmother's lives, the questions that arise with each new piece of material she finds, and the ways that information changes not only how she views her grandmothers, but how she views herself as well. Initially, Sim believed that her family history was actually a series of rather "dull" stories about average, uninteresting people. After her grandmother Ellen dies, a friend of her grandmother's calls with the genealogical research Ellen had asked her friend to do. Sim soon learns the secret Ellen was trying to keep by suppressing this research, and it spurs Sim to dig even deeper into other historical records.

Originally published in American Heritage *(May–June 1999), this piece is an excellent example of how research can lead to new insights about our families, our history, and ourselves. As you read, consider how effective it is for Sim to organize the essay around the process of finding more and more information on her grandmothers. How else might she have organized this piece? Would a different organizational pattern change the essay in any way (in terms of tone, reader interest, subject matter, the writer's conclusions, etc.)? How would the essay change if the writer chose not to use "I"? Note the places where Sim pauses to offer insights and conclusions she's made based on her research, and then notice how her conclusions change with each new piece of information.*

April 1997

I peered down a narrow alley separating big houses that overlook Pleasant Bay in South Orleans, Cape Cod, part of a row of brand-new summer homes so close-built that they prevented me from seeing the dunes and the water beyond. Then I turned around and gazed at the meager little apron of a field this subdivision of grand houses shared. I spotted a gnarled apple tree and wondered if my grandmother had climbed it as a child.

My grandmother Ellen had gone to camp here for many summers back in the teens and twenties. Camp Quanset, it was called. In the days after the Great War, she had sailed the waters of Pleasant Bay, slept in a comfortable bunkhouse, sat by the broad main field, and laughed and quarreled with her friends. She had performed in the Camp Quanset Indian Pageant in 1922 not far from where I was standing, and I imagined all the young girls dressed in Indian garb, eager and self-conscious in the Quanset interpretation of Native American people.

I gave the place a last look and headed back to my little blue house on the mid-Cape. As soon as I got home, I reached for my grandmother's old Camp Quanset brochure.

My grandmother had told me about the camp many times. It was a fine camp, a place where—for the stiff tariff of $350—well-heeled young ladies from as far south as Virginia and as far north as Canada learned to sail, and swim, and ride horses—their own horses, which they boarded for the two summer months.

The brochure boasts that "parents, each year in increasing numbers, valued wise leadership and loving care, with the right companions and environment for their daughters." My grandmother often spoke of the cotton gloves the girls wore on hot day outings to Provincetown and of the *white* kid leather shoes that pinched swollen summer feet. She described her billowy camp bloomers, a precursor to shorts. They were uncomfortable; one had to wear half-stockings with them and forever worried about getting the dress *whites* dirty.

My grandmother Ellen died on a muggy day in June of 1994. She died in New York City, at the age of eighty-nine. Grandma had arrived in New York with her parents at the age of two, and she was a New Yorker for the rest of her life.

Born of strict Bostonians, she grew up just outside the Columbia College campus on the Upper West Side and attended the rigorous Horace Mann School. Grandma graduated from Vassar College in 1927, immediately entered a dramatics school in Paterson, New Jersey, and went on to work steadily for more than thirty years on Broadway. She opened in *Oklahoma!* She had a stage presence powerful enough to allow her to hold her own with the active locomotives in the highly popular Railroads on Parade show at the 1939 World's Fair. She even tested for the role of Scarlett O'Hara (and was told she didn't get the part because her waist was too large).

During the last seventeen years of her life, my grandmother Ellen lived modestly—as so many stage veterans must—in a midtown hotel close to the theater district she had worked in and loved.

She and I would sit for several hours every couple of weeks in her room and talk about subjects ranging from theater, music, and books to clothing styles, languages, and favorite desserts (hers was called a gremlin, a mint and chocolate confection that no longer exists).

Though she suffered from ongoing health problems, Grandma retained her steeltrap memory, sharp wit, and innate elegance. She could recite every line from every play she had ever performed; I once sat in silent admiration while standing before me in her tiny room, she performed a song she'd sung in a 1933 production, complete with all the original stage directions.

I would often ask her about her family. Who were they? Where did they come from originally—before Boston?

"Virginia" was always the curt reply.

My grandmother told me her mother was born Anita Hemmings. She had attended Vassar College a generation before her daughter did, and was a strong student there. Anita married a Dr. Andrew Love, whom she met while working at the Boston Public Library not long after she had graduated. She could speak seven languages and did not know how to cook when she married. She came from French and English stock.

My grandmother recited this information to me again and again, as if by rote. I thought, over the years, "What an upright—what a dull—family. How could it produce someone as lively and interesting as grandma?" Perhaps she'd inherited her vitality from her father. I asked about Dr. Love. The information about him and his origins was just as carefully worded and yielded even less than was revealed about Anita Hemmings. She said only that Dr. Love was Southern born, had graduated from Harvard Medical School and later gone on to Columbia's College of Physicians and Surgeons, and that he was proud, dignified, strict. Another dull bird.

Here is a story my grandmother told me about her father, Dr. Love. My grandmother detested eggs. Her father, being a medical doctor in the earlier part of the century, believed strongly that eating eggs daily was key to a good constitution. Dr. Love forced eggs on his family every single morning. One morning my grandmother rebelled against the egg despotism and left her breakfast untouched. She went to school on an empty stomach.

Several hours later, sitting in her classroom, Ellen noticed her mother at the door. She held a plate with a napkin draped over it. Anita had tears in her eyes as she explained to her daughter's teacher that Ellen would have to eat her eggs. It was a decree from her father. Mortified and weeping, Ellen ate the eggs outside her classroom.

Dr. Love had sent his nice wife to do his bidding. This tale did not endear my great-grandfather to me.

Yet another story about Dr. Love involved his strenuous objections to his daughter becoming an actress. He likened the profession to that of prostitution. He was appalled my grandmother would choose acting after a Vassar education and after such a careful upbringing: eggs and Camp Quanset.

After much protest and outrage, Dr. Love did go to one production my grandmother performed in—unfortunately a play titled *Ladies' Night in a Turkish Bath*. Dr. Love never saw his daughter on the stage again.

That was as intimate as the revelations ever got. When my grandmother died—a fall in her bathroom killed her—she took her family secrets with her. Although I considered myself quite close to her, I never thought I knew who she was. And now it seemed that many questions would remain unanswered.

Not long after my grandmother's death, a very good friend of hers phoned me at the Brooklyn apartment where I was living. I will call her Alice. She lived a few blocks away from my grandmother and visited her often. Alice made weekly grocery runs for Ellen and picked up and dropped off library books for her. She also conducted genealogical searches in her spare time and offered to perform one for my grandmother.

After we said hello to each other, Alice blurted, "I feel so awful about your grandmother. I just feel awful."

At a loss for words I mumbled, "There was nothing anyone could have done. She lived alone. It was an accident."

"But I feel responsible. I'd done some genealogical research on Ellen's family, and the results did not sit well with her at all."

"What were the results?"

"I promised I wouldn't tell her family."

Alice kept insisting she was in some way to blame for my grand-mother's death. I kept reassuring her that she wasn't—and pressed her for information about what she had discovered. At the end of the conversa-tion, Alice grew quiet and then she said thoughtfully, "Now if I tell your mother what I found, I haven't broken my promise to your grandmother. I'll tell your mother and then she can decide whether or not she should tell you."

I should mention that Ellen was my father's mother. I saw my father infrequently after my parents separated when I was two, but my mother had remained very close to her ex-mother-in-law. Alice knew what good friends they were.

Two weeks later my mother called me, excited. "I found out what the secret was—what your grandmother's secret was."

"What's that?"

"Grandma's grandfather was a black man."

Oh.

I was surprised by how little surprise I felt.

My husband tells me I voiced such a suspicion years ago. After a visit to my grandmother, and frustrated by her evasions when she was quizzed about family, I wondered aloud if there might be black blood. My hus-band laughed at me: "Your family is the whitest family I've ever met!" I don't remember this conversation.

I have reddish brown hair, and it is very fine. I have blue eyes, and you can easily see the blue veins under my yellow-pale skin. I was igno-rant enough to think of blackness in the arbitrary way most of white soci-ety does: One must have a darker hue to one's skin to be black. I look about as black as Heidi.

If my grandmother's grandfather was black, then he was surely the only one in the family. Was this why my grandmother, during our hun-dreds of talks over the years, invariably changed the subject whenever I asked about family? Because of this one man? My beloved, educated, and Christian grandmother was a racist.

A few months after I learned of the black great-great-grandfather in the family line, I moved to New Mexico with my husband and son, to get the East out of my blood. I wanted to be a pioneer in my family—a family (part of it, at least) dating back from the Mayflower and which had spent several generations, after arriving in Massachusetts, in upstate New York. I would write a novel and take pictures.

I returned east eighteen months after I left. I'd taken some pictures; I never wrote the ending to my novel. I'd realized that what I wanted was to start a serious search for my family.

We moved to Cape Cod, near Boston and research sites. At my desk in New Mexico, I found on the Internet a winter rental in a small settlement called Bass River. My husband and I arrived with our son and cats the day after Christmas 1996.

I decided to begin my search by writing Vassar. In fact this would have to be my starting point: I knew little else about my grandmother and her mother other than that they both had gone to school there. I accessed the Internet on the evening of March 3, 1997, and looked for Vassar's home page. Once I'd found it, I checked for alumnae associations and got an address for the editor of the *Vassar Quarterly*, Georgette Weir. Ms. Weir might know how I could track down records for a Vassar graduate. I tapped out a few lines of e-mail inquiry and was surprised by the quickness of the reply. I received the following note the next day:

"Dear Ms. Sim:

I have been able to find some information from the alumnae records that I hope will be helpful to you in your research. According to biographical register forms she filled out for the alumnae association, your great-grandmother's full name was Anita Florence Hemmings and she was born in Boston to Dora Logan and Robt. Williamson Hemmings. She listed their nationalities as American and she identified English and French as other nationalities in her ancestry.

"Prior to her marriage, Anita worked for the Boston Public Library as a cataloguer in their foreign, incunabula, and the Brown music collections. She listed her religious affiliation as Protestant Episcopal. She prepared for college at Girls High School in Boston and Northfield Seminary. Vassar does claim Anita Hemmings as the first African-American graduate of the college, although apparently for most of her college career, she 'passed' as white."

My great-grandmother was the first black graduate of Vassar College.

And there was the real secret. This was why my grandmother would not, could not, speak of her family. Grandma's mother had been born black, and she had left her black family behind to become white. An irreversible decision. A decision that would affect all the future generations of her family. I thought of my faceless black ancestors who watched their daughter Anita leave them behind for better opportunities, for a better life, as a white woman. She had to pass as white to educate herself. She had to abandon the very core of who she was to educate herself. My great grandmother was the first black graduate of Vassar, and if the family had had its way, I never would have known about it.

But now I had names for those faceless ancestors. Anita's father was Robert Williamson Hemmings, and her mother was Dora Logan. So Robert was the black man Alice had found. The anonymous black grandfather of my grandmother.

I knew his name.

Two days later Ms. Weir contacted me again. She told me she had a colleague at Vassar, an associate professor of education and African studies, who was very eager to speak with me. Would I give Ms. Weir my phone number? I did.

A couple of days after that I received a call from Dr. Joyce Bickerstaff. "This is just amazing!" she said. "At long last, one of Anita's descendants!"

Dr. Bickerstaff went on to tell me she had become fascinated by the story of Anita Hemmings and had been researching my great-grandmother's life for eight years. Her interest began in 1989, when she was putting together an exhibit for Vassar about the black experience at the school. She wondered who the first African American to attend Vassar was and, after some digging, came up with my great-grandmother's file. The photo of the beautiful young lady, who graduated in 1897, was intriguing. What was even more interesting was that this young lady had spent almost her entire stint at Vassar passing as a white woman. Anita's true identity was discovered only days before commencement.

By all accounts Anita was an impressive student who had mastered Latin, ancient Greek, and French and, as a soprano in the college choir, had been invited to sing solo recitals at the local churches in Poughkeepsie. She was also known around the college for her *exotic* beauty. Many of her classmates tried to guess at Anita's origins; some thought she might be of Native American descent.

According to the *New York World,* "Yale and Harvard men [were] among those who sought favor with the 'brunette beauty.' "

Joyce asked me if I had any photographs of Anita. I admitted I'd never seen a picture of my great-grandmother when she was young.

"Oh, she's absolutely beautiful!"

This fact may have fomented some jealousy in Anita's roommate, who had begun to have suspicions regarding Anita's racial identity. Joyce told me that shortly before Anita was set to graduate, the roommate persuaded her own father to investigate the Hemmings. He traveled to Boston to look up Anita's family.

He found what he was looking for.

The father of Anita's roommate returned to Vassar College to drop a bomb: The beautiful and tawny fellow student Anita Hemmings was indeed a Negress.

The students felt betrayed and embittered by Anita's deceit, and a school board went into special session to decide if Miss Hemmings should be allowed to graduate after perpetrating such a falsehood.

There are no school minutes that survive to tell the tale of that board meeting. But Anita did graduate, and that summer the news of a black woman at white Vassar echoed through major cities in the United States and to "all corners of the globe," according to one paper covering the scandal.

"Society and educational circles in this city," wrote the *World*, "are profoundly shocked by the announcement in the local papers today that one of the graduating class of Vassar College this year was a Negro girl, who concealing her race, entered the college, took the four year's course, and finally confessed the truth to a professor a few days before commencement.

"The facts were communicated to the faculty, which body in secret session decided to allow the girl to receive her diploma with her class. . . .

"She has been known as one of the most beautiful young women who ever attended the great institution of learning, and even now women who receive her in their homes as their equal do not deny her beauty. . . .

"Her manners were those of a person of gentle birth, and her intelligence and ability were recognized alike by her classmates and professors. Her skin was dark but not swarthy. Her hair was black but straight as an Indian's, and she usually gathered it in a knot at the back of her head. Her eyes were coal black and of piercing brilliancy. Her appearance was such that in other environments she might have been taken for an Indian. Indeed, not a few of the students whispered that Indian blood flowed in her veins."

When Dr. Bickerstaff finished her story, I was overwhelmed by a feeling of pride for my great-grandmother, for the courage and strength she had shown in her quest for education. How alone she must have felt at the moment, almost exactly a century earlier, when the news hit the college. I could only imagine the resources she had to draw on to weather the scandal and the subsequent affront felt by the Vassar community.

What white students and faculty might have seen merely as an insolent charade was in reality an agonizing and split existence. All through her college years Anita shuttled back and forth between elite white Vassar and migrant black Boston, between rich white strangers and her poor black family.

A natural question after learning about all this was: What was that family like? Anita must have had extraordinary parents who would have encouraged her to pursue her dream of becoming "thoroughly educated" (as she put on her application to Northfield Seminary in Massachusetts) as the sole black among many whites. Anita's parents and siblings would have agonized along with her, been afraid for Anita, for all four years when she was passing as white.

I now had more information about my family than I had gotten in a lifetime of chatting with my grandmother. I felt embarrassed in front of Joyce. I had to admit to her that my family had wholly suppressed their black experience, their blood, because they were ashamed of it.

Then I realized perhaps the blame for this denial lay at the feet of my grandmother's father, Dr. Love. Anita had married a true Victorian, a strict white physician. Probably it was he who had mandated that little be said of Anita's Vassar experience and nothing about her family's true origins. Maybe he even married my great-grandmother out of pity—or, worse, a white man's mixture of pity and prurient, creepy designs on a beautiful young black woman! Horrible. Yes, this portrait fit for me. The man responsible for forcing eggs on grandmother, who was so strict and wholesome, felt he'd done the Christian thing by marrying my scandalous, lowly great-grandmother.

"There was a brother," Joyce Bickerstaff told me when we were finishing up another phone call. "A brother of whom Anita was very proud. I heard he went to MIT."

I called the Massachusetts Institute of Technology the next day and inquired at the registrar's office about a Hemmings who would have attended the school in the late nineteenth century. I was put on hold. After a moment the person at the registrar's came back on, confirmed that a Frederick John Hemmings had graduated in 1897, and offered to send me what he could about him.

A few days later the mail brought a packet containing photocopies of a group picture of MIT's 1897 graduating class and Frederick Hemmings's class portrait. I also received a copy of a page from the *MIT 1897 Class Book,* which revealed Frederick's, and thus Anita's, home address in Boston: 9 Sussex Street.

The very helpful archivist was kind enough also to send me a copy of Frederick's grades and the title of his thesis: *The Changes That Glucose Undergoes During Fermentation, and the Speed of Hydrolysis of Different Starches.* I saw that Frederick John Hemmings had done rather poorly at school. No matter; he was one of MIT's first black graduates. He was listed as "Colored" in the school records. I read that he went on to work all his life at the Boston Navy Yard as a chemist.

Frederick, unlike his sister, never passed for white. Gazing on the copy of his school photograph, I saw a man whose physical features were much like my older brother's, but decidedly darker. I was looking at the first image of my black family.

I stared for a long time at Frederick's MIT picture. Above a neat little bow tie and starched collar, his skin was smooth, his hair thick and wavy. He had a dreamy-eyed look about him that I recognized in several of my family members. Frederick appeared introspective and hesitant. In the photocopy of his class picture, he is the only black amid seventy or so whites. He stands in the last row of his class, leaning against the side of an imposing MIT building. He looks very much apart from his peers.

I checked 9 Sussex Street on a Boston map. Sussex Street still exists and is located in the city's Roxbury area. So the family lived in what to-day, as then, is a black enclave next door to the Back Bay section, close to the very white and wealthy part of the Hub.

In May I went to Vassar. I stayed at Alumni House, a Tudor building I remembered my grandmother speaking of; it had been built while she at-tended Vassar, in 1924. And indeed, I learned from Joyce Bickerstaff, they used to make gremlins—my grandmother's favorite dessert—in the Alumni House coffee shop.

Joyce Bickerstaff is a black woman. Gracious, sweet, wise, and sharp, she reminded me of Ellen. We met each other in my Alumni House hotel room. We talked, and I showed her Frederick's MIT file and a photo my grandmother had given me of Anita and Dr. Love: a view of an aging white couple in the late 1930s enjoying a piece of cake at some kind of event, an anniversary or a reunion.

Joyce and I talked and laughed well into the night. I told her everything I could about my family, and then the discussion turned to black history— to the events that were happening around the time Anita and Frederick Hemmings were in college. I had rather prided myself on my knowledge of American history, but that night at Vassar with Joyce I realized that in fact I possessed only a fair grasp of the subject, and it was confined to white American history.

I knew next to nothing about Jim Crow laws and "separate but equal." I cringed when I remembered writing a college paper about W. E. B. Du Bois. I believed Du Bois was a well-meaning white man who had encour-aged the black race in the early part of this century. (I'd seen a picture of him in a textbook, and he looked white to me.) My professor had been flabbergasted when he read my essay.

In Joyce I found a friend and a patient teacher. I felt I found more family too, not only because she reminded me of Ellen but because we shared an intense admiration for Anita Hemmings.

I went to Vassar Special Collections the next day, and Joyce showed me a picture of a young Anita Hemmings for the first time. In May the Vassar campus was glorious, the fragrance of the Hudson Valley spring all around. It was a day for falling in love. And I fell in love with my great-grandmother's picture. Seeing the young Anita was like finding another missing link, the spine of the skeleton.

Nancy MacKechnie, the archivist at Vassar Special Collections, showed me a second image of Anita she had managed to find in the depths of the holdings, a picture that had been included in one student's scrapbook of the kind young ladies used to make: photographs of friends, lines of poetry, decoupage, and playbills. This second image of Anita was even lovelier than the first. It was her graduation photograph and showed a woman more filled out than the previous image: more mature, more graceful, if that was possible, and perhaps lacking the dreamy gaze of the earlier image.

I took a walk around the campus before I left. One hundred years before, exactly, my great-grandmother Anita Hemmings was exposed before the school. Yet she stayed the course. And she did another brave thing. She sent her daughter, my grandmother Ellen, to Vassar. My grandmother successfully passed as white at Vassar, graduating exactly thirty years after her mother.

During the weeks after the Vassar trip, I sent letters of inquiry to various libraries and genealogical organizations. Soon after, in the course of subsequent phone conversations with Joyce after the Vassar visit, I learned that Anita's mother, Dora Logan Hemmings, had run a boarding-house on Martha's Vineyard every summer for more than forty years.

I also learned at this time of a letter my grandmother sent to Vassar when I was seven years old. It was her fervent wish, she said, that her granddaughter Jillian attend Vassar to "avail" herself of the "magic" one could experience there. My grandmother never said a word to me about this wish. My own college career had been less than exemplary. I did not risk anything for an education, as Anita had done. In fact I hadn't finished my education at all; I pretty much hid from the world during my three years of college and never pursued scholastic excellence as I ought to have. When my grandmother died, I still had not completed my education, that symbol of advancement so dear to her, and so dear to her mother.

In June 1997 my husband gave me an early birthday gift of three hours of research from a genealogist. I wrote to the New England Historical Genealogical Society and requested the hours from them. The genealogist assigned to my case, a man named Neil Todd, quickly dispatched to me census figures and death records from the Massachusetts Department of Health.

From these I learned that Anita and Frederick had two other siblings: Elizabeth and Robert Junior. Elizabeth died in an asylum; she was clinically insane. The death records also told me that Robert, Anita's father, died in 1908 at the age of fifty-five. The cause of his death was given as "exhaustion." According to the 1880 and the 1900 census, Robert Senior worked as a "coachman" and a "janitor." His wife, Dora, during these years was "at home."

The census records also reported that both Dora and Robert Hemmings had been born in Virginia, Dora in Bridgewater, Robert in Harrisonburg. I took out a map and saw that the two towns are not so far apart.

On Robert's death certificate his father was listed as "unknown." The name given for his mother was simply "Sarah." There were no parents' names at all listed for Dora.

I did some quick mental arithmetic and realized Anita's father died not too long after Anita's first child had died of diphtheria, in 1907, at the age of three. I knew from my grandmother that Anita had contracted measles during her second pregnancy. She remained sick and went into premature labor, giving birth to my great-aunt while five months along. The attending physician said to put the baby on a sofa to let it die; no infant could survive at five months, and it was more important to try to save the mother. But the newborn girl's cries were so loud and so strong that Dr. Love realized it was possible the baby ("no bigger than a grapefruit") could live. He turned to his wife and issued his decree: "Mrs. Love, tend that baby!" Sick, exhausted, and grief-stricken, Anita did.

On July 10 I received a copy of the marriage record for my great-grandparents, Anita Hemmings and Dr. Andrew Love. I looked at it with growing amazement. Anita is listed as "Col." And so is Dr. Love.

I immediately wrote Harvard, explaining that Andrew Love had attended Harvard Medical School and asking for any copies of his records. An archivist wrote back promptly, saying there was no evidence that Dr. Love had ever been to Harvard.

I thought about Dr. Love for a time, trying to remember where he had come from. One member of my family had said North Carolina; another, Tennessee. The marriage document said, "Canton." I checked North Carolina and Tennessee; there were Cantons in both states. I researched medical schools in the two states on the Internet and came up with a good candidate for Dr. Love's education: Meharry Medical College, a historically all-black school in Tennessee.

I contacted Meharry. The reply came two months later, in December. Andrew Jackson Love graduated from Meharry in 1890. He was listed there as colored.

The man I saw as white, cold and condescending, the man who had saved Anita from the sin of her blackness, was himself black—a passing, educated black who conducted a medical practice on Madison Avenue for rich white people.

This fact, of course, greatly complicated my easy assumption that it was he who had made Anita turn her back on her black family. I also had to discard my image of him as the licentious white savior of my black great-grandmother. A very white view, I'm afraid. Now I had to envision both Anita and Andrew as equals, partners in a lifelong deception that was courageous, desperate—and so effective that I might very well have gone to my grave without ever learning of it.

April 1998

It is April on Cape Cod—a reluctant month, its windy might resisting the coming summer. I've returned to what was Camp Quanset, which has now become, for me, an emblem of the family's fading to white. It was here, eighty summers ago, that my grandmother squeezed her feet into those white kid leather boots, cursing her bloomers, while watching her friends cantering across sunny fields on their horses.

My husband wonders aloud as we study the landscape how Anita was able to send her daughters here. She packed them off on a long journey bound for this snooty Cape Cod camp every summer, an arduous trip requiring, by my grandmother's account, both trains and boats. An all-day journey to send two black children to a white camp that was not far from Boston, from Anita's origins. A short distance from Anita's old black neighborhood. A shorter distance from Martha's Vineyard, where Anita's mother, Dora, was still alive and working at her boardinghouse while Ellen and her sister were in the bracing waters of Pleasant Bay, pale arms and legs dutifully working to keep their bodies afloat. Anita must have sent her girls there so that she could visit her mother. Summer must have been the only time Anita ever saw her family.

The wind blows over the new houses, over the sad little field that was once part of a summer camp for well-to-do white girls. I imagine that same wind, softer with summer, blowing across Ellen and lifting the laundry on the line behind her grandmother's boardinghouse, the wind that is the single most tangible bond between a family separated by the color of their skin.

Personal Investigations: Inquiry Projects

1. Few of us have family secrets as dramatic as the one Jillian Sim shares in "My Secret History," but we all have people in our families who are woven into family stories and legends. The truth of these stories is often assumed. In your research notebook, make a fast list of family stories you've heard, including those about people you may have never met or

didn't know well. Choose one of these stories as the starting point for a genealogical investigation, a project that might rely not only on interviews with family, but historical documents and records. The Internet has become a great source for genealogical researchers. The Mormon Church site, Family Search, is a great starting place for such a project. Point your browser to http://www.familysearch.org/.

2. Another starting point for a research project on your family is photographs. Find a photograph of family members that inspires you to write. Begin the project by simply fastwriting about what the photograph makes you think about, then what does it make you think, and then, and then, and then, in a kind of narrative of thought. From this initial exploration, interview other family members about the time and place of the picture, and their own recollections. Use this to fill out your own understanding. If possible, research the photograph's location. Locate it geographically as well as in memory. Write an essay that explores what that photograph helps you to see.

Craft and Conventions: Explaining and Exploring

3. "My Secret History" tells two stories: the story of the writer's great-grandmother, and the story of the research that unearthed that family narrative. How effective is this as a method for structuring the essay? What are its advantages and disadvantages?

4. One of the challenges of genealogical research is discovering a reason for sharing it with people who aren't your Aunt Ellen, or your mother, or your cousin Eddie. Does Sim manage to find a larger purpose in this essay that makes her story relevant to you? How does she do that? How might you if you were to write a piece like this one?

5. Discuss the beginning and the end of the essay. Taken together, do you find them effective? Why?

Inquiries on Inquiry: Exploring and Reflecting

6. This is an exploratory research essay. It's clear in the beginning that Jillian Sim has questions about her family that she doesn't have the answers to, and each step of the way, Sim revises her understanding of herself and her family. Most academic research papers are not exploratory in this way. How would you describe the difference between the two types of research papers? If you were asked to write an exploratory essay rather than a research paper, how might that influence your choice of topics, your use of sources?

7. Tell the story of reading this essay: What did you think first? And then? And then? What were you thinking and feeling? What other ideas and/or memories came to mind? What did it make you think about?

8. Describe your view of Sim's approach to learning (review Chapter 3). Which features of inquiry do you see her using in her discovery and writing process?

Let Them Eat Fat

The Heavy Truths about American Obesity

Greg Critser

An increasing number of books, articles, and news stories have focused on American's obsession with food and weight, but Greg Critser's article in Harper's Magazine *(March 2000) will surprise you with the analyses he draws from his research on obesity. He opens the essay with a scene in a hospital that causes him to wonder—with both sadness and revulsion—how a country so focused on health could produce a 500-pound 22-year-old man. As he looks into statistics on obesity, his questions lead him to restaurants, pharmaceutical companies, and research on eating disorders. Like several other essays in this chapter, "Let Them Eat Fat" relies on a narrative backbone. One of the stories here—perhaps the most important one—is the story of Critser's research, his passion for discovering why obesity in America persists. Notice how Critser shifts back and forth between this story and exposition of information he discovered from the research. A good writer knows that narrative keeps a piece moving and that exposition can slow it down. Does Critser achieve an effective balance between the two? Does he shift into storytelling at about the time the factual information is beginning to slow things down for you as a reader?*

In the end, Critser's conclusions about how America creates so much obesity are provocative and challenging, illustrating how much more important it can be for researchers to have their sources question each other and accepted knowledge rather than to simply amass facts on a subject. "Let Them Eat Fat," more than most of the other essays in this chapter, makes an argument. Do you find it persuasive? How does Critser's argument differ from other argumentative pieces you've read?

Not long ago, a group of doctors, nurses, and medical technicians wheeled a young man into the intensive care unit of Los Angeles

County–USC Medical Center, hooked him to a ganglia of life-support systems—pulse and respiration monitors, a breathing apparatus, and an IV line—then stood back and collectively stared. I was there visiting an ailing relative, and I stared, too.

Here, in the ghastly white light of modern American medicine, writhed a real-life epidemiological specter: a 500-pound 22-year-old. The man, whom I'll call Carl, was propped up at a 45-degree angle, the better to be fed air through a tube, and lay there nude, save for a small patch of blood-spotted gauze stuck to his lower abdomen, where surgeons had just labored to save his life. His eyes darted about in abject fear. "Second time in three months," his mother blurted out to me as she stood watching in horror. "He had two stomach staplings, and they both came apart. Oh my God, my boy. . . . " Her boy was suffocating in his own fat.

I was struck not just by the spectacle but by the truth of the mother's comment. This *was* a boy—one buried in years of bad health, relative poverty, a sedentary lifestyle, and a high-fat diet, to be sure, but a boy nonetheless. Yet how surprised should I have been? That obesity, particularly among the young and the poor, is spinning out of control is hardly a secret. It is, in fact, something that most Americans can agree upon. Along with depression, heart disease, and cancer, obesity is yet another chew in our daily rumination about health and fitness, morbidity and mortality. Still, even in dot-com America, where statistics fly like arrows, the numbers are astonishing. Consider:

- Today, one fifth of all Americans are obese, meaning that they have a body mass index, or BMI, of more than 30. (BMI is a universally recognized cross-measure of weight for height and stature.) The epidemiological figures on chronic corpulence are so unequivocal that even the normally reticent dean of American obesity studies, the University of Colorado's James O. Hill, says that if obesity is left unchecked almost all Americans will be overweight within a few generations. "Becoming obese," he told the *Arizona Republic,* "is a normal response to the American environment."

- Children are most at risk. At least 25 percent of all Americans now under age 19 are overweight or obese. In 1998, Dr. David Satcher, the new U.S. surgeon general, was moved to declare childhood obesity to be epidemic. "Today," he told a group of federal bureaucrats and policymakers, "we see a nation of young people seriously at risk of starting out obese and dooming themselves to the difficult task of overcoming a tough illness."

- Even among the most careful researchers these days, "epidemic" is the term of choice when it comes to talk of fat, particularly fat children. As William Dietz, the director of nutrition at the Centers for Disease Control, said last year, "This is an epidemic in the United States the likes of which we have not had before in chronic disease." The cost to the general public health budget by 2020 will run into the hundreds of billions, making HIV look, economically, like a bad case of the flu.

Yet standing that day in the intensive care unit, among the beepers and buzzers and pumps, epidemic was the last thing on my mind. Instead I felt heartbreak, revulsion, fear, sadness—and then curiosity: Where did this boy come from? Who and what had made him? How is it that we Americans, perhaps the most health-conscious of any people in the history of the world, and certainly the richest, have come to preside over the deadly fattening of our youth?

The beginning of an answer came one day last fall, in the same week that the Spanish language newspaper *La Opinión* ran a story headlined "Diabetes epidemia en latinos," when I attended the opening of the newest Krispy Kreme doughnut store in Los Angeles. It was, as they say in marketing circles, a "resonant" event, replete with around-the-block lines, celebrity news anchors, and stern cops directing traffic. The store, located in the heart of the San Fernando Valley's burgeoning Latino population, pulsed with excitement. In one corner stood the new store's manager, a young Anglo fellow, accompanied by a Krispy Kreme publicity director. "Why had Krispy Kreme decided to locate here?" I asked.

"See," the manager said, brushing a crumb of choco-glaze from his fingers, "the idea is simple—accessible but not convenient. The idea is to make the store accessible—easy to get into and out of from the street—but just a tad away from the—eh, mainstream so as to make sure that the customers are presold and very intent before they get here," he said, betraying no doubts about the company's marketing formula. "We want them intent to get at least a dozen before they even think of coming in."

But why this slightly non-mainstream place?

"Because it's obvious. . . ." He gestured to the stout Mayan doñas queuing around the building. "We're looking for all the bigger families."

Bigger in size?

"Yeah." His eyes rolled, like little glazed crullers. *"Bigger in size."*

Of course, fast-food and national restaurant chains like Krispy Kreme that serve it have long been the object of criticism by nutritionists and dietitians. Despite the attention, however, fast-food companies, most of them publicly owned and sprinkled into the stock portfolios of many striving Americans (including mine and perhaps yours), have grown more aggressive in their targeting of poor inner-city communities. One of every four hamburgers sold by the good folks at McDonald's, for example, is now purchased by inner-city consumers who, disproportionately, are young black men.

In fact, it was the poor, and their increasing need for cheap meals consumed outside the home, that fueled the development of what may well be the most important fast-food innovation of the past twenty years, the sales gimmick known as "supersizing." At my local McDonald's, located in a lower-middle-income area of Pasadena, California, the supersize bacchanal goes into high gear at about five P.M., when the various urban caballeros, drywalleros, and jardineros get off work and head for a quick bite. Mixed in is a sizable element of young black kids traveling between school and home, their economic status apparent by the fact that they've walked instead of driven. Customers are cheerfully encouraged to "supersize your meal!" by signs saying, "If we don't recommend a supersize, the supersize is free!" For an extra 79 cents, a kid ordering a cheeseburger, small fries, and a small Coke will get said cheeseburger plus a supersize Coke (42 fluid ounces versus 16, with free refills) and a supersize order of french fries (more than double the weight of a regular order). Suffice it to say that consumption of said meals is fast and, in almost every instance I observed, very complete.

But what, metabolically speaking, has taken place? The total caloric content of the meal has been jacked up from 680 calories to more than 1,340 calories. According to the very generous U.S. dietary guidelines, 1,340 calories represent more than half of a teenager's recommended daily caloric consumption, and the added calories themselves are protein-poor but fat- and carbohydrate-rich. Completing this jumbo dietetic horror is the fact that the easy availability of such huge meals arrives in the same years in which physical activity among teenage boys and girls drops by about half.

Now consider the endocrine warfare that follows. The constant bombing of the pancreas by such a huge hit of sugars and fats can eventually wear out the organ's insulin-producing "islets," leading to diabetes and its inevitable dirge of woes: kidney, eye, and nerve damage; increased risk of heart disease; even stroke. The resulting sugar-induced hyperglycemia in many of the obese wreaks its own havoc in the form of glucose toxicity, further debilitating nerve endings and arterial walls. For the obese and soon to be obese, it is no overstatement to say that after supersized teen years the pancreas may never be the same. Some 16 million Americans suffer from Type 2 diabetes, a third of them unaware of their condition. Today's giggly teen burp may well be tomorrow's aching neuropathic limb.

Diabetes, by the way, is just the beginning of what's possible. If childhood obesity truly is "an epidemic in the United States the likes of which we have not had before in chronic disease," then places like McDonald's and Winchell's Donut stores, with their endless racks of glazed and creamy goodies, are the San Francisco bathhouses of said epidemic, the places where the high-risk population indulges in high-risk behavior. Although open around the clock, the Winchell's near my house doesn't get rolling until seven in the morning, the Spanish-language talk shows frothing in the background while an ambulance light whirls atop the Coke dispenser. Inside, Mami placates Miguelito with a giant apple fritter. Papi tells a joke and pours ounce upon ounce of sugar and cream into his 20-ounce coffee. Viewed through the lens of obesity, as I am inclined to do, the scene is not so *feliz*. The obesity rate for Mexican American children is shocking. Between the ages of five and eleven, the rate for girls is 27 percent; for boys, 23 percent. By fourth grade the rate for girls peaks at 32 percent, while boys top out at 43 percent. Not surprisingly, obesity-related disorders are everywhere on display at Winchell's, right before my eyes—including fat kids who limp, which can be a symptom of Blount's disease (a deformity of the tibia) or a sign of slipped capital femoral epiphysis (an orthopedic abnormality brought about by weight-induced dislocation of the femur bone). Both conditions are progressive, often requiring surgery.

The chubby boy nodding in the corner, waiting for his Papi to finish his *café,* is likely suffering from some form of sleep apnea; a recent study of 41 children with severe obesity revealed that a third had the condition and that another third presented with clinically abnormal sleep patterns. Another recent study indicated that "obese children with obstructive sleep apnea demonstrate clinically significant decrements in learning and memory function." And the lovely but very chubby little girl tending to her schoolbooks? Chances are she will begin puberty before the age of ten, launching her into a lifetime of endocrine bizarreness that not only will be costly to treat but will be emotionally devastating as well. Research also suggests that weight gain can lead to the development of pseudotumor cerebri, a brain tumor most common in females. A recent review of 57 patients with the tumor revealed that 90 percent were obese. This little girl's chances of developing other neurological illnesses are profound as well. And she may already have gallstones: obesity accounts for up to 33 percent of all gallstones observed in children. She is ten times more likely than her nonobese peers to develop high blood pressure, and she is increasingly likely to contract Type 2 diabetes, obesity being that disease's number-one risk factor.

Of course, if she is really lucky, that little girl could just be having a choco-sprinkles doughnut on her way to school.

What about poor rural whites? Studying children in an elementary school in a low-income town in eastern Kentucky, the anthropologist Deborah Crooks was astonished to find stunting and obesity not just present but prevalent. Among her subjects, 13 percent of girls exhibited notable stunting; 33 percent of all kids were significantly overweight; and 13 percent of the children were obese—21 percent of boys and 9 percent of girls. A sensitive, elegant writer, Crooks drew from her work three important conclusions: One, that poor kids in the United States often face the same evolutionary nutritional pressures as those in newly industrializing nations, where traditional diets are replaced by high-fat diets and where labor-saving technology reduces physical activity. Second, Crooks found that "height and weight are cumulative measures of growth . . . reflecting a sum total of environmental experience over time." Last, and perhaps most important, Crooks concluded that while stunting can be partially explained by individual household conditions—income, illness, education, and marital status—obesity "may be more of a community-related phenomenon." Here the economic infrastructure—safe playgrounds, access to high-quality, low-cost food, and transportation to play areas—was the key determinant of physical-activity levels.

Awareness of these national patterns of destruction, of course, is a key reason why Eli Lilly and Company, the $75 billion pharmaceutical company, is now building the largest factory dedicated to the production of a single drug in industry history. That drug is insulin. Lilly's sales of insulin products totaled $357 million in the third quarter of 1999, a 24 percent increase over the previous third quarter. Almost every leading pharmaceutical conglomerate has like-minded ventures under way, with special emphasis on pill-form treatments for non-insulin-dependent forms of the disease. Pharmaceutical companies that are not seeking to capture some portion of the burgeoning market are bordering on fiduciary mismanagement. Said James Kappel of Eli Lilly, "You've got to be in diabetes."

Wandering home from my outing, the wondrous smells of frying foods wafting in the air, I wondered why, given affluent America's outright fetishism about diet and health, those whose business it is to care—the media, the academy, public-health workers, and the government—do almost nothing. The answer, I suggest, is that in almost every public-health arena, the need to address obesity as a class issue—one that transcends the inevitable divisiveness of race and gender—has been blunted by bad logic, vested interests, academic cant, and ideological chauvinism.

Consider a story last year in the *New York Times* detailing the rise in delivery-room mortality among young African American mothers. The increases were attributed to a number of factors—diabetes, hypertension, drug and alcohol abuse—but the primary factor of obesity, which can foster both diabetes and hypertension, was mentioned only in passing. Moreover, efforts to understand and publicize the socioeconomic factors of the deaths have been thwarted. When Dr. Janet Mitchell, a New York obstetrician charged with reviewing several recent maternal mortality studies, insisted that socioeconomics were the issue in understanding the "racial gap" in maternal mortality, she was unable to get government funding for the work. "We need to back away from the medical causes," she told the

Times, clearly exasperated, "and begin to take a much more ethnographic, anthropological approach to this tragic outcome."

In another example, a 1995 University of Arizona study reported that young Black girls, who are more inclined towards obesity than White girls, were also far less likely to hold "bad body images" about themselves. The slew of news articles and TV reports that followed were nothing short of jubilant, proclaiming the "good news." As one commentator I watched late one evening announced, "Here is one group of girls who couldn't care less about looking like Kate Moss!" Yet no one mentioned the long-term effects of unchecked weight gain. Apparently, when it comes to poor Black girls the media would rather that they risk diabetes than try to look like models.

"That's the big conundrum, as they always say," Richard MacKenzie, a physician who treats overweight and obese girls in downtown L.A., told me recently. "No one wants to overemphasize the problems of being fat to these girls, for fear of creating body-image problems that might lead to anorexia and bulimia." Speaking anecdotally, he said that "the problem is that for every one affluent white anorexic you create by 'overemphasizing' obesity, you foster ten obese poor girls by downplaying the severity of the issue." Judith Stern, a professor of nutrition and internal medicine at UC Davis, is more blunt. "The number of kids with eating disorders is positively dwarfed by the number with obesity. It sidesteps the whole class issue. We've got to stop that and get on with the real problem."

Moreover, such sidestepping denies poor minority girls a principal, if sometimes unpleasant, psychological incentive to lose weight: that of social stigma. Only recently has the academy come to grapple with this. Writing in a recent issue of the *International Journal of Obesity,* the scholar Susan Averett looked at the hard numbers: 44 percent of African American women weigh more than 120 percent of their recommended body weight yet are less likely than Whites to perceive themselves as overweight.* Anglo women, poor and otherwise, registered higher anxiety about fatness and experienced far fewer cases of chronic obesity. "Social stigma may serve to control obesity among white women," Averett reluctantly concluded. "If so, physical and emotional effects of greater

---

*Certainly culture plays a role in the behavior of any subpopulation. Among Black women, for example, obesity rates persist despite increases in income. A recent study by the National Heart, Lung, and Blood Institute concludes that obesity in Black girls may be "a reflection of a differential social development in our society, wherein a certain lag period may need to elapse between an era when food availability is a concern to an era of affluence with no such concern." Other observers might assert that Black women find affirmation for being heavy from Black men, or believe themselves to be "naturally" heavier. Such assertions do not change mortality statistics.

pressure to be thin must be weighted against reduced health risks associated with overweight and obesity." In other words, maybe a few more black Kate Mosses might not be such a bad thing.

While the so-called fat acceptance movement, a very vocal minority of super-obese female activists, has certainly played a role in the tendency to deny the need to promote healthy thinness, the real culprits have been those with true cultural power, those in the academy and the publishing industry who have the ability to shape public opinion. Behind much of their reluctance to face facts is the lingering influence of the 1978 best-seller, *Fat Is a Feminist Issue,* in which Susie Orbach presented a nuanced, passionate look at female compulsive eating and its roots in patriarchal culture. But although Orbach's observations were keen, her conclusions were often wishful, narcissistic, and sometimes just wrong. "Fat is a social disease, and fat is a feminist issue." Orbach wrote. "Fat is not about self-control or lack of will power. . . . It is a response to the inequality of the sexes."[†]

Perhaps so, if one is a feminist, and if one is struggling with an eating disorder, and if one is, for the most part, affluent, well-educated, and politically aware. But obesity itself is preeminently an issue of class, not of ethnicity, and certainly not of gender. True, the disease may be refracted though its concentrations in various demographic subgroupings—in Native Americans, Latinos, in African Americans, and even in some Pacific Island Americans—but in study after study, the key adjective is *poor:* poor African Americans, poor Latinos, poor whites, poor women, poor children, poor Latino children, and so on. From the definitive *Handbook of Obesity:* "In heterogeneous and affluent societies like the United States, there is a strong inverse correlation of social class and obesity, particularly for females." From *Annals of Epidemiology:* "In White girls . . . both TV viewing and obesity were strongly inversely associated with household income as well as with parental education."

Yet class seems to be the last thing on the minds of some of our better social thinkers. Instead, the tendency of many in the academy is to fetishize or "postmodernize" the problem. Cornell University professor Richard Klein, for example, proposed in his 1996 book, *Eat Fat,* "Try this for six weeks: Eat fat." (Klein's mother did and almost died from sleep apnea, causing Klein to reverse himself in his epilogue, advising readers:

[†]At the edges of the culture, the inheritors of Susie Orbach's politics have created Web sites called FaT GIRL and Largesse: the Network for Size Esteem, which claim that "dieting kills" and instruct how to induce vomiting in diet centers as protest.

"Eat rice.") The identity politics of fat, incidentally, can cut the other way. To the French, the childhood diet has long been understood as a serious medical issue directly affecting the future of the nation. The concern grew directly from late-nineteenth-century health issues in French cities and the countryside, where tuberculosis had winnowed the nation's birth rate below that of the other European powers. To deal with the problem, a new science known as puériculture emerged to educate young mothers about basic health and nutrition practices. Long before Americans and the British roused themselves from the torpor of Victorian chub, the French undertook research into proper dietary and weight controls for the entire birth-to-adolescence growth period. By the early 1900s, with birth rates (and birth weights) picking up, the puériculture movement turned its attention to childhood obesity. Feeding times were to be strictly maintained; random snacks were unhealthy for the child, regardless of how "natural" it felt for a mother to indulge her young. Kids were weighed once a week. All meals were to be supervised by an adult. As a result, portion control—perhaps the one thing that modern obesity experts can agree upon as a reasonable way to prevent the conditions—very early became institutionalized in modern France. The message that too much food is bad still resounds in French child rearing, and as a result France has a largely lean populace.

What about the so-called Obesity Establishment, that web of researchers, clinicians, academics, and government health officials charged with finding ways to prevent the disease? Although there are many committed individuals in this group, one wonders just how independently minded they are. Among the sponsors for the 1997 annual conference of the North American Association for the Study of Obesity, the premier medical think tank on the subject, were the following: the Coca-Cola Company, Hershey Foods, Kraft Foods, and, never to be left out, Slim Fast Foods. Another sponsor was Knoll Pharmaceuticals, maker of the new diet drug Meridia. Of course, in a society where until recently tobacco companies sponsored fitness pageants and Olympic games, sponsorship hardly denotes corruption in the most traditional sense. One would be hard-pressed to prove any kind of censorship, but such underwriting effectively defines the parameters of public discussion. Everybody winks or blinks at the proper moment, then goes on his or her way.

Once upon a time, however, the United States possessed visionary leadership in the realm of childhood fitness. Founded in 1956, the President's Council on Youth Fitness successfully laid down broad-based fitness goals for all youth and established a series of awards for those who excelled in the effort. The council spoke about obesity with a forthrightness that would be political suicide today, with such pointed slogans as "There's no such things as stylishly stout" and "Hey kid, if you see yourself in this picture, you need help."

By the late 1980s and early 1990s, however, new trends converged to undercut the council's powers of moral and cultural suasion. The ascendancy of cultural relativism led to a growing reluctance to be blunt about fatness, and, aided and abetted by the fashion industry's focus on baggy, hip-hop-style clothes, it became possible to be "stylishly stout." Fatness, as celebrated on rap videos, was now equated with wealth and power, with identity and agency, not with clogging the heart or being unable to reach one's toes. But fat inner-city black kids and the suburban kids copying them are even more disabled by their obesity. The only people who benefit from kids being "fat" are the ones running and owning the clothing, media, food, and drug companies. In upscale corporate America, meanwhile, being fat is taboo, a surefire career-killer. If you can't control your own contours, goes the logic, how can you control a budget or a staff? Look at the glossy business and money magazines with their cooing profiles of the latest genius entrepreneurs: to the man, and the occasional woman, no one, I mean *no one,* is fat.

Related to the coolification of homeboyish fat—perhaps forcing its new status—is the simple fact that it's hard for poor children to find opportunities to exercise. Despite our obsession with professional sports, many of today's disadvantaged youth have fewer opportunities than ever to simply shoot baskets or kick a soccer ball. Various measures to limit state spending and taxing, among them California's debilitating Proposition 13, have gutted school-based physical-education classes. Currently, only one state, Illinois, requires daily physical education for all grades K–12, and only 19 percent of high school students nationwide are active for twenty minutes a day, five days a week, in physical education. Add to this the fact that, among the poor, television, the working-man's baby-sitter, is now viewed at least 32 hours a week. Participation in sports has always required an investment, but with the children of the affluent tucked away either in private schools or green suburbias, buying basketballs for the poor is not on the public agenda.

Human nature and its lazy inclinations aside, what do America's affluent *get* out of keeping the poor so fat? The reasons, I'd suggest, are many. An unreconstructed Marxist might invoke simple class warfare, exploitation fought through stock ownership in giant fast-food firms. The affluent know that the stuff will kill them but need someone (else) to eat it so as to keep growing that retirement portfolio. A practitioner of vulgar social psychology might argue for "our" need for the "identifiable outsider." An economist would say that in a society as overly competitive as our own, the affluent have found a way to slow down the striving poor from inevitable nipping at their heels. A French semiotician might even say that with the poor the affluent have erected their own walking and talking "empire of signs." This last notion is perhaps not so far-fetched. For what do the fat, darker, exploited poor, with their unbridled primal appetites, have to offer us but a chance for we diet- and shape-conscious folk to live vicariously? Call it boundary envy. Or, rather, boundary-free envy. And yet, by living outside their boundaries, the poor live within ours; fat people do not threaten our way of life; their angers entombed in flesh, they are slowed, they are softened, they are *fed*.

Meanwhile, in the City of Fat Angels, we lounge through a slow-motion epidemic. Mami buys another apple fritter. Papi slams his second sugar and cream. Another young Carl supersizes and double supersizes, then supersizes again. Waistlines surge. Any minute now, the belt will run out of holes.

Personal Investigations: Inquiry Projects

1. Greg Critser's article, like a lot of pieces that look at a social problem, uses an effect-cause method of development. He looks at the problem of obesity in America, and then wonders what some of the causes of overeating might be. He ends up with a pretty unexpected claim: that obesity may have more to do with class than anything, and a reason the problem is getting worse is corporate irresponsibility toward the poor. As a research project, identify a social problem that interests you, and investigate various causes looking for the one that might be most *surprising* to your classmates. Develop an essay—or an argument—that uses the effect-cause structure as Critser did to inform your readers about this surprising—or least understood—cause for the problem.

2. One of the interesting things Critser does in this essay is look again at the explanations most Americans accept about why so many of us are obese. He also challenges common beliefs about eating disorders. Individually or as a class, make a list of ideas, claims, and facts concerning eating in America that we seem not to question very much. Think about health issues we seem to accept, such as eating red meat can lead to heart attacks or too many eggs will increase cholesterol. Think of admonitions you were given as children: don't play in the street; don't talk to strangers; eat everything on your plate. Then, circle the items on your list that you'd be curious to learn more about, to challenge and investigate.

Craft and Conventions: Explaining and Evaluating

3. Like a lot of fact-based articles on a social problem, "Let Them Eat Fat" provides a substantial amount of background information early on about the extent of the problem the piece examines. Critser does this in a bulleted list of facts on pages 135 and 136. This background information, while necessary, can really weigh down the reading. But that doesn't seem the case here. How does Critser manage to share a great deal of information in the beginning of his article about the problem of obesity in America and not bore the reader?

4. What do you notice about how Critser handles quoted material from his interviews? Where does it appear? How does he handle his own role as the interviewer? What questions might he have asked to get his subjects to say the things they said?

5. What are the many ways that Critser manages to get his opinions in his article?

6. How persuasive do you find Critser's argument, and why? Look at specific claims he asserts and the evidence he uses.

Inquiries on Inquiry: Exploring and Reflecting

7. Though the process of academic inquiry often involves exploration, the dominant approach in academic writing is argument, not "essaying," or attempting *to prove* rather than *to find out.* In this chapter, "Let Them Eat Fat" is one of the most explicitly argumentative. The more exploratory essays are Sanders's "Looking at Women" and Sim's "My Secret History." Choose one of those pieces to compare to "Let Them Eat Fat." Draw a line down the middle of a notebook page, and compare the features of Critser's argumentative article with a more exploratory essay. Are sources used differently? Are there differences in structure, or the writer's presence? As a reader do you experience an exploratory essay differently from an argumentative article?

8. Imagine that you were using Critser's article for your own research on a different topic, say, anorexia. How would you read "Let Them Eat Fat" differently from how you just read it? How might you use Critser's article if you were trying to figure out whether images of women in advertising have a significant impact on how they see their bodies?

9. Fastwrite about your personal response to this essay: How did it make you feel? What did it make you think about? What resonated with your own experience? What did not? What made you think differently about your own experience and beliefs? Why?

10. Reflect on what you've learned about writing a research essay from reading this article. Make a quick list of five strategies or ideas you've gained that you'd like to use in your own work.

Student Essay

An Experience in Acronyms

Jay Holmquist

Jay Holmquist, the writer of this essay, likes his drugs. And that's what inspired him to take a closer look at them—that and the fact that his friend Eric's heart stopped three times on the way to the hospital after an overdose. Personal motives are often the inspiration for a research essay, and "An Experience in Acronyms" is a good example of a work driven by curiosity. It's also well-researched. One of the remarkable qualities of this essay is that the information Jay uncovers about drugs popular with ravers almost always seems to attach itself naturally to the narrative backbone of his essay. When Jay tells a story, his move to explain his findings or cite a fact is often timely; he answers a question at about the time we might ask it.

The topic of drug use is much discussed, of course, and this essay in its most familiar form might be an argument for or against certain laws or certain drugs. But like the rest of the writers in this chapter, Jay decides to essay his subject. Rather than taking a particular position or making a specific claim at the outset, Jay decides to explore the evidence about the hazards of three particular drugs popular with ravers. As a result, "An Experience in Acronyms" is the story of what he discovers as well as an account of his personal experiences. The essay is honest, and never surrenders to preachiness.

Consider as you read this essay how the writer's approach to an exploratory essay might be different from his approach to an argumentative essay on the same topic. What are the limitations to such a mode of inquiry? What are the advantages? When Jay arrives at his conclusion toward the end of this essay, are you prepared for it? Does it follow logically from the information Jay shares? Is he convincing?

The beat pounded against the walls like the ocean against a cliff. Lights of every color imaginable traced imaginary figures across the floor. A green laser made an artificial ceiling through the dense man-made fog. The energy level was at an all time high, as people of all kinds danced in that old dusty warehouse. I was in one corner of the room showing my friend Eric a few dance moves I had learned the week before. It was a typical Saturday night for both of us. I had been in the rave scene for a few years and Eric had been going for about three months. But this night would prove to be not so ordinary. A few moments later, our friend Ben came up to us.

"Hey," he said as he looked around to see if anyone could hear him, "you guys want any acid?" I gracefully declined. I was never much into the drug scene that occurs at raves, but Eric had a look on his face that I had never seen before.

Just before we had gone to the rave we were down at our favorite hangout, the Shari's in Garden City, discussing that exact issue—whether or not we would do acid or any other "party drugs" at the rave we were going to. Most of our other friends had done it in the past but both Eric and I never had. Sure we were curious, but the opportunity had never presented itself.

Eric looked at me with a gleam in his eye, "I want to do it Jay. Will you do it with me?"

I was shocked. There I was, hit right in the face with something that I had been thinking about for such a long time. After a short battle with my conscience my curiosity got the best of me and I decided to do it. I was worried at first, but I had a lot of friends at the party who had done acid before and I was sure that they wouldn't let things get out of hand.

This was the beginning of a crazy year for me. It also was the point I was able to understand the "great safe drug debate." This has been a long, ongoing argument amongst many of my friends for quite some time now. It mainly involves three drugs: lysergic acid diethylamide (LSD), methylenedioxymethamphetamine (MDMA), and gamma-hydroxybutyrate (GHB). To my pro-drug friends, these drugs are completely safe to the body and have no adverse long-term effects, while my anti-drug friends insist that my pro-drug friends are blind to what really happens to them and they are going to kill themselves in the long run.

After another night of casual conversation a few weeks ago down at Shari's, the debate started up again. This time two of my friends, Jarret and Jesse, got into a heated debate about LSD. Eventually, the debate became a shouting match until things got out of hand and a fistfight almost broke out. What would make these people feel so passionately about their pro- or anti-drug views? Is something that the government finds harmful, yet so many people say is harmless, really that bad for you?

To understand this completely I think we need to first understand why people even do these drugs. For me personally it was an overwhelming curiosity, as it was with my friend Eric. We felt no peer pressure to do it. I had originally said no and Ben moved on. No one had pressured me into doing it before, though I had offers. A lot of the young people are taking these drugs without prior drug histories. These are the first drugs that they have done, sometimes even before alcohol or smoking (Pederson, 1999). William Pedersen (1999) describes three main groups of people that use these drugs: "New age seekers: those seeking knowledge and a better relationship to others. Dancers: supporters of the band The Grateful Dead and rave participants. And Yuppie Hedonists: students and resourceful young people in independent occupations" (p. 1696). To a majority of party drug users, they are seen as nonaddictive, a craving for them doesn't exist. The user takes the drug when he or she wants to, not when the drug wants to be taken (Pechnick & Ungerleider, 1997; McDowell, 1999).

Most users also view party drugs as being "safe." For LSD and MDMA, the amount needed for an overdose is extremely high, much higher than someone would need or want to take. There have been reports of people taking 100 times the normal dose of LSD without overdosing (Pechnick & Ungerleider, 1997; McDowell, 1999).

They are also extremely easy to get. In a recent survey, 51 percent of twelfth graders could easily get MDMA (Ecstasy use up sharply, 2001) and I know LSD and GHB are a lot easier to get.

And finally, these drugs are believed to not show up on urine tests, therefore the fear of losing one's job or getting caught in that manner are nonexistent (Glass & Henderson, 1994).

In my experience, for the most part, these drugs are taken at "raves" or "parties," hence the name. According to one observer of the scene, "A rave transcends—in spite of its lack of words and its sense for the external. Primitive impulses are interwoven with new technology" (Collin qtd. in Pederson, 1999, p. 1698). To me a rave is a place where I can escape from reality, a place where I can get out my aggression through dance and music. It's a place I am the master of my own world and no one can take anything from me. If we take a look at what these drugs do to a person we can see how these drugs have fit perfectly into the rave scene.

First, let's take a look at LSD. The way LSD works is still unknown. Its illegal status makes it difficult for scientists and doctors to do studies on human subjects (Glass & Henderson, 1994). LSD (also called "acid," "Uncle Sid," or "fry") is a hallucinogen by nature but rarely causes true hallucinations. A true hallucination manifests itself from thin air, but what LSD does is cause "illusions," distorting objects that are already there to do unnatural things such as melting or "breathing" (Pechnick & Ungerleider, 1997, p. 195). These "illusions" vary wildly. I've been known to dance uncontrollably as I stop hearing the music in my ears but instead I hear it throughout my whole body. I no longer see light but instead feel it as it enters my eyes. I am able to move objects around with the power of my mind; I once changed the rotation of the Earth. These effects are not uncommon, shapes are often misshapen and tend to "undulate and flow." Sounds are not as common but the sense of hearing is usually intensified, as are the senses of touch, taste, and smell. The sense of time also is affected (Pechnick & Ungerleider, 1997). For me everything associated with time doesn't exist, including speed (as in miles per *hour*). I can recall one instance in which I was driving on the highway and it seemed that I was the one standing still while the world moved underneath me to get me to where I was going.

MDMA, or more commonly known as ecstasy or just simply "E," is technically an amphetamine but also carries with it some stimulant and hallucinogenic effects (Ecstasy use up sharply, 2001). MDMA affects the serotonin and dopamine centers of the brain. Serotonin is a chemical in the brain that affects one's mood; when you are happy it is because a stimulant has caused serotonin to be released, and when you are depressed, serotonin is absorbed. MDMA makes the brain release all the serotonin and dopamine it has stored up (McDowell, 1999). According to Pederson (1999), "The substance has become popular because of its ability to create companionship and attachment for young people who are seeking, but feel weak ties to society" (p. 1704). Ecstasy makes you feel completely at ease with your surroundings. You are instantly friends with everyone around you. The sense of touch is heightened to such a degree that energy pulses through you if someone else just grazes you (McDowell, 1999). Massages are a common sight at raves as others try to raise the level of the high. Rubbing the neck, ears, face, and hands are the most common. Hugging and cuddling are associated with the effects of the drug (Pederson, 1999). "Cuddle puddles" and "Ecstasy tar pools" are a common at raves. The only difference in the two is the number of participants. A "cuddle puddle" usually has between five to fifteen people in it. An "ecstasy tar pool" can have many more. I once saw one at a rave in Seattle that had at least two hundred people in it, cuddling, caressing, and kissing.

The final drug I would like to take a look at is GHB. It is not totally illegal either. Possession is legal but the manufacture of it is not. It can be bought by prescription under the name *Xyrem* (Gamma Hydroxybutrate, 1999). It stimulates the release of growth hormones in the pituitary gland and causes the release of dopamine into the body, but the overall cause of GHB is unknown (McDowell, 1999). GHB is a naturally formed chemical found in most animal cells, but only in small amounts (McDowell, 1999). When taken in large amounts it acts as a sedative and creates a state of "euphoria" and "tranquility." It has some of the same effects as alcohol, such as lessened inhibitions and "a tendency to verbal-ize" (McDowell, 1999, p. 302). I personally have never tried it but I have some friends who swear by it. They say that it's like being drunk without the bad effects of being under the influence of alcohol such as the spins and nausea.

All three of these drugs are seen as nonaddictive. A tolerance is quickly built up and if the drug is taken the next day or even up to a week later no effect will be felt. Because of this tolerance, users tend to use the drugs on a periodic basis, only using them for "recreation and fun" in-stead of the need for a "fix" (Pechnick & Ungerleider, 1997, McDowell, 1999). However, sometimes cravings do develop. During my research for this paper there have been countless times that I've wanted LSD or MDMA because I was reminded of the times I've done them in the past and I'm sure this holds true for a lot of people.

But as with all drugs, there *are* bad side effects. First, I'll start with LSD. Although no one is known to have died from the direct use of LSD, behavior associated with LSD has killed people, as when people think they can break the laws of physics and try to fly by jumping out of a win-dow (Pechnick & Ungerleider, 1997). The closest I've had to this experi-ence is when I had to coerce a friend down from the crane that was erected downtown when a local hotel was being built. He had gotten halfway up before I talked him into going down to the park to chase the ducks. Flashbacks, or the reoccurrence of the drug-induced state, can of-ten occur after use. The flashbacks can last anywhere from a few seconds to several hours and can happen at any time (Glass & Henderson, 1994). Whether or not the person knows what's going on can affect how "scary" a flashback can be. If one doesn't know what's going on, a panic attack might ensue and the person may become extremely frightened (Glass & Henderson, 1994). And then there is the famous "bad trip." A bad trip is set on because the intensity of emotions is greatly magnified, including bad emotions (Glass & Henderson, 1994). Say someone is in a bad mood before they take LSD. That mood will be intensified by the drug and will bring on more unpleasant reactions. The most common that I have en-countered are what I call "ghost webs" and "ghost spiders." When some-one experiences these it feels like invisible spiders and their webs are all over your body, going into your ears and mouth and no matter how hard you try to brush them off they won't. Then there is the worse case sce-nario, the "perma-fry." In this the person never comes down from the LSD episode. They are stuck for days, weeks, sometimes years in an LSD-induced state (Pechnick & Ungerleider, 1997). My friend Chris is one such case. Chris was 18 and brilliant. He was an artist and often gave poetry readings down at the Dreamwalker Coffee House. He was headed for greatness until about three years ago one of our friends thought it would be "fun" to drop a vial (about 100 hits) of liquid LSD into his drink. He never came down from that trip. He no longer responds to his name but instead insists on being called "Tweak." He often talks about how Satan is chasing him and describes the planes of color that run parallel to the ground.

MDMA has even worse effects. MDMA suppresses the production of serotonin up to a week after taking a pill. This is the "ecstasy hangover" which can involve severe depression, loss of appetite, tiredness, "hot flashes," and "tremors" (McDowell, 1999, p. 297). Raves can make MDMA deadly. Since raves are not usually regulated, they are held in underventilated buildings where water is in short supply. People can get overheated and if not treated immediately death is possible (Boot, 2000). The biggest hazard of MDMA use is that MDMA is rarely sold in a pure form. It is usually cut, or mixed, with other substances (Baggott, 2000). "H-bombs," MDMA cut with heroin, and "smurfs," MDMA cut with PCP, are two of the more common kinds.

In a recent study by Dance Safe, people were asked to send in samples of Ecstasy pills. In their results they found that none of the pills sent in were pure MDMA and almost 30 percent of the pills sent in had no MDMA in them at all. Eight percent of the samples had no form of drug in them either (Baggott, 2000). This is what really scares me about MDMA. You might be thinking you are getting this drug that will send you to a new level of happiness, but you are actually getting who knows what; it could be rat poison for all you know.

GHB is the worst of them all. At higher doses one "may experience loss of bladder control, temporary amnesia, and sleepwalking" (McDowell, 1999, p. 302). Since GHB acts as a sedative it "slows down processes in the brain" (Haworth, 1998, p. A31) causing other systems to slow down as well. "Seizures, and cardiopulmonary depression can occur. Coma and persistent vegetative states have been reported" (McDowell, 1999, p. 302). What makes GHB worse than the other party drugs is that someone can overdose on just five times the typical dose and when mixed with other drugs, especially alcohol, that amount is considerably less.

The fact that these drugs are so dangerous, yet a lot of my friends do them, scares me. They know, for the most part, the dangers of doing drugs but they see these as "safe," which they are, compared to heroin, cocaine, and other harsher drugs. But the fact is still there—they will kill you.

I personally stopped my drug use about a year and a half ago. I was pretty much scared into it after I had to call an ambulance for Eric. He had taken all three drugs. He was so out of it he couldn't talk or even hold his head up. His breathing became sporadic so I called an ambulance. They let me ride with him on the way to the hospital because I was the only one who could calm him down. On the way to the hospital I held his hand as his heart stopped pumping three times on the ride there. We spent the next ten hours in the hospital waiting out the course of the drug.

After that we stopped doing drugs. Two months later we were at a rave and someone once again came up to us offering us drugs. I declined, but Eric accepted. He said that he could handle it this time and he would be more careful. I couldn't believe that after almost dying he was going to do it again. I immediately left the rave and haven't been back to one since, for two reasons. First, I can't stand seeing my friends in states of uncontrollable behavior. They don't act like themselves. It was different when I did it with them because we were in the same state of mind. Second, I don't go because the temptation to do these drugs is way too high. I admit it. I like my drugs. That's why I don't do them any more. I like them too much. I have my whole life ahead of me still and I don't want to end up as another statistic or have one of my friends write a paper like this because of me.

References

Baggott, M., Heifets, B., Jones, R. T., Mendelson, J., Sferios, E., & Zehnder, J. (2000, November 1). Chemical analysis of ecstasy pills. *JAMA, The Journal of the American Medical Association,*285(17), 2190.

Boot, B. P. (2000, May 20). MDMA (ecstasy) neurotoxicity: Assessing and communicating the risks. *The Lancet,* 355(9217), 1818–1821.

Ecstasy use up sharply, use of other illegal drugs steady, or declining. (2001, January 4). *Medical Letter on the CDC and FDA.*

Gamma hydroxybutrate. (1999, December 6). *Chemical Market Reporter,* 10.

Glass, W., & Henderson, L. (Eds.). (1994). *LSD: Still with us after all these years.* New York: Lexington.

Haworth, K. (1998, July 10). The growing popularity of a new drug alarms health educators. *The Chronicle of Higher Education,* A31.

McDowell, D. (1999). MDMA, ketamine, GHB, and the "club drug" scene. In M. Galanter & H. Kleber (Eds.), *The American Psychiatric Press textbook of substance abuse treatment.* (2nd ed., pp. 295–308). Washington DC: The American Psychiatric Press.

Pechnick, R., & Ungerleider, T. (1997). Hallucinogens. In J. Lowinson (Ed.), *Substance abuse: A comprehensive textbook* (pp. 195–202). Baltimore: Williams & Wilkins.

Pederson, W. (1999, November). Ecstasy and new patterns of drug use. *Addiction,* 1695–1706.

Discussion Questions: An Experience in Acronyms

1. Jay Holmquist seems to arrive at his decision to quit drugs as a result of his research about their dangers and his experience with his friend, Eric. The essay genre frequently has a delayed thesis like this. Suppose Jay wanted to revise the essay, using much of the same information, as a more conventional argument against the use of these three drugs. How would you suggest he restructure the essay? In what ways could he reorder the information? For example, how would you recommend that he begin?

2. In the middle of the essay, Jay interrupts his narrative and explains some background on each of the three drugs—LSD, ecstasy, and GHB. Do these explanations slow the movement of the essay? There is a lot of information in those few pages. How does Jay try to keep things interesting? Does he succeed?

3. The writer confesses to drug use. Does this undermine the authority of the essay?

4. When writing or reading about a controversial social issue, it's particularly important to critically evaluate sources. Are the sources in "An Experience in Acronyms" credible?

5

The Personal Academic Essay: Boundary Crossing as a Mode of Inquiry

[The research paper's] style is usually rather impersonal and even formal. Amiable chitchat, extensive use of the pronoun I, and the serene informality which often characterizes other writings are seldom regarded as appropriate. . . . Its major stylistic trait should be clarity.[*]

To say "I" in a term paper is like swearing in church. It just isn't done. That, at least, is what the great majority of students seem to believe. And no wonder. The injunction to write academic research as if it is "objective"—*this paper will argue that . . .* —is repeated often enough by teachers and textbooks that most of us have internalized the notion as an immutable law: *Thou shalt not use the first person singular in a research paper.*

But why?

Spend five minutes writing about it.

Exercise 5.1   *Shalt I?*

STEP 1: In your research notebook or journal, spend at least three minutes brainstorming a list of reasons why it's a bad idea to use "I" in an academic paper. If you happen to resent the ban against the first person, it's particularly important that you try to come up with some reasons why it might be a reasonable and logical idea to avoid using "I" in a term paper. Remember, in a brainstorm you'll write down whatever comes into your head, even if it seems stupid at first. Make your list as long as you can in three minutes.

---

[*]From J. N. Hook and William Ekstrom, *Guide to Composition* (Chicago: Lippincott, 1953) 232.

STEP 2: Rewrite your list to highlight the *three* best reasons you came up with for avoiding the first person in academic writing.

English teachers, especially, hate clichés. But one of the interesting things about a cliché is that it somehow survives as commonplace for describing some aspect of our experience, in spite of red-penned assaults from teachers and editors. What makes a cliché endure? It must be, in part, that there is a germ of truth to a cliché. While the saying "no pain, no gain" can be annoying because it is used more often as a stopping place than as a starting place for analyzing the usefulness of doing difficult things, you have to admit that there is some truth to the cliché; when we push ourselves beyond what we think we can do, we are often able to make advances that surprise us.

We resort to clichés because they (too) neatly and conveniently describe our experience or beliefs. They're the perfect fit, right off the rack. The belief that academic research should never use "I" hasn't quite carried the status of cultural cliché—for one, not enough people care enough about academic writing to give it that status—but the belief is certainly common in schools, so much so that it is rarely questioned. It seems appropriate to begin this chapter by questioning the rule about using first person. For one, the readings here will challenge your beliefs about how academic writing is *supposed* to be done. At the same time, it's important to explore why the rule against a writer talking about herself in academic writing isn't arbitrary—there is a logic and a history to that convention even though the writers in this chapter work against it.

You probably discovered some of that logic in the list you generated in Exercise 5.1. If one of the items on your list was that the rule against using first person makes scholarship seem more "objective," then consider why this might be so important. Why might you want to write a paper that seems as if it doesn't have an author?

OBJECTIVITY AND THE RESEARCH IDEAL

Part of the answer concerning the use of the first person is historical. Since the late nineteenth century, American universities embraced science and scientific methodology as the best way for arriving at truth. What is surprising is how widely this was applied to disciplines beyond the natural and physical sciences, including the humanities and the social sciences. One of the most exalted principles of scientific research is that studies are designed to remove or minimize the influence of the experimenter, and this extended to the writing of scientific research as well. Objectivity is an important principle, of course, but is it truly possible to achieve it? For example, when a physicist writes up a study, can he call on some separate pool of language that is purely descriptive, free from social influences? Words, after all, are a social resource; "proper" English is not determined by divine law but certain social agreements about the right way to say things, and what's right changes because social agreements change. Even Albert Einstein recognized this when he noted that "[p]hysical concepts are free creations of the human mind, and are not, however it may seem, uniquely determined by the external world." We have to create theories, Einstein said, in order to interpret what we see, and those theories are always subject to doubt, are always hypothetical.

In a now-famous essay, Stephen Jay Gould powerfully illustrates how a researcher's theories influence what he does and doesn't see: Gould recounts the studies done in the nineteenth century which measured the brains of African Americans and of women, finding them both smaller than white male brains. The researcher concluded that this evidence supported existing beliefs that blacks and women were inferior in intelligence to white males. What happened, of course, was that the researchers had a theory that they wanted to find support for and so did not question the reasoning they were using to equate brain size to intelligence. A host of racist and sexist laws and social conventions, however, were bolstered by this "scientific, objective" study.

Things get even more complicated when scientific principles like objectivity are applied to disciplines that aren't normally considered sciences, such as English or sociology. Many of these disciplines at least adopted the language of science when they talk about the need for a "thesis" in a critical essay, or "objectivity" in an ethnography. But can an observer of headhunters in the Philippines really strip away his own particular biases and presumptions—the uniquely personal background that fogs the lens through which he sees others?

Social scientists readily acknowledge the impossibility of this, but many are reluctant to take the step that Renato Rosaldo does in "Grief and the Headhunter's Rage" (see page 178)—talk openly in his essay about how his wife's tragic death helped Rosaldo understand why taking a head might help an Ilongot man deal with the anger of losing a loved one. On the other hand, a small, but growing number of literary critics are willing to do what Melody Graulich does in "Somebody Must Say These Things" (see page 201)—write a scholarly essay on several books by women about the American West that includes Graulich's confessions about her blindness to her own grandmother's suffering at the hands of a grandfather Graulich revered. These writers tell their own stories because they believe their personal narratives cannot be separated from the stories that unfold before them, in the jungles of the Philippines or in the pages of the novel *Old Jules.* They also believe that readers deserve to know why and how they came to the understandings they have, inviting readers to reflect with them on how persuasive their conclusions are.

Most of the essays in this chapter use the first person. But that is only an aspect of what makes them stand apart from traditional scholarship. Some openly challenge the methods of academic research, others boldly avoid the usual language of their disciplines, several call on nonacademic genres to explore their subjects. As you read and discuss the essays in this chapter, consider how they challenge your own thinking about the "correct" way to do academic research, but also be open to the problems these approaches present. For example, critics of so-called personal scholarship warn that there is always a danger that the writer overindulges in confession at the expense of her subject. Without some attempt to be objective, will the researcher be blinded to other interpretations, other ways of seeing? To help you explore these issues, we've paired personal academic essays with formal academic essays by the same author. You'll see an individual writing in two different styles, though for the same academic audience.

While many scholars across many disciplines are writing personal academic essays, in this chapter we've chosen to focus on three in particular from business, anthropology, and English. The first piece, "Learning About Work from Joe Cool" is a case study of one worker excerpted from a longer article, written in a narrative form from Gib Akin's observations and interviews. Following it are analyses of the piece by prominent members of Gib Akin's field of organization studies and then Akin's response to those articles. Altogether, these four short pieces illustrate the strengths, possibilities, and limitations of personal academic scholarship that we hope will frame your reading of the other pieces in this chapter. Renato Rosaldo's essay, "Grief and a Headhunter's Rage," is paired with an excerpt from his formal academic study of the Ilongots, the study he is reflecting on in "Grief." Then Melody Graulich's essay, "Somebody Must Say These Things," is paired with one of the essays she is reflecting on, "Every Husband's Right," which was published ten years earlier. You will witness these writers examining their original scholarship and then assess that original scholarship yourself. Our hope is that with these pairings you will be able to define the very boundaries that Akin, Rosaldo, and Graulich are crossing, as well as the modes of inquiry that the essays share.

All writing, including academic research, operates within the constraints and opportunities of rhetoric. What *can* be said, and *how* it might be said is always governed by the situation: What is the writer's subject? For whom is he writing? What is his purpose? But there is also another element at work: tradition. The readings in this chapter, to a greater or lesser extent, all propose an alternative rhetoric for research writing. What these writers are working against is *the way things are usually done.* Tradition is not arbitrary, or even necessarily unfair. It arises because it meets people's needs at a particular time and place. But we shouldn't mistake tradition for rules that should never be broken.

The readings in Chapter 4, "The Researched Essay," hopefully convinced you that it is possible for a good writer with a keen eye and a hunger to discover can produce an interesting researched essay, even if it does include facts. The readings that follow may strain your belief even more. Scholars in a variety of fields not only can write compelling and interesting research, they can also bend or break the rules and still make significant contributions to knowledge in their disciplines.

What should you take away from this for your own writing? A sense of possibility. You see it is possible, after all, to write serious research that can make a difference in your life. One of the things most of these writers insist on is that it is not always necessary to pretend that your personal experiences and feelings have no bearing on your academic work. In a now-famous essay, literary critic Jane Thompson declared that she'd had it with the academic conventions that separated intellectual analysis "from what is happening outside my window or inside my heart." She writes, "The reason I feel embarrassed at my own attempts to speak personally in a professional context is that I have been conditioned to feel that way. That's all there is to it."

It takes courage to cross boundaries. But the trip is almost always worth it.

TANDEM READINGS: BUSINESS

In this section, you will read Gil Akin's essay on "Joe Cool." Then, you'll hear three scholars in the author's field of organizational studies address questions about creative nonfiction as a method of research and inquiry. Akin's response to the commentaries then follows. These readings about Akin's portrayal of a man and his work are models for the kind of analysis we hope you will do with all the tandem readings in this chapter.

Learning About Work from Joe Cool
Gib Akin

Gib Akin is a business professor who thinks that the subject of business needs "the vision of art." There are no shortage of studies on the workplace, he says, and many of them—despite their impressive statistics, flowcharts, and models— fail to provide a rich vision of work as a human experience. What does work really mean *to people, asks Akin, and what is the best way to find that out?*

One answer is the article you are about to read. First published in the Journal of Management Inquiry, *"Learning About Work from Joe Cool" is*

Akin's effort to bring subjective interpretation to the business of business scholarship. Interpretation, he argues, is artistic if open-ended, a means of seeing a range of possible truths from the evidence provided. In this case, the evidence comes in the form of a story about Lonnie Beasley, also know as Joe Cool, a motorcycle-riding, fast-talking, master of the produce section at a supermarket. Joe Cool is also fifty-five.

Akin admits that his profile of Joe Cool is incomplete. "Right now I'm long on attitude and short on skill, but willing to put my work out anyway," he writes. But he is convinced that creative nonfiction provides scholars with a useful method for getting at complicated meanings rather than simple truths. Akin took a course in creative nonfiction during a sabbatical from his duties as a professor of business, and the essay you are about to read is a product of that experience.

As you read "Joe Cool," see if you agree that a nonfiction profile like this one can tell scholars things about their subjects that quantitative or scientific studies cannot. To begin with, what does the essay tell us about the meaning of work to Joe Cool, and possibly to others like him? What does Akin leave out that might give us more insight into this question? Do you sense that Akin had a methodology when he wrote this? What might be the limitations of this approach?

Because Akin quite deliberately does not make his own interpretations explicit, reading scholarship like this is a lot like reading any other story. Consider the choices that Akin made. What did he choose to emphasize in his profile? What did he seem to leave out? What do these suggest about Akin's intentions? Most important, though, if this story is a kind of evidence, what do you think it adds up to?

The announcement over the supermarket PA system cut through the anonymous burble of shopping talk: "Hey folks, this is Joe Cool and my manager's jumpin' all over me 'cause I done stacked too many beans out here. Old Joe won't be COOOOL no more if he don't get these things movin'. So, please—come on over and buy some of these beans so I can get my manager off my back. And while you're here we've got a great buy on California navel oranges."

Here's Joe Cool himself: slim, angular, small turned-up nose on a face that is slightly dished, older than what you would expect from the name. But that's part of what makes him cool, acting so youthful, even at 55, and sporting an intensely white beard. The hair is striking in its contrasting black, and is parted in the middle, with a wing-like sweep back over each temple, plastered flat. It gives him an old fashioned look, like your jolly barkeep from the 1890s. A name tag on his denim apron makes it official that he really is Joe Cool. He's constant motion and constant talk, moving produce, keeping the customers, especially women customers, happy.

Lonnie Beasley became Joe Cool in the Kroger produce department, first only behind the scenes and then out front with the customers. He started produce work in 1971 and by 1975 his coworkers had begun to corroborate the Joe Cool persona. They gave him a pair of sunglasses to emulate the Peanuts cartoon showing Snoopy as Joe Cool. Stickers of the cartoon character began appearing on his locker, as well as near the water fountain and the time clock. The back room was becoming Joe Cool's domain. The work there was physically demanding, and all were amazed at Lonnie's youthful strength and endurance—lifting, unloading trucks, and stacking and moving large four-wheeled carts of produce.

But the idea that Lonnie was cool came mainly from his constant joking, talking, and relentlessly youthful attitude. "He would say anything." The mostly younger coworkers liked it that someone older could be like them, always fooling around, not serious, "a nut." But he also retained his seniority, and was paternal as well. He helped everybody. Susan Marsh remembers that "he always made me feel like a daughter he hadn't seen in quite a while." (She didn't know the circumstances that give her simile its keenness.)

And, he rode a motorcycle to work, the crash helmet worn for protection also creating his nineteenth-century hairdo. He didn't ride a mean machine as an aging outlaw biker, but a friendly, playful one as the fresh-air kid. That was really cool. He had a sly affection for the slightly wild image of a motorcyclist, even though he claimed he started riding motorcycles because of the good gas mileage.

When the store moved to a new location, a system of weighing and pricing produce in the section rather than at the register was started, and Lonnie was given the "out front" job as scale man. That's when grocery shoppers got to meet Joe Cool. Donald Linke, who also worked in produce and like Lonnie had come from the other store, now made an "official" name tag that read JOE COOL.

From his new job out front, Lonnie also became the idol of the airwaves. When he got on the PA system to announce some special promotion, people in the store would be quiet so they could hear what Joe Cool was going to say. On one Fourth of July holiday, the store manager, in response to running out the year before, had overstocked hamburger and hot dog rolls. As the day wore on and there were mountains of unsold buns remaining, Lonnie gave the play-by-play: "Folks, the manager has gone crazy, flipped his lid, gone bananas. He's giving away rolls, two for the price of one." And ten minutes later, "He's getting worse, now the poor fool has gone completely over the edge. He's giving four for the price of one. Y'all better get over here and stop this before we have to carry him off." As people arrived, Lonnie would load their baskets and whisk them off. What to do with all the buns? Nobody worried; it was Joe Cool.

Someone said to the manager, "Do you hear what that guy is saying about you?"

"Don't bother me none. Them rolls are moving aren't they?"

Lonnie was especially attentive to the ladies. He claimed that his beard had turned white as a result of all the smooching he had done (wink, touch your shoulder). Women shoppers always knew that both they and their vegetables were beautiful. Having been raised on a farm and always having his own garden even when living in town, Lonnie knew about produce and would help women pick the best vegetables and then advise on preparation.

Attention to women was also about kids. Kids loved Joe Cool and would have their mothers take them to see him.

The grocery store job was a second one, even though for most of the time it was a 40-hour-a-week commitment, a full-time job in its own right. Lonnie had always been a two-job man. "I guess working is just my thing." He had worked as a salesman at Sears and drove a Yellow cab as a second job. He sold life insurance as a first job and sold tires at the B. F. Goodrich store as a second. In 1971, he joined the University of Virginia police department working the graveyard shift and soon after began working days at the supermarket.

The police job had a lot of the same opportunities to help people. Lonnie claimed only 30 percent was crime fighting, and 70 percent was helping people and doing PR. And especially with University police, you got to deal with better people. Still, the people in produce were an antidote to some of the unfixable unhappiness he saw as a police officer.

Coworkers at the store would wonder how, and why, he would do it. "How much sleep you get?"

"Three or four hours."

"You call that living?"

"Depends on your aim."

Lonnie had two aims in work. One was simple, conventional, economic, and easy to talk about. Lonnie described himself as a depression baby, born in 1931. His parents separated when he was five, and his mother carried him back to the country where her people were. They never had anything but always worked to pay their way. You didn't want to owe anything or anybody. And what you did was work.

He had always wanted to go back to the country, and the work earnings eventually allowed the purchase of a house and seven acres—not really a farm, but a place that could be lived on farm-like. In an open, ramshackle barn, is stored his second motorcycle, a blue 500cc Yamaha that replaced the Honda 350 he started with in 1976. They look faded and scrawny next to his current ride, a huge Honda Gold Wing with a sidecar. There's also a little-used RV. Three old cars live on the acreage, only three of many projects in various states of completion.

Depression babies, who never had anything, don't throw things away. Lonnie and Nancy's house was full of things collected deliberately or just impossible to part with. And they all had stories connected with them. Lonnie told the stories while Nancy listened. She sometimes interjected to show physical traces of the story, a photo, a card, a toy, a piece of clothing. (There was quite a collection of icons of the Snoopy Joe Cool character, modeled in banks, T-shirts, soap, a radio.) In retrieving one thing, something else always surfaced, and that kicked off another story. It wasn't having the things themselves it was that they provided a kind of archaeology, the shards in which their life was encoded, an aid to the remembering and telling that make things real.

The accumulation has now attained some sort of critical mass so that there is not the same need to work so much. (Nancy, who Lonnie always calls "Mamma" or "doll," has never worked.) Part of the fullness has been achieved by inheriting some money, primarily from Nancy's side of the family. The farmers who were her kin may have lived poorly, but in the end their land had substantial cash value, which helped Lonnie and Nancy finally have something.

The other aim of Lonnie's work was less conventional and harder to tell.

Lonnie and Nancy referred to their son, James Irvin, as the achievement of their life. He was born in 1954, two years after they were married. At the age of two, James Irvin was taken sick with encephalitis and spent the rest of his life in need of special care. He died in a hospital in Lynchburg, 60 miles away from his family, in 1976. While he was alive, Lonnie, always devoted to helping people, couldn't really help as he would have liked.

During the time when James Irvin was alive and after his death, work was a form of therapy. "Cheaper than a psychiatrist," Lonnie claimed. It was a way to keep busy, a way to keep from worrying himself into the hospital.

Nancy quietly did most of the direct care giving, while Lonnie, feeling more and more distressed, took a second job and spent more time working. A friend admonished Nancy that Lonnie was running away and not helping. But Nancy, uncharacteristically, stood up strong, defending that Lonnie was doing his part by working to pay the bills, doing what he could do in his own way for James Irvin.

When his son died, Lonnie cried, but he kept on working.

Lonnie also couldn't help his daughter as he would have liked. Born seven years after James Irvin and named Nancy like her mother, she always knew her dad was cool. What was really cool was being delivered to school by taxi, a regular treat when Lonnie worked a second job as a driver for Yellow Cab. She recalled motorcycle trips to visit relatives in the Tidewater and that her dad would do anything to help someone in need, including her and her stricken brother.

The younger Nancy was married before finishing high school. Her dad didn't exactly approve ("I may be Joe Cool, but I'm a square"). He remained supportive of her, nevertheless. Nancy and her husband had a daughter, but soon separated, and Nancy went to California—a place that for Lonnie was mysterious and dangerous, a place that changed people and made his daughter into someone he didn't know. He worried that she was drawn to men who were bad for her. But he was still there for her, even helping her move back to California after some time back at home. When she left with "her fellah" (Lonnie still can't say the name of the man he so disliked), Nancy's daughter Amber stayed with her grandparents.

Later, Lonnie and Nancy sued for custody of Amber, who was living with them. At the time, the younger Nancy was angry that her parents were trying to take her daughter away. She now sees it differently, that Lonnie had to make this arrangement to be able to get Amber into school and to be able to provide medical care. Her reframing keeps alive the father she knows as helping people, as being supportive of her even if not approving.

When the younger Nancy's "fellah" was killed in an accident, Lonnie paid for the funeral and helped Nancy get resettled. And Nancy, exactly as her father would have done, managed the pain and confusion by going to work. Employed as a receptionist at a psychiatric hospital, she was back at her job the next day. When a fellow employee, surprised that she was working so soon after the loss, asked what she was doing there, she replied, "To keep from going crazy. And if I do go crazy here you can just put me in one of the rooms down the hall." Work as therapy seemed to be an idea with genetic connections.

Lonnie doesn't like to talk about these times. It's as if he doesn't know how, that there is no understandable face to put on it, no way to make anyone happy. It's not like what he could do at work.

There is less pain now, and there are fewer bills to pay. Lonnie wants to spend time with Amber. And with the two Nancys. Be at home more. Lonnie is so social at work you might expect him in retirement to want to be around other people. He's a self-declared "people person," but that doesn't mean just being social; it means being personal. Sociability covers much of the pain that comes from not being able to help, to make someone else happy. There's less of that now, so there isn't as much need for work as therapy.

When an early leave plan was offered by the grocery company in late 1986, Joe Cool could retire. He still worked the graveyard shift as a university police officer, but spent more time at home with Amber and

Nancy, his wife of 41 years and a "right cute chick" he still likes to do things for.

On a recent Sunday, as Lonnie, Amber, and the two Nancys were strolling the local shopping mall, they were approached by a young mother. "Aren't you Joe Cool? I want you to say hello to my son."

Personal Investigations: Inquiry Projects

1. The profile is a creative nonfiction genre that is based on often extensive interviews. The writer sorts through the material and attempts to create a dominant impression of her subject. What the profile subject says is especially important evidence to consider, but so, too, is what others say about him, and even seemingly insignificant details such as how he dresses, what type of books line his shelves, and how he handles himself can be remarkably telling. In a sense, a profile is an extended case study; it may also be a great way to explore a topic because the genre captures the complexity of experience in ways that conventional scholarship cannot. Might this approach help you to research a topic? For example, suppose you wanted to write about midwifery or homelessness. Might a profile of a local midwife or staff member at the homeless shelter be an effective way to reveal important aspects of each subject?

2. As an exercise, generate a list of people you know who stand out in your mind for some reason. Choose one whose personality can be described in a word—arrogant, kind, flirtatious, short-tempered, flaky, and so forth. Compose a detailed description of that person, perhaps in a scene or particular situation that *shows* that quality so a reader might guess it. Do not do any explaining or interpretation—and particularly don't use the word you chose to render.

Craft and Conventions: Explaining and Evaluating

3. In a profile, seemingly little details can sometimes reveal big things about the person portrayed. Go through "Learning About Work from Joe Cool" and make a list in your notebook of the details—specific quotes, descriptive or sensory information, and so forth—that stand out in this respect. Which details are *most* revealing?

4. To get a sense of the kind of questions Akin might have asked Lonnie Beasley to get the information Akin used to write this story, try to work backward. Begin with a passage and speculate what questions might have produced the information. For example, consider the anecdote

about the overstock of hamburger and hot dog buns on the Fourth of July (see page 160). What questions might Akins have asked to bring out the anecdote? What kinds of questions will help the interviewer discover useful information for a profile?

5. What is your interpretation of this story? What does it seem to say about the meaning of work?

Inquiries on Inquiry: Exploring and Reflecting

6. A reviewer of "Joe Cool" wrote that "good research, that which is . . . published in the field's most respected outlets, may be recognized as much by its form as by its content, and the analytical form symbolizes the right stuff for many of us." The form of this essay is anything but analytic. It's a clear departure from the scientific methods that are generally in favor. What do you think are the risks, then, for scholars like Akin who choose such an unconventional approach? How might Akin respond to his critics?

7. One of the limitations of the case study as a research method is that it has meaning in context. It is always risky to generalize too much from the particulars of a specific case. What, then, are the case study's advantages? Why would you want to include them in your research?

8. Fastwrite about your personal response to this article: What were you thinking and feeling as you read it? What did you find most and least convincing? Then explore *why* you responded as you did, what in your experience affected how you read this article.

Responses to Gib Akin's "Learning About Work from Joe Cool"

Do you wonder how "Joe Cool" was received by other scholars in the field of business? The academic journal that published it in 2000, the Journal of Management Inquiry, *invited three leading scholars to evaluate Akin's essay, and we've included their commentaries here so you can literally see the kind of academic conversation we've been emphasizing throughout the book. It's common, in fact, for academic journals to have a "Comment" section where readers respond to the work that has been published, evaluating and critiquing it, and where writers can address those critiques. In these commentaries, scholars are discussing the very question at the heart of this chapter: How does traditional academic inquiry change when scholars cross boundaries between the academic and the personal, between quantitative and qualitative research methods, between creative nonfiction and formal academic reports or arguments?*

In "Storytelling and Organizational Studies: A Critique of 'Learning About Joe Cool,'" John Jermier and Theresa Domagalski discuss how literary criticism can significantly change and inform traditional research methods in the field of organizational studies. In doing so, they are careful to explain what researchers gain and lose in adopting each of these approaches. What do traditional methods of research exclude? What can we not see if we use those methods? What do they allow us to see? What does an article like Akin's help us know that traditional research cannot?

These questions are also addressed in, "Learning About Work from Creative Nonfiction," except that Gary Alan Fine evaluates Akin's article based not on traditional research criteria, but on criteria from other "subjective" modes of research such as ethnography and case study. Akin himself responds to the issues raised by his peers in "Response to Commentaries on 'Learning About Work from Joe Cool," acknowledging some criticisms and defending the essay against others. Together, these pieces are a productive dialogue about the nature of inquiry within organizational studies, one we hope will inform the way you read and analyze the other articles in this chapter.

As you read, pay attention to the points on which these writers agree and disagree. Note, as well, what they argue is gained and lost in each approach to research.

Storytelling and Organizational Studies
A Critique of "Learning About Work from Joe Cool"

John M. Jermier
Theresa Domagalski

The analytical style of much organizational literature (replete with methodological description, tabulated statistics, calculated interpretations, inductive conclusions, and other scientific pronouncements) remains fashionable and conforms well with expectations of researchers who favor the traditional, scientific model of inquiry. This style often evokes a sense of authoritativeness and plays a role in leaving reviewers and critics feeling assured of the truth value of the knowledge claims set forth. Apart from detailed considerations of the rigor and generalizability of the work, for the reader who is well socialized in positivist epistemology, this genre of organizational literature resonates well with traditional background expectations and subtextual preferences. Good research, that which is elevated to the status of exemplar and published in the field's most respected outlets, may be recognized as much by its form as by its content, and the analytical form symbolizes the right stuff for many of us.

The monopoly of the traditional scientific approach to producing good organizational research has, however, begun to erode during the past three decades. Scholars have rediscovered participant observation and other qualitative methodologies. Legitimate and even exemplary organizational research can now be conducted from a base in phenomenological or critical epistemology, and the form in which this research is presented might have little or nothing in common with the traditional analytical style. Today, organizational scholars tend to accept a blurring of the line separating the humanities from the sciences. They tend to understand that insights about people, work, and organizations can be produced and presented with or without positivist methods and analytical symbols.

Some organizational scholars have even begun to turn to literary methods in the quest to understand organizational behavior more fully. They believe that students of organization can benefit from exposure to great literature and to the methods found in the field of literary criticism. Literature can convey insights about the world of organizations in a way that is not simply vivid and memorable, but that also expands understanding of deeper and subtler realms of experience. The argument for learning about organizations and their members from literature and related genres has been stated eloquently by others who underscore the unique contributions of this domain, namely, the ability to capture the emotional, sensual, and subjective features of organizations (e.g., Czarniawaska-Joerges & Guillet de Monthoux, 1994; Waldo, 1968). It has been suggested that it is easier to present, in a compelling and evocative way, the impact of work organizations on the conditions of humanity through literary methods (Jermier, 1992).

By reading a flowing story that addresses the emotional life of a character depicted at work, for example, a scholar may become similarly emotionally engaged and begin to identify with the experiences of the character. Through this process of identification, a phenomenological type of knowledge is conveyed that may not be possible to acquire when reading reports about organizations that are written in the more partitioned, analytical style of the scientific tradition. Literary expression has a spherical quality that generates pictures and other imagery that facts do not typically generate. And, equally importantly, literary expression can move people emotionally and even morally as both empathy and imagination expand.

The field of literary criticism becomes very relevant once we move toward experimentation with the range of literary methods in developing organizational studies. Literary criticism is a practice aimed at distinguishing and developing good literature. For example, literary critics comment on stories, often bringing deeper understanding of and appreciation for a piece of work while identifying certain limitations and weaknesses. What does distinguish a good story? All stories share common elements. Characters are set within a story line or some sort of plot, and there is typically a moral conveyed that is usually presented in a symbolic rather than concrete fashion. A good story brings the reader in. It creates identification with the characters or with the message. The reader embraces the possibilities created by the writer as authentic reflections of that which exists or that which might be. The craft of storytelling requires skilled use of imagination and creativity to present an image that is at one and the same time convincing, informative, and entertaining.

In a sense, we have been asked to act as literary critics in commenting on Gib Akin's tale about "Joe Cool" and the meaning of work. Akin uses the method of creative nonfiction writing to present an image of the life of a working class character who is partially trapped by an unsatisfactory personal history. Joe Cool (also known as Lonnie Beasley) is presented as a likeable chap—sociable, humorous, and hard working. He is portrayed as somewhat comedic and eccentric and, inexplicably, seems to have a mystique that sets him apart from others who toil in the bowels of the capitalist juggernaut. For Joe Cool, work seems to serve dual purposes. It is a source of financial security, but it also serves as an arena for escaping from personal travails.

In our view, the main strength of this story is that it represents a more holistic view of work and other spheres of existence than is usually the case in studies of organizational behavior. Akin pushes us to consider how work and other life activities may be inseparable. We do have theories of work and nonwork that propose connections between and among the various spheres of life activities (and also those that propose compartmentalization and independence of the spheres), but this area of research has not been very active lately. Akin's story reminds us that in real life, nonwork often spills over into work (and vice versa) and that thinking psychoanalytically, work sometimes compensates for deficiencies in other parts of our lives. This is a valuable contribution on which future research could build. The field of organizational studies would be more relevant if it contained insights into connections among the various domains of experience in people's lives rather than focusing exclusively on connections among various aspects of work experience. Often, it is difficult or impossible through traditional methods of inquiry to open up for discussion and study the nonwork domains of people's lives. Organizational surveys that contain such content are often censored by gatekeepers, and even interviewers and participant observers sometimes feel uncomfortable delving into the personal worlds of research subjects. Literary methods provide more flexibility when it comes to learning about and representing the lives of organizational participants.

Any short story will emphasize some things and leave other things in the background, but many who write creative nonfiction tend to emphasize the emotional, sensual, and subjective aspects of life. In reading Akin's tale, what do we learn about human emotion and its expression? What is revealed about the deeper realms of subjective experience from exposure to the life and times of Joe Cool? What feelings of agony and suffering, joy and ecstasy, or other more middling emotions are part of the sensuous life experiences of Joe Cool? When we attempt to answer these questions with reference to Akin's text, we see that he has mostly left this realm to our imaginations.

Joe Cool, as a character in Akin's story, seems to be wounded emotionally but we are not quite sure why. The character lacks emotional experience or at least we are not given much access to the color and intensity of his experience. Akin hints at Cool's pain but does not provide a character profile with which it is easy to identify, empathize, or understand. We are not provided with a credible rationale for the image of the deeply habituated, happy worker because Cool's past (theoretically the source of sublimated impulse in the workplace) is sketched so superficially. We learn nothing of the processes through which pain and suffering experienced earlier in a person's life later lead to work involvement and life adjustment. Perhaps there is an attempt to convey a message that Joe Cool's buoyant exterior self overshadows any deeper emotion or even prevents Akin, the researcher, from learning about Cool's subsurface being. Without information about the method Akin used to learn about Cool's life, it is difficult to know if the subject was impenetrable or if the researcher stopped short in his inquiry.

Many writers of creative nonfiction base their stories on in-depth research similar to that conducted by ethnographers or interviewers, whereas others base their stories more on imagination intermingled with snippets of data. As a literary writer, Akin was under no obligation to describe his method of research. He did, however, offer a reflexive preamble to the story in which other details were presented, raising a question about why he did not provide the reader with background information on his data-gathering practice.

A related concern about Akin's portrait is that the workplace, the primary setting of the story and another possible source of the meanings Cool attaches to work, is left unstated. The story line, or more precisely, the organizational context, is largely missing from the portrait. The implication is that all meaning attributed to work is derived from extra work sources. Although this may be the point Akin wishes to convey—suggesting that alienation from the work itself and form the contemporary workplace is so deep and pervasive that the experience is meaningless without sublimation and other unconscious processes—it does not seem that he is attempting to lead us to this perspective. A number of questions of interest to organizational researchers are left unanswered. What is it about the supermarket and the university police department that contribute to the character's feelings about work? Moreover, why has this character chosen these two settings to invest so much of his time and energy, and how do these settings construct the character? On what basis does Joe Cool's work at the supermarket come to the foreground in establishing the character's essence, whereas the university police job is consigned a lower priority? The implicit theoretical model of organizations that underwrites Akin's story is rather weak. It is difficult to imagine any contemporary theory of organization that does not focus attention on relations of power. It is curious that there is no mention of this central feature of the work experience in Akin's tale.

Finally, what moral is one to take from this story? Is the lesson that damaged lives can be repaired and "normalized" through immersion in work, regardless of the type of work and organization? Is the message deeper? Are we to conclude that although events and impersonal forces beyond our control often cast our lives in less than satisfactory ways, we can overcome? Through heroic personal agency we can at least partially escape the prisons destined for us by oblivious cosmic forces? Whatever its literary, methodological, and theoretical shortcomings, "Learning About Work from Joe Cool" is a tale worth reading. It presents a memorable hypothesis about the meaning of work and another example of how organizational researchers can expand method and style.

References

Czarniawaska-Joerges, B., & Guillet de Monthoux (Eds.). (1994). *Good novels, better management. Reading organizational realities in fiction.* Chur, Switzerland: Harwood Academic.

Jermier, J. M. (1992). Literary methods and organizational science: Reflection on "When the sleeper wakes." In P. Frost & R. Stablein (Eds.), *Doing exemplary research* (pp. 207–226). Newbury Park, CA: Sage.

Waldo, D. (1968). *The novelist on organization and administration: An inquiry into the relationship between two worlds.* Berkeley, CA: Institute of Governmental Studies.

Learning About Work from Creative Nonfiction

Gary Alan Fine

The thing that would astonish anyone coming for the first time into the service quarters of a hotel would be the fearful noise and disorder during the rush hours. . . . At meal-times everyone is doing two men's work, which is impossible without noise and quarreling. Indeed the quarrels are a necessary part of the process, for the pace would never be kept up if everyone did not accuse everyone else of idling. It was for this reason that during the rush hours the whole staff raged and cursed like demons. . . . What keeps a hotel going is the fact that the employees take a genuine pride in their work, beastly and silly though it is.

—George Orwell, *Down and Out in Paris and London* (1961)

Perhaps the most profound depiction of work ever written was that of the great leftist journalist Eric Blair (a.k.a. George Orwell). Orwell's depiction of his personal experiences of Parisian restaurant life has few peers in the manner it allowed one to vicariously experience working as a plongeur (dishwasher) in the subterranean kitchens of the grand restaurants of Paris. *Down and Out in Paris and London* is perhaps not to be labeled new journalism, but surely it is profoundly creative nonfiction. From Orwell we sense—smell, taste, touch, hear, and see—work life in culinary furnaces.

Orwell would surely never claim to be a member of the academic guild, nor would he have wanted to. In contrast, Gib Akin is a member of the scholarly trades. We are not to take his writing—in this distinguished, if quirky, academic journal—as journalism. It is a management study, a study of work.

If the title speaks of "Learning About Work from Joe Cool," its subtitle is "Learning About Work from Gib Akin." Akin presents an account of a laboring eccentric and then adds a set of uncertain and nondefinitive psychodynamic explanations for his actions. Joe Cool (Lonnie Beasley) is an American original. If he is a working stiff, he is surely no stiff worker. Cool is a man who through force of personality and cultural style carved out a distinctive and treasured role for himself in the produce department of a local supermarket. With his motorcycle, white beard, swept-back black hair parted in the middle, and running patter, Cool surely served effectively as an ironic icon of corporate salesmanship in an academic community in which such ironic self-parody was comfortable to consumers. As a "nutty" pitchman for beans and buns, he put a personal face on an impersonal industry.

Of course, Joe's patter was not wholly original. No form of creativity ever is. He was a bricoleur, modifying those television advertisements of the "Crazy Eddie" type: the mad manager whose insanity (with an ironic wink) is supposed to provide economic benefit to the consumer, the Hell's Angel with a heart of gold.

One of the virtues of this type of analysis is that it focuses a spotlight on a particular case: a microscopic and bounded life history. Indeed, with the presenting of profiles of work lives as a goal, one might take issue with the decision of Akin to provide such a thin slice of daily activity. Although we are presented with a few illuminating examples, the daily routines of Joe Cool are glossed over. We are essentially provided with two brief, yet compelling, instances of Cool's labor. However, as Akin surely would readily admit, these humorous and striking doings are not all there is and perhaps are not fully typical. We never get a sense of what work life in the store entails, what the emotional contours of Cool's day involves, and how standard interactions with customers are pulled off strategically, particularly with those shoppers who desire nothing more than a mundane, predictable transaction. Rather than a profile, we receive a caricature.

To expand the caricature, readers are given motive. The illness of Lonnie's son, his disappointment at his daughter's choices, the conscientious raising of his granddaughter, and his compulsion to work as a means of providing his family with income and, perhaps, himself with satisfying companionship. The claims are plausible in creating a story, and yet, perhaps because of the sketchy observations, they have something of the feel of armchair psychiatry. Creative nonfiction does not require excess brevity.

What is particularly useful about "Learning About Work from Joe Cool" is that it underlines both the virtues and drawbacks of creative nonfiction data collection and presentation. Akin's discussion is powerful in reminding us that the analysis of work is ultimately etched in the life experiences of particular workers, and he is quite right to assert that scholars often examine work as a generic feature of life, rather than a particular feature. The account of the work life of Joe Cool amounts to a powerful case study that permits the reader to understand the power of agency, even in fairly routinized, bureaucratic, and controlling workplaces. Similar to this, his intense (perhaps excessive) commitment to work as a psychological salve suggests that labor is not merely an instrumental domain, but equally an expressive realm in which personal needs for sociability and mastery are being met.

However, inevitably, weaknesses follow strengths. The account is both sketchy and its provenance is uncertain. What was the methodology through which Akin conducted his research? Did he follow Cool around, observing his moves? Was the research grounded on interviews? What does "creative nonfiction" mean in practice?

Furthermore, the article attempts to do much and to do it quickly. It begins with an account of Akin's personal perspective on work and on his career, sliding into an analysis of the phenomenological meaning of work. He then briefly describes Joe Cool's work life and finally provides an account of Cool's motivation. Yet, the story is brief and the descriptions are rushed. My concern is not with the attempt to achieve any of these tasks, but the insistence on doing all of them without depth. As a result, we are left with a few memorable images but nothing that is fully persuasive. Magazine articles have their place, but so do research monographs.

As a long-time ethnographer, I am delighted to see other scholars attempt to devise novel approaches to social life. I welcome Akin's attempt. Yet, I have long believed that qualitative research is a demanding skill: If we do not demand large-scale financial resources to conduct research, we do demand a large investment in time and in care of analysis. Had Akin attempted, much as Studs Terkel has done in his masterwork, *Working* (Terkel, 1974), to present a pantheon of workers, the lightness of being of each portrait could easily be excused. Joe Cool is cool, but he demands a cohort of other workers who stand by his side, laboring with him. Otherwise, this account, filled with gossamer insight, will merely float away, too airy for our own good.

References

Orwell, G. (1961). *Down and out in Paris and London.* New York: Harcourt Brace Jovanovich.

Terkel, S. (1974). *Working.* New York: Avon.

Response to Commentaries on "Learning About Work from Joe Cool"

Gib Akin

I had at first thought I would not write a response to the commentaries on the Joe Cool piece, reasoning that the story, with my introduction, should stand on its own and didn't need any further explanation from me. Though

I still do, for the most part, see it that way, it also seemed not in the spirit of discussion that *JMI* [*Journal of Management Inquiry*] has encouraged. Besides, no response is still a response, just a more ambiguous one.

First, however, I would like to thank Karen Golden-Biddle for her interest in this work and her invitation to participate in this forum. I also thank Gary Fine, Theresa Domagalski, and John Jermier for their thoughtful and incisive commentaries. I found it a little scary, though, to have such direct response to my work out in public, without the chance to revise and resubmit. Usually, things are published after a lot of behind-the-scenes work, which can also be painful, as was documented by Peter Frost and Larry Cummings in their fascinating *Publishing in the Organizational Sciences* (Cummings and Frost, 1995). But I agreed to this format, and even though I don't have the opportunity to revise the Joe Cool piece itself, I will take the opportunity to respond to some of the concerns of the commentators, who I think are like me in wanting to develop literary sensibility in our field.

Gary Fine is surely right: The story is not just Joe Cool on work, but also Gib Akin on work. And now it is also Gary Fine on work and Theresa Domagalski and John Jermier, too. And that, it seems to me, is exactly as it should be. The story is there to be interpreted, to get the reader thinking about and seeing, perhaps in new ways, people at work. If successful, it might enrich what we can see for ourselves in the settings we engage.

I think the criticism that the profile is not extensive enough, that it is too light, is right. I hope, however, that it is better reframed as a sketch and not as a caricature (though Lonnie might be said to have caricatured himself to achieve the Joe Cool persona). Furthermore, I hope that the story, apart from its content and what it says, has a compelling shape, satisfying rhythms, and can stand as a thing in itself, a colorful and enhancing artifact. Fine acknowledges that he gets "a few memorable images." And that may be enough, especially if we take his suggestion to collect many such images to be arranged into a more substantial workscape. It is the collection that might eventually approach being "fully persuasive."

I found Domagalski and Jermier's discussion of the path to qualitative and on to literary methods to be a useful and even-handed introduction. It sets the stage for the role that they adopt, that of literary critics. And that, it seems to me, is exactly the right role, one that could be adopted even if the text to be critiqued is not explicitly offered as a story or as literature. (Some take this to be the postmodernist agenda, with all sorts of things treated as text.)

The substance of Domagalski and Jermier's critique mainly takes the form of a number of questions that they would like answered in or by the story. Not having a way to get satisfying answers from the story itself is arguably a shortcoming (one that Fine also identifies), particularly if you are looking at the piece as research. That is not so crucial if you treat the story as a palpable thing of its own, with its own expectations, promises, and logic. In that case, you would be concerned about questions and answers in the story itself, not from the outside. Nevertheless, I think the story could have and should have been richer in detail and provided the reader with more information from which to draw relationships and explain things. Remember, though, that my task was not to promote my own explanations, but rather to document Joe Cool's explanations.

Addressing one of Domagalski and Jermier's unanswered questions may serve to clarify. They were puzzled that no mention was made of relations of power because power, for them, is a "central feature of the work experience." I didn't mention it because Joe Cool didn't mention it, nor did he constitute his action or his interpretation of others' actions in terms of power. But if you do want to say something about power, you could look at the dialogue between the customer and Joe Cool's manager. The customer thinks the manager will reprimand Joe for what appears to be criticism of the manager; that is, he would use the power of his position. However the manager eschews the expected exercise of power and expresses appreciation that the goods are moving. That is the manager's statement about power, that he doesn't use it. Joe Cool himself transcends the power question, not didactically, but by continually framing his world in terms of helping. Power is a construct from the outside, one that is notable in its absence as a construct used by those in the story.

Finally, Domagalski and Jermier ask what moral (the bottom line?) one is to take from the story and suggest three possibilities. I like all three. So go for any one of them, or another that may appear for you, and see where it might lead.

Emily Dickinson cast literature as a ship, a vessel to take you on a trip. We read not just to get the facts, but to be transported. And we write not just to give the moral, but to make it compelling to find one. I would not be so presumptuous as to cast my sketchy story as literature, but I will continue trying to launch some voyages.

Reference

Cummings, L. L., & Frost, P. J. (1995). *Publishing in the organizational sciences.* Thousand Oaks, CA: Sage.

Personal Investigations: Inquiry Projects

1. How common is it for researchers to talk to each other in the pages of academic journals? To find out, look at some journals in an academic field you are majoring in or that is of interest. Do they have a "Comment" section? If so, read at least three of them and write what you've learned about academic inquiry in that field. How do these writers talk to each other? What do they focus on? What is the nature of the critiques they are discussing? What tone do they adopt? What kind of format is used? How is it similar to or different from the academic articles in that journal?

2. How credible are the commentators here? Using your library's bibliographic databases, look up the work of at least one of these scholars and compare his or her research writing to what he or she says here about the nature of research, writing, and knowledge in the field. Does this person's academic writing lend credibility to what he or she says about Akin's work?

Craft and Conventions: Explaining and Evaluating

3. Reread "Storytelling and Organizational Studies" and "Learning About Work from Creative Nonfiction" with the purpose of summarizing what each commentary defines as traditional research in organizational studies. Mark passages, terms, and details that will help you understand the standard convention for writing about research in this field that is contrasted with Gib Akin's approach in "Joe Cool." You may need to look up terms (such as quantitative and qualitative research, for example). What kinds of things can traditional research in this field tell us? What can it *not* tell us?

4. Reread "Storytelling and Organizational Studies" and "Learning About Work from Creative Nonfiction," focusing on what each says about the strengths and benefits of using creative nonfiction/literary criticism/case study as a way of researching questions about work. What do scholars gain from the perspective offered in Akin's approach? What questions can't be answered from this approach?

5. After you've answered Questions 1 and 2 above, create two columns in your notebook, one titled "Traditional Research" and the other "Nontraditional Research." In each column, list qualities that apply to each:

   - What kinds of writing conventions are used (for example, narrative structure, traditional argument, sensory detail, statistical detail)?

- What perspective or angle on a subject does each emphasize (for example, a broad sweep, a narrow focus, an emphasis on emotional and subjective experience versus objective and countable information)?
- Which methods of inquiry (explaining, evaluating, exploring, reflecting) are emphasized?
- What counts as evidence?

Then, as you compare each column, circle the features that are common to both methods of research. In what ways, for example, is each using academic inquiry? Next, put a star by the most significant differences between the two. Last, use these seed sentences to begin a seven-minute fastwrite about what you've learned from this exercise: *The personal academic essay (in the field of organizational studies/business) is "academic" because _____. The personal academic essay (in the field of organizational studies/business) breaks these academic conventions for these reasons _____.*

6. You may be asked to evaluate the strengths and weaknesses of the other personal academic essays in this chapter, using these commentaries as examples. What have you learned about how to evaluate personal academic essays? About how to compose such a commentary? What will you do when you are assigned such a critique?

Inquiries on Inquiry: Exploring and Reflecting

7. Which reading strategies did you use as you read these commentaries? Why? What did you struggle the most with while reading? The least?
8. You will often have to read material that you personally may not find very interesting, but that has been assigned for a course. If you found these articles to be relatively uninteresting to you, what strategies did you use to accomplish the goals your instructor set in assigning them?
9. What did you find most convincing about these pieces? Least? Why? Were you persuaded that there is some academic value to the approach Akin uses? Why or why not? What in your own experience affected your response?

TANDEM READINGS: ANTHROPOLOGY

The first essay in this section created quite a stir when it originally was published. Critics wondered if anthropology could survive as a respected discipline if standardized methods and principles of objectivity were abandoned for the personal and subjective. The second piece in the section served as the foundation for first; it is an earlier, more traditionally academic work by the same writer on the same topic. Both are strong academic works, with a difference in voice.

Grief and a Headhunter's Rage
Renato Rosaldo

Renato Rosaldo, a Mellon Professor of Interdisciplinary Studies at Stanford University, is a well-known anthropologist who, with his wife Michelle Rosaldo, studied a number of cultures by living with the natives. In the piece given here, Rosaldo is reflecting on research he and his wife did in the Philippines, particularly on his interpretations of the Ilongot people's tradition of taking a human head out of grief for the death of a loved one. "Grief and the Headhunter's Rage" is the introduction to Rosaldo's book Culture and Truth: The Remaking of Social Analysis *(1989), in which he argues for a new method in researching cultures that will account for the researcher's subjectivity. Like Melody Graulich's article, which appears later in the chapter, on the violence of men against women, this piece draws on personal experience and feelings to* revise *the author's prior conclusions from his research and to raise questions about the research methods in his field. Rosaldo asserts that his own experience of grief is so intimately linked with every other way of interpreting this ritual that it cannot be taken out. He proposes, in fact, that ethnographic method should be revised to account for the ethnographer's own feelings and experiences. Until he experienced grief, Rosaldo argues, he misrepresented the Ilongot ritual, doing the group an injustice; experiencing grief enabled him to see what he missed all those years before.*

The entire essay is not included here; we have cut sections that address methodology, theory, and ethnographic knowledge that might be unfamiliar and is not critical to your study of this work. As you read this piece, pay attention to how Rosaldo makes his case for including his personal experience in his analysis of this ritual. Consider as well how his use of the first person affects your sense of trust in him as a researcher and writer. You may run into concepts and phrases that are unfamiliar to you, so mark them as you read. Later we'll give you the opportunity to find out more about them and consider how important those concepts are to your understanding of the essay. Then, as we've done with the other essays in this chapter, we'll ask you to read a section of the very

study Rosaldo is reflecting on here and compare that formal academic writing
to this personal academic essay.

If you ask an older Ilongot man of northern Luzon, Philippines, why he cuts off human heads, his answer is brief, and one on which no anthropologist can readily elaborate: He says that rage, born of grief, impels him to kill his fellow human beings. He claims that he needs a place "to carry his anger." The act of severing and tossing away the victim's head enables him, he says, to vent and, he hopes, throw away the anger of his bereavement. Although the anthropologist's job is to make other cultures intelligible, more questions fail to reveal any further explanation of this man's pithy statement. To him, grief, rage, and headhunting go together in a self-evident manner. Either you understand it or you don't. And, in fact, for the longest time I simply did not.

In what follows, I want to talk about how to talk about the cultural force of emotions. The *emotional force* of a death, for example, derives less from an abstract brute fact than from a particular intimate relation's permanent rupture. It refers to the kinds of feelings one experiences on learning, for example, that the child just run over by a car is one's own and not a stranger's. Rather than speaking of death in general, one must consider the subject's position within a field of social relations in order to grasp one's emotional experience.

My effort to show the force of a simple statement taken literally goes against anthropology's classic norms, which prefer to explicate culture through the gradual thickening of symbolic webs of meaning. By and large, cultural analysts use not *force* but such terms as *thick description, multi-vocality, polysemy, richness,* and *texture.* The notion of force, among other things, opens to question the common anthropological assumption that the greatest human import resides in the densest forest of symbols and that analytical detail, or "cultural depth," equals enhanced explanation of a culture, or "cultural elaboration." Do people always in fact describe most thickly what matters most to them?

The Rage in Ilongot Grief

Let me pause a moment to introduce the Ilongots, among whom my wife, Michelle Rosaldo, and I lived and conducted field research for thirty months (1967–1969, 1974). They number about 3500 and reside in an upland area some 90 miles northeast of Manila, Philippines. They subsist by hunting deer and wild pig and by cultivating rain-fed gardens (swiddens) with rice, sweet potatoes, manioc, and vegetables. Their (bilateral) kin relations are reckoned through men and women. After marriage, parents and their married daughters live in the same or adjacent households. The largest unit within the society, a largely territorial descent group called the *bertan,* becomes manifest primarily in the context of feuding. For themselves, their neighbors, and their ethnographers, headhunting stands out as the Ilongots' most salient cultural practice.

When Ilongots told me, as they often did, how the rage in bereavement could impel men to headhunt, I brushed aside their one-line accounts as too simple, thin, opaque, implausible, stereotypical, or otherwise unsatisfying. Probably I naively equated grief with sadness. Certainly no personal experience allowed me to imagine the powerful rage Ilongots claimed to find in bereavement. My own inability to conceive the force of anger in grief led me to seek out another level of analysis that could provide a deeper explanation for older men's desire to headhunt.

Not until some fourteen years after first recording the terse Ilongot statement about grief and a headhunter's rage did I begin to grasp its overwhelming force. For years I thought that more verbal elaboration (which was not forthcoming) or another analytical level (which remained elusive) could better explain older men's motives for headhunting. Only after being repositioned through a devastating loss of my own could I better grasp that Ilongot older men mean precisely what they say when they describe the anger in bereavement as the source of their desire to cut off human heads. Taken at face value and granted its full weight, their statement reveals much about what compels these older men to headhunt.

In my efforts to find a "deeper" explanation for headhunting, I explored exchange theory, perhaps because it had informed so many classic ethnographies. One day in 1974, I explained the anthropologist's exchange model to an older Ilongot man named Insan. What did he think, I asked, of the idea that headhunting resulted from the way that one death (the beheaded victim's) canceled another (the next of kin). He looked puzzled, so I went on to say that the victim of a beheading was exchanged for the death of one's own kin, thereby balancing the books, so to speak. Insan reflected a moment and replied that he imagined somebody could think such a thing (a safe bet, since I just had), but that he and other Ilongots did not think any such thing. Nor was there any indirect evidence for my exchange theory in ritual, boast, song, or casual conversation.

In retrospect, then, these efforts to impose exchange theory on one aspect of Ilongot behavior appear feeble. Suppose I had discovered what I sought? Although the notion of balancing the ledger does have a certain elegant coherence, one wonders how such bookish dogma could inspire any man to take another man's life at the risk of his own.

My life experience had not as yet provided the means to imagine the rage that can come with devastating loss. Nor could I, therefore, fully appreciate the acute problem of meaning that Ilongots faced in 1974. Shortly after Ferdinand Marcos declared martial law in 1972, rumors that firing squads had become the new punishment for headhunting reached the Ilon-got hills. The men therefore decided to call a moratorium on taking heads. In past epochs, when headhunting had become impossible, Ilongots had al-lowed their rage to dissipate, as best it could, in the course of everyday life. In 1974, they had another option; they began to consider conversion to evangelical Christianity as a means of coping with their grief. Accepting the new religion, people said, implied abandoning their old ways, including headhunting. It also made coping with bereavement less agonizing because they could believe that the deceased had departed for a better world. No longer did they have to confront the awful finality of death.

The force of the dilemma faced by the Ilongots eluded me at the time. Even when I correctly recorded their statements about grieving and the need to throw away their anger, I simply did not grasp the weight of their words. In 1974, for example, while Michelle Rosaldo and I were living among the Ilongots, a six-month-old baby died, probably of pneu-monia. That afternoon we visited the father and found him terribly stricken. "He was sobbing and staring through glazed and bloodshot eyes at the cotton blanket covering his baby." The man suffered intensely, for this was the seventh child he had lost. Just a few years before, three of his children had died, one after the other, in a matter of days. At the time, the situation was murky as people present talked both about evangelical Christianity (the possible renunciation of taking heads) and their grudges against lowlanders (the contemplation of headhunting forays into the surrounding valleys).

Through subsequent days and weeks, the man's grief moved him in a way I had not anticipated. Shortly after the baby's death, the father con-verted to evangelical Christianity. Altogether too quick on the inference, I immediately concluded that the man believed that the new religion could somehow prevent further deaths in his family. When I spoke my mind to an Ilongot friend, he snapped at me, saying that "I had missed the point: what the man in fact sought in the new religion was not the denial of our inevitable deaths but a means of coping with his grief. With the advent of martial law, headhunting was out of the question as a means of venting his wrath and thereby lessening his grief. Were he to remain in his Ilongot way of life, the pain of his sorrow would simply be too much to bear." My description from 1980 now seems so apt that I wonder how I could have written the words and nonetheless failed to appreciate the force of the grieving man's desire to vent his rage.

Another representative anecdote makes my failure to imagine the rage possible in Ilongot bereavement all the more remarkable. On this oc-casion, Michelle Rosaldo and I were urged by Ilongot friends to play the tape of a headhunting celebration we had witnessed some five years be-fore. No sooner had we turned on the tape and heard the boast of a man who had died in the intervening years than did people abruptly tell us to shut off the recorder. Michelle Rosaldo reported on the tense conversation that ensued:

> As Insan braced himself to speak, the room again became almost uncannily electric. Backs straightened and my anger turned to nervousness and something more like fear as I saw that Insan's eyes were red. Tukbaw, Renato's Ilongot "brother," then broke into what was a brittle silence, saying he could make things clear. He told us that it hurt to listen to a head-hunting celebration when people knew that there would never be another. As he put it: "The song pulls at us, drags our hearts, it makes us think of our dead uncle." And again: "It would be better if I had accepted God, but I still am an Ilongot at heart; and when I hear the song, my heart aches as it does when I must look upon unfinished bachelors whom I know that I will never lead to take a head." Then Wagat, Tukbaw's wife, said with her eyes that all my questions gave her pain, and told me: "Leave off now, isn't that enough? Even I, a woman, cannot stand the way it feels inside my heart."

From my present position, it is evident that the tape recording of the dead man's boast evoked powerful feelings of bereavement, particularly rage and the impulse to headhunt. At the time I could only feel apprehensive and diffusely sense the force of the emotions experienced by Insan, Tukbaw, Wagat, and the others present.

The dilemma for the Ilongots grew out of a set of cultural practices that, when blocked, were agonizing to live with. The cessation of headhunting called for painful adjustments to other modes of coping with the rage they found in bereavement. One could compare their dilemma with the notion that the failure to perform rituals can create anxiety. In the Ilongot case, the cultural notion that throwing away a human head also casts away the anger creates a problem of meaning when the headhunting ritual cannot be performed. Indeed, Max Weber's classic problem of meaning in *The Protestant Ethic and the Spirit of Capitalism* is precisely of this kind. On a logical plane, the Calvinist doctrine of predestination seems flawless: God has chosen the elect, but his decision can never be known by mortals. Among those whose ultimate concern is salvation, the doctrine of predestination is as easy to grasp conceptually as it is impossible to endure in everyday life (unless one happens to be a "religious virtuoso"). For Calvinists and Ilongots alike, the problem of meaning resides in practice, not theory. The dilemma for both groups involves the practical matter of how to live with one's beliefs, rather than the logical puzzlement produced by abstruse doctrine.

How I Found the Rage in Grief

One burden of this introduction concerns the claim that it took some fourteen years for me to grasp what Ilongots had told me about grief, rage, and headhunting. During all those years I was not yet in a position to comprehend the force of anger possible in bereavement, and now I am. Introducing myself into this account requires a certain hesitation both because of the discipline's taboo and because of its increasingly frequent violation by essays laced with trendy amalgams of continental philosophy and autobiographical snippets. If classic ethnography's vice was the slippage from the ideal of detachment to actual indifference, that of present-day reflexivity is the tendency for the self-absorbed Self to lose sight altogether of the culturally different Other. Despite the risks involved, as the ethnographer I must enter the discussion at this point to elucidate certain issues of method.

My preparation for understanding serious loss began in 1970 with the death of my brother, shortly after his twenty-seventh birthday. By experiencing this ordeal with my mother and father, I gained a measure of insight into the trauma of a parent's losing a child. This insight informed my account, partially described earlier, of an Ilongot man's reactions to the death of his seventh child. At the same time, my bereavement was so much less than that of my parents that I could not then imagine the overwhelming force of rage possible in such grief. My former position is probably similar to that of many in the discipline. One should recognize that ethnographic knowledge tends to have the strengths and limitations given by the relative youth of field-workers who, for the most part, have not suffered serious losses and could have, for example, no personal knowledge of how devastating the loss of a long term partner can be for the survivor.

In 1981 Michelle Rosaldo and I began field research among the Ifugaos of northern Luzon, Philippines. On October 11 of that year, she was walking along a trail with two Ifugao companions when she lost her footing and fell to her death some 65 feet down a sheer precipice into a swollen river below. Immediately on finding her body I became enraged. How could she abandon me? How could she have been so stupid as to fall? I tried to cry. I sobbed, but rage blocked the tears. Less than a month later I described this moment in my journal: "I felt like in a nightmare, the whole world around me expanding and contracting, visually and viscerally heaving. Going down I find a group of men, maybe seven or eight, standing still, silent, and I heave and sob, but no tears." An earlier experience, on the fourth anniversary of my brother's death, had taught me to recognize heaving sobs without tears as a form of anger. This anger, in a number of forms, has swept over me on many occasions since then, lasting hours and even days at a time. Such feelings can be aroused by rituals, but more often they emerge from unexpected reminders (not unlike the Ilongots' unnerving encounter with their dead uncle's voice on the tape recorder).

Lest there be any misunderstanding, bereavement should not be reduced to anger, neither for myself nor for anyone else. Powerful visceral emotional states swept over me, at times separately and at other times together. I experienced the deep cutting pain of sorrow almost beyond endurance, the cadaverous cold of realizing the finality of death, the trembling beginning in my abdomen and spreading through my body, the mournful keening that started without my willing, and frequent tearful sobbing. My present purpose of revising earlier understandings of Ilongot headhunting, and not a general view of bereavement, thus focuses on anger rather than on other emotions in grief.

Writings in English especially need to emphasize the rage in grief. Although grief therapists routinely encourage awareness of anger among the bereaved, upper-middle-class Anglo American culture tends to ignore the rage devastating losses can bring. Paradoxically, this culture's conventional wisdom usually denies the anger in grief at the same time that therapists encourage members of the invisible community of the bereaved to talk in detail about how angry their losses make them feel. My brother's death in combination with what I learned about anger from Ilongots (for them, an emotional state more publicly celebrated than denied) allowed me immediately to recognize the experience of rage.

Ilongot anger and my own overlap, rather like two circles, partially overlaid and partially separate. They are not identical. Alongside striking similarities, significant differences in tone, cultural form, and human consequences distinguish the "anger" animating our respective ways of grieving. My vivid fantasies, for example, about a life insurance agent who refused to recognize Michelle's death as job-related did not lead me to kill him, cut off his head, and celebrate afterward. In so speaking, I am illustrating the discipline's methodological caution against the reckless attribution of one's own categories and experiences to members of another culture. Such warnings against facile notions of universal human nature can, however, be carried too far and harden into the equally pernicious doctrine that, my own group aside, everything human is alien to me. One hopes to achieve a balance between recognizing wide-ranging human differences and the modest truism that any two human groups must have certain things in common.

Only a week before completing the initial draft of an earlier version of this introduction, I rediscovered my journal entry, written some six weeks after Michelle's death, in which I made a vow to myself about how

I would return to writing anthropology, if I ever did so, "by writing Grief and a Headhunter's Rage. . . ." My journal went on to reflect more broadly on death, rage, and headhunting by speaking of my "wish for the Ilongot solution; they are much more in touch with reality than Christians. So, I need a place to carry my anger—and can we say a solution of the imagination is better than theirs? And can we condemn them when we na- palm villages? Is our rationale so much sounder than theirs?" All this was written in despair and rage.

Not until some 15 months after Michelle's death was I again able to begin writing anthropology. Writing the initial version of "Grief and a Headhunter's Rage" was in fact cathartic, though perhaps not in the way one would imagine. Rather than following after the completed composi- tion, the catharsis occurred beforehand. When the initial version of this introduction was most acutely on my mind, during the month before actu ally beginning to write, I felt diffusely depressed and ill with a fever. Then one day an almost literal fog lifted and words began to flow. It seemed less as if I were doing the writing than that the words were writ- ing themselves through me.

My use of personal experience serves as a vehicle for making the quality and intensity of the rage in Ilongot grief more readily accessible to readers than certain more detached modes of composition At the same time, by invoking personal experience as an analytical category one risks easy dismissal. Unsympathetic readers could reduce this introduction to an act of mourning or a mere report on my discovery of the anger possible in bereavement. Frankly, this introduction is both and more. An act of mourning, a personal report, *and* a critical analysis of anthropological method, it simultaneously encompasses a number of distinguishable processes, no one of which cancels out the others. Similarly, I argue in what follows that ritual in general and Ilongot headhunting in particular form the intersection of multiple coexisting social processes. Aside from revising the ethnographic record, the paramount claim made here con- cerns how my own mourning and consequent reflection on Ilongot be- reavement, rage, and headhunting raise methodological issues of general concern in anthropology and the human sciences.

Personal Investigations: Inquiry Projects

1. Renato Rosaldo writes that he could not understand the headhunter's rage at the death of a loved one until he had tragically lost his own brother and wife. He adds that while it is risky business to generalize

from one's own experience and use those generalizations to understand another culture, it is crucial to recognize those connections if
they exist. Consider a research project that encourages a similar kind
of relevant subjectivity. Most of us have experienced loss, for example. Some of us have also experienced the joys of childbirth or the
ambivalence of entering adolescence and leaving childhood. Choose a
stage in your life, or an experience that aroused strong feeling, and
study how another culture deals with the same stages or experiences.
Write an essay that attempts to explore connections and differences
between a life experience of yours and how that illuminates your
understanding of another culture.

Craft and Conventions: Explaining and Evaluating

2. In the beginning of his essay, Rosaldo announces that he wants to write
   about the "cultural force of emotions." What do you think he means by
   that?

3. Based on your readings of "Grief and the Headhunter's Rage," who
   would you say is the primary audience for this piece? Did you feel as if
   it were written for someone like you? If not, how might the essay be
   rewritten to make it compelling for such an audience?

4. This essay is an introduction to a book by Rosaldo that explores anthropology's research methods. What questions does his introduction raise
   that you suspect might (or should) be addressed in later chapters?

5. Choose at least one passage from this essay that seems to best capture
   Rosaldo's argument. Then, fastwrite about why that is the best passage
   and what Rosaldo is trying to convey. What is his main argument, and
   how do you know?

6. Choose three passages that best exemplify what you consider to be
   "academic" about this essay. Where is he using methods of academic
   inquiry? What seems academic about his voice and style? Then retype
   those passages and, in the margins, point out to your instructor the specific things that seem academic to you and why.

Inquiries on Inquiry: Exploring and Reflecting

7. On page 184, Rosaldo writes about the dangers of a researcher applying
   his own experiences and values "to members of another culture." The
   researcher should always presume, he says, that there are "wide-ranging
   human differences." But he adds that "such warnings against facile

notions of universal human nature can, however, be carried too far." Do you see any problems with the idea that there are at least some common human qualities that exist between cultures, and that these can be the basis for interpretation?

8. Research and researchers should be objective, or so we often assume. How does this essay change your understanding of objectivity and research?

9. Even though this essay is quite personal, it is also rather difficult to understand in places. If you struggled to read this piece, write about why. What about the text itself and your own background seemed to contribute to this struggle? Or, choose at least one passage you found challenging and write about why, specifically, it was challenging and how you worked to understand it.

10. Rosaldo argues that our subjective responses and experiences should be a part of our analysis of a subculture. But when does that go too far? When does our personal response hinder our interpretations, and when does it help? How might we know when to trust them? Does Rosaldo offer any guidelines for you, as a writer, about how to use your personal response while doing academic inquiry?

The Politics of Headhunting, 1945–1954
Renato Rosaldo

Anthropologist Renato Rosaldo spent several years in the field studying Ilongot culture in the Philippines. From 1967 to 1969, he and his wife, Michelle Rosaldo, lived with the Ilongots and conducted an ethnographic study of their culture, keeping a field journal with observations, conversations, and notes, as well as many other artifacts and material records of the culture. In 1974, Rosaldo returned for further study and eventually wrote the book, Ilongot Headhunting, 1883–1974: A Study in Society and History, *published in 1980. We've chosen a very small portion of that book for you to read here, two excerpts from the same chapter that specifically address headhunting and Rosaldo's initial interpretations of its purpose and meaning. These sections directly relate to his later essay "Grief and a Headhunter's Rage," in which Rosaldo reflects on this earlier analysis and realizes that his own experiences and feelings are integral to his ethnographic inquiry.*

In what follows, Rosaldo first explains the significance of headhunting in the male Ilongot life cycle—most specifically, as part of the period he calls "Youth"—a ritual that marks a young man's initiation into adulthood. It is important to remember that headhunting had not been a consistent ritual throughout Ilongot history. Three different times over several generations the practice ceased, and then was renewed. As more and more Ilongot people converted to Protestantism, fewer of them participated in or even admitted to having taken someone's head. It took Rosaldo several years to earn the trust of the Ilongot men so they would share their stories of headhunting, and the second excerpt here narrates one of those stories in graphic detail. You may find it hard to suspend your own judgments about headhunting as you read, but it's important that you try, just as Rosaldo did, in order to understand Ilongot culture on their terms rather than your own.

As you read, we hope you'll note the places where Rosaldo offers his interpretations of the ritual—its meaning and purpose in the larger culture and in the male life cycle. Note as well how he justifies and explains those interpretations. On what are they based? How much of his own experiences and feelings are in this account as compared to his later essay, "Grief and a Headhunter's Rage?" You'll see that Rosaldo uses several writing strategies to convey his research, from academic argument—making a claim and supporting it with evidence—to narrative and sensory detail. In what ways are those strategies academic?

Youth. Youth is a time of beauty, ordeals, and stress. Paragons of beauty, as vain as they are uneasy about their ever-changing bodies, young men adorn themselves with bright red kerchiefs, tight metal armbands, and delicately crafted calflets, belts, necklaces, and earrings. They are called the "quick ones," for they are energetic, light of step, and free to travel widely and often. Those years, for Ilongots, are the prime of life.

I often saw unmarried young men clustered away from the rest, where they would wrap their arms and legs around one another as they whispered secrets, giggling and blushing now and again. If at those moments they seemed bent on nothing more than the cultivation of their own vanity and silliness, at other moments they lived lives of intense emotional involvement. As a group they would go through a series of ordeals—their *rites de passage*—from teeth-filing (out of fashion from about 1960) through head-taking to marriage. Subject as they are to such severe tests of manhood, it is little wonder that youths are regarded as volatile. Indeed, their moods and passions are subject to dramatic ups and downs; and many youths describe themselves in song and story alike as weeping in their fierce, as yet frustrated, desire to "arrive" and take a head.

A six-year-old boy beneath a rice granary.

The source of the weeping youths' fierce desire is above all envy of their peers and elders, those men who no longer are novices (*siap*) because they have taken a head and thus won the coveted right to wear finely curved red hornbill earrings dangling from their upper lobes. During a raid it is the older men, with their greater stamina and knowledge, who "care for" and "lead" the youths through their critical life passage. In fact, an older man is usually the first to reach the victim, and it is often he who severs the head so it can be thrown away by the youth, who thus ceases to be a novice. The point in Ilongot headhunting is not for one man to take more heads than others, but for all men who are peers to take at least one head and thereby lose once and for all their status as novices. To take a head is, in Ilongot terms, not to capture a trophy, but to "throw away" a body part, which by a principle of sympathetic magic represents the cathartic throwing away of certain burdens of life—the grudge an insult has created, or the grief over a death in the family, or the increasing "weight" of remaining a novice when one's peers have left that status.

Regarded as a ritual, headhunting resembles a peculiar sacrifice: it involves the taking of a human life with a view toward cleansing the participants of the contaminating burdens of their own lives. Taking a head is a symbolic process designed less to acquire anything (whether so-called soul stuff or fertility) than to remove something. What is ritually removed, Ilongots say, is the weight that grows on one's life like vines on a tree. Once cleansed through participation in a successful raid, the men are said to become "light" in weight, "quick" of step, and "red" in complexion. Thus youths accentuate and older men recover—if only for a relatively short and gradually fading span of time—their characteristic youthful vigor as "quick ones." In other words, the raiders regress through this ritual process to a culturally idealized phase of life.

When a victim is beheaded, older men discard the weight of age and recover the energy of their youth, whereas youths advance from novice status and adorn themselves with red hornbill earrings. To wear such earrings, they say, is to gain the admiration of young women and to be able to answer back when other men taunt. And taunt they do. Novices who marry, for instance, must somehow withstand the culturally stereotyped "insult" that they have designs on beheading their wives. Maniling put the matter more broadly: "Others will scorn you if you marry without taking a head." While at certain historical moments they have married without doing so, it is little wonder that young men have usually hoped to take a head as a prelude to marriage. In effect, by taking a head the young man has cleared his path toward marriage: he has become at once more attractive to women and better able to defend himself by "answering back" throughout the ordeals imposed on him by his girlfriend's father and brothers.

Lest there be confusion, let me emphasize that it is not obligatory for Ilongot men to take a head before marriage. The view that the former is a necessary precondition for the latter is as mistaken as it is widespread in Philippine ethnography and popular culture. After a brief visit to the region, Albert Jenks reported that, among the Ilongots, "no man may marry who has not first taken a head" (1905: 174); thus this mistaken view made its appearance in the modern ethnographic literature. Jenks's version, however, was little more than a sober rendition of the lurid tale that has circulated in the valleys surrounding Ilongot territory from at least the late nineteenth century (see Campa 1891: 568–69; Savage 1904: 329).

When the firetree blossoms, the tale has it, the Ilongot mating season arrives and lustful unmarried young men go on the warpath in search of Christian heads. Those who find victims present the severed heads (or other body parts) to their prospective brides as a gift. On June 8, 1963, for example, the *Chronicle* of Manila reported: "It is during the summer months when Ilongots observe their mating season. It is part of the Ilon-

A young man uprooting clumps of runo grass to
clear a garden site.

got's marriage ritual to present a Christian head to his prospective bride."
Like other stereotypes of supposedly alien peoples, this tale endows Ilongots with a bestial character (their mating season) and barbaric folkways
(their wedding gift; see R. Rosaldo 1978a). Suffice it to add that the victim's head is presented neither to the bride nor to anyone else; it is, as I
said, simply thrown away.

    It is through taking a head (if he does so) that the young man takes the
first major step from his childhood and youth, centered in his family of
origin, toward his adult and elderly life, centered in his family of marriage. Headhunting and marriage are the two critical moments in a period
conceived of as the only significant rupture in the otherwise continuous
course of the life cycle. Unlike the gradual transition from childhood to
youth, the young man who marries ceases definitively to be a youth and

becomes a man. Celebrated in ritual, story, song, and oratory, this change in social status is culturally elaborated to a greater extent than any other throughout the Ilongot lifetime. . . .

The Renewal of Raiding, 1950–52

In the rest of this chapter, the process by which the ten young men took heads is viewed against the background of the male life cycle. The reader should notice that details of the following narratives are designed to show the sense of politics and history embodied in headhunting. When, in 1952, five of the young men took heads in quick succession, their conduct was seen, looking backward, as one realization of the Ilongot historical sense that peers move in the same direction at the same time. At the same time, participation in raiding parties and the unfolding of the Butag-Rumyad feud were major determinants of shifting political alignments, manifested in residential moves and broken marriages.

While all of the ten young men were old enough to remember the events of 1945, only two of them were over 21 at the time, and the average age for the group was 17. Nonetheless, three of the ten succeeded in taking Japanese heads in 1945: Tukbaw (then 22) beheaded the hapless Japanese who had come to fetch water at dawn; Bayaw (16) decapitated one of the troops who had driven his people, along with those from Tenga and Butag, from their place of refuge; and Dinwag (27) was among those who beheaded the last three soldiers who remained in central Rumyad. Dinwag, as it turned out, was the last Rumyad man to take a head for five years, until Insan did so in 1950.

How Insan took a head, 1950. Insan had good reason to be especially eager to "arrive" and take a head. His "fierce" desire dated from 1945, when his father, Lakay, had slashed the Japanese soldier to death by the sweet potato patch. At the time Insan (then only 13) had begged his father to let him take the head and throw it away; but instead the first throw had gone, as was only proper, to his older brother, who had thereby gained the much envied right to adorn himself with red hornbill earrings. Not until 1950 could Insan persuade his father to organize a raid on his behalf.

Insan in the end was able to persuade his father that they should no longer remain "still," because the tenor of the times in the surrounding lowlands had in fact changed. By early 1950 what had started some eight years before as the Anti-Japanese People's Army (popularly known as the Hukbalahap, or Huks) had re-emerged in central Luzon and the Sierra Madre Mountains just south of Ilongot territory as a powerful people's guerrilla movement. It was in January 1950 that "all units of the people's army were ordered to make simultaneous attacks on provincial capitals, cities and enemy camps on March 29, August 26 and November 7, 1950"

(Guerrero 1970: 70). During April and May of that year, towns in Nueva Ecija near the southwestern margin of Ilongot country were successfully attacked by the Huks. In the aftermath of these raids, news of an imminent Huk takeover of Manila was given credence in the Ilongot hills. Ilongots heard other news as well: late in 1949 they learned that companions of the Huks had been victorious in the homeland of the Chinese (whom they knew as well-to-do shopkeepers in lowland barrios and towns); and by late June 1950 word was spreading about the outbreak of the Korean War. It was evident in retrospect that "mid-1950 marked the flood tide of the Huk rebellion" (Lachica 1971: 131). Lakay and the others could no longer deny that yet another epoch of lowland violence was upon them. These years of 1950–54 were later known as *ka'ukbu,* "the time of Huks."

By July or August 1950, Lakay and his younger brother from Kakidugen had organized a raiding party, as Insan had asked. In doing so they recruited their brethren from Pengegyaben. When he asked the Pengegyaben people to join him on the raid, Lakay made a public statement confirming that Baket was his "sister" and that her son, Tukbaw, was his "son" as well. In thus consecrating their kinship, Lakay and Baket were setting the stage for what surely was their unspoken hope that their children might intermarry, as happened some five years later.

Those of the ten young men who participated in that raid of 1950 follow: from Pengegyaben, Tukbaw (then 27), who had taken a head in 1945, along with the novices Tawad (25) and his younger brother, Adēlpig (22); from Kakidugen, Bayaw (then 21), who had taken a head in 1945 and whose family had just joined that local cluster, along with the novices Ta'at (19), Radu (19), and Insan (18). The three youths who did not take part in the raid were Dinwag (32), who had taken a head in 1945 and was ill at the time, and the two youngest members of the group, Tepeg (17) and Maniling (15), who were regarded as "still children" and hence unable to withstand the hunger and deprivation that a long-distance raid would entail. In all, the raiding party was 18 strong. Five men were from Pengegyaben and the rest from Kakidugen; there were six married men, of whom only one was a novice, plus 12 unmarried men of whom seven were novices. Lakay was planning to "lead" his son Insan in taking a head, and Tukbaw was hoping to do the same for his classificatory brother Tawad.

The customary agreement about the sequence in which victims would be "shared" was more critical than usual. In the first place, all the men were pent up with "anger" as a result of the grief they had not yet "thrown away" over deaths suffered in their families in 1945. And Lakay was still mourning the sudden death of his eldest son only two years before. Second, the presence of so many eager novices who had been restrained from acting out their "envy" of older brothers who had earned red hornbill earrings in 1945 meant that the older men present had to keep the youths from cutting one another up in attempting to realize their desires to take a head.

After discussion of their plans, the men reached a consensus about the order in which the youths would "follow" one another in taking heads. The first victim was to be for Insan from Kakidugen, because his father had initiated the raid. The second victim (had there been one) was to be for Tawad for the following reasons: he was from Pengegyaben, and one of the guests should be "next in line"; he was the oldest novice among the group, and it was felt that he had remained an "unmarried young man" (*buintaw*) for too long; he had to throw away the grief from having been orphaned by his father's arrest in 1940 and by the killing of his mother, his grandmother, and his sister in 1945. The third victim was for the married novice from Kakidugen, because he was long past due to "arrive" and because the pattern of sharing should alternate between the Kakidugen hosts and their Pengegyaben guests. Regarding the victims, Tukbaw said: "Should they be many, it seems that there is no other kind (bērtan) among us, so if we get more we will give them to the other novices among us." Rumyads all, they would not fight over victims the way they might if their raiding party were mixed with other bērtan.

The plan was set. They were to head downstream on unfamiliar paths as far from Kakidugen as possible, in order to avoid reprisals for this, the first Rumyad raid of the post-1945 era. After their decimation in 1945, the raiders were more than ever determined to kill without being killed. They held no notion of the valor of death in open combat, for they could not conceive of asking a brother, a son, or a father to lay down his life—"to sell his body," as they said of soldiers, less in contempt than out of sheer moral incomprehension.

The day before the raiders left Kakidugen, all the signs they sought out were auspicious for their departure. At high noon that day, the men gathered on the cleared yard of Lakay's house and there implanted a woven bamboo basket in which they had placed betel nut, sugar cane, and sweet potato as a food offering for the spirit they called "from the forest." As the offering was made, an Aymuyu man (whose gun two years later accidentally killed Lakay's father) chanted the invocation in a loud voice: "Now, you, eye of the sun; there now, you are on high." Abruptly, "tightening" his voice to its highest pitch, he tweeted, he clucked, he warbled— *'uu kudēkudek*—and lured the "heart" of the victim, which was likened to a bird. Finally, his voice loosened and became deep in pitch because the hearts of the victims had come; they hovered for a time near their beheaders-to-be and then perched on the upper lobes of their ears (the very spot where, if he succeeded, the headhunter would place his red earrings). The "person of knowledge" drew near and grabbed the hearts where he found them perched, the first on Insan, the second on Tawad, and the third on the married novice from Kakidugen. All was as it should be, and the hearts were then placed in the bamboo basket; drawing their bolos, the men encircled the hearts in the basket. The person of knowledge looked to see whether any of the men was destined to be wounded on that raid. Their fates appeared favorable. That night in the forest, the men softly played their stringed instruments, the violin and the bamboo zither, and listened for the calls of omen birds. All signs were propitious, and they decided to leave the next day.

Moving toward their victim slowly and with deliberation, as was done in hunting and fishing as well, the men waded downstream along stretches of shallow water, peering downward through their homemade goggles as they went. Though the first of the seasonal sporadic rains had come, the waters were still low enough for fishing. Ever searching for small river fish, tiny crabs, or frogs, the men repeatedly stretched their elastic strips (cut from automobile inner tubes) and released the attached sharpened umbrella rods toward their targets. At the still, deep pools they stopped and dove with longer spears, peering into crevices and holes where mudfish and eels might have hidden for the day.

Along with the men were ten women. They had come to sing farewell, inspiring the men and lending beauty to their departure. Though two were married, none of the women had children to care for and they all were regarded, in this loose sense, as "quick ones"; six of them later married six of the young men. The women carried the supply of rice for the raiders in rattan baskets held by tumplines, freeing the men to wade, to dive, to leap from rock to rock, to run in short bursts, spurred on to display their prowess by the competitive ethos of foraging and by the very presence of the women.

More or less in coordination with the men, walking steadily along the banks or crossing the river here and there, the women went downstream along the Kakidugen to the fork of the Tubu River, and there they stopped to cook the rice. Most of the cooked rice was stuffed inside bamboo tubes for future consumption, so the raiders could avoid having their presence known by the smoke from their fires. What rice remained was eaten along with the fish in a tender feast of farewell. After the meal, each woman handed her "brother" or husband or lover a neatly tied betel quid to save and chew in the moment before attacking the victim. The women said, "Take this now, it is my betel quid," and the men answered with this ritual incantation: "May you [the betal offering] make me light of foot. Let all the reeds blossom [an allusion to the feather headdress worn only after taking a head]." Then the headhunters departed downstream while the women stood singing, one after the other, their melodious farewells.

The men walked slowly, in single file and in silence. On this long-distance raid, walking in a direction where they had neither hunted nor raided before, they knew neither where to walk nor how far it would be—only that they were certain to suffer hunger and fatigue before they reached their lowland victims. Often moving on hands and knees, their progress was painfully slow as they sought out the most forbidding thickets along the highest ridges, hoping to avoid attention.

The first day out they found a rifle with still usable parts dating from 1945; clearly, no Ilongot had walked by that spot for at least five years, probably longer. But the next day they discovered that the game trails farther downstream were riddled with pits filled with sharpened bamboo stakes, and everywhere there were rattan triggers set to release arrows pulled taut for the kill. The raiders saw that these traps were freshly erected and deduced (correctly, as Kugkug and others later confirmed) that a hunting party of Tamsi people from far downstream was in the vicinity. They redoubled their caution, for as Insan said, "We were afraid of the Tamsi people." Tukbaw explained that they had heard the "story" of how certain Rumyads and Tamsis had long ago lived together in Ulawi, a place on the Tubu, but "we thought it [the story] was a lie because it didn't make sense to us; we thought it was just a story, a mere story." In those days there was no social intercourse between Rumyads and Tamsis, for they had not yet even "walked back and forth" and "seen one another." Five years were still to pass before the two peoples became neighbors and began a process of union through joint raiding and four intermarriages.

Once they had safely skirted the Tamsis, the men walked on downstream for about ten days more. Aside from a fawn that Tukbaw shoved off a cliff, they ate only the rice from the bamboo tubes and whatever fruits and nuts they happened to find on their path. So short did their tempers become as they walked that they began to fight among themselves. In that crisis (by no means unique for long-distance raids) it was the tubercular older half-brother of Tukbaw—by then himself so thin that, Insan said, "he looked like a monkey"—who calmed the men's "thumping hearts" as he played his soothing flute and thus dissipated their twin feelings of hunger and anger. At last they spied the weeks-old footprints of lowland hunters, and soon after, as it started to rain, they reached the grasslands at the edge of the forest nearly 25 miles from Kakidugen.

That day they spent hiding in the brush at the top of a hill above a swidden, while two of their members went to scout and determine where to set up the ambush. Before sunrise the next morning the men thought of their "sisters" or wives or lovers as they chewed their parting gifts of betel nut; with their manhood thus inspired, their hearts were further moved by anger. The older men then advised the youths to be cautious, saying, "Do not cut one another; do not let yourselves be seen by the people [lowlanders]." Certain men agreed to keep track of one another during the attack. The Ilongots purposely distinguished themselves from the lowlanders (who would be dressed in pants and shirts) by wearing only G-strings and white kerchiefs tied for easy visibility in the buns of their long hair. Those who had already taken heads adorned themselves with their feather headdresses, thereby stirring the hearts of the novices by exciting their envy. It was shortly after dawn when the men fanned out and took their positions in the ambush.

While the sun rose higher and higher they waited and waited, neither speaking nor moving. It must have been noon or a little after when they saw a man come riding along on a carabao. He was a lowlander, all alone and whistling a cheerful tune to himself. As the raiders watched from above, he tied his carabao by the bank of the river, then took off his pants, waded into the water, and began to fish with a net. Lakay's younger brother took careful aim at the fisherman. It had been agreed that he would fire the first shot because, after his infant daughter's death earlier that year, he had vowed never to use his weapon until he shot a victim with it, thereby, in Ilongot terms, dissipating and tossing away the weight of his grief. When the shot rang out the victim fell over on his face and the raiders, 18 strong, charged forward at a full run with their vision "focused" (*'upug*) solely on the victim. Tukbaw said, "There is no other than that they [the raiders] see, except for the victim." In a taped story of the raid told to Maniling, Insan recalled the confusion of the moment he reached the victim:

> Father said to me, "Baah, hold on to it [the head]." Then father said, "Cut it off. Uh, let me do it. I'll cut it off."
>
> Then our uncle said, "Leave it to me. I'll cut it off." Then the two of us, father and son, held on to it while our uncle cut it off. . . .
>
> Then the old man [Insan's father, Lakay] said to me, "Throw it away," and I threw it away. I just threw it out there where there were no people.
>
> Then I just said, "Booh, male victim I beheaded, I snatch away your life."

The men vented their pent-up anger on the cadaver and chopped it up until "it had no body and you couldn't see its bones," until "it was like ashes."

Tukbaw then spotted a 20-year-old member of their party who had become so sick, as sometimes happens, from the chaos and the smell of gore that he was wandering vaguely away from the scene. As he staggered along, dizzy and dazed, his wide eyes rolling in circles, the more experienced Tukbaw ran and grabbed him brusquely and cut a lock of his hair. Then together the two shouted 'a 'ee 'u 'u until the youth recovered his senses. In the meantime, Tawad had climbed to the top of a tall tree nearby and began shouting to his companions that he had spied houses just a short way downstream. The men bolted off and vanished into the forest.

The raiders fled without stopping. From the moment of decapitation they paused only now and again to shout and to sing the song of celebration. In so doing, they said, they lifted the weight from their bodies and made themselves light of foot; through their celebratory song they sought to acquire the speed and grace that epitomized Ilongot versions of health and well-being. Close to where they stopped that first night, they collected the leaves from a sweet-smelling fern and tucked them into their metal armbands in order to modify and preserve the smell of the victim.

The following morning on the Tubu River the men tried to dive for fish, but gave up because they were too weak from hunger. They had eaten the last of the rice before the attack, and as Insan said, "Alas, our ribs stood out like so many sticks placed side by side for sitting in the forest." That afternoon they shot a doe by a salt lick, and then Tukbaw's older half-brother killed a large male wild pig. As they ate the game, their bodies, by then pale ("white") from the rain and deprivation, once again took on color ("red"). Indeed, in other such narratives men claimed that taking a head, pure and simple, gave their bodies color as a visible sign of health.

As the raiders neared Kakidugen shortly before sunset on the second day of their return trip, they shouted out 'a 'ee 'u 'u just once to indicate that they had taken only one head. An old woman met the raiders, and she asked them and they in turn asked her whether everybody was alive and well: "Are you all there? Are all of you alive?" They were all in good health. No sooner had they entered Lakay's house than the women, in chorus, began to sing the song of celebration; the men replied in unison to their verses. The women took up the gongs (stringed instruments were forbidden at that moment); and one at a time the men and women took turns dancing, their bodies arched and arms spread wide. Their "hearts lengthened with joy" as they sang and danced and played the gongs through the night and into the early morning. Even a few people from Butag who happened to be visiting at the time joined in and sang and danced in celebration for Insan.

After resting for a day, the raiders walked to Adiw, where the Pengegyaben people lived. They and the women there "answered one another" in song, and they all danced and played the gongs far into the night. The clanging gongs were audible through central Rumyad, and word spread quickly that Insan had taken a head. It was not until the next day that the raiders dispersed to their separate homes.

Personal Investigations: Inquiry Project

1. After you've spent time answering the Craft and Conventions questions below that ask you to analyze the academic features of both of Renato Rosaldo's essays, write an essay that explains what makes Rosaldo's work (that is, both essays) "academic." What seem to be the key features of academic inquiry and the academic conventions expected in anthropology based on just these two pieces? Do some research about the field of anthropology and see what you can learn about the research methods that are emphasized, the kinds of evidence that researchers need to collect, and the expectations of an anthropological audience. You might interview some anthropology faculty at your university or college, as well.

Craft and Conventions: Explaining and Evaluating

2. Rosaldo refers to himself frequently in this "The Politics of Headhunting" excerpt, and in fact throughout the book-length ethnography from which it is taken. Compare his references to himself in this essay and in "Grief and a Headhunter's Rage." Are both of these pieces personal? Why or why not?

3. Like the essays in Chapter 4, this piece uses narrative, vivid detail, and dialogue to bring Rosaldo's research to life. Choose a passage that is especially vivid and engaging, and (1) explain why you find this passage so engaging, and (2) imagine *how* Rosaldo got the information he needed to reconstruct this story.

4. Using a colored pen or pencil, reread this essay and mark the phrases, sentences, and sections that indicate to you this is a formal academic piece in contrast to the personal academic piece you read earlier. What kinds of academic moves does Rosaldo make here? Develop a working definition of academic writing to guide you as you read, possibly using ideas we've discussed in this book or definitions you find on the

Internet that focus specifically on anthropology. What makes this a piece of academic research and *not* a personal academic essay?

5. How does Rosaldo integrate the voices of others in this account—the voices of the Ilongot people, the voices of other scholars in his field, and so on? Choose two passages as illustration and note in the margins *how* he uses quotes, summaries, and paraphrases.

Inquiries on Inquiry: Exploring and Reflecting

6. It's likely that you found this excerpt disturbing to read. Explore your experience reading this ethnographic account, describing the feelings it evoked, the memories or associations you have, the judgments you made, and so on. Then, return to the text and look closely at how Rosaldo guides us, as readers, toward a particular understanding of Ilongot headhunting. How does he want us, as readers, to think and feel about this violent behavior? How does that compare with what you actually thought and felt while reading?

7. What reading strategies did you use when reading "The Politics of Headhunting"? How do those compare with the strategies you used with "Grief and a Headhunter's Rage"? Be as specific as you can about what you struggled with in each essay, what you found engaging, and what approaches you chose to take with each. Did you mark them both equally? Did you find one easier to read? And so on.

8. As an ethnographer, Rosaldo needs to sort out what is "true" from all the interview accounts he collects and all his observations. What does he do, as a writer, to convince us that his assessment of Ilongot culture is true? Why should we trust him?

9. As a researcher, what sources of information does Rosaldo use?

TANDEM READINGS: ENGLISH STUDIES

As noted earlier in this chapter, a small but growing number of scholars in English are writing about literary works from a more personal perspective, believing that their own experiences cannot be separated from their professional work. As anthropologist Renato Rosaldo argued in the previous section, a scholar's background and experiences do influence his or her interpretations and analyses, so writers should acknowledge and explore those connections. The first two essays in this section demonstrate one writer's path toward this more openly subjective type of academic inquiry; the third, a student essay, shows autobiography mingling with literary study.

Somebody Must Say These Things:
An Essay for My Mother
Melody Graulich

Why research something? Melody Graulich offers one answer: because it can change your life. This essay, written by Graulich, a Utah State University professor, is a serious piece of literary scholarship, but it's also a moving account of how her study of a certain tradition in the literature of the American West helped Graulich to understand her own mother, and perhaps to love her more deeply.

Graulich arrives at this insight using a similar approach to personal scholarship seen in anthropologist Renato Rosaldo's "Grief and a Headhunter's Rage," earlier in this chapter. Rosaldo's personal experience with loss helped him to understand how he misread the grief rituals of a tribe of Philippine natives in an anthropological study he conducted years earlier. Like Rosaldo, literary critic Graulich returns to an earlier research project she has done on women, violence, and literature of the American West, and explores how her knowledge of her own grandfather's violence against her grandmother affected how Graulich felt about herself, her mother, and the larger arguments feminist literary critics were making about women in the West.

Graulich is among a large number of literary critics who are writing autobiographical literary criticism. This essay was originally published, in fact, in The Intimate Critique: Autobiographical Literary Criticism, *a 1993 collection of essays that focused solely on autobiographical criticism. Feminists such as Graulich have encouraged this kind of criticism for a number of reasons, one of them being, as she says in this piece, that "women often cannot understand the significance of their own experience until they see it mirrored in literature." She adds that "the dialogue we establish with women writers as we read and write about their works inevitably alters our perceptions and . . . leads to an examined life."*

As you read this article, mark the places where Graulich shifts from her personal experience to literary texts and think about what conclusions she is able to draw by bringing personal experience and those texts together. Consider, as well, where she expresses her feelings and what effect that expression has on you as a reader and on her research more generally. Do you find yourself trusting her as a writer and scholar? Note, too, the kinds of research sources she draws on and how well she supports her conclusions. How might the essay and its conclusions be different if Graulich left out her experience with her grandfather? What does her experience enable her to see and not see about women and violence in the West? Is autobiographical criticism more important for women, as Graulich asserts?

Before you read Graulich's essay try to define for yourself (and possibly as a class) what makes this essay both personal and academic. What are the boundaries that it is crossing, specifically?

This essay begins with a digression, with a personal rather than a literary experience. I have spent several years seeking the conclusion to this experience, so it is apt that I wander toward my thesis. The real story often emerges in a narrative digression, as I learned from my grandfather, who may have learned it from Twain's Jim Blaine. Born in the Badlands of South Dakota, or so he said, my tall, handsome grandfather was a western drifter who rode buffalo, sang songs about a girl named Duckfoot Sue, and was descended from Geronimo—or, on alternate days, Sitting Bull. Rambling with me in the western mountains, Gramps taught me through his "prevarications" the freedom of self-definition that cornes in storytelling. Informing me daily that *he* had wanted to name me Rebel, he let me know that I could do anything I set my mind to.

Gramps himself had a lot more control over his tall tales than over his life. As I grew older and recognized some of his failings, such as alcoholism, my view of him was shaped by the name he had intended for me: I saw him as a flawed visionary, an outlaw from a seedy, conformist society, a man who would "go to hell" before he'd compromise his values. In my own stories, he became the quintessential American hero. His rebellious, freedom-seeking footsteps led me directly to American studies, and I began a dissertation on male writers and their narrative escapades about the West.

A few years after his death, I was confronted with some unwelcome implications of the rebellious western myth my grandfather had personified for me. One night my mother described for me a scene that had occurred many times throughout her childhood: my grandfather beating up on my grandmother. Recalling details of 35 years earlier, details she had never before talked about—"he yanked her from the car by her hair"— she recounted how she had felt powerless, embarrassed, responsible. In retrospect I find it surprising that I didn't protest the truth of the story she was telling me about the man I knew to be affectionate and loving, the man who had twice cried through *The Incredible Journey* with me, but somehow I could see the beatings happening, as if I shared my mother's eyes. Although parts of myself seemed to have been yanked raggedly apart, settling into new, uncomfortable relations, I accepted this information about my grandfather calmly, meanwhile gathering all my unconscious psychological strategies to hold onto my feelings about him. When I saw my still-living grandmother the next day, I was appalled to discover that I could not identify with her suffering, that I wanted to keep my distance from her. Her experience recalled for me only the dark side of my beloved grandfather, whom I had to find a way to explain and excuse.

As a literary critic, I naturally turned to literature about violence against women in an effort to understand my mother's story and what it meant. I discovered, however, that feminist critics can be resisting readers of female as well as male texts and that there are parts of our mothers' stories that we sometimes evade hearing. I have opened this essay with a convention long established in feminist criticism, the personal voice, not simply to establish my relationship to my subject but because the engagement between critic and subject and how it shapes both reader and text *is* my subject. The revisions in thinking and in feeling I went through in writing two essays about how violence affects women testify that women often cannot understand the significance of their own experience until they see it mirrored in literature, that the dialogue we establish with women writers as we read and write about their works inevitably alters our perceptions, and that our best reading, like psychoanalysis, leads to an examined life. It leads also to an acknowledgment of our connections to other women and to an awareness of how those connections shape our insights and conclusions.

As abuse of women has been until recently invisible within our society, an embarrassing "abnormality" to be concealed, so has it been absent from our literary canon. None of the books on my graduate school reading lists touched the subject. In fact, the American studies tradition, as Nina Baym has shown, has been dominated by a fascination with "melodramas of beset manhood," fantasies in which men escape into the wilderness in search of their own moral values, their relations to women presented in only the barest and most romanticized ways. This tradition provided the story, the melodrama, in which I made my grandfather the star. It was at least two years after my mother told me her secrets before I came across a book little known outside of western history circles, Mari Sandoz's *Old Jules* (1935), ostensibly the biography of her father, Jules Sandoz, a "prophet" who came west seeking his "promised land" (406): "free land, far from law and convention," where he could "live as he liked" (4). In his daughter's eyes, Jules is a "big man," the typical visionary frontiersman who pervades our literature and history. He possesses the heroic virtues of the romanticized masculine West: a desire for absolute free will and self-determination.

Yet hidden within this biography of her father, Sandoz wrote a woman's history of the West, focusing on the widespread physical and emotional abuse of women, suggesting that the "promised land" did not pay off on its promises to women, that women were often the victims of the frontier's celebrated freedom. Her portrayal of the frontiersman's attitudes toward women and marriage dominates her father's biography. Married four times, Jules beat each of his wives. When his first wife disobeys an order, "Jules closed her mouth with the flat of his long muscular hand" (5).

When his second wife asks why he does nothing, "his hand shot out, and the woman slumped against the bench. . . . [Later] he pretended not to notice [her] swollen lip, the dark bruises on her temple, and the tear-wearied eyes" (102). Sandoz concentrates on his relationship to his fourth wife, her mother Mary, and on the power dynamics in their marriage:

> Mary avoided crossing him or bothering him for help in anything she could possibly do alone. But there were times when she must have his help, as when the roof leaked or the calves had to be castrated. It took weeks of diplomatic approach to get him to look after the two bull calves before they were too big for her to handle at all. And when she couldn't hold the larger one from kicking, Jules, gray-white above his beard, threw his knife into the manure and loped to the back door. "I learn the goddamn balky woman to obey me when I say 'hold him.' " He tore a handful of four-foot wire stays from the bundle in the corner of the shop and was gone towards the corral, the frightened grandmother and the children huddled at the back window.
>
> They heard the banging of the gate. Jules's bellow of curses. Then Mary ran through the door, past the children and straight to the poison drawer. It stuck, came free . . . the blood dripping from her face and her hand where she had been struck with the wire whip, the woman snatched up a bottle, struggled with the cork, pulling at it with her teeth. The grandmother was upon her, begging, pleading, clutching at the red bottle with the crossbones.
>
> Jules burst in. "Wo's the goddamned woman? I learn her to obey me if I got to kill her!"
>
> "You!" the grandmother cried, shaking her fist against him. "For you there is a place in hell!"
>
> With the same movement of her arm she swung out, knocking the open bottle from the woman's mouth. . . . Then she led Mary out of the house and to the brush along the river. (230–231)

But Jules is no more brutal than most other men in his community, as Sandoz demonstrates through repeated example until *Old Jules* becomes a catalog of male-caused tragedies in women's lives. One of the grisliest examples suggests that sons learn violence from their fathers: When Mrs. Blaska summons the nerve to leave her husband, he uses her love for her sons to "coax" her back. After she is found dead, "stripped naked, in the open chicken yard," her husband admits he whipped her. "She started to run away again and, handicapped by his crutch, he sent her sons to bring her back. They held her while he pounded her" (412). Although Sandoz respects her mother and other pioneer women, she presents their lives as violent and circumscribed and the frontier marriage as institutionalizing male power; Mr. Blaska considers his behavior "every husband's right." Sandoz never suggests that Jules or the other men are mentally ill, nor that their behavior is motivated by their personal lives. The causes for their brutality lie in their society's attitudes about women and marriage. The conflict between men and women is clearly unequal, and the women's physical victimization symbolizes the social and institutional power men hold over them. Sandoz implies that there were two Wests, her father's and her mother's, one characterized by the qualities of Frederick Jackson Turner's classic description of power, freedom, and vision, the other by powerlessness, fear, and accommodation.

As these few quotations suggest, *Old Jules* is a powerful and disturbing book. I was initially interested in Sandoz's book for its historical evocation of time and place. She was born the same year as my grandfather and grew up only a few hundred miles from his birthplace. I imagined my great-grandfather as another Old Jules, training his sons to behave like the Blaska boys and saw my grandfather's behavior as the inevitable consequence of the society in which he was reared. But I soon realized that Sandoz's story was really about the teller, that she had not resolved her feelings about her father and mother. For me, *Old Jules* came to be the story of Sandoz's uncertainty about whether to identify with her father's or her mother's West, her ambivalent attachment to, admiration for, and fear of each parent shaping her narrative. I know now that I attended carefully to Sandoz's conflicted feelings, overlooked by other critics, because I too had been unable to resolve my own feelings about my grandfather and grandmother. I didn't project my feelings onto her, but she allowed me to externalize them, to examine them in another guise.

Throughout her book, Sandoz shows how she was forced during her childhood to take on a woman's responsibilities while being confronted with her community's attitudes about women. She recognizes that she is identified with her mother and what womanhood will bring her when Jules, unable to beat the pregnant Mary, turned to his daughter as substitute and "whipped [her] until he was breathless" (279). Yet Sandoz eventually comes to blame her mother for attempting to make her into a copy of her own victimized self. She characterizes Mary as resenting her husband's behavior and her own powerlessness, but as expecting and even forcing her daughter to accept her own burdened and unrespected role. Mary Sandoz had an idea of what it meant to be a woman, and she tried to pass it on to her daughter; Sandoz could not see that had Mary not done so, she would have undermined her own life.

Yet it is easy to understand why the daughter rejects her mother's powerlessness in search of her own self-esteem and identifies with her father's West. She sees as the central difference between her parents that her mother "preferred the smaller, the more familiar things, while her Jules saw only the far, the large, the exalted canvas" (191). Recognizing her kinship to her mother, she finds her life filled with situations to avoid, not to aspire to. She presents pioneer women as heroic within their obvious limitations, as making "the best of the situation," but their lives are filled with drudgery. (Sandoz, "Pioneer Women" 60) Her "visionary" father's dying words to her reveal what kind of esteem she can expect— from herself and others—so long as she remains woman-identified: "'There is nobody to carry on my work. . . . If [Mari] was a man she might—as a woman she is not worth a damn' " (418). Forced to see women as deficient, desiring her father's freedom, his imagination, his defiant and stubborn self-confidence, his reknown—all traits promised to the western male—Sandoz turns away from women in her later histories to explore the classic masculine West and its themes, to what she calls "the romantic days" ("Pioneer Women" 59).

I had done this myself, though my dissertation's title suggests that I had already begun to see, as indeed Sandoz had, some of the problems with the masculine western myths: "The Frontier Self: Freedom and Its Limitations." Sandoz revealed to me my own rebellious feelings about being a woman, my desire to escape from what I unconsciously defined as a confined life. She and I followed the pattern of many other successful women writers, which Carolyn Heilbrun describes in *Reinventing Womanhood:* "those women who did have the courage, self-confidence and autonomy to make their way in the male-dominated world did so by identifying themselves with male ideals and role models . . . by not identifying themselves . . . as women" (31). I differed from Sandoz, however, in that I defined myself as a feminist, and I *thought* I was woman-identified. It seemed healthy and natural to resist victimization, so powerfully symbolized by physical abuse. Yet I didn't realize that I was resisting much more than that until I found myself profoundly moved and disturbed by a fine essay by another western feminist, "Eve among the Indians," in which Dawn Lander describes her own "liberated" childhood in the West:

> I did not identify myself with houses, churches, and fences. I loved to be outdoors. I loved the space, energy and passion of the landscape. . . . Repeatedly, however, I could find no place for myself and for my pleasure in the wilderness in the traditionally recorded images of women on the frontier. Tradition gives us the figure of a woman, strong, brave and often heroic, whose endurance and perseverance are legendary. It may seem strange that I find it difficult to identify with this much-praised figure. But I can almost hear her teeth grinding behind her tight-set lips; her stiff spine makes me tired and her clenched fists sad. Victimization and martyrdom are the bone and muscle of every statue, picture, and word portrait of a

pioneer woman. She is celebrated because she stoically transcended a situation she never would have freely chosen. She submits to the wilderness just as—supposedly—she submits to sex.
But she needn't enjoy it, and her whole posture is in rigid opposition to the wilderness experience: to the land, to the Indians. Her
glory, we are told, is that she carried the family, religion, fences,
the warmth of the hearth and steaming washtubs inviolate to the
middle of the American desert. (195–196)

Initially I felt as if Lander voiced my own feelings as a well-read western
tomboy who had always felt ill at ease with party dresses and social en-
gagements—my own versions of her "churches and fences." We had felt
the same frustration with the Molly Woodses and Miss Watsons our literary tradition had given us as female models, naturally we had both hun
gered to be Huck. Our literary tradition, as Judith Fetterley has demonstrated, had demanded of us that we identify with a selfhood that defined
itself in opposition to us, and we had responded by resisting the stereotype of the civilizing woman, by attempting to claim male territory as our
own. Our feminism had led us to seek—and discover—women writers
who themselves resisted the stereotype.

Yet something always nagged at me about Lander's response. It had
to do with that single phrase "the warmth of the hearth," which she uses
so ironically. This was not an institutional image but one that inevitably
recalled for me the female body and its capacity for nurturance and
"warmth," which I couldn't help but link to female values by turning the
phrase into "the warmth of the heart." Lander's irony pained me, and I
gradually realized that it seemed to me self-hating, that she—and I, and
Sandoz—had too readily accepted the denigration of female values inherent in the stereotypes of our western myths, that her anger at the stereotype, like Sandoz's rejection of her mother, suggested an unwillingness to
acknowledge and seek to understand the limitations in our mothers' lives.
Mary Sandoz and many other pioneer women did grind their teeth and
clench their fists; if my own grandmother occasionally acted like a fearful
victim, she had good cause.

When I got this far—not nearly far enough, as some of you will have
noticed—I wrote the essay about Sandoz I have summarized. (See
Graulich, "Every Husband.") My conclusions tied in nicely with what
were then, and continue to be, central questions in western women's history: Did the frontier liberate women, as Turner and many other historians
allege it liberated men? Sandoz and many other contemporary feminist
historians would clearly answer no; several important books and essays
have argued that the pioneer woman went West reluctantly and analyzed
why. These historians portray western women in terms of what Lander

claims is a stereotype created by men; like Sandoz, they suggest that most women "made the best of the situation," that their heroism is characterized, largely, by endurance and innovation within constraints. My reading and my experience had taught me that many pioneer women had indeed been victims of men, of male violence, but I sought a different personal response than those of Sandoz and Lander. My rhetoric was pretty dramatic, I now see:

> It is natural for feminist scholars who yearn, like Sandoz and Lander, for the freedom promised the frontiersman to search for women who share their feelings of rebellion because the promise of the frontier is, after all, a *human* fantasy. But as feminists we must not purchase our self-esteem—our freedom—at our mothers' expense, or, as [the passage I quoted from Nancy] Chodorow suggests, we will turn against our very selves. (19)

I hid my personal response in a universal "we," just as I stated my final declaration abstractly (even quoting an authority): *Old Jules* "reveals the difficulties of writing about women while aspiring to male freedom and the importance, in Heilbrun's words, of learning to aspire '*as women,* supporting other women, identifying with them, and imagining the achievement of women generally' " (20). That sounds pretty good. But it *was* an abstract response and not an emotional one; I had intellectually acknowledged my—or rather "our"—affinities but I had not felt them. I could see the difficulties Sandoz had had, and I admitted that her confusion was shared by many female scholars, but I had not overcome my own difficulties. I could see how my experience, and particularly my literary tradition, had led me to be male-identified. I could empathize abstractly with women's victimization, but it would still take me a while to imagine and redefine the achievement of women.

Although I removed my personal story from my published essay, I manipulated essays with it when I presented my research at conferences, telling the story about my grandfather with which I began this essay, a story that inevitably charms the audience into smiling at the familiar image of this endearing American tale-teller and then smacks them with his violence. Sometimes I passed around a favorite photo of mine: with the bare California foothills in the background, I, aged one, sit atop a horse; my grandfather, tanned, shirtless, blue-jeaned and booted, ready to catch me if I fall. I was quite aware of the power of this manipulative story, and I milked it. Yet it is also an honest story, focused as it is on my grandfather and then on me and my response. It took me too long to realize that there was a silenced person in the story, someone who got left out, the person who told the truth: my mother.

But I'm getting ahead of myself. My mother's voice came to me a year later, as I typed the conclusion to another paper on violence, in a digression that started out as yet another retelling of the story about my grandfather. I didn't want to write another paper about violence; it was depressing and disturbing, and my grandparents were both dead. But I saw that Sandoz had turned away from the subject too readily, had escaped too quickly. Learning from her example, I began to think about other western books and to look for links. I realized that it was daughters who broke the silence, who wrote autobiographical narratives about their pioneer mothers' victimization. While researching the Sandoz paper, I had asked several social scientists, experts on violence against women, about studies on the effect of such violence on daughters, and received no suggestions. Not surprisingly, the research has until recently concentrated on men, on how sons of abusers become abusers themselves. Obviously this is useful research, but it does not address the psychological consequences for women who grow up watching their mothers be victimized. How would that affect a girl's self-esteem? Was Sandoz typical in her response? It did not occur to me to wonder if my mother was typical in *her* response.

My second essay, "Violence against Women in Literature of the Western Family," explores the autobiographical narratives of four western women: Sandoz's *Old Jules,* Agnes Smedley's *Daughter of Earth,* Tillie Olsen's *Yonnondio,* and Meridel Le Sueur's *The Girl.* The conclusion of these writers that violence against women is the result of patriarchal definitions of gender and marriage rather than of individual pathology anticipates the analysis of the most recent feminist scholars, and the first part of my essay explores this point in detail. But I eventually focused on what the books themselves stress: the effect of the violence on the mothers' lives and how watching a mother become a victim of male aggression affects a daughter's complex identification with and resistance to her mother's life. The books reveal the struggles women face growing up female in a world where women are victimized and devalued.

Reading these books gave me a different ending to my neat little story about how I learned about storytelling from my grandfather. The women writers, the daughters, showed me how I had missed the point. My mother told me the secrets she and my grandmother had kept for 35 years, yet I used these secrets not to understand their lives but to explore my continued identification with my grandfather, to evade the most painful identification a woman experiences. I learned—at first and unconsciously—that because I am a woman there is "something wrong with me . . . something too deep even to cry about" (Smedley 12). I did not conceal the story, but like Sandoz I thought it was about the man, and I could not see that the story was really about the teller, my mother, about her deep, abiding attachment to my grandmother and how it affected her feelings about herself. I could not see that that attachment and the feelings and values it expresses were the richest "secret" my mother had to give me, that her story was meant to let me know—finally—that a woman's strengths—nurturance, love, interdependence, vulnerability—make her, in Le Sueur's word, a "treasure." Although I am a feminist, I rendered my foremothers invisible and thoughtlessly covered up the real costs of abuse of women.

I can remember the pain I felt when I first wrote that final sentence two years ago. But confessions mean little in isolation, and although I was ready to "say these things," I was still attempting to distance myself from the emotional implications of what I had discovered. Preparing to present my paper at the Women's West conference that year, I told myself that, like my mother, I am a very private person, and I would not cry when I got to the paper's conclusion. I was determined to resist the image of the weeping woman. Yet as I neared the end of my talk, I saw a woman in the audience begin to cry, making no effort to wipe the tears that welled out of her large, brown eyes. Certain that her tears were in response to her own experience, that she had confronted violence in her own or her mother's life, I began to cry in response to her tears. In front of 65 people, I cried for her, for my mother, for my grandmother, for myself, and for what connected us all. (The brown-eyed woman later told me that she had never experienced violence, but cried because she identified with the pain of the women I discussed—and with my own.)

I made this public emotional acknowledgment of my failure to understand nearly two years ago, but I did not tell my mother about my tears or about my essay. Like her, I find secrets tempting to keep. I was afraid that she would feel I had exposed her, afraid of the anger I know she too often has been unable to express, afraid that she, who has often claimed not to understand my essays, would not understand. I thought I would wait until the essay, dedicated to her and my grandmother, was published, and when it was published I decided to wait until I saw her. I took it with me on the next trip—and I couldn't find the right moment. I was afraid, really, of acknowledging the connections between us. Finally a friend, Barbara White, told me that though she too thought it might upset my mother, it was clear that I was going to send it someday so I might as well send it now. Knowing that there are things that Barbara regrets having left unsaid to her own mother, now dead, I mailed the essay that same day.

A few days later my mother called from California. "I got your essay," she said neutrally. "It seemed from your note that you'd been afraid to send it to me. Why?"

"Oh, I was afraid you'd be upset that I'd told your secrets."

"I think it's important for somebody to say these things, and I really understood what you were saying," she said. "I spent the afternoon crying. I'm so proud of you. I only wish your grandmother were still alive."

Starting to cry, as she was, I said, "That means so much to me. I wanted you to know that you and Grandma were in my mind while I was writing it. I wanted you to know that I've tried to understand."

As I have written these essays on violence, I have often thought in terms of how much the work was costing me emotionally, but in reading a recent essay by Bell Gale Chevigny, I realized more fully that it was my resistance, and not my conclusions, that was costly and painful. "Our difficulty in knowing our mothers dominates us as daughters and to some extent, blocks our growth and self-knowledge," she writes (372).

One day almost two weeks ago as I sat making lists about what I wanted to say in this essay, I thought about my mother's comment that she wished my grandmother were still alive to read the essay I dedicated to her. As my mind wandered inevitably back to my grandfather, I realized that still, after all this, *I* wished *he* were alive to read it, that still I needed to communicate with him. After a few painful hours of soul-searching, I decided that while it would be too bad to end where I began, with my grandfather, I would have to conclude my essay with this admission. Now, only a short time later, writing this essay has made me realize—emotionally and not merely intellectually—that he isn't my audience any longer. In telling my story I've tried to attend to and tell my mother's story, to claim and be proud of—and no longer keep secret—my connections to her. To you, Mom.

Works Cited

Baym, Nina. "Melodramas of Beset Manhood: How Theories of American Fiction Exclude Women Authors." *American Quarterly* (Summer 1981): 123–139.

Chevigny, Bell Gale. "Daughters Writing: Toward a Theory of Women's Biography." *Between Women.* Ed. Carol Ascher, Louise De Salvo, and Sara Ruddick. Boston: Beacon Press, 1984.

Fetterley, Judith. *The Resisting Reader: A Feminist Approach to American Literature.* Bloomington: University of Indiana Press, 1978.

Graulich, Melody. "Every Husband's Right: Sex Roles in Mari Sandoz's *Old Jules.*" *Western American Literature* 18 (May 1983): 3–20.

Graulich, Melody. "Violence Against Women in Literature of the Western Family." *Frontiers* 7.3 (1984): 14–20.

Heilbrun, Carolyn. *Reinventing Womanhood.* New York: W. W. Norton, 1979.

Lander, Dawn. "Eve Among the Indians." *The Authority of Experience: Essays in Feminist Criticism.* Ed. Arlyn Diamond and Lee R. Edwards. Amherst: University of Massachusetts Press, 1977.

Sandoz, Mari. *Old Jules.* 1935. Lincoln: University of Nebraska Press, 1962.

Sandoz, Mari. "Pioneer Women." *Hostiles and Friendlies*. Ed. Virginia Faulkner. Lincoln: University of Nebraska Press, 1959.

Personal Investigations: Inquiry Projects

1. People sometimes explain their preference for reading nonfiction rather than fiction this way: You can learn so much more from reading a "true" story rather than one that's made up. It's interesting, then, when Melody Graulich observes in the beginning of her essay that she turned to literature to discover the meaning of her mother's story about Graulich's violent grandfather. She turned to novels that deal in some way with violence against women, and "Somebody Must Say These Things" is the story of her discoveries. Think about some aspect of your life that you'd like to understand better. Perhaps it's a longing for wild places or your feelings about a friend's death. Maybe it's anger about racism or confusion about who you are or who you want to be. Interview a literature professor, and ask him or her what novel or stories might give you insight into your personal mysteries. Use literature as Graulich does here—as a way of seeing.

2. Alternatively, select a poem, short story, novel, or essay you've read over the years that reflected your feelings or experiences at some stage in your life. Perhaps it was a Mary Oliver poem or Salinger's *Catcher in the Rye*. Read the work again, but this time look for lines or passages that really struck (or strike) home. What is it that was (is) so moving or powerful? Underline those passages so you can find them again. Draft a collage essay that alternates with lines or passages from your favorite text and scenes or moments from your past experiences that seem connected to them.

Craft and Conventions: Explaining and Evaluating

3. A common convention in academic writing is a summary of what has already been said by scholars and others about the topic being investigated. Though "Somebody Must Say These Things" is unconventional in many ways, Graulich does try to place her discussion in the larger context of what has been said about violence against women and women in the frontier West. Where exactly does she do this in the essay?

4. Using a story or a novel as a source in a research essay can be quite different than using an informational article in a research paper. Rather than

using the source for ideas or facts, the writer of the essay based on literature looks for relevant *parts of the story*. Find a passage where Graulich does this (there are several). What are the ways that Graulich uses passages from the novel *Old Jules,* and what are her purposes for using them?

5. How would you argue that this essay is academic? To answer this question, begin by fastwriting for several minutes about the qualities of academic writing. How can you tell what is and is not academic writing? Do some online research to find out how others define it and review what we've said about it in this textbook. Then come up with a working definition of academic writing to apply to Graulich's essay.

6. Reread this essay with the purpose of identifying the places where Graulich is using various methods of inquiry—what we call here exploring, explaining, evaluating, and reflecting. Which ones does she seem to use? Use specific passages to explain her modes of inquiry. How many of the places you've identified draw on both personal or emotional knowledge as well as scholarly or literary knowledge (that is, other scholars in the field and literary texts)? What conclusions might you draw about how Graulich uses inquiry in this essay?

Inquiries on Inquiry: Exploring and Reflecting

7. A feature of the essay as a mode of inquiry is that it allows the writer to say things and then report that she no longer believes them, or at least revise and qualify what she thought initially. Is this a move Graulich makes in her essay? What do you think of such a move, especially from an "expert"? Does it make an essay seem less persuasive for an expert to demonstrate that she disagrees with herself, that her ideas have changed?

8. Emotion is not thought to be the province of academic writing. That's obviously not the case in this essay, where Graulich confesses that she read the piece at a conference and wept. Does this confession strengthen or weaken the essay? Perhaps both?

9. Using the dialogue journal approach, play the believing and doubting games with this essay (see Chapter 2 and Chapter 3).

10. Write a personal response to this essay, reflecting on your initial thoughts and feelings, the associations you made with what Graulich says, and the experiences that influenced your reading of this essay. If you found this difficult to read—or "boring" or hard to get through emotionally—explore *why*. Then finish this sentence: *As I reflect on my reading experience of this essay, I now understand _____ about my initial responses because _____.*

Every Husband's Right: Sex Roles in Mari Sandoz's *Old Jules*

Melody Graulich

You may remember Graulich referring in "Somebody Must Say These Things: An Essay for My Mother" to essays she had written on the same subject years before as she was studying the writer Mari Sandoz's work, domestic violence, and Western women's writing. The piece you find here is excerpted from one of those essays; we've included it because we believe you can learn a great deal about both *academic writing and personal academic essays by comparing and contrasting the work one author has done in both genres. You may have to make choices yourself as an academic writer about how much of the personal to include in a history paper, a chemistry report, or a sociology paper; so we hope this comparison can offer criteria for making such a decision.*

From the original article, we've included the lead paragraphs and then a long section at the end of the essay that is directly related to what Graulich argues in "Somebody Must Say These Things." Even though you've probably never read Old Jules, *you'll be very familiar with the story as you read this article because Graulich includes both summaries and detailed passages from the work. In fact, doing so is one requirement of academic writing in literary studies; passages from the text itself are the most important pieces of evidence for the claims made in a literary analysis, and the writer must read them very closely.*

What else might you need to know about formal literary criticism to help you read this essay? Generally, essays are structured as formal arguments, which means you'll find very direct claims supported by textual evidence or by the research of other literary critics. In addition, literary scholars need to explain why their research question is significant to the field given what other specialists in the area have said. They also need to analyze the quotes they use, commenting on what is being said, extending it, contrasting it with something else, connecting it to a larger theme or a larger context. You won't find Graulich, for example, simply dropping in quotations and moving on. Her analysis frames every quotation. And yet, we don't get strong insertions of her feelings and experience in this essay as we do in "Somebody Must Say These Things." That's because formal literary criticism (or at least some theories within that category) demands the author focus on the subject of the essay itself, not on the author's relationship to that subject. And yet you may find that Graulich's voice is relatively familiar to you in this essay.

Originally published in 1983, "Every Husband's Right" was the first article Graulich published on Old Jules, *so it shows her initial thinking about the*

*themes of domestic violence and women's roles in Western literature. As you
read, we hope you'll do so with the following questions in mind: What qualities
make this a formal academic essay compared to Graulich's personal academic
essay, "Somebody Must Say These Things"? How does Graulich register her
presence in this essay without using "I" frequently or referring to her experience and feelings? What kinds of research did Graulich do as she wrote this
essay? How did your reading of the personal academic essay Graulich wrote
influence how you read this one?*

> In the end the Plains woman might be as weatherbeaten and wrin-
> kled as an old boot top but still standing firm beside her husband
> and children, grown strong together while overcoming the
> calamities that dog the vulnerable—the wiry old settler at her side
> deserving the ultimate accolade of the Plains as a good husband:
> "He never laid a hand on his wife."[1]

When Mari Sandoz wrote this passage near the end of her life, she
returned to one of the subjects of her first book, *Old Jules* (1935): the widespread physical and emotional abuse of pioneer women. Ostensibly a biography of her father, Jules Sandoz, a "prophet, . . . a sort of Moses working
the soil of his Promised Land,"[2] and a husband who does not deserve the
Plains' "ultimate accolade," *Old Jules* is one of the very few western histories to explore the pioneer West's dominant institution, marriage, and to imply that relations among women and men are a significant historical theme.[3]
Sandoz's award-winning book anticipates many of the conclusions of recent scholarship on pioneer women and, with its focus on violence against
women, presents unique insights on the lives of western women.[4]

Old Jules can also help to illuminate the problems women scholars
face as they reconstruct women's history. Feminist critics have been

---

[1]Mari Sandoz, *Love Song to the Plains* (Lincoln: Univ. of Nebraska Press, 1961), p. 125.

[2]Mari Sandoz, *Old Jules* (Lincoln: Univ. of Nebraska Press, 1962, originally published, 1935), p. 406.
Page numbers follow subsequent quotations in text.

[3]Other than those focusing on Mormon life, few histories until recently have explored these areas, al-
though some western writers like Wallace Stegner have written about marriage and sex stereotypes.
Several recent studies use demographics to suggest that the pioneer West was occupied largely by
married couples. See Christine Stansell, "Women on the Great Plains, 1865–1890," *Women's Studies,*
Vol. 4 (1975), 87–98: Johnny Faragher and Christine Stansell, "Women and Their Families on the
Overland Trail to California and Oregon 1842–1867," *Feminist Studies,* Vol. 2 (1975), 150–66; and
John Faragher, *Women and Men on the Oregon Trail* (New Haven: Yale Univ. Press, 1979).

[4]For a brief and more generalized treatment of violence in *Old Jules,* see Rosemary Whitaker, "Violence in *Old Jules* and *Slogum House*," *Western American Literature,* Vol. XVI, No. 3 (Nov., 1981),
215–224. Although Whitaker mentions Jules's treatment of his wives, she does not explore the implications of his violence against women.

sorely confused about how to judge the lives of western women. Some search for literary and historical foremothers who defy the traditional roles of the nineteenth century's "women's sphere" to achieve in their lives the measure of freedom our cultural myths associate with the frontier; others acknowledge the truth in the stereotype of the reluctant woman pioneer, accepting that most women were confined within restrictive definitions of their character, often powerless, though perhaps creating order and meaning in their lives through connections to other women and to a woman's subculture.[5] While Jules Sandoz found the freedom Frederick Jackson Turner described, the West did not offer Mary Sandoz, his wife, the same bargain. After exposing in *Old Jules* the violent and circumscribed lives of her mother and other plains women, Sandoz turns in her later histories to the classic masculine West and its themes, to what she calls "the romantic days."[6] Interested in heroism, individualism, and power, which she sees as the natural subjects of history, Sandoz never again gives a woman a starring role in western history, though women sometimes are protagonists in her fiction. Sandoz's uncertainty about whether to identify with her father's or her mother's West clearly separate worlds in *Old Jules,* and her struggles to assess the relative heroism of her pioneer parents' lives help elucidate central questions raised by contemporary feminists. . . .

Sandoz's male-dominated women lead seemingly unbearable lives. Through her numerous examples, she exposes many aspects of pioneer women's lives recently discussed by scholars, showing that they often moved out of the nineteenth century's "women's sphere" to do male chores, while there was seldom any reciprocal change in the work patterns of men; that the lack of birth control, the yearly pregnancy, took a heavy toll not only on the pioneer woman but also on her eldest daughter; that husbands often forced isolation upon their wives; that men and women did not marry for companionship but turned to members of their own sex for society.[7] *Old Jules* contains many insightful passages which stress the differences in men's and women's lives.

---

[5]See works by Stansell and Faragher, as well as Christiane Fischer, *Let Them Speak for Themselves: Women in the American West, 1849–1900* (New York: Dutton, 1978); Julie Roy Jeffrey, *Frontier Women: The Trans-Mississippi West, 1840–80* (New York: Hill & Wang, 1979); Joanna Stratton, *Pioneer Women: Voices from the Kansas Frontier* (New York: Simon and Schuster, 1981); and Susan Armitage, "Western Women's History: A Review Essay," *Frontiers,* Vol. V, No. 3. (Fall, 1980), 71–73. I will return to these works throughout this essay.

[6]Mari Sandoz, "Pioneer Women," an unpublished essay excerpted in Mari Sandoz, *Hostiles and Friendlies,* edited by Virginia Faulkner (Lincoln: University of Nebraska Press, 1959), p. 59. Sandoz eventually turned this essay into a much sanitized and cheerier version of her mother's life, entitled "The New Frontier Woman" (1936), reprinted in *Hostiles and Friendlies* as "Marlizzie," 60–66.

[7]These topics are generally discussed by Fischer, Stansell, Faragher, and Jeffrey.

> But as soon as the storms let up, the men could get away from the
> isolation. They could go to the warm, friendly saloons to talk, to
> drink if they had a few cents in their pockets. . . . But not their
> women. They had only the wind and the cold and the problems of
> clothing, shelter, food and fuel. Sometimes their voices shrilled,
> sometimes they died to dark silence. (82)

Throughout the book Sandoz demonstrates what Susan Armitage has argued in a review essay on western women's history: "there were two
Wests, a female and a male one."[8] In her rich treatment of the marriage of
Jules and his fourth wife, Mary, the heart of the book, Sandoz honestly
describes the conflict and violence within her own family and explores
the difference in power in her father's and mother's lives.

Mary, a town woman, marries Jules when she finds herself abandoned
by her brother and unable to homestead alone. "Brought up in a tradition of
subordination to man, she gave Jules her savings, a hundred dollars," and
finds herself without money to run away (187). Soon she is pregnant, feeling she is trapped forever, in bondage to a "difficult, but . . . intelligent"
man who expects her to do all the farm work and wait on him whenever he
orders. He denies her any social contact and ridicules her feelings and
opinions; the effect of such isolation is to undermine her sense of herself.
He controls their money, often spending it impractically, never consulting
her in any decision. He believes that "women got to have children to keep
healthy," and when she has children, he abuses them (110).

Jules threatens Mary constantly with curses and beatings. She finds
"the back door to the lean-to was a convenient avenue of escape when she
must run to the brush" to avoid a beating (193). She feels safe only when
she is pregnant, when "he would hesitate to kick or strike her too hard"
(204). He punishes her arbitrarily, often for his own mistakes. Powerless
against Jules and desperate, Mary seeks escape through self-destruction in
a scene which reveals the terse power and tension in Sandoz's style:

> Mary avoided crossing him or bothering him for help in anything
> she could possibly do alone. But there were times when she must
> have his help, as when the roof leaked or the calves had to be cas-
> trated. It took weeks of diplomatic approach to get him to look af-
> ter the two bull calves before they were too big for her to handle
> at all. And when she couldn't hold the larger one from kicking,
> Jules, gray-white above his beard, threw his knife into the manure
> and loped to the back door. "I learn the goddamn balky woman to
> obey me when I say 'hold him.' " He tore a handful of four-foot

---

[8]Armitage, p. 73.

wire stays from the bundle in the corner of the shop and was gone towards the corral, the frightened grandmother and the children huddled at the back window.

They heard the banging of the gate, Jules's bellow of curses. Then Mary ran through the door, past the children and straight to the poison drawer. It stuck, came free, the bottles flying over the floor. Her face furrowed in despair, blood dripping from her face and her hand where she had been struck with the wire whip, the woman snatched up a bottle, struggled with the cork, pulling at it, with her teeth. The grandmother was upon her, begging, pleading, clutching at the red bottle with the crossbones.

Jules burst in. "Wo's the goddamned woman. I learn her to obey me if I got to kill her!"

"You!" the grandmother cried, shaking her first against him. "For you there is a place in hell!"

With the same movement of her arm she swung out, knocking the open bottle from the woman's mouth. . . . Then, she led Mary out of the house and to the brush along the river. . . .

And hidden far under the bed the three children cowered like frightened little rabbits, afraid to cry. (230–31)

Although her mother prevents Mary's suicide, her children do witness the obliteration of their mother's selfhood throughout their childhood. To survive, Mary must constantly compromise herself. She gives up her values and principles, like Henriette, and begins to fight back. And she gives up her own needs to pander to Jules's character and desires.

Although Mary manages to encourage Jules's "mellowing" by accepting him as he is, this "choice" is another kind of self destruction. Her past self gone, all stimulation denied her, Mary has nothing in her life but work, which focuses her attention away from herself and solaces her because "if she worked hard enough and long enough she could sleep" (195). The beautiful and cultured woman "had three [eventually six] anaemic, undernourished children very close together, without a doctor. She lost her teeth; her clear skin became leathery from field work; her eyes paled and sun-squinted; her hands knotted, the veins of her arms like slack clotheslines" (215). Intelligent, strong, capable, determined, Mary must turn all her energy to sheer drudgery; because she does so, she and her husband eventually "got along well enough now" (279). But even when he stops beating her, Jules has the power in the family: he controls the money; he makes the decisions; he harrasses Mary constantly; and he refuses to work, though he claims the credit for Mary's work. Without him, Mary possesses the strength to be independent, but married to him, she must squelch her character and her ambitions; she must bend to his authority and find ways to circumvent his power. (After Jules's death Mary would become a shrewd businesswoman, in fact, and make her children rich.) As *Old Jules* shows, none of this was lost upon her daughter, who knew what it meant to take her mother's place as whipping girl: unable to beat the pregnant Mary, Jules turned to his daughter as substitute and "whipped Marie until he was breathless" (279).

Sandoz sees the violence, the horror, in women's lives as the result of physical and institutional power. She never tries to suggest that Jules or the other violent husbands are mentally ill, nor does she explain their behavior as caused by their personal lives. The causes for their brutality are embedded in the fledgling society's attitudes about women and marriage, many imported from the Old World. Her portrayal of the pioneer West confirms what some recent studies of battered wives have shown, that wife-beating has been far more widespread than generally acknowledged, that western culture has until recently covertly sanctioned the husband's right to beat his wife.[9] On the lawless frontier, Sandoz believed, physical power was more significant than in settled regions; there was nothing to limit a husband's "rights."[10] Jules only defines women as his society does. Sandoz presents a few kind husbands (and several positive male figures), but most men see women as something to exploit. A man needs a wife to work, obey, and bear children, and the laws and culture support his attitudes.

Given this portrayal of the power dynamics in the Sandoz family, it is difficult to understand Sandoz's introduction to her subject:

> As I read, the stories of my childhood came back to me with new significance. . . . Not one character . . . would I have one whit different, not my mother, who had the courage and the tenacity to live with this man so many years, or [a list of other characters], or Old Jules himself. These people endured, and as I review them from the vantage point of twice knowledge, my eyes mist. A gallant race, and I salute them.[11]

She would not change this father? Or her mother's life? This is hard to believe, even granting Sandoz's stoicism, and most readers would probably

---

[9]See R. Emerson Dobash and Russell Dobash, *Violence Against Wives* (New York: Free Press, 1979). Recent data collected in the United States, Britain, and Canada suggest that "more than half of all married women are beaten by their husbands," reported in *The Boston Sunday Globe* (June 6, 1982), p. 17.

[10]Some studies have shown that in communities that policed moral behavior, neighbors were more likely to get involved in wife-beating cases. See Laurel Ulrich's analysis of puritan New England in *Good Wives: Image and Reality in the Lives of Women in Northern New England, 1650–1750* (New York: Knopf, 1982).

[11]Foreword to *Old Jules*, p. ix.

imagine another cause for her "misty" eyes. Given her obvious sympathies and identification with her mother, why does Sandoz, who once said that "the story of the pioneer woman had yet to be written," focus her story on her father?[12] The answer to this question lies in Marie's relationship to her mother and her efforts to reject her mother's devalued role.

While Sandoz freely enters Jules's point of view throughout her book, the second half is influenced much more by her mother's viewpoint and, increasingly, by that of Marie as she grows up. She explores with particular insight and compassion her mother's inner thoughts and feelings.

> Often Jules and his friends sat about the kitchen as she worked; sometimes they sang, now and then in German. Then she joined them and was happier. But usually they laughed and talked in French, looking at her, maybe, saying things she could not understand. . . . Often she slipped away into the unheated bedroom and stayed there until she was wooden with cold. But Jules's friends were glad enough to eat her well-cooked meals, to throw ashes over her meat floor. By this time Mary had given up trying to get Jules to spit into a can or a box of sand. When he left the house she wiped up the great nauseating splotches and a deep, dark anger against him grew within her. (206–7).

Although Sandoz, the historian, identifies with a woman's feelings, the narrative child Marie has a conflict-filled relationship with her mother. While the historian will try by the book's end to see her mother's life as heroic, her parents' marriage as a successful pioneer union, the recreated self, Marie, resists her mother's role and looks for a way to escape it.

From her childhood, Marie is forced to take on women's responsibilities while being confronted with her society's attitudes about women. She recognizes that she is identified with her mother and what womanhood will bring her when she is beaten as her mother's substitute. She is confronted with the powerlessness of her sexuality when she is attacked by a convict her father boards, hiding his offense, sexual assault on girls. And the constant babies, despite Mary's efforts to avoid pregnancy by nursing each for several years, show Marie the consequences of sexuality for women. Mary forces her daughter to take on her burden, assigning her the care of each new baby. "Never Jule or James, always Marie" (296). Finally, after the fifth baby, the desperate child, "driven to words" by yet another pregnancy, suggests to her mother that they both suffer from her "condition": " 'I should think you'd be tired of having babies—I'm tired of watching them—' " (341). Mary's response to her daughter is one of the saddest moments in the

---

[12]Excerpts from "Pioneer Women," p. 60.

book: she slaps her across the face. Although she recognizes the truth in her daughter's words and refuses to sleep with Jules after the baby is born, she never acknowledges Marie's feelings or helps her to cope with the limitations of her womanhood, though she heaps its responsibilities upon her. She hits this mirror image of herself, and she belittles her, just as the child's father does. Mary resents her husband's behavior and her own powerlessness, but she expects and even forces her daughter to accept her own burdened and unrespected role. And the child does: while the boys run away from their father, "usually Marie stayed, accepting the abuse silently, without the spirit to rebel" (374).

Christine Stansell has suggested that pioneer mothers felt a sense of failure when their daughters rejected their definitions of woman's role. If they were unable to pass on their own subculture and tradition, they would "disappear behind the masculine preoccupations and social structure which dominated the West," becoming invisible.[13] Women clung to what they thought of as their sphere in an effort to hold on to a few shreds of identity from a more satisfying past. Although the family was often filled with conflict and dominated by the father, women still believed that within the home they exercised their influence. Mary Sandoz had an idea of what it was to be a woman, and she passed it on to her daughter. Not to do so would be to undermine her whole life.

Marie finally rebels, escaping to a school teaching job and to the University. She becomes a writer, wins a prize, and begins her first book, which grows out of her "emotional identity." And her treatment of her subject matter reveals her confusion about growing up female in a society which victimizes women. Theorist Nancy Chodorow has described the problems girls face in developing self-esteem when a patriarchal society forces them to undervalue their mothers:

> Most psychoanalytic and social theorists claim that the mother inevitably represents to her daughter (and son) regression, passivity, dependence, and lack of orientation to reality, whereas the father represents progression, activity, independence, and reality orientation. Given the value implications of this dichotomy, there are advantages for the son in giving up his mother and identifying with his father. For the daughter, feminine gender identification means identification with a devalued, passive mother whose own self-esteem is low. Conscious rejection of

---

[13]Stansell, pp. 88–89. Fischer has also pointed out that there are often significant differences in the feelings expressed about western life by original settlers and their daughters, who were raised without such strong female networks.

her oedipal maternal identification, however, remains an unconscious rejection and devaluation of herself. . . .[14]

Rejecting her mother's powerlessness in her search for self-esteem, Sandoz shifts her "emotional identity" to her father's vision, to the heroic
virtues of the masculine West.

She believes that her mother is heroic, but hers is a qualified heroism,
subordinate to Jules's, an everyday kind of heroism. She respects Mary,
who, like other pioneer women, "made the best of the situation," but her
life was filled with situations to avoid, not to aspire to.[15] She sees as the
central difference between her parents that her mother "preferred the
smaller, the more familiar things, while her Jules saw only the far, the
large, the exalted canvas" (191). Jules is a powerful prophet, with time to
dream because his women do all the work. He is the romantic visionary,
about whom settlers say things like:

> "Yeah, maybe he see what we don't. He is like the tree that grow
> on the bluff of the river—the pine. He get the wind and the storm
> that do not touch us who are the cottonwood and the willow near
> the water. But his root is strong and he see the cloud far off—and
> the sun before she shine on us. (39)

In contrast, Sandoz makes Mary and her life of drudgery dull and unap-
pealing. Her "visionary" father's dying words to her reveal what kind of
esteem she can expect—from herself and others—so long as she remains
woman-identified: " 'There is nobody to carry on my work. . . . If the
Marie was a man she might—as a woman she is not worth a damn' " (418).

Old Jules shows how Sandoz was torn between her parents' worlds,
recognizing her kinship to her mother but desiring her father's freedom,
his imagination, his defiance, his stubborn self-confidence, all traits
promised to the western male. Only he could be the hero of history. Says
Helen Stauffer, Sandoz's biographer:

> She sees her heroes as vital forces, often larger-than-life, per-
> forming on a vast landscape—actually an epic view . . . shared by
> most western writers. Epic has been defined as, ". . . a narrative
> of some length that deals with events which have a certain
> grandeur and importance and come from a life of action, espe-
> cially of violent action such as war. It gives a special pleasure be-

---

[14]Nancy Chodorow, "Family Structure and Feminine Personality," in *Women, Culture and Society,*
edited by Michelle Z. Rosaldo and L. Lamphere (Stanford: Stanford Univ. Press, 1974), 43–65, p. 65.
See also Chodorow's *The Reproduction of Mothering: Psychoanalysis and the Sociology of Gender*
(Berkeley: Univ. of California Press, 1978).
[15]Excerpts from "Pioneer Women," p. 60.

cause its events and persons enhance our belief in the world of human achievement and in the dignity and nobility of man."[16]

The irony of this definition in terms of Mary's life is apparent, and Sandoz can find grandeur in her father's life only by squelching her identification with her mother, by suppressing judgment of his affronts against the "dignity and nobility" of woman. The great themes of western history belong not to Mary but to Jules, and here too, they are representative pioneers. In western diaries, John Faragher has noticed one major difference: "Women were concerned with family and relational values—the happiness and health of the children, family affection, home and hearth, getting along with the traveling group, and friendship, especially with other women. Men were concerned with violence and aggression—fights, conflicts, and competition, and most of all, hunting."[17] Men's activities are "epic," no matter how brutal, and women's are not. Men can be heroes; women cannot.

Many women readers have told me that they find *Old Jules* a very depressing book; perhaps Sandoz herself found pioneer women's lives depressing and dull. She recognized that *Old Jules* contained a woman's history of the West, composing a paper entitled "Pioneer Women" (1934) out of passages from it, and she saw that women had been stereotyped by being presented only through men's eyes, arguing that in male documents men mention wives only in connection "with calamity," but the rest of her histories overlook women's lives.[18] She turned away from a "virgin land" she was uniquely qualified to explore, and in this she follows the pattern of many other successful women writers described by Carolyn Heilbrun in *Reinventing Womanhood:* ". . . those women who *did* have the courage, self-confidence, and autonomy to make their way in the male-dominated world did so by identifying themselves with male ideals and role models, . . . by not identifying themselves . . . as women."[19]

In "Eve Among the Indians," Dawn Lander has confronted this problem in identification by challenging what she feels is the depressing and oppressive stereotype of the pioneer woman in American literature and literary criticism, and her reaction helps illuminate Sandoz's. After describing her own liberated childhood in the West, she says,

---

[16]Helen Stauffer, "Mari Sandoz and Western Biography," in *Women, Women Writers and the West,* edited by L. L. Lee and Merrill Lewis (Troy, N.Y.: Whitston Press, 1980), 55–69, p. 63. Stauffer's biography, *Mari Sandoz: Story Catcher of the Plains,* has just been published (Lincoln, Nebraska: Univ. of Nebraska Press, 1982).

[17]Faragher, p. 14.

[18]Excerpts from "Pioneer Women," p. 59.

[19]Carolyn Heilbrun, *Reinventing Womanhood* (New York: Norton & Co., 1979), p. 31.

I could find no place for myself and for my pleasure in the wilderness in the traditionally recorded images of women on the frontier. Tradition gives us the figure of a woman, strong, brave and often heroic, whose endurance and perseverance are legendary. It may seem strange that I find it difficult to identify with this much-praised figure. But I can almost hear her teeth grinding behind her tight-set lips; her stiff spine makes me tired and her clenched fists sad. Victimization and martyrdom are the bone and muscle of every statue, picture and word portrait of a frontier woman. She is celebrated because she stoically transcended a situation she never would have freely chosen. She submits to the wilderness just as—supposedly—she submits to sex. But she needn't enjoy it, and her whole posture is in rigid opposition to the wilderness experience; to the land, to the Indians. Her glory, we are told, is that she carried the family, religion, fences, the warmth of the hearth and steaming washtubs inviolate to the middle of the American desert.[20]

Believing that a stereotype which did not reflect her own experience, her love for the "space, energy, and passion" of the West, must also distort that of other women, Lander searches for women writers who form a countertradition. Today many such women have become feminist heroines: Caroline Kirkland, Eliza Farnham, Laura Ingalls Wilder, Abigail Scott Duniway, Elinore Pruitt Stewart. Lander finds male writers and critics responsible for creating "the discrepancy between women's actual feelings and the received tradition."[21]

Lander discovers liberated western women whose lives satisfy her own needs, but her anger at the stereotype, like Marie's rejection of her mother, suggests an unwillingness to accept—and come to understand—the real limitations in our mother's lives. Although scholars of western women's history are still arguing about the "central question" of whether the frontier liberated women, as Susan Armitage has shown, most seem to agree with Sandoz that the answer is no.[22] Fischer says that "One has the constant sense that moving West for them did not mean that a new dimension was given to their lives or that new horizons opened to them."[23] Faragher concludes that women went west "not [with] enthusiasm but en-

---

[20]Dawn Lander, "Eve Among the Indians," in *The Authority of Experience: Essays in Feminist Criticism,* edited by Arlyn Diamond and Lee R. Edwards (Amherst: Univ. of Massachusetts Press, 1977), 194–211, pp. 195–6.
[21]Lander, p. 197.
[22]Armitage, p. 71.
[23]Fischer, p. 13.

durance."[24] Coming to accept the reality of what Lander sees as a stereotype, Jeffrey discovers a different personal response:

> My original perspective was feminist: I hoped to find that pioneer women used the frontier as a means of liberating themselves from stereotypes and behaviors which I found constricting and sexist. I discovered that they did not. More important, I discovered why they did not. Though my own ideological commitment remains the same, I now have great sympathy for the choices these women made and admiration for their strength and courage. I have continually wondered whether any of us would do as well.[25]

While Lander is right that it is important for women to resist stereotypes, Jeffrey's empathy, her ability to identify with women whose lives turn them into victims and pawns and to understand their choices, allows her to question her culture's definition of heroism and to challenge the epic virtues that helped to circumscribe the pioneer woman's identity and power. As Nina Baym has shown, the American Studies tradition has been dominated by a fascination with "Melodramas of Beset Manhood," fantasies of masculine escape to the wilderness in search of male identity, in rejection of the civilized world of women,[26] and, as a result, feminist critics nurtured in this rebellious tradition have been encouraged, as Judith Fetterley has persuasively argued, to identify with characters who define themselves in opposition to women, to identify against themselves.[27] It is natural for feminist scholars who yearn, like Sandoz and Lander, for the freedom promised the frontiersman to search for women who share their feelings of rebellion because the promise of the frontier is, after all, a *human* fantasy. But as feminists we must not purchase our self-esteem—our freedom—at our mother's expense or, as Chodorow suggests, we will turn against our very selves.

   Old Jules is valuable to students of women's history because it explores the power dynamics within the pioneer marriage and undercuts the myth of the heroic frontiersman, but also because it reveals the difficulties of writing about women while aspiring to male freedom and the importance, in Heilbrun's words, of learning to aspire "*as women,* supporting other

---

[24]Faragher, quoted in Armitage, p. 73.
[25]Jeffrey, pp. xv–xvi.
[26]Nina Baym, "Melodramas of Beset Manhood: How Theories of American Fiction Exclude Women Authors," *American Quarterly* (Summer, 1981), pp. 123–39.
[27]Judith Fetterley, *The Resisting Reader: A Feminist Approach to American Literature* (Bloomington: Univ. of Indiana Press, 1978).

women, identifying with them, and imagining the achievement of women generally."[28] Sandoz's confusion about her "emotional identity" as a woman scholar is one that all women share, though we may not realize it.

Personal Investigations: Inquiry Projects

1. You may have been surprised to read about domestic violence in an article by an English professor, especially if you have always thought the field mainly was concerned about novels and poems rather than sociological issues. What does this article add to your understanding of domestic violence? Begin a research project that focuses on some aspect of domestic violence you find interesting—whether that means looking at it historically or in the present, through statistical data, or in fiction, poetry, or nonfiction.

2. If you found yourself interested in learning more about feminist analyses of literature, or about women's writing in general, begin a research project on the subject, focusing on the questions you find most compelling.

Craft and Conventions: Explaining and Evaluating

3. In both this essay and "Somebody Must Say These Things," Graulich uses the first person, referring to herself and her experiences. Does that mean both essays are personal academic essays? Why or why not? Look closely at the passages where Graulich refers to herself in this essay, and compare them to at least two passages from "Somebody Must Say These Things" where she refers to herself. Is she using her experiences, feelings, and thoughts the same way in both of these essays?

4. Now that you've read both of these essays, do you agree with Graulich's self-criticism in "Somebody Must Say These Things" about her earlier attitude toward her mother in "Every Husband's Right"? Why or why not?

5. Skim through the essay again and note all the long quotations. Then look closely at what Graulich says before and after them. What purposes do the quotes serve in her argument? How would you describe what Graulich is doing before and after each quote? Is she restating the quote? Comparing it to an earlier one? Analyzing it from the perspective of another theory or argument? Raising questions about it?

---

[28]Heilbrun, p. 32.

6. If you had to create a handout for students in a literature class that out-lined the writing conventions and methods of inquiry used in formal lit-erary criticism—based on this essay—what would you include? You won't be able to cover all of them, but you may be able to explain what kinds of evidence are valued, what kinds of questions are typically asked, which of the methods of inquiry we've discussed seem to be emphasized, what kinds of organizational and argumentative structures are used, how quotes are handled, and so forth. See what you can come up with and then compare notes with your small group.

Inquiries on Inquiry: Exploring and Reflecting

7. Before you read these two essays, what beliefs and associations did you have with feminism? Why? What in your own experience has influ-enced that? How is feminism defined in this essay? Use specific pas-sages to illustrate. Then discuss whether this essay and/or "Somebody Must Say These Things" has affected your understanding of feminism.

8. Both of Graulich's essays in this chapter examine the same novel and draw on many of the same critics (such as Dawn Lander). What does it mean that one person can read the same evidence in very different ways? Is one interpretation more true than another? How can we decide?

9. When you began reading this essay, what were your initial impressions? What kept you reading? What made you want to stop? What strategies did you use to finish reading it? If you did not find it engaging, explore why in a fastwrite. If you did find it relatively engaging, explore that. What in the essay made you respond that way? In your own background?

Student Essay

In Search of Grace

Peggy Jordan

Autobiographical criticism is like singing along with a text. Your voice mingles in some kind of harmony with the author's words, and the result is music that enriches them both. The essay by Peggy Jordan you are about to read is about singing, too; it's about the courage to keep singing in the mornings when the voice has gone south and there is no one to hear you except you. This is an essay about coming to terms with aging. But what makes Peggy's piece so poignant is the way the work of the poet Grace Butcher becomes the occasion for this reflection, and how Peggy returns again and again to Butcher's words for illumination. The light that is cast gives us a deeper understanding of several of Butcher's poems as well as Peggy's story.

Personal scholarship is sometimes criticized as self-indulgent, or solipsistic. But at their best, autobiographical-critical essays like "In Search of Grace" enchant us because the writer makes the connection between the research and the personal seamless, almost essential. It is impossible to imagine this essay without the words of Grace Butcher (and others) and the personal narrative Peggy weaves around them.

We also like this essay because the writer is a nontraditional student, returning to school in her forties, and finding in academic study both cage-rattling changes and a new sense of fulfillment. "In Search of Grace" speaks to that experience. But of course the essay transcends that, too, finding in the life and words of an aging poet a sense of hope that we can all appreciate.

As you read her essay, notice how effectively Peggy incorporates analyses of the poems with her personal narratives. This is difficult to do well. One central question to ask is this: Are there any parts of the essay in which Peggy's personal narratives and the critical analysis of the texts she is studying seem disconnected? In other words, does she ever stop singing along with those texts?

When I was in high school, three visiting poets showed up one day to read their work for my English class. I can't remember anything at all about two of them except for the foggy impression that they were men and that even though I tried hard to get some idea of what they were talking about, it all just sounded like blah blah blah blah blah. The only poetry I really knew at the time was that of Robert Frost, because we had discussed it in class, and my big sister's books by Rod McKuen—which I considered ridiculously self-indulgent. At that time, I believed that any poetry without rhyme was just an excuse to cheat, to write any old thing and break it into odd lines.

Then the third poet stepped to the podium. I still remember her name, Grace Butcher. I remember the sound of her voice. She was a marathon runner, and probably about as old then as I am now, but she didn't look, sound, or act like somebody's mom. She was timeless, she had somehow remained her real self through several phases of life that turn most women dumpy and resigned. She was built like a wood nymph. And her words flowed like music, sweet and full of power and even subtly suggestive.

I was so taken with her, but somehow I missed something in her reading, because at the end of one poem having to do with landscape, she smiled wickedly at us and said, "Now wasn't that a nice poem about farming?" Everyone laughed in a way that told me the poem must have really been about sex. I had missed that. I was mortified to have taken the poem literally. Of course, I laughed and pretended to get the joke. I was even more in love with her now that she had treated a bunch of high school kids as if we were mature enough to be trusted with such a joke, as if it were somehow our little secret from the uptight faculty. She assumed our intelligence and won me over forever.

But even though her name was clear in my mind, along with her soft, lovely voice, I remembered not a single word of her work when asked recently to list my favorite authors. I wanted to go back, to see what made her so memorable, to see if whatever impressed me so at 16 would still ring true at 44. I wanted to find out if any lines sounded familiar, if some poem of hers might contain a time capsule message sent to me by my own younger self.

None of the local libraries had anything she had written. I searched online for any trace of her under authors, women authors, poetry, women poets, Ohio poets, poems about running, and on and on in vain until it finally dawned on me to just start a search with her name. There she was, on my screen, smiling out from her own Web site. In the photo her hair is a deep, rich brown and she still looks just like a wood nymph, albeit a slightly more wrinkled one. I scrolled around and learned that she was born in 1934 and is still running and still writing, currently working on "a book-length poem about my relationship with my Canadian boyfriend." I also learned that her work was published in two anthologies, *Rising Tides* and *When I Am an Old Woman I Shall Wear Purple,* and amazingly enough, both were on my bookshelf.

I couldn't believe I still had *Rising Tides,* because at one point in 1982 I gave away or sold everything I owned, including my books, except for what would fit in the back of a Volkswagen Squareback. Most of the stuff was easily replaced and not hard to part with, but I still regret selling one of the guitars and I still miss every single book.

Somehow, *Rising Tides* had survived the big purge. It was a paperback published in 1973. It smelled like a grandmother's attic and the pages were yellowed and stiff, but there it was in my bookcase, in my hands. The blurb on the back cover proclaimed, "Rising out of the same growing consciousness that spawned the Women's Liberation Movement, this book is a feminist statement in the largest sense: it expresses a belief in the full humanity of woman and her right to define herself." The price on the cover was $1.95. It was a shock to realize that I've been around long enough to have bought a book at a time when feminism was still a new idea to most people, and was still being referred to as Women's Liberation.

There were three of Grace's poems inside. I skimmed hurriedly over the first two, looking for something specific and recognizable and not finding it. The third made me stop. It is about the different ways that girls and boys learn to love horses—or maybe learn to love.

Results of the Polo Game

> The young boys forget about cars awhile,
> saunter carefully casual to touch the lathered shoulder,
> wait for the sweet monotony of walking the wet ones dry.
> The ponies are tough and tired and friendly,
> walk docilely for a hundred different hands
> around the circuit of cities and grass.
> The young girls love easily:
> the sweet smell of the silken coats,
> the immense deep moving of hidden muscle,
> the fumbling soft lips, the fine boney heads.
>
> But the boys are slower, reluctant to react
> to the uncoiling of this unfamiliar love.
> They carry the smell in their nostrils for hours,
> stronger, stranger than perfume or gasoline.
> In bed before sleep they walk the wet horses,
> the heads still loom at their shoulders,
> their fingers curve to the sweated leather.
> There is the neck to touch, to arch with the arm;
> comparisons to make: a thousand pounds of power
> held by thin reins, the alien metal in the soft mouth.
>
> The thighs ache to curve around this new body.
> There is confusion about the meanings of love,
> embarrassment at boundaries that will not stay put,
> ambiguous language that always leads to lust:
> the curves, the shine, the power, the deep sweet smell,
> the capturing, taming, gentling; the moving together.
> The girls already know. Their thighs are open.
> It is a satisfactory substitute, this love.
> The boys, in sleep, run a hand through the thick mane,
> lay their faces against a shining shoulder, and decide. (232)

I felt my own body ache for the touch and smell and sheer massiveness of a real live horse. I was horse crazy as a child, got my own horse at 11, and managed to find ways to keep riding and stay connected with horses all my adult life until I moved to Idaho with my then-fiancé. I left their world behind, moving responsibly toward marriage and a picket fence and a settled, urban life. I still dream of horses all the time. When I took a six-week writing course one summer, the first thing I wrote about was being 3 years old and wanting a horse more than anything. It took months and months to write and made me cry almost every time I picked it up. I started it as part of that workshop, and finished it as part of my first freshman English composition class. It concluded with the observation that horses had always been guiding spirits for me, they always show up when I need direction in life, and now they had appeared once again to tell me that looking for Grace Butcher was a really good idea.

"Results of the Polo Game" alerted me in many ways and proved that Grace knew what she was talking about and exactly how to put it, but this was not the poem I was looking for. It spoke to me powerfully about who I once was, but was no help with where I live now. There is little chance of my finding real, live horses at this point. There is no time for that these days. I'm divorced, I live alone, I work and go to school and write and study and worry a lot about deadlines and money and grades and running out of time and getting old. Since I'm in my forties, people always speak of me as being "back" in school and I usually don't bother to correct them, but I never went when I was younger. I moved to Boston right after high school and started singing and playing guitar in bars and coffeehouses. My college career didn't begin until I was 40, the same year I had to give up being a professional musician because my back gave out—two bad disks wouldn't let me carry all my gear from gig to gig anymore. I had been thinking about giving it up anyway, for many reasons, mostly because it was so discouraging to still be playing in smoky bars for 50 bucks a night after all those years. I wanted to do something else, but what? Who would I be if I didn't play and sing? How would I attract love and attention, what purpose would guide and drive me, what would I do with all the passion I had poured into practicing and composing and performing? I was afraid I might disappear if I stopped playing.

My body decided for me, finally. I was in so much pain for several months that I couldn't even hold an instrument if someone else picked it up for me. So I finally did what I had been talking about doing for years and started college, seeking an English degree. I quit my office job and began waiting tables at night.

I took out my copy of the other anthology, *When I Am an Old Woman I Shall Wear Purple.* This is another book I bought when it was new in 1987, but I've never read all of it, only pieces. I couldn't help recoiling from the photos of old shriveled-up women with skin like faded crepe paper. And most of the stories were so dark—there was no reassuring message saying, "Don't worry, there is nothing to be afraid of, we're perfectly happy here, we feel much better than we look." The book's aggregate effect is more one of, "This happens to everyone eventually. It will happen to you and you will hate it bitterly and feel like you have to hide away in embarrassment. Tough shit. We're sick of hiding—here, look at these shrunken ankles, see if you can stand it."

But there was a poem of Grace's, one I didn't remember but must have read before because the page was marked (with a postcard advertising one of my own concerts):

Athlete Growing Old

> The caution is creeping in:
> the step is hesitant
>   from years of pain;
> a soft grunt bends the body over,
>   and straightens it.
> The skin loosens; everything moves
>   nearer the ground.
>
> To overcome the softening,
>   the yearning towards warmth,
> she exercises,
>   makes her muscles hard,
>   runs in the snow,
>   asks herself when she is afraid,
> "What would you do now if
>   you were *not* afraid?"
>
> She listens for the answer
>   and tries to be
>   like that person who speaks,
> who lives just outside
>   all her boundaries
>   and constantly calls her
>   to come over, come over. (73)

Good question: "What would you do now if you were *not* afraid?" But who is the voice urging the speaker to "come over, come over?" Is it death? That must have been what I thought when I first read it, because I had penciled in big question marks at the bottom of the page. Maybe the voice is that of one who says "Don't look down, keep *going* already."

Keep going, keep going, keep going, come *on*—these are the words I speak to myself almost constantly because I have so much to do. I've made big changes; left my sad, empty marriage and the little house I was so attached to, went through a frightening depression, bought my own little house and through it all still got straight A's.

I love being in school. I love the rich intellectual life I have at last after so many years of pretending to be less intelligent than I am—I was raised to think that showing off is bad and that girls are not supposed to speak up. Now I get to rant and vent and examine deep thoughts on paper and earn college credit for it. I even get to talk to other students and instructors about ideas and philosophies and meanings. I love not having to dress up or worry much about how I look. I love having guidance and being part of a *bona fide* system of learning rather than having to figure everything out on my own, the hard way, as I did with music.

But it costs me. I have only one night a week off and a schedule at odds with that of most people I know. I am lonely and horny and tired. I feel as if I am dragging a heavy load up a steep hill that keeps getting steeper and there is no one to help me. I worry that I'll miss a deadline or forget a promise or sit down at the computer and suddenly be incapable of generating anything at all, even for the easy assignments. I am afraid that I'll get depressed again. I drink too much, I should exercise more, I hardly ever have time to take a walk. I worry that even though I look pretty good for my age, my attractiveness has an expiration date, and what if by the time I graduate that date will be past and I will have missed the chance to find true love? I know this sounds ridiculous, but there it is.

And my house feels empty and way too quiet.

I looked up another of Grace's poems in the *Literary Review,* published in 2000:

What the Crow Does Is Not Singing

On winter mornings
when no bird sings
the crow represents all ideas.
On fire with purple and green,
blazing black against the snow,
its feathers eat the sun.
The silence is pure as
the ring of the rim
of a crystal glass.

The crow stands alone
in the white field, fills my eye
with its oval shape.
I will look out darkly
and sing the morning myself:
all consonants with no
split in my tongue.

> I'll leave the lightsome vowels
> to the wren, the wood thrush
> when they return in the simple spring,
> unaware of how it was here
> for us in the snow, how harsh
> the song we had to sing,
> how cold the words.

I didn't know what to think. It didn't knock me out; it didn't have anything to do with horses and was definitely not the time-capsule poem. It just seemed like an unstructured description of winter and starkness. I didn't feel my heart pound or hear the Hallelujah Chorus or anything—I was so caught up in trying to decide whether it was "good" or not, too wrapped up in my own static and mental noise. It was like the photos in . . . *I Shall Wear Purple.* I didn't want to think about it.

Thomas Moore writes in *Care of the Soul* that "Growing old is one of the ways the soul nudges itself into attention to the spiritual aspect of life. The body's changes teach us about fate, time, nature, mortality, and character. Aging forces us to decide what is important in life." (216)

I put this essay about Grace aside for the next few days, but I kept thinking about "What the Crow Does Is Not Singing." I keep doing my assignments and chores and going to work and ironing my tuxedo shirts and saying in my head, "I will look out darkly / and sing the morning myself." It made sense in a way I struggled to explain to myself. What I do these days is not singing, either, but just as the crow belongs in the landscape as much as cuter birds, so do I still have a purpose and a place here. I still want to make some noise. Pretty or not, there needs to be singing, it has to get done. The idea gave me strength and patience; though my outlook was bleak, I would sing the morning, I would speak and work and write from right here, daring anyone within earshot to stand it.

I thought about the wren and the wood thrush, singing "lightsome vowels in the simple spring," and had to admit that even as I complain about my situation and hate how quiet and solitary my life has become, I am somehow still proud. I have lived through much and made brave choices and done daring things. I realized that there was considerable bragging in my complaining, I felt somehow deeper and more soulful than the pretty birds singing happy songs of resurrection in the "simple spring."

I think of the young women in this writing class, who unintentionally keep reminding me of my age and of how old I must seem to them. They say things like, "But he's so *old,* he's like, *forty. . . .* " I am older than their parents. I must be like the crow to them, a dark omen of what it might be like for them someday—oh horror! To be aging and single! And I'm grinning as I write this because I imagine they think it won't happen to them because they'll do all the right things and wear the right clothes, and work out, and put on makeup every day. *They* won't ever "let themselves go"—such a revealing expression. I know, because I used to think similar things. Just as I used to think that if someone got cancer, they must be guilty of not eating right or taking proper care of themselves.

Now I don't judge that easily.

A friend and I put together a small house concert for some other friends last winter. We played some songs together and some individually, but, without really planning to, we ended up with a whole program of early Joni Mitchell songs. Vicki is one year younger than I, and her hair is completely gray in beautiful, striking shades of ethereal silver and gleaming iron. We both learned those songs when we were in our early teens, when the songs were brand new. It was eerie to be singing them again in our forties—we both felt like we were *exactly the same* as we had been then. I think I even joked between songs that, when I first learned to play "A Case of You," I was 13 and had no idea what my future would be like after high school and wished I could lose about ten pounds and wondered if I would ever find true love. And now I'm 44 and I have no idea what my future will be like after college and I wish I could lose about ten pounds and I wonder if I will ever find true love.

Like the crow, eating road kill, living on dead things, I keep mentally rehashing the trials of the past few years. I carry around all this baggage, afraid to get rid of any of it, digging through it like an archeologist looking for clues, in the hope that I can learn to live differently and more bravely and not repeat the same old dumb patterns. But this personal exile is also a gift. It is a five-year chance to grow a new kind of voice and figure out who I will be from now on and how I will fit in to my community, how I will make a living, literally.

When I first began paying attention to the crow poem, I was caught up in "how hard it was for us in the snow, how harsh the song we had to sing, how cold the words." It was only after memorizing it and saying it to myself as I worked or walked through the halls that I noticed the part about "The crow represents all ideas," and is "blazing black against the snow." The more I reread and said the lines to myself, the more I became convinced that the poem is about hope, not despair.

In Joni Mitchell's song, "The Last Time I Saw Richard," the speaker relates a conversation between two old friends who have gone in different directions. One gives up and joins the Establishment, one insists on living as an Artist. They argue . . .

Last time I saw Richard was Detroit in '68
and he told me: All romantics meet the same fate
someday—cynical, and drunk,
and boring someone in some dark cafe. (*Blue* 1973)

By the end of the song, the speaker, the Artist, finds herself in exactly that position, but even though the prophecy has come true, she refuses to believe that the story ends here. She says:

Dark cafes—only a dark cocoon
before I get my *gorgeous* wings and fly away
Only a phase, these dark cafe days . . .

There is no way to type the way Joni Mitchell sings the word "gorgeous." She leans on it, insisting that those wings will be incredible and worth every second of what it cost her to grow them.

I thought when I began working on this essay that I needed to reconnect with my old self, to find out who I once wanted to be when I grew up. Now I think that the point of all this is not the looking backward, but the looking ahead. I am not, technically speaking, old. But I will be soon. I want to know what it is like in that far country, whether I'll still be myself in my sixties and seventies. I don't know what "growing up" means. A friend of mine—forty-something—who never gave up music and is still living on the road from concert to concert—wrote in a song:

Do I have to act my age?
I don't know how old I am. (Conoscenti 1997)

Indeed. Neither do I. I am obsessed with it and yet I keep forgetting. I don't *feel* middle-aged. I jump on my cruiser bike and ride to class, standing up on the pedals, and feel the same as I did riding around my Strub Road neighborhood on the Schwinn cruiser bike that I got for a First Communion present. This bike is even a remake of that same model, except that this one is green instead of pink and white. Maybe I'll get some of those shiny, plastic, streamer things to blaze from the ends of the handlebars.

On winter mornings
when no bird sings,
the crow represents all ideas.
On fire with purple and green,
blazing black against the snow.

I don't have horses, I don't have a lover, I don't have even the regular company of friends because we're all so busy and they all have other loved ones at home to swallow up their attention. I don't have time to care for my yard, weed my flower beds, or keep my house as clean as my sensibilities require. I have piles of binders and paper and textbooks and floppy disks cluttering every surface that is waist-high or above. I am spending money that was supposed to be saved for retirement to support myself through college.

Everywhere I look this afternoon, there is something crying for attention, some task I can't address, some evidence of how far behind I am. I want to go back to bed. Who would notice if I did? Who would care? But though I look out darkly, I will sing the morning myself.

> the crow represents all ideas.
> On fire with purple and green,
> blazing black against the snow.

The ideas, the possibilities are still all around. Spring is coming and the days are getting longer. I will sing the morning myself—I've been singing since before I could talk, surely I know how to do *that* by now.

> I will look out darkly
> and sing the morning myself:
> all consonants with no
> split in my tongue.

I won't pretty it up. This is a rough and halting song of all consonants. Nor will I sing with the proverbial "forked tongue" of the hidden-agenda-white-man. For those of you who come after me: You will hate getting older. No matter how diligently you exercise, your tits will sag, your butt will sag, you, too, will grow a mustache, you will sometimes pee your pants when you sneeze. You won't feel like you are at a fork in the path at all, it will be more a case of the path disappearing completely as you find yourself on the edge of the Enchanted Dark Forest with no idea what it's like in there and no possible way to go back.

I can't reassure you. I hate it here. I hate that it is not only my attitude that dictates my reality; there are also very real physical and temporal limitations. No amount of positive thinking will regenerate damaged cartilage or stop presbyopia.

I see the same crow that you are probably seeing when you look at me, but I can look ahead. I can look at the photo of a poet on the home page of her Web site and see a woman of 66 still smiling a charmingly crooked smile, who still runs, still writes, still falls in love, and calls her man her "boyfriend." Who is feisty enough to fight with time by dying her gray hair brown.

This transition through middle age into old age is much scarier than I would've guessed. I hate to admit how much the wrinkles in my neck bother me. It is hard for us geezers-to-be here in the snow and, like Grace Butcher's crow, I am singing cold words through lips that move imperfectly and grudgingly. But I crack jokes. I lift weights. I get A's. I am growing a new kind of voice, and maybe I'll come out of this with new wings, too—*gorgeous* ones. I'll just have to be careful about using them, on account of my bad back.

Works Cited

Barba, Sharon and Laura Chester, ed. *Rising Tides: 20th Century American Women Poets.* New York: Washington Square Press, 1973. Back cover.

Butcher, Grace. "Athlete Growing Old." *When I Am an Old Woman I Shall Wear Purple.* Ed. Sandra Martz. Watsonville, California: Papier-Mache Press, 1987. 73.

———. Home page. 3 March 2001. <http://www.geocities.com/athens/3716/about.html

———. "Results of the Polo Game." In *Rising Tides.* Ed. Sharon Barba and Laura Chester. New York: Washington Square Press, 1973. 232.

———. "What the Crow does Is Not Singing." *The Literary Review.* Spring 1998. 23 March 2001. http://webdelsol.com/tlr/tlrsp98/butcher.html

Conoscenti, Don. "Mrs. Whitney." My Brilliant Masterpiece. *Cogtone Records.* 1997.

Frost, Robert. "Dust of Snow." *Selected Poems.* New York: Gramercy Press, 1992. 113.

Mitchell, Joni. "The Last Time I Saw Richard." *Blue.* Reprise Records. 1971.

Moore, Thomas. *Care of the Soul.* New York: HarperCollins Publishers, Inc. 1992. 216.

Discussion Questions

1. Like many essays, "In Search of Grace" does not *seem* to make a conventional argument in which the writer begins by establishing a claim and then attempts to make it convincing. Does the essay make an argument at all? If so, what is it?

2. This student essay is autobiographical literary criticism. Another example of this genre is Melody Graulich's piece, "Somebody Must Say

These Things," earlier in this chapter. Compare the two essays. Do they take essentially the same approach to personal criticism? Do they use outside sources and texts in similar ways?

3. In the crudest sense, autobiographical criticism is an extension of the familiar comment, "I can really relate to this" poem, story, essay, article, book. That may, of course, be a starting point for a work like "In Search of Grace," but how does strong autobiographical-critical writing go beyond merely "relating" to a text?

4. The crow becomes a rich symbol for Peggy Jordan in this essay. What is your understanding of some of those meanings?

6

The Ethnographic Essay: Ethnography as a Mode of Inquiry

The claim to attention of an ethnographic account does not rest on its author's ability to capture primitive facts in faraway places and carry them home like a mask or a carving, but on the degree to which he is able to clarify what goes on in such places, to reduce the puzzlement—what manner of men are these?—to which unfamiliar acts emerging out of unknown backgrounds naturally give rise.[*]

"The Sandman is a Manhattan biker gang," begins Anne Campbell's ethnographic study of "girl gangs." "It is arguable whether or not biker is an appropriate description, since while I was in contact with them there was only one functioning motorcycle (a BSA 650), although there was much discussion of the purchase and renovation of other bikes." From the first line of Campbell's account of her study of this girl gang we're hooked, curious about what she observed, what happened while she was studying them so closely. As we continue reading, we find out that Campbell has literally been right in the middle of this group, watching its activities, from packaging pot to sell to initiating new members into the group, to warding off potential fights on the subway.

This is not a research essay where the writer only spends her time in the library reading about gangs or sits on the sidelines secretly observing the group. Instead, Campbell tells us about the gang from the inside, from firsthand experience. In the end, Campbell's entire study, *The Girls in the Gang,* challenges the research of experts on the role of women in gangs, raising questions about the gender bias of that research and the lack of detailed knowledge about why girls join gangs.

---

[*]Clifford Geertz, "Thick Description: Toward an Interpretive Theory of Culture," *The Interpretation of Cultures.* New York: Basic Books, 1973.

Like the other essays in this book, Campbell's began with a question, something she was curious about, and that question took her to observing the workings of a culture. Ethnographic research like Campbell's relies on observations and interviews as primary sources of information and often uses narrative, concrete details, and the experience of the researcher to compose an engaging account of the culture under study. As you read the ethnographies in this chapter you'll notice that, like the pieces in the last two chapters, they borrow from the tradition of the essay, beginning their study in order *to find out* about their subject instead of *to prove* something about it. In fact, well-known anthropologist Clifford Geertz notes that "the essay, whether of 30 pages or 300, has seemed the natural genre in which to present cultural interpretations and the theories sustaining them."

The ethnography, then, is one form of academic research that has clearly broken with traditional structures for scientific writing. The people in the cultures come alive as we hear stories about them and come to understand their culture, their values, their motivations for belonging in ways we would not understand with a study that seeks statistics on girl gangs, for example, or tabulates the amount of money the gang makes selling illegal drugs.

As you read the pieces in this chapter, keep notes on how the writers choose to structure their pieces. While some writers will use a narrative approach as Anne Campbell does, detailing "a day in the life" of the group they're studying, others may choose a topical structure, organizing around the main conclusions they've drawn about the group.

Pay attention, as well, to whether the writers put themselves in their study. Do they talk about the assumptions and biases they bring to their research and how those may affect their conclusions? Do they try to assume a more objective stance by keeping themselves out of the narrative? Sometimes ethnographers are quite self-reflective about how they came to the conclusions they have, showing us the way their knowledge has evolved over time.

The credibility of the researcher's conclusions are always an issue in ethnographic research, so you'll want to consider how well these writers corroborate their conclusions with other sources, relying on patterns in behavior and research from others to interpret what is happening.

You'll find that these pieces have much in common with the research essays from Chapter 4 and the academic essays from Chapter 5, but their approach to research is quite different. A few of the pieces included in this chapter are not considered "academic ethnographies" but adopt an ethnographer's perspective in writing about research, so you'll want to consider how explicit ethnographies may be different from and yet similar to essays that borrow from ethnographic ways of seeing. Maybe you'll even be persuaded to do an ethnography of your own.

EXPOSING THE WEB OF CULTURE

Think about the culture of your high school. What kind of cliques did your high school have? The popular kids, the jocks, the skaters, the bikers? We bet you could tell us what kinds of clothes each group wore, how they talked to each other and to outsiders, and what kinds of cars they drove or where in town they lived. If you ever wanted to belong to one of the groups, you probably can also recall what it took to become a member. You might not think about these kinds of groups as subcultures, but they are; these are groups whose members have certain shared values and common ways of behaving, dressing, talking, seeing themselves and the world. They are all part of a larger culture of high school students and an even larger culture of the United States.

The world is an intricate mosaic of cultures, and anthropologists spend most of their time trying to study the ways those various cultures and subcultures work. Obviously, you don't have to travel overseas to investigate the workings of cultures and subcultures; you can practice the ethnographic way of seeing by staying right where you are.

Before we talk more about what it means to use an ethnographic way of seeing, let's spend some time thinking about what we mean by "culture." What comes to mind when you hear that word? Here are some ideas our students came up with: *Asian culture; Native American culture; ethnic groups; things associated with "having culture" like wine, symphonies, Shakespeare.*

What you'll notice is that cultures are groups of people who share common values, backgrounds, histories, traditions, reasons for belonging. They also tend to have spoken and unspoken rules for their members, guidelines for behavior, and certain languages that reflect the values of the group (for a great example of an "insider" language, read the beginning of the next chapter). Most cultures also have "artifacts" or objects that have special meaning and use within the culture. If you're a Roman Catholic, for example, you know that what identifies that culture are things such as holy water, statues of the Virgin Mary, rosary beads, and the confessional, and each of these "artifacts" reflects specific religious beliefs of Catholicism. You also know that this culture teaches certain ways of behaving and has several ceremonies or rituals that not only reinforce the group's values, but are used to initiate people into the group: Baptism, First Communion, Confirmation.

When we look at a culture we examine individuals who belong, but also everything that makes up the culture: members' behaviors, rules for behavior and relationships with others (including outsiders), artifacts, use of space, and language. In looking at all these elements we can then interpret the values of the group and what gives it meaning. One popular metaphor for culture is that it is a kind of spider web, often unnoticeable unless you're looking for it, and held together by nearly invisible strands. Anthropologists often discover the web by studying the strands that give it meaning.

Exercise 6.1 may alert you to the possibilities of ethnographic research in your own community, a project that may emerge from your reading of this chapter. But a successful field project depends on careful observation, good notes (see "Approaches to Field Notes" on page 245), and lots of information. This chapter ends with an essay from just such a project by Tammy Anderson, one of our former students, who finds herself entangled in the cultural web of the women who sell Mary Kay cosmetics.

Exercise 6.1   *Under Our Very Nose: Subcultures in the United States*

You may not have thought before about the different cultures you have just in your own hometown, but the United States includes myriad cultures and subcultures.

STEP 1: To help you begin thinking as an ethnographer, brainstorm with the whole class lists for the following prompts:

- List all the most current fads you can think of (*coffeehouses, chat rooms, dot-com companies, Tommy Hilfiger, computer bars, etc.*)
- List all the activities people engage in for which they meet in groups (*team sports like football, mountain climbing, religious services, etc.*)
- List subcultures you currently find on your campus, in your city, in your state (*fraternities, sororities, Young Republicans, Management Club, Gay/Lesbian/Bisexual Alliance, Basque culture, etc.*)
- List all the subcultures each member of the class belongs to

STEP 2: Choose one from the list to focus on more specifically and put these categories on the board: *Artifacts, Language, Rituals.* See how much you already know about this culture by naming the artifacts that are particular to that group, the words and phrases they use, and the rituals they seem to engage in frequently. Here's a list that one of our classes made on "golfers":

Artifacts	Language	Rituals
golf ball	par	caddying
nine-iron	birdies	making business deals
golf shoes	putt	silence while playing

STEP 3: As you look at all the things you already know about the culture, create another category on the board, *Interpretations,* and brainstorm a list of conclusions you might draw about this group based on what you've put on the board. For example, what might you say this culture most values in its

members? What artifacts or objects hold the greatest meaning? How do group members view outsiders? These conclusions will be limited because you haven't spent time observing the group and analyzing their artifacts and rituals, but you can make some preliminary interpretations. What is important is that you connect the interpretations to specific parts of the culture that you've put on the board.

ETHNOGRAPHIC WAYS OF SEEING

As we said earlier, social scientists like anthropologists find these kinds of subcultures fascinating and they've developed a research method called "ethnography" to study them. In an ethnography, a researcher spends a lot of time observing a culture, trying to understand it from the inside and describe it with as much detail and respect as possible. She looks at the elements of a culture we've described above: artifacts, behaviors, rituals, language, space, and treatment of insiders and outsiders.

You may remember Renato Rosaldo's essay in Chapter 5 where he describes his research on Philippine headhunters and their ritual for dealing with grief. Rosaldo spent a number of months observing this tribe, taking copious notes on what he saw and heard, and then he tried to interpret what he saw and describe the way the culture works. For someone who finds head-hunting a rather extreme means of revenge, Rosaldo had to suspend his judgment while he was researching and try to explain to his audience why, given this culture's values, rituals, and beliefs, headhunting makes sense. He looks for the patterns in their behavior, the "webs of significance" as anthropologist Clifford Geertz calls them, that distinguish a culture from an individual.

What Rosaldo found, however, was that he couldn't simply try to be objective in his observations—he had to recognize how his own experiences and beliefs consciously and unconsciously affected what he did and didn't see. In this way the ethnographic essays in this chapter often bring the writer's experience into the essay, recognizing that they cannot separate what they see from who they are. Like the essays in Chapter 4 and Chapter 5, these pieces complicate the idea that research should be objective, highlighting the way that subjectivity is a more ethical way of interpreting a culture one knows little about.

We often ask our students to use ethnographic research methods for one of their essays because they introduce other ways of gathering research: direct observation, interview, and published sources. They also emphasize a way of looking at research that is quite different from what you may be used to. Instead of distilling conclusions down to succinct phrases or generalizing about what one has researched, ethnographies rely on what Geertz calls "thick description." If we go back to Campbell's research on girl gangs we

Approaches to Field Notes

The double-entry style notebook is useful for field notes because, as always, it encourages you to not just collect information but reflect on it. Consider using opposite pages in your notebook, rather than the usual line down the middle of the page. You'll probably need the room.

ON THE LEFT SIDE:

- Specific observations of how people in the group interact
- Specific observations of individuals and what exactly they're doing
- Fragments of distinctive language, "insider phrases," sayings, jargon
- Notes of overheard conversations or from interviews
- Specific descriptions of the place
- Rough sketches of the layout of the space
- Specific descriptions of objects used by the participants
- Specific observations of how group members come and go
- Specific observations of how group members respond to outsiders
- Specific observations of clothing, and other cosmetic features of group members
- Specific accounts of stories members tell each other

ON THE RIGHT SIDE:

Reflect on whether you see any patterns in the data you collected on the opposite page.

- Are certain behaviors repeated by group members?
- Do group members seem to use the space in a characteristic way?
- Is the language they use distinctive? In what situations do they use it?
- Do group members seem to reproduce certain ways of interacting with each other?
- What are "typical" situations that seem to recur?
- How do members learn from each other? How is knowledge passed along?
- What kind of behaviors is most valued by the group? What kinds of knowledge?
- How do group members view outsiders?
- What motivates members to want to belong?

find an excellent example of "thick description": We learn what the gang patches mean to members and what the penalties are for touching them; we see the ways each member protects the others and punishes them for violating gang rules; we see Connie behaving as a good mother one moment and then learn she's packaging marijuana to sell and allowing her teenage daughter to drink alcohol. With each artifact and behavior in the culture, Campbell gives us several ways of interpreting it. Beer, for example, is not just something the group drinks when it parties; it is also used in initiation rituals, poured over a person in celebration. At the same time, spilled beer is always cleaned up, suggesting a fastidiousness about the gang's space that seems contrary to their ritual of pouring beer over someone.

"Thick description" is not just about giving as many specific details about a culture as you can, but about discovering all the meanings the group has for something as simple as beer. Seeing as an ethnographer means observing what seems natural or ordinary and analyzing the significance of those observations. It means practicing all the habits of mind of academic inquiry: asking questions, suspending judgment, tolerating ambiguity, thinking dialectically, and taking responsibility for one's ideas.

In practicing these habits Campbell is able to see that something as ordinary as beer can represent a girl gang's values—their sense of loyalty to their members, the importance for members of meeting the challenges of initiation, their respect for having clean living spaces, their desire to be both uninhibited and yet in control of themselves. Even if your instructor does not ask you to write an ethnography, we hope you will be able to use observation and interview in your research process and to analyze what you see from this cultural perspective, engaging in a valuable academic skill of interpreting your subject within larger contexts. If nothing else, seeing ethnographically will make the world come alive for you, as the ordinary and the commonplace are suddenly charged with meaning.

Fifteen

Bob Greene

"Fifteen," Bob Greene writes. "What a weird age to be male. Most of us have forgotten about it, or have idealized it. But when you are 15 . . . well, things tend to be less than perfect." With this lead, journalist and columnist Greene takes us into the culture of two 15-year-old boys and shows, through careful

detail, how weird it can be to be male, without a car, and between boyhood and manhood.

Greene is a former columnist for the Chicago Tribune *and has also published a number of books and won awards for his work as a writer. "Fifteen" was published in the magazine* Esquire *in 1982. While this short piece is not explicitly an ethnography, it has elements of the ethnographer's perspective: paying attention to what characterizes a culture—in this case, the culture of 15-year-old boys in 1982. Greene follows Dan and Dave, two teenaged boys who have been dropped off at the mall on the weekend. In the narrative he creates, Greene focuses on what is important to Dan and Dave, the kinds of things they do (like hanging over the railing on the second floor and trying to get the attention of the girls below and cruising through a pet store), the kinds of things they say, and what is important to them.*

As you read this piece, pay attention to how Greene uses detail to convey the culture of 15-year-old boys. What key artifacts does he focus on? What conclusions does he draw about their culture? What does he help us see that we wouldn't otherwise pay attention to?

"This would be excellent, to go in the ocean with this thing," says Dave Gembutis, 15.

He is looking at a $170 Sea Cruiser raft.

"Great," says his companion, Dan Holmes, also 15.

This is at Herman's World of Sporting Goods, in the middle of the Woodfield Mall in Schaumburg, Illinois.

The two of them keep staring at the raft. It is unlikely that they will purchase it. For one thing, Dan has only twenty dollars in his pocket, Dave five dollars. For another thing—ocean voyages aside—neither of them is even old enough to drive. Dave's older sister, Kim, has dropped them off at the mall. They will be taking the bus home.

Fifteen. What a weird age to be male. Most of us have forgotten about it, or have idealized it. But when you are 15 . . . well, things tend to be less than perfect.

You can't drive. You are only a freshman in high school. The girls your age look older than you and go out with upperclassmen who have cars. You probably don't shave. You have nothing to do on the weekends.

So how do you spend your time? In 1982, most likely at a mall. Woodfield is an enclosed shopping center sprawling over 2.25 million square feet in northern Illinois. There are 230 stores at Woodfield, and on a given Saturday those stores are cruised in and out of by thousands of teenagers killing time. Today two of those teenagers are Dave Gembutis and Dan Holmes.

Dave is wearing a purple Rolling Meadows High School Mustangs Windbreaker over a gray M*A*S*H T-shirt, jeans, and Nike running shoes.

He has a red plastic spoon in his mouth, and will keep it there for most of the afternoon. Dan is wearing a white Ohio State Buckeyes T-shirt, jeans, and Nike running shoes.

We are in the Video Forum store. Paul Simon and Art Garfunkel are singing "Wake Up Little Susie" from their Central Park concert on four television screens. Dave and Dan have already been wandering around Woodfield for an hour.

"There's not too much to do at my house," Dan says to me.

"Here we can at least look around," Dave says. "At home I don't know what we'd do."

"Play catch or something," Dan says. "Here there's lots of things to see."

"See some girls or something, start talking," Dave says.

I ask them how they would start a conversation with girls they had never met.

"Ask them what school they're from," Dan says. "Then if they say Arlington Heights High School or something, you can say, 'Oh, I know somebody from there.' "

I ask them how important meeting girls is to their lives.

"About 45 percent," Dan says.

"About half your life," Dave says.

"Half is girls," Dan says. "Half is going out for sports."

An hour later, Dave and Dan have yet to meet any girls. They have seen a girl from their own class at Rolling Meadows High, but she is walking with an older boy, holding his hand. Now we are in the Woodfield McDonald's. Dave is eating a McRib sandwich, a small fries, and a small Coke. Dan is eating a cheeseburger, a small fries, and a medium root beer.

In here, the dilemma is obvious. The McDonald's is filled with girls who are precisely as old as Dave and Dan. The girls are wearing eye shadow, are fully developed, and generally look as if they could be dating the Green Bay Packers. Dave and Dan, on the other hand . . . well, when you're a 15-year-old boy, you look like a 15-year-old boy.

"They go with the older guys who have the cars," Dan says.

"It makes them more popular," Dave says.

"My ex-girlfriend is seeing a junior," Dan says.

I ask him what happened.

"Well, I was in Florida over spring vacation," he says. "And when I got back I heard that she was at Cinderella Rockefella one night, and she was dancing with this guy, and she liked him, and he drove her home and stuff."

"She two-timed him," Dave says.

"The guy's on the basketball team," Dan says.

I ask Dan what he did about it.

"I broke up with her," he says, as if I had asked the stupidest question in the world.

I ask him how he did it.

"Well, she was at her locker," he says. "She was working the combination. And I said. 'Hey, Linda, I want to break up.' And she was opening her locker door and she just nodded her head yes. And I said. 'I hear you had a good time while I was gone, but I had a better time in Florida.' "

I ask him if he feels bad about it.

"Well, I feel bad," he says. "But a lot of guys told me, 'I heard you broke up with her. Way to be.' "

"It's too bad the Puppy Palace isn't open," Dan says.

"They're remodeling," Dave says.

We are walking around the upper level of Woodfield. I ask them why they would want to go to the Puppy Palace.

"The dogs are real cute and you feel sorry for them," Dan says.

We are in a fast-food restaurant called the Orange Bowl. Dave is eating a frozen concoction called an O Joy. They still have not met any girls.

"I feel like I'd be wasting my time if I sat at home," Dan says. "If it's Friday or Saturday and you sit home, it's considered . . . low."

"Coming to the mall is about all there is," Dave says. "Until we can drive."

"Then I'll cruise," Dan says. "Look for action a little farther away from my house, instead of just riding my bike around."

"When you're 16, you can do anything," Dave says. "You can go all the way across town."

"When you have to ride your bike . . . " Dan says. "When it rains, it ruins everything."

In the J. C. Penney store, the Penney Fashion Carnival is under way. Wally the Clown is handing out favors to children, but Dave and Dan are watching the young female models parade onto a stage in bathing suits.

"Just looking is enough for me," Dan says.

Dave suggests that they head out back into the mall and pick out some girls to wave to. I ask why.

"Well, see, even if they don't wave back, you might see them later in the day," Dan says. "And then they might remember that you waved at them, and you can meet them."

We are at the Cookie Factory. These guys eat approximately every 20 minutes.

It is clear that Dan is attracted to the girl behind the counter. He walks up, and his voice is slower and about half an octave lower than before.

The tone of voice is going to have to carry the day, because the words are not all that romantic:

"Can I have a chocolate-chip cookie?"

The girl does not even look up as she wraps the cookie in tissue paper. Dan persists. The voice might be Clark Gable's:

"What do they cost?"

The girl is still looking down.

"Forty-seven," she says and takes his money, still looking away, and we move on.

Dave and Dan tell me that there are lots of girls at Woodfield's indoor ice-skating rink. It costs money to get inside, but they lead me to an exit door, and when a woman walks out we slip into the rink. It is chilly in here, but only three people are on the ice.

"It's not time for open skating yet," Dan says. "This is all private lessons."

"Not much in here," Dave says.

We sit on benches. I ask them if they wish they were older.

"Well," Dan says, "when you get there, you look back and you re-member. Like I'm glad that I'm not in the fourth or fifth grade now. But I'm glad I'm not 25, either."

"Once in a while I'm sorry I'm not 21," Dave says. "There's not much you can do when you're 15. This summer I'm going to caddy and try to save some money."

"Yeah," Dan says. "I want to save up for a dirt bike."

"Right now, being 15 is starting to bother me a little bit," Dave says. "Like when you have to get your parents to drive you to Homecoming with a girl."

I ask him how that works.

"Well, your mom is in the front seat driving," he says. "And you're in the back seat with your date."

I ask him how he feels about that.

"It's embarrassing," he says. "Your date understands that there's nothing you can do about it, but it's still embarrassing."

Dave says he wants to go to Pet World.

"I think they closed it down," Dan says, but we head in that direction anyway.

I ask them what the difference is between Pet World and the Puppy Palace.

"They've got snakes and fish and another assortment of dogs," Dan says. "But not as much as the Puppy Palace."

When we arrive, Pet World is, indeed, boarded up.

We are on the upper level of the mall. Dave and Dan have spotted two girls sitting on a bench directly below them, on the mall's main level.

"Whistle," Dan says. Dave whistles, but the girls keep talking.

"Dave, wave to them and see if they look," Dan says.

"They aren't looking," Dave says.

"There's another one over there," Dan says.

"Where?" Dave says.

"Oh, that's a mother," Dan says. "She's got her kid with her."

They return their attention to the two downstairs.

Dan calls to them: "Would you girls get the dollar I just dropped?"

The girls look up.

"Just kidding," Dan says.

The girls resume their conversation.

"I think they're laughing," Dan says.

"What are you going to do when the dumb girls won't respond," Dave says.

"At least we tried," Dan says.

I ask him what response would have satisfied him.

"The way we would have known that we succeeded," he says, "they'd have looked up here and started laughing."

The boys keep staring at the two girls.

"Ask her to look up," Dan says. "Ask her what school they go to."

"I did," Dave says. "I did."

The two boys lean over the railing.

"Bye, girls," Dave yells.

"See you later," Dan yells.

The girls do not look up.

"Too hard," Dan says. "Some girls are stuck on themselves, if you know what I mean by that."

We go to a store called the Foot Locker, where all the salespeople are dressed in striped referee's shirts.

"Dave!" Dan says. "Look at this! Seventy bucks!" He holds up a pair of New Balance running shoes. Both boys shake their heads.

We move on to a store called Passage to China. A huge stuffed tiger is placed by the doorway. There is a PLEASE DO NOT TOUCH sign attached to it. Dan rubs his hand over the tiger's back. "This would look so great in my room," he says.

We head over to Alan's TV and Stereo. Two salesmen ask the boys if they are interested in buying anything, so they go back outside and look at the store's window. A color television set is tuned to a baseball game between the Chicago Cubs and the Pittsburgh Pirates.

They watch for five minutes. The sound is muted, so they cannot hear the announcers.

"I wish they'd show the score," Dave says.

They watch for five minutes more.

"Hey, Dave," Dan says. "You want to go home?"

"I guess so," Dave says.

They do. We wave goodbye. I watch them walk out of the mall toward the bus stop. I wish them girls, dirt bikes, puppies, and happiness.

Personal Investigations: Inquiry Projects

1. Go to a local mall and spend time at the eating area, taking note of the largest age groups you see. Do you see any patterns to the kinds of people who are at the mall? Then, wander around the rest of the mall and see what you notice about who frequents it. What seem to be their ages? Is there a way each age group dresses? Can you tell anything about people's social class from what they're wearing or buying? How do people seem to treat each other at the mall, especially strangers? What conclusions can you draw about the kind of people you see at the mall?

2. Bob Greene decided to focus on the lives of two fifteen-year-old boys to see what he could learn about their culture, but this piece isn't a traditional ethnography. Instead, Greene begins with a question about boys in this age group and then follows them around to see what he might learn. Make a list of (1) people you'd like to know more about, (2) age groups you're curious about (Forgot what it was like to be five? Wonder what it will be like to be considered a senior citizen?), and (3) current fads you've seen people embrace. As you review what you listed here, pick one or two items you're interested in and find someone to interview about the subject. Consider following that person around to see what you can observe about the questions you have.

Craft and Conventions: Explaining and Evaluating

3. Look at the first two paragraphs of Greene's essay. What would you expect the essay to be about based on just these paragraphs? What questions drive Greene's observations of these two young men? How

well does the rest of the essay meet the expectations set by the opening paragraphs?

4. Look at how Greene decides to organize this essay. The a-day-in-the-
life structure is similar to that Anne Campbell uses in her essay later in
the chapter. How else might Greene have organized this essay to
emphasize his conclusions? As you look at each section, separated by
white space, what do you notice? How does each section relate to the
essay as a whole?

5. Greene occasionally mentions himself in this piece, but most of his
focus is on the dialogue and activity of Dan and Dave. How would the
essay be different if Greene didn't mention himself at all? Where does
Greene register his presence in the essay without using "I"?

6. Make a list of all the phrases you'd say are part of the culture of fifteen
year-old boys. Then, list all the artifacts that you'd point to as part of
their culture. Based on these lists, what theories would you pose about
the culture of fifteen-year-old boys? If you were to turn Greene's essay
into a larger ethnography, what other sites would you visit? Who would
you interview? What would you research in the library to answer some
of your questions about this culture?

Inquiries on Inquiry: Exploring and Reflecting

7. "Fifteen" was published in *Esquire* and is clearly not an academic piece.
In what ways is it not academic? In what ways might it be? What kinds
of moves is Greene making that you might consider academic? What
kinds of thinking is he doing that you might be asked to do in your
other classes in college?

8. Compare your experience reading this essay to that of reading another
in this chapter. Which reading strategies did you use and why? How do
your personal responses to both essays compare? Why?

9. What do you find least convincing about this essay and why? If you
were to update Greene's research, what would you do? Why? What
might he have left out or unconsciously ignored?

10. How does Greene's depiction of the world of fifteen-year-old boys compare to your own experience?

The American Man at Age Ten

Susan Orlean

Taken together, the preceding essay and the piece you are about to read pro-
vide a portrait of the culture of certain young American males during a period
in their lives that profoundly shapes how they later view women, money, class,
and race. It's a time that's worth a close look. In "The American Man at Age
Ten," literary journalist Susan Orlean spends time with Colin, an afficionado
of Nintendo, recycling, and the lottery. He's not keen on girls, and thinks his
Mom is the most beautiful woman in the world. Colin is saving money to buy a
ranch in Wyoming, a place he visited once with his family. Like Dave and Dan
in Bob Greene's essay "Fifteen," Colin is white and middle class, but these
facts don't seem quite relevant to him yet. He does, however, spend a lot time
thinking about money.

*   "The American Man at Age Ten" is not a formal ethnography. In fact,*
Susan Orlean is a journalist, not an academic, but like other selections in this
chapter ("Fifteen" and "The Cave"), this work is easily seen as an informal
study of the culture of some young American males. You'll notice immediately
that Orlean is a keen observer of her subject, richly detailing conversations,
specific descriptions of the places Colin values, and the weight he puts on cer-
tain artifacts and attitudes. Obviously, Susan Orlean spent considerable time
with Colin doing the kind of "immersion" reporting that literary journalists are
known for. But her methods could just as easily be likened to ethnographic
fieldwork; she carefully documents and interprets what she sees.

*   As the title implies, "The American Man at Age Ten" promises to profile a*
typical ten-year-old, and here's where this essay and the work of social anthro-
pologists Anne Campell and Timothy Simpson, whose work you'll read later in
this chapter, seem to depart. Most ethnographers are very careful to say that
they only attempt to describe a particular culture in a particular place and at a
particular time. As you read this essay, think about whether Orlean's implied
claim that Colin is representative of all ten-year-olds seems convincing. Since
we all know ten-year-olds—and some of us were ten-year-old American
males—our own experiences and observations will certainly influence our reac-
tions to the piece.

If Colin Duffy and I were to get married, we would have matching super-
hero notebooks. We would wear shorts, big sneakers, and long, baggy T-
shirts depicting famous athletes every single day, even in the winter. We
would sleep in our clothes. We would both be good at Nintendo Street
Fighter II, but Colin would be better than me. We would have some

homework, but it would never be too hard and we would always have just finished it. We would eat pizza and candy for all of our meals. We wouldn't have sex, but we would have crushes on each other and, magically, babies would appear in our home. We would win the lottery and then buy land in Wyoming, where we would have one of every kind of cute animal. All the while, Colin would be working in law enforcement—probably the FBI. Our favorite movie star, Morgan Freeman, would visit us occasionally. We would listen to the same Eurythmics song ("Here Comes the Rain Again") over and over again and watch two hours of television every Friday night. We would both be good at football, have best friends, and know how to drive; we would cure AIDS and the garbage problem and everything that hurts animals. We would hang out a lot with Colin's dad. For fun, we would load a slingshot with dog food and shoot it at my butt. We would have a very good life.

Here are the particulars about Colin Duffy: He is ten years old, on the nose. He is four feet eight inches high, weighs 75 pounds, and appears to be mostly leg and shoulder blade. He is a handsome kid. He has a broad forehead, dark eyes with dense lashes, and a sharp, dimply smile. I have rarely ever seen him without a baseball cap. He owns several, but favors a University of Michigan Wolverines model, on account of its pleasing colors. The hat styles his hair into wild disarray. If you ever managed to get the hat off his head, you would see a boy with a nimbus of golden-brown hair, dented in the back, where the hat hits him.

Colin lives with his mother, Elaine; his father, Jim; his older sister, Megan; and his little brother, Chris, in a pretty pale blue Victorian house on a bosky street in Glen Ridge, New Jersey. Glen Ridge is a serene and civilized old town 20 miles west of New York City. It does not have much of a commercial district, but it is a town of amazing lawns. Most of the houses were built around the turn of the century and are set back a gracious, green distance from the street. The rest of the town seems to consist of parks and playing fields and sidewalks and backyards—in other words, it is a far cry from South-Central Los Angeles and from Bedford-Stuyvesant and other, grimmer parts of the country where a very different 10-year-old American man is growing up today.

There is a fine school system in Glen Ridge, but Elaine and Jim, who are both schoolteachers, choose to send their children to a parents' cooperative elementary school in Montclair, a neighboring suburb. Currently, Colin is in fifth grade. He is a good student. He plans to go to college, to a place he says is called Oklahoma City State College University. OCSCU satisfies his desire to live out west, to attend a small college, and to study law enforcement, which OCSCU apparently offers as a major. After four years at Oklahoma City State College University, he plans to work for the

FBI. He says that getting to be a police officer involves tons of hard work, but working for the FBI will be a cinch, because all you have to do is fill out one form, which he has already gotten from the head FBI office. Colin is quiet in class but loud on the playground. He has a great throwing arm, significant foot speed, and a lot of physical confidence. He is also brave. Huge wild cats with rabies and gross stuff dripping from their teeth, which he says run rampant throughout his neighborhood, do not scare him. Otherwise, he is slightly bashful. This combination of athletic grace and valor and personal reserve accounts for considerable popularity. He has a fluid relationship to many social groups, including the superbright nerds, the ultrajocks, the flashy kids who will someday become extremely popular and socially successful juvenile delinquents, and the kids who will be elected president of the student body. In his opinion, the most popular boy in his class is Christian, who happens to be black, and Colin's favorite television character is Steve Urkel on *Family Matters,* who is black, too, but otherwise he seems uninterested in or oblivious to race. Until this year, he was a Boy Scout. Now he is planning to begin karate lessons. His favorite schoolyard game is football, followed closely by prison dodge ball, blob tag, and bombardo. He's crazy about athletes, although sometimes it isn't clear if he is absolutely sure of the difference between human athletes and Marvel Comics action figures. His current athletic hero is Dave Meggett. His current best friend is named Japeth. He used to have another best friend named Ozzie. According to Colin, Ozzie was found on a doorstep, then changed his name to Michael and moved to Massachusetts, and then Colin never saw him or heard from him again.

He has had other losses in his life. He is old enough to know people who have died and to know things about the world that are worrisome. When he dreams, he dreams about moving to Wyoming, which he has visited with his family. His plan is to buy land there and have some sort of ranch that would definitely include horses. Sometimes when he talks about this, it sounds as ordinary and hard-boiled as a real estate appraisal; other times it can sound fantastical and wifty and achingly naive, informed by the last inklings of childhood—the musings of a balmy real estate appraiser assaying a wonderful and magical landscape that erodes from memory a little bit every day. The collision in his mind of what he understands, what he hears, what he figures out, what popular culture pours into him, what he knows, what he pretends to know, and what he imagines, makes an interesting mess. The mess often has the form of what he will probably think like when he is a grown man, but the content of what he is like as a little boy.

He is old enough to begin imagining that he will someday get married, but at ten he is still convinced that the best thing about being married will be that he will be allowed to sleep in his clothes. His father once observed that living with Colin was like living with a Martian who had done some reading on American culture. As it happens, Colin is not especially sad or worried about the prospect of growing up, although he sometimes frets over whether he should be called a kid or a grown-up; he has settled on the word *kid-up*. Once, I asked him what the biggest advantage to adulthood will be, and he said, "The best thing is that grown-ups can go wherever they want." I asked him what he meant, exactly, and he said, "Well, if you're grown-up, you'd have a car, and whenever you felt like it, you could get into your car and drive somewhere and get candy."

Colin loves recycling. He loves it even more than, say, playing with little birds. That 10-year-olds feel the weight of the world and consider it their mission to shoulder it came as a surprise to me. I had gone with Colin one Monday to his classroom at Montclair Cooperative School. The Coop is in a steep, old, sharp-angled brick building that had served for many years as a public school until a group of parents in the area took it over and made it into a private, progressive elementary school. The fifth-grade classroom is on the top floor, under the dormers, which gives the room the eccentric shape and closeness of an attic. It is a rather informal environment. There are computers lined up in an adjoining room and instructions spelled out on the chalkboard   BRING IN: 1) A CUBBY WITH YOUR NAME ON IT, 2) A TRAPPER WITH A FIVE-POCKET ENVELOPE LABELED SCIENCE, SOCIAL STUDIES, READING/LANGUAGE ARTS, MATH, MATH LAB/COMPUTER; WHITE LINED PAPER; A PLASTIC PENCIL BAG; A SMALL HOMEWORK PAD, 3) LARGE BROWN GROCERY BAGS—but there is also a couch in the center of the classroom, which the kids take turns occupying, a rocking chair, and three canaries in cages near the door.

It happened to be Colin's first day in fifth grade. Before class began, there was a lot of horsing around, but there were also a lot of conversations about whether Magic Johnson had AIDS or just HIV and whether someone falling in a pool of blood from a cut of his would get the disease. These jolts of sobriety in the midst of rank goofiness are a 10-year-old's specialty. Each one comes as a fresh, hard surprise, like finding a razor blade in a candy apple. One day, Colin and I had been discussing horses or dogs or something, and out of the blue he said, "What do you think is better, to dump garbage in the ocean, to dump it on land, or to burn it?" Another time, he asked me if I planned to have children. I had just spent an evening with him and his friend Japeth, during which they put every small, movable object in the house into Japeth's slingshot and fired it at me, so I told him that I wanted children but that I hoped they would all be girls, and he said, "Will you have an abortion if you find out you have a boy?"

At school, after discussing summer vacation, the kids began choosing the jobs they would do to help out around the classroom. Most of the jobs are humdrum—putting the chairs up on the tables, washing the chalk-board, turning the computers off or on. Five of the most humdrum tasks are recycling chores—for example, taking bottles or stacks of paper down to the basement, where they would be sorted and prepared for pickup. Two children would be assigned to feed the birds and cover their cages at the end of the day.

I expected the bird jobs to be the first to go. Everyone loved the birds; they'd spent an hour that morning voting on names for them (Tweetie, Montgomery, and Rose narrowly beating out Axl Rose, Bugs, Ol' Yeller, Fido, Slim, Lucy, and Chirpie). Instead, they all wanted to recycle. The recycling jobs were claimed by the first five kids called by Suzanne Nakamura, the fifth-grade teacher; each kid called after that responded by groaning, "Suzanne, aren't there any more recycling jobs?" Colin ended up with the job of taking down the chairs each morning. He accepted the task with a sort of resignation—this was just going to be a job rather than a mission.

On the way home that day, I was quizzing Colin about his world views.

"Who's the coolest person in the world?"

"Morgan Freeman."

"What's the best sport?"

"Football."

"Who's the coolest woman?"

"None. I don't know."

"What's the most important thing in the world?"

"Game Boy." Pause. "No, the world. The world is the most important thing in the world."

Danny's pizzeria is a dark little shop next door to the Montclair Cooperative School. It is not much to look at. Outside, the brick facing is painted muddy brown. Inside, there are some saggy counters, a splintered bench, and enough room for either six teenagers or about a dozen 10-year-olds who happen to be getting along well. The light is low. The air is oily. At Danny's, you will find pizza, candy, Nintendo, and very few girls. To a 10-year-old boy, it is the most beautiful place in the world.

One afternoon, after class was dismissed, we went to Danny's with Colin's friend Japeth to play Nintendo. Danny's has only one game, Street Fighter II Champion Edition. Some teenage boys from a nearby middle school had gotten there first and were standing in a tall, impene-trable thicket around the machine.

"Next game," Colin said. The teenagers ignored him.

"Hey, we get next game," Japeth said. He is smaller than Colin, scrappy, and, as he explained to me once, famous for wearing his hat backward all the time and having a huge wristwatch and a huge bedroom. He stamped his foot and announced again, "Hey, we get next game."

One of the teenagers turned around and said, "Fuck you, *next game*," and then turned back to the machine.

"Whoa," Japeth said.

He and Colin went outside, where they felt bigger.

"Which street fighter are you going to be?" Colin asked Japeth.

"Blanka," Japeth said. "I know how to do his head-butt."

"I hate that! I hate the head-butt," Colin said. He dropped his voice a little and growled, "I'm going to be Ken, and I will kill you with my dragon punch."

"Yeah, right, and monkeys will fly out of my butt," Japeth said.

Street Fighter II is a video game in which two characters have an explosive brawl in a scenic International setting. It is currently the most popular video-arcade game in America. This is not an insignificant amount of popularity. Most arcade versions of video games, which end up in pizza parlors, malls, and arcades, sell about 2000 units. So far, some 50,000 Street Fighter II and Street Fighter II Championship Edition arcade games have been sold. Not since Pac-Man, which was released the year before Colin was born, has there been a video game as popular as Street Fighter. The home version of Street Fighter is the most popular home video game in the country, and that, too, is not an insignificant thing. Thirty-two million Nintendo home systems have been sold since 1986, when it was introduced in this country. There is a Nintendo system in seven of every ten homes in America in which a child between the ages of eight and twelve resides. By the time a boy in America turns ten, he will almost certainly have been exposed to Nintendo home games, Nintendo arcade games, and Game Boy, the hand-held version. He will probably own a system and dozens of games. By ten, according to Nintendo studies, teachers, and psychologists, game prowess becomes a fundamental, essential male social marker and a schoolyard boast.

The Street Fighter characters are Dhalsim, Ken, Guile, Blanka, E. Honda, Ryu, Zangief, and Chun Li. Each represents a different country, and they each have their own special weapon. Chun Li, for instance, is from China and possesses a devastating whirlwind kick that is triggered if you push the control pad down for two seconds and then up for two seconds, and then you hit the kick button. Chun Li's kick is money in the bank, because most of the other fighters do not have a good defense against it. By the way, Chun Li happens to be a girl—the only female Street Fighter character.

I asked Colin if he was interested in being Chun Li. There was a long pause. "I would rather be Ken," he said.

The girls in Colin's class at school are named Cortnerd, Terror, Spacey, Lizard, Maggot, and Diarrhea. "They do have other names, but that's what we call them," Colin told me. "The girls aren't very popular."

"They are about as popular as a piece of dirt," Japeth said. "Or, you know that couch in the classroom? That couch is more popular than any girl. A thousand times more." They talked for a minute about one of the girls in their class, a tall blonde with cheerleader genetic material, who they allowed was not quite as gross as some of the other girls. Japeth said that a chubby, awkward boy in their class was boasting that this girl liked him.

"No way," Colin said. "She would never like him. I mean, not that he's so . . . I don't know. I don't hate him because he's fat, anyway. I hate him because he's nasty."

"Well, she doesn't like him," Japeth said. "She's been really mean to me lately, so I'm pretty sure she likes me."

"Girls are different," Colin said. He hopped up and down on the balls of his feet, wrinkling his nose. "Girls are stupid and weird."

"I have a lot of girlfriends, about six or so," Japeth said, turning contemplative. "I don't exactly remember their names, though."

The teenagers came crashing out of Danny's and jostled past us, so we went inside. The man who runs Danny's, whose name is Tom, was leaning across the counter on his elbows, looking exhausted. Two little boys, holding Slush Puppies, shuffled toward the Nintendo, but Colin and Japeth elbowed them aside and slammed their quarters down on the machine. The little boys shuffled back toward the counter and stood gawking at them, sucking on their drinks.

"You want to know how to tell if a girl likes you?" Japeth said. "She'll act really mean to you. That's a sure sign. I don't know why they do it, but it's always a sure sign. It gets your attention. You know how I show a girl I like her? I steal something from her and then run away. I do it to get their attention, and it works."

They planned four quarters' worth of games. During the last one, a teenager with a quilted leather jacket and a fade haircut came in, pushed his arm between them, and put a quarter down on the deck of the machine.

Japeth said, "Hey, what's that?"

The teenager said, "I get next game. I've marked it now. Everyone knows this secret sign for next game. It's a universal thing."

"So now we know," Japeth said. "Colin, let's get out of here and go bother Maggie. I mean Maggot. Okay?" They picked up their backpacks and headed out the door.

Psychologists identify ten as roughly the age at which many boys experience the gender-linked normative developmental trauma that leaves them, as adult men, at risk for specific psychological sequelae often manifest as deficits in the arenas of intimacy, empathy, and struggles with commitment in relationships. In other words, this is around the age when guys get screwed up about girls. Elaine and Jim Duffy, and probably most of the parents who send their kids to Montclair Cooperative School, have done a lot of stuff to try to avoid this. They gave Colin dolls as well as guns. (He preferred guns.) Japeth's father has three motorcycles and two dirt bikes but does most of the cooking and cleaning in their home. Suzanne, Colin's teacher, is careful to avoid sexist references in her presentations. After school, the yard at Montclair Cooperative is filled with as many fathers as mothers—fathers who hug their kids when they come prancing out of the building and are dismayed when their sons clamor for Supersoaker water guns and war toys or take pleasure in beating up girls.

In a study of adolescents conducted by the Gesell Institute of Human Development, nearly half the 10-year-old boys questioned said they thought they had adequate information about sex. Nevertheless, most 10-year-old boys across the country are subjected to a few months of sex education in school. Colin and his class will get their dose next spring. It is yet another installment in a plan to make them into new, improved men with reconstructed notions of sex and male-female relationships. One afternoon I asked Philip, a schoolmate of Colin's, whether he was looking forward to sex education, and he said, "No, because I think it'll probably make me really, really hyper. I have a feeling it's going to be just like what it was like when some television reporters came to school last year and filmed us in class and I got really hyper. They stood around with all these cameras and asked us questions. I think that's what sex education is probably like."

At a class meeting earlier in the day:

Suzanne: "Today was our first day of swimming class, and I have one observation to make. The girls went into their locker room, got dressed without a lot of fuss, and came into the pool area. The boys, on the other hand, the *boys* had some sort of problem doing that rather simple task. Can someone tell me what exactly went on in the locker room?"

Keith: "There was a lot of shouting."

Suzanne: "Okay, I hear you saying that people were being noisy and shouting. Anything else?"

Christian: "Some people were screaming so much that my ears were killing me. It gave me, like, a huge headache. Also, some of the boys were taking their towels, I mean, after they had taken their clothes off, they had their towels around their waists and then they would drop them really fast and then pull them back up, really fast."

Suzanne: "Okay, you're saying some people were being silly about their bodies."

Christian: "Well, yeah, but it was more like they were being silly about their pants."

Colin's bedroom is decorated simply. He has a cage with his pet parakeet, Dude, on his dresser, a lot of recently worn clothing piled haphazardly on the floor, and a husky brown teddy bear sitting upright in a chair near the foot of his bed. The walls are mostly bare, except for a Spiderman poster and a few ads torn out of magazines he has thumbtacked up. One of the ads is for a cologne, illustrated with several small photographs of cowboy hats; another, a feverish portrait of a woman on a horse, is an ad for blue jeans. These inspire him sometimes when he lies in bed and makes plans for the move to Wyoming. Also, he happens to like ads. He also likes television commercials. Generally speaking, he likes consumer products and popular culture. He partakes avidly but not indiscriminately. In fact, during the time we spent together, he provided a running commentary on merchandise, media, and entertainment:

"The only shoes anyone will wear are Reebok Pumps. Big T-shirts are cool, not the kind that are sticky and close to you, but big and baggy and long, not the kind that stop at your stomach."

"The best food is Chicken McNuggets and Life cereal and Frosted Flakes."

"Don't go to Blimpie's. They have the worst service."

"I'm not into Teenage Mutant Ninja Turtles anymore. I grew out of that. I like Donatello, but I'm not a fan. I don't buy the figures anymore."

"The best television shows are on Friday night on ABC. It's called TGIF, and it's *Family Matters, Step by Step, Dinosaurs,* and *Perfect Strangers,* where the guy has a funny accent."

"The best candy is Skittles and Symphony bars and Crybabies and Warheads. Crybabies are great because if you eat a lot of them at once you feel so sour."

"Hyundais are Korean cars. It's the only Korean car. They're not that good because Koreans don't have a lot of experience building cars."

"The best movie is *City Slickers,* and the best part was when he saved his little cow in the river."

"The Giants really need to get rid of Ray Handley. They have to get somebody who has real coaching experience. He's just no good."

"My dog, Sally, costs 72 dollars. That sounds like a lot of money but it's a really good price because you get a flea bath with your dog."

"The best magazines are *Nintendo Power,* because they tell you how to do the secret moves in the video games, and also *Mad* magazine and *Money Guide*—I really like that one."

"The best artist in the world is Jim Davis."

"The most beautiful woman in the world is not Madonna! Only Wayne and Garth think that! She looks like maybe a . . . a . . . slut or something. Cindy Crawford looks like she would look good, but if you see her on an awards program on TV she doesn't look that good. I think the most beautiful woman in the world probably is my mom."

Colin thinks a lot about money. This started when he was about nine and a half, which is when a lot of other things started—a new way of walking that has a little macho hitch and swagger, a decision about the Teenage Mutant Ninja Turtles (con) and Eurythmics (pro), and a persistent curiosity about a certain girl whose name he will not reveal. He knows the price of everything he encounters. He knows how much college costs and what someone might earn performing different jobs. Once, he asked me what my husband did; when I answered that he was a lawyer, he snapped, "You must be a rich family. Lawyers make $400,000 a year." His preoccupation with money baffles his family. They are not struggling, so this is not the anxiety of deprivation; they are not rich, so he is not responding to an elegant, advantaged world. His allowance is five dollars a week. It seems sufficient for his needs, which consist chiefly of quarters for Nintendo and candy money. The remainder is put into his Wyoming fund. His fascination is not just specific to needing money or having plans for money: It is as if money itself, and the way it makes the world work, and the realization that almost everything in the world can be assigned a price, has possessed him. "I just pay attention to things like that," Colin says. "It's really very interesting."

He is looking for a windfall. He tells me his mother has been notified that she is in the fourth and final round of the Publisher's Clearinghouse Sweepstakes. This is not an ironic observation. He plays the New Jersey lottery every Thursday night. He knows the weekly jackpot; he knows the number to call to find out if he has won. I do not think this presages a future for Colin as a high-stakes gambler; I think it says more about the powerful grasp that money has on imagination and what a large percentage of a 10-year-old's mind is made up of imaginings. One Friday, we were at school together, and one of his friends was asking him about the lottery, and he said, "This week it was $4 million. That would be I forget how much every year for the rest of your life. It's a lot, I think. You should play. All it takes is a dollar and a dream."

Until the lottery comes through and he starts putting together the Wyoming land deal, Colin can be found most of the time in the backyard. Often, he will have friends come over. Regularly, children from the neighborhood will gravitate to the backyard, too. As a technical matter of real-property law, title to the house and yard belongs to Jim and Elaine Duffy, but Colin adversely possesses the backyard, at least from 4:00 each afternoon until it gets dark. As yet, the fixtures of teenage life— malls, video arcades, friends' basements, automobiles—either hold little interest for him or are not his to have.

He is, at the moment, very content with his backyard. For most intents and purposes, it is as big as Wyoming. One day, certainly, he will grow and it will shrink, and it will become simply a suburban backyard and it won't be big enough for him anymore. This will happen so fast that one night he will be in the backyard, believing it a perfect place, and by the next night he will have changed and the yard as he imagined it will be gone, and this era of his life will be behind him forever.

Most days, he spends his hours in the backyard building an Evil Spider-Web Trap. This entails running a spool of Jim's fishing line from every surface in the yard until it forms a huge web. Once a garbageman picking up the Duffys' trash got caught in the trap. Otherwise, the Evil Spider-Web Trap mostly has a deterrent effect, because the kids in the neighborhood who might roam over know that Colin builds it back there. "I do it all the time," he says. "First I plan who I'd like to catch in it, and then we get started. Trespassers have to beware."

One afternoon when I came over after a few rounds of Street Fighter at Danny's, Colin started building a trap. He selected a victim for inspiration—a boy in his class who had been pestering him—and began wrapping. He was entirely absorbed. He moved from tree to tree, wrapping; he laced fishing line through the railing of the deck and then back to the shed; he circled an old jungle gym, something he'd outgrown and abandoned a few years ago, and then crossed over to a bush at the back of the yard. Briefly, he contemplated making his dog, Sally, part of the web. Dusk fell. He kept wrapping, paying out fishing line an inch at a time. We could hear mothers up and down the block hooting for their kids; two tiny children from next door stood transfixed at the edge of the yard, uncertain whether they would end up inside or outside the web. After a while, the spool spun around in Colin's hands one more time and then stopped; he was out of line.

It was almost too dark to see much of anything, although now and again the light from the deck would glance off a length of line, and it would glint and sparkle. "That's the point," he said. "You could do it with thread, but the fishing line is invisible. Now I have this perfect thing and the only one who knows about it is me." With that, he dropped the spool, skipped up the stairs of the deck, threw open the screen door, and then bounded into the house, leaving me and Sally the dog trapped in his web.

Personal Investigations: Inquiry Projects

1. The first two essays in this chapter provide a portrait of certain American males, ages ten and fifteen. What's missing, obviously, is a similar close look at girls at those same ages. Consider a project that would do just that. Arrange to spend time with a ten- or fifteen-year-old girl. Take elaborate notes. Consider using Susan Orlean's essay and Bob Greene's "Fifteen" as an opportunity to draw comparisons between the experiences, worldviews, and rituals of young girls and boys.

2. Make a list of groups that seem to gather based on age, or that share particular characteristics because of their ages. For example, if you're around young children a lot, you've probably noticed similarities and differences in how different age groups play together. After you've made your list, choose a group to study further that is accessible to you and that you know little about. Then see what you discover.

Craft and Conventions: Explaining and Evaluating

3. On several occasions in this essay, Susan Orlean explicitly interprets what she sees, trying to draw larger conclusions about the culture of ten-year-olds. Where are these interpretations? Do you agree with them? What evidence does Orlean provide that convinces you of their validity? Where is there insufficient evidence?

4. One of the methods of literary journalism—and ethnography, for that matter—is the use of scene-by-scene construction. Choose a scene from this essay and study how Susan Orlean crafts dialogue, uses description, and selects details. Each scene must work purposefully toward implying something about what it means to be ten. Analyze these implications for the scene you chose.

5. Probably the most common shortcoming of the student ethnographies we've assigned is that the writer collects too little information and is ultimately compelled to use everything. The result is an unfocused essay. Speculate about the kind of field work and research that Susan Orlean used to write this longish profile of Colin Duffy. Who did she interview? Where did she go to observe? Did she resort to reading research?

Inquiries on Inquiry: Exploring and Reflecting

6. We've said that academic inquiry often involves dialectical thinking, a moving back and forth from your observations of things and your ideas about them, between evidence and interpretation, and showing and

telling. This movement is also evident sometimes in the published work itself. Can you detect that dialectical movement in "The American Male at Age Ten?" Where does Orlean move from experience to reflection?

7. Susan Orlean's essay is a work of creative nonfiction; there are no citations, no bibliography, and no effort to connect her investigation to the previous work of others. If "The American Male at Age Ten" was to be a starting point for a more academic investigation of this culture of boys, what are some of the things a research project might entail? How might the methods differ?

8. Remember yourself at age ten. In your journal, describe your bedroom at that time. Brainstorm a list of details of everything you see, hear, smell, and touch. Make this list very specific and as long as you can. After five minutes of list making, review the items you generated. Circle one that you think says something about who you were back then. Use this as a prompt for a seven-minute fastwrite. Let the writing lead you back into thinking about that time. Finish by skipping a line and completing the following sentence: *As I look back on that time in my life. I now realize that _____.*

9. As you read this essay, what did you find most convincing and why? What makes those parts believable to you? What would make them convincing to a parent or a psychologist? How do you decide how valid Orlean's claims are when different kinds of readers need very different kinds of evidence and proof?

Connie and the Sandman Ladies
Anne Campbell

In 1979, researcher Anne Campbell went to New York City to study the role of girls in local gangs; the essay here is an excerpt of what she observed. "I wanted to observe and interact with girl gang members," she says, "and to represent their own views of their situations. The literature [on gangs] abounds with rich accounts of the lives of street corner men and street corner gangs, but women appear at second hand and only through the reports of male speakers. I wanted to redress the balance and to hear girls speak for themselves."

The form of the ethnography was best suited for researching her questions, so Campbell spent six months with three very different female gangs, becoming as much of an insider as she could. She was open with the groups about her project, knowing the groups might lie to her but believing she couldn't lie to them about her purposes. The book she wrote based on this research is entitled The Girls in the Gang *and it was published in 1991. Still influential, Campbell's book is central to academic research on girl gangs. Today, she teaches social psychology at Rutgers University, and the excerpt from her book that follows is an excellent example of ethnographic research written by an academic.*

Campbell uses a "day in the life" structure to introduce readers to Connie, the leader of the Sandman Ladies, but in this selection doesn't explicitly state the conclusions she's drawn about this culture. As you read, mark the artifacts, rituals, and specialized language that are particular to this group. Note as well the places where Campbell refers to herself and her interactions with the group. Think about your own assumptions about girl gangs and how Campbell's observations address those assumptions. But most of all, marvel at the richness of the portrait that Campbell renders of these women; you won't be surprised that ethnography, in the hands of a writer like this, can easily be compared to the best creative nonfiction.

The Sandman is a Manhattan biker gang. It is arguable whether or not biker is an appropriate description, since while I was in contact with them there was only one functioning motorcycle (a BSA 650), although there was much discussion of the purchase and renovation of other bikes. However, biker seems appropriate in the light of the age of the leading member (30 years old), the sense of brotherhood the gang felt with other biker gangs (such as the Wheels of Soul), and the conversational preoccupations and attitudes of the members. Discussions of drug experiences and trips to the country "runs" and the predominance of Satanic and Nazi badges and emblems were very reminiscent of descriptions of the Hell's Angels. But the members in general had little sympathy for this group. They rejected their size, criminality, and fascistic political views, arguing that the Sandman, by contrast, was a social club and an unofficial family. Local biker clubs were seen as very different from the national, almost institutionalized, structure they attributed to the Hell's Angels.

Although they described themselves as a club, the Sandman was designated as a gang by the New York City Police's Manhattan Gang Intelligence Unit #1. In the final report by this unit in 1979 it is identified only as a Hispanic gang with an alleged membership of thirty five and a verified membership of ten. No information on its activities is available. Many members did not live locally but commuted in to Manhattan from the Bronx or Brooklyn to hang out. The membership was not particularly stable because of this and also because some of the members, especially girls, periodically drifted back to the Times Square area where they were involved in drugs or prostitution.

The major source of income for the gang when I was in contact with them was drug dealing. Prior to establishing their own area of operation, they had worked downtown, keeping the streets of another drug-selling group "safe." They were also involved in an ongoing dispute with the Chosen Ones (a group from uptown Manhattan), which seemed to be related to drug sales and to other gangs' belief that the Sandman had provided the police with information that led to the imprisonment of their members. After the incident reported by the *New York Post,* in which a chase occurred along the subway tracks, the dispute continued. Two of the Sandman were shot at (one escaped injury, the other had four bullet wounds) and Connie's teenage daughter was the object of a shooting, although she escaped unharmed. Connie continued to care for her four children, support her husband, and lead the Sandman Ladies throughout.

A Day with Connie

Connie lives in the Upper West Side of Manhattan on the thirteenth floor of a project apartment building. You can spot her windows easily from the ground. A Puerto Rican flag hangs from one and heads bob in and out of the other to check what's happening on the street. Inside, the lobby is painted a pale lavatorial green and echoes with the laughter and shrieks of children in the nursery on the ground floor. It smells of a musty scent that covers the odor of chemical used to control cockroaches. The two elevators operate spasmodically. A ten-minute wait is not unusual.

No one answers Connie's door at first because the knocking is drowned out by the thundering bass of the rap disco blasting out of radio speakers. The door's spyhole cover opens, swings shut, and OK is standing there. He waves me through, smiling with exaggerated politeness. In the corner of the living room, the color television is on with the sound turned down, and quiz-show hosts grin and chatter idiotically. JR is stretched out luxuriously on the sofa beneath a giant Sandman insignia depicting a hooded face on an iron cross, which hangs on the wall. He wears a yellow T-shirt that proudly states "I love Brooklyn," in graffiti writing and a leather vest. A bottle of Colt 45 beer rests on the floor next to him. Mico is in the kitchen, helping Connie bag up marijuana for the day.

Connie, perched on a stool, looks up and smiles. She wears no makeup and her hair, scrupulously clean, falls around her face. She is small—five feet two—but the tall stool gives her a certain stature. Up high by the window, she can see down onto the street. She is wearing a check blouse, jeans, and two belts, one with a demonic goat's head and the other apparently a chain from a BSA motorcycle. At the side of one belt is a small leather case that holds a knife. Connie always carries a flick knife and always in a visible place—as long as it is not a switchblade (which shoots the blade forward from the handle) and it is not concealed, the police will leave her alone. I pull up a chair and the three of us talk over the blare of the radio, yelling to make ourselves heard or leaning together conspiratorially to catch some complicated story.

In the mornings, Connie and Suzie, her daughter, get up early at 7:30. Suzie is 14, taller than her mother, and very capable. The girlfriend of Connie's 6-year-old son Raps comes by to pick him up and often she dresses and feeds him as well. He is out of the house by 8:30. JJ, Connie's youngest son, has to be dressed and given breakfast along with baby Dahlia. She and Suzie take him to school, put Dahlia in the nursery downstairs, and sometimes manage to eat breakfast together in a donut shop. By 9:30 the kids are usually dispatched for the day.

This particular Friday, Suzie has stayed home to help out and hang around. Gino, Connie's husband and leader of the Sandman, is not going to work today and is sleeping through the early morning hubbub. Connie is happy to have all her family around her. As we talk, she bags up with a dexterity she has developed over years—snipping up the grass and packing it into tiny yellow envelopes. She seals each with Scotch tape and then, with a small piece of cardboard, scrapes another bagful from the white plastic bowl. We talk about jealousy. Connie leans over and pulls a notebook out of the kitchen drawer. Each page has neat paragraph entries, the visible results of years of sitting, thinking, bagging, and talking. She writes down each new insight about life and relationships.

This morning she announces that she has to get on with her "automated routines," so she gets up, washes the dishes, puts a pile of dirty T-shirts into the washing machine, and lights a cigarette. OK is now listening to the radio through headphones, but the volume is so loud that we can all hear it. JR has turned up the television and sits absorbed by a soap opera. Connie runs out of cigarettes and OK is sent to the store to buy a pack of Kools. Connie tells me about when she had Suzie at 15. After her fourth child at 28, Connie "closed down the factory." "I felt like a damn incubator. There has got to be some balance in life, but who should decide who's to live and who's to die?" she ponders as she slaps Scotch tape onto the tiny bags.

At one o'clock, Wolfy from the Satan's Wheels in the South Bronx arrives. He has a black handkerchief around his head, held in place by a piece of string, and wears a T-shirt and a cut-off denim jacket without gang insignia or "patches." Patches seen on the subway cause trouble. The guys get up to greet him as he comes into their clubhouse. They exchange news from different clubs, and Connie and I sit by, half-listening from the kitchen. From the bedroom comes a warm roar and Gino appears with arms outstretched to Wolfy. "Hey, hey, what's up?" They embrace and Gino's presence as leader is felt.

Connie divides the plastic bags and hands them to some of the guys who pull on their leather jackets and denim patches with SANDMAN MC NYC on the back and go out for the day to the street. Gino, wearing a black leather biker's cap with his leather jacket, jeans, and motorcycle boots, comes over and kisses Connie. Then he leaves to go down with the guys.

At 1:30, Shorty arrives. She is small and curly-haired, perhaps only 19. She is gang member Sinbad's girlfriend and wears her denim jacket over a blue sweatshirt. To be Sinbad's girlfriend is not a direct entry into the Sandman Ladies, however. She must prove her capability, just like anyone else who wants to join, and she has not yet earned her patches. Connie will decide when she deserves the title Sandman Lady. Connie says that she doesn't care about a girl's fighting history; what she looks for in a possible member are brains. Shorty is still learning. Later, when she answers the door and leaves it ajar as she tells Connie who it is, Connie tells her never, never to leave the door open. How does she know that someone they don't want to see isn't out there about to walk right in? Shorty nods. She sits in the living room quietly watching and listening to everything.

Connie's favorite song plays on the radio. She jumps up and whistles for Suzie to come in from the bedroom. Together they take over the living room floor, doing the hustle. Suzie acts the male's part perfectly, with minimum body movement and an expression of total boredom. At the end of the song, Suzie walks back to the bedroom and Connie, out of breath, laughs to herself. At 1:45, Connie's mother phones from Queens. Connie talks with her mother frequently on the phone but does not see her often. Her mother disapproves of the club, and Connie feels caught between duty and love.

Everything is quiet now. Family members have gone their ways for the day, and only Shortly sits quietly in the next room, clutching a hankie. Connie tells me more of her life story. When she was 19—11 years ago—her father died. She shows me one of the letters he wrote to her while he was in the hospital for drug treatment. The handwriting is scrupulously neat. He complains that the doctors think he is crazy and tells Connie that if anything should happen to him, she should investigate it. He writes with great pride about Connie's new career in nursing and about his beautiful granddaughter (Suzie). Among his letters, Connie finds some official papers. One is a charge sheet from the police or a court, signed by a doctor, testifying that her father was found unfit to plead because of "imbecility." The other is a telegram from the hospital telling her that he is dead and asking her to make funeral arrangements. Connie never saw the death certificate and never knew what her father died from. Now she remembers his injunction and feels guilty. She never did check the circumstances of his death. She looks at the clock; it's time to go pick up the kids.

Halfway to the elevator Connie runs back to the apartment to get her sunglasses. Last week she got beaten up. Her nose was broken, she had stitches, and both her eyes puffed out. The swelling has gone down, but two plum-colored circles remain around her eyes. Until they go, the sunglasses are compulsory public wear. She has also changed into a pair of dark red boots—lovingly cared for with daily doses of cold cream—that are pulled over her jeans. Over her blouse, she wears a fur-lined leather jacket, a couple of sizes too big, and on top of that her patches. Sewn on the denim jacket are the full colors of the club: SANDMAN NYC LADIES. With Shorty, we go into the weak afternoon sunshine.

Outside on a bench, Gino is recounting to the gang how the police beat him up when he had tuberculosis: "They beat the TB right out of me!" Sitting on the stone bench and the wall are seven club members all with their colors on. Wolfy and Lalla, a girl of 20 who deals around the area, are there too. Lalla wears a baseball cap back to front and a red jacket. She looks young and jumpy in comparison to Connie, severe and feminine, who sits on the stone chess table listening quietly while her husband speaks. Gino's story gets increasingly boisterous, and there is much laughter as they slap one another's hands in appreciation of the tale. The group appears insulated and self-contained. Their uniform jacket patches and their red bandannas divide them from the rest of the world. Nevertheless, neighbors, janitors, social workers, mothers of children who share Dahlia's nursery greet them as they pass, and Gino and the group wave back or shout "Hi. What's up?"

Dahlia stumbles out of the front lobby, watched by her teacher. She heads straight for Connie who picks her up, kisses her, and switches her shoes, which Dahlia has put on the wrong feet. Gino kisses Dahlia hello, and he and Connie decide who will go to pick up JJ from school. Gino goes, since he is usually at work these days and misses the daily ritual.

Every so often, someone approaches one of the group—the guy who is "holding" that day. The drug deal is transacted quietly. The girls sit separately. We talk about the neighborhood, about fights, about men. Now and again one of the guys asks for a cigarette or tells Connie something in Spanish connected with today's business. At the end of the day, all the money goes to Connie, who does the bookkeeping. Connie gives Suzie a couple of dollars from the roll of bills in her pocket to take Dahlia to the store to buy some candy. Today Dahlia gets some marshmallows, but Connie doesn't generally approve. She doesn't want her to get a taste for too much sugar.

Gino returns, and now the whole family is together. Raps, 6 years old, tells about a fight he had at school: "Yeah, I really dogged him. I fucked up his shit." Gino teases him about his 10-year-old girlfriend, offering some fatherly advice: "You tell that bitch that she can't carry your gaddam books to school no more." Everyone laughs except Raps, who looks down, embarrassed. He likes the attention but doesn't really know what is so funny. The teenage girls from the project are coming home from junior high school. As they pass, they greet Connie with a kiss, exchange a few words, kiss her cheek again, and go inside. They all know her and Suzie. Members of the club who have been at work or school arrive one at a time until there are 15 of us. We each throw in a couple of dollars, and JC goes off to the liquor store. He returns with small plastic cups, a bottle of Coke, and some Bacardi rum. The girls' drinks are poured into the cups and are very strong. Sinbad notices me sipping at mine and instructs me to "Drink like a *woman*." The guys pass the liquor bottle around, drinking theirs neat. Before each one drinks, he pours a little of the rum on the ground in memory of those who are dead or in jail. The bottle ends up on the stone chess table in front of the girls, and the guys gravitate toward it. Gino and Wolfy speak half to each other and half to the kids who climb on and off the benches, threatening to upset the liquor. Raps drops his lollipop on the ground, and Gino picks it up, wipes it off, and pours Bacardi over it to sterilize it. Raps puts it back in his mouth and grimaces.

The conversation turns to Gino's time in Vietnam, where, he tells us, he was a combat photographer. He tells how many of the injuries he saw were perpetrated by the Americans on themselves when incendiary bombs were dropped short of target or when machines backfired. He was injured in the leg, but when the U.S. Army withdrew, his medical papers were lost. Now he has no way to prove that he is entitled to veteran's compensation, unless he were to take his case to court and that would cost him thousands. "If I had that kind of money, I wouldn't need their damn compensation, right?" Gino interrupts the story to wave and yell at a guy across the street who is something of a local celebrity because he had a role in *The Wiz*. Gino also sees two guys in surplus army jackets crossing the street—plainclothes cops. Gino watches as they enter a flower shop, which is a local drug-dealing center. Later, a local guy comes over to tell Gino that he followed them but they split up and went different ways.

It's 4:50 and it's getting colder. Gino announces we are going to a party tonight at the house of the president of Satan's Wheels in the Bronx. Upon hearing of the party, Connie, who has been standing back with Shorty, occasionally chatting to her, decides it is a good time to give Shorty her first patches. They disappear upstairs to sew them on her jacket and to check that Suzie can baby-sit. As we sit drinking, the daylight fades quickly. People coming home from work pass the apartment building in a steady stream. Some stare curiously at the group. Others, more familiar, simply hurry past. The light in the lobby spills out onto the concrete in front and the yellow street lights come on.

Connie and Shorty return. Shorty spins around triumphantly to show off her new patches: LADY NYC. Later she will earn her final patch: SANDMAN. The guys yell and whistle and, led by Gino, pour bottles of beer over her head in traditional gang congratulations. She squeals. It's very cold by now and her hair is soaking wet, but she smiles and flicks back her curls with the back of her hand. Sinbad hugs her proudly.

Connie disappears and returns with a sandwich wrapped in silver foil from a local Spanish store. We pass it around and share it with the kids who have come downstairs. By now there are about 20 of us. From time to time, one of the guys comes over and looks through my notebook, curious to see what I have written down today. They borrow my pen to make illustrations, additions, or subtractions. Connie and I stand together. She points out females who pass by, some friends and some potential enemies. I am shivering from the cold, but Connie teases me that my knees are knocking at the thought of going to the South Bronx. There is talk that the Satan's Wheels will send a van to pick up everyone. That would be better than going by subway. On the subway, 20 people dressed in gang colors attract attention, which often leads to problems with the police. But the Sandman must wear their colors as a sign of pride in their club if they are going to another club's turf. Maybe they'll carry them over their arms on the train and put them on when they get out. Some of the guys who have come from work look tired. Gino tells them to watch out for being burned. If they fall asleep at the party he will set fire to their pants, a disciplinary custom that reminds members always to be on their guard when they are away from their own area.

Gino announces that we will go by subway but no one is to wear colors on the train. Five of us take the kids and their various toys and carts up to the apartment. Suzie has two girlfriends over for the evening and is playing disco music. Connie leaves a small bag of grass for them. Suzie tries for a pint of Bacardi too, but Connie refuses. Dahlia cries for her mother but quiets down when Suzie picks her up. We go downstairs after I have been given a plain denim jacket so I won't look completely out of place.

OK and Shorty carry down motorcycle helmets, which they offer to Gino. Gino asks what the hell they are for. OK protests that Gino told him to bring them. Gino says he didn't. OK mumbles some curse and turns away. Gino loses his temper and begins yelling at him. Everyone freezes and watches to see what will happen. OK does not say a word. Gino berates him for not listening, for not following orders, for being insolent. Wolfy, even though it is not his gang, joins in: "He's your leader. You'd better damn well respect him." OK, head down, walks away. Gino does not let up: "And don't you be sulking like that neither." OK seems to look happier afterward. Gino's threat to leave him chained to the iron fence at the edge of the project buildings is forgotten.

We walk in twos and threes to the subway station five or six blocks away. Gino stops to urinate behind a wall. I walk on with the Hulk, talking about his future, his school, his clothes. Connie calls out, "Hey, where's Annie?" She is looking out for me all the time. At the subway, Wolfy and I walk down the steps while the rest of the group gathers at the entrance. I put my token in the stile, but Wolfy walks through the swing doors without paying. The subway clerk calls him back, but he walks on. When Gino and the others appear, the clerk has already picked up the phone to call the transit police. Gino intervenes and pays everyone's fare, including Wolfy's. On the platform, he bawls Wolfy out, telling him it's crazy to get the cops down for the measly fare. Gino shows a roll of money in his pocket to reinforce the point. This is, after all, their turf. They have to use the subway all the time, so why make trouble? Wolfy is a guest and, as such, he should respect their turf.

Gino tells us to split up because we look too conspicuous in a group. Connie, Shorty, and I walk down the platform. Near us two black girls are casually rolling a joint. Connie watches them—there is something about their manner that she doesn't like. When we get on the train, one of them leans on the center post of the car, ignoring the available seats. Connie walks over and leans on the opposite post four feet away, staring at her through her dark glasses. They stare each other down, but the other girl breaks first. She looks away, then at her feet, then gets off the train. We change trains at 182nd Street. A train pulls in, but it's not the one we want to take. Inside a car, a man in his thirties, dressed in a suit, smiles at us. It isn't clear to me whether he is leering or laughing at us. As the train pulls away, Shorty smashes her fist at the window where his face is. He jumps back and the train disappears. Shorty clutches her hand. In a few minutes, it begins to swell and turn red, but she does not mention it.

We board our train. Two Puerto Rican girls are standing by the door, whispering and laughing. Connie watches them, wondering whether to "bug them out." She approaches them, but I cannot hear what is said. One girl reaches into her bag and pulls out some gum, offering Connie a stick. She takes one and offers it to me. I decline. Connie pops it in her mouth and leans over to kiss the girl on the cheek. Connie is smiling. The girls look pleased, embarrassed, and confused. The guys walk up and down the train in ones and twos, checking that everybody is on and knows where to get off. Although they are carrying their colors over their arms, they look conspicuous in their chains, boots, and bandannas. Some have sheath knives in their waistbands. Passengers watch their comings and goings uneasily.

We get off the train and climb the unlit stairs to the street. The guys take the girls' arms to guide us up. Several young girls are standing by the subway entrance. They seem excited at our arrival and particularly interested in Connie and Shorty with their patches. As we cross the street, Sinbad authoritatively holds up his hand to halt the oncoming traffic. We straggle along a side street, and Gino peers down an alleyway to a handball court where some kids are playing by floodlight. The game breaks up, and after a few seconds one of them appears in patches: FLAMES NYC. It is Felix, a friend of Gino. He greets all of us and cordially offers a small plastic cup of vodka and grapefruit juice, which we pass around. He has recently redesigned his club patches—from a swastika into a more complex design with a skull set in red and orange flames—and turns around so we can admire them. I reach out to touch them, wondering how he got such a complicated design so professionally done. Connie pulls my hand back and tells me that it is forbidden to touch someone's patches. And there are rituals surrounding them: they can never be taken off carelessly, but must be folded and laid down safely, they must always be worn with boots, never with sneakers.

Felix decides to escort us through his turf to the party, which is several blocks away. He is on good terms with Satan's Wheels. We walk on down dark streets with huge empty tenements on either side. Doorways are covered heavily with graffiti and smell of urine. Connie, Shorty, and I walk at the rear, and Sinbad turns every few yards to make sure we are keeping up. Connie advises me to sit quietly at the party and be careful that nothing I do be misunderstood. I am white and, as such, am considered to be available property. Don't say too much and stick close to her, Connie says. We gaze around at the buildings. We are both completely out of our territory, although Connie points a few blocks downtown to where she lived briefly years ago. She tells me this isn't a real nice area. Broken bottles crunch under our feet. Finally we halt outside a grocery store, waiting while Gino and Felix finish their discussion.

We walk into an old tenement building. The huge hallway is painted crimson and lit by long fluorescent tubes. Initials and names are emblazoned on the walls. We walk up one flight of stairs and ring a doorbell. After a few minutes, we are let in and walk down a hallway. Three or four girls are sitting in a bedroom through some French doors. Gino greets the guys in the club who are in the kitchen drinking, and Connie goes into the bedroom. In perfect Spanish and very politely she introduces herself as head of the Sandman Ladies and thanks the girls for their hospitality. They are much younger than she is and struggle to summon an equally dignified reply. They are dressed casually, but when they reappear several minutes later, they have put on sweatshirts that say PROPERTY OF SATAN'S

WHEELS NYC with the name of their particular man underneath. Connie tells me that *her* girls don't belong to any man.

We all assemble in the living room. Connie points out that the room is "typically Spanish"—velour-patterned sofa and many mementos on the tables and shelves; dolls, candles, crucifixes. The Satan's Wheels move the sound system into the room. Bottles of beer and Bacardi are passed around, interspersed with joints. When the music comes on, it is heavy rock— Stones, Led Zeppelin, Pink Floyd—and is deafening. Conversation is possible only by leaning right up against the other person's ear. The main lights go out, and the room is lit only by three ultra-violet lights, which illuminate eyes, teeth, and the white in jacket patches. One by one people begin to dance. Connie sits next to me on the sofa with her back straight.

It is the Hulk's sixteenth birthday. Suddenly the lights are switched on and he is drenched by several bottles of beer. He waves his arms, apparently enjoying the experience. The floor is awash with liquid, but one of the Satan's Wheels later mops up. Everyone is also scrupulously careful to flick their cigarette ashes into ashtrays, rather than on the floor. Amid the apparent chaos, there is a definite order. The Hulk moves around the room, embracing every member of the club, and by the end, we are all nearly as wet as he is. Gino spends most of the evening in the kitchen, discussing club business with the Flames and Satan's Wheels. Connie and I sit together drinking. Everybody is loosening up. Chino gets his beard set alight as a reminder that he is getting a little too loose. He climbs onto the fire escape and peers down, announcing that he is contemplating suicide. Then he laughs.

Connie and I, as we drink more, consider the implications of everything in the world being a product of our imagination. If we wished it all away now, only *we* would remain, suspended 60 feet in the air, discussing this very thought. A guy next to me searches vainly for some matches. I hand him some and Connie warns me about body contact. If you touch someone accidentally, they may take it the wrong way. I move away from him, suddenly aware that I have been half-leaning on him. Connie motions me to lean forward and tells me that if we keep talking together, maybe the guys will assume that I'm with her. That way, I'll be safe. Gino returns to sit by us. He and some other guys are throwing a bottle back and forth with eyes closed, a kind of test of everybody's reaction speed. I notice Connie's hands loose in her lap but ready in case it is thrown her way. The music changes to disco—a whole album side of it—and Connie gets up to dance alone.

It is after midnight and I decide to leave. Connie forces 20 dollars into my hand for a cab. Gino assigns two guys to walk me to the taxi office. Everybody yells goodnight, and I make my way back home.

Personal Investigations: Inquiry Projects

1. Anne Campbell's ethnography is based on her firsthand experience with the Sandman Ladies, experience as an outsider who has been allowed into the group. Think about the groups in your area where you might be welcomed as an observer and make a list of them in your journal. Which of these groups interests you the most? Which would be the riskiest group to research? The easiest? The one you know the most about? Try to choose a group that is challenging but doesn't pose a risk to your safety, one that you are interested in and yet don't know very much about. Set up times to observe this group, using the suggestions on page 245 for taking field notes, and write an ethnography that combines your observations, interviews, outside sources, and analysis of artifacts.

2. Return to the lists you made in Step 1 of Exercise 6.1. Choose a group or activity from the list and visit a site where you can observe that group or people engaging in that activity for an hour or two. When you're done taking notes, spend some time fastwriting about what you've seen. Then, write up the scene as a narrative, using as much detail as you can, much as Campbell does in her essay. When you're done, brainstorm a list of questions you have about the group or the activity that you'd like to know more about. See where those questions take you in your research. You may not end up doing a full ethnography, but you can use your observation as a basis for generating ideas for a research paper you're about to write.

Crafts and Conventions: Explaining and Evaluating

3. Unlike some of the other essays in this chapter, "Connie and the Sandman Ladies" doesn't have explicit statements about what Campbell concluded from her observations. The piece is primarily a carefully detailed narrative about one day in Connie's life. However, ethnographers do pose theories about cultures based on their observations. What can you infer from this narrative about the conclusions Campbell has come to? What does she seem to be telling us about this culture? Point to places in the narrative that lead you to these conclusions.

4. Ethnographers look carefully at a group's artifacts, language, rituals, and use of space. What would you say the key artifacts are in Connie's culture? What words or phrases seem to be used only by insiders? What do you notice about the ways this group uses their space—that is, how do they treat their apartment, the subway, the apartment of the gang having the party? What rituals does this group seem to have? What theories can you pose about this culture's values based on these artifacts, rituals, language, and space?

5. How would you describe Campbell's presence in the essay? Occasionally she refers to herself, but she primarily stays in the third person. What is the effect of only mentioning herself once or twice in the piece? Why might she have chosen not to discuss how she was feeling while she was with the group or what she thought about them?

6. Campbell chooses a day-in-the-life structure to convey her findings. What do you find effective about this approach? How does this structure help Campbell present her implicit conclusions about this culture? What are the limitations of using this structure? Choose one section of the essay to illustrate your points if you discuss this question in class.

Inquiries on Inquiry: Exploring and Reflecting

7. In order to make sense of what is being observed, an ethnographer often needs to compare her observations, interviews, and conclusions to other things that have been written on the subject. If you were to advise Campbell where she might look, what would you suggest? What sources might Campbell use at the library to obtain information for comparison with her observations?

8. Unlike large research projects that look at a large number of gangs and create tables and statistics to use to generalize about all gangs, Campbell's essay here focuses only on one girl gang in New York. If she can't generalize yet about girl gangs across America, then how useful do you think her research is? What might we learn from the details of only one group?

9. Explore your personal response to this essay: What struck you about it? What in your own background affects the way you read it? What assumptions about or experiences with gangs in general did you bring to reading this essay? What effect, if any, did the essay have on those assumptions? What questions does the essay raise for you?

The Cave

Jon Katz

In 1999, Rolling Stone *writer Jon Katz had returned to the magazine after a stint with* Wired, *which under the editorship of Louis Rossetto had earned a reputation as a renegade magazine promoting the cultural power of the*

Internet. Katz was discouraged. Wired *had been purchased by a conglomerate, which quickly muted its radicalism, and Rossetto was replaced. But Katz had already earned something of a reputation as a renegade himself through his* Wired *columns and an earlier book,* Virtuous Reality, *an essay collection that touted the virtues of "screen culture—the Net, the Web, TV, and movies."*

Needless to say, Katz got a lot of e-mail from geeks, a subculture he had taken a keen interest in. One night, "sorting through the geek outpouring," Katz received an e-mail from a teenager from Caldwell, Idaho, a small town near Boise.

"He'd written to tell me about a Geek Club that a sympathetic teacher had founded . . . , and how the club had quickly become an institution at their rural school," Katz writes in Geeks, *the book that tells the story of the Idaho teen, Jesse Dailey, and his friend Eric. "The idea of a Geek Club in . . . Idaho amazed me in itself. But I also responded to the kid's tone; his mixture of vulnerability, pride, and defiance."*

The excerpt you are about to read, "The Cave," is the second chapter of Katz's book Geeks: How Two Lost Boys Rode the Internet Out of Idaho. *Like several other selections in this chapter, it's not an academic ethnography, but it offers a surprisingly rich glimpse at a geek subculture—the patterns of behavior, the familiar artifacts, and the belief systems of two adolescents fresh from high school who belong to this "accidental empire" of young people in love with the Internet.*

Ethnographies are often revealing because of their local context. The writer looks very closely at particular people, at a particular time, in a particular place. But the question is always this: Can we generalize from this picture? To what extent, for example, does Katz's sketch of Jesse and Eric in Caldwell, Idaho, inform us about other geeks in other places? Academic ethnographers are often careful to avoid making claims beyond the local context they are studying; popular writers like Katz often imply more general claims. What do you think? Are Jesse and Eric typical of geek subculture?

From: Jesse Dailey
To: Jon Katz

When I was looking on the Tribune, there were 433 jobs under Computer/Info Systems, under every other category I looked in there was an average of 15–20. . . . A total of about 40 percent computers. The problem now isn't finding a place in which those jobs are in demand, because like you say . . . they are everywhere. The problem is finding a place that wants to hire someone like me. In a Human Resources kinda way I'm defined as 19 w/ one year of experience. . . . In reality, I am an ageless geek, with years of personal experience, a fiercely aggressive intelligence coupled with geek wit, and the education of the best online material in the world. Aarrgghh!! too much stress being a geek on the move. :)

Jesse and Eric lived in a cave—an airless two-bedroom apartment in a dank stucco-and-brick complex on the outskirts of Caldwell. Two doors down, chickens paraded around the street.

The apartment itself was dominated by two computers that sat across from the front door like twin shrines. Everything else—the piles of dirty laundry, the opened Doritos bags, the empty cans of generic soda pop, two ratty old chairs, and a moldering beanbag chair—was dispensable, an afterthought, props.

Jesse's computer was a Pentium II 300, Asus P2B (Intel BX chipset) motherboard; a Matrix Millenium II AGP; 160 MB SDRAM with a 15.5 GB total hard-drive space; a 4X CD-recorder; 24X CD-ROM; a 17-inch Micron monitor. Plus a scanner and printer. A well-thumbed paperback—Katherine Dunn's novel *Geek Love*—served as his mousepad.

Eric's computer: an AMD K-6 233 with a generic motherboard; an S3 video card, a 15-inch monitor; a 2.5 GB hard drive with 36 MB SDRAM. Jesse wangled the parts for both from work.

They stashed their bikes and then Jesse blasted in through the door, which was always left open since he can never hang on to keys, and went right to his PC, which was always on. He yelled a question to Eric about the new operating system. "We change them like cartons of milk," he explained. At the moment, he had NT 5, NT 4, Work Station, Windows 98, and he and Eric had begun fooling around with Linux, the complex, open-source software system rapidly spreading across the world.

Before settling in at his own rig, Eric grabbed a swig of milk from a carton in the refrigerator, taking a good whiff first. Meals usually consisted of a daily fast-food stop at lunchtime; everything else was more or less on the fly. There didn't seem to be any edible food in the refrigerator, apart from a slightly discolored hunk of cheddar cheese.

Jesse opened his MP3 playlist (MP3 is a wildly popular format for storing music on computer hard drives; on the Net, songs get traded like baseball cards) and pulled down five or six tracks—Alanis Morissette, John Lee Hooker, Eric Clapton, Ani DiFranco. He turned on his Web browser, checked his e-mail, opened ICQ chat (an also-rapidly growing global messaging and chat system) looking for messages from Sam Hunter, fellow Geek Club alumnus, or his mother or sisters.

He and Eric networked their computers for a few quick rounds of Quake II. Racing down hallways and passages on the screen, picking up ammo and medical supplies, acquiring ever bigger guns and blasters, the two kept up their techno-patter about the graphics, speed, and performance of their computers. "My hard drive is grungy," Eric complained. Jesse gunned Eric down three times in a row, then yelped, "Shit, I'm dead." A laser burst of bullets splattered blood all over the dungeonlike floor.

Meanwhile, the two of them continued to chat with me over their shoulders, pausing every now and then to kill or be killed. All the while, Jesse listened to music, and answered ICQ messages. Somebody called and asked about ordering an ID card, the cottage industry that at 50 bucks a pop will help underwrite their contemplated move to Chicago. Somebody e-mailed a few additional MP3s; somebody else sent software and upgrades for Quake and Doom. I was dizzied and distracted by all the activity; they were completely in their element.

The game was still under way when Eric moved over to the scanner and printer and printed out something semi-official-looking.

"Too dark," was Jesse's assessment, without seeming to look away from the screen. So Eric went back to his computer and called up a graphic program. Jesse took another phone call, still playing Quake, as Joni Mitchell gave way to Jane's Addiction, then the Red Hot Chili Peppers.

At any given point, he was doing six things almost simultaneously, sipping soda, glancing at the phone's caller ID, watching the scanner and the printer, blasting away at menacing soldiers, opening mail from an apartment manager in Chicago, fielding a message from his sister in Boise.

He wasn't just a kid at a computer, but something more, something new, an impresario and an Information Age CEO, transfixed and concentrated, almost part of the machinery, conducting the digital ensemble that controlled his life. Anyone could have come into the apartment and carted away everything in it, except for the computer, and Jesse wouldn't have noticed or perhaps cared that much. He was playing, working, networking, visiting, strategizing—all without skipping a function, getting confused, or stopping to think.

It was evidently second nature by now, which explained why he looked as if he hadn't been out in the sun for years. It was more or less true: A couple of weeks earlier, he'd gone hiking along the Idaho River on a bright day and landed in the hospital emergency room with his arms and legs severely sunburned.

He carried himself like someone who expected to get screwed, who would have to fend for himself when that happened, and who was almost never surprised when it did. Trouble, Jesse often declared, was the building block of character. Without the former, you didn't get the latter.

Of the two, Jesse was more social, more outward-looking. He sometimes read novels or, when he had no other means of communication, yakked on the phone (though almost always while online); he was on the lookout for a few good friends, though not highly sanguine about finding any. Eric rarely socialized, e-mailed, or chatted, at least about non-techie topics. Jesse claimed that if his computer were ever stolen or unplugged, he would read obsessively; Eric didn't know what he would do, and hoped never to find out.

Both had had difficult adolescent lives, in complex families under unstable circumstances. Eric, who hadn't seen or spoken with his father in years, had emerged darker, angrier than his friend, a part of him beyond the reach of teachers, peers, and well-intended adults. Jesse, hooked on arguments and ideas—he often describes himself as a fighter—could usually be drawn out of his shell.

Although they were forever getting into raging late-night debates about the nature of cable modem access, the longevity of Microsoft, or what constituted pass interference, and despite enormous philosophical and social differences, the two saw the world in essentially the same way.

That was, they were outsiders. They'd spent virtually all their 19 years on the periphery of various things—families, teams, churches, school cliques—and had developed a profound suspicion of hierarchies, authorities, institutions, bureaucracies, and anything connected with them. Those things represented the other world, the road not taken, the domain of suits and yuppies. This shared philosophy, plus their mutual poverty, prompted them to rent the Cave together a year earlier. They might as well be broke and isolated together.

At times hurt and anger radiated from them like heat rising from Idaho blacktop in the sun. You could practically see the scars left by years of rejection and apartness. "I never went to one single high school party until graduation," Jesse told me once. "And if I'd been invited, I would've said yes, then not showed up. . . . I had that mutual inclination toward nerdiness." If Eric sometimes seemed to see this as his fate, a part of Jesse never quite accepted it.

Living with his divorced mom and two sisters in one Montana town or another, sometimes in dire poverty, Jesse always felt like an outcast. He grew up very much apart from the jocks who dominated the schools, the towns, his world. Sometimes his reading was to blame, sometimes his ponytail, sometimes his aversion to sports.

"He wasn't popular. He didn't have a lot of friends," his mother, Angela Dailey, recognized. "He was out cruising the cosmos with Stephen Hawking while the other kids were playing."

Despite the name of the club that so shaped them, there was nothing nerdy about Jesse or Eric. Both were tough, smart, resilient, and independent. In fact, before the Geek Club, Jesse had some ugly bouts with gangs and drugs, and several run-ins with local cops.

From the time he entered middle school, though, Jesse had also always had a computer—first a hand-me-down from someone he could no longer recall, then one left behind by his mother's departing boyfriend—and through them, his own portable and growing cyber-community. Perhaps he didn't really need the world of high school games and dances and crowds. He was too busy taking part in the creation of his own.

White, working-class kids are as invisible in media and politics as the poorest toddlers in the worst slums. They're nobody's children, really, nobody's constituency. Politicians don't worry about them and interest groups don't lobby for them. Thrown mostly on their own by divorce (four already among Jesse and Eric's families, with more possible) and by financial precariousness, Jesse and Eric knew the score: When you're out of high school, you're on your own. If you want more education, you work to pay for it. You find your own career track, or don't.

"For most of my friends, life is liquor, drugs, and bad jobs with no hope of escape," Jesse had told me. "That's what I grew up seeing. It's just life here, for some kinds of people." When he ticked off the names of friends he grew up with, it was a litany of trouble: one was an alcoholic and divorced at 20, with a child and no job. Another, unemployed, was perpetually blasted on drugs. One lived from party to weekend party; he was in a beery stupor much of the time in between. They all worked at bottom-rung jobs in "big-box" superstores and fast-food franchises for $7 an hour.

For Jesse and Eric, therefore, getting out of Idaho was less a lifestyle choice than a matter of survival. There was no net beneath these kids, only the Net. It had guided much of their lives—how they thought, what they did, what kind of a future they could have. It was the only thing they trusted absolutely and relied on continuously. So far, it was one of the few things that had never really failed them. "The Net isn't work and it isn't play," Jesse explained. "It's work *and* play."

Not surprisingly, both harbored smoldering class resentment at people whose parents bought them computers and $100 pairs of Timberlands and unquestioningly paid for their college expenses. Unhappiness and suffering builds character, Jesse told himself—and me—again and again, repeating one of his Nietzschean mantras. What doesn't kill you makes you stronger.

They'd learned to expect little from bosses and other authority figures, with the single and crucial exception of a teacher named Mike Brown, whom they both credited with having changed their lives.

Personal Investigations: Inquiry Projects

1. The Internet offers enormous potential for research. An ethnographer could focus on the culture of chat rooms, for example, or the use of e-mail in particular kinds of groups. "The Cave" takes a different

approach. Rather than observe the behavior of his subjects exclusively online, Katz chooses to exploit his journalistic skills by hanging out with subjects at their apartment, observing how they inhabit real, not just virtual, space. This seems to be a particularly revealing approach because we get at least a glimpse of the subjects' behavior in two worlds, not one. But how do these worlds overlap? Are they really so distinct? Katz's book might be a starting place for an investigation of those research questions. Where else might you take it?

2. Geeks are but one, though admittedly a quite large, subculture that inhabits the Internet. What other subcultures can you name? Are they worthy subjects for an ethnography project?

Craft and Conventions: Explaining and Evaluating

3. What do you infer is Katz's definition of "geeks" from reading this excerpt?

4. In several places, Katz makes interpretations or claims about what he is observing. Find a passage where he does this, and then evaluate the evidence he provides that seems to have led to this interpretation or claim. Is Katz convincing? Might there be other interpretations about Jesse or Eric that would be equally valid? On what basis would you argue that those other interpretations are more valid?

5. Strong ethnographies—and strong writing, for that matter—require an almost compulsive attention to detail. In this account, which details about "The Cave" or its occupants stand out? What makes a particular detail or observation more powerful than another?

Inquiries on Inquiry: Exploring and Reflecting

6. "The Cave," like Bob Greene's essay "Fifteen" that opened this chapter, are both general nonfiction pieces rather than academic ethnographies. How would you distinguish nonfiction essays and academic ethnographies? What are the advantages and disadvantages of an academic ethnography versus a creative nonfiction essay like "The Cave" or "Fifteen"?

7. Ethnographies, as you've gathered by now, challenge the idea that all research is objective. On the other hand, creative nonfiction, like Katz's piece, isn't held to that academic standard. Reflect on what you now see as the key questions regarding academic objectivity and research. What *is* objectivity? What seems like a responsible standard for a researcher in the humanities and social sciences?

8. Your own assumptions about "geeks," young men, and computer users might have affected how you read this essay. Explore those assumptions in a seven-minute fastwrite, describing the beliefs and experiences that influenced your interpretation, and then question them.

Snake Handling and Redemption
Dennis Covington

Whether you've attended a snake-handling religious service or only heard about them, you probably share writer David Covington's questions about the religious subculture that believes poisonous snakes are important to their faith. Covington himself has some connections to this subculture, and that means he takes a different stance than writers like Susan Orlean, Anne Campbell, and Jon Katz. While not a formal ethnography, this excerpt from his 1995 book, Salvation and Sand Mountain, *reflects ethnographic ways of inquiry: an immersion in a subculture in order to understand its values, beliefs, rituals, language, and behaviors.*

In this piece, Covington shares his experiences handling snakes in a church on Sand Mountain in Alabama. He goes to Sand Mountain to reconnect with his Southern roots, but along the way he encounters a conflict between spiritual ways of knowing and science. How do we explain the fact that snakes rarely bite their handlers during religious services? How does that compare with his own experience with snakes as a child and with scientific information about how dangerous and unpredictable they are? As you'll see, Covington has a personal stake in the research he's doing, and he chooses to experience a snake handling service as a part of his research. That experience presents another way to understand the "truth" about snakes, as well as the members of this subculture.

Before you read this excerpt, spend some time in your notebook fastwriting about the times in your own life when your experience with something conflicted with scientific knowledge. Think of moments, as well, when your spiritual beliefs conflicted with other kinds of knowledge. Then, fastwrite about the assumptions you have about snake handling in religious services. What do you know about them? What in your own upbringing influences your interpretations of these services?

As you read the essay, note the all the ways Covington tries to get at the "truth" about snakes. Note, as well, the places where reason seems to conflict

with spirituality. How does he resolve these conflicts? Does he? In what ways
does this excerpt seem like an ethnographic essay, and in what ways is it not?
How does Covington's personal experience affect the interpretations he has of
this group?

When I was a kid, the best snakes—the absolutely best snakes of all—
came from Ruffner Mountain, a foothill of the Appalachians that overlooked East Lake. It was just out of walking distance from my house. We
only tried walking it once. Other times, my father drove and dropped us
off. We said we were hiking to the fire tower at the top of the mountain,
but I always had my eyes peeled for snakes.

The first one I caught on Ruffner Mountain was a corn snake I saw
wrapped around the trunk of a pine tree. Docile and graceful, it had scarlet
blotches and an intricately patterned head, as surprising as if it were a piece
of Arabian carpet dangling in the Alabama woods. The corn snake ate mice,
but I couldn't bear to keep it long, even though my father made me a first-
rate snake cage with the power tools he'd bought after someone told him he
needed a hobby. I let that corn snake go one day in our neighbors' cauliflower field and always hoped that I would see it again. I never did.

My friend Bert Butts gave me my second Ruffner Mountain snake.
It was a speckled king, big and black, freshly shed, with yellow speckles
from head to tail, as though a paintbrush had been shaken lightly over it.
King snakes are famous for their placid dispositions. Like marine mam-
mals, they seem to wear a perpetual smile, and they happen to eat rattlesnakes. I named this king snake Kuebert Wood after a track star at a
local high school. He would sunbathe on my stomach. I swore I'd never
let him go. But then I caught a gigantic five-and-a-half-foot gray rat
snake—a record, I thought. I gave that snake the cage my father had
built and relegated Kuebert Wood to a number ten washtub with a
screen on top, held down by rocks. During the night, Kuebert escaped—
or, I prefer to think, wandered off. I have hated the memory of that rat
snake ever since.

A final gift came from a friend named Galen Bailey, who lived closer
to the mountain than I did. This snake was very delicate and rare, a scarlet
snake, with alternating rings of red, black, and yellow. Except for the broken rings and the order of the colors, it looked exactly like a coral snake:
quite perfect, but it wouldn't eat. I kept it longer than I should have, because of its beauty. I hope it survived after I released it in the cauliflower
field. With snakes, you never know.

The poisonous snakes came later, when I was an adult. I have caught
only three, and I did not keep any of them overnight. The first was a
pygmy rattlesnake I found sunning on a grave in a cemetery in southwest
Louisiana, where I was stationed while in the Army in the early seventies.

The pygmy is a small, stout species, rarely over two feet in length. It is ill-tempered and can deliver a painful bite. Its venom is as powerful as that of larger rattlesnakes, but since less venom is injected at a time, the bites of pygmy rattlers are rarely life threatening.

This particular snake looked plenty dangerous to me, though. I was hung over. My first wife Susan and I had taken a Sunday drive to visit old cemeteries. It was springtime, and tarantulas were crossing the road in droves. When I saw the pygmy rattlesnake on the grave, it seemed to be a sign: I had to conquer my fear of it. My heart beat faster. My palms ached. I found a stick, pinned the snake behind the head, and picked it up. Susan was horrified when I told her what it was. She'd hunted nonpoisonous snakes with me, but this was a little much.

The problem, I discovered, was not in catching the snake, but in releasing it. How do you let a rattlesnake go without risking a bite? I wound up taking the steps in nearly reverse order: putting it on the ground, pinning it with the stick, and only then releasing my grip. It worked. I had accomplished something.

The second poisonous snake I found was a copperhead, the last of the summer, stretched out on a road on Red Mountain in Birmingham. I was married to Vicki by then and teaching at the university. Again I was hung over. I brought the snake home, stretched between my hands, and told Vicki to find an empty ice chest to put it in. She, too, was horrified, but she drove with me into the country to let it go away from houses. I wrote a short story that talked about the way it looked coming out of the ice chest and disappearing into the dark woods.

In the years following, I sobered up. We had our girls and built a house in the woods on the side of Sand Mountain. The last poisonous snake I caught was a canebrake rattlesnake crossing the pavement at the bottom of our driveway. I brought it up to the house so the girls could get a good look and know what kind of snake to avoid. Then I said I was going to let it go in the woods—but I killed it instead. I do not believe it is necessary for a man to allow a poisonous snake to cross his property while his children are young. The canebrake snake is the only snake I have ever killed like that. It still bothers me some.

Around eight thousand people in the United States are bitten each year by poisonous snakes, but only a dozen or so die. There are two families of poisonous snakes in this country, both of them native to our part of the South. The first, Elapidae, which includes cobras, mambas, and other deadly Old World snakes, is represented in the New World by Eastern and Western coral snakes—shy, beautiful, and extremely dangerous. Their venom is a neurotoxin which attacks the central nervous system, particularly such autonomic functions as breathing and heartbeat. Fortunately, coral snakes are reclusive by nature. They seldom bite, and when they do, their small mouth and fixed fangs make it difficult for them to successfully latch on to humans.

The second family of poisonous snakes, the Crotalidae, contains the pit vipers—rattlesnakes, copperheads, and cottonmouths. The pits for which these snakes are named are infrared heat sensing organs which lie between the nostrils and eyes. With them, the snakes hunt their warm-blooded prey by seeking out body heat. The pit vipers are efficient killers with large, flexible mouths, big retractable fangs, and venom that attacks and destroys cell tissue. Victims die of internal hemorrhaging, cardiovascular shock, or kidney and respiratory failure.

The least dangerous of the pit vipers to humans is the copperhead, although its bite can kill children. The *most* dangerous is the Eastern diamondback rattlesnake, which can grow to a length of eight feet and has a combative temperament and a large reservoir of venom. Somewhere in between lies the timber rattler, often called the canebrake in our part of the country. Herpetologists disagree about whether the canebrake is a color variation or a distinct subspecies. The timber rattler is often seen in serpent-handling churches, because it is the poisonous snake most readily available on the rocky hillsides and grassy valleys of the Appalachians. It shares its range with the copperhead but appears to me more sociable, often found in large numbers in dens or burrows. The timber is somewhat smaller and less aggressive than the diamondback, but it is still a dangerous snake, unpredictable and with venom that can easily kill an adult.

The timber rattler is also, to me, the loveliest of the rattlesnakes, varying in color from pink to straw to nearly uniform black, with sharp, dark chevrons on its back. Its neck is narrow, and its head is as finely defined as an arrow. Oftentimes the tail is velvety in appearance; in such cases, the handlers will call the snake a "satinback." Encountered in the wild, a large timber rattler, *Crotalus horridus,* is an impressive and frightening sight. When cornered, it rattles energetically and coils to strike. But its first impulse is to flee, and perhaps that too is a source of its beauty: a dangerous animal, exquisitely made, turning away from a fight.

In captivity, timber rattlers can live up to thirty years. Their tenure among the handlers is much shorter, rarely exceeding a season. I have seen timber rattlers die while being handled; they are not made to be jerked around. On the other hand, some of the snakes are well cared for, and simply released back into the wild after a few months. Handlers are always in search of new snakes, always trading specimens back and forth. It appears to be a ritual after services for handlers to give snakes to one another, like an offering of brandy or after-dinner mints or hand-rolled cigars in other circles. Some of the handlers regularly catch their own snakes, most of the time in the conventional ways, with a snake stick and a burlap bag or pillowcase. Others buy snakes from professional exhibitors at prices the handlers complain are getting more outrageous every year, as much as forty-five dollars at last reckoning.

However the snakes are obtained, they often become objects of affection in the homes of the handlers and their families. The first rattlesnake that Charles McGlocklin's wife Alice took up, for instance, was called Old Crooked Neck, because of the injury it had received during capture. The big copperhead in the terrarium on the McGlocklins' kitchen counter used to be called Mr. Hog, Charles said, until it had eight babies and they had to start calling it Miss Piggy instead. But no amount of affection or care can ensure that a rattlesnake or copperhead won't bite when handled. They do not tame in a conventional sense. No one can predict what will happen when a handler reaches into the serpent box. And contrary to popular misconception, multiple bites do not result in immunity to snake venom, but may even increase the risk of death because of allergic reaction.

I came to know snake handlers in February of 1992, when I covered the trial of Reverend Glenn Summerford for *The New York Times*. Summerford, the pastor of The Church of Jesus with Signs Following in Scottsboro, Alabama, was convicted and sentenced to ninety-nine years in prison for attempting to murder his wife Darlene with rattlesnakes. The trial had echoed themes from a troubled secular society   marital infidelity, spousal abuse, and alcoholism—but it also raised questions about faith, forgiveness, redemption, and of course, snakes. The Church of Jesus with Signs Following, a converted service station on Wood's Cove Road, seemed to me to be the emblem of a submerged and disappearing population. I wasn't content just to report the outcome of its preacher's trial. I had to find out more about the handlers themselves—who they were and why they did what they did.

After Summerford's conviction, his church in Scottsboro split. Some members of the congregation began meeting outdoors on top of Sand Mountain. They invited me to worship with them, and we entered that unspoken conspiracy between journalist and subject. The handlers had something they wanted to show me, and I was willing to be shown. I went to scores of services in Alabama, Georgia, Tennessee, Kentucky, and West Virginia. I wanted something more than a story, but I didn't know exactly what it was.

The handlers eventually taught me there were two kinds of handling, one done as a simple demonstration of faith and the other as the result of a specific anointing by the Holy Ghost. During an anointing, the Holy Ghost would descend on them, they said, and give them power to take up serpents without fear. They described this altered state as "joy unspeakable. . . perfect love." I handled a rattlesnake myself once in Georgia on faith, but I did not experience an anointing until the summer of 1993.

That spring, Charles McGlocklin told me that Glenn Summerford's cousins, Billy and Jimmy, had started a new church on top of Sand Mountain, near a place called Macedonia. Charles didn't worship with them, though.

"Why not?" I asked.

Brother Charles was a big man with hands the size of waffle irons. He took a deep breath and surveyed the land around him, yellow and gray in the afternoon light. We were on the deck behind his and Aline's trailer in New Hope, Alabama. Beside the trailer was a doghouse for their bluetick hound named Smokey, and behind it was a corral for their horse, a buckskin mare named Dixie Honeydew.

"I know enough about some of those people to know I ought not to worship anymore with them," Charles said. As a snake handler, he had set himself apart from the world, and sometimes he even set himself apart from other snake handlers. It was part of the Southern character, I thought, to be always turning away like that toward some secret part of oneself.

"You know how much I love you," Charles said. He put one of his big hands on my shoulder and shook it. "You're my brother. But anytime you go up there on Sand Mountain, you be careful."

We could hear the sound of the wind through trees, a soughing, dry and hesitant, and then Dixie Honeydew neighed.

"You might be anointed when you take up a serpent." Charles continued, "but if there's a witchcraft spirit in the church, it could zap your anointing and you'd be left cold turkey with a serpent in your hand and the spirit of God gone off of you. That's when you'll get bit."

We walked around the corner of the trailer, where photographer and friend Jim Neel was waiting for me in his pickup truck.

"So you really watch and remember what Brother Charles tells you," Charles whispered. "Always be careful who you take a rattlesnake from."

This sounded like solid advice.

I got into Jim's truck, and Charles motioned for us to roll a window down. "Y'all come back any time," he yelled.

So my journey had come back around to the congregation on Sand Mountain, the remnant of Glenn Summerford's flock that had left the converted service station on Wood's Cove Road in Scottsboro and then met under a brush arbor in back of J. L. Dyal's house until the weather got too cold. After worshiping for a while in the basement of an old motel, they finally found a church for sale on the mountain. It was miles from nowhere, in the middle of a hay field south of Section, Alabama—home of Tammy Little, Miss Alabama of 1984. The nearest dot on the map, though, was Macedonia, a crossroads consisting of a filling station, a country store, and a junk emporium. It was not the kind of place you'd visit of your own accord. You'd have to be led there. In fact, Macedonia had gotten its name from the place in the Bible that Paul had been called to go to in a dream. Paul's first European converts to Christianity had been in Macedonia. But that was, you know, a long time ago and in another place.

Glenn's cousins negotiated the deal for the church. Billy was friendly and loose-limbed, with a narrow red face and buck teeth. He'd worked mostly as a carpenter, but he'd also sold coon dogs. Jimmy was less amiable and more compact. Between them, they must have been persuasive. They got the church for $2,000. A guy down the road had offered $5,000, Billy said, but the owner had decided to sell it to them. "God was working in that one," he concluded.

It was called the Old Rock House Holiness Church in spite of the fact that it wasn't made of rock. But it was old in contrast to the brick veneer churches out on Highway 35, the ones with green indoor/outdoor carpet in the vestibules and blinking U-Haul It signs out front.

The Old Rock House Holiness Church had been built in 1916, a few years before Dozier Edmonds first saw people take up serpents in Jackson County at a church in Sauty Bottom, down by Saltpeter Cave. I'd met Dozier during the brush arbor meetings, outdoor revivals held under temporary shelters framed with timbers and topped with brush. A rail-thin old man with thick glasses and overalls, Dozier was the father-in-law of J. L. Dyal and the husband of Burma, the snake handling twin. (Burma's sister, Erma, was always in attendance at the services, but didn't handle serpents herself.) Dozier said he'd seen men get bit in that church in Sauty Bottom more than seventy years ago. They didn't go to a doctor, just swelled up a little bit. He also remembered a Holiness boy at the nearby one-room school who would fall into a trance, reach into the pot-bellied stove, and get himself a whole handful of hot coals. The teacher would have to tell the boy to put them back.

There was also a Baptist church in that area called Hell's Half Acre, Dozier said. They didn't take up serpents, but they'd do just about anything else. They were called Buckeye Baptists. They'd preach and pray till midnight, then gamble and fight till dawn. One time a man rode a horse into the church, right up to the pulpit. Out of meanness, Dozier said. Everything was different then. "They used to tie the mules up to a white mulberry bush in the square," he said. Why, he remembered when Scottsboro itself was nothing but a mudhole. When the carnival came through, the elephants were up to their bellies in mud. There wasn't even a road up Sand Mountain until Dozier helped build one.

Dozier came from a family of sharecroppers who lived on the property of a Confederate veteran, Colonel Mance, who had a bullet hole through his neck. He'd built his own casket. Every Easter, Colonel Mance invited the children of the families who lived on his property to come to the big house for an egg hunt. One Easter, he wanted the children to see what he'd look like when he was dead, so he lay down in the casket and made the children march around it. Some of the grown-ups had to help get him out. "It was a pine casket with metal handles on it," Dozier said. Colonel Mance eventually died, but he wasn't buried in the casket he'd made. He'd taken it apart years before and given the handles to the families who lived on his property, to use as knockers on the doors of their shacks.

That was the kind of place Sand Mountain had been when the Old Rock House Holiness Church was in its heyday. By the time the Summerford brothers bought in the winter of 1993, it had fallen onto hard times. It didn't even have a back door. Paper wasps had built nests in the eaves. The green shingles on the outside were cracked, and the paint on the window frames had just about peeled off. Billy Summerford and some of the other men from the congregation repaired and restored the church as best they could. It'd be another year, though, before they could get around to putting in a bathroom. In the meantime, there would be an outhouse for the women and a bunch of trees for the men. The church happened to be sited in the very center of a grove of old oaks. Fields of hay surrounded the grove and stretched to the horizon. As you approached the church along a dirt road during summer heat, the oak grove looked like a dark island in the middle of a shimmering sea of gold and green.

That's the way it looked to me, anyway, on a bright Sunday morning in late June, six months after the Summerfords had bought the church, when Jim Neel and I left the McGlocklins' place and drove up for the first annual homecoming. Brother Carl Porter from Georgia had invited us by phone and given us directions; he was scheduled to preach at the homecoming. Other handlers were coming from all over—from east Tennessee and south Georgia, from the mountains of Kentucky and the scrublands of the Florida panhandle. If we hadn't had Carl's directions, we'd never have found the place, though. The right turn off the paved road from Macedonia was unmarked, one of several gravel roads that angled off into the distance. Where it crossed another paved road there finally was a sign, made of cardboard and mounted at waist level on a wooden stake. After that, the gravel turned to dirt. Dust coated the jimsonweed. The passionflowers were in bloom, and the blackberries had begun to ripen in the heat. There were no houses on this road, and no sound except for the cicadas' steady din, like approaching rain.

Jim and I were early. We stepped up on a cement block to get through the back doorway of the church. The door itself was off its hinges, and none of the windows in the church had screens. There were no bathrooms, no cushions on the pews, no ornaments of any kind except a portrait of Jesus etched into a mirror behind the pulpit and a vase of plastic flowers on the edge of the piano bench, where a boy with a withered hand sat staring at the keys. We took our places on a back pew and watched the handlers arrive. They greeted each other with the holy kiss, women with women, men with men, as prescribed by Paul in Romans 16. Among them was the legendary Punkin Brown, the evangelist who I'd been told would wipe the sweat off his brow with rattlesnakes. Jamie Coots from Kentucky and Allen Williams from Tennessee were also there; they sat beside Punkin on the deacons' bench. All three were young and heavyset, the sons of preachers, and childhood friends. Punkin and Jamie both wore scowls, as though they were waiting for somebody to cross their paths in an unhappy way. Allen Williams, though, looked serene. His father had died drinking strychnine in 1973, and his brother died of snake bite in 1991. Maybe he thought he didn't have anything more to lose. Or maybe he was just reconciled to losing everything he had. Within six months of sitting together on that deacons' bench at the Old Rock House Church, Jamie, Allen, and Punkin would all be bit.

The church continued to fill with familiar faces, many from what used to be The Church of Jesus with Signs Following (over in Scotts boro), and as is customary in spirit-led churches, the music began without an introduction of any kind. It sounded like a cross between Salva tion Army and acid rock: tambourines, an electric guitar, drums, cymbals, and voices that careened from one note to the next as though they were being sawn in half. James Hatfield of Old Straight Creek, a Trinitarian church on the mountain, was on drums. My red-haired friend Cecil Esslinder from Scottsboro was on guitar, grinning and tapping his feet. Cecil's wife Carolyn stood in the very middle of the congregation; as was her habit, she faced backwards to see who might come in the rear door. Also in the congregation were Bobbie Sue Thompson, the twins Burma and Erma, J. L. Dyal and his wife and in-laws, and just about the whole Summerford clan. The only ones missing were Charles and Aline McGlocklin. Charles was still recovering from neck surgery on an old injury, but I knew from the conversation we'd had in New Hope that even if he'd been well he wouldn't have come.

One woman I didn't recognize told me she was originally from Detroit. This came as some surprise, and her story seemed equally improbable. She said her husband used to work in the casinos in Las Vegas, and when he died she moved to Alabama and started handling rattlesnakes at the same church on Lookout Mountain where the lead singer of the group Alabama used to handle. "Didn't you see the photo?" she asked. "It was in *The National Enquirer*."

I told her I'd missed that one.

Children were racing down the aisles. With high foreheads, eyes far apart, and gaps between their front teeth, they all looked like miniature Glenn Summerfords. Maybe they were. He had at least seven children by his first wife, and all of them were old enough to have children of their own.

About that time, Brother Carl Porter walked in with a serpent box which would prove to contain the biggest rattlesnake I'd ever seen. Carl smelled of Old Spice and rattlesnake and something else underneath: a pleasant smell, like warm bread and cider. I associated it with the Holy Ghost. The handlers had told me that the Holy Ghost had a smell, a "sweet savor," and I had begun to think I could detect on people and in churches—even in staid, respectable churches like the one I went to in Birmingham. Anyway, that was what I smelled on Brother Carl that day as he talked about the snake in the box. "I just got him today," he said. "He's never been in church before." Carl looked over his glasses at me an smiled. He held the serpent box up to my face and tapped the screen until the snake started rattling good.

"Got your name on him," he said to me.

A shiver went up my spine, but I just shook my head and grinned.

"Come on up to the front," he said. I followed him and sat on the first pew next to J. L. Dyal, but I made a mental note to avoid Carl's eyes during the service and to stay away from that snake of his.

Billy Summerford's wife Joyce led the singing. She was a big woman with a voice that wouldn't quit. *Re-member how it felt, when you, walked out of the wilderness, walked out of the wilderness, walked out of the wilderness. Re-member how it felt, when you, walked out of the wilderness . . .* This was one of my favorite songs because it had multiple meanings now. There was the actual wilderness in the Old Testament that the Israelites were led out of, and there was the spiritual wilderness that was its referent, the condition of being lost. But there was also the wilderness that the New World became for my father's people, the Scotch-Irish immigrants who settled in the Appalachians. When I say wilderness, I don't mean the mountains, though. I mean the America that grew up around them, that tangled thicket of the heart.

Re-member how it felt, when you, walked out of the wilderness . . . My throat tightened as I sang and remembered how it had felt when I'd sobered up in 1983. It's not often you get a second chance at life like that. And I remembered the births of my girls, the children Vicki and I thought we'd never be able to have. Looking around at the familiar faces in the congregation, I figure they were thinking about their own wildernesses and how they'd been delivered out of them. I knew I was still coming out of mine. It was a measure of how far I'd come, that I'd be moved nearly to tears in a run-down Holiness church on Sand Mountain, but my restless and stubborn intellect was still intact. It didn't like what it saw—a crowd of men dancing up to the serpent boxes, unclasping the lids, and taking out the poisonous snakes. Reason told me it was too early in the service. The snakes hadn't been prayed over enough. There hadn't even been any preaching yet, just Billy Summerford screaming into a microphone while the music swirled around us like a fog. But the boys from Tennessee and Kentucky had been hungry to get into the boxes. Soon, Punkin Brown was shouting at his snake, a big black-phase timber rattler that he had draped around his neck. Allen Williams was offering up his copperhead like a sacrifice, hands outstretched. But Brother Carl had the prize, and everyone seemed to know it. It was a yellow-phase timber as big as they ever come. Carl glanced at me, but I wouldn't make eye contact with him. I turned away. I walked to the back of the church and took a long drink of water from the bright yellow cooler propped up against a portrait of Jesus with his head on fire.

"Who knows what this snake is thinking?" Carl shouted. "God knows! God understands the mind of this snake!" And when I turned back around, Carl had laid the snake down and was treading barefoot on it from tail to head, as though he were walking a tightrope. Still, the snake didn't bite. I had heard about this, but never seen it before. The passage was from Luke: *Behold, I give unto you the power to tread on serpents and scorpions, and over all the power of the enemy; and nothing shall by any means hurt you.* Then Carl picked the snake back up and draped it around his neck. The snake seemed to be looking for a way out of its predicament. Carl let it nuzzle into his shirt. Then the snake pulled back and cocked its head, as if in preparation to strike Carl's chest. Its head was as big as a child's hand.

"Help him, Jesus!" someone yelled above the din. Instead of striking, the snake started to climb Carl's sternum toward his collarbone. It went up the side of his neck but then lost interest and fell back against his chest.

The congregation was divided into two camps now, the men to the left with the snakes, the women to the right with each other. In front of Carl, one of the men suddenly began jumping straight up and down, as though he were on a pogo stick. Down the aisle he went and around the sanctuary. When he returned, he collapsed at Carl's feet. One of the Summerford brothers attended to him there by soaking a handkerchief with olive oil and dabbing it against the man's forehead until he sat up and yelled, "Thank God!"

In the meantime, in the corner where the women had gathered, Joyce Summerford's sister Donna was laboring in the spirit with a cataleptic friend. She circled the friend, eyeing her contortions carefully, and then, as if fitting her into an imaginary dress, she clothed her in the spirit with her hands: an invisible tuck here, an invisible pin there, making sure the spirit draped well over the flailing arms. It took her a while. Both of the women were drenched in sweat and stuttering in tongues by the time they finished.

"They say we've gone crazy!" Brother Carl shouted above the chaos. He was pacing in front of the pulpit, the enormous rattlesnake balanced now across his shoulder. "Well, they're right!" he cried. "I've gone crazy! I've gone Bible crazy! I've got the papers here to prove it!" And he waved his dogeared Bible in the air. "Some people say we're just a bunch of fanatics!"

"Amen. Thank God."

"Well, we are! *Hai-i-salemos-ah-cahn-ne-hi-yee!* Whew! That last one nearly took me out of here!"

It's not true that you become used to the noise and confusion of a snake-handling Holiness service. On the contrary, you become enmeshed in it. It is theater at its most intricate and improvisational—a spiritual jazz. The more you experience it, the more attentive you are to the shifts on the surface and in the dark shoals underneath. For every outward sign, there is a spiritual equivalent. When somebody falls to his knees, a specific problem presents itself, and the others know exactly what to do, whether it's oil for a healing, or a prayer cloth thrown over the shoulders, or a devil that needs to be cast out.

The best, of course, the simplest and cleanest, is when someone gets the Holy Ghost for the first time. The younger the worshiper, the easier it seems to be for the Holy Ghost to descend and speak—lips loosened, tongue flapping, eyes rolling backward in the head. When a thirteen-year-old girl gets the Holy Ghost, the moment transcends the erotic. The older ones often take time. I once saw an old man whose wife had gotten the Holy Ghost at a previous service. He wanted it bad for himself, he said. Brother Charles McGlocklin started praying with him before the service even started, and all through it, the man was in one attitude or another at the front of the church—now lying spread-eagle on the floor while a half-dozen men prayed over him and laid on hands, now up and running from one end of the sanctuary to the other, now twirling, now swooning, now collapsing once again on the floor with his eyes like those of a horse who smells smoke and with the unknown tongue spewing from his mouth. "He got the Holy Ghost at last! He got the Holy Ghost!" you think—until you see him after the service eating a pimento cheese sandwich downstairs. His legs are crossed. He's brushing the crumbs from his lap. He agrees it was a good service all right, but it sure would have been better if he'd only gotten the Holy Ghost.

Maybe he means you can never get enough of the Holy Ghost. You can never exhaust the power when the Spirit comes down, not even when you take up a snake, not even when you take up a dozen of them.

The more faith you expend, the more power is released. It's an inexhaustible, eternally renewable resource. It's the only power some of these people have.

The longer you witness such a service, unless you just aren't able to respond to the spontaneous and unexpected, the more you become a part of it. *I* did, and the handlers could tell. They knew before I did what was going to happen. They saw me angling in, and they were already making room for me in front of the deacons' bench. I'd always been drawn to danger. Alcohol. Psychedelics. War. If it made me feel good, I'd do it. I was always up for a little trip. I figured that if I could trust my guide, I'd be all right. I'd come back to earth in one piece. I wouldn't really lose my mind. That's what I thought, anyway. I couldn't be an astronaut, but there were other things I could do and be.

So I got up there in the middle of the handlers. J. L. Dyal, dark and wiry, was standing on my right; a clean-cut boy named Steve Frazier was on my left. Who would it be? Carl's eyes were saying, *You.* And yes, it was the big rattler, the one with my name on it, acrid-smelling, carnal, alive. And the look in Carl's eyes seemed to change as he approached me. He appeared embarrassed. The snake was all he had, his eyes seemed to say. But as low as it was, as repulsive, if I took it I'd be possessing the sacred. Nothing was required except obedience. Nothing had to be given up except my own will. This was the moment.

I didn't stop to think about it. I just gave in. I stepped forward and took the snake with both hands. Carl released it to me. I turned to face the congregation and lifted the rattlesnake up toward the light. It was moving like it wanted to get up even higher, to climb out of that church and into the air. And the experience was exactly as the handlers had told me. I felt no fear. The snake seemed to be an extension of myself. And suddenly there seemed to be nothing in the room but me and the snake. Everything else had disappeared. Carl, the congregation, Jim—all gone, all faded to white. I could not even hear the earsplitting music. The air was silent and still and filled with that strong, even light. And I realized that I, too, was fading into the white. I was losing myself by degrees, like the incredible shrinking man. The snake would be the last to go, and all I could see was the way its scales shimmered one last time in the light, and the way its head moved from side to side, searching for a way out. I knew then why the handlers took up serpents. There is power in the act of disappearing; there is victory in the loss of self. It must be close to our conception of paradise, what it's like before you're born or after you die.

I came back in stages, first with the recognition that the shouting I had begun to hear was coming from my own mouth. Then I realized I was holding a rattlesnake, and the church rushed back with all its clamor, heat, and smell. I remembered Carl and turned toward where I thought he might be. I lowered the snake to waist level. It was an enormous animal, heavy and firm. The scales on its side were as rough as calluses. I could feel its muscles rippling beneath the skin. I was aware it was not a part of me now and that I couldn't predict what it might do. I extended it toward Carl. He took it from me, stepped to the side, and gave it in turn to J. L.

"Jesus," J. L. said. "Oh, Jesus." His knees bent, his head went back. I knew it was happening to him, too.

Then I looked around and saw that I was in a semicircle of handlers by the deacons' bench. Most had returned their snakes to the boxes, but Billy Summerford, Glenn's bucktoothed cousin, still had one, and he offered it to me—a medium-sized canebrake that was rattling violently. I took the snake in one hand without thinking. It was smaller than the first, but angrier, I realized circumstances were different now. I couldn't seem to steer it away from my belt line. Fear had started to come back to me. I remembered with sudden clarity what Brother Charles had said about being careful who you took a snake from. I studied the canebrake as if I were seeing it for the first time and then gave it back to Billy. He passed it to Steve Frazier, the young man on my left. I watched Steve cradle it, curled and rattling furiously in his hands, and then I walked out the side door of the church and onto the steps, where Bobbie Sue Thompson was clutching her throat and leaning against the green shingles of the church.

"Jesus," she said. "Jesus, Jesus."

It was a sunny, fragrant day, with high-blown clouds. I looked into Bobbie Sue's face. Her eyes were wide and her mouth hooked at the corner. "Jesus," she said again.

I thought at first she was in terrible pain, but then I realized she wasn't. "Yes, I know, Jesus," said I.

It's hard for me to talk about myself. As a journalist, I've always tried to keep out of the story. Yet look what happened to me. I loved Brother Carl, but sometimes I suspected he was crazy. Sometimes I thought he was intent on getting himself, and maybe the rest of us, killed. Half the time I walked around saying to myself, "This thing is real! This thing is real!" The other half of the time, I walked around thinking that nothing was real, and that if there really was a God, we must have been part of a dream he was having, and when he woke up . . . *poof!* Either way, I worried I'd gone off the edge, and nobody would be able to pull me back.

One of my uncles by marriage was a Baptist minister, one of the kindest men I've ever known. I was fifteen, though, when he killed himself, and I didn't know the whole story. I just knew that he sent his family and friends a long, poignant, beautiful letter about how he was ready to go meet Abraham, Isaac, and Jacob. I believe he ran a high-voltage line from his basement to a ground floor bedroom. He put "How Great Thou Art" on the record player. Then he lay down on the bed, reached up, and grabbed the live wire. He left a widow and two sons. My uncle's death confirmed a suspicion of mine that madness and religion were a hair's breadth apart. My beliefs about the nature of God and man have changed over the years, but that one never has. Feeling after God is dangerous business. And Christianity without passion, danger, and mystery may not really be Christianity at all.

Personal Investigations: Inquiry Projects

1. Depending on your own experience with a religious organization, you may have wondered about the meaning of various rituals you've participated in, seen, or heard about. Make a list of the religious rituals you've only heard about. Then make a list of the rituals you've seen or participated in yourself. Choose one item from either list and fastwrite about it, exploring the questions you have, your beliefs about it, your understanding of its meaning. Do this for a couple more of the items on your list until you've found a ritual that raises a lot of questions for you.

   Then, do some searching in the library and on the Internet and see what you can find out about what that ritual means for the members of the particular religious community who perform it. At the same time, search for the scientific, rational explanations for the ritual. Try to explore what the ritual means within religious ways of knowing as well as within secular, rational ways of knowing. Your purpose here is not necessarily to decide which explanation of the ritual is true, but to explore the bases for the different ways of understanding what truth means.

2. Our culture has a lot of stereotypes for Southern culture, many of them less than flattering: Appalachians are sometimes called "hillbillies" or "rednecks," and participants in religious communities like the one in this story are often called Holy Rollers, and so on. In your notebook, make a list of all the words and images that come to mind about the events and the people in this essay. Then, fastwrite for five minutes about what all those terms mean. What do they imply about the people and the culture they are describing? Then fastwrite for another five minutes about why dominant culture might use these words to describe this particular group of people. What are these stereotypes based on? Where did they come from?

   For a research project, consider exploring the roots of these stereotypes. You could, for example, consult the rest of Covington's book, *Salvation on Sand Mountain.* You might also read *Into the Heart of Appalachia,* by John O'Brien, a book rich in history about Appalachia and how many Americans came to have so many misconceptions and prejudices about the region.

Craft and Conventions: Explaining and Evaluating

3. This essay is essentially broken up into three sections: first, a description of Covington's personal experiences with snakes; second, some historical and scientific information about snakes; and third, a narrative about his experience among snake handlers. Why might Covington have separated the essay into these sections? How would the essay be different if he wove the three together as Jillian Sim does in "My Secret History" (Chapter 4)?

4. Does Covington have an underlying research question that is guiding this essay? How might you phrase it? What conclusions do you think he comes to about it?

5. What are the key artifacts within this subculture, and what do they signify to the members of it? To Covington?

6. Covington must have done a lot of interviewing to be able to gather so much information. Look back over the essay and mark the places where you think he used an interview as a source. How does he transform the interview into a narrative with dialogue? How does he make that information come alive rather than simply stating it?

7. Covington has a difficult task in this essay: In a section we did not include here, he acknowledges his audience's possible misconceptions and prejudices about Southern culture. How does his writing reflect his awareness that his audience may find the ritual of snake handling outside the mainstream? How does he address those possible prejudices?

Inquiries on Inquiry: Exploring and Reflecting

8. In your notebook, make a list of all the sources of information Covington uses in his essay. Then, label three columns: first section, second section, and third section. Under those headings, jot some notes about what we learn about snakes from each section. In particular, look closely at the explanations various characters in the story have for why snakes will bite. (How do the snake handlers explain it? How do the scientists?) How do the sources of information Covington uses affect what he knows about snakes? What conclusions does he draw, implicitly or explicitly, about snakes in each section?

   As you look at the conclusions in each column, see if there are any contradictions. Do any of the sources of information he uses lead him to quite different truths about snakes and snake handling? If so, how does he resolve those conflicts? Or does he?

9. This essay is as much about Covington as it is about his fascination with snake handling. How does Covington seem to change as a result of his experiences? What does he understand about himself now, do you think, that he didn't understand before he went through the snake handling ceremony?

10. On pages 294 to 295, Covington says, "my restless and stubborn intellect was still intact. It didn't like what it saw—a crowd of men dancing up to the serpent boxes, unclasping the lids, and taking out the poisonous snakes. Reason told me it was too early in the service. The snakes hadn't been prayed over enough." In this passage we see reason conflicting with spirituality, with religious beliefs, with the unknown. How does Covington reconcile this conflict? What does this essay seem to say about the power of reason to explain religious beliefs?

11. Use Exercise 2.3 on page 24 to play the believing and doubting games with this essay. Explore, as well, your personal response to this piece. Try to articulate the beliefs and associations that you had before you read it, as well as the roots of those beliefs and assumptions. What do you understand now about this essay that you didn't before you used these approaches?

Subcultures, Pop Music, and Politics: Skinheads and "Nazi Rock" in England and Germany

Timothy S. Brown

When you hear the term "skinhead," what comes to mind? More than likely you don't think about particular kinds of music that are associated with this subculture, though you probably have a visual image of what "skinhead style" looks like. You may have even seen skinhead rallies somewhere in the United States and know in general what their central values are. You might be surprised, then, to read this academic article about skinhead subcultures in England and Germany. In it, historian Timothy Brown explains that skinheads originally defined themselves by a particular style of dress and an interest in music by black immigrants, particularly Jamaican reggae. How then did skinheads come to be associated with racism and white pride? That's one of the many questions Brown tries to answer.

Although Brown is not as immersed in skinhead culture as an anthropologist might be, he still analyzes this subculture by studying its rituals, behaviors, values, and language. We have excerpted a small portion of a much longer essay that shows how "Nazi rock" came to be in England and Germany, and it is important that you remember Brown is not talking about skinheads in the United States. For the purposes of this chapter, we decided to focus on Brown's analysis of skinhead style and dress. He explains the historical roots of the combat boots and cropped hair, for example, and what values they signify to the group. But he also illustrates that skinhead identity itself is not easy to define because it is in conflict: The original skinhead identity is in conflict with the groups that have embraced extreme right-wing politics in England and Germany. As you read this article, we hope you'll learn more about how to analyze the artifacts and behaviors of members in a subculture. Where does Brown move from describing the specific details of skinhead style to interpreting their meaning and significance to the subculture? What other sources of information does he use beyond his own observations of skinheads in these two countries? How does that information affect his interpretations of what he observes?

Right-wing extremist rock music—so-called "Nazi rock"—is one of the most problematic of popular musical genres. Emerging from the skinhead youth subculture in Britain at the end of the 1970s, and spreading to the continent and across the Atlantic in the following decade, it has served as accompaniment to a rising tide of racist and anti-immigrant violence in Germany, and become a focus of recruiting for the radical right worldwide. Yet as a generic category, "Nazi rock" is inherently unstable. A phenomenon that is at once artistic and political, it sits uneasily across analytical boundaries. The area of overlap between music genre and political content is, for one thing, far from complete. Right-wing extremist ideas are not strictly confined to skinhead rock music, but have found their way into a variety of other musical genres and youth subcultures.[1] The spread of Nazi rock beyond its original social boundaries—it is no longer simply "skinhead music"—means that the genre and the skinhead subculture are, if still intimately linked, by no means synonymous. Conversely, the various genres that make up "skinhead music" are by no means exclusively right-wing. Although Nazi rock arose out of the skinhead subculture, the subculture is—as will be seen—heavily divided about the meaning and value of the genre.[2]

The original skinhead movement of the late-1960s was a multicultural synthesis organized around fashion and music. The first skinheads were offshoots of the British "mod" subculture of the early 1960s. The mod was stylish, dedicated to cultivating the right look; upwardly mobile, very likely the son or daughter of a worker moving up into the white-collar realm of the bank or advertising firm. Above all, the mod was a music fan, obsessed with dancing to American soul music at all-night parties.[3] From the 1960s, the split implicit in the mod scene—between its working-class origins and its upper-class pretensions; between its subcultural subversiveness and its obvious appeal for boutique-owners and advertisers—began to widen. With the mod subculture swerving ever closer to the commodified, Carnaby-street hippie style of "swinging London," certain mods began to emphasize the more proletarian aspects of the look, cutting their hair shorter and replacing dandified suits and expensive shoes with jeans and heavy boots. These no-frills "hard mods" prefigured the arrival of the first skinheads.[4] Whereas appreciation for black culture—above all American soul music but also Jamaican ska—had stood at the center of the mod way of life, the skinheads took the connection a step further; their reference point was a local symbol of cool, young Jamaican immigrants who modeled themselves on the authority-defying "rude boy" of the Kingston ghettos. The clean, hard look of these transplanted "rude boys" fit nicely with the stripped-down elements of the hard mod style, and their evening wear echoed the earlier mod emphasis on expensive suits and nice shoes. But by far the most critical element in the symbiotic relationship between skinheads and black immigrants was music. Skinheads embraced the reggae music of Jamaican performers like Desmond Dekker as their own. Reggae artists and labels, in turn, actively courted the skinheads, producing songs and albums aimed at this young white audience. The resulting genre—"skinhead reggae"—fueled the rise of the skinhead subculture while jump-starting the careers of many Jamaican performers in Britain. The identity of the original skinhead was thus constructed in dialogue with black immigrants and organized around music created by black performers.[5]

The decline of the original skinhead subculture by the early 1970s, and its rebirth later in the decade under the influence of punk rock, opened the way for new influences. Not only did fresh musical genres arise around which skinhead identity could coalesce—above all so-called "street punk," or "Oi!" music—but, for reasons to be discussed below, right-wing politics became fashionable and were embraced by increasing numbers of skinheads. This politicization—which became prominent at the end of the 1970s and reached a peak in the early 1980s—produced a crisis of identity in the skinhead scene. A schism developed between—on the one hand—right-wing skins ambivalent toward, or dismissive of, the subculture's black roots, and—on the other—left-wing or "unpolitical" skins who upheld these roots as being central to skinhead identity. The conflict between the two sides in this debate became a struggle to define the essence of the subculture, a fight over *authenticity*.[6] . . .

A second site in the struggle over authenticity was personal style. The original skinhead subculture was created out of distinctive elements of clothing organized around the cropped hair: Tight Levi's jeans or StaPrest pants, Ben Sherman button-down and Fred Perry tennis shirts, work boots, suspenders (braces), and Levi's or Harrington jackets. Suits modeled on those of the Jamaican rude boys were often worn in the evening, but day or night, the skinhead look was hard, masculine, and working-class. With his boots, sturdy clothing, and cropped hair, the skinhead became, in the words of Phil Cohen, a "caricature of the model worker."[7] Like the "right" music, the "right" clothing signified taste and authenticity. But as new influences crept into the skinhead subculture during the revival of the late-1970s, style, like music, became a source of conflict as well as unity. In order to match the shock value of punk, these second-generation skins—many of them themselves ex-punks—took the style to new extremes, emphasizing the threatening aspects of the look at the expense of the sharp stylishness prized by the original skins. Boots became taller, military surplus MA-1 jackets replaced earlier more "civilian" looks, tattoos—previously confined to the arms or torso—began to crop up above the neckline, and hair became shorter to the point of baldness. These changes in style mirrored, to an extent, changes in the content of the subculture, with the more extreme looks coming to signify affiliation with the radical right.[8]

Reacting against this trend—which they considered a bastardization of the original skinhead style—numbers of skins began to stress the cultivation of the "original" look, making fashion, like music, a litmus test for authenticity. Violators of the proper codes were not skinheads, but "bald punks," a category to which racists—who, in the eyes of purists, failed completely to understand what the subculture was about—were likely to belong. The connection between right-wing politics and "inauthentic" modes of dress was personified in the figure of the "bone head," a glue-sniffing, bald-headed supporter of the extreme right, sporting facial tattoos, a union-jack T-shirt, and "the highest boots possible."[9] Although the emphasis on correct style was not explicitly political, it grew—like insistence on the subculture's black musical roots—out of a concern with the authentic sources of skinhead identity. As such, it was heavily associated with the attempts of left-wing and so-called "unpolitical" skins to "take back" the subculture from the radical right in the early 1980s.

Hard-and-fast political divisions were, however, never fully encoded in style; outward appearance never corresponded 100% to political viewpoint. To understand why, it is necessary to think about the factors around which the cohesion of the subculture was based. Queried about what belonging to the subculture means to them, skinheads inevitably cite things like drinking, hanging out with their friends, and—more ominously— "aggro" (violence). Less frequently cited, because so obvious, is the fact that they like the skinhead "look;" that is, they choose to belong to a community organized around a shared personal style. The style is, to be sure, connected with meaning(s). During the original wave of the late-1960s, the short hair of the skinhead represented a working-class reaction against changes in class and gender roles, especially the feminization of men represented by the hippie movement. The adoption of traditionally proletarian clothing, attitudes, and behaviors, at precisely the moment when these were beginning to disappear, was, according to Dick Hebdige, "a symbolic recovery of working class identity" that sought to preserve the boundaries of class through culture.[10] This maneuver was a type of resistance: Against the "coming man" of the late-1960s—the middle-class, peace-loving, long-haired student—the skinhead—short-haired, violent, and working-class—became the rebel *par excellence*.

But whatever the semiotic content of the skinhead "look"—and however subjectively important notions of skinhead as "a way of life" may be to its adherents—being a skinhead is, at the most basic level, a matter of adopting a certain outward appearance. The author of a work on gay skinheads, noting the irony represented by the presence of significance numbers of homosexuals in a scene based on an image of traditional masculinity, and citing the appropriation of the skinhead look as another in a series of urban gay stereotypes—i.e. a uniform for "clubbing" rather than part of a "way of life"—argues that being a "real" skinhead was, in the final analysis, little more than a matter of "looking the part."[11] While this view is, I believe, mistaken gender is, after all, only one element in the skinhead's system of meaning, and the complex relationship among music, politics, and notions of "authentic identity" in the skinhead subculture suggest that much more than fashion is at work—it brings up an important point: skinhead is, above all else, a *style community*. That is to say, it is a community in which the *primary* site of identity is personal style. . . .

A Style of Politics or a Politics of Style? The Struggle over Skinhead Identity

The increasing role of skinheads in violence against immigrants makes them a sought-after constituency for right-wing extremist parties in Germany. Yet the origins of the skinhead phenomenon in a youth subculture organized around fashion and music makes such recruitment problematic, and not just because it is inherently difficult to bind disaffected and frequently alcohol-besotted young men into a disciplined regimen of rallies and demonstrations. Youth subcultures—organized as they are around an internal logic that reconfigures select commodities or elements of style into symbolic weapons against the dominant society—are inherently unstable; the meaning of the elements that signify membership are, as we have seen, open to interpretation.

This is particularly true of the skinhead subculture, and in order to understand why it is useful to think about one of the key concepts that has been used to explore how the various elements of subcultural identity fit together, that of *homology*. A subculture is homologous when all the elements of identity—music, fashion, drugs, politics—combine to form a unified whole. The classic homologous subculture is the hippie movement of the 1960s and '70s. Here, everything—drug use ("dropping out" of society in the search for altered states of consciousness and corresponding new modes of relating to the world), clothing (favoring relaxed standards of personal appearance as an antidote to the business "uniforms" of the capitalist "rat-race," and exhibiting a preference for natural fabrics as a rejection of the perceived artificiality of industrial society), and hair length (signaling, again, the identification with nature and "the natural")—expressed and reinforced the hippie world view. The history of youth subcultures can, to an extent, be interpreted as the history of the search for homology. The skinhead subculture, like the others, tends in the direction of homology: the short hair and sturdy clothing portray an image of proletarian manliness which expresses and reinforces an exaggerated conservatism of outlook; the practice of violence is an exaggerated "proletarian" response to the presence of the Other; the chief drug—alcohol—is a perfect fit with the "traditional" mores supposedly expressed by the subculture. Yet, the homological fit at the level of world-view is partial at best. The skinhead "look"—unlike, say, the hippie look—is open to more than one meaning. There is, as noted earlier, a rudimentary kind of politics encoded in the skinhead style; but the governing conceit of the skinhead "style community" is that to be a skinhead means to dress sharp, have fun, listen to good music, and go to parties. The introduction of right-wing politics into the style community—something that occurred, for reasons discussed above, to this particular youth subculture at a certain historic conjuncture—created a situation in which it was impossible for members to share an unproblematic identity, especially when a key focus of identity—music—expressed diametrically opposing points of view and assigned diametrically opposed meanings *to the same fetish items of identity*. It is, in other words, precisely the skinhead subculture's *inability* to be homologous that makes skinhead identity a site of conflict.[12]

It is then hardly surprising that the politicization of the subculture in a right-wing direction has not been achieved without resistance. Indeed, forces within the movement have sought to combat the subculture's association with the radical right, emphasizing, on the one hand, the movement's multicultural roots (with their implied anti-racism), and on the other, the supposed original purity and *authenticity* of skinhead style and taste (alleged to exist in a purely aesthetic realm outside of politics). These two potentially-contradictory impulses come together in the most central focus of efforts to take back skinhead identity from the extreme right, *Skinheads Against Racial Prejudice,* or S.H.A.R.P. Founded in New York City in 1986—the same year that *Skrewdriver* records began to be imported into the US—S.H.A.R.P. was brought to the UK by Roddy Moreno, owner of Oi! Records, and frontman for the Oi! band *The Oppressed,* after a trip to the States. It subsequently moved to Germany where it became a focus of attempts to re-site the skinhead subculture in a cultural, rather than political, space. The idea behind S.H.A.R.P. was quite simple: "S.H.A.R.P. skins" professed no political affiliation, they merely insisted that the original skinheads had not been racists, pointed out that appreciation for Jamaican culture had been central to the formation of skinhead identity, and argued that, therefore, no *true* skinhead could be a racist. In practice, Skinheads Against Racial Prejudice did come to fill a "left-wing" function, partly because racist skins accused S.H.A.R.P. skins of being leftists, and partly because S.H.A.R.P.'s policy of allowing non-skinheads to join meant that punks and anarchists—to the scorn of most skinheads—often joined S.H.A.R.P. as a means of fighting Nazis. S.H.A.R.P.'s refusal to embrace any politics—other than being anti-Nazi—meant that its battle to reclaim skinhead identity had to be based on culture. Thus the counter-offensive against the "Nazification" of the scene of which S.H.A.R.P. was the most vocal proponent was organized more around style than it was around politics. The reaction against right-wing extremism was as much a reaction against bad style as it was against bad politics; the two were seen to be, in a way, the same thing. This was a reflection of the nature of the skinhead subculture as a "style community." . . .

Endnotes

1. More than one genre of music has been infiltrated by right-wing and racist beliefs. The 1990s have seen the emergence of Nazi techno and Nazi folk to name just two. See the essays in Devin Burghardt, ed., *Soundtracks to the White Revolution. White Supremacist Assaults on Youth Subcultures* (Chicago, 1999).

2. Indeed, the Oi! genre is home to a number of self-consciously anti-racist and even socialist-leaning bands that place themselves in open opposition to racist and Nazi bands. See George Marshall, *Spirit of '69. A Skinhead Bible* (Dunoon, Scotland, 1991), 143.

3. See Dick Hebdige, "The Meaning of Mod," in Stuart Hall and Tony Jefferson, eds., *Resistance Through Rituals* (London, 1993), 87–96.

4. Dick Hebdige, *Subculture. The Meaning of Style* (London and New York, 1979), 55; Stanley Cohen, *Folk Devils and Moral Panics: Thirtieth Anniversary Edition* (New York, 2002).

5. See Hebdige, *Subculture,* chapters 3–4; Marshall, *Spirit of '69,* pp. 44–49. Roger Sabin has recently argued that the claims of the affinity between punks and skinheads and blacks in Britain have been overstated; Roger Sabin, " 'I Won't Let That Dago By': Rethinking Punk and Racism," in Roger Sabin, ed., *Punk Rock: So What? The Cultural Legacy of Punk* (London and New York, 1999), 199–218, 202. Jack Moore makes a similar but less nuanced argument in Jack Moore, *Skinheads Shaved for Battle: A Cultural History of American Skinheads* (Bowling Green, Ohio, 1993), 57.

6. Frank Cartledge has emphasized, with respect to punk rock, the highly contingent nature of "authenticity;" see Frank Cartledge, "'Distress to Impress?,' Local Punk Fashion and Commodity Exchange," in Sabin ed., *Punk Rock: So What?,* 143–153, 149.

7. Phil Cohen, "Subcultural Conflict and Working Class Community," *Working Papers in Subcultural Studies 2,* University of Birmingham: Centre for Cultural Studies (1972).

8. Marshall, *Spirit of '69,* 136.

9. See the caricature in Ibid., 142.

10. Hebdige, *Subculture,* 31.

11. Murray Healy, *Gay Skins: Class, Masculinity and Queer Appropriation* (London, 1996), 197. For a different reading of the gay-skinhead connection see Ashley Dawson, " 'Do Doc Martins Have a Special Smell?' Homocore, Skinhead Eroticism, and Queer Agency," in Kevin J. H. Dettmar and William Richey, *Reading Rock and Roll, Authenticity, Appropriation, Aesthetics* (New York, 1999), 125–143.

12. Originally introduced by Claude Levi-Strauss, the concept of homology was first applied with respect to youth subcultures by Paul Willis; Paul E. Willis, *Profane Culture* (London, 1978). See discussion of the concept's use in Hebdige, *Subculture,* 133–117.

Personal Investigations: Inquiry Projects

1. Many subcultures are defined by—or easily identified by—members' style of dress. Make a list in your notebook of groups in which a particular kind of attire and appearance mark one as an insider. Uniforms for private schools may come to mind. What about groups you observed in high school, such as Goths or skaters? Once you have several groups on your list, choose one and list all the features of that group's style. Then skip a few lines and fastwrite about what each feature suggests about

the group's beliefs and values. Why those clothes and not others? What does that style react against and/or imitate? Consider researching this group for your ethnography project.

2. The role of music in the development of skinhead culture is briefly referred to in this excerpt. You're probably familiar with how music has influenced other subcultures—like hip hop, the blues, jazz, early rock and roll. The counter-cultural movements of the 1960s and 1970s, for example, were closely connected to particular songwriters. In your notebook, brainstorm a list of the groups who seem to be formed around or defined by the music that they listen to, like punk rockers, moshers, and so on. Choose one group that you find most interesting and develop a research project where you study the importance of music to a particular subculture—to its history, its identity, its response to dominant culture, its values. You might use interviews as well as observation of the group, in addition to library and Internet research, to develop a full picture of this group and the relationship of the music that seems to be central to their sense of identity and/or purpose.

Craft and Conventions: Explaining and Evaluating

3. Reread the excerpt and mark the place where Brown reflects on or theorizes about skinhead style. In your journal, draw a line down the middle of the page. On the right side, list the theories or conclusions Brown asserts about skinhead style and culture. On the left, list the evidence he gives for his conclusions. Then, fastwrite about how persuasive you find Brown's conclusions given the evidence he provides. Does Brown draw on the same elements of culture (language, use of space, artifacts, behavior, rituals, values) as Anne Campbell or any of the other writers in this chapter do?

4. In your own words, explain the term "homology" (on page 306) and why it is significant to studying a subculture. First, fastwrite about what you think it means after reading the essay once. Then reread only the passages where Brown discusses it and quickly explain what you believe it means. Return to the passage as many times as you need before composing a brief paragraph of your understanding.

5. On page 305, Brown asserts, "Youth subcultures—organized as they are around an internal logic that reconfigures select commodities or elements of style into symbolic weapons against the dominant society—are inherently unstable; the meaning of the elements that signify membership are, as we have seen, open to interpretation." Fastwrite for seven minutes about what you understand this passage to mean. Use

the reading strategies we discussed in Chapter 2 to help you with this difficult passage. Once you feel you have a grasp on what Brown means, summarize the passage in your own words.

6. In what ways does this essay reflect academic ways of inquiring and academic forms of writing? To answer this question, make two columns in your notebook. On the right side list the academic features you see—features that *you* associate with academic writing and that we've discussed in Chapters 1 through 3. On the left side, copy passages from the essay that illustrate each feature and then discuss what you've found in small groups. If it helps, talk about the features in this essay that are more characteristic of the researched essays in Chapter 4. Then, come to consensus about how you would finish this statement (in specific terms): *Brown's essay is an example of academic research writing because _____.*

7. This essay is not officially an ethnography, but it uses ethnographic ways of seeing and interpreting a subculture. Given your understanding of ethnographic research from this chapter, what makes this essay ethnographic?

Inquiries on Inquiry: Exploring and Reflecting

8. Use Exercise 2.5 (page 28) as a guide for responding to this difficult essay. Which strategies in Exercise 2.5 helped the most? The least? What more do you need to know to understand this article?

9. Fastwrite about the beliefs and associations you brought to this essay about skinhead culture. How much did you know about skinheads in England and Germany? Were you familiar with the music mentioned in this piece? How did your personal background experience affect your of reading this essay? Your interpretation of it?

10. Tell the story of your reading experience with this essay: *When I first started, I thought _____. And then _____.*

11. This essay focuses on the conflicts within skinhead culture over what constitutes authentic skinhead identity. Group members don't agree on what is true or authentic. Why? What do you make of that? Should they all agree? Why or why not?

12. Did you find Brown's analysis convincing? Why or why not? Fastwrite your response using as much detail as possible. Then return to the essay and focus on one passage you find especially convincing (or not). Fastwrite again about *why* you find it believable or not.

Student Essay

Mary Kay: American Dream in a Bottle

Tammy Anderson

Pink Cadillacs, pendants, pink silk roses. These are some of the "artifacts" that hold meaning for the women who sell Mary Kay cosmetics. In the following essay, composition student Tammy Anderson describes her entry into this world as part of an assignment to study a local subculture. But to the women of Mary Kay, Tammy was a potential recruit. As she attempts to negotiate the awkward position of being both an ethnographer and a potential initiate, Tammy finds it hard to be objective. In fact, it's virtually impossible for an ethnographer to see her subjects impassively and without bias. But how, then, can we trust the researcher's findings?

As you read "Mary Kay: American Dream in a Bottle" give this some thought. Are Tammy's observations and interpretations credible? This seems a particularly important question to ask about research on the Mary Kay subculture, a group that seems particularly vulnerable to criticism. In this fascinating essay, Tammy participates in some of the key initiation rituals of the group, and reports that what she finds is an incredibly well-organized system that appeals to a very particular group of women. Artifacts abound to signal status, including the ultimate reward for compliance with the group's values and goals: a pink Cadillac. Tammy finds herself put off by all of this, but she works hard to document what she sees as an ethnographer.

Unlike some of the other pieces in this chapter, "Mary Kay: American Dream in a Bottle" is not a formal work of ethnographic research. In some ways, it reads like a personal essay. But as you read the piece, notice how the effort to see Mary Kay through the lens of culture shapes Tammy's observations and interpretations. Imagine other lenses that might be used to look at the same things. What else might you see?

Laura is driving down I-84 doing 80 miles an hour. She has just realized she forgot her make-up kit in Caldwell that she would need for a skin care class the next morning, and has turned around, angry that she will waste an hour going back for it. As she grumbles to herself, she sees a woman standing on the shoulder of the freeway beside a running car. Laura drives on, but then feels something prompting her to stop and offer assistance. At 80 miles an hour, she is well past the woman before she even makes up her mind to stop. In order to get to her, she backs up several hundred yards on the freeway during rush hour. Other drivers honk their disapproval as they fly past. The woman comes up to Laura's van and thanks her for stopping. She explains she'd stopped to remove something that was dragging from the outside of her car, and had accidentally locked the door when she got out. She had been out there for 30 minutes, watched hundreds of cars pass, including two state police cars and only Laura had stopped.

"Can I give you a ride somewhere?" Laura asks.

"I would really appreciate it if you could take me to get the other set of keys to my car," the woman answers. Laura is already resigned to losing an hour going back for her make-up kit, so she agrees to go the extra mile for this stranger.

"By the way, my name is Christine. Thanks again for stopping," she says as they wait to get back on the freeway.

"It's nice to meet you. I'm Laura," she replies.

Christine studies Laura very carefully, and after few minutes, asks, "Do you sell Mary Kay?" When Laura answers in the affirmative, Christine suddenly exclaims, "I am so tired of my make-up!"

As they drive on chatting, Laura smiles quietly to herself, unable to believe her good fortune. She knows she has a captive audience for at least the next hour, and she hadn't even brought up the subject of Mary Kay. The next morning at 7:30, Christine calls to say she wants to be a Mary Kay consultant too. Laura is not surprised. She has only been in the business two and a half months, but she already knows it is the best career in the world.

Mary Kay Cosmetics was founded on September 13, 1963, by Mary Kay Ash. She had already retired after a 25-year career as a professional saleswoman, but decided to start a company that would allow women to set their own hours, be their own bosses, and have better opportunities than they would find anywhere else in the work force, which seemed to be designed *by* men *for* men (Ash, *Mary* 4). The company was built on three cornerstones: the first is the "Go-Give Spirit" which is expressed as the consultants "cheerfully give of their time and experience without thought of what they might receive in return"; the second cornerstone is a common list of priorities, simply stated, "God first, family second, and career third"; the last foundational belief is that "seeds of greatness are planted within us all, and God expects each of us to bring them into fruition" (Ash, *Mary* 174).

Mary Kay had purchased the formulas for the homemade skincare products she had been using for many years. The products were developed first by a man who tanned hides for a living. He had become aware of the fact that his hands were more youthful than his face, and he assumed it was because his hands were always in the tanning solutions. He experimented on his own face, and was impressed by the result. After he died, his daughter continued to perfect his formulas, and began selling them out of her home, where Mary Kay became acquainted with them (Ash, *Mary* 24, 25).

In the early planning stages of what Mary Kay refers to as her "dream company," her husband was intimately involved, and planned to handle the administrative end of the business. One month before they were scheduled to open, Mary Kay's husband died of a heart attack while going over the company's percentages with her. Mary Kay wrote, "I believe that work is often the best antidote for grief. And despite my shock, I decided to open the business as planned" (Ash, *Mary* 4). This was the beginning of a cosmetic empire and Mary Kay's dream.

Women who become Mary Kay consultants are given the opportunity to make 50 percent of everything they sell. They also receive 10 to 15 percent of the sales of those they recruit. Today, their "national sales directors" make over $200,000 a year and are held up as an example of what every woman in Mary Kay can accomplish. For many women, this is an offer too good to refuse.

My first encounter with Mary Kay Cosmetics came in 1983 when I was a young mother with two small daughters and a husband who was constantly encouraging me to supplement his income. I was old-fashioned in my thinking, and believed my girls needed me at home; my husband thought they would be content with nicer clothes and new toys. My sister-in-law (who is always looking for an easy way to make money and still have time for more important things) invited me to a Mary Kay party at her home. I agreed, thinking I was simply going to have a facial, not realizing I would be offered a new and exciting career in the field of cosmetics. Though I was unaware of it, my lifestyle was considered perfectly suited to becoming a Mary Kay representative: I was a young mother, with low self-esteem, who needed money, and wanted to set my own hours.

I went to the facial feeling confident that I generally looked pretty nice. I didn't wear much make-up, but I always did my hair, and I thought that should be enough to please my husband. After all, I was only 22 years old, and looking back, I realize I really didn't need a lot of make-up. However, the consultant seemed slightly appalled by my casual attitude toward my looks, and I suddenly felt ashamed. I, too, wanted to feel good about myself; I wanted my husband to be proud of the wife he came home to everyday, and I knew I could only accomplish this with Mary Kay Cosmetics. I was very tempted to become a consultant then, but couldn't quite afford the start-up costs. I left that evening with $100 worth of products, which I used for six months before returning to my "over-the-counter" routine. My sister-in-law took out a $1500 loan and embarked on a new career that night, which would last a mere eight months when she decided she just wasn't pushy enough to make it in Mary Kay.

I crossed a threshold that evening: for the rest of my life, I would be prey to overzealous, relentlessly optimistic Mary Kay consultants, who were convinced they were doing me a great service by trying to recruit me to sell Mary Kay. To these women, life, outside of the confines of Mary Kay, is simply not worth the bother, but with my winning personality, and stunning good looks (courtesy of their product), I could be driving a pink Cadillac into a brand new life in no time at all. Unfortunately for these ambitious women, I never took the bait.

However, I recognized that the premise of the Mary Kay business was very cunning indeed. There are established rituals used first to draw women into the business, and then those used to keep them in it. These women go into the homes of their clients, and tailor the offer to the apparent needs in the woman's life. Does she have small children? If so, they emphasize flexible hours and minimal effort. Does she seem lonely? Then they might share about the familial atmosphere of their meetings and the new relationships they have made through the business. Is it apparent that money could be an issue? In this case, they are pleased to communicate how easy it is to earn a car, and to explain the amazing earning potential of the business. Is the woman unschooled in glamour or is she aging? This is when focusing on the wonderful cosmetic benefits, and the cost of the product becomes a wise move, because it is cheaper to use the product if you are also selling it. Addressing areas of vulnerability has been a key to the success of this corporation, and in some ways, this method delivers what it promises. Women do make money and friends, and also receive unique opportunities through Mary Kay.

Recently, I found myself a "Mary Kay target" once again when Sue, a woman from my church, approached me with an exciting new career opportunity. I inwardly cringed when she mentioned the words "Mary Kay." I realized a promising friendship had just ended, because I was no longer an acquaintance, I was a prospect. I would be forced to come up with somewhat dishonest excuses (in church, no less) just to avoid being dragged to another Mary Kay meeting. I was concerned I might offend her if I just said "no."

Yet, when I was assigned an essay on a subculture in our community, I began to think of my past experiences with Mary Kay, for it is an organization rich in rituals and artifacts. These women shared a deep belief in their product and in Mary Kay herself. At some of the early meetings I had attended, they even sang rousing melodies akin to high school spirit songs to help raise the gathering's momentum. They spoke a language of Mary Kay facials and achievements I could not quite understand, such as "business debuts," "perfect starts," "star consultants," and some sort of "adoption" of a consultant whose director was living out of town. They were cheerfully driven by one another, as well as by a deep desire to emulate Mary Kay Ash. The world of Mary Kay consultants seemed to be a worthwhile subject for my essay. I decided I would kill two birds with one stone. I would appease Sue by going to a meeting, and gather information for my paper at the same time.

I knew enough about Mary Kay to know I would encounter an air of excitement and almost unrealistic enthusiasm. Even as some very cunning figures in history were aware, enthusiasm is contagious and can actually be orchestrated. These meetings are designed to give the ladies a sense of belonging, to remind them they are part of a worldwide organization of women with the same love of God and family, and to motivate them to schedule more skin care classes and sell more products. I was also prepared for some high-pressure sales pitches that would seem deceptively low pressure, and might even be tempting for me. Though Mary Kay believes in discouraging "aggressive selling," and stressing skin care education (Ash, *Mary* 48), the underlying resolve is to enlist as many women as possible to increase sales and the emphasis in every Mary Kay activity is, in fact, recruiting. In the past, I had been offered an opportunity that was glamorous, extremely profitable, easy, and would provide me with new friends and lots of fun. I could travel and even fund our future retirement. This network of women represented an inviting trap for me, so I knew I would have to watch out or risk becoming one of them.

I arranged to go to a regular weekly meeting, and Sue was more than helpful. I wondered if this was part of the "Go-Give Spirit" I'd heard about, but I was uncomfortable because I knew inwardly that Sue was hoping to gain a new recruit in me. I sincerely hoped in this instance, according to the "Go-Give" philosophy, that Sue would get nothing in return.

I felt very conspicuous when I first arrived at the meeting; all the women turned to stare, wondering who I was, what I was doing there, and who had invited me. I found the highly motivational setting almost suffocating. There were performance charts all over the walls proclaiming the consultants' accomplishments and challenging them to even greater pursuits. There were also pictures of the much sought after "pink Cadillac," manufactured exclusively for Mary Kay Cosmetics, with the caption, "Drive the Dream." At front and center was a picture of the great Mary Kay Ash herself, and I was almost disappointed to see there was no altar beneath it, adorned with burning candles and flowers. Had I entered the world of a cult or secret sisterhood? I almost thought I had.

I observed the women in attendance, and saw that they were predominantly very excited, friendly and eager. They chatted and seemed to genuinely care for one another. Yet, no one could be so naturally cheerful; I wondered if any of them ever had a bad day, and resented the optimistic front they had to put on for these meetings. Still, I didn't hear one complaint, or sense even a hint of negativity. Mary Kay wrote of the importance of putting your own problems aside and not inflicting your problems on others, and she told of going to a national sales conference just days after her third husband, Mel Ash, died of lung cancer. She felt obligated to speak as scheduled at the conference, and even managed to "put on a happy face" (Ash, *Mary* 56), so her consultants have set before them a strong example of hiding disturbing emotions. I wondered if this approach to handling difficulty got in the way of developing open, honest relationships within these groups, and maybe even in other areas of life. Feeling out of place, and fearful that my own critical attitude might be apparent, I put on a smile and sat quietly in the back, determined to put my preconceived prejudices aside for a while.

As I continued to scrutinize the ladies, I began to feel I could tell those who had not been selling Mary Kay very long. They were a tad dowdy and less polished. In my experience, these were the very women Mary Kay targets: somewhat insecure, with lots of room for improvement. Many of these women had a wistful, lonely demeanor, and they seemed to look at the senior consultants with awe, wondering if they might actually have the same self-confidence and sense of camaraderie someday. They were in the early throes of joining a business, and seemed a little unsure of their ability to be successful; perhaps even wondering if they had gotten in over their heads. True Mary Kay consultants are absolutely convinced they have the best possible careers, and they honestly believe in the genius of Mary Kay Ash. Experienced consultants have been schooled in the great importance of good grooming and exhibiting their product in the best light possible. These new consultants were in the early stage of a process that, if successful, would transform them in many ways. Not only would their outward appearance change, but inwardly they would become almost oblivious to possible rejection. As new consultants, they will first be encouraged to offer the Mary Kay opportunity to all of their relatives and acquaintances because these people are less likely to turn them down. As they become more self-assured, they will then begin to eye every human encounter as an opportunity to recruit others to sell the product. Of course, until they recruit several members on their own sales teams, they won't realize how much money their efforts will bring to those above them on the Mary Kay echelon.

I turned my attention to the other women. They had impeccable faces, heavily made up with that unmistakable "Mary Kay look." These women had been in the business for quite some time. All of them wore nice dresses and skirts, and I would learn that this is something Mary Kay Ash insists upon, believing women should always present themselves in the most feminine, professional manner possible (Ash, *Mary* 109, 110). I have heard that in Mary Kay's home state of Texas, there is a saying that you can catch more flies with honey than vinegar, and this seems to apply to her philosophy of business. Women need to look their best because it gives them an advantage. She tends to disagree with the usual Southern Baptist view of women as merely subservient, and feels they can be just as successful as men without compromising their femininity.

The senior consultants wore red jackets adorned with all kinds of pendants; the jackets are a status symbol, and signify women who have recruited at least three to four members on their teams. I learned that each piece of jewelry also has special significance and tells of accomplishments and sales. One initiation rite included gold necklaces, given for fulfilling the entry-level goals of Mary Kay. These are then filled up one bead at a time for every class and minor goal achieved. The sales directors wore a rhinestone pin spelling out "DIQ," which stands for "director in qualification"; these women have chosen to move up in the ranks of leadership in Mary Kay and have several members on their teams. My friend, Sue, wore so many pendants I was unable to keep track of all their meanings.

The first order of business was to announce upcoming events. The list was so long, that it seemed to violate the principle of "God first, then family and finally, career" because attending even a few would take a tremendous amount of time on top of that already given to Mary Kay daily; I found the inconsistency disturbing. Next came the introduction of the guests, myself and one other woman. I explained my academic reason for attending, but had the feeling these women really believed I was there because I wanted to become a consultant. The speaker's eyes rested on the other guest and me so often, I was concerned we might not make it out until we had signed on the dotted line. I was once more reminded we were not just guests; we were fair game!

I was initially impressed by some of the speaker's words of encouragement and felt she had some original ways to motivate the women. However, when I later read some of Mary Kay Ash's books, I realized that the speaker and even some of the other women were only "parroting" the words of Mary Kay. They talked of the importance of helping women to feel better about themselves, and how Mary Kay could change a woman's destiny. Another important theme addressed dreams, goals, and ideas, as well as the privilege of being in charge of not only one's business but also one's life. Perhaps without even knowing it, they took her personal and business philosophies as their own; they certainly seemed to believe the words they spoke. Every word I heard that evening, whether formally or in private conversation, was first written by Mary Kay Ash.

My friend, Sue, began the long process of handing out that week's awards. Mary Kay believes in celebrating every accomplishment, no matter how small, because she feels a little encouragement goes a long way (Ash, *On* 19, 20). The newest consultants (the women I had already identified as new to Mary Kay) were called to the front for an interesting ritual: each one received a pink silk rose, signifying their new beginning and comparing them to rosebuds that will come into full bloom. One of these women gave her testimony and shared, almost tearfully, that she was receiving the recognition and encouragement she'd never known in any other endeavor. Several women shared their initial doubts about becoming consultants, but none of them mentioned the drawback that was foremost in my mind: I would hate to have other women wince when I call or approach them because of my association with the smiling, pushy world of Mary Kay Cosmetics. By ignoring this negative aspect, they are able to focus only on why they believe they made the right decision in joining the company; and sharing this with others serves to take them one step further into this exciting world, and makes it that much harder to back out. Backing out would mean an admission of failure in a field they are constantly told they can succeed in, and these fragile personalities certainly don't need another failure on their conscience. Mary Kay is a form of salvation to them, and they will do everything necessary to hold on to it.

The awards continued for everything from giving 15 facials in 14 days to one director in line to receive her first car. Most of the acknowledgements were in the form of jewelry, given to those who recruited others to sell Mary Kay. Laura, the consultant I mentioned earlier, was awarded a gold pendant called a "Pearl Enhancer" for sharing the "Mary Kay opportunity" with Christine in her van that day. The sales director, who was about to earn her red Grand Am, was given a scarf signifying this important achievement, and nicely complementing her red jacket. The scarf will tell other Mary Kay consultants at regional and national meetings of her accomplishment. When she finally receives her car, Mary Kay will make the lease payment, pay for the registration, personalized, success-oriented license plate (such as OPR2NTY or FUN2WIN) and up to 85 percent of the insurance. Each ritual here is used to draw the consultants deeper into the network, and each artifact received is to remind them of their successes and to entice them to go after more.

The Cadillacs were particularly intriguing to me as artifacts of this subculture. For many years these were the only Mary Kay cars I had seen, and though recent cars awarded on the lower echelon of the corporation now include the aforementioned red Grand Ams, and red Blazers, the pink Cadillacs are still the award that says "Mary Kay" all over. The shade of pink is used exclusively to package the company's cosmetics, and there is something about a big, fancy car that seems to fit well with Mary Kay's image of a self-made, wealthy, Southern woman. There are many other cars that Mary Kay could choose from today that might denote riding in the lap of luxury, but the Cadillac was the Lexus of her generation, and will probably remain the company's ultimate status symbol for many years to come.

After the awards, the other guest and I were taken to a room where we were given facials, showcasing Mary Kay's new spring colors. When we returned to the meeting room, the women's response left me wondering how hideous I had looked before Mary Kay worked her magic on me. Yet, the new colors I wore were strikingly similar to those I normally wear; there was actually little difference in my appearance. These women, however, were sales consultants to the core; their job was to make me feel good about my "new" look and to encourage me to buy their products. Their enthusiasm was painfully embarrassing and, I felt, unwarranted. In one last attempt to manipulate our desire to sign up as consultants, we were then given ribbons that read, "I am special," and the speaker presented us each with one red-velvet rose holding a pair of earrings. I was relieved to realize that the meeting was over and I quickly left, triumphant in the knowledge that I had once again escaped becoming a Mary Kay consultant.

As I drove home, I thought about the women I had met; it was apparent Mary Kay offered them something they couldn't find anywhere else. Mary Kay takes self-esteem, beauty, privately owned business, flexible hours, nice cars, unimaginable wealth, faith, marriage and family life, and puts them all in a lovely pink bottle. Yet this wonderful benefit package can only be obtained by selling it, one bottle at a time, to other women who need a dream.

Works Cited

Ash, Mary Kay. *Mary Kay.* 3rd ed. New York: Harper, 1994.
_____. *On People Management.* New York: Warner, 1984.

Discussion Questions

1. The opening anecdote of the essay tells the story of a Mary Kay salesperson named Laura rescuing another woman with car problems. This is a clever way to draw the reader into the essay, but leads must do more than that—they must at least hint as the writer's purpose and motives. Analyze the opening anecdote. What does it imply about what the essay is about? What does it suggest about the Mary Kay subculture?

2. Tammy Anderson acknowledges her own earlier involvement with Mary Kay, and it is these experiences that seem to shape her response to the group when she later studies it as an ethnographer. Is this a problem?

3. Can you imagine a different way of interpreting some of the things that Tammy observes?

4. Read Renato Rosaldo's essay in Chapter 5, "Grief and a Headhunter's Rage," along with this essay. Though on the surface they seem to be a very unlikely pairing, Rosaldo seems to speak to an issue raised by some of the previous questions: How should Tammy's previous experiences shape her response to Mary Kay?

5. Though Tammy only uses the word once in her essay, it isn't difficult to read the word "cult" into much of her account of Mary Kay. Is this fair? When does a subculture become a cult? What line needs to be crossed?

7

Fields of Writing: Making Sense of Formal Research

Jeremy: What's the dily yo?
Brian: Chillin like a villain. Hey, did I see you pushin up Lisa? You know I've been
peepin' her!
Jeremy: That skoochie? Slow yo roll, dude. I may be pimpin' but not with her. She's
tore up from da floor up. Bump that.
Brian: Oh. Sorry, man. I guess somebody was just in my lunch. I'm straight. I'm
gonna bounce this place.

> *Our translators explain that Brian was concerned because he heard*
> *that Jeremy was flirting with Lisa, a student he finds attractive. But*
> *while Jeremy has indeed dated many female students, he feels Lisa is*
> *not very pretty. Brian admits it was all just gossip anyway and says*
> *he's leaving.* *

Depending on how you look at it, the conversation between Brian and Jeremy is just plain goofy or richly revealing. Outsiders to such teen talk—and
that's most of us—tend to be put off when people talk to each other in a way
that seems deliberately exclusionary or obtuse.

However, as you know from Chapter 6, an ethnographer would see Brian
and Jeremy's dialogue as an intriguing example of "insider language," talk
that can be analyzed to reveal a culture's affinities, origins, and ideas about
itself. For example, a linguist commenting on the jargon of teens observed
that the culture is currently influenced by hip-hop music, and that adolescent
conversation, particularly in the white suburbs, is heavily laced with urban
street talk. (Interestingly, the appropriation of words and phrases seems to
work in only one direction—while suburban white kids seize on the language
of the inner city, African American teens seem uninterested in the language
of the suburbs.) That music is a major source of slang for American teenagers

---

*From Bill Briggs, "'What's the Dily Yo?' Send for a Translator." *Denver Post Online*. 25 April
2000: 6 pgs. 24 July 2000. <www.denverpost.com/life/lang0425.htm>.

suggests how the music industry's influence in the culture continues to be profound, but that influence is always changing as certain artists and musical movements command certain young audiences.

In other words, a researcher studying teen culture would read Brian and Jeremy's conversation quite differently than, say, the boys' parents—or quite possibly—you.

In this chapter we'd like you to try to read academic writing with an ethnographer's eyes. This won't be easy. After all, most of us are outsiders to the so-called *academic discourse* of the university, and our initial reaction when we encounter an academic article in a journal or book is sometimes to feel like Brian and Jeremy's parents likely do: confused, maybe even frustrated, and suspicious that somehow the writer is trying to hide something from us. Like American teenagers, academics have their own languages— phrases or words that may be a shorthand for something else that only others in a particular field would know—as well as certain *conventions* for writing about ideas, discoveries, studies, or experiments. That you don't know these languages or conventions makes sense—you're new to the neighborhood.

An Outsider at the Dog Show

The academic neighborhood isn't always friendly to a newcomer. In fact, it's a place that sometimes seems filled with fences rather than doors, where arguments abound, and where a great deal is assumed. What does this feel like? It's unsettling. "I don't understand what he means by the word *discourse*," one student complains. "Why all this mumbo jumbo?" Another complains that the assigned readings in an art history class are all "boring." A third wonders what one class has to do with another: "All of my professors want me to write my papers differently. Why can't they all agree?" When understanding comes it's a huge relief, but it's hard to avoid the sense that it's all a game, an academic game.

This might be easy to dismiss if the stakes weren't so high. You have a paper due and you want to do well on it. You have a plan for your life, and success in college is a key part of it. And besides, you've always liked learning new things; that's one of the main reasons you're in college in the first place.

If any of this sounds familiar, what you're experiencing is very similar to how an ethnographer feels at the dog show when she's a cat person. What may be different, however, is that the ethnographer thoroughly expects to begin as an outsider and has a method for quickly learning what she needs to know to overcome the cultural distance between herself and her study subjects. She pays attention to certain rituals and conventions—such as whether it's appropriate to talk with a trainer before she enters the show ring or pet the pooch before it performs—and she is careful to respect and, at times, use those conventions herself.

The university is hardly a dog show, and you may not be an ethnographer, but we can borrow that approach to study academic culture, focusing on one moment that often makes students feel most like outsiders: reading academic articles and essays. This is when students are most likely to complain that what they have to read is boring, that it uses jargon, or that it is hard to follow. Trying to read academic articles for a research project is, for many students, the closest thing to being dropped into a dog show and charged with making sense of what they see. But you don't have to feel stupid. You just have to learn the culture.

How? Look for the clues like an ethnographer would. The local dog show we went to recently, for example, was a pretty laid-back affair, but there were many conventions that were immediately apparent. In the ring, only the judge has the authority to speak, and much of what she communicates is through hand signals, gestures that were easily decoded by the handlers who ran or walked or posed their dogs on the judge's cues. The participating animals, in most cases, had bloodlines that could be traced to predecessors that earlier had established success (and authority) as competitors. The breeders and handlers frequently used these bloodlines as evidence of the championship potential of their dogs. While these casual ethnographic observations of a dog show don't seem to have much to do with decoding an academic article, there are many similarities. Our observations had to do with conventions such as who has authority and how it is established, as well as how information is communicated. Similar questions are crucial to understanding how to read a difficult journal article. For example,

- How and when does the author introduce the topic, question, or problem of interest?
- Does the author acknowledge, in some way, others who have already said something about this topic in other books and articles?
- What is the manner of presentation? Does certain information come first? Second? Last? What about the tone?
- What kinds of evidence are offered to support an opinion or claim? What does this suggest about that discipline's notions of the kinds of facts that suggest something is true?

CASE STUDY: DISSECTING ACADEMIC ARTICLES

To provide you with a glimpse at how an ethnographic reading of an academic articles might go, Michelle tells the story of her own research on a topic that most of us have at least thought about a little: Can a man or a woman simply be friends without romantic complications or sexual tension? To start with, we'd like you to do some of your own exploration of this question.

Exercise 7.1 *Can a Man and a Woman Just Be Friends?*

STEP 1: Begin with a focused fastwrite in your journal, using one or more of the following prompts. Write for seven to eight minutes, longer if the writing runs away with you.

- Think about a *friendship* you've had with someone of the opposite sex. Try to remember a particular moment or scene in which that friendship was tested, revealed its strength or weakness, or created some tension. Put yourself back in that moment and describe in detail what is happening. At the end of eight minutes, finish this sentence: *As I look back on this now, I realize that . . .*

- Begin with a list. For thirty seconds, brainstorm a list of assumptions people often make about male-female friendships. Choose one or more of these assumptions, and fastwrite about your own experience with it. Does it complicate, confirm, or challenge the assumption? Finish by composing a sentence or two that summarizes your own beliefs about cross-gender friendships.

STEP 2: After this exploratory writing, discuss in small groups or in the full class the kinds of perspectives, insights, or feelings that emerged in your journal. Generate a class list of these ideas, beliefs, or assumptions about friendships between two people of the opposite sex. What are the most common? What questions do these assumptions and beliefs raise for you? What do they say about American culture, or about gender roles, or our expectations of friendship?

STEP 3: Imagine how your experiences with cross-gender friendships and these assumptions and questions might lead to a research project. What might that look like? What might be the opening questions of such an investigation?

STEP 4: When you've finished this exercise, you'll be standing shoulder to shoulder with Michelle as she begins the story of her own inquiry into her close friendship with a man who is not her husband. In the pages that follow, look over her shoulder as she begins reading and writing about this topic. Notice how an experienced reader tries to navigate material outside of her own academic discipline. We think you'll find this a story you can relate to in many ways.

Michelle's Inquiry: The Story Begins with an Itch

My essay began, like most essays, with an itch: I had recently taken up fly fishing and so had been spending entire days on a river in the summer with someone who was more expert than I was, one of my closest friends. It just so happens that this friend is a man, and I soon found that the only comment some people would make when I talked about my joy in finally catching a wily trout was, "How does your husband feel about you spending a full day with Bruce alone?"

Bruce and I have been friends for more than ten years, and like my brothers and my father, he had naturally become one of my teachers as I took to the water and tried to learn the art of casting, reading the river, and figuring out the hatch. Neither my husband nor Bruce's wife are interested in fishing, but because they know it's important to us, they encourage us to take a day when we can. When some of my friends started asking questions, though, I was surprised: Why did we perceive male-female friendships so differently? I had thought that our culture had moved, even if only slightly, away from the belief that men and women's relationships were always and only about sexual or romantic intimacy. I wanted to find out more about male-female friendships: How common are they? How many of them do indeed fit our stereotype that sexual tension is inevitable? As I thought about my friendship with Bruce, I realized all the ways he had, like my close women friends and my husband, enriched my life, and I wanted to know more about the dynamics and psychological benefits of friendships between men and women.

Those questions led me to several fascinating articles, mostly from the field of psychology, but also from sociology, business, English, and communications. I'll share a few of them with you here, beginning with one from psychology. I'm not a psychologist so I'm new to the kind of research and writing psychologists do. I knew I would have to read these articles like an ethnographer so I could figure out the unfamiliar language, structure, and ideas being discussed. In just quickly flipping through the pages I discovered a lot of charts and statistics that made me a little nervous—I never quite got statistics in school, so when I read about variances and means, everything gets muddled. I'd rather just skim over that part. But the researchers wouldn't be putting these charts and statistics in their articles without good reason, so I need to find a way to understand how to read them. Just the fact that every article I read has statistics tells me that in the field of psychology numbers are persuasive. Those in the field value measuring things and rely on an accepted way of doing that. In my field of English we rarely measure things using statistics—or measure anything, for that matter—so I really am an outsider when it comes to knowing how to use those numbers in my own essay.

Before I read these articles closely, though, I wanted to get a sense of whether they are all organized in similar ways. I know that some disciplines have specific forms they expect their members to use when writing (such as a lab report; a proposal; a clear statement of a hypothesis, method, and results), so I wonder what those forms might be for psychology. Immediately I noticed that most of them had a summary of the article right below the title—typically called an *abstract*—but the summaries didn't really explain what the researchers had concluded. They described the research questions, the way the researchers gathered their data, and the writers' general conclusions about their research. Why would they need an abstract at the beginning, I wondered? Reading these summaries did help me decide whether an article was connected to my own research question, but I clearly needed to read the entire article to get the details.

As I flipped through the ten articles I'd gathered, I noticed that many of them were organized in sections with the same headings: *Methods, Results, Discussion.* I saw that the others used the same structure but didn't use those terms for the headings. I wonder why the discipline of psychology expects their researchers to use the same form for all of their articles. Certainly for me as a reader, those headings made it easier to follow the process of inquiry the researchers used to arrive at their conclusions. I also suspected the structure reflected what psychological researchers value: A research project must begin with questions and then

*Preliminary Question:
What do researchers in this discipline seem to value most as a form of evidence?*

speculate on hypotheses (or expected answers to the questions); then it has to be clear about the methods used so other researchers can determine how valid the conclusions are (a bad survey or experiment will produce bad results). Most of the studies used surveys to gather information, so I can probably assume that surveys are valid forms of evidence in this field, too. I'm probably not going to read about someone's theories or speculations about male-female friendships; instead, I want to read about one or two issues in those friendships that the researchers can actually measure. This would seem to be pretty difficult to accomplish because of the fluid interactions and feelings between friends, so I'm initially a little skeptical that these studies will answer my questions. But I read on because I'm curious about what they have to say.

Before I read any of the articles closely, I flip through them again and look only at the bibliographic citations, the names of other researchers that

Preliminary Question:
Who gets mentioned most as
an expert on this topic?

are in parentheses throughout the article [for instance, (Rubin, 1985)]. I look for often-cited names because that will tell me who psychological researchers consider experts in their field. I notice that Lillian Rubin comes up in every article, as do Michael Monsour, Donald O'Meara, Robert Bell, and Paul Wright. I quickly jot those names down in my notebook in case I want to look up their research, too. The simple fact that their research is used in all these articles tells me that they are considered credible, respected researchers, and that I should be able to rely on their work for my own project, too.

So what do I know so far? More than you might imagine after simply breezing through a few articles without reading much of any of them. I know, for example:

1. Who the insiders are in the psychology community on this particular topic.

2. How some psychologists organize and present research.

3. What kind of evidence or facts they value.

Of course, that isn't much of an introduction to this culture, but it's a good start. Now it's time to read one article a little more closely and see what I can find.

Entering the Conversation: A Psychology Article

The following is one of the first articles I found while doing library research on cross-gender friendships. (There was really an amazing amount of information on the topic.) Join me in reading the first section of "Challenges Confronting Cross-Sex Friendships." As you do, pay attention to your own reactions to what you read—both the content and the way the information is presented. It's a formal academic paper from a respected journal, and it is pretty intimidating at first. But I have a method for discovering what I want to know. You'll notice, for example, that I've underlined ideas that seem important and I've made comments and asked questions in the margins. I also pause after reading short sections to talk to you about what I'm seeing and learning. You'll find my comments boxed throughout this and the next essay, and I've underlined key passages.

Challenges Confronting Cross-Sex Friendships

Much Ado About Nothing?

Michael Monsour, Bridgid Harris, Nancy Kurzweil, and Chris Beard

Sex Roles: A Journal of Research, July 1994 v31 n1-2 p55(23)

Author's Abstract: Copyright Plenum Publishing Corporation 1994.

This research was an investigation into four challenges purported to confront cross-sex friends. One hundred and thirty eight individuals (*females = 86, male = 52*) completed two surveys designed to explore the extent to which the "sexual," "emotional bond," "audience," and "equality" challenges were present in their cross-sex friendships. Over 98 percent of the participants were heterosexual, 99 percent were Caucasian, and approximately 5 percent were Hispanic. Data gathered from the first survey were analyzed using a three-way analysis of variance, with gender, type of friendship, and romantic status as the independent variables, and three of the four challenges as the dependent variables. The first survey also included open-ended questions designed to explore the nature and existence of the challenges. The second survey was in a diary format. Respondents kept a frequency count for three weeks of discussions they had with their cross-sex friend concerning the challenges, and thoughts that they had as individuals concerning those challenges. Results from both surveys indicate that though the challenges exist and have powerful effects on a small percentage of individuals in cross-sex friendships, for the majority of participants the challenges are not perceived as salient.

Full Text: Copyright Plenum Publishing Corporation 1994.

Cross-sex friendships occupy a unique place in the relational fabric of society. Though they lack the prominence of same-sex friendships and romantic relationships, they still provide participants with advantages that are hard to obtain in other relationships (Rubin, 1985; Sapadin, 1988). Despite a growing recognition of the importance of cross-sex friendships, they have been relatively neglected by social scientists (O'Meara, 1989). Though information on these relationships is sparse, we do know that friendships between women and men can be complicated affairs. As a result of gender role socialization, men and women tend to view one another as sexual and/or romantic partners, rather than friends (Bem, 1981; Brain, 1976; Chafetz, 1974). Individuals internalize societal expectations into gender-based cognitive schemata, which encourages the interpretation of cross-sex interaction according to cultural guidelines. Those guidelines suggest male-female interaction should be predominantly romantic or sexual in nature (Bem, 1981).

The ambiguous nature of cross-sex friendships leads to a number of problems that relational partners may have to confront. In a long overdue call for researchers to pay more attention to this ignored relationship, O'Meara (1989) delineated four 'challenges' that participants may face during negotiation of a cross-sex friendship (also see Rawlins, 1982). O'Meara contends that there may be other challenges endemic to cross-sex friendship, and that the challenges he does identify are in need of further empirical verification. The central purpose of this research was to ascertain to what extent the four challenges identified by O'Meara exist in cross-sex friendships. Let us briefly review the nature of each challenge before outlining the methodology utilized to investigate those challenges.

The Emotional Bond Challenge

Cross-sex friends need to arrive at some mutual agreement concerning what type of emotional bond exists in the relationship (O'Meara, 1989). This may be particularly problematic because males and females have been socialized to see one another as potential romantic partners, which in turn increases the likelihood of viewing the emotional bond as one of romantic love. Indeed, studies have revealed that romantic undertones are present in many cross-sex friendships (Monsour, 1988), and that some individuals find those undercurrents intriguing (Rubin, 1985). Closely related to the emotional bond challenge is the sexual challenge.

The Sexual Challenge

For decades scholars have argued that society conditions males and females to view one another as potential sexual partners (Chafetz, 1974; Lepp, 1966; Monsour, 1988). Consequently, many individuals in cross-sex friendships perceive sexual overtones in those relationships (Rubin, 1985). Though women and men frequently detect sexual tension in their friendships, not all individuals react to that tension in the same way (Sapadin, 1988). Some cross-sex friends report that they enjoy the sexual tension because it adds zest to the relationship, while others express a concern that sexual intimacy could destroy a friendship, and thus should

What has already been said?* *As I read the opening section of this article, I'm looking for the key question that is driving the study. My first clue is when I read the line, "The ambiguous nature of cross-sex friendships leads to a number of problems that relational partners may have to confront." Now I'm intrigued— I have my own ideas about what those problems might be (people thinking you're romantically involved; negotiating how emotionally close you are willing to be, especially if you are married; and so on), so I keep reading. I discover that other researchers have categorized these challenges in pretty interesting ways, and have called for more research. Then the writers explicitly state the purpose of their own study. More about that later.*

What comes next is what is usually called a literature review—*a summary of what has already been said about the issue you are studying. As a reader— and an outsider to the psychology community—I want to know more about what people in this field have said about my topic, so this summary is very helpful. They almost always are to an outsider. The literature review shows that the writers know what they're talking about—they've done their homework. But I also remember that all the other articles make the same move—begin with a review of what is already known about their subject—so insiders in this field* expect it. For people in the field, this kind of review signals insider status: I know this subject and who the experts are and I have authority to speak about it. *You'll find the literature review is a pretty common move in many disciplines.*

Such a review of what has already been said on a topic demonstrates a basic idea of most research: We do our work standing on the shoulders of others. *Academic articles often begin this way both as a courtesy to those authors whose earlier contributions are relevant to the topic,* and *as a way to introduce how this project will extend their vision. As you read the following section, try to visualize these authors methodically climbing on the backs of one previous researcher after another, working toward a view of the topic they can claim adds something new to what has already been said.*

---

be actively avoided (Bell, 1981; Rubin, 1985). Research also indicates that males are more likely than females to define intimacy in their cross-sex friendships as involving sexual contact (Monsour, 1992), and that some males interpret friendly interaction from females as sexual in nature (Abbey, 1982; Shotland & Craig, 1988).

---

*Michelle's comments are shown in the boxes throughout this reading. Underlined passages show key points she wanted to highlight.

What's the question? *Sometimes reading an article like this is similar to waiting at a railroad crossing while a freight train goes through. You watch railroad car after railroad car rumble by while you wait impatiently for the caboose. In the last paragraph of this section, the caboose finally appeared, listing the questions* these *writers are studying. This is something I'm always looking for because, measured against my own purposes, I can begin to decide if this article is going to do me any good. Are they trying to answer a question that I'm interested in?*

In this case, the authors are challenging some of the conclusions other researchers have come to and are wondering, "Does it matter if you're close friends? If you're committed to a partner? If you're male or female?" This kind of approach is what we might call the "yeah, but" tradition: "Yeah, it makes sense that cross gender friends have these challenges, but are those challenges affected by gender? By being in a committed relationship? By the quality of your friendship?" These researchers have looked for possible questions that other people have missed in an effort to examine a subject more closely. Most academic researchers use this "yeah, but" tradition in their work. To better understand a subject, they believe, we need to constantly question what others have said and discovered, not settling for what eventually becomes conventional wisdom about a subject. Just think what would have happened if no one questioned the conventional wisdom that the earth was flat, or beliefs that women were less intelligent than men. This kind of questioning leads to new knowledge.

The Equality Challenge

Equality is a central element of friendship (Paine, 1974; Rawlins, 1992). O'Meara (1989) argues that establishing and maintaining equality is a challenge that must be met in cross-sex friendships. He further contends that this challenge is best met by creating a communal relationship (Clark & Mills, 1979) rather than one based upon exchange principles. Males have more resources to barter with than females, presenting the possibility of males having the upper hand in cross-sex friendships (Lipman-Blumen, 1976).

The Audience Challenge

The first three challenges are concerned with the private and dyadic negotiation of the definition of the relationship. Once the cross-sex friends have arrived at some mutual definition of their relationship, and frequently while they are struggling at agreeing on that definition, they must present the correct picture of the relationship to relevant audiences (O'Meara, 1989). Rawlins (1982) characterized this challenge as a continual one that is strategically met in different ways by trying to balance the public and private nature of the friendship. It is reasonable to assume that certain factors might impact the degree to which friends are concerned with public perception of their relationship. One such factor is the propensity of an individual to self-monitor his or her behavior. Self-monitoring is the extent to which an individual monitors his or her behavior in accordance with what he or she thinks is suitable for a particular situation (Synder, 1974). The lack of research into challenges perceived by cross-sex friends lead to the following research questions.

Research Question 1: To what extent do the four challenges identified by O'Meara exist in cross-sex friendships? Research Question 2: What effect does gender (female and male), type of friendship (casual and good), and romantic status (single and attached) have on the perception of the sexual, audience, and equality challenges? Research Question 3: What effect does level of self-monitoring have on perception of the audience

How to answer it   *Next comes the "Methods" section, which seems pretty standard for these kinds of psychological and other quantitative studies. It's really tempting to skip this section. It goes into sometimes excruciating detail about who, what, when, where, and how. But skimming the methods section of an academic article is always worth it because it helps give you a sense of context for the study. In this case, for example, I find it interesting that the study focuses exclusively on university students. Focusing on only college-age, college-educated people would shape, I think, the results. Since most of the students are single, I immediately wonder whether the results of this study will connect with my own experience as a married woman. I also suspect that education level and social class influence how cross-gender relationships are perceived and the kind of challenges the friends face, but those issues aren't addressed here.*

Psychologists reading this article are in a much better position than I am to evaluate whether the methods of the study are sound, but that's the beauty of the so-called peer reviewed *or* refereed *article like this one—I don't have to worry about that question. Before this article was published in the journal, other experts in the field reviewed it, and among the things they evaluated was the soundness of the authors' methods.*

Read along with me. As you do, I've shared some of the notes I made in the margins or in my journal as I read. Is there anything else that is revealed in the following section about how the study was conducted that might influence the way you see the results? You might want to discuss this in class.

challenge? Research Question 4: To what extent will data gleaned from retrospective accounting of a particular friendship concerning the four challenges be verified by diary data concerning that same friendship?

Method

Subjects

What does "n" mean here?

Data were collected during the 1992–1993 academic school year in thirteen communication classes from two western universities. One hundred and thirty eight respondents were solicited. Thirty eight percent of the respondents were male (n = 52), and 62 percent were female (n = 86). Participants received extra credit in their classes for engaging in the research. Individuals who chose not to be involved were given an opportunity to receive extra credit in another way. Ages ranged from 17 to 58, with a median age of 25. Seventeen percent of the respondents were married, 41 percent were dating someone steadily, and 42 percent were single and not dating anyone steadily. Over 98 percent of the participants were heterosexual, and 99 percent were Caucasian. Approximately 5 percent of the respondents were Hispanic.

So the conclusions of this study are limited to heterosexual Caucasians around the age of 25?

Procedures

During solicitation of respondents the general parameters of the research project were explained. Individuals were told that the project was designed to study cross-sex friendships, that is, friendships between members of the opposite sex, excluding romantic, marital, and family relationships. They were informed that if they were interested in participating in the study they would need to complete two surveys, and give a third survey to a cross-sex friend to be mailed back to the department. Data collected from the respondents' cross-sex friends is not presented in this report.

It sure would be interesting to know what the friends said . . .

Seventy randomly selected respondents from the 138 participants completed a revision of Synder's (1974) Self-Monitoring Scale (Synder & Gangestad, 1986). Data was gathered from this smaller sample to see if there was a relationship between self-monitoring and the audience challenge. All 138 participants were given a survey to complete at home and return the next class period. The survey consisted of eight open-ended and 22 closed-ended items designed to investigate respondent perception of the four challenges in a specific cross-sex friendship. The first 12 items were comprised of demographic information and forced-choice questions covering such things as where the friends met, where they

> # Skimming Strategies
>
> In a scientific article like this one, your reading can slow to a crawl, and a painful one at that. Skimming is often a good idea if there's a method to it. Skim *strategically*.
>
> 1. Seize the handles provided, like headings, italicized and boldfaced text, and abstracts.
> 2. Remember that introductions and endings usually contain the most important information.
> 3. Read the first sentence of every paragraph.
> 4. Check out charts, tables, and graphics.
> 5. Look for key words, like *therefore, because, in conclusion, suggests*, and *reveals* that imply a move toward interpretation.

most frequently interacted, how many same and cross-sex friends they had, and so on. Individuals were instructed to categorize the friendship they were reporting on as new, casual, good, or best.

Once the first survey was completed and returned, individuals were given another survey to keep for a three week period. The survey was in a structured diary format, with 10 closed-ended and 13 open-ended items. The same type of questions were used for all four challenges. For example, closed-ended items would ask: "Approximately how many times over the past three weeks have you and your friend talked about the sexual dimension of your friendship?" and "How many times over the three week period did you find yourself thinking about the sexual dimension of your friendship?" Due to space limitations, data from the open-ended questions cannot be presented in this report.

Data Analysis

The first research question was explored through descriptive examination of open-ended questions from the first survey. There was one global open-ended question designed to investigate the existence of any and all challenges that might occur in the context of a cross-sex friendship. That question preceded all closed-ended questions pertaining to the four challenges under investigation. Open-ended questions employed to investigate the nature of each specific challenge were placed at the end of the survey. Though placement of these questions at the end of the survey allowed for the possibility that previous closed-ended questions might impact responses to the open-ended ones, the same problem would present itself regardless of where the open-ended questions were placed in the survey. In other words, irrespective of whether open-ended questions follow or pre-cede closed-ended ones, respondents can add to or change their replies if they are so inclined. However, there is little reason to suspect that respon-dents would have any motive for changing an initial response unless they thought the change represented a truer accounting of the relationship.

Additionally, the open-ended questions at the end of the survey were aimed at exploring the nature of each of the four primary challenges, whereas the global open-ended question in the beginning of the survey that preceded the closed-ended items was employed to test for the exis-tence of the challenges. For all open-ended questions in the first survey a preliminary perusal of half the surveys and a literature review was conducted to arrive at category systems for replies. Inter-coder re-liability was computed by calculating per-centage agreement between the two coders. Inter-coder reliability was above .8 for each of the utilized open-ended questions throughout this research.

> *I have no idea what "inter-coder reliability" means. I assume other psychological researchers do, and that this number somehow helps them understand how reliable the data is.*

In regards to the second research question, a three-way analysis of variance was conducted with gender (male and female), type of friendship (casual and good), and romantic status (single and attached) as the inde-pendent variables, and the sexual, audience, and equality challenges as the dependent variables. Single individuals were respondents who were not dating anyone steadily, and attached individuals were those who were either married or dating someone steadily. Only good and casual friend-ships were included in the analysis of variance because not enough indi-viduals categorized their friendship as "new" or "best" for an adequate testing of those categories of friendship. For purposes of the ANOVA, two of the closed-ended items on the first survey were de-signed to explore the sexual challenge, six were tailored to apply to the audience challenge, and three were geared towards investigation of the equality challenge.

> *What is "ANOVA"? I see this a lot in the articles I'm reading.*

Strategies for Dealing with Unfamiliar Language

Mark the words you don't know, remembering that they are probably insider terms and that you may have to talk to an insider to learn what they mean and/or go to the dictionary; skim the section and return to it after reading the entire article.

In this section I find a lot of language that I'm not familiar with (ANOVA, median-split procedure, t-test). Some of the processes used to analyze data are alien to me, so I'm not going to be able to critically analyze the results the way I'd like. I really feel like an outsider. I have to admit I'm quickly skimming this part because I don't fully understand it. I'll remember my difficulty and return to this section after I've read the article through. I may have to talk with someone in the psychology department who can explain these procedures to me. I have searched the Internet using a search engine that focuses more on academic sites (northernlight.com), and I've discovered that ANOVA means "analysis of variance":

> *Analysis of Variance (ANOVA): A test of the statistical significance of the differences among the mean scores of two or more groups on one or more variables or factors. It is an extension of the t-test, which can only handle two groups, to a larger number of groups. More specifically, it is used for assessing the statistical significance of the relationship between categorical independent variables and a continuous dependent variable. (John B. Green, Jr., Ph.D.: School of Business & Mass Communication at Brenau University; http://faculty.brenau.edu/green/anova.htm)*

Now, this definition only clears up a little of my confusion. When I looked up "t-test" with northernlight.com I became even more confused. These are processes only insiders know, and I need to do more than simply look up definitions in the dictionary or on the Internet.

Sorting through the details: what's most important? *As I flip through the "Results" section, I notice that it's organized around the research questions that motivated the study. That clear organization makes it easier for me to read, but the length of this section suggests an incredible level of detail. How much of this should I read carefully? Well, I want to focus on the research questions that interest me most. Much of the rest, I'll skim (see sidebar on page 334). I also know that if I'm tired right now, I probably should wait to read this section. As you read along with me, mark the sections that you think have the most to do with my research question. I've highlighted the information that stands out to me.*

The third research question was explored through an inspection of the self-monitoring data collected from 70 of the respondents. A median-split procedure was utilized to divide the group into high and low self monitors, and a t-test was employed to detect differences. High self-monitors were differentiated from low self-monitors on two of the six items designed to investigate the audience challenge. The fourth research question concerned the extent to which data gleaned from the three week diary survey would verify what was uncovered in the first survey. Only closed-ended questions were utilized from the diary data, specifically items pertaining to the frequency of discussions and thoughts about each of the four challenges.

RESULTS

Research Question 1

There were a number of open-ended items from the first survey designed to investigate the four challenges. The first open-ended question asked: "What 'challenges' (i.e., obstacles and/or problems) have you (or you and your friend) had to overcome in order to establish and maintain this friendship? Please number your replies (1, 2, 3, etc.)." Replies to this item were placed into one or more of seven categories. As shown in Table I, in addition to the audience, emotional, sexual, and equality challenges, there were the "significant other" challenge, the "logistics" challenge, and an "other" category. The "significant other" challenge refers to a situation where a significant other of one of the friends applies pressure on the friendship. The significant other challenge was the only additional challenge uncovered that flowed from the cross-sex nature of the friendship.

The "logistics" challenge refers to problems that friends encountered because they lived so far apart or had such busy schedules that it was difficult to spend time together. Originally the logistics challenge was placed into the "other" category because it was not unique to cross-sex friendships. However, a decision rule was adopted concerning categorization of other challenges. If a specific challenge was reported by more than 10 percent of any of the groups under examination it was given its own category.

Six groups of individuals were examined throughout inspection of the descriptive data gleaned from the open-ended questions: all females in the study (n = 86), all males in the study (n = 52), casual cross-sex friends (n = 38), good cross-sex friends (n = 67), single individuals (n = 57), and attached individuals (n = 79). Table I gives the total number of challenges reported by each of the six groups, the average number of challenges reported by each group and the percentage of the total number of challenges that fell into a particular category.

As shown in Table I, some individuals perceive "no challenges" in their cross-sex friendship. Of the four challenges under examination, the emotional bond challenge comprised the highest percentage of the

At this point I'm wondering what the researchers make of what I've underlined. What does it mean that the emotional bond challenge got the most hits, so to speak? What does it mean that friends found the audience challenge greater than the sexual or equality challenge?

Now I'm wondering why more women than men thought their friend wanted more intimacy. What does that mean? Are those percentages really meaningful? I'm also confused by their assertion that most participants said they had no emotional bond challenges. How does that compare with what they said earlier, that the emotional bond challenge was the one people struggled with the most? This is confusing me.

challenges listed by the various groups. A representative reply is the following given by a single male in a good cross-sex friendship: "Sometimes I am confused about how I really feel about her." Only a minuscule percentage of the challenges reported relate to perceived inequality in the friendship. A typical reply of a respondent who did perceive inequality is the following given by a female in a good cross-sex friendship: "Its hard to say—sometimes I feel as if my friend is trying to boss me around." A larger percentage of challenges fell into the sexual challenge category than the equality category, though percentages were still quite small. A characteristic reply is the following given by a single male who had once had sex with his cross-sex friend: "Sex is a problem—the fact that we once had it!" The percentage of challenges falling into the audience category was higher than the equality and sexual categories. A typical response is the following given by a male in a casual friendship: "Sometimes other people get the wrong impression of what's going on (or not going on) in our relationship." To further investigate the nature of the four challenges open-ended questions were included which specifically addressed each challenge. In reference to the audience challenge respondents were asked: "How do you indicate to others (friends, fellow employees, family members, spouses, lovers, etc.) that you and your friend are friends and not dating. . . . In your reply indicate who you communicate the message to and how you do it." Table II presents six groupings of respondents and what percentage of each group reported that they communicate to a specific type of audience that they are just friends. Large percentages of individuals from each group indicated that they "do not explain their friendship to anyone." Substantial percentages of individuals in each group reported that they tell "everyone" that their relationship is just a friendship. For example, one male phrased it this way: "If anyone asks I tell them she and I are just friends and that I am dating someone."

To further investigate the emotional bond challenge individuals were asked: "Briefly explain problems (if any) that you and your friend have had concerning what type of emotional bond exists between you? Please number your replies." Three types of problems associated with the emotional bond challenge emerged. As shown in Table III, in addition to some participants indicating that they had "no problems" with the emotional bond, respondents reported that they and their friend "were previously dating partners," that one member of the friendship "wanted more intimacy than the other," and/or that there was "romantic and sexual tension" in the friendship. Table III gives the percentages of each group who specified each type of problem.

The vast majority of individuals reported that there were no emotional bond problems in their friendship. Only small percentages of each group reported one or more of the three problems, some of which are worthy of special note. For example, 12 percent of the females reported that one partner wanted more intimacy than the other, compared to 2 percent of the males. Another noteworthy comparison is that 10 percent of the attached individuals reported that one partner wanted more intimacy than the other, whereas 5 percent of the single individuals had this perception.

To investigate the sexual challenge respondents were asked: "Briefly describe problems (if any) you and your friend have encountered concerning the sexual dimension of your relationship. Please number your problems (e.g., 1, 2, 3, etc.)." As shown in Table IV, replies fell into one of five categories. Once again, the vast majority of individuals in each group reported that there were "no problems" in the relationship concerning the sexual challenge. The four problem areas were mentioned by tiny percentages of each group. The second, third, and fourth problems listed in Table IV were specific problems easily identified by coders because they were clearly expressed by respondents. For example, a typical response falling into the category "one wants more intimacy than the other" is the following given by a single female: "It's obvious to me that my friend would like this relationship to become a sexual thing." The last problem area in Table IV, "sexual tension," was reserved for responses that dealt with sexual tension, and yet were too general to be placed in one of the other categories. For example, a single male in a good cross-sex friendship indicated "Since about the seventh month of our friendship (the brief romantic period), the sexual dimension has been limited to talk and rare light teasing." Though the percentages for each specific type of problem were small, all four problems concern sexual tension of some sort. Combining the percentages for each type of sexual problem indicates that 20 percent of the males in the study, and 10 percent of the females reported the existence of some type of sexual tension.

I wonder what these sets of numbers mean? That men think about sex more than women? If most people felt the sexual challenge was minimal in their friendship, then what do these percentages mean?

To further investigate the equality challenge the following item was included in the survey: "Current research suggests that some males and females in cross-sex friendships struggle with who has more power and control in the relationship, and who has more status. Please briefly explain to what extent this is true in your cross-sex friendship." Inclusion of the word "some" (i.e., "some males and females") was meant to insure that respondents recognized that some friends struggle with the problem of power and control, but some do not. As shown in Table V, replies were categorized into one of five ways. Despite the fact that the item was somewhat leading in nature, most individuals in each group reported that they and their friends "do not struggle with power and control." Three percent or less of each group reported that one person has more power than the other and that it causes problems.

In regards to the equality challenge individuals were also asked to indicate "who has more power in the relationship?" They were given four choices: "I do," "my friend does," "there is equal power and control," and "I never really thought about it—it does not seem relevant." Table VI shows the percentages of each group that replied in each of the four ways. Large percentages of all groups had the perception that there was equal power and control in the relationship, and even larger percentages of each group reported that they never really thought about the issue of power and

I'm not sure I believe this . . . control in the relationship and that it did not seem relevant.

Research Question 2

The second research question concerned the extent to which gender (male and female), type of friendship (good and casual), and romantic status (attached and single) would impact perception of the sexual, audience, and equality challenges. With <u>significance levels set at P < .05, a three-way analysis of variance</u> resulted in eight <u>main effects</u> and <u>three interaction ef-</u>

What do these terms mean? <u>fects.</u> Table VII reports all main effects, and Table VIII reports the interaction effects.

There were two main effects in regards to the sexual challenge, one pertaining to romantic status, and one to type of friendship. When asked "How much difficulty do you and your friend have in dealing with the sexual dimension of your relationship?" <u>single individuals reported having slightly more difficulty than did attached individuals</u> (1 = none at all, 4 = moderate difficulty, 7 = extreme difficulty; attached = 1.23, single = 1.83; F = 9.598, P <.003. When asked "How often do you and your friend discuss the issue of sexuality in your friendship?" <u>good cross-sex friends reported having those discussions more often than did casual cross-sex friends</u> (1 = never, 4 = sometimes, 7 = frequently; CCSF = 1.61, GCSF = 2.71; F = 10.132, P <.002).

This is where I take out my journal and begin taking the notes you'll find on pp. 347–348. I keep rereading the same sentence because I don't know why these conclusions are significant, so I try to group the conclusions in my journal.

There were three main effects in regards to the audience challenge, and one interaction effect. All main effects were associated with type of friendship. When asked "How often do you and your cross-sex friend discuss the perceptions that others (e.g., friends, family) have of your friendship?" good cross-sex friends reported having these discussions more often than did casual cross-sex friends (1 = never, 4 = sometimes, 7 = frequently; CCSF = 1.51, GCSF = 2.29, F 7.761, P <.006). There was a Sex by Type of Cross-Sex Friendship interaction (F = 5.851, P < .017). Though females in good cross-sex friendships reported having these discussions more often than females in casual cross-sex friendships (CCSF = 1.19, GCSF = 2.48), there was no difference between males in good and casual cross-sex friendships (CCSF = 1.94, GCSF = 1.96).

When asked "How often do you find yourself explaining to your family (parents, siblings, relatives) that your cross-sex friendship is not a dating relationship?" good cross-sex friends reported doing so more often than did casual cross-sex friends (1 = never, 4 = sometimes, 7 = frequently; CCSF = 1.61 GCSF = 2.75, F = 10.382, P <.002). A similar item asked: "How often do you find yourself explaining to your same-sex friends that your cross-sex friendship is not a dating relationship?" Good cross-sex friends reported engaging in those explanations more often than did casual cross-sex friends (CCSF = 1.79, GCSF = 2.63; F = 6.296, P < .014).

There were three main effects associated with the equality challenge, all concerned with type of friendship. When asked "In this friendship to what extent are you and your friend equals?" there was a marginally significant difference between casual and good cross-sex friends (1 = to no extent, 4 = to a moderate extent, 7 = to a great extent; CCSF = 5.26, GCSF = 5.78, F = 3.114, P < .08). There was also a marginally significant interaction effect between Sex and Type of Cross-Sex Friendship (F = 3.555, P < .06). Whereas there was little difference between females in casual and good cross-sex friendships (5.5 and 5.7, respectively), there was a considerable difference between males in casual and good cross-sex friendships (4.8 and 6.0, respectively). There was also an interaction effect between Type of Cross-Sex Friendship and Romantic Status (F = 3.766, P < .05).

Two additional main effects for the equality challenge were associated with type of friendship. Several items in the survey were designed to investigate the communal aspects of cross-sex friendships. In communal relationships there is a concern for the welfare of one's partner, more than

TABLE I Total and Average Number of Challenges Reported and the Percentage of Each Type of Challenge Reported by Males, Females, Good Cross-Sex Friends (GCSF), Casual Cross-Sex Friends (CCSF), Single Individuals, and Attached Individuals[a]

	Males	Females	GCSF	CCSF	Single	Attached
Total number of challenges	75	141	111	59	83	109
Average number of challenges	1.4	1.6	1.6	1.5	1.4	1.3
1. Audience challenge	11%	22%	13%	18%	5%	19%
2. Sexual challenge	6%	8%	7%	2%	7%	4%
3. Emotional challenge	21%	20%	14%	13%	13%	15%
4. Equality challenge	1%	3%	3%	1%	2%	1%
5. Significant other challenge	8%	13%	7%	8%	7%	6%
6. Logistics challenge	19%	35%	17%	31%	17%	21%
7. No challenges	17%	16%	10%	23%	14%	20%
8. Other challenges	60%	46%	39%	58%	48%	33%

[a]Males n = 52, females n = 86, GCSF n = 67, CCSF n = 38, singles n = 57, attached n = 79. For example, females reported a total of 141 challenges, an average of 1.6 challenges, and of those 141 challenges, 22% fell into the category of the audience challenges, and 46% fell into the "other" category.

TABLE II Percentages of Individuals in Each of Six Groups Who Explain the Nature of Their Cross-Sex Friendship to Specific Audiences[a]

Audiences	Females	Males	CCSF	GCSF	Single	Attached
1. Parents	10%	13%	5%	10%	12%	10%
2. Family	8%	11%	10%	12%	14%	6%
3. Significant other	12%	8%	10%	15%	0%	19%
4. Friends	20%	19%	18%	22%	16%	24%
5. Co-workers	3%	6%	2%	3%	7%	2%
6. Everyone	39%	33%	39%	33%	40%	34%
7. Nobody	26%	21%	24%	27%	19%	26%

[a]Females n = 86, males n = 52, CCSF = casual cross-sex friends n = 38, GCSF = good cross-sex friends n = 67, single individuals n = 57, attached individuals n = 79. For example, this Table Indicates that 5% of CCSF indicate to their parents that they and their cross-sex friend are not dating partners.

there might be in an exchange relationship (Clark & Mills, 1979). When asked "To what extent are you concerned about the welfare of your friend?" individuals in good friendships reported concern for the welfare of their friend to a greater degree than did individuals in casual friendships (1 = to no extent, 4 = to a moderate extent, 7 = to a great extent;

TABLE III Percentages of Individuals in Each of Six Groups Reporting Specific Types of Problems Associated with the Emotional Bond Challenge[a]

Type of Problem	Females	Males	GCSF	CCSF	Single	Attached
1. No problems	66%	76%	57%	94%	66%	70%
2. Were previously dating partners	1%	4%	11%	0%	7%	0%
3. One wants more intimacy than other	12%	2%	11%	0%	5%	10%
4. Romantic and sexual tension	5%	6%	8%	3%	9%	4%

[a]Females n = 80, males n = 52, GCSF = good cross sex friends n = 65, CCSF = casual cross-sex friends n = 34, single individuals n = 54, attached individuals n = 77, For example, the table indicates that 2% of the males reported that one of the cross-sex friends wanted more intimacy than the other did.

TABLE IV Percentages of Individuals in Each of Six Groups Reporting Specific Types of Problems Associated with the Sexual Challenge[a]

Type of Problem	Females	Males	GCSF	CCSF	Single	Attached
1. No problems	76%	78%	72%	77%	67%	84%
2. Were previously dating partners	1%	6%	5%	0%	7%	0%
3. One wants more intimacy than other	5%	2%	5%	3%	3%	4%
4. Sexual attraction but one is attached	2%	2%	3%	0%	3%	0%
5. Sexual tension	2%	10%	5%	8%	5%	3%

[a]Females n = 82, males n = 50, GCSF = good cross-sex friends n = 64, CCSF = casual cross-sex friends n = 36, attached individuals n = 24, single individuals n = 57.

GCSF = 5.69, CCSF = 4.47, F = 22.314, P < .001). When asked to what extent they thought their friend was concerned about their welfare the average response for casual friends was 5.0, compared to 6.09 for good friends (F = 20.840, P < .001).

Research Question 3

To investigate the third research question 70 randomly selected individuals from the 138 respondents completed the revised Self-Monitoring Scale. When asked "How often do you find yourself explaining to family that your cross-sex friendship is not a dating relationship?" high self-monitors indicated doing this more often than low self-monitors (1 = never, 4 = sometimes, 7 = frequently; HSM = 2.6, LSM = 1.6, F = 2.26, P < .01). In a similar fashion, when asked "How much do comments from your parents and/or siblings about your cross-sex friendship affect how

TABLE V   Percentages of Individuals in Each of Six Groups Reporting a Specific Situation Associated with the Equality Challenge[a]

Situation	Females	Males	GCSF	CCSF	Single	Attached
1. Do not struggle with power and control	77%	81%	79%	87%	75%	93%
2. I have more power but that does not cause a problem	7%	11%	10%	3%	12%	7%
3. My friend has more power but that does not cause a problem	5%	2%	4%	5%	5%	3%
4. I have more power and it causes problems	1%	2%	1%	0%	2%	1%
5. My friend has more power and it causes problems	1%	2%	1%	0%	3%	0%

[a]Females n = 86, males n = 52, GCSF = good cross-sex friends n = 67, CCSF = casual cross-sex friends n = 38, single individuals n = 57, attached individuals n = 74.

TABLE VI   Replies to the Question "Who has More Power and Control?" Arranged According to the Percentage of Each Group Who Gave a Specific Reply[a]

Type of Reply	Females	Males	CCSF	GCSF	Single	Attached
1. I do	8%	11%	10%	4%	16%	6%
2. My friend does	6%	4%	5%	7%	7%	4%
3. There is equal power	35%	35%	24%	37%	28%	40%
4. Never really thought about it, not relevant	51%	50%	60%	51%	49%	49%

[a]Females n = 86, males n 52, CCSF = casual cross-sex friends n = 38, GCSF = good cross-sex friends n = 67, single individuals n = 57, attached individuals n = 79.

you view that friendship?" high self-monitors reported that such comments affected them more than did low self-monitors (1 = not at all, 4 = some, 7 = a great deal; HSM = 1.8, LSM = 1.3, F = 2.9, P < .003).

Research Question 4

The fourth research question asked to what extent diary data gathered over a three week period would corroborate the results of the first survey. Diary data tended to verify information gleaned from the first survey concerning the four challenges. Table IX presents the average number of times that members in each of the six groups discussed each challenge with their cross-sex friend, the average number of times that individuals

TABLE VII *F* Values for Main Effects Associated with the Sexual, Audience, and Equality Challenges in Cross-Sex Friendships[a]

	Factor			
	Cross-Sex Friendship Type		Romantic Status	
Challenges	*F* value	Significance	*F* Value	Significance
Sexual Challenge				
1. Frequency of discussing sexual issues	10.132	p < .002	—	—
2. Difficulty in dealing with sexual issues	—	—	9.598	p < .003
Audience Challenge				
1. Frequency of explaining CSF (cross-sex friend) to family	10.382	p < .002	—	—
2. Frequency of explaining CSF to same-sex friends	6.296	p < .01	—	—
3. Frequency of discussing perceptions of others with CSF	7.761	p < .006	—	—
Equality Challenge				
1. Degree to which CSF perceives equality in the friendship	3.114	p < .08	—	—
2. Degree to which respondent is concerned about welfare of CSF	22.314	p < .000	—	—
3. Degree to which respondent feels his/her CSF is concerned about his/her welfare	20.840	p < .000	—	—

[a]Both reported factors had two levels. Type of cross-sex friendship was casual and good, romantic status was single and attached. Gender as a factor (female and male) had no significant effects on any operationalizations of the three challenges. Nonsignificant *F* values are indicated by a dash.

thought about the challenges while alone, and the total number of times that a respondent and his or her partner did something and/or communicated over the three week period. Let us examine each challenge.

As shown in Table IX, all six groups reported talking about the sexual dimension of their friendship less than once over the three week period, but thinking about it on average from one to three times. Though averages were small, a few individuals reported discussing or thinking about the sexual dimension with considerable frequency. For example, a few females reported discussing the sexual challenge with their cross-sex friend 20 times. One female respondent reported that she thought about the sexual dimension of her cross-sex friendship 80 times during the three week period.

TABLE VIII Interaction Effects Associated with the Audience and Equality
Challenge in Cross-Sex Friendships[a]

	Interaction			
	Gender × type of CSF		Type × of CSF × RS	
	F Value	Significance	*F* Value	Significance
Audience Challenge				
1. Frequency of discussing perceptions of others with CSF	5.851	$p < .01$	—	—
Equality Challenge				
1. Degree to which CSF perceives equality in the friendship	3.555	$p < .06$	3.766	$p < .05$

[a]CSF = cross-sex friendship. RS = romantic status. Each of the three factors had two levels.
Levels for gender were male and female, levels for type of cross-sex friendship were casual
and good, levels for romantic status were single and attached. Nonsignificant *F* values are
indicated by a dash.

TABLE IX Average Number of Times that Individuals in Each of Six Groups
Discussed Each of the Four Challenges with Their Cross-Sex Friend,
and Average Number of Times Individuals in Each Group Thought
About Each of the Four Challenges, and Average Number of Contacts
During Three Week Period[a]

	Females	Males	CCSF	GCSF	Single	Attached
1. Talked about sex	.78	.71	.37	.95	.70	.85
2. Thought about sex	2.71	3.30	1.17	2.02	3.3	1.55
3. Talked about audiences	1.47	.53	.52	.45	.71	.66
4. Thought about audiences	1.48	2.03	.88	1.34	2.23	1.27
5. Talked about emotions	.65	1.23	.40	.51	1.31	.38
6. Thought about emotions	3.02	3.36	2.00	1.93	3.41	1.89
7. Talked about power	.12	.33	.16	.15	.16	.22
8. Thought about power	.66	.60	.52	.61	.92	.43
9. Average number of times of contact during three week period	8.5	12.7	8.8	8.9	12.6	8.0

[a]Females n = 82, males n = 35, CCSF = casual cross-sex friends n = 21, GCSF = good cross-
sex friends n = 51, singles n = 41, attached n = 58.

The same pattern that existed for the sexual challenge was manifested
for the audience challenge. Though averages were low, the number of discussions reported by some individuals indicated that in their cross-sex
friendship talking about how others view their relationship occupied a

---

Strategies for Dealing with Lists of Data

Take notes in your journal about what *you* notice about the results, what interpretations you might have, so you can better understand the "Discussion" that comes later; understand that it is a convention in this field to separate data from interpretation

---

significant portion of their time. For example, one female reported having 10 such discussions, while another reported having 63 of them. Table IX indicates that all groups except for males and single individuals reported discussing the emotional bond less than once during the three week period. As was true of the previous two challenges, some individuals reported having frequent discussions with their friends about their emotional bond, with several reporting having such discussions 20 or more times, and thinking about it even more frequently.

In regards to the equality challenge, individuals were asked to indicate how many times they and their cross-sex friend discussed who has more power and control in the relationship, and how often they thought about the issue. Averages were extremely small here, and lower than the other challenges. However, there were a few isolated individuals who reported having such discussions as many as four times during the three week period, and found themselves thinking about it as often as 20 times.

I had to skim this section twice. It seems mostly to list the results of the surveys and offer little interpretation of the results. That means I don't know what to make of their results. Now, I could be patient and read on to the "Discussion" section, but I want to know what I think of the results before I read theirs. I'm a little frustrated at this point, so I take out my journal and begin to take notes on each of the research questions:

RESEARCH QUESTION 1 (see p. 337)
When prompted to list challenges
Emotional bond has highest %
Larger % in sexual than equality
When asked specifically about a challenge
No emotional bond problem
  Gender differences: 12% fem
              2% male

one partner wanted more intimacy
    attachment diff: 10% attached
                    5% single

most reported no problems w/sexual challenge

    gender: 20% males   *reported existence of*
            10% females   *some type of problem*

most saw no problem w/ power + control
    never thought about, didn't seem relevant—hmm

                    RESEARCH QUESTION 2 (see p. 340)
I'm unfamiliar w/ "three-way analysis of variance"
                    "main effects"
                    "interaction effects"
at this point I have to slow down bec unfam w/ #s + how to read/
    interpret
women more concerned about people's perceptions?
good cross-gender friends had discussions more often (sexual challenge)—the
more intimate, the more diff w/sex?
good cross-sex friends:
    talk about issue of sexuality more
    discuss perceptions of others more (women > men)
    spend more time explaining that they aren't dating
    more concerned about welfare of friend
I get lost on equality challenge

                    RESEARCH QUESTION 3 (see p. 343)
Self monitoring Scale—I'm unfamiliar w/ + they don't explain
    diff. betw high + low self monitors
High self monitors   *Low self monitors*
    explain more that not dating
    views of the friendship affected
    more by comments from family

                    RESEARCH QUESTION 4 (see p. 344)
diary info corroborates other data

    After organizing their results like this, I have a few questions and
comments:

- *I wonder why more women than men thought their friend wanted more intimacy? Is that based on women's definitions of intimacy vs. men's?*
- *Why would more men report that there were some problems with sexual tension than women?*
- *I'm not sure I believe that cross-gender friends have little if any problems with power and control. Given our socialized gender roles, it would seem that men would inherently have more power in the relationship. If the participants in this study were not conscious of the power differences in our culture between men and women—in other words, if they wanted to believe they were equal—then they would have this response. Is this true in my relationship with Bruce?*
- *I'm not surprised that good cross-gender friends have more discussions about the sexual challenge than casual friends—it makes sense that the closer you are emotionally, the more willing you'd be to talk about those issues. Of course, this study is assuming a heterosexual perspective on sexuality—if a gay man and a heterosexual woman were friends, would they discuss sex as a challenge in their relationship?*

How to Interpret the Results *If the "Results" section of a scientific article serves up the meat, the "Discussion" section is where it gets chewed. This is the real meal. So I'll linger a little more in this section, skimming less and, since I have some specific questions, scanning more (see sidebar on page 351). As you read this section, mark the places where the writers are telling us how their results are significant.*

Discussion

Our central research question concerned the extent to which the four challenges identified by O'Meara (1989) exist in cross-sex friendships. <u>Evidence gathered in this research reveals that though the four challenges present significant problems for some cross-sex friends, the majority of individuals do not have difficulty in these areas.</u> Nevertheless, results from both surveys provide limited support for all four challenges, enough to warrant explication of some of the implications of these findings and to justify further research. Throughout this discussion data from both surveys will be examined simultaneously, and conclusions about each of the four research questions will be explored as we discuss each individual challenge.

Ah, here we have a clear thesis statement: "Evidence gathered in this research reveals that though the four challenges present significant problems for some cross-sex friends, the majority of individuals do not have difficulty in these areas." I also notice in this paragraph that the writers explain what they are about to do next. This move seems pretty common in the other articles I've read, too. The essays from Chapter 3 in this book don't often make such explicit statements about their thesis or the direction the article is going, so insiders in this field must expect such statements. They sure help me as an outsider.

Sexual Challenge

Though many argue that society conditions males and females to view one another as potential sexual partners (e.g., Chafetz, 1974), the results of both surveys suggest that this conditioning presents a sexual challenge in only a small percentage of cross-sex friendships. That challenge is typically manifested as subjective impression of sexual tension in the relationship. There were mixed results concerning the possibility of gender differences in the perception of that challenge. Though the analysis of variance did not support gender differences, 20 percent of males reported sexual tension of some type in their cross-sex friendship, compared to 10 percent of the females. Males also thought about the sexual dimension more often than did their female counterparts. These results indirectly support research which suggest that men sometimes misjudge a woman's friendly behavior as an indication of sexual interest and that men perceive more situations as sexually oriented than do women (Abbey, 1982; Shotland & Craig, 1988).

Ah, here they've given me something to think about when I look at the 20 percent of men and 10 percent of women who suggested sexual tension exists in their relationship.

Data from the diary survey supported what was found in the first survey concerning pervasiveness of the sexual challenge. Each of the six groups under examination discussed the sexual challenge less than once during the three week period. Of course the frequency of discussions of this challenge may not be indicative of the seriousness of the challenge. Perhaps it is not discussed because it is so sensitive. In addition, a few individuals appeared to be almost obsessed with the sexual component of their friendship—discussing and thinking about it significantly

Here I realize why they're used the "diary data"—it's more information to either support or challenge their results using different methods. It makes sense that survey results could be different from the daily details people would put down in their diaries.

more often than the typical respondent. These results also support recent research indicating that males and females in cross-sex friendships agree with one another that sexual and romantic overtones in their friendships are moderately low (Monsour, Betty, & Kurzweil, 1993).

<u>Though the results of the ANOVA reveal that romantic status and type of friendship have a significant impact on the perception of the sexual challenge, none of the groups reported having even moderate difficulty with that challenge.</u> Single individuals reported having more difficulty in dealing with the sexual dimension of their friendship than did attached individuals. We hesitate to make too much out of these differences. Though they were statistically significant, the mean differences were relatively small (1.2 compared to 1.8). Wright (1988) correctly cautions researchers against reifying statistical significance, especially when the practical differences have not been fully addressed. In a similar fashion, though good friends did report that they had discussions about the sexual dimension significantly more often than did casual friends, the practical implication of those differences is debatable.

Now this information supports my own experiences with cross-gender friends, that the challenge of sexual tension is minimal. I didn't know whether this was true for other male-female friendships, as well.

Emotional Bond Challenge

As revealed in the first survey, the emotional bond challenge comprised the largest percentage of all the challenges reported by cross-sex friends. <u>Approximately 20 percent of the challenges mentioned by males and females</u>

Scanning Strategies

If skimming is a bit like a leisurely stroll, trying to get the lay of the land, scanning is a more deliberate hunt for particular things in an article's landscape. Obviously, you have to know what you want to find—perhaps a certain statistic, interpretation, case study, or quotation—or possibly an answer to a particular question. How do you scan strategically?

1. Use the map provided. Studies usually provide titles and subheadings that cue you to content.

2. Look where the kind of information you're after is located. For example, if you're after numerical data, focus on lists and charts.

3. Scan after you've skimmed. Once you understand the organization and logical development of the article, you'll know where to concentrate the hunt.

were categorized as an emotional bond challenge, suggesting a lack of gender differences in perception of the prevalence of this challenge. However,
when specific emotional bond problems are examined the possibility of
gender differences becomes apparent. For example, whereas only 2 percent
of the males reported that one partner wanted more intimacy than the other,
12 percent of the females had this perception. Information gleaned from the
diary reveals that individuals in the various groups talked about their emotional bond less than once a week, but thought about the challenge more often than that. As was true of the other challenges, some individuals reported
having frequent discussions with their friends about their feelings for one
another, and thinking about it even more frequently.

Despite the fact that the emotional bond challenge was more common
than the other three challenges, the vast majority of individuals reported
having no problems in that area. The most striking difference in percentages is that 94 percent of casual cross-sex friends reported that they had
no difficulties of this type compared to only 57 percent of the individuals
in good cross-sex friendships. One possible explanation for this discrepancy can be found in a developmental approach to friendship formation.
Stage models of friendship development contend that as a friendship
evolves the participants become more intimate (Perlman & Fehr, 1986).
Development of intimacy would certainly involve discussions of how

*These ideas seem rather
obvious to me.*

partners feel about one another. Perhaps casual friends have not yet reached the developmental stage of friendship that would
make the emotional bond challenge relevant.

It is necessary to make one final qualification concerning our results
as they pertain to the emotional bond challenge. Unfortunately the Likert
item dealing with the emotional bond challenge was unintentionally
deleted from the final version of the survey, which meant that the challenge could not be included as part of the analysis of variance. This over-
sight weakens any conclusions we might draw concerning the effects of
type of friendship, gender, and romantic status on the emotional bond
challenge. However, as noted in the preceding two paragraphs, there is
still fairly strong evidence that gender and type of friendship impact perception of the emotional bond challenge. Nevertheless, conclusions
would certainly have been more convincing had that challenge been included in the ANOVA.

Audience Challenge

There was mixed support for existence of the audience challenge, though
it appears clear that level of self-monitoring does impact that challenge.
High self-monitors are more concerned with public perception of their relationship than are low self-monitors. Future research might further

explore what communicative strategies are used by high self-monitors to insure that the "correct" picture of the relationship is communicated to relevant audiences.

Depending upon the group, the audience challenge comprised anywhere from five to 22 percent of the total number of challenges reported. Though fairly large percentages of individuals from each group reported that they do not explain their relationship to members of their social network, even larger percentages replied that they let "everyone" know that they and their cross-sex friend were not dating partners. One unanticipated finding was that of the six groups under examination, the single individuals reported the lowest percentage of challenge falling into the audience dimension (5 percent). One might think that individuals who are not spoken for would be natural targets for the assumption by audiences that "something else is going on."

| I think this is interesting, too. I wonder why that is? |

No clear picture presents itself as to the possibility of gender differences in perception of the audience challenge. In the diary survey females reported having discussions about the audience challenge more often with their cross-sex friends than did males, and yet males thought about the audience challenge more often than did females. On the open-ended question from the first survey, the percentage of challenges falling into the audience challenge was twice as high for females as it was for males. Though these findings suggest that gender might have an impact on perception of the audience challenge, the ANOVA did not support the existence of gender differences.

Though the results of the ANOVA revealed that type of friendship had a significant impact on the perception of the audience challenge, caution should be applied in the interpretation of those results. For example, though good cross-sex friends had discussions about audience perception of their friendship more often than casual friends, even good cross-sex friends fell short of "sometimes" having such discussions.

Equality Challenge

The same pattern reveals itself in connection to the equality challenge as was manifested with the other challenges. The major difference is that the equality challenge is less of a problem than the other three challenges. As revealed in the first survey, only minuscule percentages of the total number of challenges reported were categorized as an equality challenge. This finding supports the contention made by Roberts (1982) that cross-sex friendships are characterized by "symmetrical eligibilities" meaning that cross-sex friends have equal eligibilities in their friendships.

These results also further verify findings by Monsour (1988), that the issue of power and control (as manifested in conversational control and decision making) does not appear to be a concern in cross-sex friendship. Data from the diaries verified findings from the first survey in that the vast majority of individuals never discussed the issue of power and control, and hardly ever thought about it.

> *I was skeptical that cross-gender friends had few challenges with power and control, but it seems that another study has found the same thing. I guess I'll have to think about this issue more.*

The ANOVA did reveal some interesting effects in regards to the equality challenge, all pertaining to the type of cross-sex friendship. Though the difference between casual and good friendships reached statistical significance the practical difference was negligible. Individuals in both types of friendship reported that they and their friend were equals to a slightly greater than moderate extent. Good cross-sex friends also reported to a significantly greater degree than casual cross-sex friends that they and their cross-sex friends were interested in promoting one another's welfare. This suggests that good cross-sex friends are more likely than casual cross-sex friends to approach their relationship from a communal orientation. Such an orientation might lessen the chances of male domination in the friendship (Lipman-Blumen, 1976).

> *After reading this "Discussion" section, I look back at the questions I came up with when I tried to interpret the material, and I find that only one of them is answered (why men might report more problems with sexual tension than women). Otherwise, I find myself not surprised by what I read, and I often find myself saying that some of their conclusions seem obvious. But if I've learned anything from being a professor, it's that every field takes up research on questions that may seem obvious to outsiders, but aren't to those on the inside, so I'm cautious in my criticism.*
>
> *The "Conclusions" section I'll read word for word, for obvious reasons.*

Conclusions

Have researchers made "much ado about nothing" in regards to purported challenges facing cross-sex friends? We conclude that scholars have been justified in their study of these challenges, but perhaps have overestimated their prevalence. Our research indicates that the chal-

> *Here the writers are rephrasing their "yeah, but" move.*

What does this mean, then? That these challenges are inaccurate and we should be figuring out what the actual challenges are? This statement makes me wonder about how seriously I can take the four types of challenges. If these aren't relevant, then which ones are?

lenges enumerated by O'Meara (1989) were not relevant to many individuals in cross-sex friendships. However, for some respondents the challenges were of central importance, and a few cross-sex friends even became preoccupied with certain challenges. There is also the possibility that some respondents self-selected a nonchallenged friendship to report on, which would give the impression that the challenges were less common than they actually are. However, the reverse argument could also be made, that is, respondents are more prone to report on cross-sex friendships in which there are challenges because those friendships are more salient and easier to remember.

One direction for future research seems obvious. As a first step, investigators need to identify cross-sex friends who are struggling with particular challenges. This might be accomplished through survey research utilizing open-ended questions. Once those individuals are identified, then perhaps a different methodological strategy than the one used in this research should be employed. For example, in-depth qualitative interviews might be the appropriate step to take once individuals dealing with the challenges are located. In-depth interviewing would allow the researcher to more fully explore various dynamics involved in the negotiation of challenges, and to investigate important questions that were not explored in this research. For example, what role (if any) does nonverbal communication play in the recognition and negotiation of challenges? In what ways are the emotional bond and sexual challenges related to one another? To what degree, if any, does mass media impact perceptions concerning appropriate female-male friendships? How might sexual orientation impact perception of challenges in cross-sex friendships? The investigation of these questions, and many more, would make substantive contributions to an area that has been relatively ignored by social scientists.

In closing, as scholars develop research strategies to explore numerous questions pertaining to cross-sex friendships they must be cognizant of the impact that such study might have on those friendships. Relationship research does not occur in a vacuum, meaning that the studied relationship might be changed by the research endeavor. This is particularly true of cross-sex friendships because of the struggle (sometimes manifested as challenges) that characterizes some of those relationships. Consequently, researchers must make an effort in their designs to minimize the impact that those designs will have on the studied relationship.

References

Abbey, A. (1982). Sex differences in attributions for friendly behavior: Do males misperceive females' friendliness? *Journal of Personality and Social Psychology, 42,* 830–838.

Bell, R. (1981). *Worlds of friendship.* Beverly Hills, CA: Sage.

Bem, S. L. (1981). Gender schema theory: A cognitive account of sex typing. *Psychological Review, 88,* 354–364.

Brain, R. (1976). *Friends and lovers.* New York: Basic Books.

Chafetz, J. S. (1974). *Masculine/feminine or human?* Itasca, IL: Peacock.

Clark, M. S., & Mills, J. (1979). Interpersonal attraction in exchange and communal relationships. *Journal of Personality and Social Psychology, 37,* 12–24.

Lepp, I. (1966). *The ways of friendship.* New York: Macmillan.

Lipman-Blumen, J. (1976). Toward a homosocial theory of sex-roles: An explanation of the sex segregation of social institutions. In M. M. Blaxall & B. Reagan (Eds.), *Women and the workplace.* Chicago: University of Chicago Press.

Monsour, M. (1988). Cross-sex friendships in a changing society (Doctoral Dissertation, University of Illinois-Champaign, 1988). *Dissertation Abstracts International.*

Monsour, M. (1992). Meanings of intimacy in cross and same-sex friendships. *Journal of Social and Personal Relationships, 9,* 277–295.

Monsour, M., Betty, S., & Kurzweil, N. (1993). Levels of perspectives and the perception of intimacy in cross-sex friendships: A. balance theory explanation of shared perceptual reality. *Journal of Social and Personal Relationships, 10,* 529–550.

O'Meara, D. (1989). Cross-sex friendship: Four basic challenges of an ignored relationship. *Sex Roles, 21,* 525–543.

Paine, R. (1974). An exploratory analysis in "middle class" culture. In E. Leyton (Ed.), *The compact. Newfoundland social and economic papers No. 3,* Institute of Social and Economic Research. Toronto: University of Toronto Press.

Perlman, D., & Fehr, B. (1986). Theories of friendship: the analysis of interpersonal attraction. In V. J. Derlega and B. A. Winstead (Eds.), *Friendship and social interaction.* New York: Springer-Verlag.

Rawlins, W. K. (1992). *Friendship matters: Communication, dialectics, and the life course.* New York: Walter de Gruyter.

Rawlins, W. K. (1982). Cross-sex friends and the communicative management of sex-role expectations. *Communication Quarterly, 30,* 343–352.

Roberts, M. K. (1982). Men and women: Partners, lovers, friends. In K. E. Davis and T. O. Mitchell (Eds.), *Advances in descriptive psychology, 2,* 57–78.

Rubin, I. (1985). *Just friends.* New York: Harper & Row.

Sapadin, L. (1988). Friendship and gender: Perspectives of professional men and women. *Journal of Social and Personal Relationships, 5,* 387–403.

Shotland, R. L., & Craig, J. M. (1988). Can men and women differentiate between friendly and sexually interested behavior? *Social Psychology Quarterly, 51,* 66–73.

Synder, M. (1974). The self-monitoring of expressive behavior. *Journal of Personality and Social Psychology, 30,* 526–537.

Synder, M., & Gangestad, S. (1986). On the nature of self-monitoring: Matters of assessment, matters of validity. *Journal of Personality and Social Psychology, 51,* 125–139.

Wright, P. H. (1988). Interpreting research on gender differences in friendship: A case for moderation and a plea for caution. *Journal of Social and Personal Relationships, 5, 361–313.*

In the conclusion I find the authors going back to the experts they mentioned in the beginning: "Our research indicates that the challenges enumerated by O'Meara (1989) were not relevant to many individuals in cross-sex friendships." The authors never forget the context within which their research fits. I can imagine them asking themselves, "So, now that we've done this research, what have we learned about O'Meara's research, the categories we used to generate our own research questions? How well do his categories reflect the difficulties in male-female friendships?" They are in dialogue with the other researchers in their field, not out on their own ignoring what other people have said. They see themselves as contributing to the knowledge in their field that was begun by the experts they draw upon.

I'm particularly struck in this section by the list of questions for future research. This is also a common aspect of the articles I read, describing what researchers can do next. It reinforces that idea of dialogue, of a group of people talking together to figure things out and constantly looking for new directions to seek out new ideas. I'm happy to see that these writers are thinking about the issue of sexual orientation as I was earlier.

I'm also curious about the connection between the emotional bond and the sexual challenges, and disappointed that this study didn't explore that. But all in all, this article was a good way to enter the conversation in psychology about my topic. I know a lot more than I did about how psychologists write up research, what evidence they value, and most importantly, who are some of the key people in the field who have said something about cross-gender friendships. I have an initial sense of the questions they're asking, too, which is helping me revise my own questions. There is a dialogue going on in my notebook and in my head with these experts, which is exactly what I'm after.

Exercise 7.2 *Reader Reflections*

Join Michelle as she reads another academic article on this topic, and as you do, explore along with her your own reactions to the ideas and findings, possibly working toward an essay of your own.

STEP 1: Spend five minutes fastwriting about your own reaction to the article you just read, focusing on how it might have changed your thinking about cross-gender friendships. Begin the fastwrite with this phrase: *When I began the article, I thought _____ but now I think _____.* Follow that "seed" sentence and see where it goes.

STEP 2: We'd also like you to keep track of *how* you're reading this kind of material. You've witnessed Michelle's struggles and strategies for reading "Challenges Confronting Cross-Sex Friendships." What about your own? In your journal, take a moment to explore in a fastwrite one or more of the following questions:

- What was the hardest part about reading the article? What did you do if you got frustrated?
- If you have never read an article like this one before, what two or three reading strategies helped you most to get through the piece? If you are familiar with this kind of article, how did you approach the reading differently this time?
- What do you understand about reading scientific articles that you didn't understand before?
- Did you feel like an outsider reading this article? Describe how that felt.

What's Alien and What's Not

No one wants to read stuff that makes them feel stupid. But if you read like an ethnographer, you will see that you're not stupid at all; you've just been thrust into an alien culture. In the beginning, you simply pay attention. How do these people do things? What is distinctive about their language? But also consider the ways this culture isn't alien at all. This book began with essays and articles that didn't seem very academic, often personal pieces that some people call creative nonfiction. If you think about it, the article you just read on cross-gender friendship and, say, the piece by Greg Critser, "Let Them Eat Fat," in Chapter 3 have some things in common. Each has a specific focus or angle, each brings in the voices of others, and each is testing a proposition about the way some small part of the world seems to work.

What distinguishes these pieces more than anything else is that they were written for very different audiences—one a group of specialists who belong

FIGURE 7-1   The Range of Fact-Based Writing

Popular Nonfiction		Academic Article
General Audience		Specialized Audience
Flexible Rules of Evidence		Stict Rules of Evidence
Form Open-Ended		Form Prescribed
Writer Usually a Nonexpert		Writer an Expert

to a subculture called psychology, and the other for a larger group of generalists, people not too unlike us. If you imagine research writing located on a continuum, with an essay such as Hodgman's "No Wonder They Call Me a Bitch" in Chapter 4 on one end, and "Challenges Confronting Cross-Sex Friendships" on the other, you can see the wide range of fact-based writing (see Figure 7-1). Move to the right, and the language becomes more specialized, the audience more exclusive, valid evidence more limited, and the structure more prescribed. Shift to left, and the opposite happens—things loosen up, the language becomes more familiar, and the pieces often develop in unexpected ways.

The point is this: *Good readers are able to move more easily back and forth on this continuum, adjusting their reading strategies in response to different kinds of texts, consciously aware of when they're outsiders or insiders equipped with the tools to lower the barriers to understanding.*

Now that you've reflected on your own reading strategies for academic articles, let's return to the research Michelle is reading.

Men and Women at Work: A Business Article

Having looked at research about the challenges men and women face when they are friends, I wanted to see what studies had been done about the psychological and emotional effects of those friendships. I found two articles that were interesting, one on male-female friendships in the workplace and another on the effect of sex-roles on friendships. The more I read, the more I realized that the fields of psychology and sociology were beginning to do more research on cross-gender friendships, and what they were finding challenged the conventional wisdom that men and women can only be sexual or romantic partners. I had to be careful, though, that I was not simply reading articles that supported the beliefs I came into the research with.

As you read the following article, have your journal and a pen handy. We'll be asking you to practice reading this piece as an ethnographer, and I'll be focusing more of my own comments on the ideas presented in the study rather than my reading strategies. This article, like the others I looked at, is organized loosely around the *Hypothesis, Methods, Results, Discussion* organizational pattern, but these terms aren't all used. Things to focus on when marking up the article:

- Mark the terms and phrases that are unfamiliar, that seem part of the insider language for this community of psychologists.

- Mark the places in the text where you see the authors "entering the conversation"—that is, acknowledging what others have had to say about this subject.

- Underline the places where the authors introduce their research questions and state their "thesis" or main findings. What do you notice about where those statements are placed?

- In the margins, begin making a list of the kind of evidence the researchers use to support their findings. What does this suggest about the information that is considered valid in this field?

Love Without Sex

The Impact of Psychological Intimacy Between Men and Women at Work

Robert Quinn, Sharon A. Lobel, and Lynda St. Clair

In past decades, close working relationships most often developed between members of the same sex: on the assembly line or in the boardroom, for men; and within the secretarial pool or the nurses' station, for women. Male-female friendships were relatively infrequent since fewer women worked, occupations tended to be either "male" or "female," and social norms discouraged close friendships between men and women outside of marriage.

Today, however, with more and more women entering formerly male-dominated professions and assuming positions involving frequent interactions with men, circumstances are ripe for psychologically intimate relationships between men and women to develop. Moreover, as organizations continue to embrace such management strategies as team building, networking, and coalition building, the intensity of co-worker interactions and the need for employees to gain co-worker support will increase, which will make male-female relationships stronger than ever.

This development is likely to raise new concerns for employees, who, according to published reports, are already confused about what consti-

Ah, I hadn't thought of that before—team building and collaboration would affect the nature of the relationships in the workplace, and if we only believe that men and women can be sexual/romantic partners, then we should go back to sexist practices years ago that keep them separated in the workplace (if they're heterosexual, that is). Certainly in my case, I collaborate a great deal with my co-workers, and the kind of relationship I develop with them affects everything—my own feelings about work, how well a project will succeed, and whether my colleagues will listen to my ideas.

tutes "appropriate" male-female attitudes and behaviors at work—a confusion fueled by the sexual-harassment hearings conducted during the confirmation proceedings for Supreme Court Justice Clarence Thomas. Moreover, in attempting to discourage sexual harassment among employees, organizations also have questions: Should they seek to eradicate sexuality entirely from the workplace? Should they encourage men and women to relate to one another in an impersonal, "professional" manner—that is, merely as holders of work roles? Does it make sense to encourage team building among co-workers on the one hand, but discourage personal relationships between men and women on the other? Or is it acceptable for opposite-sex co-workers to connect with one another as individuals?

Of course, much media and public attention has focused on workplace relationships involving sexual attraction and/or sexual harassment. However, close psychological relationships between men and women at work deserve increased analysis as well. A national survey of professionals, conducted by the authors, reveals that psychologically intimate workplace relationships have both costs and benefits for the individuals involved, as well as for co-workers and the organization as a whole. As these relationships grow in number, it will become essential for managers to have a better understanding of their cause and impact, so they will be able to prevent them from undermining organizational morale and performance.

A Study of Close Relationships at Work

To help managers understand the effects of emotionally intimate relationships between men and women in the workplace, the authors designed a study involving male and female professionals. Our first step was to gather data and analyze themes derived from a number of cases. We began by sending a letter to 900 randomly selected members of a national professional training and development association, asking if they had experienced "nonsexual love relationships" at work and, if they had, to describe in writing:

---

*Michelle's comments are shown in the boxes throughout this reading. Underlined passages show key points she wanted to highlight.

1. The participants;

2. The way the relationship began and the key events that subsequently occurred;

3. The characteristics of the relationship that indicated its closeness, and the factors that deterred sexual involvement;

4. The personal and organizational payoffs and costs of the relationship;

5. Unique characteristics of the relationship; and

6. The perceived frequency of similar relationships in the organization.

Of those we contacted, 50 people responded—a satisfactory response rate, we believed, considering the highly personal nature of the questions, the length of time it would take to write out the answers, and the fact that we did not expect the majority of our sample to have experienced this kind of relationship.

We examined the 50 responses for common themes and selected the sentences we would include as questionnaire items for further survey research. We then mailed a survey, which included the new questionnaire items, to 1,709 people, all of whom resided in the United States and had participated in the executive education program at the business school of a large midwestern university during the previous three years. All of the 709 female program participants were included in the survey sample; because a large number of program participants came from Illinois, Indiana, Michigan, and Ohio, we decided that every third male from these states and every male from all other states would receive a survey, for a total of 1,000 males.

We sent each recipient the 12-page survey along with a cover letter inviting participation in a nationwide study of friendships between male and female co-workers. The survey asked people to describe their closest relationship with a person of the opposite sex at work, and, even if that relationship was actually quite superficial, to indicate the extent of their agreement with such statements as "We feel love for each other," "We deeply trust one another," and "If I were in a situation of need, I could freely ask for this person's help even if it would inconvenience him or her." For purposes of comparison, we also asked married people and people involved in a romantic relationship to respond again to these statements, this time thinking about their spouse or partner. Anonymity was guaranteed.

Here I find that these researchers specifically focused on people who were both married and single. I also notice that the median age of the participants is closer to my own than those in the previous study (who were 18- to 21-year-olds). This article might have more to do with my research questions than some of the others I've read.

We received 1,044 completed surveys (569 males, 475 females), yielding a 61 percent response rate (57 percent for males, 67 percent for females). Because we were interested in close relationships that were nonsexual, we also asked respondents to indicate how physically intimate their relationship was. Some 968 respondents indicated their relationship was not sexually intimate. This subsample included 527 males (54.4 percent) and 441 females (45.6 percent); the median age was 38, with a minimum of 23 and a maximum of 69. Some 776 respondents in this subsample (80.2 percent) indicated they were married, 87 (9.0 percent) said they were "unmarried but committed to a relationship," and 104 (10.7 percent) said they were "uncommitted." Also within this subsample, 82.3 percent (n = 797) had at least a bachelor's degree, and 87 percent (n = 842) held managerial positions. The median salary was $50,000, with a minimum of $18,000 and a maximum of $680,000.

In addition, 20.0 percent (n − 194) of the respondents in this subsample said their relationship was with a superior; 37.1 percent (n = 359) said a peer; and 37.4 percent (n = 362) said a subordinate. The remainder (n = 53, 5.5 percent) selected "other" to describe the position of the other person in relation to themselves. The median number of years the individuals in the relationship had been acquainted was three.

The Nature of Psychological Intimacy

I'm grateful here that they define what they mean by psychological intimacy. I haven't thought about my own definition of it yet, so I'll keep this one in mind as I read more articles and think about how full this definition is.

The 50 responses to our initial, open-ended questionnaire suggested that psychologically intimate work relationships are chara cterized by affection and concern for one another, shared attitudes, and affirmations of one another's worth and accomplishments. Communication takes place in deep, rich ways, and involves high levels of self-disclosure, a sense of trust, and sometimes the ability to predict the reactions of the other. Said a male respondent:

> This is an opportunity for a man to talk to someone who is experiencing the same pressures and issues at work. [There is] better understanding without threats of vulnerability that another man might present.

In addition, statistical analyses of our follow-up survey responses uncovered a series of factors most closely associated with psychological intimacy, which we grouped by theme using factor analysis. Three themes emerged that characterized close relationships, a deep emotional bond, mutual interest and respect, and a willingness to devote time and energy to another person in the absence of any obligation to do so.

These three themes were highly interrelated but distinct. For example, the individuals who expressed a deep emotional bond with their co-workers also indicated mutual interest and respect—but those expressing the latter did not always indicate the former.

Co-workers vs. Spouses

Statistical analyses of respondents' descriptions of their psychological intimacy with their spouses or partners revealed a different set of factors. Therefore, we cannot make direct comparisons between feelings of closeness for a spouse or partner versus a co-worker. We did observe, however, that as psychological intimacy with a co-worker increased, psychological intimacy with a spouse or partner also increased, except when the co-worker relationship involved "charged" emotions, the desire to be together, and "exhilarating chemistry." As feelings of this type for the co-worker increased, the reported degree of psychological intimacy with the spouse or partner decreased.

Because our study was designed to measure people's perceptions at one point in time, we cannot determine if intense feelings for an opposite-sex co-worker arose because of a decline in these types of feelings for the spouse or partner; nor can we say if the relationship with the spouse or partner became less intense because of growing psychological intimacy with the co-worker. The kinds of feelings respondents had about their co-workers and spouses were reflected in two comments from respondents:

The only cost I can think of has been some resentment and/or conflict with our spouses who may not trust us as much as we deserve. I think relationships of this type are happening often, but the only ones we hear about are the sensational ones which include an extramarital affair. My loyalty to my marriage makes relationships like

Now this is intriguing. So many people I talk to seem to assume that a marriage will suffer if the partners are emotionally close with someone of the opposite sex. Clearly, as they say here, if romantic or sexual feelings are involved, the marriage will suffer. I wish they'd talk more about why they think male-female friendships increase intimacy with a spouse. I have my own ideas. . . .

I would agree that you need a good marriage to make close relationships with someone of the opposite sex work. To me, a good marriage is one based on trust, love, and respect for the differences in your spouse. Too much pressure is put on spouses in marriages to be the only source of emotional support for the other. The relationship is richer, in my experience, when each spouse has close relationships with a few other people.

this possible in any job setting I have been in, and I see it often in co-workers who are faithful. I believe the character of the individual influences his/her ability to be faithful. However, this is of course contingent upon a good marriage.

How Do Psychologically Intimate Relationships Develop?

Participants gave a variety of explanations for how their relationships began. One said the friendship was originally a formal mentoring relationship, while another mentioned common interests:

> We met at work. . . . We soon realized that we had a lot in common (likes, dislikes, parental relationships, childhood hardships, birthdays, etc.) and we soon became very close friends. . . . Key events were moments of sharing, hours of talking, and the realization that we could say anything about ourselves, each other, and others. We did not judge each other. A truly honest relationship was established.

Another described a more dramatic beginning:

I read somewhere a long time ago that the workplace was becoming the new family in our culture—a lot of people prefer to go to work and not stay at home because they feel more accepted and experience less interpersonal conflict than they do at home. Plus, for so many of us, our work is a central part of our identity, so sharing it with someone else is satisfying. I wonder how true this is in nonprofessional settings? This study is clearly focused on a particular social and educational class, and so these conclusions are limited, I suspect.

The minute the new vice president walked into the personnel office and introduced himself and [we] shook hands, it was like an electric shock passed between us. It was instant attraction [in terms of] both appearance and personality . . . [he] took me to lunch and we compared our childhoods and found we had much in common.

Although some participants mentioned special circumstances that led to the development of their relationships, many just said they had worked together over a period of time and came to know one another. Thus, work itself was frequently seen as central to the development of psychological intimacy.

Effects of the Relationship on Behaviors and Attitudes

In developing our survey, we decided to assess whether and how psychological intimacy with a co-worker was associated with work-related factors, such as support for the other's career, motivation, commitment to the organization, and the size of the respondent's most recent merit increase. We first examined previous research on four types of social support that exist in

> *Since Bruce is someone I work with, I can say that we offer each other all of these kinds of support. I'm not sure what to do with this information, however. It further clarifies the kind of psychological effects that men and women have as friends, and that answers one of my research questions. But I don't have any questions to ask about these ideas.*

the workplace: *emotional support*, which includes behaviors that contribute to another's well-being, such as nurturing, providing empathy, caring, loving, trusting, listening to problems, and promoting the other's happiness; *instrumental support*, which involves directly helping people in need, such as doing their work for them; *informational support*, which involves providing advice or other information individuals can use to help themselves cope with problems; and *appraisal support*, which involves providing feedback about performance or other information individuals can use to evaluate themselves.

Our survey responses showed that psychologically close relationships were characterized by all four types of support:

> My friendship with my male co-worker is my first true friendship with a male. . . . We truly trust each other and enjoy what this friendship has given us as individuals. . . . Because of the time people spend at work, a true friend can be just the person that is needed to share and vent those things that occur in our day-to-day lives. [Emotional Support]

> The relationship matured as time passed, to the point where she was quite indispensable. . . . She looked out for my welfare, from keeping track of my daily activities to getting my lunch when I was too busy to get my own. [Instrumental Support]

> I have had three "cross-gender" relationships in the workplace. . . . In each case it enhanced my [understanding] of my job, how I was doing and how the company worked. I think it is important (and healthy) for women in business to have cross-gender relationships to learn how to "play the game." [Informational Support]

> She helped me see myself better. . . . She boosted confidence in my own abilities. [Appraisal Support]

In addition, in analyzing our results, we expected that psychological intimacy with a co-worker would be associated with positive work-related outcomes, an expectation based in part on previous research that suggests that emotional support from a supervisor or co-worker directly minimizes interpersonal tensions and satisfies a worker's needs for affiliation and ap-

Wow, I didn't realize there was previous research which detailed how close friendships with co-workers positively affected the individuals and their performance. It would seem that these close friendships enhance the workplace rather than create problems, as some might think.

proval. And, in fact, participants in psychologically intimate relationships <u>said they helped each other reach work goals, shared career information, and provided useful feedback.</u> Increasing psychological intimacy with a co-worker was also associated with <u>greater commitment to the organization, more involvement with one's job, positive self-evaluations of performance, and higher merit increases.</u> Said one female respondent:

He helped my career enough that I'm now a VP (and became one at 33). I worked like a dog and made him look good. We had lots of success

Effects on the Work Group

Office romances, which include sexual involvement, have been shown to engender negative consequences, such as gossip, jealousy, resentment, and even lawsuits. This is especially true when the relationship involves a superior and a subordinate. Co-workers tend to perceive that personal/sexual resources are being exchanged for career advancements. In the cases of psychologically intimate relationships, even though the participants are not sexually involved, co-workers may think that they are, or may still resent the special privileges that seem to stem from the closeness. Said one respondent:

A couple must be very mature to have a serious relationship [at work]. You must be able to separate your work and personal lives. Even if the couple demonstrates this ability, there will be others at the workplace who will be nonbelievers [and will be convinced that one individual in the relationship is receiving special favors].

Said another:

I sometimes worry about this issue at work, but good friends—whether male or female—need to be aware that others might feel like outsiders. The friends need to go out of their way to include others and minimize those feelings.

Benefits to the organization are substantial [because we have] an excellent work relationship with open communication. . . . [However] it is known that we are very close so there may be some feeling that "outsiders" don't get an equal playing field.

Indeed, when survey respondents characterized their relationship in terms of "love," "chemistry," and a desire to be with the co-worker, they also indicated that the relationship generated gossip and rumors, complaints and gripes, hostilities, and distorted communications in the work group:

> Both of our bosses constantly said to us individually that it didn't look good and that people were wondering and talking about us since we spent so much time together, including lunch in the company cafeteria or out at a restaurant.

In some cases the consequences were reported to be quite serious:

> A colleague (also a personal friend) and her boss were fired for having an alleged affair. I have no way of knowing the truth, but she has told me that they were not having an affair . . . it's not worth it if appearances can influence one's position at work.

On the other hand, some respondents said the relationship's impact on the group was mostly positive:

> *Bruce and I work closely on a lot of projects, and I do see that we get more work done of a higher quality, in part because of the strengths we each bring, but also because of our friendship. We don't mess around with ego, hostilities, competition, hurt feelings. And the people who are around our office have said they feel very comfortable around us.*

> There's no friction on the job . . . [the good working atmosphere] not only enhances our ability to perform but seems to extend to our co-workers. They seem to vicariously share our love/affection for each other. We work for a large communication company where the culture is usually highly competitive and secretive—[but] this does not exist in our department.

The respondents reported that their relationships had payoffs for the organization, such as perceptions of improved teamwork and work-group productivity. These payoffs increased as psychological intimacy with the co-worker increased.

Deterrents to Sexual Intimacy

Among the most obvious and significant questions we had as we researched our subject was this: Why weren't these relationships sexual? Some 12.9 percent of our respondents agreed or strongly agreed with the statement "We feel love for each other," while 6.2 percent said they had openly decided not to act on their feelings of sexual attraction. When asked why their relationship had not led to sexual intimacy, 49.7 percent of the sample said a lack of sexual attraction was not the reason. Thus, even in cases where sexual attraction was present (and in some cases that attraction was strong), many respondents held back. Sexual attraction had more of an impact in relationships with "charged" emotions than in those characterized by deep trust and respect but no intense emotions. These data suggest that sexual attraction may be present in psychologically intimate relationships, and may be either openly acknowledged or not discussed. Said one respondent:

> In the 20 years I have been working, there have been various amounts of sexual tension between myself and others in the organization. I have not acted upon these tensions, but I have dreamed and fantasized about the other person. These feelings eventually go away.

Said another:

> Men and women can be . . . just friends [at work, even if they have] a sexual interest in each other.

Those findings really blow the stereotype that men and women can only be sexual partners. It's heartening to me that so many people consciously choose not to act on sexual attraction because they value the friendship and their own ethics about monogamy (if they're in a committed relationship). These researchers are suggesting that sexual attraction exists in male-female relationships, but that attraction doesn't control or define them.

Commitment to a spouse or partner, a strong sense of ethics, and the desire to keep one's personal and professional lives separate were the factors participants cited most often as deterrents to sexual intimacy. For relationships in which sexual attraction was relatively strong, fear that sex might kill the relationship, fear of company policies, and fear of rejection were also frequently cited. One male respondent said:

> I have few people in my life that I trust and confide in like her. . . . The only reason it isn't sexual is our respect for each other, as well as our marriages. We don't believe in "stepping out" and surely would lose respect for each other (and ourselves) if we did.

One female respondent noted:

> We soon realized we wanted a sexual relationship . . . [But] he was married and I was engaged, [and] he was not ready to break the commitment to his wife so we both respected that. We remained just as close, and continued our relationship as it had been.

Gender Differences

Studies suggest that women, compared with men, provide not only more emotional support, but better emotional support to their friends. Women are also assumed to be the primary support providers to spouses, children, and co-workers. Therefore, we were not surprised to find some gender differences in the responses to our questionnaire.

That certainly wasn't true in my case—Bruce had lots of close women friends, but I hadn't had many close friendships with men beyond my husband, so I think I was more worried about it than he was. And that helped me worry less.

First, <u>men were more likely to perceive barriers to opposite-sex friendships than women were.</u> For example, the male respondents were more likely to agree that people of the opposite sex have different interests and needs, and that they did not know how to develop friendships with the opposite sex—even though they felt a greater desire to form such friendships than the female respondents did. <u>Men were also more likely than women to agree that "Men-women relationships are sexual for me, not just friendships" and that friendships with the opposite sex should be reserved for marriage.</u>

This finding is consistent with the previous study I read. Men seem, if only slightly, to have more worries about how to deal with sexual tension than women do in these relationships.

In addition, women reported higher levels of intimacy in their workplace relationship than men did, and they were also more likely to agree that as a result of the relationship, they and their "significant other" were able to provide one another with career-related support by sharing information, providing feedback, and helping one another reach work goals. Women also indicated more often that they communicated with their workplace friend about non-work-related subjects, talking about spiritual matters, for example, or having long discussions on private matters. Although we were not measuring the perceptions of both members of each pair, these data seem to <u>imply different conceptions of psychological intimacy between men and women, rather than actual differences in the characteristics of the relationships.</u>

This is interesting that women perceive the intimacy differently, even though the research didn't see many differences. I think this issue of perception needs more research.

Implications for Managers

We have described the kind of psychologically intimate relationship that often exists between men and women at work, and have determined the associated payoffs and costs for participants and their organizations. Our

This paragraph is a nice summary of their main points. The writers imply in the last two sentences that male-female friendships at work have these challenges: the "audience challenge" as Monsour and his co-authors describe it, and the "sexual challenge." These writers seem to get more at how cross-gender friends manage those challenges than the previous researchers did. I wonder if anyone else has looked closely at how male-female friends negotiate these issues?

study shows that male and female co-workers develop bonds of varying types, and that deep feelings for one another may include an element of sexual attraction. In some cases, this attraction is openly acknowledged; in others, individuals work through these issues alone. According to many of the case study respondents, men and women who become psychologically intimate but decide not to act on their sexual attraction walk a fine line that demands self-discipline and active restraint. Even if they walk the line successfully, the reaction of co-workers is yet another challenge they must face.

So how can organizations reap the benefits of psychological intimacy while reducing the costs?

First, it is important to recognize that, with the exception of relationships involving sexual harassment, personal relationships do not necessarily involve conflicts of interest with organizational aims. As the data presented illustrate, participants believe their psychologically intimate relationships bring about career benefits. In addition, they feel that their enhanced motivation, job involvement, and organizational commitment also benefit the organization and are reflected in higher merit increases.

As our respondents indicated, participants may spend work time engaged in nonwork activities, such as long, private discussions. In addition, such relationships may spur office gossip, causing downtime and declines in morale.

This part of the article is less relevant to my research questions, but it's interesting. What kind of conversations do enhance relationships in the workplace?

At this point, it may be time for the manager to step in. But in assessing whether or not to intervene, managers need to recognize that clear standards for determining whether a specific relationship conflicts with organizational aims are indeed elusive. Surely, same-sex conversations occur over non-work-related subjects, such as sports. Do these conversations contribute to relationship building, which is important for organizational vitality? At what point is a person spending too much time talking about nonwork topics?

These questions can best be answered by objective evaluations of each individual's work performance. If performance is not up to par, managers must determine if the problem is related to the relationship or not. It is not appropriate to assume that the performance deficit must be due to an existing close relationship with a member of the opposite sex. Clear evidence that the relationship is having a negative effect on performance—for example, that participants are unable to meet deadlines because of the excessive amount of time they are spending discussing nonwork matters—must exist.

What if the negative impact is on the performance of co-workers, rather than participants? It is possible, for example, that co-workers may be adversely affected by the relationship—especially when it involves a superior and a subordinate—because they are denied equal access to information and privileges. In these cases, interventions should emphasize the value of top-notch management practices, such as the development of all subordinates. Evaluation against standards can help the organization determine whether a manager involved in a psychologically intimate relationship is being fair to all of his or her employees. At the same time, observers of these relationships need to retain a certain amount of skepticism about appearances, especially since close relationships between man and woman do not necessarily include sexual involvement. Intervention is not necessary unless clear negative impacts on the work group can be identified.

> *I'm glad someone has finally said this. Male-female relationships really highlight our cultural and gendered assumptions about relationships, and we need to be more skeptical of what we think is going on.*

Managers should also be trained to understand the differences between office romances, sexual harassment, and nonsexual, psychologically intimate relationships. Office romances are sexually intimate relationships that may or may not involve psychological intimacy; sexual harassment involves unwelcome, negative attention; and psychologically intimate relationships involve positive, reciprocated interactions. Despite these distinctions, however, managers should be alerted to several cautionary flags:

First, as noted above, if psychological or sexual intimacy is perceived to give the participants an unfair advantage in employment decisions, co-workers may take legal action.

Second studies by other researchers show that men and women differ in their interpretations of what constitutes sexual harassment, while our study indicates that women and men differ in their perceptions of what constitutes psychological intimacy. Thus, attempts to draw boundaries between different kinds of relationships will clearly not apply to men and women in the same manner.

Third, although it is quite unlikely that a relationship involving sexual harassment may develop into an office romance or a nonsexual, psychologically intimate relationship, the reverse is possible if a once-close relationship sours for one of the participants.

These caveats might encourage managers to opt for the conservative approach in managing relationships between men and women—that is, to attempt to eradicate sexuality from the workplace. In fact, some organizations encourage employees to behave in an impersonal "professional" manner, assuming that this behavior is an antidote to sexual harassment, and that the elimination of personal relationships from work life will reduce conflicts of interest. However, while we recognize the seriousness of sexual harassment, we would argue that such a strategy is not practical, and that a preferable approach would be to identify the positive and negative impacts of nonsexual, psychologically intimate relationships and intervene only as necessary.

> I agree that trying to get rid of all close relationships in the workplace is not an answer to sexual harassment. How we feel at work is crucial to our sense of well-being and our productivity, and these researchers have pointed out that close friendships at work can have some benefits for everyone.

We believe that managers must also recognize that the presence of sexual attraction that is not acted upon may either energize employees or preoccupy and distract them, depending on their individual characters and needs. Since commitment to a spouse or partner was seen as a deterrent to sexual intimacy in our study, we can assume that the quality of each participant's relationship with his or her spouse or partner, as well as the depth of their commitment to their marriage or outside-of-work relationship, clearly plays a role in determining the effects of unfulfilled desires in the workplace. For single, uncommitted individuals, key factors determining the effect of their unfulfilled desires include their interest in developing a serious relationship outside of work and the availability of potential partners other than their co-worker. Whether feelings of love and trust at work are reciprocated may also determine the impact of the work relationship on individuals and their work groups.

> Yes!

Finally, managers must be careful not to apply different standards to opposite-sex relationships, compared to same-sex friendships. <u>Specifically, when they perceive an interaction between a male employee and a female employee that makes them suspicious, they should ask themselves whether they would have the same reaction or assessment if the participants were both men or both women, and there was no possibility of sexual intimacy.</u>

Issues for Further Study

We examined psychologically intimate workplace relationships at one point in time; longitudinal research is needed to determine if the impacts of these relationships change as time passes. Particularly in cases where sexual attraction is involved, it's important to determine whether these relationships are likely to become sexual over the long term. Sexual involvement may bring about a variety of consequences, such as a sexual harassment charge if the relationship should terminate, or disciplinary action if the relationship violates organizational policy.

We also need research to uncover more about why and under what circumstances psychologically intimate relationships emerge. We already know that the effects of intimacy are related to the prevailing climate at the workplace, as well as the differing needs and values of the individuals. Future research should examine the effect of such individual variables as marital status, age, religious commitment, and occupation, and of such organizational variables as culture, size, structure, and the relative positions of the co-workers involved. The relationship between workplace intimacy and marital intimacy is intriguing. Considering today's high divorce rate and other social factors, such as fear of AIDS, workers may increasingly choose to develop close personal relationships with co-workers.

Developments within and outside of the workplace are likely to produce an increase in the prevalence of psychologically intimate relationships between men and women at work. Because this type of relationship can have both positive and negative consequences, managers have a vital role to play: fostering positive outcomes while intervening to minimize any negative repercussions.

Selected Bibliography

J. Blustein, *Care and commitment: Taking the personal point of view,* New York: Oxford University Press, 1991.

D. R. Eyler and A. P. Baridon, "Far more than friendship: The new rules for reckoning with sexual attraction in the workplace," *Psychology Today*, May-June 1992, pp. 59–67.

J. S. House, *Work stress and social support* (Reading, MA: Addison Wesley, 1981).

J. S. House, D. Umberson, and K. R. Landis, "Structures and process of social support," *Annual Review of Sociology, 14*, 1988, pp. 293–318; A. S. Wharton and R. J. Erickson, "Managing emotions on the job and at home," *Academy of Management Review, 18*, 1993, pp. 457–486; D. Belle, "Gender differences in the social moderators of stress," in R. C. Barnett, L. Beiner, and G. Baruch (Eds.), *Gender and*

Stress (New York: Macmillan, 1987), pp. 257–277; A. R. Hochschild, *The Managed Heart* (Berkeley: University of California, 1983).

S. A. Lobel, "Sexuality at work: Where do we go from here," *Journal of Vocational Behavior, 42,* 1993, pp. 136–152.

S. A. Lobel, J. E. Dutton, and R. O'Neill, "Nurturing: Elaborating our understanding of important roles, skills and contexts in organizations," Conference of Women and Work, May 7–8, 1992, Arlington, Texas.

R. E. Quinn, "Coping with cupid: The formation, impact and management of romantic relationships in organizations," *Administrative Science Quarterly, 22(1),* 1977, pp. 30–45; Bureau of National Affairs, *Corporate Affairs: Nepotism, Office Romance, and Sexual Harassment* (Washington, DC: BNA, 1988); Clawson, J. G., & Kram, K. E., "Managing cross-gender mentoring, *Business Horizons,* May-June, 1984, pp. 22–32; and E. G. Collins, "Managers and lovers," *Harvard Business Review, 61* (Sept-Oct), 1983, pp. 142–154.

C. Solomon, "Romancing coworkers gets riskier," *The Wall Street Journal,* October 18, 1991, p. B2; and M. Ingrassia, "To flirt or not to flirt," *Newsday,* October 17, 1991, p. 73.

Exercise 7.3   *Reader Reflections*

STEP 1: You've done some initial fastwriting (Exercises 7.1 and 7.2) on your own feelings and beliefs about male and female friendship, and now you've read two academic articles on the subject. We'll admit it—these were tough pieces to read, and you may have had to struggle a bit to get through them. But the more you think about your reading process the more likely you'll get control over it. Take 20 minutes to reflect on what you've learned so far. First, look over your notes and write fast for five to seven minutes about what has struck you so far about cross-gender friendship after reading these two articles and looking over Michelle's shoulder as she responded to them.

Begin again with this "seed" sentence: *What I understand now that I didn't understand before I read these articles is . . .*

As you write, explore how your feelings or ideas about friendship have been challenged, qualified, or reinforced.

STEP 2: Now that you've practiced reading like an ethnographer, take some time to reflect on your reading process. In your journal or in small groups, respond to the following questions:

1. It's always a challenge to read an article that you may not be interested in. Were you able to overcome that resistance? How?

2. Make a quick list of the things you've learned so far about techniques for reading formal research.

3. What seemed to be the most difficult about reading like an ethnographer? What did you struggle with when you tried to identify the conventions of writing like a psychologist?

4. Compare the conclusions you've reached about this article with your group members or the whole class. What did you notice about how these writers show they are insiders in this subculture, for example? What kind of evidence do they value? How does that compare with the previous article that Michelle read?

Romance and Attraction:
Two Communication Studies Articles

In her essay "Just Friends: Can Men and Women Do It—without Doing It?" writer Abby Ellin remarked that:

> It's the . . . sexual energy that's so alluring—and frustrating—about cross-gender friendships. The inevitable flirtations and sexual tensions add a certain spice to the relationship, and excitement that often can't be found in same-sex friendships. Because, truth be told, there's usually some sort of attraction between any two people who become friends, and if you're straight, it's that much more intense with people of the opposite sex. (My gay male friends, by the way, say they encounter the same problem with gay male friends.) Whether you choose to act on the attraction is something else, but the issue is bound to pop up at some point.

Is she right? It seems to be a common perception that if you're straight you can't avoid sexual tension in such a friendship. But as I did more research, I discovered two communications professors who have done extensive research on cross-gender friendships, particularly in terms of the role attraction plays, and they've discovered how complex that sexual tension actually is. They also address the role of sexual orientation in studies of cross-gender friends. This was different from most of the other studies I'd already read, which assumed a heterosexual perspective on the subject that I found rather limiting. So here I've taken some long excerpts from their articles within the communications field. At this point I'm going to step back and not make any more of my own comments so you can practice the reading strategies I've been using. As you read, use what you've learned so far about reading academic research and:

- Mark the terms and phrases that are unfamiliar, that seem part of the insider language for this community of communications scholars.

- Mark the places in the text where you see the authors "entering the conversation"—that is, acknowledging what others have had to say about this subject.

- Underline the places where the authors introduce their research questions and state their thesis or main findings. What do you notice about where those statements are placed?

- In the margins, begin making a list of the kind of evidence the researchers use to support their findings. These studies are both using what is called "qualitative research methods"—that is, approaches to studying human interactions that do not focus on statistical information, but instead rely on interviews and observations that can be interpreted without statistical formulas. What does this suggest about the information that is considered valid in this field?

"I Like You . . . As a Friend": The Role of Attraction in Cross-Sex Friendship

Heidi M. Reeder

ABSTRACT

This study investigated attraction in heterosexual cross-sex friendships. Study I used in-depth interviews with 20 dyads (40 participants) to uncover four types of attraction that occur in cross-sex friendships—subjective physical/sexual attraction, objective physical/sexual attraction, romantic attraction, and friendship attraction. These types of attraction are subject to being symmetrical or asymmetrical, and may incur changes over time. Study II ($N = 231$) used a questionnaire to assess the frequency of each type of attraction and the frequency with which types of attraction are perceived to change. The most prevalent form of attraction was friendship attraction, and the least prevalent form was romantic attraction. The implications of these results for understanding both cross-sex friendships and the process of attraction are discussed.

KEY WORDS: attraction • "cross-sex friendship" • relational development

Little is known about friendships between men and women. In fact, only recently has "cross-sex friendship" been considered its own relational category (Gaines, 1994). As late as 1986, such relationships were still considered under the rubric of romantic relationships. This is perhaps not surprising given the normative expectation that male–female bonds are primarily romantic and sexual. Indeed, the pervasive norm of heterosexual attraction is likely to influence how men and women experience cross-sex friendship. While many studies have looked at variables related to attraction in general, few have investigated attraction in male–female friendship specifically.

The assumption that attraction is prevalent in cross-sex friendship is revealed in many sources. Two recent movies (*When Harry Met Sally*, 1989; *My Best Friend's Wedding*, 1997) have sent the message that sexual and romantic attraction is a strong possibility in male–female friendships, and that such relationships cannot stay platonic for long. Similarly, several television shows (e.g., *Three's Company*, 1977–1984; *Friends*, 1994–present) have indicated that romantic attraction underlies male–female interactions, even if the participants are friends or roommates. The media is not the only place, however, that suggests this view. Much of the research on cross-sex friendship tends to take the perspective that attraction is a potential part of the experience. For example, O'Meara's (1989) definition of cross-sex friendship is quite different from the standard definition of friendship, which is assumed to be between same-sex people. O'Meara defines male–female friendship as a:

> Nonromantic, nonfamilial, personal relationship between a man and a woman. The relationship is nonromantic in the sense that its function is purposefully dissociated from courtship rites by the actors involved. Nonromantic does not mean, however, that sexuality and passion are necessarily absent from the relationship (p. 526).

O'Meara's definition serves primarily to distinguish cross-sex friendships from the standard of male–female relationships as romantic. He indicates that cross-sex friendships do have the potential for sexuality and passion, but that these features are not emphasized. This is quite different from Rawlins' (1992) definition of friendship. Synthesizing the early studies on friendship, Rawlins asserts that friendship is characterized as a voluntary, personal tie, with a spirit of equality, mutual involvement, and positive affect. This definition does not mention the opportunity for romance or passion. Although not directly stated, Rawlins' definition appears to pertain to friendships between same-sex heterosexuals where the potential for attraction (other than "liking") is not an issue.

What does it mean that attraction is a potential issue in cross-sex friendship? Does attraction in this context mean "sexuality and passion," as O'Meara suggests? Does male–female friendship provide a ripe opportunity for a committed romantic relationship? Or is attraction simply experienced as "liking," as it is in heterosexual same-sex friendship? This study seeks to answer these questions by discovering how attraction is experienced subjectively in cross-sex friendships. . . .

Study Rationale and Theoretical Framework

Cross-sex friendships are a relatively recent area of enquiry and many gaps in our knowledge still exist. The studies that have been conducted on attraction in cross-sex friendship thus far are limited in several respects. First, previous studies have typically limited their investigations to sexual attraction and have, therefore, overlooked other features of attraction. Second, past research has been criticized for investigating friendship as if there were one standard form. Allan (1989) claimed that a range of elements exist in any given friendship, and what is important in one friendship may not be relevant in another. When this variation is not investigated sufficiently, researchers are likely to gain limited understanding of those relationships. Third, in his review of the cross-sex friendship literature, Monsour (1997) pointed out that most studies investigate the perspective of only one member of the dyad. Researchers of personal relationships (e.g., Duck, 1990) are suggesting that a more complete picture of the relationship is gained from assessing the perspective of both people. Indeed, friends do not always hold the same definition or understanding of their relationship. Fourth, most previous studies have investigated narrow, specific questions with quantitative methods (e.g., "Are men or women more likely to perceive a cross-sex friendship to be potentially sexual?"). The drawback of studies that begin with predetermined categories or have a very narrow focus is that they may inadvertently overlook other experiences that are significant to participants.

The purpose of this study was to correct these limitations by beginning with a qualitative method to investigate the subjective experience of attraction in cross-sex friendship from the perspective of both friends. According to Strauss and Corbin (1990), qualitative research is beneficial for providing intricate and varied details about the nature of a phenomenon, particularly in areas where little is known. For Study I, I conducted in-depth interviews with 40 heterosexual friends (20 cross-sex pairs). I looked specifically at heterosexual people because one's sexual orientation was expected to be relevant in an investigation of male–female friendship and attraction. A broad and exploratory research question was proposed in this initial investigation: How is attraction experienced in heterosexual cross-sex friendships?

Study 1

Method

Interview Procedures

Members of close, heterosexual cross-sex friendships were recruited to participate in individual in-depth interviews. A call for respondents was announced in undergraduate communication courses at a large southwestern university. Potential interviewees were told that only those persons who are truly interested in discussing this topic should volunteer. Similar to the snowball technique, respondents were asked if their cross-sex friend would also be willing to come in for an interview. Only relationships where both friends were interviewed were included in the analysis.

Interviews were scheduled at the participants' convenience and were conducted either in my office or in an empty classroom. Friends were interviewed individually rather than in pairs so that they would not influence one another's answers and would feel more free to share private or negative information about the relationship. Participants were guaranteed confidentiality, and are referred to by pseudonyms in the results section to protect their identities. Interviews were audio-recorded and lasted 30–60 minutes. In addition to tape-recording, I took shorthand notes to remember the parts of their story I wanted to probe further.

The following process was used to gather participants' in-depth narratives (see Appendix on page 391 for interview questions). Before each interview, I told participants that I considered them "co-researchers" and that my questions would simply be used to assist them in describing what they think is important about their relationship. In fact, my first interview question was "If you were conducting research on friendship between men and women, what would you want to find out? What do *you* think would be important?" Interestingly, half of all participants mentioned "attraction" as a key issue when prompted with this broad initial question. I then asked them to recall specific events in the friendship, such as how they met and how their friendship developed. Near the end of the interview I asked why they had or had not considered dating or having a sexual relationship with their friend, if they had not addressed this question already. In addition to these guiding questions, follow-up questions were asked as determined by the participants' responses. At the conclusion of the interview, participants were asked if there was anything they would like to add that had not yet been covered in the interview. The completed interviews were transcribed verbatim, with average transcription containing 11.5 pages and 5377 words.

Participants

Forty people (20 cross-sex pairs) participated in the study. These friendships ranged in length from 4 months to 7 years, with a mean of 2 years. The sample was primarily European American (36 of 40 participants), with middle or upper-middle class backgrounds (34 of 40 participants), and an age range of 19–36, with a mean of 21 years. Almost half of the interviewees were single at the time of the interview, almost half were in committed but non-marital relationships, and one was divorced. Most of the participants were full-time students, approximately half of whom held outside jobs as well. One interviewee was a recent graduate.

Analysis

While the original purpose of the interviews was to gather narratives that would be used to generate themes of cross-sex friendship in general, for this study I focused specifically on those categories that reflected issues of attraction. As solo-analyzer, I began by using Strauss and Corbin's (1990) open coding process to simplify the transcribed interview data. Open coding consisted of labeling each piece of data, with each distinct idea or concept spoken by the participant as the unit of analysis. For example, the statement, "Diane's the first girl who's an attractive girl who I actually have no sexual feelings for" received the code "thinks she's attractive, but not sexually attracted to her," which I believed reflected the essential meaning of the participant's statement. Hundreds of codes were acquired in this manner and each one was subsequently placed on an index card so that they could be constantly compared with each other and sorted into categories. Codes with the same meaning (e.g., "thinks she's cute, but not attracted to her" and "knows he's attractive, but she doesn't feel attracted") were placed in the same group, and these groupings received category names that reflected their content. Each new code was compared with previously created categories to determine whether the new piece of data should belong in one of the existing categories, or whether a new category should be created. After placing an item in a category, the other items in that grouping were re-examined.

The purpose of coding and categorizing was to identify meta-categories, or themes, in the participants' experience of attraction in cross-sex friendship. Themes were determined using Owen's (1984) interpretive theme criteria. The first criterion is recurrence. A theme is said to recur when a given meaning can be observed again and again in the data. The second criterion is repetition. This refers to key words, sentences, or phrases that are repeated throughout the data set. The third criterion is forcefulness. A forceful theme is one that stands out in the interview data as a significant descriptive property of attraction in cross-sex friendship. This significance was based on how much importance it was given by the participants. While not every theme was recurring, repetitive, and forceful in each interview, each met these criteria when the data were analyzed as a whole.

Results

Three primary themes emerged that explain both the common and varied experience of attraction in cross-sex friendship. The first theme refers to the types of attraction that are present in cross-sex friendships. In this study four types emerged—subjective physical/sexual attraction, objective physical/sexual attraction, romantic attraction, and friendship attraction. The second theme refers to whether the types of attraction are symmetrical or asymmetrical between friends. The third theme refers to the changes in attraction that may occur over time.

Types of Attraction

The narratives repeatedly revealed that participants differentiated between types of attraction. While past cross-sex friendship research has investigated only sexual attraction, these friends took pains to explain that their friendship had one kind of attraction, but not another. It was discovered that there are four qualitatively different types of attraction (see Table 1): subjective physical/sexual attraction, objective physical/sexual attraction, romantic attraction, and friendship attraction. These forms of attraction could exist separately or together, in varying degrees, to create different experiences in friendship.

Objective and subjective physical/sexual attraction.   The first two types of attraction occurred when one's friend was perceived to be good-looking or sexy. Physical/sexual attraction could be experienced either subjectively or objectively. Subjective physical/sexual attraction occurred when one found oneself feeling physically or sexually attracted to one's friend. For example, Robert said, "I was physically attracted to Millie. I thought she was very good looking." Ray said, "I had some mixed feelings, sexually." Rena said, "When I first saw Rob I was like, 'Wow, he's cute'." Sean claimed, "I wouldn't mind going to bed with Dorothy. I mean, she's a good looking girl." In most cases, these feelings of physical/sexual attraction were strongest at the beginning of the friendship.

Objective physical/sexual attraction occurred when one acknowledged that one's friend was physically attractive in general, but one did not feel the attraction oneself. In these cases, respondents thought their friend was physically attractive, but they did not feel attracted to him or

TABLE 7-1 Types of Attraction

Types of Attraction	Definition	Example
1. Subjective physical/sexual	Feeling physically or sexually attracted to the other.	"I was physically attracted to Millie. I thought she was very good looking."
2. Objective physical/sexual	Thinking that the other is attractive in general, but not to oneself.	"Marylin's really attractive and I see that and I can relate to that, but I just don't feel the attraction myself."
3. Romantic	Wanting to turn the friendship into a romantic relationship.	"I still think of her as really cool and so that would make her a good girlfriend."
4. Friendship	Feeling close and connected as friends.	"I adore the guy and I really value his friendship."

her. For example, Carla said, "I think Ray is a physically attractive person, I just do not have any level of attraction towards him whatsoever." Similarly, Greg said, "Marylin's really attractive and I see that and I can relate to that, but I just don't feel the attraction myself."

Other participants did not experience either subjective or objective physical/sexual attraction. They did not feel physically attracted to their friend, nor did they suggest that others may find them attractive. Physical attraction was not a relevant experience for these participants in any way. Participants usually explained the non-relevance of physical/sexual attractiveness quite simply. Chuck said, "I'm not physically attracted to Lily." Kraig said, "Beattie's not the kind of girl that I look at in a bar or anything like that." Even when there was some form of physical attraction, however, a romantic relationship was not necessarily desired.

Romantic attraction.   The next type of attraction that occurred in this sample was romantic attraction. Romantic attraction is different from physical/sexual attraction. Romantic attraction occurred when a participant was attracted to the idea of turning the friendship into a romantic relationship (i.e., the participant believed that his/her friend would make a good boyfriend, girlfriend, or spouse). While romantic attraction was rare in this sample, a few participants reported experiencing it. Robert said, "I was interested in her . . . I wanted more than just a friendship." Tim claimed, "I thought it was going to blossom into a relationship." Rob said, "I still think of her as really cool and so that would make her a good girlfriend."

What was more typical in these narratives, however, was an acknowledgment of the lack of romantic attraction. Participants often identified many things about their friend, such as being "wild" or "anal," that made them fine for friendship, but unsuitable for romance. Michael said, "Molly's really wild . . . that's not what I'm looking for in a relationship." Molly's perspective was, "We could never date because Michael is too serious for me . . . I'd kill him." Carla explained, "I am not attracted to Ray's personality. We get along real well as people and we relate on the same level . . . but he is kind of anal in different ways and there are just things about him that I am not attracted to." Vanessa said, "I think Jim is too wild. I wouldn't want somebody in a relationship that was so outspoken and wild." Eric said, "I've known Leah for a long time and there are certain qualities about her that I'm not looking for in an intimate relationship . . . she smokes, she complains too much, and she's too dependent on people."

In all of these cases, the participant described the reasons his/her friend was not attractive for a romantic relationship. This did not mean, however, that the friend was unattractive for friendship. In fact, participants often described their friendship attraction by differentiating it from romantic attraction.

Friendship attraction.   The last type of attraction was friendship attraction. Most of the friends in this sample had grown to like each other, and sometimes love each other, as friends. They reported that they adored one another, and felt close and connected. Millie said, "I adore the guy and I really value his friendship." Jeff said, "There's definitely a connection there. A certain chemistry. I'd say [friendship] chemistry is where you can sit down with someone and talk." Nina said, 'We look like we're best friends, it's the cutest thing. I love Austin." Chuck reported about Lily, "She's like a best girl friend, like platonically." Michael said about his friend, "I love her like a sister. . . . There's a lot of care involved."

Friendship attraction was often described as finding the friend's behavioral characteristics attractive for friendship, but not attractive for a romantic relationship. For example, Greg liked his friend's talkativeness for friendship, but not romance, "She talks a lot, which I love that as a friend, but not that I'd want that as a girlfriend." Mac specified Frank's "spastic" behavior as inappropriate for a romantic partner, but good for friendship:

> I could never picture myself coming home and just having a spastic person never letting me get a moment's peace. . . . But I like Frank because as a friend he can always keep me going, like always keep me in a good mood. I rely on him for that. So it's kind of nice to have a spastic person for a friend.

Friendship attraction was experienced throughout the sample, except in a few cases where the friendship was limited or rocky. In two cases, the friends actually had primarily negative things to say about each other. For example, Dave criticized Suzanne, "She is really overbearing and she's rather rude. At times she gets on my nerves to where I can't handle to talk to her." Beattie had a similar friendship with Kraig. She said, "I hate him, but he's still like my good friend. He bugs me."

Overall, however, friendship attraction was the strongest form of attraction experienced in this sample. Even participants who felt subjective physical/sexual and/or romantic attraction explained that those feelings were not strong enough to warrant jeopardizing the friendship. In most cases, friendship attraction was prioritized above the other forms. For example, Michael mentioned that while he had thought of his friend Molly sexually, he would not want to act on his feelings and risk ruining the friendship:

> I'm not going to sit here and lie and say I've never thought about sleeping with her. . . . But for the most part those are boundaries I'm not willing to overstep just because of the fact that I've got too much invested in [the friendship], she's got too much invested in it, [and] it would just go out the window.

Molly felt similarly. She had put aside romantic intentions in favor of the friendship:

> All my girlfriends are like, "You guys should date" you know, they'll say stuff like that of course. So, you know, I've thought about it, but then I just don't think it'll work. I think we would ruin the friendship. . . . I think that it is perfect as it is, and if we even attempted to kiss or anything I think the relationship would probably be doomed.

Summary and integration of attraction types.   These narratives revealed that attraction in cross-sex friendship is not a unidimensional variable. Rather, there were many different kinds of attraction. Finding one's friend "cute" or "handsome" (objective physical/sexual attraction) did not mean that one was attracted *to* one's friend (subjective physical/sexual attraction). As Vanessa put it, "I might think [my male friends] are cute, but that doesn't mean I want to sleep with them." Liking someone's personality for friendship (friendship attraction) did not mean that personality was attractive for a romantic relationship (romantic attraction). In Rona's experience, "Rob's just a little too immature for me as a boyfriend, but as a friend I love it." Thinking that someone is attractive as a friend (friendship attraction) is not the same as feeling physically attracted to him or her (subjective physical/sexual attraction). As Lily explained, "There was never any physical attraction, it was just kind of buddy–buddy." Being physically attracted to someone (subjective physical/sexual attraction) is not the same as wanting to be in a romantic relationship with that person (romantic attraction). From Mae's perspective, "We've both admitted that we have found each other attractive . . . but we probably couldn't do very well at dating." These different forms of attraction created qualitatively different experiences in cross-sex friendship. Adding to the complexity, some friendships had symmetrical forms of attraction, while other friendships had asymmetrical attraction.

Symmetrical or Asymmetrical

Interviewing both parties revealed that some friends are symmetrical in their forms of attraction, while others are not. Symmetrical attraction occurred when both friends experienced the same type(s) of attraction. For example, in some friendships, both people felt friendship attraction, and no other form of attraction. In other cases, both people experienced friendship attraction plus subjective physical/sexual attraction. Asymmetrical feelings occurred when friends had different experiences of attraction in the friendship. For example, in some cases, one person had friendship attraction and subjective physical/sexual attraction, while the other had only friendship attraction. In other cases, one person felt romantic attraction plus friendship attraction, while the other experienced only friendship attraction. The symmetry or asymmetry of different forms of attraction created varied experiences in cross-sex friendship.

Asymmetrical romantic attraction.   When it was experienced, asymmetrical romantic attraction was the most detrimental condition for cross-sex friendships. The pressure of one person wanting to make the friendship romantic often caused these friendships to become strained and ultimately less close. For example, Tim had at one time thought his friendship with Tammy would become romantic, but in the interview he claimed, "Our relationship is kind of take it or leave it [now], to tell you the truth." Tammy agreed, "We're friends, but we pretty much keep our distance now." Maya, who had thought of Josh as a potential boyfriend, now found herself questioning their friendship, "I know there have been a couple of times I've said, 'Why are we friends?'" Robert explained that being romantically attracted to Millie without her returning his interest was taking its toll, "I shouldn't be spending so much time with her because I'm hurting myself by not looking for somebody else."

Asymmetrical subjective physical/sexual attraction.   When it was experienced, asymmetrical subjective physical/sexual attraction was rarely detrimental to these cross-sex friendships because, unlike those with romantic attraction, those with physical attraction did not typically feel a desire to change the friendship. First, there was little motivation to make the friendship into a sexual relationship because without symmetrical subjective physical attraction, the relationship had no "spark." For example, although Ray was physically attracted to Carla, the lack of a spark held him back from pursuing it, "Even though I had some mixed attractions sexually. . . . There's just no spark, no drive. . . . If there's not a spark you can't move on to the next level." The asymmetrical attraction from Carla explained why this spark was likely missing, "I just do not have any level of attraction towards Ray whatsoever." Similarly, Sean couldn't figure out why it didn't "click" with Jesse, "I think she's physically attractive, [but] it just doesn't click for some reason." That "some reason" may have been Jesse's feelings, "I mean I think he's adorable, but attracted to him like sex? . . . I couldn't even imagine kissing him." Without the simultaneous mutual attraction needed to create a "spark," the relationship often felt friendly rather than passionate. A second reason participants with subjective physical/sexual attraction were not motivated to alter their friendship, spark or not, is that they tended to value their friendship more than their feelings of physical attraction. They did not want a sexual encounter to jeopardize an important friendship. Vanessa explained, "I guess maybe if we were really trashed out of our minds we might sleep together. But I would never want to because I really like the friendship that we have."

Attraction between friends could also be symmetrical. A few friendships experienced symmetrical subjective physical/sexual attraction. This was rarely threatening to the friendship because, again, physical attraction was not perceived to be important enough to risk the friendship. Symmetrical romantic attraction was revealed in a few of the friendships. Participants in this condition indicated that they were open to the possibility that the nature of the relationship may change in the future.

Changes in attraction
What became clear through the narratives is that the experience of attraction in cross-sex friendship could remain constant, or it could vary. This finding differs from past research on attraction, which has typically measured whether attraction exists at a given point in time, rather than discovering how one's experience of attraction can change. Some participants in this study consistently felt romantic and/or subjective physical/sexual attraction throughout the friendship. Robert said, "I had strong feelings for her, and in fact I still have strong feelings for her." Other participants consistently lacked any physical or romantic attraction toward the other. Nina said, "I have never thought 'more than a friend' of Austin." Kelly said, "I've never really been attracted to David." Tammy said, "I've never had any feelings for Tim."

In other cases, however, participants experienced a certain form of attraction that later changed. While a few participants reported that their romantic attraction had grown at some point during the friendship, the most common change was dissipating romantic attraction. For example, Diane changed her mind about being romantically attracted to Thomas, "I was kind of thinking 'Maybe Thomas should be more than my best friend,' [but now] I know him so well, it's like I know exactly how he would be as a boyfriend and I just know that wouldn't be right." The same thing happened to Maya, "When Josh took me to my prom I thought he would be the perfect boyfriend. . . . I considered it once and then it never came up again." Frank changed his mind on this issue as well, "Over the summer I had some ideas. I liked Mae, she's very attractive and I was thinking, well maybe I should pursue trying to go out with her. . . . I tried to feel out the situation a little bit. I just realized it was more comfortable with us just being friends."

It was also possible for the other forms of attraction to change. For example, Nina did not like Austin when they first met, but friendship attraction developed over time, "I thought he was annoying at first. But later I realized he was caring and funny." Tim's feelings of subjective physical/sexual attraction changed, "I don't find her sexually attractive anymore." For Suzanne, when physical and romantic interest went away there was not much left to the friendship, "When we first started hanging out together we would go eat and talk and we would call each other on the phone all the time, and it seemed like there was a little bit of a spark there, but there wasn't. . . . Now we never talk just to talk."

Summary

The themes discovered in this study reveal that cross-sex attraction is quite complicated. There were four different types of attraction (objective physical/sexual, subjective physical/sexual, romantic and friendship) that could be symmetrical or asymmetrical and that could be perceived to change over time or stay consistent throughout the friendship.

Study II was conducted to validate and quantify the qualitative data in Study I. The purpose of the second study was to discover the frequency of each type of attraction, how types of attraction are related to length of relationship, the perceived change in each type of attraction, and the frequency with which participants experienced more than one type of attraction within a given cross-sex friendship. . . .

References

Abbey, A. (1982). Sex differences in attributions for friendly behavior: Do males misperceive females' friendliness? *Journal of Personality and Social Psychology, 42*, 830–838.

Adams, R. (1985). People would talk: Normative barriers to cross-sex friendship for elderly women. *The Gerontologist, 25,* 605–611.

Allan, G. (1989). *Friendship: Developing a sociological perspective.* New York: Harvester Wheatsheaf.

Bell, R. (1981). *Worlds of friendship.* Beverly Hills, CA: Sage.

Berscheid, E., & Walster, E. (1974). Physical attractiveness. In L. Berkowitz (Ed.), *Advances in experimental social psychology* (Vol. 7, pp. 157–215). New York: Academic Press.

Caldwell, M., & Peplau, L. (1982). Sex differences in same-sex friendship. *Sex Roles, 8,* 721–732.

Duck, S. (1990). Relationships as unfinished business: Out of the frying pan and into the 1990s. *Journal of Social and Personal Relationships, 7,* 5–28.

Festinger, L., Schachter, S., & Back, K. (1950). *Social pressures in informal groups: A study of human factors in housing.* New York: Harper.

Gaines, S. (1994). Exchange of respect-denying behaviors among male-female friendships. *Journal of Social and Personal Relationships, 11,* 5–24.

Gottman, J. (1994). Why can't men and women get along? In D. Canary & L. Stafford (Eds.), *Communication and relational maintenance* (pp. 203–229). Orlando, FL: Academic Press.

Green, S., Buchanan, D., & Heuer, S. (1984). Winners, losers, and choosers: A field investigation of dating initiation. *Personality and Social Psychology Bulletin, 10,* 502–511.

Griffit, W. (1970). Environmental effects on interpersonal affective behavior: Ambient effective temperature and attraction. *Journal of Personality and Social Psychology, 15,* 240–244.

Hatfield, E., & Sprecher, S. (1986). *Mirror, mirror . . . The importance of looks in everyday life.* Albany: State University of New York Press.

Lin, Y., & Rusbult, C. (1995). Commitment to dating relationships and cross-sex friendships in America and China. *Journal of Social and Personal Relationships, 12,* 7–26.

May, J., & Hamilton, P. (1980). Effects of musically evoked affect on women's interpersonal attraction toward and perceptual judgments of physical attractiveness of men. *Motivation and Emotion, 4,* 217–228.

McCrosky, J., & McCain, T. (1974). The measurement of interpersonal attraction. *Speech Monographs, 41,* 261–266.

Monsour, M. (1992). Meanings of intimacy in cross-sex and same-sex friendships. *Journal of Social and Personal Relationships, 9,* 277–295.

Monsour, M. (1997). Communication and cross-sex friendship across the lifecycle: A review of the literature. *Communication Yearbook, 20,* 375–414.

Monsour, M., Betty, S., & Kurzweil, N. (1993). Levels of perspectives and the perception of intimacy in cross-sex friendships: A balance theory explanation of shared perceptual reality. *Journal of Social and Personal Relationships, 10,* 529–550.

Monsour, M., Harris. B., & Kurzweil, N. (1994). Challenges confronting cross-sex friendships: "Much Ado About Nothing?" *Sex Roles, 31,* 55–77.

Moyer, A., Hojjat, M., & Salovey, P. (1994, May). *Attitudes towards cross-sex friendships.* Paper presented to the International Network on Personal Relationships conference, Iowa City, IA.

Nahemow, L., & Lawton, M. (1975). Similarity and propinquity in friendship formation. *Journal of Personality and Social Psychology, 32,* 205–213.

O'Meara, J. D. (1989). Cross-sex friendship: Four basic challenges of an ignored relationship. *Sex Roles, 21,* 525–543.

Owen, W. (1984). Interpretive themes in relational communication. *Quarterly Journal of Speech, 70,* 274–287.

Rawlins, W. (1992). *Friendship matters.* New York: Aldine de Gruyter.

Rickelman, K. E. (1981). *Childhood cross-sex friendships: An investigation of trends and possible explanations.* Unpublished honors thesis, University of Illinois, Champaign.

Rose, S. (1985). Same- and cross-sex friendships and the psychology of homosociality. *Sex Roles, 12,* 63–74.

Rubin, L. (1985). *Just friends.* New York: Harper & Row.

Sapadin, L. (1988). Friendships and gender: Perspectives of professional men and women. *Journal of Social and Personal Relationships, 5,* 387–403.

Segal, M. (1974). Alphabet and attraction: An unobtrusive measure of the effect of propinquity in a field setting. *Journal of Personality and Social Psychology, 30,* 654–657.

Simpson, J., & Harris, B. (1994). Interpersonal attraction. In A. Weaver & J. Harvey (Eds.), *Perspectives on close relationships* (pp. 45–66). Needham Heights, MA: Allyn & Bacon.

Strauss, A., & Corbin, J. (1990). *Basics of qualitative research.* Newbury Park, CA: Sage.

Thorne, B., & Luria, Z. (1986). Sexuality and gender in children's daily worlds. *Social Problems, 33,* 176–190.

Werking, K. (1997). *We're just good friends.* New York: Guilford Press.

Appendix

Study I Questions (asked of participants during interviews)

1. What do you think is important to ask in a study of friendships between women and men?
2. How did you meet?
3. How did the relationship develop?
4. How would you describe this relationship? [Probes: How do you feel toward this person and the relationship? How do you/would you describe it to your friends/dating partner? What activities do you do together? What are the topics of your conversation?]
5. Do you have any same-sex friends? When you think of these friendships, how are they the same/different from your cross-sex friendship?
6. During your cross-sex friendship have you been seeing anyone romantically? How is/was that relationship the same/different from your cross-sex friendship?
7. (If applicable) What does/did your romantic partner think of your relationship with your friend?
8. Have you ever talked about your friendship with your friend? Can you describe what you've talked about in those conversations?
9. Have you ever considered dating/having a sexual relationship with this person? Why? Why not? What about your friend or the circumstances contribute to you not being in a romantic relationship with this person?
10. Is there anything you would like to add that we have not covered?

Heterosexism in Studies of Cross-Gender Friends

One of the issues often ignored in studies of cross-gender friendships is the role of sexual orientation. Is sexual attraction an issue between gay men and heterosexual women? Between gay women and heterosexual men? I wanted to find out what kind of research has been done to address these issues, and I found this summary of existing research from the book *We're Just Good Friends: Women and Men in Nonromantic Relationships* by Kathy Werking. The book itself contains valuable material for my research project, but too much to reproduce here, so I've only chosen short excerpts that directly address some of the questions I'm now asking based on the earlier research I've done.

We're Just Good Friends

Romance and Sexuality in Friendships Between Homosexual and Heterosexual Partners and Between Homosexual Women and Men

Kathy Werking

Cross-sex friendships in the homosexual community have rarely been researched. Existing studies have investigated same-sex friendships within the homosexual and lesbian communities (see Nardi, 1992; Nardi & Sherrod, 1994). However, friendships between the two communities remain unstudied. One form of cross-sex friendship that has received attention (although quite limited) is friendship between gay men and straight women. Conventional wisdom has been that friendships between gay men and straight women are common (Altman, 1982); however, the frequency of this form of friendship is not really known.

A recent survey conducted by Nardi (1992) indicates that gay male–heterosexual female friendships may not occur frequently since less than 10% of gay men in his sample stated that their best friends were heterosexual females while 82% of the men said that their best friends were gay or bisexual men. Nardi explains these numbers by citing the emergence of a gay-identified community where close relationships are forged primarily with other gay persons.

Other researchers (Malone, 1980; Whitney, 1990) have conducted studies specifically targeting the relationships between gay men and heterosexual women. This research has not been limited to friendships but also encompasses married and "committed" relationships. Paradoxically, both research projects reveal that although many of the participants viewed their friendships as a safe haven from the perils of sexual and romantic relationships initially, sexual attraction and activity between the friends existed. The people in these studies managed this attraction in different ways. A woman participating in Whitney's (1990) study summed up her frustration with this issue by stating:

> "I don't know whether my gay friend and I qualify as a 'gay-straight love match.' We're not lovers, but we do love each other, and it seems that there is some sexual energy between us that is disconcerting to us both. It has caused some problems between us, and I can't say with any certainty that we've come to terms with it yet, although we are both more comfortable with it than we were three years ago. Our relationship has survived a lot of confusion and frustration." (p. 115)

What is interesting about these results is that they question the assumption that sexual attraction occurs only in friendships between heterosexual men and women. In other words, these results defy dichotomous thinking about heterosexuality and homosexuality and suggest fluidity between the two concepts. These studies also suggest that the participants grappled with defining their relationships since their relational experiences stood apart from the "normal" man–woman bond. Much like the heterosexual cross-sex friends whom I have interviewed, these participants struggled with definitions of love, commitment, sex, and long-term relational goals.

Dichotomous thinking about sexual orientation may also be challenged by friendships between gay women and men. An interesting collection of essays about friendships between these communities, written by persons engaged in these friendships, highlights the close and complex relationships between gay men and women (Nestle & Preston, 1994). These essays reveal the societal forces of oppression that propel gay women and men toward friendships, with one another and expose the forces of sexism that drive a wedge between the two communities. Further, the writings of gay men and women about their friendships with one another uncover the sensual nature of cross-sex homosexual friendship. In this way, these friendship stories add further evidence questioning our heterocentric assumption that expressed or unexpressed sexual attraction occurs only between heterosexual men and women.

There is much to be learned about cross-sex friendships in the homosexual community as well as cross-sex friendships between homosexual and heterosexual men and women. Such study is worthwhile because ignoring these forms of cross-sex friendship truncates our knowledge of the diversity of norms, rules, and societal contexts within which men and women forge friendships (Duck, 1994). The following questions may be explored by researchers: To what extent does cross-sex friendship occur between gay men and women? What facilitates or impedes its formation? What issues are important in this form of cross-sex friendship? How do these concerns correspond with cross-sex friendship in the straight community? What is the nature of cross-sex friendship between homosexual and heterosexual persons? Is this type of cross-sex friendship viewed as somehow more legitimate by outsiders because this type of friendship is considered "definitively" nonsexual?

Again, the above questions and comments are meant to be generative in nature. In the future, researchers need to expand their investigations to include a wider variety of cross-sex friendship forms if they are to make valid claims about the nature of such friendship in American society.

Kathy Werking's book, *We're Just Friends*, also studies the affect of male-female friendships on marriage, something I haven't found anywhere else. This question came up in the article I read from business, "Love Without Sex" (pages 360–375), so I wanted to pursue it more. Here's another small excerpt from Werking's book that summarizes what she's found in her interview-based study about the role of cross-gender friendships in marriage.

Cross-Sex Friends and "Marriage Work"
Kathy Werking

My participants echoed Oliker's (1989) finding that female best friends perform "marriage work." She defines "marriage work" as "reflection and action to achieve or sustain the stability of a marriage or a sense of its adequacy" (Oliker, 1989, p. 123). The marriage work of female friends involved listening to marital problems, suggesting solutions, offering criticism, and probing emotions. One result of engaging in marriage work with a female friend was a heightened commitment to the marriage.

In the accounts I heard, cross-sex friends also engaged in marriage work. Though the nature of the marital work may have differed somewhat from that done in same-sex friendships, it did not undermine the marital bond, as has been suggested by other researchers (e.g., Francoeur & Francoeur, 1977; Lampe, 1985), but reinforced it.

These cross-sex friends performed marriage work when they talked about marital relationships and spouses. Several male friends said that their female friends often talked to them about problems in their marriages many times before they talked with their husbands about them (if they talked over the problems with their husbands at all). The male friends believed that when problems were discussed, their married friends walked away with possible solutions or insights into problems. Thus, friends saw their cross-sex relationships as a positive influence on marriage. One woman stated that one of the biggest rewards of talking with her male friend was that he provided a different perspective on the situation. She said:

> "If you are having a difficult time understanding your relationship with your spouse, another male can say, 'Well, now wait a minute. You know, he's not so far off. He sees it this way.' "

Another woman testified to the importance of talking over problems with her male friend:

"Getting to see what the other side is like. *(Laughs)* You kinda think, you know, see how the men think about things. You know, I won't get that out of my husband. But I will hear that outta Bob."

According to all of these married interviewees, and to several of their cross-sex friends, it seemed that involvement in a cross-sex friendship lessened the emotional burden placed on the marital relationship. This relief was an important way in which the cross-sex friendship nourished the marital bond. Emotional burdens were diminished because the married person was able to experience the companionship of the opposite sex, gain the opposite-sex perspective, and share similar interests with a member of the opposite sex without experiencing romantic involvement or encompassing marital responsibilities. Consequently, these interviewees did not expect their spouses to fulfill their emotional needs to the extent to which they might have expected if their cross-sex friendships did not exist. Further, these men and women recognized that there were aspects of their lives that their spouses were not interested in or that their spouses were unwilling to share with them. The married women also believed that it was healthier to share those things with male friends than it was to continue to heap expectations on their spouses. A woman expressed this awareness nicely when she stated:

"And I've often said that I feel like there are two halves of me. This mother-wife half that my husband gets and then the music half that my friend gets. There is . . . no, my husband cannot understand that. He loves me dearly, but there is just . . . he can't share that. I mean, that is just not a passion of his.

"Just like figuring out how things grow is not a passion of mine. That's the difference and that's fine, but it is a passion. I can turn to my friend and say, 'God, did you hear that in the music?' And I look over and he's crying too. And that's an immediate emotional link that I can't share with my husband."

One man saw his cross-sex friendship as enabling his marital relationship to continue:

"I can talk to her [his friend] about things I can't talk to my wife about. In fact, because I have her friendship, I can continue my marriage without expecting to talk to my wife about everything. And that's good, because there are some things I shouldn't talk to my wife about—even though I love my wife more than anything in the world. Telling her certain things might hurt her feelings or make her think less of me. My marriage is *better* because of my friendship."

In addition to providing emotional support or the opportunity to share interests, these cross-sex friendships also provided a break from the everyday routine of marriage. One man characterized his role in his friend's marriage as providing a "diversion from everyday life." Similarly, another man spoke of his friendship as giving his cross-sex friend a "break" from her marriage. A woman said that with her cross-sex friend she did not have the "financial crap . . . the kid crap . . . the in-law crap." Cross-sex friendship was viewed by these interviewees as an arena in which they could have fun and receive emotional support, which ameliorated marital demands as it rounded out their interpersonal lives.

Cross-Sex Friendship and Marriage: Summary

For the most part, the positive influences of engaging in a close cross-sex friendship while married have been overlooked. My interviews with close cross-sex friends not only point to the beneficial contributions that cross-sex friendships can make to marriage but also begin to uncover cracks in the assumption that cross-sex friendship subverts marriage. This negative assumption was clearly reflected in the questions that outsiders asked these friends. Yet, it was within such a context that these cross-sex friends had to orchestrate their relationships. Their task was not easy. It was filled with tension and ambiguity and required ongoing effort and commitment from the involved parties. These friends, however, seemed committed to trying to "make it work" even though they were aware that it might not. This awareness was clearly reflected in their responses to the question, "Can you think of a reason that would cause your friendship to end?" *All* of the participants cited their spouses' objection to the friendship as a possible reason.

References

Altman, D. (1982). *The homosexualization of America*. Boston: Beacon.

Duck, S. (1994). A topography of relationship disengagement and dissolution. In S. W. Duck (Ed.), *Personal relationships: Vol. 4. Dissolving personal relationships* (pp. 1–30). London: Academic.

Francoeur, R., & Francoeur, A. (1977). Hot and cool sex: Fidelity in marriage. In R. Libby and R. Whitehurst (Eds.), *Marriage and alternatives: Exploring intimate relationships* (pp. 302–318). Glenview, IL: Scott, Foresman.

Lampe, P. E. (1985). Friendship and adultery. *Sociological Inquiry, 55* (3), 310–324.

Malone, J. W. (1980). *Straight women/gay men.* New York: Dial.

Nardi, P. M. (1992). Sex, friendship, and gender roles among gay men. In P. Nardi (Ed.), *Men's friendships* (pp. 173–185). Newbury Park, CA: Sage.

Nardi, P. M., & Sherrod, D. (1994) Friendship in the lives of gay men and lesbians. *Journal of Social and Personal Relationships, 11,* 185–199.

Nestle, J., & Preston, J. (1994). *Sister and brother: Lesbians and gay men write about their lives together.* San Francisco: HarperCollins.

Oliker, S. J., (1989). *Best friends and marriage: Exchange among women.* Berkeley: University of California Press.

Whitney, C. (1990). *Uncommon lives: Gay men and straight women.* New York: New American Library.

Exercise 7.1 Reader Reflections

These researchers provided even more ideas for me to consider, and they've even answered some of the questions I had from reading the psychology articles.

STEP 1: What did you think? What did you make of the way researchers in communications write up their studies compared to those in psychology and business? Spend some time fastwriting in your journal about what you've learned so far, using the following questions as prompts:

1. What are the two most significant ideas or pieces of evidence that surprised you or challenged your initial assumptions about cross-gender friendships?

2. What did you find challenging about reading these excerpts? What reading strategies did you use to help you deal with that?

STEP 2: Make a list of all the things you've learned about the research writing that is done in the communications subculture: What kinds of evidence are valued? How do researchers show they are insiders? What kind of organizational structure seems most common? How does this subculture compare to those you've read earlier in this chapter?

How Social Context Affects Friendships: A Sociology Article

So far the research I've read focuses on the particulars of friendships—the strategies friends use to stay friends, the different kinds of attraction cross-gender friends experience—but I don't have a sense, yet, of how culture and history affect friendship. I know from my background in nineteenth-century

American women writers that women in the late 1800s had intimate female friends with whom they shared feelings and thoughts that we in the twenty-first century tend to reserve for our spouses and romantic partners. Marriage in the nineteenth century was based on a belief that men and women had separate "spheres," separate roles and obligations, and so spouses did not expect the emotional intimacy that I, for example, expect in my marriage—or that Bruce expects in his. So how have my attitudes toward friendship and marriage been affected by my time period, my identity as an American, my young adulthood as part of second-wave feminism? Sociology answers those kinds of questions, and I've included below excerpts from a wonderful article by Graham Allan, a professor in the United Kingdom, who summarizes what sociology "knows" at this point about friendship. As with the other readings in this chapter, we hope you'll mark this text with two purposes in mind: (1) to read as an ethnographer of this subculture of sociological research and academic writing; and (2) to read in dialogue with the ideas Allan presents about friendship and how they inform my research so far. Again, I will not comment on this essay myself so you will have space for your own comments.

Friendship, Sociology, and Social Structure

Graham Allan

ABSTRACT

This article is concerned with the contribution that sociology has made to our understanding of the ways in which friendships are socially patterned. Rather than treating these ties as individual or dyadic constructions, it examines how the social and economic contexts in which they develop influence their form. It focuses particularly on the impact that social location has on friendship, arguing that both class and status divisions are important for understanding the character of informal solidarities. However, both of these must be seen as dynamic, for neither class nor status characteristics are fixed; both alter biographically and historically, and as they alter the pattern the friendships individuals sustain. The final section of the article attempts to explicate how structural change at the end of the 20th century will affect friendship. While some theories of privatization imply that informal relationships are becoming less significant socially, the argument developed here is that the transformations of late modernity are likely to result in informal solidarities of friendship becoming more central.

KEY WORDS • class • context • friendship • late modernity • status

. . . [This article's] focus is explicitly on friendships rather than personal relationships more generally. Within this, its purpose is to explore what sociological perspectives have to offer the general analysis of friendship as a form of personal tie, and in the process highlight why studying friendships (and other equivalent informal relationships) is more central to dominant sociological concerns than is usually recognized. This is a project with which I have been involved for some 25 years, but the invitation to write a review paper provides an appropriate vehicle for reflection about these issues. It will be an added bonus if this helps in any way towards a fuller integration of different perspectives on personal relationships. . . .

Working-Class Male Sociability: An Illustration

In the 1950s and early 1960s a good deal of research was conducted on kinship and community ties in Britain. Informed by concerns that family and neighbourhood solidarities were breaking down, these studies investigated patterns of informal support and sociability, particularly within working-class localities. These were of special interest because of the impact that housing regeneration and geographical mobility was thought to be having on 'traditional' ways of life. Although their main focus was usually on kinship ties, their community orientation resulted in many of these studies containing a good deal of material pertinent to friendship (for reviews of this research, see Klein, 1965 and Allan, 1979). From these studies it was possible to identify a style of working-class non-kin sociability, especially amongst men, which was quite different from the dominant mode of middle-class friendship.

In essence, working-class male non-kin sociability was heavily framed by interactional settings. That is, the relationships tended to be restricted to the particular contexts in which people met, with little attempt being made to extend the boundary of the ties by incorporating them into other settings. Whereas middle-class sociability typically entailed developing friendships by involving people in a number of activities, this was largely absent in working-class sociability. Thus, for example, within middle-class circles, compatible people who met at work would often arrange to go to the theatre or to a concert together, or they might be invited home to a dinner party or a barbecue. Their mode of friendship was to reveal wider aspects of the self by incorporating friends into a range of shared activities, often including couple- or family-oriented ones. Such a broadening of the activities and settings seen as relevant for friendship was uncommon within working-class patterns of sociability. These ties were generally kept quite tightly framed around specific activities and places—a bar, a particular hobby, a sports club—with little effort being made to broaden them in the way the middle class routinely did. Their emphasis was on sociability within that setting rather than a broader reve-lation of the self through a gradual extension of the relationship's situa-tional boundaries. Importantly within this, the home was rarely used as a means of developing or strengthening friendships. More commonly, the home was implicitly defined as a "private" arena, one reserved for "fam-ily"—however defined—and not taken to be an appropriate site for so-cializing with non-kin.

As a result of these factors, working-class men frequently claimed to have few, if any, friends. What they had were "mates," people who they saw more or less frequently and with whom they enjoyed interacting. But because these relationships tended to be situationally defined, they did not fit easily into the culturally dominant (middle-class) model of what "friendship," as such, entailed. Some researchers took this to indicate that working-class respondents generally lacked the necessary social skills to develop friendships (Klein, 1965). However, it seems more likely that dif-ferent modes of organizing sociability were dominant in working- and middle-class culture. Middle-class patterns, with their emphasis on indi-vidual relationships over specific settings, matched cultural criteria of friendship in a way that working-class sociability, with its prioritizing of setting, did not. (For a fuller discussion of these different modes of socia-bility, see Allan, 1979; 1989.)

But why was working-class sociability framed as it was? What was it about people's circumstances that fostered this way of managing informal ties and, in effect, discouraged the adoption of the middle-class model? The most compelling factor was material deprivation. Particularly in the type of locality most frequently studied, households were dependent on relatively poorly paid and insecure employment, with few having much income above that required for weekly survival. The management of re-sources was a matter of significant concern. As a consequence, while there might be money for some sociability and leisure—generally un-equally distributed between husband and wife—there was a need to keep control over expenditure. One way of doing this was not to become in-volved in series of open-ended exchanges in which money was spent. Yet to some degree this is what middle-class friendship patterns encouraged. The underlying basis of most friendships is an equality of exchange; what one friend does now is reciprocated in some equivalent form by the other later. In an economy of poverty and insecurity, avoidance of such obliga-tion can be important, if not for particular individuals, then at least collectively within the culture. The dominant mode of working-class sociability facilitated this. By prioritizing setting over relationships, people were able to control their commitments more readily. They were freer to enter and leave a particular arena of sociability without incurring expense than they would have been if the relationship itself was prioritized, as was the case in the middle-class mode.

However, it is not simply issues concerned with controlling reciprocity when resources are limited, which are relevant here. Other material and social conditions also shape the patterns that emerge. In particular, the poverty of people's housing was important. In many of the localities studied, people were living in inadequate housing that lacked basic amenities, even by the standard of the times. Many, for example, still had outside toilets, lacked fixed baths and even shared cooking facilities, as well as being overcrowded. In these circumstances, the home was often reserved for family. Especially for those who valued respectability, maintaining some degree of privacy around the domestic sphere was important, particularly as inadequate housing combined with close knit social networks made the control of gossip difficult. In this environment, it is hardly surprising that the home was not defined as an appropriate arena for entertaining others or as a site for developing friendships. Effectively, keeping non-kin ties out of the home again gave people a level of control over the reciprocities in which they were involved.

In addition, though, there was another domestic consideration that influenced friendship patterns: the dominant form of marital relationship. Generally marital roles were highly segregated; there was a marked division of labour, and to quite a large degree husbands and wives led separate lives, rarely being involved in shared sociability outside of kinship. In this regard, men's relationships tended to be removed from the domestic sphere and to be independent of their wives, thereby consolidating the perspective that the home was an inappropriate arena for male sociability. Thus, in the context of limited resources, these comparatively segregated marital roles also helped foster the differences that existed between working-class and middle-class modes of ordering ties of friendship and sociability.

But what happens as social and material conditions alter, as they have been doing over the last 40 years? While some households continue to be in poverty, in particular those who through lack of employment are dependent on state benefits, standards of living have risen for the majority of working-class couples. Changes in married women's labour market participation mean that domestic economies are increasingly built around two incomes, albeit one often significantly smaller than the other. Linked in with this, there have been major changes in housing circumstances. Not only have rates of owner-occupation almost tripled since 1945, but more importantly, average standards of comfort and amenity are far higher than they were. Despite the continuing inequalities and inadequacies that exist in the housing market, for men, especially, improvements in domestic ambience have fostered greater commitment to the home as an arena for leisure and sociable activity.

Although it is easy to romanticize, re-definitions of what constitutes an acceptable marriage or partnership have also been significant here. Within current marital "blueprints" (Cancian, 1987), there is a greater emphasis than previously on notions of "partnership," emotional fulfilment and intimate disclosure (Duncombe & Marsden, 1993; Hawkes, 1996). Encapsulated in this are ideas that wives and husbands should value spending time together. Increasingly, from a cultural viewpoint, a marriage in which the spouses do not want to be together sociably is perceived—rightly or wrongly—as a marriage "in difficulty," in a way that would have little resonance among couples two generations earlier (Mansfield & Collard, 1988).

These changes have had an impact on dominant modes of male, working-class sociability. Although the number of pertinent studies conducted recently is limited compared with the range of family, occupational and community studies from the mid-century period, the sociable relationships that working-class men now sustain do appear to be ordered differently from then. In part, this has involved elements of privatization: a shift in the focus of social activities from neighbourhood and community to the private sphere of the home. Yet what has happened is more complex than simply a move from community participation to a life centred predominantly on domestic and familial concerns (Allan & Crow, 1991). First, while there has been a loss of local involvement, this has not meant that sociability itself has necessarily declined. Instead, congruent with Wellman's (Wellman et al., 1988; Wellman & Wortley, 1990) analysis of changing networks in north America, sociable ties are now more geographically dispersed than they were.

Second, the shift from "the public" to "the private" has modified understandings of the nature of the domestic sphere and the role of the home in men's lives. As a result, working-class men are more likely to use the home as a site for sociability. That is, whereas previously ties of sociability were typically framed by specific activities and took place in public settings, now it is more likely that the home will play a part in the development and servicing of these ties. For most, some interaction continues to take place in public settings but this will not be exclusively the case. Whether or not such ties become couple friendships, the boundaries constructed around them are more permeable than in the past. They are not defined by setting in the way they were; changes in material resources, domestic ambience and marital ideologies have resulted in the home being more "open" for non-kin sociability.

The point here is not that working-class men's ties are becoming more like traditional middle-class friendships, though this does appear to be happening to a degree. Rather the point is to demonstrate how the material and social environments in which informal relationships develop have an impact on the construction of these relationships. The patterns that were dominant for male, working-class sociability in mid-century are no longer so typical as the circumstances that framed them have altered. The material and ideological shifts that have been outlined briefly here are such as to make change likely. In particular, the altered need to manage reciprocity as poverty reduces, the changed home ambience, and emerging ideologies of partnership and marriage make for different ways of ordering sociable ties. Patterns rooted in previous social and economic environments become modified as a new conditions emerge offering different opportunities and constraints. . . .

Friendship and Identity in Late Modernity

It was noted above that the patterns of friendship that emerge within a given social formation are shaped by the character of economic and social relationships within that formation. In turn, there is an articulation between the social location individuals occupy and the identity that their friends help them construct and sustain. The issue for this final section of the paper is how the transformations currently occurring in social structure influence friendship patterns and their significance in identity construction. These transformations—reflected in terms such as postmodernity or late modernity (Giddens, 1991)—are typically held to entail new forms of solidarity with an emphasis on individual fulfilment rather than collective commitment or constraint. With changes in the economic sphere, including rapid technological development, globalization of markets, high levels of job change, and new constellations within the division of labor, old patterns and old certainties no longer apply so securely to the world that people experience. . . .

As writers such as Beck (1992) and Giddens (1991; 1992) have theorized, these changes have an impact on the ordering of personal relationships. This is most apparent in terms of partnership, family and household constructions where there is far more diversity now than there was even a generation ago. In Britain this is most evident in terms of household demography where increases in divorce, cohabitation, births to unmarried mothers and step-families have been dramatic since the mid-1970s. At the same time, age at first marriage has increased while the number of people marrying has been in significant decline. For example, in 1991, less than three-quarters of the female population had married by the time they were

30 compared with over 90 percent in 1971. Similarly the number of households in which there are openly gay partnerships has been increasing (Allan & Crow, 1999; Haskey, 1996).

Overall these household arrangements represent a change in the character of commitment in personal and sexual relationships. We are witnessing a strong social endorsement of more flexible and less permanent relationships. Even though many people still believe in life-long heterosexual marriage as an ideal, there is now not only more tolerance of alternatives, but also an acceptance that diversity is inevitable given the character of present-day life-styles. Thus, while Giddens (1992), for example, can be criticized for overstating the ease with which people can make changes in their personal lives, nonetheless his central thesis about the direction of change is compelling. Compared with mid-century there is now a much deeper cultural acceptance that adults should not be bound to each other in relationships that are no longer providing satisfaction or fulfilment. In Britain in many respects, the most powerful symbol of this perspective was the 1969 Divorce Reform Act, which recognized "irretrievable breakdown" as the only rationale for ending a marriage. Of course, what "irretrievable breakdown" signifies at a popular level—what in other words people accept as satisfactory within such a relationship—has itself altered since the Act was passed, with some behaviour that was previously tolerated now being seen as unacceptable.

The question to be posed here is what happens to other informal relationships, such as friendship, given the kinds of social and economic shifts outlined above. With increased flexibility in personal life and the actual or potential growth of alliances based around life-style interests, does friendship become any more or less important socially? Contrary to some theories of privatization, which have suggested that individuals will become increasingly detached from non-domestic ties of sociability, it is likely under the developing social formation of late modernity that the significance of informal ties will, if anything, be heightened (O'Connor, 1998). That is, to the extent that the changes that are occurring are fostering individuality, the significance of the self, and identity as a personally and socially constructed life-choice issue, then the realm of the informal will become increasingly significant. It is here, rather than in membership of more formal organizations and associations that the self will find both expression and identification. . . .

Though family relationships continue to be of major significance in people's lives, there is, as we have seen, a sense in which family ties, and in particular domestic and sexual partnerships, are not as secure as they were. But equally, self-identity will also be constituted through other types of informal relationship, especially friendships. The processes discussed above, in which friends help establish a sense of self, individuality

and worth, are likely to become the more important as other aspects of social organization (including, arguably, partnerships) become less permanent and more fragmented.

That is, relationships with friends will continue to be one of the main
arenas in which we express ourselves as the people we are. Friends know
"the real self," and not just a self that is being portrayed in a particular
way for instrumental purposes. Of course, different friends may perceive
that "reality" differently, but each, by the nature of their friendship, is
thought to have a privileged gaze at the other's character. Indeed because
of the types of social and economic transformation that late modernity
heralds, friendship may increasingly hold together the "centre" of self.
Thus far from being peripheral, the sphere of personal relationships may
become of increasing significance. This is where we "find" ourselves,
where we celebrate most clearly who we are, where indeed we *become*
who we are. With the possibility of greater levels of diversity in people's
experiences and a heightened emphasis on life-style issues, friendships
may be recognized increasingly as one of the main sites of activity giving
life meaning, just as family relationships have for many, though not all,
given the increased heterogeneity of domestic arrangements. . . .

Importantly though, neither these identities nor the friendships that
help sustain them are likely to be unchanging. The very processes that en
courage an emphasis on personal relationships as a significant sphere of
life are the ones that generate diversity and fragmentation in experience.
As people's commitments, interests and social location alter, so too their
personal networks of friends will be modified accordingly. As argued
above, this is inherent in friendship because of its basis in equality. Increasingly, then, the sense of self will be established through ties of personal solidarity, but these ties will not of themselves be stable. Perhaps
more accurately, the network of ties will not be stable. Particular friendships will wax and wane as people's circumstances and interests alter, but
the role of friendship remains important.

Clearly there is a tension in this. There are limits to the extent friends
can be replaced while still promoting an overarching sense of self. However, in practice, neither the process of changing self-identity nor that of
modifying friendship networks is likely to be particularly rapid. Each
goes hand-in-hand with the other. As circumstances alter, as new interests
emerge, as a new perspective on what we are as people develops, so the
people with whom we associate also alter. As we redefine ourselves in the
light of fresh understandings of who we are (and who we are not), new
friendships that are consonant with these understandings will replace existing ones. As we devote more time to these new friendships, so they
help cement our refurbished identities. The process is much as described

in the discussion of divorce above. What is altering, according to theories of late modernity, is simply the frequency with which individuals experience these sorts of change and the reduced importance of monolithic structural configurations that inform our understanding of our social location. In a world that is becoming more diverse and fragmentary, personal solidarities in general come to have greater significance, though individual relationships are liable to fade. . . .

References

Acitelli, L.K. (1995) "Disciplines at Parallel Play." *Journal of Social and Personal Relationships* 12: 589–96.

Adams, R. & Allan, G. (1998) *Placing Friendship in Context*. Cambridge, UK: Cambridge University Press.

Allan, G. (1979) *A Sociology of Friendship and Kinship*. London: George Allen & Unwin.

Allan, G. (1989) *Friendship: Developing a Sociological Perspective*. Hemel Hempstead, UK: Harvester Wheatsheaf.

Allan, G. & Crow, G. (1991) "Privatization, Home-centredness and Leisure", *Leisure Studies* 10: 19–32.

Allan, G. & Crow, G. (1999) *Families, Households and Society*. London: Macmillan.

Anderson, M. (1980) *Approaches to the History of the Western Family, 1500–1914*. London: Macmillan.

Beck, U. (1992) *Risk Society: Towards A New Modernity*. London: Sage.

Bell, C. & Newby, H. (1973) *Community Studies*. London: Allen & Unwin.

Cancian, F. (1987) *Love in America: Gender and Self-development*. Cambridge, UK: Cambridge University Press.

Duck, S. W. (Ed.) (1993) *Social Context and Relationships*. Newbury Park, CA: Sage.

Duck, S.W. (1994) *Meaningful Relationships: Talking, Sense, and Relating*. Thousand Oaks, CA: Sage.

Duck, S.W., West L. & Acitelli, L. (1997) "Sewing the Field: The Tapestry of Relationships in Life and Research," in S.W. Duck, K. Dindia, W. Ickes, R. Milardo, R. Mills & B. Sarason (Eds) *Handbook of Personal Relationships, Second Edition*. London: Wiley.

Duncombe, J. & Marsden, D. (1993) "Love and Intimacy: The Gender Division of Emotion and 'Emotion Work,'" *Sociology* 27: 221–41.

Feld, S. & Carter, W. (1998) "Foci of Activity as Changing Contexts for Friendship," in R. Adams & G. Allan (Eds) *Placing Friendship in Context*. Cambridge, UK: Cambridge University Press.

Giddens, A. (1991) *Modernity and Self-Identity*. Cambridge, UK: Polity.

Giddens, A. (1992) *The Transformation of Intimacy: Sexuality, Love and Eroticism in Modern Societies*. Cambridge, UK: Polity.

Harrison, K. (1998) "Rich Friendships, Affluent Friends: Middle-Class Practices of Friendship," in R. Adams & G. Allan (Eds) *Placing Friendship in Context*. Cambridge, UK: Cambridge University Press.

Haskey, J. (1996) "Population Review: (6) Families and Households in Great Britain," *Population Trends* 85: 7–24.

Hawkes, G. (1996) *A Sociology of Sex and Sexuality*. Buckingham, UK: Open University Press.

Hess, B.B. (1972) "Friendship," in M.W. Riley, M. Johnson & A. Foner (Eds) *Aging and Society (Vol. 3): A Sociology of Age Stratification*. New York: Russell Sage Foundation.

Jerrome, D. (1984) "Good Company: The Sociological Implications of Friendship," *Sociological Review* 32: 696–718.

Klein, J. (1965) *Samples from English Cultures*, Vol. 1. London: Routledge & Kegan Paul.

Mansfield, P. & Collard, J. (1988) *The Beginning of the Rest of Your Life? A Portrait of Newly-Wed Marriage*. London: Macmillan.

Marks, S. (1998) "The Gendered Contexts of Inclusive Intimacy: The Hawthorne Women at Work and Home," in R. Adams & G. Allan (Eds) *Placing Friendship in Context*. Cambridge, UK: Cambridge University Press.

Milardo, R. (1987) "Changes in Social Networks of Women and Men Following Divorce: A Review," *Journal of Family Issues* 8: 78–96.

Milardo, R. & Wellman, B. (1992) "The Personal Is Social," *Journal of Social and Personal Relationships* 9: 339–42.

O'Connor, P. (1998) "Women's Friendships in a Post-modern World," in R. Adams & G. Allan (Eds) *Placing Friendship in Context*. Cambridge, UK: Cambridge University Press.

Oliker, S. (1989) *Best Friends and Marriage: Exchange among Women*. Berkeley, CA: University of California Press.

Oliker, S. (1998) "The Modernization of Friendship: Individualism, Intimacy and Gender in the Nineteenth Century," in R. Adams & G. Allan (Eds) *Placing Friendship in Context*. Cambridge, UK: Cambridge University Press.

Silver, A. (1990) "Friendship in Commercial Society: Eighteenth Century Social Theory and Modern Sociology," *American Journal of Sociology* 95: 1474–504.

Suitor, J. (1987) "Friendship Networks in Transitions: Married Mothers' Return to School," *Journal of Social and Personal Relationships* 4: 445–61.

Wellman, B., Carrington, P. & Hall, A. (1988) "Networks as Personal Communities," in B. Wellman & S. Berkowitz (Eds) *Social Struc-

tures: A Network Approach. Cambridge, UK: Cambridge University Press.

Wellman, B. & Wortley, S. (1990) "Different Strokes by Different Folks: Community Ties and Social Support," *American Journal of Sociology* 93: 558–88.

Zorn, T. (1995) "Bosses and Buddies: Constructing and Performing Simultaneously Hierarchical and Close Friendship Relationships," in J. Wood & S.W. Duck (Eds) *Understanding Relationship Processes 6: Under-studied Relationships: Off the Beaten Track.* Thousand Oaks, CA: Sage.

Exercise 7.5   *Reader Reflections*

STEP 1: Spend some time writing in your journal, reflecting on what you've just read:

1. What do you understand about friendship now that you didn't before you began reading this piece?

2. How does the research Allan presents contribute to Michelle's research questions about cross-gender friendships? Of the other studies you've read in this chapter? Which seem to connect to this article or address similar things?

3. How does sociological research writing seem similar to and different from that in psychology, business, and communications? Be specific.

STEP 2: Describe the story of your reading of this piece: *When I began reading, I thought . . . and then . . . and then . . . Now I think/wonder . . .*

Blame It on the Sexual Revolution: An English Studies Article

Graham Allan's summary of sociological research on friendship made me wonder if it was only possible for men and women to be friends with the advent of feminism and sexual revolution, once social and economic pressures began to change the nature of both marriages and friendships. I also wondered whether disciplines besides the social sciences studied friendship in any way. What I found was a lengthy article about Margaret Fuller and James Freeman Clarke, two nineteenth-century figures who were close friends who wrote copious letters to one another. Most of their letters still exist for scholars to study, which is just what English professor Barbara Packer does in the following essay. And because English studies is more concerned about language than about human interactions or sociological effects, this essay looks closely at the friendship between Fuller and Clarke based on the textual evidence in these letters. How did cross-gender friends navigate their socially defined gender roles of the time to forge an intellectually and emotionally intimate friendship? And what can that tell me about cross-gender friendships in general? About mine in particular? Let's see what you think. And remember, continue to read as an ethnographer of this academic culture, English studies, as well as a researcher on the subject of cross-gender friendships.

Dangerous Acquaintances: The Correspondence of Margaret Fuller and James Freeman Clarke

Barbara Packer

The correspondence of Margaret Fuller and James Freeman Clarke, which began early in 1830 and lasted almost to the end of Fuller's life, was a determined experiment in conducting friendship across gender lines.[1]

Could a sensitive young Harvard student innocently carry on a candid correspondence with a brilliant young woman to whom he was not engaged? Could a brilliant woman reveal her intimate thoughts to a young man without fear of compromising her reputation? Could both of them discuss life, self, ambition, sensibility, and moments of despair with one another as if the obvious differences between them did not exist or at least did not matter? When Margaret Fuller visited the Emersons in 1837 she spoke on the subject of "Woman" in a way that seemed to dismiss the notions of separate roles or separate spheres for women: "Who would be a goody that could be a genius?"[2]

Yet Fuller would discover during the course of her correspondence with Clarke that traditional roles were not so easily abandoned, while Clarke, who wanted to address Fuller with masculine frankness yet still find in her feminine receptiveness, blundered repeatedly into cruelties he did not even know that he was committing. These painful moments form only a small part of a correspondence that is overwhelmingly brave, generous, and high-spirited. But they seem all the more significant for that. With genuine affection on both sides, with mutual esteem, with the boundaries of their relationship apparently agreed upon from the start, Fuller and Clarke could not help arousing feelings that drew them away from camaraderie into displays of malice, into mutual lacerations and then into shamefaced apologies. To witness them try to regain their composure after one of these lapses is both moving and disturbing: moving, because their determination to treat one another simply as friends is so important to both of them; saddening, because they keep being warped away from high-mindedness toward the deviousness and reproachfulness of ordinary erotic life.

The correspondence began in the form of notes passed between a pair of intellectually ambitious nineteen-year-olds when they both lived in Cambridge. James Freeman Clarke, a graduate of the Harvard class of 1829 who was just beginning studies at the Divinity School, met Margaret Fuller at social gatherings in Cambridge where he quickly became impressed by the brilliance of her conversation and by the range of her reading. While Clarke had been plodding through the prescribed curriculum at Boston Latin and then at Harvard, where the Greek professor forced students to wade through the *Iliad* as if it were a bog, Fuller had been educated by a series of tutors.[3] Her first tutor was her father Timothy, a lawyer who in Margaret's youth had been a congressman from Cambridge. He started her out when she was six with lessons in Latin and English grammar. He continued to direct her progress by letter when he was absent in Washington during congressional sessions. Her first letter to him there, written when she was seven-and-a-half, suggests the ambitiousness of the program he expected her to follow. She dutifully reports: "I have been reviewing Valpy's Chronology. We have not been able to procure any books on either Charles 12th of Sweden or Philip IId of Spain but Mama intends to send to Uncle Henry. I hope to make greater proficuncy [*sic*] in my Studies I have learned all the rules of Musick but one."[4] Later she had periods of formal schooling—at the new Cambridge Port Private Grammar School, at Dr. John Park's Boston Lyceum for Young Ladies, at Miss Susan Prescott's Young Ladies' Seminary at Groton. But since the age of fifteen she had conducted her own ambitious program of self-improvement. Though Harvard's classes were closed to her she used all its resources—books, friendly professors, lecturers—to learn more about the Romantic writers who increasingly fascinated her: Coleridge, Shelley, Byron, de Staël, Rousseau.[5] Since these were the writers whom the Harvard undergraduates also revered, Fuller appeared to them as a kind of adjunct professor, master of that unofficial curriculum that played so large a part in the lives of nineteenth-century American undergraduates.[6] Fuller's social position in Cambridge added to her air of authority. Although her father had declined to seek a fifth term in Congress and had resumed his law practice in Boston, hoping for a diplomatic appointment that never materialized, Margaret Fuller still enjoyed the prestige and wide acquaintanceship that her father's prominence gave her.

James Freeman Clarke, on the other hand, was the son of a hapless speculator whose schemes for raising money to support a family of thirteen children all went badly awry. The senior Clarke practiced medicine, served as a judge, tinkered with various inventions, tried raising merino sheep in Vermont (the sheep sickened and died), and experimented with bleaching beeswax in Boston (the factory burned down just after the insurance policy on it had expired). At last the family came to depend upon a boardinghouse Mrs. Clarke opened in Boston.[7] James had been spared the worst of his family's misfortunes. Since the age of five he had been raised in the rural home of his maternal grandmother and step-grandfather, the celebrated Unitarian minister James Freeman, in whose honor he had been named. James Freeman raised the young Clarke with affection and tutored him with skill; he agreed to finance Clarke's first year at Divinity School. Still, the anomalous position Clarke occupied as the dependent of an elderly relative while his immediate family struggled to survive contributed to his tendencies toward insecurity.[8]

Fuller's air of queenly self-confidence seemed enviable to Clarke, though it might have been put on to carry her through a social world that judged her arrogant, sharp-tongued, and very unattractive. His first surviving note to Fuller, written early in 1830, made it clear that he saw himself as a suitor for her attention and affections. He brought her a copy of Sheridan's play *The Rivals*, apparently in response to her request, and then made a playful request of his own: "I desire that you would investigate our relationship, for I believe I am as much your cousin as George is, and if so there is no reason why you should not answer my notes, and indeed there is no reason at any rate."[9]

Although Clarke's maternal grandfather had been named Fuller, Robert Hudspeth, the editor of Margaret Fuller's letters, has determined that Clarke's grandfather did not come from the same branch of the Fuller family as Margaret Fuller.[10] But Clarke's claim of cousinship was convenient even if it was false. It licensed the frankness he hoped to find in her letter. Personal confidences were permitted to courting couples, and family members might be frank within the family circle. But for two unrelated young people to indulge in uninhibited self-revelation without the protection of an engagement was more than faintly scandalous; it could be dangerous. Clarke's note of March 1830, with its curious mixture of deference to opinion and defiance of it, was meant to announce to Fuller that she could trust him. He suggested at once that they were both too advanced to need the excuse of cousinship for a correspondence and that they could always claim the excuse when needed.

Fuller's reply of 16 March 1830 shows that she understood Clarke very well. Her answer to his reassurances about the propriety of their correspondence took the form of Johnsonian parody: "'t is neither conformable to the spirit of the nineteenth century, nor the march of mind, that those churlish reserves should be kept up between *the right and left hands*, which belonged to ages of barbarism and prejudice, and could only have been inculcated for their use." As to the claim of relationship, Fuller replied mockingly that she found upon inquiry that it was by no means to be compared with the closeness of her relationship to George Davis, and hence "of course, the intimacy cannot be so great. But no matter; it will enable me to answer your notes." She signed the letter, "your cousin only thirty-seven degrees removed."[11]

This first letter from Fuller to Clarke is interesting for other reasons. It began by giving the time of day with unusual precision: "*Half-past six, morning.*" Indeed, Fuller told Clarke that she had gotten up at sunrise in order to have leisure to answer his note. The flattery implicit in this quick response to Clarke's plea for a note shows that Fuller was more than willing to answer warmth with warmth. But her eagerness was alarming. Clarke was a close friend of George Davis, a brilliant conversationalist who reminded Fuller of Richardson's Lovelace.[12] Davis, though flattered by Fuller's attentions, was drawing away from her, and Clarke may have felt that by his own gallantries and demands for intimacy he had unwittingly nominated himself to fill Davis's place. Clarke's next surviving letter to Fuller asked her pointedly to send him her ideas on his "Louisa affair"—his unsuccessful suit of a woman who, despite Clarke's belief that she would have (as he says) "been benefitted by coming in contact with a *really* powerful intellect," had nonetheless married another man.[13] The letter is written in a style that young American men in the first half of the nineteenth century tended to affect when speaking to other men about women: half-mocking, half-sentimental, full of fashionable cynicism, redolent of comfortable clubs where women were present only as the subject of toasts: the style of Tommo's description of the beauteous Fayaway in *Typee* or of Miles Coverdale's estimate of Zenobia's full-blown womanhood in *The Blithedale Romance*. Clarke's letter serves as both an invitation and a barrier to Fuller. "See, I am treating you as I would one of my Harvard friends," it says; "but please remember that I consider an erotic relationship with you out of the question."

Fuller refused Clarke's invitation to discuss other women. She told him curtly that she could not comply with his wish to discuss "the Louisa affair": she asked him to excuse her "caution," but said firmly that she dared not "be generous in these matters," though she promised to talk to him about the subject when a "fitting opportunity" presented itself.[14] To be invited to exchange confidences with a flattering young man and then to be asked immediately to serve as a confidante in his affairs of the heart was to be dismissed with unnecessary brutality. She had already made clear that she understood exactly where she stood in Clarke's affections; in an early letter she wrote: "I should rejoice to cultivate generosity, since (see that *since*) affections gentler and more sympathetic are denied me."[15] Why then did he insist upon dragging her into painful discussions about the charms of other women?

Clarke's insensitivity on this point can seem exasperating. But his attempts to recruit Fuller as a confidante may also reflect a genuine perplexity about how to address a woman who had renounced hopes for tenderness, declared herself free of conventional delicacy, and laid claim to masculine freedom in thought and self-assertion. Clarke was in awe of her brilliance and full of admiration for her refusal to be confined within the limits thought proper for her sex. But if Fuller did not want to be treated like a frivolous girl, did she want to be treated like one of his Harvard classmates? How did one address a woman with whom one wanted intimacies but with whom one did not mean to flirt?

Clarke understood that he had offended Fuller by writing about the "Louisa affair." He immediately tried to mend fences. Tactfully, he concentrated only on the part of her note that expressed social fear. "You fear to show me vagaries, from the forevision of my hour of cooler judgment. I might tell you that in my coldest mood I could not criticize words which were dictated by a confiding spirit." He went on to insist with firmness that she not hide behind social conventions, that she match his candor with her own:

> . . . I cannot expect to argue down your feelings. But what I do say is this—that you cannot expect from me that which you do not return. There are enough who rejoice in relieving their full bosoms, by telling you their sorrows and joys, seeking nothing but an attentive ear, and an intelligent heart. The case is different, as you know, with me. It is only when I know that those to whom I write or speak are ready to give me an equal store of treasured emotions, that the ice-bars break from the depths of my nature, and the hidden fountains well upwards. I am not 'heroic,' if heroism consists in throwing away your buckler before one cased in armor.

He listed each of his friends and said "how far" he had gone with each in that "disclosure of weaknesses" he identified as the "highest confidence." And he told her: "I should have been happy in going further with you than with all before," but he cannot do that without an "answering store" of disclosures from her.[16]

Clarke's letter sounds remarkably like the letters discussed by Karen Lystra in *Searching the Heart*, which studies romantic love among nineteenth-century Americans. She says that "appropriately disclosing and explaining the self formed the foundation of nineteenth-century American romantic love," and she quotes a letter written by a man named Albert Janin to his beloved: "if you would not grieve and distress me, do not treat me with reserve and want of confidence—I mean, do not employ toward me the caution that you use in correspondence with others." Indeed, Lystra argues, "self-revelation became the primary symbol of intimacy" in nineteenth-century America.[17]

Fuller's startling response to this letter of Clarke's suggests that she saw his demand for candor as erotic in itself, a substitute for the gentler affections she felt were elsewhere denied her. She told Clarke in the language of erotic romance how his demand for self-revelation had affected her: "Ten minutes before I received it, I scarcely thought that anything again would make my stifled heart throb so warm a pulse of pleasure. Excuse my cold doubts, my selfish arrogance." She rejoiced to find a friend who was unwilling to put up with the kind of unequal relationship to which her superiority to other people had usually condemned her. If she could not yet promise limitless confidence, she promised that "no timid caution, no haughty dread shall prevent my telling you the truth of my thoughts on any subject we have in common."[18] . . .

The double exile of Fuller and Clarke from Cambridge initiated the major phase of their correspondence. While they both lived in Cambridge the notes they passed back and forth supplemented a friendship that brought them together nearly every day. Now they were cut off not only from one another but from everything that had sustained them intellectually. The letters they sent grew longer, more detailed. Their candor, which had once been flaunted as the proof of spiritual distinction, now served to bring relief from isolation among uncongenial companions. In the absence of other friends, surrounded by adult responsibilities that often daunted them, Clarke and Fuller now needed someone to whom they could speak the simple truth.

Clarke's situation was in many ways more painful than Fuller's, at least at first. She had always been subject to her father's whims, and though she felt homesick for Cambridge and her friends she had her family around her. The scenery around Groton was lovely, and the town was close enough to Cambridge that determined friends could still come for visits. Clarke paid her one such visit in 1833, during which he read her translation of Goethe's *Tasso* and spoke to her with such freedom that he felt that their minds "were embracing, and found no discord at their center."[29] The memory of the meeting had given him strength.

He needed the strength, for emigration to Louisville brought Clarke nothing but homesickness and humiliation. He had chosen it as the site of his emergence as an independent agent in creation. But already on the journey West he had felt grumpy and sluggish rather than responsive to sublimity. "I passed along with the gravity of an Alderman from city to city, through valley, over mountain—like the lady who said 'How rural' in the vale of Chamouni."[30]

If the journey was bad the arrival was worse. Louisville was bleak and treeless; the Westerners whom he had hoped to convert with his liberal religion had little interest in anything beyond hunting or farming; and the only parishioners he had were a handful of Unitarian exiles from New England. He was dreadfully homesick. He admitted that his courage was "oozing out of the end of his fingers." He confessed that half a dozen women walked out of his first Louisville sermon. And he implored Fuller not to reveal to anyone back in Cambridge how miserable he was.[31]

The next letter carried even bitterer self-mockery. "*I*, whose pride has scoffed at the thought of being under the sway of circumstances, yes, I have been miserable because I was suddenly torn from my *Umgebung*: my room and books and routine of daily work and daily relaxation—prayers, bells, recitations, chats with minds of *culture* and *polish* and *refinement*—(Alas, Margaret, I miss them)." He explained how he planned to recreate some semblance of his former life by putting familiar objects around his room. Then he broke out in a sad apostrophe: "Oh! my beloved, carpeted, curtained, astral lighted, Cambridge home! This will be but a poor mockery of thy little elegancies."[32]

Gently, Fuller reminded him about a conversation they had had the preceding summer, when she had deplored the power of circumstance in shaping life and he had denied it. "You then professed the faith which I resigned with such anguish,—a faith in the power of the human will. Yet now, in every letter, you talk to me of the power of circumstances." She wanted him to understand that she was not chiding him for inconsistency, merely trying to recall him to his earlier faith. She urged him to stop apologizing for his letters. "Why do you apologize? I think I know you very, very well; considering that we are both human, and have the gift of concealing our thoughts in words. Nay further—I do not believe you will be able to become anything which I cannot understand."[33] Clarke had confessed that without her "confidence and intimacy" he would have "a very machine-like feeling" in going about his duties.[34] She replied that if he had become a machine she expected to find him "a grand, high-pressure, wave-compelling one—requiring plenty of fuel." She too would become a machine, she promised, then suddenly changed the metaphor: "No! upon second thoughts, I will not be a machine. I will be an instrument, not to be confided to vulgar hands,—for instance, a chisel to polish marble, or a whetstone to sharpen steel!"[35]

In another letter written while she was visiting Boston in October of 1833 Fuller matched his confessions of inadequacy with her own: "I wish to study ten-thousand, thousand things this winter—Every day I become more sensible to the defects in my education—I feel so ignorant and superficial. Every day hundreds of questions occur to me to which I can get no answer and do not know what books to consult."[36] Despite her lack of professional training and the new burdens she felt as the eldest child of a family on a working farm, Fuller found time to continue her voracious reading.

In 1834 she again visited Boston and Cambridge. Clarke, too, had obtained leave from his Kentucky congregation to make a visit home. The intimacy that had grown up between them ought to have made their reunion happy, but in fact Clarke's behavior toward Fuller was puzzling and hurtful. The revelations he had made to her from Louisville of his misery and professional inadequacy may have embarrassed him when they met in the crowded world of Cambridge. For whatever reason, he was standoffish to her when they met. At a party on their last evening together he ignored her and talked to a pretty woman who had already alienated the affections of a man Fuller had herself once been in love with.[37]

Some kind of angry scene between Clarke and Fuller took place before Clarke left Cambridge; Fuller evidently told him that she neither expected nor wanted to hear from him again. By the time Clarke reached Louisville in September of 1834 he was not only repentant but desperate. He confessed his rudeness at the party, pleaded with Fuller for forgiveness and reinstatement. "I feel grateful for the high intellectual culture and excitement of which you have been to me the source," he wrote. "Do not determine that if we are not *all* to each other we shall be nothing," he pleaded, "I can never find such another as you."[38]

The relationship Clarke wanted with Fuller—the progressively deepening intimacies of courtship without its termination in union—was inherently unstable, and though Fuller agreed (without retracting anything she had said to him in anger) to welcome Clarke back as a correspondent in the hopes that they might "begin a new era and . . . alter the *nature* of our friendship without altering the soul," little had really changed between them.[39]

Clarke continued to depend on Fuller for brilliant descriptions of nature and emotion, of German and English Romantic poetry. He felt invigorated by her passionate intellectual attentions. "It gives me a glow of encouragement to receive a letter from you," he told her in 1835. "I feel stronger and much more daring after one of your letters."[40] Still, this very sense of obligation gave rise in Clarke to a mean wish to strike back at her, if only to preserve some sense of self-respect. When Fuller published a short story called "Lost and Won," based loosely on the characters and love affairs of her Cambridge acquaintances, Clarke, under the guise of praising it, told Fuller he had procured extra copies of the story and sent them to the originals of her characters. Fuller was so distressed by this bit of treachery that she fell seriously ill. Clarke did not even dare to answer the furious letter she wrote to him; he enlisted his sister to write an apology for him.[41]

Clarke's flare-ups of unconscious hostility caused Fuller pain, but his genuine encouragement of her literary ambitions—and his willingness to offer constructive criticism of the things she wrote—were as important to her as her brilliant provocations were to him. When he took over the editorship of the fledgling Unitarian periodical *The Western Messenger* and moved it from Cincinnati to Louisville, he pestered her for essays and reviews. "The Bulwer, and Crabbe, and More, and Artevelde—all will be very acceptable . . . As for the Hebrew tales you mention, could you not write one as a specimen and let me publish it? You see I grow rapacious like other editors."[42]

When she told him of her ambition to write a life of Goethe, he offered to lend her his forty-volume set of Goethe's works, and added: "Go on with your task, fear not, you can do it."[43] When she became convinced that she could never understand Goethe without understanding something about the history of German metaphysics, a subject she had always avoided, he answered quickly with a long letter providing a history of English and German philosophy in the two centuries leading up to Kant's *Critique of Pure Reason*, and added encouragingly: "I think you had better read some of the *Kritik*. You will find it very intelligible."[44] When she complained that she lacked access to primary sources about Goethe's life, Clarke sympathized with her frustration: "I wish I could be the jackal for the lion, and procure for you all the other sources of information which you ought to have from abroad."[45]

The flattery implicit in Clarke's metaphor suggests why Fuller was as dependent on him as he was on her. In a world that denied her entrance to schools, colleges, and professions, Clarke treated her as an intellectual equal and served as a grateful audience for all of her ideas and emotions. Clarke's endless receptivity to her gorgeous and intimidating epistolary self-display may have been more important than anything he said in reply, for Fuller at that time wrote well only when she was sure of the affections of her audience. Her published writings at that time were stilted and hieratic or else lush with overripe romanticism. Her letters were brilliant, witty, and supple. They contain the best writing she did during these years, and the best of these letters are the ones she wrote to Clarke. . . .

Their friendship survived Clarke's marriage and subsequent return to Boston. They continued to exchange occasional letters, though only

Clarke's half of the later correspondence still survives. He was as generous in praise of her preface to her 1839 translation of *Eckerman's Conversations with Goethe* as he had been critical of her reviews for the *Western Messenger*. He told her he had read her preface on the terrace of the Clifton House overlooking Niagara Falls, "with the thundering cataract foaming over in full sight." He took back everything he had said about the deficiencies of her style. "Your preface seemed to me a masterpiece of composition, clear yet cogent, dignified yet playful, with *point* to attract attention and weighty matter to occupy the thought."[57] He sympathized with her sufferings when she served as editor of the *Dial* with a fellow-feeling born of experience. When she was visiting Chicago in 1843, he sent her fifty dollars, knowing that she was seriously short of funds, with the prayer that she should "have no more scruple in taking this from me than I should in receiving it from you under like circumstances."[58] Her articles for the New York *Tribune* in the mid-1840s earned praise from him for their new "ease, grace, and freedom."[59] When Fuller was in Italy in 1848 he wrote her a final kind, funny letter giving an account of the religious vagaries of present-day Boston and urging her to "leave revolutions to revolve alone." He closed by saying: "Farewell. God bless you."[60]

The correspondence between Fuller and Clarke testifies both to the strength and the precariousness of friendships between men and women. Still, if the two correspondents could not always keep their friendship on an even keel, they usually managed to right it before it foundered. The strongest impression their correspondence makes is one of shared excitement, and the many kinds of aid they gave one another helped sustain them through painful experiences. Their letters to one another were momentary liberations from drudgery and loneliness, reminders of intellectual companionship, and acts of love. What the correspondents really wanted from one another was the vivifying shock of intimacy that Clarke requested in one of his earliest letters to Fuller: "Electrify my stupor with your generosity."[61]

Notes

1. James Freeman Clarke's letters to Margaret Fuller have been collected in a single volume, *The Letters of James Freeman Clarke to Margaret Fuller*, ed. John Wesley Thomas (Hamburg: Cram, de Gruyter, 1957). Fuller's letters to Clarke survive in various stages of completeness, since many of her letter manuscripts were cut up for use by the three editors of *The Memoirs of Margaret Fuller Ossoli*, 2 vols. (Boston, 1852). Clarke edited the first third of the *Memoirs* and included paragraphs from Fuller's letters to him. These letters or fragments of letters may now be

found throughout volumes 1 and 2 of Robert Hudspeth's six-volume edition of *The Letters of Margaret Fuller* (Ithaca, N.Y.: Cornell Univ. Press, 1983–94). (All letters cited from this volume are from Fuller to Clarke, unless otherwise specified.) Hudspeth's account of the editing of the *Memoirs* and the role Clarke played in them can be found in his introductory account of "The Sources," 1:59–65.

2. Fuller's remark to Emerson is quoted by Charles Capper in *The Private Years*, vol. 1 of *Margaret Fuller: An American Romantic Life* (New York: Oxford Univ. Press, 1992), 216. The remark can be found in *The Journals and Miscellaneous Notebooks of Ralph Waldo Emerson*, ed. William Gilman and others, 16 vols. (Cambridge: Harvard Univ. Press, 1960–82), 5:407.

3. James Freeman Clarke, *Autobiography, Diary, and Correspondence*, ed. Edward Everett Hale (Boston: Houghton, Mifflin and Company, 1891), 36. In addition to the tutoring she received from her father and uncles, Fuller was tutored at one time by a young divinity student, Ezra Stiles Gannett, future president of the American Unitarian Association. Fuller also attended at various times the Cambridge Port Private Grammar School, Dr. Park's Boston Lyceum for Young Ladies, and Miss Susan Prescott's Young Ladies' Seminary at Groton. See Capper, 1:29–83.

4. Margaret Fuller to Timothy Fuller, 13 January 1818, in *Letters of Margaret Fuller*, 1:81. My account of Fuller's childhood follows Capper, 1:29–41.

5. See Capper, 1:93.

6. For an account of the "extracurriculum" at nineteenth-century American colleges, see Frederick Rudolph, *Curriculum: A History of the American Undergraduate Course of Study since 1636* (San Francisco: Jossey-Bass Publishers, 1977), 94–98.

7. See Clarke, *Autobiography*, 8–10. The boardinghouse, however, had a distinguished clientele. According to Clarke's biographer Arthur S. Bolster, Jr., Mrs. Clarke's boarders at one time included Elizabeth Peabody, Horace Mann, and Jared Sparks, the future president of Harvard. See Bolster, *James Freeman Clarke: Disciple to Advancing Truth* (Boston: The Beacon Press, 1954), 63.

8. See Capper, 1:105.

9. 1830, in *Letters of James Freeman Clarke*, 9. The letter is there marked as "post-dated" 1829. Clarke added dates to many letters, not always accurately, after Fuller returned them to him. Fuller's reply to Clarke's note, printed in *Letters of Margaret Fuller*, 1:160–61, suggests that the correct date of Clarke's note should be 1830.

10. See Hudspeth's note to letter 63 (16 March 1830) in *Letters of Margaret Fuller*, 1:161.

11. 16 March 1830, in *Letters of Margaret Fuller*, 1:160–61.

12. See Capper, 1:104.

13. 19 March 1830, in *Letters of James Freeman Clarke*, 10.

14. [28? March 1830], in *Letters of Margaret Fuller*, 1:162.

15. [28? March 1830], in *Letters of Margaret Fuller*, 1:163.

16. 27 March 1830, in *Letters of James Freeman Clarke*, 11.

17. Karen Lystra, *Searching the Heart: Men, Women, and Romantic Love in Nineteenth-Century America* (New York: Oxford Univ. Press, 1992), 15. Lystra notes that middle-class men, who were expected to remain strongly self-controlled in most public situations, saw love-letters as places in which they could reveal their inner emotions freely and without fear of censure.

18. [28? March 1830], in *Letters of Margaret Fuller*, 1:162–63. . . .

29. [post-dated] 1833, in *Letters of James Freeman Clarke*, 43.

30. 9 September 1833, in *Letters of James Freeman Clarke*, 59.

31. 12 August 1833, in *Letters of James Freeman Clarke*, 57.

32. 9 September 1833, in *Letters of James Freeman Clarke*, 59, 60.

33. [September? 1833?], in *Letters of Margaret Fuller*, 1:192.

34. 9 September 1833, in *Letters of James Freeman Clarke*, 60.

35. [September? 1833?], in *Letters of Margaret Fuller*, 1:192–93.

36. 25 October 1833, in *Letters of Margaret Fuller*, 1:196.

37. See Capper, 1:140–41.

38. 8 September 1834, in *Letters of James Freeman Clarke*, 80.

39. 28 September 1834, in *Letters of Margaret Fuller*, 1:206.

40. 12 April 1835, in *Letters of James Freeman Clarke*, 91.

41. The apology begun by Sarah Clarke, headed 29 September and later post-dated 1835, was finished by James; the double letter can be found in *Letters of James Freeman Clarke*, 104–6.

42. 12 April 1835, in *Letters of James Freeman Clarke*, 91.

43. 28 March 1836, in *Letters of James Freeman Clarke*, 117.

44. The long letter of 26 February 1836 containing Clarke's brief history of German metaphysics is printed in *Letters of James Freeman Clarke*, 113–16. He is writing in reply to Fuller's letter dated [ca. 14 February 1836] in *Letters of Margaret Fuller*, 1:244–45.

45. 7 January 1836, in *Letters of James Freeman Clarke*, 113. . . .

57. 8 October 1839, in *Letters of James Freeman Clarke*, 137.

58. 10 July 1843, in *Letters of James Freeman Clarke*, 143. Clarke accompanied Fuller and his sister, Sarah Ann Clarke, on the first leg of their midwestern journey, as they traveled first to Niagara Falls and then to Buffalo, where they caught the steamboat for Chicago. He arranged for his brother, William Hull Clarke, to accompany them around Illinois. See Susan Belasco Smith's "Introduction" to Margaret Fuller's *Summer*

on the Lakes, ed. Belasco Smith (Urbana: Univ. Illinois Press, 1991), viii, xxi, n.4.

59. 26 July 1845, in *Letters of James Freeman Clarke*, 145.

60. December 1848, in *Letters of James Freeman Clarke*, 146–47.

61. 11 April 1830, in *Letters of James Freeman Clarke*, 13.

Exercise 7.6   *Reader Reflections*

Spend some time fastwriting in your journal about the following questions:

1. What seems to distinguish research writing in English studies from the other disciplines you've read in this chapter? What constitutes evidence, for example? How do writers establish authority to speak on their subject? How is research presented? How is it organized? What kind of presence is expected from the writer?

2. What has this examination of one friendship added to your developing ideas about cross-gender friendship? What ideas does it raise that are similar to or different from the other pieces in this chapter? What questions does it raise for you?

3. If you were assigned to write a research essay on cross-gender friendships, what do you think you'd want to focus on? Why?

4. What have you learned from this chapter about reading formal academic research? Make a list of the five to ten things you've learned, attitudes and strategies you plan to use in your other courses when you read academic sources.

How Does the Story End? Reflections on Michelle's Inquiry Project

Throughout this chapter we've had two story lines going: Michelle's inquiry into her questions about male-female friendships, and Michelle's encounters with unfamiliar academic research writing. We wanted to immerse you in one person's research project so you could witness academic inquiry at work, one way that a writer and researcher applies what we've been emphasizing throughout the book. Where, for example, did you see Michelle applying the modes of inquiry—exploring, explaining, evaluating, and reflecting? How did she respond to confusing ideas or conflicting "opinions"? How did her understanding about her research project develop with each article? What surprised you about Michelle's approach?

At the same time, we wanted you to witness one person using "ethnographic reading" strategies as she entered into five different academic subcultures. Academic research articles can be a challenge for outsiders to read, and yet you will be expected to use such articles in other college courses. Michelle demonstrated how she identifies the rhetorical conventions of a discipline's research writing—what constitutes evidence, what organizational structures are expected, how a writer establishes credibility, what the larger conversation has been about the particular subject of the article, who the key people are in the field. Once she understood the general conventions of the subculture, she could better figure out what was most significant to her research question.

We began this chapter with a story about how Michelle became interested in researching cross-gender friendships, and after she commented on the first two articles, Michelle's voice disappeared from the margins of the other readings so you could practice what you were learning. But we don't know what she made of all that she read. Where will she go next? How would she begin an essay on this subject? Here are her reflections on those questions:

> When I began researching cross-gender friendships, I had a very personal connection to the subject. I believed men and women could be friends as long as they both were committed to protecting the boundaries between their friendship and their marital relationships (if they were a factor). I also had never had a close male friend, so I sometimes wasn't sure, for example, if a display of affection I'd share with a female friend, like Bruce's wife, was okay in my friendship with a male. I wanted to understand the friendship better. I was prompted to do this research because of the questions friends and family members raised about having a man as my best friend. On some level, of course, I wanted to prove them wrong—I wanted to find research that showed I was right. Of course men and women can be friends, and romance or sexual attraction either isn't a factor or, if it is, can be controlled. I'm sure you've approached many research projects with similar kinds of convictions or motivations to prove something you believe but don't have evidence for. To truly inquire into my research question, though, I had to be aware of my personal motivations to simply illustrate my own experience. I had to suspend my judgment and see what I found. Once I did that, I was more open to the research I discovered and the new questions each of them created for me.
>
> I didn't want to believe, for example, that attraction was a factor in male-female relationships, even though the members of my faculty writing group kept encouraging me to look into it. I decided to pursue it, tentatively, and stumbled on more information than I could reasonably read. Heidi M. Reeder's article, " 'I like you. . . as a friend' " (pages 377–391) impressed me immediately because her

study began with interviews from actual friends, and from those interviews emerged four very different ways of defining attraction and how each affects friendship. In this article I suddenly saw pairs of friends who did in fact have to deal with sexual attraction, some of whom also felt what Reeder calls "romantic attraction," and they were making conscious decisions not to "ruin the friendship" by choosing not to act on those impulses. Most friendships don't have those combinations, as Reeder illustrates; in fact, it is more typical for cross-gender friends NOT to feel romantic attraction to each other.

This article prompted me to think more about the differences between friendship and romance. The letters between Margaret Fuller and James Clarke were an example of two friends trying to figure out that line. I also saw many similarities to my relationship with Bruce, particularly in terms of the intellectual and emotional exchanges Fuller and Clarke had. I didn't get the sense they were, in Reeder's terms, attracted to each other in a subjective way, but were certainly drawn to each other's friendship qualities. And they struggled a bit with whether their emotional intimacy was that of a romantic relationship—in nineteenth-century terms, that is. That essay highlighted for me what Graham Allan talks about in the twentieth and twenty-first centuries: definitions of romantic and marital relationships change over time and influence the ways friendships develop. I was especially struck by Allan's argument that, currently, friendships are one of the primary ways we express who we are. I began thinking about my friendships in a whole new way. How *do* they express who I am? How much of my identity is shaped by my friendships? By my marriage? By my family? Are cross-gender friendships, no matter our sexual orientation, more possible now because (1) of the ways we define marriage and (2) the changes in friendship patterns and its affect on our sense of identity? And how does my social class, as well as Bruce's, affect not only our friendship with each other, but with our other friends? My husband, who comes from a working-class family, does seem to have very different approaches to friendships than I do, and I've begun wondering how much of that is class based.

As you can see, these articles have raised a lot of new questions for me. Which might I focus on if I were to write an essay about this subject? I could focus on Graham Allan's arguments about friendships shaping identity and explore how that applies to my relationship with Bruce. Or I could reflect in a personal way on how each of these essays has affected how I view cross-gender friendships, as well as how they've mirrored or challenged my particular friendship. I could take a very different approach and combine everything I've read into an essay that examines definitions of friendship and marriage/romance in the twenty-first century, defining as clearly as I can what the line seems to be that friends of the opposite sex will not cross. What other possible approaches might I take to an essay based on this research? I'm sure you have plenty of ideas yourself. I'm definitely ready to write this essay, and I've had fun getting such a broad and complex perspective on my research question.

What direction might you take with an essay about cross-gender friendships? Would you change your research question and focus on another issue that came up in the research Michelle found? Would you create your own study and conduct interviews and distribute surveys? What would *you* do with the information about male-female friendships you've learned from these different disciplines? If you're like many of our students, you've probably not considered extending the scope of your research to include multiple disciplines. Yet, as Michelle's story illustrates, an article from communication studies like Heidi M. Reeder's can apply to an article from English studies like Barbara Parker's, leading to new insights and questions. Plus, her researched essay will be more credible because it includes both the broad perspective on friendship that sociology provides and the narrow case study of one friendship from the nineteenth century, as well as large-scale, contemporary studies of actual cross-gender friends.

In Chapter 8 you'll have a chance to apply what you've learned here about reading across disciplines and genres. You'll also have a chance to develop your own researched essay on a question about the ethics of publishing disturbing photographs. But we also hope you can apply the strategies offered in this chapter whenever you encounter any piece of formal academic research. We hope you feel less intimidated, better prepared to understand some of the strange differences in each field's writing conventions, modes of inquiry, general focus, and uses of evidence. Just as importantly, we hope you've also learned how examining a subject from multiple disciplines can help you develop a rich and complex understanding of your research question.

c   h   a   p   t   e   r

8

Reading and Writing Across Disciplines: The Ethics of Publishing Disturbing Photos

ENCOUNTERS WITH DISTURBING PHOTOGRAPHS

Standard fare in high school driver education classes is the horrifying accident movie. The theory is simple: If you scare the hell out of would-be drivers, they will be less likely to drive recklessly. One of us suffered through a film titled "Death on the Highway," a thirty-minute gem that featured severed arms, mangled corpses, and bright red pools of blood amidst unimaginably crumpled cars. At least a few people always fled the darkened room, and the survivors of the film never blamed them. "Death on the Highway" was a terrible ordeal.

It's hard to say for certain whether the scare-the-hell-out-of-them strategy really works, though there is some research that suggests that it may not. But there's little argument that shocking images can disrupt, disturb, revolt, entice, frighten, horrify, and interest people. Seeing "Death on the Highway" was required to pass that driver's education class, and though students were allowed to leave the room, there was never any debate about whether, in the context of driver's ed, exposure to such images was appropriate. But is there any debate about those shocking photographs in newspapers and magazines, the ones that may greet us while we wolf down our Special K in the morning?

Many of you, for example, remember this chilling photograph of a firefighter carrying the bloodied baby from the carnage of the 1995 Oklahoma City bombing. The photo (Figure 8-1), taken by a local bank clerk and distributed to newspapers nationwide by the Associated Press, came to symbolize the tragedy, but some considered its publication tasteless and unnecessary. "Too upsetting for adults, much less children," said one complaining

FIGURE 8–1

The photograph that immortalized the Oklahoma City bombing. One-year-old
Baylee Almon later died. Photo by Charles H. Porter/ZUMA.

reader. The controversy deepened when the baby, 1-year-old Baylee Almon,
later died.

One editor who received reader complaints about the picture noted that
his newspaper recently published a similar photograph of a dead Rwandan

baby that produced only a single call. Another editor who ran the shot on page one of his large metropolitan newspaper argued that the "photo showed what happened better than anything I've seen. There wasn't a photo that better captured what happened there, so we decided to use it." The same editor also admitted that he had a child the same age, and later that night "walked out to the parking lot and cried. I have never done that before."

It's easy to summon other examples of shocking pictures that give pause. The Iraqi conflict has produced its share of them, including the controversial images of the four American contractors who were hauled from their SUVs, and then burned (see "Images of Horror from Fallujah" on page 438), and the photographs of prisoner abuse at Abu Ghraib prison. The September 11, 2001, terrorist attacks produced countless images that disturbed, helped along by digital photography that made it possible for amateurs to produce instantaneous pictures of the tragedy.

We're certain that you can remember a moment watching television or reading a paper or magazine when you encountered a picture that made you feel uncomfortable. Did you ever think to yourself in those moments that the photograph shouldn't have been aired or published? In this chapter, you'll get a chance to think about that question. This is an issue that hits almost everyone in the gut, and it's our experience that even if you've never really considered the ethics of photojournalism before, you'll find a lot to think about and a lot to say as you work through the readings in this chapter. Here are some of the things we hope you'll learn along the way:

- How to apply the strategy of inquiry you've learned in this book to a range of essays and articles all focused on a single theme.
- How to read material in a range of genres and from a range of disciplines and use them to think more deeply about an issue.
- How to draw on what you've learned from reading, writing, and discussing the ethics of disturbing photographs to write an insightful argument or essay on the topic.

Exercise 8.1   First Thoughts, First Feelings

Before you begin a research project, it's often helpful to examine any initial feelings, beliefs, or attitudes you might have toward the subject. That's particularly important on a topic like this, which often generates strong feelings and about which we have some prior knowledge. Before you begin reading the essays in this chapter, spend some time in your notebook exploring your first thoughts and feelings about the whole issue of publishing disturbing photographs.

FIGURE 8–2

Another victim of the civil conflict in Haiti between supporters and opponents of former President Aristide.

STEP 1: Look closely at the photograph shown in Figure 8-2. In your notebook, spend five minutes exploring your reaction to it. Begin by writing, *When I first look at this picture I think . . . And then I think . . . And then . . . And then . . .* Fastwrite the story of your thoughts and feelings to this image.

STEP 2: Reread your fastwrite. Then finish the following sentences in your notebook:

1. The thing I least expected to say but said in my fastwrite was . . .
2. Overall, I felt the image was . . .
3. If I encountered this picture in the newspaper, I would think . . .

Discussion Questions

1. Imagine that you're an editor trying to decide whether to publish this picture. What would you want to know before making the decision?
2. Would it make any difference if you were publishing the picture in a Haitian or an American newspaper?
3. Do you think readers who encountered this photograph might respond differently to it because it was taken in another country? Because the subjects are black?

FIGURE 8-3   The Pyramid of Generality

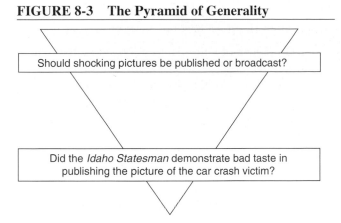

You'll know things are going well when you find yourself confused at times as you write about the material in this chapter. You'll probably start with a gut feeling about whether shocking photographs are distasteful or nec essary, art or exploitation, an essential part of a free press or unethical jour- nalism. However, this is a topic in which questions lead to more questions, and just when you feel you're ready to come to a conclusion about what you think, you discover something you haven't considered. This, of course, is why the ethics of disturbing photographs is such a great subject for inquiry: You have to struggle with ambiguity and uncertainty.

No matter how strongly you might feel initially, avoid the impulse to rush to judgment. This advice might also help:

1. *Decide whether you're writing an argument or an essay.* If you're writ- ing an argument, at some point you need to come to a conclusion: What are your assertions or claims? What reasons and evidence can you sum- mon to support them? If you're writing an exploratory essay, you may come to conclusions toward the end of your draft, but they may be tenta- tive, and they may raise even more questions.

2. *Find the right sized question.* Like all inquiry projects, this one begins with a question. An obvious one might be, "Should disturbing photo- graphs of death and dying be published or broadcast?" While this isn't a bad starting place, it's such a broad question that you'll quickly get stuck, mired in more questions. Should *all* "disturbing pictures" be banned? Should the same principle be applied to *all* media? What is the definition of a "disturbing picture," anyway? Figure 8-3 represents the challenge of working your way down the inverted pyramid to find a more manageable question that will give you some traction. Whenever

you can, find a question that focuses on a *particular* image that is used in a *particular* context, for a *particular* purpose.

You will hear a range of voices in this chapter on the issue of publishing or airing disturbing pictures: grieving parents who feel that their privacy is violated by photographers, journalists who worry about their own exposure to a steady stream of shocking images, editors who advocate ethical guidelines for photojournalism, and scholars who study the impact of shocking images. Listen carefully to these voices. Converse with them in your writing and thinking. But in the end, the most important voice is your own.

Case Study 26

Photojournalism and Tragedy

Clifford Christians, Kim Rotzoll, and Mark Farkler

What follows is a brief excerpt from a journalism textbook on media ethics. "Case Study 26: Photojournalism and Tragedy" tells the troubling story of three drowned boys, their grieving parents, and an eager photojournalist. Following the narrative is a brief analysis of the ethical issues involved.

Begin by simply reading the case study and doing some fastwriting about your own feelings about the situation described. We think it may be difficult, at first, to be at all sympathetic to the photographer here, but consider his situation—the visual opportunity that presents itself and the photojournalist's obligations—and try to see it from his point of view, too.

The second half of this brief case study provides some analysis by its authors. Do you agree with them?

The scene is a river. By the time the photographer arrives, the bodies of three boys covered with sheets lie on the bank. Firefighters are still looking for the body of a fourth boy. Three of the drowning victims are from the same family. A fire police officer intercepts the photographer and tells him to leave. Family members have asked that no pictures be taken of the bodies.

The photographer ignores the police officer. He sees the parents of the three boys talking to a state trooper. To the photographer, the parents appear too numbed by shock to care whether photos are taken. He snaps a picture of them. The trooper waves the photographer away, shouting, "Get the hell out of here with that camera!"

A second fire police officer orders the photographer to stop taking pictures. The photographer explains that he is only doing his job. He shoots two shots of the sheeted bodies. Then he waits. The picture he wants most is one of the firefighters bringing the fourth boy from the river.

The body is found. The photographer kneels to take the picture, but the fire police officer and a dozen onlookers surround him. His view blocked, he moves to shoot from another angle. The crowd follows him. He calls to the state trooper for police protection. "You don't deserve it!" shouts the trooper.

The mother of the three boys has been lying over the body of one of her sons. Attracted by the commotion, she looks up to see the photographer surrounded by the onlookers. She seizes her only surviving son, age two, holds him over her head, and shouts to the photographer, "Why don't you take a picture of him? He's all I have left!"

The crowd responds to her words by ripping the gadget bag from the photographer. The mother falls across the bodies of her sons. The photographer takes one more picture, then leaves.[1]

Michael J. Ogden, executive editor of the *Providence Journal Bulletin,* condemns photographs that capitalize on human grief:

> I can understand the printing of an auto accident picture as an object lesson. What I can't understand is the printing of sobbing wives, mothers, children. What is the value of showing a mother who has just lost her child in a fire? Is this supposed to have a restraining effect on arsonists? I am sure that those who don't hesitate to print such pictures will use the pious pretense of quoting Charles A. Dana's famous dictum that "whatever the Divine Providence permitted to occur I was not too proud to print." Which is as peachy a shibboleth to permit pandering as I can imagine.[2]

But Ogden is a rare editor. Every day in newspapers and on television, photographs and film footage emphasize grief and tragedy. In fact, pro-

---

[1] Original source: Arthur W. Geisleman, Jr., "Take Pictures of Tragic Scenes or Flee from Irate Onlookers?" *Editor and Publisher* 92 (13 August 1959): 13.

[2] John Hohenberg, *The News Media: A Journalist Looks at His Profession* (New York: Holt, Rinehart, and Winston, 1968), p. 212.

fessional awards are regularly given to grisly pictures regardless of whether they pander to morbid tastes.

The defense usually centers on newsworthiness. The broken-hearted man whose child was just run over, a shocked 8-year-old watching his father gunned down by police, the would-be suicide on a bridge—all pitiful scenes that communicate something of human tragedy and are therefore to be considered news. Photojournalists sum up a news event in a manner the mind can hold, capturing that portrayal "rich in meaning because it is a trigger image of all the emotions around by the subject."[3] The photographer in this case acted as an undaunted professional, fulfilling his role as reporter on everyday affairs including the unpleasantries. From the photographer's framework, to capture the newsworthy moment is an important self-discipline. He is trained not to panic but to bring forth the truth as events dictate. Photographers are schooled to be visual historians, and not to be freelance medics.

On what grounds, however, can the photographer condone his behavior? All the principals at the scene condemned him: police, family, and onlookers. If he were invited to justify himself morally, does any conceivable case exist? If he contends he is only doing his job—that is, providing what his editors want—that would not be an acceptable explanation. He could call on the warning bell thesis, asserting that his photos will make other parents more safety conscious; however, this utilization appeal to consequences has no genuine basis in fact. Perhaps in the name of reporting news, the photojournalist in this case is actually caught in those opportunistic professional values that build circulation by playing on the human penchant for morbidity.

No overarching purpose emerges that can ameliorate the direct invasion of privacy and insensitivity. Bruce Roberts presents a forthright position based on the ethical principle that all human beings are worthy of respect: "A photographer is first a human being with compassion for other human beings. If he arrives at the scene of an accident first before any aid has been summoned that is his first duty and a Pulitzer prize-winning picture possibility should make no difference."[4] In all jurisdictions, the reporting of events of public concern involve no legal issue of privacy invasion. But it is here that the photographer should consider the moral guideline that suffering individuals are entitled to the same respect as any

---

[3]Harold Evans, *Pictures on a Page* (Belmont, Calif.: Wadsworth, 1978), p. 5.

[4]Joseph Cosra, Lloyd B. Walcon, and Bruce Roberts, "Get the Picture or Act the Samaritan?" *Bulletin of the American Society of Newspaper Editors,* 1 June 1961, p. 7.

other human being, despite the fact that events may have made them part of the news.

Photojournalism is an extremely significant eyewitness of the humanity and inhumanity of man. In pursuing its mission, the ethical conflict typically revolves around the need for honest visual information and for respecting a person's privacy. In this case, assailed as an unfeeling voyeur, the photographer provides no evidence of wrestling with the dilemma. Perhaps he considers such judgments to be the responsibility of his editor.

Personal Investigations: Inquiry Projects

1. Compose your own analysis of the case study or change some details in the narrative that you believe would make a significant difference in how the ethics of the situation might be viewed. Alternatively, tell the story of a situation in which you believed a photographer was an intrusion, perhaps violating your sense of privacy. Do the case study and your experience shape your understandings of the ethical and moral issues involved?

2. This excerpt is from a book on media ethics, an area of much research and writing in the field of mass communications. One way to explore the issues raised by the publication of disturbing photographs is to read what scholars and journalists have written about the issues involved. Go to your campus library and search the online card catalog and a journal database such as ComAbstracts using "photojournalism and ethics" as search terms. Also use the terms to search databases of national newspapers such as *The New York Times.* Look for patterns in what you find: Are there certain ethical issues that often get raised? Are there certain arguments, both for and against publishing the photos, that are repeated? What are your reactions?

Craft and Conventions: Explaining and Evaluating

3. In this case study, the story is intended to tell all; there are no pictures. Is it difficult to make a judgment about the appropriateness of the photojournalist's actions without seeing the images?

4. In their analysis of the case study, the authors mention the "warning bell thesis," the idea that the publication of such pictures might encourage parents to be more concerned about their children's safety. This is an idea, the authors argue, that has "no basis in fact." What do you think of this claim?

5. It's hard to imagine that the victims of tragedy would *ever* want photographs taken during the moments of suffering. Certainly the mother in this story doesn't. The authors argue that photojournalists are obligated to protect the privacy of their subjects, but doesn't that mean that all unwanted pictures are likely to be seen as an invasion of privacy? Does this make tragic photos impossible to publish?

Inquiries on Inquiry: Exploring and Reflecting

6. One of the great things about a case study, a common research genre in the social sciences and business, is that it makes concepts and ideas come alive by attaching them to particulars. Here, we're no longer talking in abstractions about media ethics, but trying to apply them to the specifics of a woman, a river, and four drowned boys. But the case study does have some serious limitations. What are its virtues? What are its drawbacks?

7. This piece is quite different from the other essays in this chapter and from some in the book as a whole. What purposes guided your reading of this case study? How did you decide what was important to focus on and what you could skim or ignore? How did this piece meet and/or disrupt your expectations of what it "should" be doing?

Code of Ethics of the National Press Photographers Association

A careful search of the Web on the ethics of photojournalism might very well lead you to the pages of the National Press Photographers Association (NPPA), the group that oversees the profession. Started in 1946, the NPPA was formed because press photographers felt like "step children of the Fourth Estate."

"We've got a voice, finally, and we're going to make use of it," proclaimed the editorial announcing the formation of the group. "We're going to yell so loud—when the occasion demands, and not just for the fun of hearing ourselves shout—that those in this country who have been injuring us with scant courtesy will begin to realize that the here is a new force to be reckoned with."

From this defensive posture more than 50 years ago, the NPPA has grown to 10,000 members and the presence of the news photographer is considered commonplace at all manner of public events. We expect our news to be served up with pictures. But has the success of photojournalism turned the photographer into a pest, invading moments of tragedy and aiming lenses at things that ought not be photographed?

The NPPA's "Code of Ethics" seems a response to such criticisms. How adequate is it? Like many professional codes or by-laws, these nine points often seem abstract, designed to be general enough so as not to limit a photographer's options in a particular situation but clear enough to provide some guidance. For example, in point number 2, what does the code mean when it urges photojournalists against "mercenary considerations of any kind"?

Article XVII

Code of Ethics

A. Application

   Every member in NPPA is required to endorse the Code of Ethics.

B. Purpose

   The National Press Photographers Association, a professional society dedicated to the advancement of photojournalism, acknowledges concern and respect for the public's natural-law, right to freedom in searching for the truth and the right to be informed truthfully and completely about public events and the world in which we live. NPPA believes that no report can be complete if it is possible to enhance and clarify the meaning of the words. We believe that pictures, whether used to depict news events as they actually happen, illustrate news that has happened, or to help explain anything of public interest, are indispensable means of keeping people accurately informed, that they help all people, young and old, to better understand any subject in the public domain. NPPA recognizes and acknowledges that photojournalists should at all times maintain the highest standards of ethical conduct in serving the public interest.

C. Code of Ethics

   1. The practice of photojournalism, both as a science and art, is worthy of the very best thought and effort of those who enter into it as a profession.

   2. Photojournalism affords an opportunity to serve the public that is equalled by few other vocations and all members of the profession should strive by example and influence to maintain high

standards of ethical conduct free of mercenary considerations of any kind.

3. It is the individual responsibility of every photojournalist all times to strive for pictures that report truthfully, honestly, and objectively.

4. As journalists, we believe that credibility is our greatest asset. In documentary photojournalism, it is wrong to alter the content of a photograph in any way (electronically or in the darkroom) that deceives the public. We believe the guidelines for fair and accurate reporting should be the criteria for judging what may be done electronically to a photograph.

5. Business promotion in its many forms is essential but untrue statements of any nature are not worthy of a professional photojournalist and we severely condemn any such practice.

6. It is our duty to encourage and assist all members of our profession, individually and collectively, so that the quality of photojournalism may constantly be raised to higher standards.

7. It is the duty of every photojournalist to work to preserve all freedom-of-the-press rights recognized by law and to work to protect and expand freedom-of-access to all sources of news and visual information.

8. Our standards of business dealings, ambitions and relations shall have in them a note of sympathy for our common humanity and shall always require us to take into consideration our highest duties as members of society. In every situation in our business life, in every responsibility that comes before us, our chief thought shall be to fulfill that responsibility and discharge that duty so that when each of us is finished we shall have endeavored to lift the level of human ideals and achievement higher that we found it.

9. No Code of Ethics can prejudge every situation, thus common sense and good judgment are required in applying ethical principles.

D. Amendments

Article XVII may only be amended or repealed by a 2/3 vote of the Board of Directors present.

Personal Investigations: Inquiry Projects

1. Contact the NPPA by e-mail or by phone. Interview someone with the organization about the group's code of ethics. How effective is the

code? Have aspects of the code been tested in particular instances? Have there been recent attempts to amend the code? What were the issues involved? Contact a news photographer with your local paper. Is he or she aware of the NPPA's code? If so, does it provide some useful guidelines for how to take pictures and which pictures to pursue? Spend a day following a local photojournalist at work. What does this reveal to you about the nature of the job in terms of the extent that ethical issues are a daily problem?

2. Since the terrorist attacks on September 11, 2001, there has been a surge of research and writing about ethical issues in photojournalism. Find at least two Web sites for professional photojournalists that address these issues in some way, or search for recent articles on the subject. Then compose an essay that reviews what has been said to date about the ethical issues raised in covering terrorist attacks in the United States and abroad.

Craft and Conventions: Explaining and Evaluating

1. The third item in the NPPA code of ethics calls for news photographers to "strive for pictures that report truthfully, honestly, and objectively." What do you think is meant by an "objective" photograph?

2. Do you think the code provides enough guidance for photographers to make ethical decisions? Should it be more specific? In what ways?

3. How can a news photograph "lift the level of human ideals and achievement" (the ninth principle)? Can such an ideal be applied to the photographs taken during the attacks on September 11, 2001, or those taken of contractors being hanged in Fallujah during the war in Iraq (see "Images of Horror in Fallujah" on pages 438–447)?

Inquiries on Inquiry: Exploring and Reflecting

4. Increasingly, we turn to the Web as a source of research information even though we know how unreliable it can be. Web research requires a finely tuned crap detector. Turn your attention to the NPPA Web pages at http://www.nppa.org. How would you evaluate these pages as a source of information for an academic essay on the ethics of shocking pictures? Draw a line down the middle of a page. On the left, list the characteristics of these pages that make them authoritative; on the right, list the drawbacks of using the material for an academic paper.

Images of Horror from Fallujah

David D. Perlmutter and Lesa Hatley Major

The gruesome murder of four American contractors in Iraq in the spring of
2004 is only a recent example of the ethical dilemma facing journalists. What
should one do with pictures that show the charred bodies of the victims hanging
from the beams of a steel bridge? As you'll see from the article that follows, the
answer to that question varies. Some television stations just used video of the
burning SUV from which the men were dragged; some newspapers buried the
pictures of the hanging bodies deep in the paper, while others focused on the
cheering Iraqis.

It's comforting that the American press didn't respond monolithically to
this tragedy; it's good to know that editors don't always agree about what is
and what isn't a newsworthy picture because in a democracy we want a diverse
news media. But this varied response to publishing pictures of the event also
points to a profoundly complicated ethical dilemma that is nicely summarized
in the third paragraph of the article you're about to read. As you'll see, it isn't
just a question of whether pictures of dead bodies should be printed or not. It's
how and where and when, too.

On March 31, 2004, Iraqi terrorists, throwing grenades, killed four American civilian contractors who were driving through the city of Fallujah, Iraq. A quickly swelling crowd of civilians then beat the burned bodies (with anything in hand, including shoes), dragged them through the streets, and hung two of them from a nearby Euphrates River bridge. Many onlookers and participants danced with joy and chanted anti-American slogans.

The horror was caught on camera. Within hours, Fallujah video footage and photographs were made available to the world's newspapers, magazines and television newscasters. Almost as quickly, in nearly every U.S. newsroom, a debate on whether and how to handle these images began. "It was one of the toughest calls I've ever had to make," wrote Ellen Soeteber, editor of the *St. Louis Post-Dispatch*.

The basic questions, whether one edited a small-town daily or a network newscast, were:

- What pictures should we use, where and why?
- Which ones should we not use and why not?
- Should we digitally edit those we use to reduce their "horror" quotient?
- For print editors, should pictures go on an inside page or the front page?
- How should we caption and contextualize what we are showing?

FIGURE 8–4

Children cheer around burned bodies that had been cut down after being hung from a bridge following an attack in Fallujah. Photo by Ali Jasim/Courtesy of Reuters.

Importantly the process of addressing these quandaries was not kept secret or restricted to insiders. Many news outlets editorialized their rea sons for using one image rather than another, and media columnists and commentators throughout the country expressed their views about these decisions on air or in print. In many of their columns and stories, they quoted editors and producers about why they made the decisions they did, and several of these explanations appear below. And readers and viewers responded. Papers and broadcasters received thousands of letters, e-mails and phone calls. And it is almost certain that no journalism class escaped discussion of the ethics and professional codes affecting the editors' decisions about using these grisly news photos.

The public ferment—in many cases furor—about the photographs was no less divided. Many publications extended their usual letters section to accommodate the large number of letters and the range of opinions voiced in them. And editors listened. *U.S. News & World Report,* which published the "burned bodies" picture, received letters such as one from the wife of a military person serving in Iraq, who wrote, "You may feel inclined to report these happenings, but the photos were not necessary." She said she was "appalled and disgusted by the photos of the horrendous act." A Marine who served at Iwo Jima called the use of the photograph "blatant sensationalism." Another reader, saying the magazine "went too far," ripped the pages out and returned them with a message, "Please consider carefully how much gore and carnage your readers need to see to get the full scope of war and human suffering." In the face of such negative criticism, Brian Duffy, the editor, replied: "Our intention was not to offend but to present a faithful record of a transformative moment. In doing so, however, we did offend, and for that I apologize. We erred."

Decisions About Images

What Americans saw from Fallujah was determined by their news source. [See the table on p. 444–445 showing Fallujah photos used by American newspapers.] The *New York Times* ran on its front page The Associated Press (AP) photo (Contractors Hanging on Bridge) in color, which included the clearly visible bodies with celebrating Iraqis in the foreground. *The Times*'s executive editor, Bill Keller, said of this decision: "You can't shy away from the news, and the news in this case is the indignities visited upon the victims and the jubilation of the crowd. At the same time you have to be mindful of the pain these pictures would cause to families and the potential revulsion of readers, and children, who are exposed to this over their breakfast table." *The Washington Post* ran a cropped version on page A11 of the Ali Jasim (Reuters) photo with a smiling boy in the foreground. Len Downie, the paper's executive editor, stated: "We owed readers photographic as well as print reporting about what took place. We chose photos that actually were on the less graphic end of available photos."

For regional papers as well, the predicament was as palpable. The *Palm Beach Post* ran the AP photo (Contractors Hanging on Bridge) on its front page. John Bartosek, the paper's managing editor, claimed, "We selected that photograph, after a lot of thought and discussion, because it's a powerful news image of a dramatic, horrific and brutal day in Iraq." In contrast, Richard Tapscott, managing editor of The Des Moines Register, noted, "The photograph (Contractors Hanging on Bridge) is detailed enough that you can see the bodies hanging from the bridge and that they are charred." The Register chose to run the photo on the inside in black and white.

For the major television networks, decisions were visible in the editing. Not one network newscast showed the most graphic images, at least initially, without cropping, blurring, or using long shots of the gruesome details. CNN spokesman Matt Furman explained: "We told the story throughout most of the day using wide-angle images of the cars burning, without what we would describe as graphic images. We held off until 7 p.m. [Wednesday] for the explicit reason of giving offi-

Digital Photography and News Images

Another issue to emerge from the Iraq War coverage, as noted in recent Congressional testimony by no less than Secretary of Defense Donald Rumsfeld, is the omnipresence of digital photography. Amateur pictures have always found their way into the news stream; some have become icons of photojournalism, such as the photo of the Oklahoma City fireman and baby.

Now, with the advent of cheap digital cameras and the Internet, a dynamic is emerging in which anyone able to shoot an image can distribute it easily to the entire world. The picture of the "cargo of caskets" was transmitted via e-mail to *The Seattle Times*. Images of the abuse of Iraqi prisoners were more easily brought to public attention because, apparently, the photographs were taken with digital cameras.

This technology makes censorship harder. A photo can be "leaked" with the click of a mouse. But there is an ominous aspect to this issue as well. Digital technology—especially Photoshop-type image manipulation software—makes photo fakery by amateurs and professionals easier as well. Earlier in the Iraq War a Los Angeles Times's photographer was fired for creating a composite image from two separate pictures. And via the Internet any number of "incredible" news pictures circulate through chain mail messages. But many of these images are simply *not* credible.

So far, the number of manipulated (or faked) photographs that have been published or broadcast is low—we think! But a muddled future for war photography could lie ahead as editors will have to confront—and make quick decisions about whether to print or air—increasing numbers of amateur-produced images of sensational content but unknown truth.—D.P.

cials the opportunity to notify next of kin." Steve Capus, executive producer at NBC Nightly News, argued, "Quite honestly, it doesn't need to be seen in full in order to convey the horrors of this despicable act." Fox News Channel limited its images to shots of the burning vehicles in which the contractors had been riding and to footage of joyous crowds in Fallujah. Bill Shine, Fox's vice president of production, said: "We made the call that it [footage of the charred bodies] was too graphic in nature to put on our air."

Foreign responses were as varied. Britain's Channel 4 showed blurred images of bodies being dragged through the street, but offered clear shots of the corpses hanging from the bridge. Yet normally unabashed Al Jazeera showed only fuzzy footage of burned bodies. And, of course, unedited collections of images were available to look at on some Web sites.

Showing Images of War

For photojournalism, the decision-making dilemmas prompted by the Fallujah images are as old as war photography itself. Oliver Wendell Holmes wrote in an *Atlantic Monthly* essay in August 1863 of his reaction to photographs of the dead from the bloody Civil War battle of Antietam: "Let him who wishes to know what war is look at this series of illustrations." Yet Holmes, whose son served in the Union Army, felt the pictures were too powerful to witness more than once: "[It was] so nearly like visiting the battlefield to look over these views, that all the emotions excited by the actual sight of the stained and sordid scene, strewed with rags and wrecks, came back to us, and we buried them in the recesses of our cabinet as we would have buried the mutilated remains of the dead they too vividly represented."

For today's editors, the parameters of this debate revolved around the concerns Holmes wrote about more than 140 years ago. On one hand, there is the photographs' news value—their content as it relates to current public policy or public affairs issues. This is set against the images' sensationalism—with their disturbing images of death or violence. When photographers capture gruesome images—whether it be of mutilated civilians in the Japanese rape of Nanjing, a self-immolated Vietnamese monk, a street execution in Saigon, the charred bodies of Iraqi children killed by a U.S. bomb while in their air raid shelter in the first Gulf War, or a dead Marine in this Iraq War—journalists and the public wonder what should be shown, how it should be shown, and why.

Certainly, the pictures from Fallujah are relevant to the public debate about the Iraq War, touching as they do on both the reasons why the United States went to war and the wisdom of its present course. After all, the Iraqis rejoicing at the abuse of these Americans are people whom U.S. forces were allegedly sent to Iraq to liberate. If French citizens were dancing over the bodies of dead G.I.'s in France in 1944, the image would be similarly upsetting but it would never have been published, except by the Third Reich. The Fallujah images are also related to the debate about other issues involved with the Iraq situation—such as whether the U.S. military is stretched too thin as many quasi-military tasks are subcontracted, and the reality that civil contractors are risking death to help the Iraqis but are also earning high pay for their risks. Then there are the questions that arise from what was not in these pictures. Where were the American military while these mob actions were taking place? In short, the pictures, it can be argued, are most definitely news.

But was this news value only able to be expressed in its grisliest detail? To show horror solely for its shock value is akin to being a pornographer of war. Most editors who did not run the grimmest images cited the "breakfast table" test and "next of kin" rationale. Newspapers and television newscasters are, after all, mass marketers: Anybody can be watching at any time—including toddlers and the families of the dead. As one editor put it, "People watching [network news or reading the morning paper] with their children do not expect to be surprised." *The Dallas Morning News* editorialized, "We didn't think it was appropriate to show bodies on Page One." Many papers and networks deliberately cautioned readers or viewers about what they might see.

There are other contextual issues. Veterans and military historians could point out that such images are a part of every war. Is it problematic to show ghastliness and imply it is evidence against *this* particular war? Consider that in World War II most Americans never saw pictures of American combat deaths in the papers or newsreels. Home-front audiences had to go to a Warner Brothers movie to see a G.I. get killed at Omaha Beach, Monte Casino, or Iwo Jima. And even then, as infantry combat veteran and cultural critic Paul Fussell complained, many Hollywood images of death in the war were "Disneyfied." No blood, no guts, just heroics.

Generals and editors during World War II—the last major war involving American troops that resulted in an unequivocal victory—assumed that the public did not want to see images of war's horrors and that, indeed, the war effort would be undermined by their daily display. Would American victories, like the Normandy invasion, have been viewed differently if the American public had been shown thousands of dead G.I.'s carpeting the beaches? Perhaps it is just as important to provide readers with historical, as well as political, context in war images.

In all, the transparency of angst and indecision about the Fallujah images have been good for journalism. One reason why public esteem for and faith in the fairness, accuracy, and honesty of journalism is so low is the public's feeling that news professionals are not "people." That is, as the late columnist Mike Royko once accused, those who go into news these days are no longer working-class folks who can write, but rather upper middle-class products of top universities—elites who are just like politicians or lobbyists. This claim is no doubt true: In our combined 40 years of teaching journalism and working in the field, we've met only a handful of reporters (or journalism teachers) who were war combat veterans. The star system is another sign to the public that reporters are not qualified to be populist tribunes.

Yet many people don't appreciate that journalism is a messy process, not a conspiracy. When editors and reporters make public their gut-wrenching debates about what is news, their humanity is revealed, even more so when they admit error. Readers and viewers get the opportunity to listen in as editors say, with sincerity, how much they care about the re-

U.S. Newspapers Decide Which Images of the Fallujah Killings to Publish

Newspapers that published the photo shown in Figure 8–5.

Akron Beacon Journal
Anchorage Daily News (cropped)
The Atlanta Journal-Constitution
The Boston Globe
Chicago Sun-Times
The (Cleveland) Plain Dealer
    (cropped)
The Columbus Dispatch
Daily News of Los Angeles
The Dallas Morning News
Fort Worth (Tex.) Star-Telegram

Houston Chronicle
Newsday
Pittsburgh Post-Gazette
The (Portland) Oregonian
The Sacramento Bee
San Jose Mercury News
Seattle Post-Intelligencer
The Seattle Times
The Star-Ledger (N.J.)
The Times-Picayune
The Washington Times

Newspapers that published the photo shown in Figure 8–6.

The (Baltimore) Sun
The Buffalo News
The Charlotte (N.C.) Observer
Chicago Tribune
Daily Herald (Il.)
The Des Moines Register
Detroit Free Press
The Hartford Courant
New York Post
The New York Times
The Palm Beach Post
The Philadelphia Inquirer

St. Louis Post-Dispatch
St. Petersburg (Fla.) Times
The San Diego Union-Tribune
The Tampa Tribune

Newspapers that published the photo shown in Figure 8–7.

Asbury Park Press
The Beaumont Enterprise (Tex.)
Courier News (N.J.)
The Des Moines Register
The Dothan Eagle (Ala.)
The Greenville News (S.C.)
The Honolulu Advertiser
The Idaho Statesman
Las Vegas Review-Journal

This information was compiled by David Perlmutter and Lesa Hatley Major.

FIGURE 8–5 Cheering Iraqis with burning SUV.
Photo by Karim Sahib/AFP/ Getty Images.

FIGURE 8–6 Contractors hanging on bridge.
Photo by Khalid Mohammed/The Associated Press.

FIGURE 8–7 Man in white shirt in front of burning SUV.
Photo by Abdel Kader Saadi/The Associated Press.

actions and opinions of those they serve. For the public then to be included in the ongoing discussion and feel their voice matters makes the news delivery process appear neither inaccessible nor inflexible. Because of the Fallujah debate, bus drivers, insurance salespeople, and firefighters heard and saw that journalists, like everybody else, face tough decisions in their jobs and struggle through them with a similar reliance on professional codes, ethical constraints, and thoughtful uncertainty.

Personal Investigations: Inquiry Projects

1. An ethical issue in photojournalism is the practice of digitally manipulating photographs, changing them slightly, or even combining several images. *Newsweek,* in fact, recently published on the front page a "digital illustration" of Martha Stewart because she was about to be released from prison. The head is hers, but not the body, and the curtains she's holding were not part of the original shoot for either Martha's head or the body double. What are the ethical issues involved in using a photograph as an illustration rather than a representation of "truth"? Should such pictures be published? Research this issue and develop a researched essay/argument.

2. As this article mentions, war photographs have been around since the Civil War, and they've played an interesting role in history. Do research on the history of war photography and see what questions emerge for you. Given the current war in Iraq and the use of photographic images today, what might we learn from the history of war photographs that could influence our responses to our current situation?

Craft and Conventions: Explaining and Evaluating

3. This article was written by a professor of communications and a graduate student in communications who was first a journalist. In what ways might you consider this article academic? Was it written for an academic audience? How do you know?

4. Look closely at how this article is organized, and create an informal outline. What do you find effective and/or ineffective about this structure given its rhetorical context and purpose?

5. What kinds of evidence do the authors use to support, illustrate, or critique various claims? How persuasive do you find that evidence and why? Given the intended audience, how persuasive might it be to them?

6. Compare this essay to another in this chapter (for example, "Tragedy of the Common" pages 471–479). First, examine how each is written: Is one an argument and the other an essay? Do they use similar kinds of organizational structures? Do they use the same kinds of evidence? And so on. Then, look at how they both address the subject of disturbing photos: What angle does each take and why? How do their arguments compare?

Inquiries on Inquiry: Exploring and Reflecting

7. What did you find most convincing about this article? Why? In what ways did it change your mind about these issues, or simply prompt you to think about an issue in a different way?

8. One of the arguments the authors make is that the public is now learning that journalism is a messy process, and readers have been invited into the decision-making process for editors and photojournalists—both of which are good things. Do you agree? To what extent should the public be a part of these conversations? Why?

9. Which modes of inquiry are used in this article? Use specific examples.

10. What new questions does this article raise for you?

11. If you wanted to know more about the ideas addressed in this article, what might you investigate further?

Representing Contemporary War
David Campbell

In the aftermath of September 11, 2001, we've been inundated with images of war. Journalists have been embedded with troops, national news programs give daily reports of casualties, and the most violent images from Iraq are distributed through the Internet, even though many news agencies have chosen not to publish them themselves. Many of us tend to think of these images as a representation of the truth about the war. Photographs don't lie, after all. Or do they? Even if we're skeptical of the military's agenda in allowing embedded reporters, we're still fascinated by what those reporters show us, and we build our opinions about the war from those images. This connection between photography and politics during war is the subject of a recent book by philosopher Susan Sontag, Regarding the Pain of Others, *a reassessment and extension of the work she did fifteen years ago in* On Photography.

That is the book David Campbell reviews in the following essay as he also applies Sontag's theories to the current events in Iraq. Campbell is professor of international politics and director of the Newcastle Institute for the Arts, Social Sciences, and Humanities at the University of Newcastle upon Tyne in England. His scholarly research focuses on images of war and atrocity, so this review is a natural extension of his current work. We think you'll find this excerpted review both challenging and well-written. You'll probably also notice the extensive research Campbell has done to document his claims and evidence. As you read, mark the places where he specifically discusses Sontag's book. What is his assessment of it? Pay attention, as well, to what this article contributes to your discussions about disturbing photographs so far. What does Campbell add to the conversation that is provocative or interesting?

Despite living in an age commonly understood as being awash with images of atrocity, there are few writers who theorize the relationship between political conflict and its pictorial representation. This relative absence means that various assertions about the power of pictures have come to dominate popular understanding. Foremost among these are two fundamentally contradictory claims, which, Susan Sontag observes, are "fast approaching the stature of platitudes."[1] One, the "CNN effect," is that the power of news imagery is such that it can alter the course of state policy simply by virtue of being broadcast. The other, the "compassion fatigue" thesis, argues that the abundant supply of imagery has dulled our senses and created a new syndrome of communal inaction.

Susan Sontag's 1977 book, *On Photography,* remains one of the classic statements about the politics of representing violence, and an important starting point in working through the merits of the above claims. Although it may seem like an anachronistic practice in the contemporary pictorial economy of international news, photography remains an important portal through which the politics of images generally can be considered. While television, with its stream of video imagery, may be the premier source of news and information from distant places, its very preponderance may limit its staying power in the minds of the viewer. As Sontag argues, "photographs may be more memorable than moving images, because they are a neat slice of time, not a flow. Television is a stream of underselected images, each of which cancels its predecessor. Each still photograph is a privileged moment, turned into a slim object that one can keep and look at again."[2]

---

[1] Susan Sontag, *Regarding the Pain of Others* (New York: Farrar, Straus and Giroux, 2003), p. 104.
[2] Susan Sontag, *On Photography* (New York: Anchor Books, 1990), pp. 17–18.

Partly because of its role as contemplative moment, photography provides an important interpretative resource for television and its images, helping to set a standard by which the mundane is marked off from the significant. The famous BBC film of the 1984 Ethiopian famine—shot by Mohammed Amin and Michael Buerk at Korem in October of that year—had an impact in the United States because, in the words of William Lord, the executive producer of ABC's *World News Tonight,* "it was as if each clip was an award-winning still photo."[3] In addition to providing something of an interpretative code for the meaning of video, the ubiquity of video in the representation of the other has given the photograph a renewed role as a site for reflection. As John Taylor argues, "The immediacy and normality of television imagery have revived photojournalism."[4] . . .

Being a site for contemplation does not necessarily make the photograph an instrument for political change. According to Sontag, the image itself cannot create a possibility that otherwise does not exist: "a photograph that brings news of some unsuspected zone of misery cannot make a dent in public opinion unless there is an appropriate context of feeling and attitude." The image can, however, help develop an attitude. While a photograph "cannot create a moral position" it can "reinforce one   and can help build a nascent one."[5] As a result, the event or issue has to be identified and named as an event or issue before photography can make its contribution. This means "the possibility of being affected morally by photographs is [determined by] the existence of a relevant political consciousness. Without a politics, photographs of the slaughter-bench of history will most likely be experienced as, simply, unreal or as a demoralizing emotional blow."[6]

In Sontag's 1977 account, however, the question of an image's power was also a product of its repetition and usage as much as the previously existing political context through which it was read. Indeed, Sontag went as far as to suggest that "concerned photography"—the self-consciously humanistic work of recognized documentarians—had saturated popular consciousness in the previous thirty years to such an extent that the communal conscience had been deadened rather than aroused. Because shock depended on novelty, repeated use bred familiarity and passivity if not contempt. . . .

---

[3] Susan D. Moeller, *Compassion Fatigue: How the Media Sell Disease, Famine, War and Death* (New York: Routledge, 1999), p. 117.

[4] John Taylor, *Body Horror: Photojournalism, Catastrophe and War* (Manchester: Manchester University Press, 1998), p. 46.

[5] Sontag, *On Photography,* p. 17.

[6] Ibid., pp. 18–19. . . .

Photographs and Power Reconsidered

That Sontag should return to the themes of *On Photography* in her new book, *Regarding the Pain of Others,* and that this return should be followed by the most media-saturated war in human history, provides us with a significant context for assessing Sontag's contribution to an account of war photography. For what is most significant about Sontag's *Regarding the Pain of Others* is its openly expressed doubt about the assured claims of *On Photography* concerning the power of photographs.

This revision stems from Sontag's recognition of the "dual powers of photography" to both "generate documents" (the pellets of information) and to "create works of visual art" (the clouds of fantasy).[7] This structural undecidability inherent in photography means that a number of—indeed, almost any number of—responses to a particular image is possible. Given the time for contemplation allowed by the fixing of the image, the construction of meaning arises from the complex interplay of the photographic representation, its location, accompanying text, moment of reading, as well as the frames of reference brought to it by the reader/viewer. They might turn us off, or turn us on; they might frighten us, or they might anger us; they might distance us, or make us feel proximate; they might weaken us or they might strengthen us. But whatever the response, it is not media saturation that leads to political inaction: "People don't become inured to what they are shown—if that is the right way to describe what happens—because of the *quantity* of images dumped on them. It is passivity that dulls feeling."[8]

With this observation, Sontag not only challenges the compassion fatigue thesis; she questions the notion of the CNN effect. With regard to inaction in Bosnia despite the steady stream of images of ethnic cleansing that made their way out of Sarajevo, Sontag argues that people didn't turn off because they were either overwhelmed by their quantity or anaesthetized by their quality. Rather, they switched off because American and European leaders proclaimed it was an intractable and irresolvable situation. The political context into which the pictures were being inserted was already set, with military intervention not an option, and no amount of horrific photographs was going to change that.[9]

Having been subjected in the last two years to the media-saturated events of September 11, the war in Afghanistan, and the war in Iraq, we

---

[7] Sontag, *Regarding the Pain of Others,* p. 76.
[8] Ibid., p. 102.
[9] Ibid., p. 101. For an argument against the CNN effect in relation to images of Bosnian atrocity, see David Campbell, "Atrocity, Memory, Photography: Imaging the Concentration Camps of Bosnia—The Case of ITN versus *Living Marxism,* Part II." *Journal of Human Rights* 1, no. 2 (2002), pp. 157–58; see also www.virtual-security.net/atrocity/atrocity2.htm.

might think that being immersed daily in the visuals of distant wars has been a historical constant. Up until World War II, images of atrocity were relatively rare, and conflict came to us textually and somewhat late. Up until the Vietnam War, photographs of combat and its consequences—or, at least those photographs of combat and its consequences that were released for use—were often positive in both their intent and effects. In large part, that is because these images were produced by official cameramen who were either commissioned by the military for this particular purpose (as in the case of Roger Fenton and the Crimea War) or at least had their presence sanctioned by the authorities (as with Mathew Brady during the American Civil War). Thus, our status as a "spectator of calamities," and a spectator of distant calamities in real time, is a thoroughly modern if not late-modern experience, Sontag points out. Indeed, "The understanding of war among people who have not experienced war is now chiefly a product of the impact of these images."[10] Given the structural undecidability of photographs, this centrality of images to our experiences means we can be subject all too easily to imperatives that then employ pictures in their service, trading on the sense of immediacy that comes from their documentary mode to banish any thoughts of the fantasy that springs from their role in the visual arts.

In *Regarding the Pain of Others* Sontag maintains the position established in *On Photography* that photographs can buttress and expand a previously established moral disposition, but they cannot create that disposition themselves out of nothing. This is particularly true in the context of conflict. When a war is unpopular and that feeling has come to be prior to the taking of photographs,

> The material gathered by photographers, which they may think of as unmasking the conflict, is of great use. Absent such a protest, the same antiwar photograph may be read as showing pathos, or heroism, admirable heroism, in an unavoidable struggle that can be concluded only by victory or by defeat. The photographer's intentions do not determine the meaning of the photograph, which will have its own career, blown by the whims and loyalties of the diverse communities that have use for it.[11]

Pictures and War: Iraq 2003

In the Iraq war of 2003 imagery was central to the conflict and often the subject of conflict itself. In this context, the Pentagon's strategy of "embedding" reporters and their camera crews with fighting units, and having

---

[10] Ibid., p. 21.
[11] Ibid., pp. 38–39.

them operate at the behest of that unit, continues the long-running tradition of a close relationship between the media and the military. Although the details of the arrangements and their effectiveness have changed over time—from the combination of accreditation and daily briefings in Vietnam, the restrictions on access that resulted from the dependence for transport in the Falklands, to the selected pools and video briefings in the Persian Gulf War of 1990–91, and the embedding of Iraq 2003—at no stage in the post–World War II period has the U.S. or U.K. military operated without detailed media management procedures designed to influence the information (specifically the pictorial) outcomes.

Given this, Sontag is perhaps surprisingly sanguine about the genuineness of war photography in the contemporary period. While recognizing that many of the now iconic combat images of the pre-Vietnam period were staged, she sees Vietnam as a watershed such that "the practice of inventing dramatic news pictures, staging them for the camera, seems on its way to becoming a lost art."[12] Insofar as Sontag is referring to the likelihood of individual photographers seeking to deceive, she may be right. There was, however, at least one notable instance in Iraq of digital manipulation. This resulted in the *Los Angeles Times* sacking award-winning staff photographer Brian Walski, whose altered image of a British soldier in Basra (he had combined two photos into one to improve marginally composition) was used on the paper's front page.[13]

Walski knowingly violated the *Los Angeles Times* editorial policy that expressly forbids "altering the content of news photographs," and quickly accepted responsibility for his error in "tweaking" the picture.[14] What is interesting about the Walski case is that the error he made was not in constructing the image per se, but the stage in the process of production of the image at which he did his tweaking. In essence, all photographic images, even when considered in isolation, involve substantial amounts of tweaking—reducing the three-dimensional, color-filled world to a two-dimensional, framed, flat image (often in black and white) requires the photographer to exclude much that exceeds the frame. But those tweaks inherent to the taking of a photograph occur before the shutter is clicked. Walski's error was to engage in tweaking after the shutter had been clicked. This demonstrates two key features of the relationship between photographs and reality in war. First, even in the age of the digi-

---

[12]Ibid., p. 58.

[13]Duncan Campbell, "War in the Gulf: US war photographer sacked for altering image of British soldier," *Guardian,* April 3, 2003, p. 5; and Stephen Bates, "Media: Faking it," *Guardian,* May 5, 2003, pp. 2–3.

[14]Jay DeFoore, "Brain Walski Discusses His Doctored Photo," *PDNewswire,* May 7, 2003; available at www.pdn-pix.com/news/archive/2003/050703.html#4.

tal image, where there is no negative to secure an understanding of the original photograph, Walski's case shows there remains a strong sense of the shutter freezing a moment of reality, such that this moment is privileged as the original that cannot ethically be altered.

Second, and even more important, the Walski case demonstrates that the larger and more significant ways in which pictures structure reality through exclusions are themselves excluded from the discussion about manipulation so long as the professional responsibility not to alter what the shutter secures is maintained. Taking this wider view, Sontag's belief that the age of inventing and staging war images is behind us seems seriously misplaced. That is because in the contemporary period the issue of inventing and staging dramatic news pictures has escalated from the actions of a few individuals seeking to deceive to the whole purpose and structure of the military's media management operation. . . .

Nor are such instances of overt manipulation the main problem. One of the principle effects of having journalists, cameramen, and photographers embedded with particular units was to ensure that the stream of images coming back from the front line revolved around allied military hardware and personnel. As *New York Times* staff photographer Vincent Laforet—who spent twenty-seven days aboard the USS *Abraham Lincoln* in the Persian Gulf—wrote afterward, "My main concern was that I was producing images that were glorifying war too much. These machines of war are awesome and make for stunning images. I was afraid that I was being drawn into producing a public-relations essay."[15]

Laforet's concern is well founded, but the media outlets themselves share responsibility for the glamorizing coverage of war achieved through the embedded system. The fact that reporters and photographers were embedded might have increased the prospects of favorable coverage but did not guarantee such coverage. While one *Boston Herald* reporter was so embedded he felt comfortable in calling out Iraqi positions to his military unit (and thus played a role in killing three Iraqi soldiers), a *Washington Post* story on the shooting of civilians has led to a Pentagon investigation of the unit responsible.[16] These differing outcomes have produced an ongoing debate in media circles about embedding in which journalists are clearly undecided about the costs and benefits of the arrangement.[17]

---

[15]Vincent Laforet, "Photographer Worried about 'Glorifying War,'" *Editor & Publisher,* April 23, 2003; available at www.editorandpublisher.com/editorandpublisher/headlines/article_display.jsp?vnu_content_id=1871177.

[16]Nancy Bernhard, "Embedding Reporters on the Frontline," *Nieman Reports* 57, no. 2 (2003), pp. 87, 89.

[17]For a U.K. perspective, see Roy Greenslade, "Media: Fighting talk," *Guardian,* June 30, 2003, p. 6.

Nonetheless, what is most striking about the embedded journalists' coverage of the Iraq war is the way in which the images of the conflict produced by the allies' media was so relatively clean, being largely devoid of the dead bodies that mark a major conflict. In this outcome, the media is a willing accomplice. An account of a *Time* magazine editorial meeting helps explain this:

> In the darkness of a conference room at *Time* magazine last Friday, a war of terrible and beautiful images unfurled on a screen: the steely-eyed marine taking aim, the awe-struck Iraqi pointing to bombers in the sky, the bloodied head of a dead Iraqi with an American soldier standing tall in the background.
>
> The last image was an appalling but vivid representation of American dominance in a very violent week. But Stephen J. Koepp, deputy managing editor of *Time,* dismissed the photograph as a candidate for the issue to be published today. "You want a little picture with your blood," Mr. Koepp said. The photo and editorial staff assembled in the half-light murmured in agreement.
>
> Large numbers of Iraqi soldiers have been killed, according to the Pentagon, and more than 2,000 Iraqi civilians, the government of Saddam Hussein said, many of them in the last week. But when James Kelly, the managing editor of *Time,* lays out the 20 pages of photos intended to anchor the magazine's coverage of the war, there were pictures of soldiers, battles and rubble, but no corpses.[18]

The relatively bloodless coverage of conflict (and not just that in Iraq) derives from the media outlet's invocation of the criteria of "taste" and "decency." This is most often expressed as a concern for the anticipated reaction of readers and viewers, now readily available to newspapers through the offices of ombudsmen and readers' editors. Often this concern is so strong that some U.S. newspapers have the presumptive principle that "intrusive" images containing bodies or blood will *not* be run, or, at the very least, only after extensive editorial discussion.[19] Their British counterparts demonstrated similar self-imposed restraints.[20] Television broadcasters are even more bound because of regulations, so that while their

---

[18]David Carr, Jim Rutenberg, and Jacques Steinberg, "Bringing Combat Home: Telling War's Deadly Story at Just Enough Distance," *New York Times,* April 7, 2003, p. B13.

[19]Randy L. Rasmussen, "Arriving at Judgments in Selecting Photos," *Nieman Reports* 56, no. 3 (2002), pp. 67–70; and Michael Larkin, "Deciding on an Emotion-Laden Photography for Page One," *Nieman Reports* 55, no. 3 (2002), p. 77.

[20]Annie Lawson, "Editors show restraint with war images," *MediaGuardian.co.uk,* March 31, 2003; available at media.guardian.co.uk/iraqandthemedia/story/0,12823,924949,00.html.

cameramen record the complete picture of death and destruction in war, and their reporters lament their inability to convey the full truth, the vast majority of that footage is simply deemed too gory to be shown.[21]

The media's concern for taste and decency has meshed perfectly with the military's long-established aversion to images of death. In World War I, the British War Office prohibited the appearance of bodies (regardless of whether they were British or German) in any official photograph or film, an edict that led also to the censorship of war paintings that depicted dead soldiers.[22] In the Persian Gulf War, the sensitivity was so great that in one instance pool photographers had film ripped from their cameras to prevent publication of images recording the aftereffects of a Scud missile attack on U.S. barracks in Saudi Arabia that left twenty-five soldiers dead.[23]

The same sensitivities—though now extended to the captured as well as the dead—were on display in Iraq when al-Jazeera broadcast images of U.S. prisoners of war and U.K. casualties. U.S. networks held back from showing the footage for at least a day before releasing it in very short clips with identifying features obscured.[24] Despite the Bush administration's frequent disregard for international conventions, and notwithstanding the Pentagon's earlier release of pictures from Guantánamo Bay of captives in degrading confinement, Secretary of Defense Donald Rumsfeld rushed to decry the broadcasts as a grave breach of the Geneva Conventions. While the International Committee of the Red Cross says any image "that makes a prisoner of war individually recognizable" is a violation of Article 13 of the third Geneva Convention of 1949, this issue was complicated by a number of factors.[25] First and foremost, al-Jazeera was broadcasting Iraqi TV footage rather than producing the images. Moreover, it was doing so at the same time as numerous U.S. and European

---

[21] Both reporters and cameramen in a series of U.K. documentaries discuss this conundrum openly on the media and Iraq. See Jon Snow, "The True Face of War," *The War We Never Saw,* Channel 4, June 5, 2003; and Fergal Keane, "Iraq: The Cameramen's Story," BBC4, June 30, 2003. For the view of three U.K. television news editors that reveal the restraints, see "Media: What can you show?" *Guardian,* March 31, 2003, p.7.

[22] Michèle Barrett, "Review: Shell-shocked," *Guardian,* April 19, 2003, p. 34.

[23] Patrick J. Sloyan, "What Bodies?" *Digital Journalist,* November 2002; available at www. digitaljournalist.org/issue0211/sloyan.html.

[24] Bill Carter and Jane Perlez, "The Networks: Channels Struggle on Images of Captured and Slain Soldiers," *New York Times,* March 24, 2003, p. B6. Subsequent broadcast of a seven-second clip of the bodies of two U.K. soldiers, filmed by al-Jazeera but used in a BBC documentary, drew criticism from their relatives, the Ministry of Defence, and the British prime minister, but the BBC was not deterred from its use. Jamie Wilson, "Blair fails to get BBC to remove Gulf bodies footage," *Guardian,* May 29, 2003, p. 6.

[25] Anthony Dworkin, "The Geneva Conventions and Prisoners of War," *Crimes of War Project* 24 (March 2003); available at www.crimesofwar.org/special/Iraq/brief-pow.html.

networks were broadcasting images of Iraqi POWs, some of which were provided by Pentagon and Ministry of Defence film crews in Iraq. That made Iraq and the allies (rather than the broadcasters) equally culpable, because only states are subject to the convention.

Nonetheless, this issue propelled al-Jazeera into the limelight. Al-Jazeera took an editorial decision during the Iraq war to show all the shocking images that came its way (whether taken by its eight crews inside Iraq or from tapes supplied by other sources). The fact that al-Jazeera's images were, in the words of John MacArthur, "too honest," had the paradoxical effect of making al-Jazeera the story rather than the images and what they represented.[26] Given that its cameras were the only ones outside both the system of embedded journalists and the Western media's adherence to codes of "taste," al-Jazeera's images of the conflict were unrelentingly horrific. Yet they were no more than what appeared, in actuality, before its camera lenses. The footage of civilian casualties and dead soldiers (whether Iraqi, U.S., or British) was unedited and unpackaged. The sense of immediacy and proximity that these images achieved—whether as video or still frames grabbed from that video—gave them a force unmatched by the cleaner, more distanced pictures produced by journalists at the CMC, just down the road from al-Jazeera in Qatar. Al-Jazeera's approach led some television executives to argue they had a credibility problem with worldwide audiences who see the shocking images on non-Western channels. While refraining from advocating that the BBC emulate al-Jazeera, the deputy director of BBC News, Mark Damazer, deemed his network's coverage "too conservative" and in need of a rethink with respect to the broadcasting of shocking images.[27]

The Challenges of Representation

The extensive management of the media coverage of war—as a conjunction of official restrictions and self-imposed standards—has for the most part diminished the verisimilitude of the resulting images. Constrained by the confines of the Coalition Media Center, reporters seeking an overview were (in the words of Michael Wolff) in danger of becoming little more than a series of "Jayson Blairs," constructing colorful accounts of scenes they had never witnessed.[28] Organized around imagery of the armed forces and their personnel, these reports were more than sympathetic por-

---

[26]Quoted in Snow, "The True Face of War."

[27]Jason Deans, "BBC's war coverage was too "conservative," *MediaGuardian.co.uk,* June 25, 2003; available at media.guardian.co.uk/broadcast/story/0,7493,984976,00.html.

[28]Ciar Byrne, "US TV networks 'kissed ass', says Wolff," *MediaGuardian.co.uk,* June 25, 2003; available at media.guardian.co.uk/iraqandthemedia/story/0,12823,984899,00.html. Jayson Blair was the *New York Times* reporter whose fabrications resulted in upheaval at the newspaper.

trayals of the war—they were themselves part of the war. The "media was weaponized" and the imagery was "a force-multiplier" exercising pressure on the Iraqi leadership.[29]

In this context, photography has its work cut out for it. The speed at which (dis)information circulates in the media-managed battle space means the time for contemplation and critique offered by the still image is more compressed than ever. Nonetheless, while the images are unlikely to lead to change, especially in the short time available, they become part of what Sontag calls the vast repository of pictures that make it difficult to sustain the "moral defectiveness" of ignorance or innocence in the face of suffering. Images may only be an invitation to pay attention. But the questions photographs of war and atrocity pose should be required of our leaders and us: "Who caused what the picture shows? Who is responsible? Is it excusable? Was it inevitable? Is there some state of affairs which we have accepted up to now that ought to be challenged?"[30]

The conclusion of *Regarding the Pain of Others* is itself something of a battle cry: "Let the atrocious images haunt us. Even if they are only tokens, and cannot possibly encompass most of the reality to which they refer, they still perform a vital function. The images say: This is what human beings are capable of doing—may volunteer to do, enthusiastically, self-righteously. Don't forget."[31] The *Guardian* used this Sontag quote in a short editorial to support its publication, twelve years after the event, of many previously unseen photographs from the Persian Gulf War.[32] Under the title "Blood in the Sand," and edited by Don McCullin, these unsparing images "reveal[ed] the true horror of the Gulf war," and their publication was timed to coincide with the global antiwar marches on February 15, 2003.[33]

Photographs such as these do not let us forget. But we will be allowed to forget if timely outlets for images of war are not found. That on the brink of another war in Iraq pictures of the carnage from 1991 could be published for the first time is an indictment of the amnesia and superfi-

---

[29]Lucian K. Truscott IV, "In This War, News Is A Weapon," *New York Times,* March 25, 2003, p. A17. The weaponization of the media also preceded the conflict, especially when it came to the issue of weapons of mass destruction. One of the underreported elements of the Blair crisis at the *New York Times* was that "the paper's bioterrorism expert, Judith Miller, admitted her main source on Iraq's weapons of mass destruction programme had been the Pentagon's favoured Iraqi, Ahmad Chalabi. That in turn suggested that the Pentagon and Mr Chalabi had used the paper to help create justification for war." Suzanne Goldenberg, "US paper gripped by new crisis of ethics," *Guardian,* May 30, 2003, p. 19.

[30]Sontag, *Regarding the Pain of Others,* p. 117.

[31]Ibid., p. 115.

[32]"The Pity of War: It is right to confront images of death," *Guardian,* February 14, 2003, p. 23.

[33]*Guardian (G2),* February 14, 2003, pp. 1–17.

ciality Sontag cites as indices of "moral defectiveness."[34] With that amnesia, Sontag argues, comes heartlessness. But it is not the photographs that are the problem. It is passivity—not pictures—that dull feeling. How, then, can we use the pellets of information that photographs bear to dissipate the clouds of fantasy in the official coverage of war and overcome the passivity it enables?

Personal Investigations: Inquiry Projects

1. On page 450 Campbell describes the ways we make meaning of an image:

   [T]he construction of meaning arises from the complex interplay of the photographic representation, its location, accompanying text, moment of reading, as well as the frames of reference brought to it by the reader/viewer. They might turn us off, or turn us on; they might frighten us, or they might anger us; they might distance us, or make us feel proximate; they might weaken us or they might strengthen us. . . .

   Using this passage as a guide for analyzing images, find recent photographs of current events (from newspapers, news magazines, or online sources) and spend time interpreting each one carefully. Then develop an essay around a key question that has emerged for you from this analysis and the reading you've done so far in this chapter.

2. In a section from "Representing Contemporary War" that we've cut, Campbell examines the events and images surrounding the rescue of Private Jessica Lynch during the war in Iraq. He argues, based on evidence, that the story was manipulated to advance the war effort. Do some of your own investigating of this event. See what you can find about the Lynch story from the time the story broke until now, paying attention to how it was interpreted at first and then the questions that were raised about it. Look for evidence of what was "true" and what was not. What do you make of what you've found?

Craft and Conventions: Explaining and Evaluating

3. Campbell uses several sources of information as he constructs his argument. What does he rely on for evidence? How persuasive is that evidence and why?

---

[34]Sontag, *Regarding the Pain of Others*, p. 114.

4. What seems to be Campbell's overall assessment of Susan Sontag's book, *Regarding the Pain of Others*? Draw on specific passages as you explain your understanding of his evaluation.

5. What do you think Susan Sontag means when she says, "a photograph that brings news of some unsuspected zone of misery cannot make a dent in public opinion unless there is an appropriate context of feeling and attitude" (found on page 449)? Fastwrite about your understanding of this quote, and then return to Campbell's essay to further clarify your understanding.

6. Although we've cut several paragraphs from the original review essay, you can still get a good sense of how Campbell has structured this article as an argument. Sketch a rough outline of this review to get a visual image of how he moves from one point to the next. What do you notice about how this piece is structured?

Inquiries on Inquiry: Exploring and Reflecting

7. Explore your personal response to this essay in a ten-minute fastwrite. What did you think and feel as you read Campbell's review? What did you find confusing or surprising? What did you agree with? Disagree with? Why? What in your background influences how you read this piece?

8. Given the questions you've been exploring about publishing disturbing photos, what are the three most significant ideas/perspectives/arguments that Campbell offers that have also affected your initial ideas about this subject? What has changed? What has been complicated? Reinforced?

9. As you read this review, what did you find the most challenging? Of the habits of mind we've discussed in this book, which were the most difficult for you to engage in: suspending judgment, tolerating ambiguity, engaging in dialectical thinking, beginning with questions rather than answers?

10. Toward the end of this article, Campbell points out that photographs and video from the war in Iraq were noticeably devoid of dead bodies, and that this was because of both the media's concerns for "taste" and "decency" (see page 454) and the military's "long-established aversion to images of death" (see page 455). What do you think of these decisions? Should war be an exception to the usual guidelines for publishing disturbing images? Why or why not?

11. In Chapter 4, the research essay "Did NASA Fake the Moon Landing?" examines how "truthful" photographic images can be. Explore the connections between Ray Villard's argument about the veracity of images and Campbell's arguments about representations of war.

Victims of Violence

Paul Martin Lesser

In this excerpt from his book, Photojournalism: An Ethical Approach, *journalism professor Paul Lester offers several philosophies that seem to govern the publication of shocking pictures. The Hedonistic philosophy, a view that disturbing pictures are the commercial bread and butter of American newspapers, may be the most objectionable, and the Golden Rule philosophy—do to others as you would have them do to you—the easiest to understand. But the Categorical Imperative philosophy—that dramatic pictures should be published because they powerfully communicate aspects of a story—seems most common among photojournalists.*

Among the interesting issues raised by Lester in "Victims of Violence" is information about the patterns *of reader response to shocking photographs in their local newspapers. Drawing on communications research, Lester points out, among other things, that whether the photo was in color or black-and-white seems to make a difference in how readers feel about it, as does placement in the paper and the photograph's proximity to the story.*

If you're hoping that Lester's essay might simplify the ethical dilemma of printing death pictures, the piece will disappoint you. But he does end by suggesting a range of ways that the newsroom can be more thoughtful about the dilemma of publishing disturbing photographs. Do Lester's suggestions go too far, or not far enough? That's something you'll have to figure out. But he does remind us that one of the central questions is whether newspaper readers should influence the content of their local papers. As newspaper readers, and probably not journalists, our first instinct might be to feel that reader response should matter to editors more than it seems to. But consider the implications for a free and independent press. Where would you draw the line?

Violence and tragedy are staples of American journalism because readers are attracted to gruesome stories and photographs. "If it bleeds, it leads" is an undesirable rule of thumb. Judges of contests also have a fatal attraction. Pulitzer Prizes are most often awarded to photographers who make pictures of gruesome, dramatic moments (Goodwin, 1983). *Milwaukee Journal* editor Sig Gissler summed up the newspaper profession's sometimes Hedonistic philosophy when he admitted, "We have a commercial interest in catastrophe" ("Knocking on death's door," 1989, p. 49).

Ethical problems arise for photographers and editors because readers are also repulsed by such events. It is as if readers want to know that tragic circumstances take place, but do not want to face the uncomfortable details.

After the publication of a controversial picture that shows, for example, either dead or grieving victims of violence, readers, in telephone calls and in letters to the editor often attack the photographer as being tasteless and adding to the anguish of those involved. As one writer noted, "The American public has a morbid fascination with violence and tragedy, yet this same public accuses journalists of being insensitive and cynical and of exploiting victims of tragedy" (Brown, 1987, p. 80).

The Immediate Impact of Images

Photographs have long been known to spark more emotional responses than stories. Eugene Goodwin (1983) in his book, *Groping for Ethics,* agreed. Goodwin wrote, "Pictures usually have more impact on people than written words. Their capacity to shock exceeds that of language" (p. 190). Other researchers have noted the eye catching ability of newspaper photographs. Miller (1975) wrote, "Photos are among the first news items to catch the reader's eye. . . . A photo may catch the eye of a reader who doesn't read an accompanying story" (p. 72). Blackwood (1983) argued that "People who either can't read, or who don't take the time to read many of the stories in newspapers do scan the photographs . . ." (p. 711). Nora Ephron (1978) asserted that disturbing accident images should be printed. "That they disturb readers," Ephron wrote, "is exactly as it should be: that's why photojournalism is often more powerful than written journalism" (p. 62).

When U.S. servicemen were killed in Iran during the 1980 attempt to rescue American hostages, gruesome images of the charred bodies were transmitted to American newspapers. Ombudsman George Beveridge of the defunct *Washington Star* defended his paper's publication of the photographs by writing, "newspapers were obliged to print them because they gave readers a dimension of understanding of the situation and the people involved that written words could not possibly convey" (cited in Gordon, 1980, p. 25). For Beveridge, if photographs accurately and dramatically document a news event, even though their content may be gruesome, those pictures should be printed. Beveridge is probably using the Categorical Imperative philosophy. Nevertheless, newspapers received hundreds of calls and letters protesting the use of the images. A Mississippi newspaper editor tore the pictures up when he saw them because he explained it would have been "the poorest kind of taste to display those ghastly pictures" (p. 28). The editor was most likely guided by the Golden Rule philosophy.

The Public Suicide of Budd Dwyer

Editors have noticed that when emotionally charged and gruesome pictures come from a local event, readers react the strongest. A mother grieving over a drowned child in Bangladesh will not produce the same level of reactions as an identical subject in a reader's hometown.

Pennsylvania State Treasurer Budd Dwyer had just been convicted of bribery. Journalists from several newspapers, news services, and television stations gathered around a small podium that sat on a table expecting to hear Dwyer announce his resignation from state government. What they heard were the long, rambling last words of a seriously troubled man. Dwyer pulled out a .357 magnum, long barrel pistol, waved back reporters, stuck the revolver in his mouth, pulled the trigger and ended his torment. His desperate act also created torment with editors around the country who were left with some hard questions: Should any pictures be used? Should more graphic or less graphic pictures be used? Should only one or a complete series of pictures be printed? On what page should the pictures be displayed? How large should the pictures be? Should color or black-and-white pictures be used?

Journalism researcher Robert Baker (1988) found that among the 93 daily newspapers he studied, "Newspapers more than 200 miles away from the victim's hometown were two-and-a-half times as likely to use the 'very graphic' photographs than those within 100 miles" (p. 21). Editors were more likely to use the most gruesome images the further they were from the event.

Robert Kochersberger (1988), another journalism researcher, also looked at the Dwyer suicide photo use. He found a trend toward sensitivity to the publishing of the graphic suicide pictures. For him, this result may suggest the "abandoning [of] the time-worn patterns of 'Front Page'-style journalism that would have called for using the graphic photos with little second thought" (p. 9).

As evidence of this new sensitivity, Kochersberger cited two editors. "Jess Garber, managing editor of the *Record Herald,* Waynesboro, PA, wrote, 'I believe in the public's right to know but am not sure that carries to seeing a distraught person blowing his brains out'" (p. 8). "John Wellington, managing editor of the *Meadville Tribune,* published in Dwyer's hometown, wrote . . . 'Would anyone with half a whit of common sense want graphic suicide pictures imposed on his or her children? I would not" (p. 9).

Apparently, many editors disagreed with Garber and Wellington. Baker's (1988) data shows that "very graphic" suicide photographs were used by up to 58 percent of newspapers in his survey in one of his demographic categories. Editors that used the "very graphic" images justified their publication with statements such as, " 'Photos had tremendous impact as a news story' " and " 'We used the photo to show a bizarre news event. It's not normal for a person to shoot himself at the end of a news conference'" (Kochersberger, 1988, p. 7–8). Once again, opposing philosophies are at work. One group of editors would most likely side with the Veil of Ignorance or Golden Rule philosophies. Another group would probably side with the Categorical Imperative philosophy.

Reasons for Reader Reactions

Some writers fear that readers become calloused by the many images of the dead and dying shown in the media. Bill Hodge (1989), past president of the NPPA, recently wrote, "There's a change occurring among our audiences. I see a desensitized viewer and reader that is harder to offend or shock. They seem to be more immune to—or more interested in—shocking things" (p. 14). Hodge cited such "Trash TV" shows led by Geraldo Rivera and Oprah Winfrey that regularly feature programs that test the public's sensitivity.

There is some concern among professionals that the real culprit in the controversy over gruesome images is not the content, but whether the picture is printed in color. Readers of the Minneapolis *Star Tribune* complained about several graphically descriptive pictures that were printed in color. One caller said, "Color should be something beautiful." Another reader complained that an image of a bleeding Arab mayor "needed black and white." Lou Gelfand (1989), ombudsman for the *Star Tribune*, reported that former chief photographer, Earl Seubert, "says color is the cause of most of the response. Some of the . . . pictures ran in black-and-white in an early edition and looked comparatively dull." Color may be a contributing factor to a reader's reaction, but readers are still moved by dramatic black-and-white content.

Many readers, editors note, complain when a graphically violent picture is published in the morning, rather than the evening paper. For some readers, there is a sacredness about the first meal of the day. A typical response can be found from a Minneapolis reader who admitted, "I can't handle that kind of picture with breakfast" (Gelfand, 1989, p. 12).

Another contributing factor to a reader's negative reaction to a controversial photograph is the reader's perception of the respect given to the victim and the family. An image of a photographer at a funeral wearing blue jeans and an open-collared shirt and hovering over a casket with a wide-angle lens for a close-up, gives readers the impression that the photographer has little respect for the subject. Of course, an editor will seldom print that uncomplimentary portrait.

An editor can show disrespect in the eyes of some readers, however, by running a picture extremely large on the front page or with only a brief caption explanation. Readers associate the importance given to a photograph with a story that accompanies it. When readers objected to a picture of a man killing a calf with a pistol during a mass slaughter of cattle during a protest over the cost of raising beef, Bill Cento of the St. Paul *Dispatch and Pioneer Press* said, "The story ran across the top of page one, but we ran the picture inside. A mistake, I believe. The words are needed to tell why it was done. The picture most forcefully tells that it was done" (Mallette, 1976, p. 118). Whenever possible, stories and photographs should be located on the same page.

One heartening note: Readers will voice their negative comments about a picture regardless of the victim's race or gender characteristics. Readers seem to be equal opportunity commentators. Many of the most controversial images printed in newspapers in the past 15 years have received reader wrath with subjects who were men, women, African American, Asian, Caucasian, or Hispanic.

A Family's Tragedy Becomes Public

One of the best ways for an editor to learn if readers have grown calloused and insensitive is to take note of the calls and letters produced after the printing of a controversial image. When an image offends, an editor knows of it quickly. It is almost reassuring, then, to learn that photographs still have the power to offend readers—particularly an image of a drowned child with distraught family members standing over the body.

The editors of the Bakersfield *Californian,* an 80,000-circulation newspaper, heard loud and clear the anger of readers over a remarkable photograph. The paper received 500 letters, 400 phone calls, 80 subscription cancellations, and one bomb threat. Such a reader reaction is extraordinary given the paper's size. National columnist Bob Greene (cited in Gordon, 1986) wrote, "The picture should never have been published; in a way I hope you can understand, it was pornography." For Greene the picture, "epitomized . . . everything that is wrong about what we in this business do" (p. 19).

The controversy at the *Californian* was reminiscent of other disturbing photographs that are printed from time to time and objected to by the nation's newspaper readers. Stan Forman, then with the Boston *Herald-American,* captured a tragic moment with his 135mm lens. A woman and her young niece are frozen by the fast shutter speed in a fall from a faulty fire escape's metal platform. The woman was killed, while the child was saved because she landed on her aunt's body. One critic said the picture was a "tasteless breach of privacy" ("Tasteless breach," 1986, p. 27).

Maria Rosas of the *Miami Herald* made a self-admitted shocking photograph of a lifeless, nude Haitian man from a group of 33 who were drowned while trying to reach the safety of Florida. Callers characterized the picture as "vulgar, racist, and sensationalistic" ("Readers object," 1982, p. 2). Nudity, the fact that the picture was in color, and that it was used large on the front page were contributing factors in the protest. From a helicopter's overhead perspective, George Wedding made a striking photograph of the nude body of 11-year-old Andy Carr lying face-up in the back of an ash-filled pickup truck, a victim of Mt. St. Helen's powerful force. Readers called the image "callous, insensitive, gross, cruel, tacky, in very poor taste, barbaric, unimaginable, and repulsive" (Gordon, 1980, p. 25). With all three pictures, editors most likely justified them with the Categorical Imperative philosophy—the image described the tragic even like no combination of words ever could. With all three pictures, readers more often objected to them with the Golden Rule philosophy—the images contributed to the victim's family grief or upset readers who would rather not see such tragic events.

With a caption head titled, "A family's anguish," there is no doubt that John Harte's photograph of young, lifeless, 5-year-old, Edward Romero, halfway zippered in a dark, plastic body bag with family members crying and a bystander awkwardly reaching for one of the survivors, is a powerful and disturbing image. Under the outstretched arms and objections from a deputy sheriff, Harte made the picture with a 24mm lens from about 5 feet away. Harte admitted that the family scene was a "get-at-any-cost picture" and the most dramatic moment he had ever photographed. For Harte, his motivation was probably the Categorical Imperative philosophy—a dramatic, human tragedy should always be the subject of pictures.

After a discussion with Harte's weekend duty editor and the managing editor, Robert Bentley, who was called in to make a decision on the photograph, the editors ran the picture on an inside page agreeing with Harte's Categorical Imperative philosophy. Bentley also employed the Utilitarian approach. One other young boy had drowned on the same day. Clearly the swimming area was a dangerous spot that the editors felt the public needed to know about with Harte's dramatic image (Gordon, 1986).

A storm of protest from readers immediately followed and Bentley changed his position. In a column titled, "What should give way when news values collide with reader sensibilities?" Bentley admitted, "We make mistakes—and this clearly was a big one." Wrote Bentley, "The damage done to the memory of the late Edward Romero . . . and to the offended sensitivities of *Californian* readers cannot be undone. It can only be followed by sincere apologies and deep company-wide introspection"

(Gordon, 1986, p. 19). Bentley now advocated the Golden Rule philosophy, shared by a majority of his readers, to justify his changed position.
Not all the letters were negative, however. Connie Hoppe wrote:

> I was horrified [by Harte's photograph], but I felt the item was
> newsworthy . . . that picture was real—maybe a little more real to
> me because my own 2-year-old son drowned . . . If maybe just
> one parent saw that picture of the grieving family and drowning
> victim and has taken more precautions around pool and beach ar-
> eas because of it, then that picture may have saved another child's
> life. (Gordon, 1986, p. 23)

Bill Hodge (1989) reported that in the two months prior to the boy's
death, 14 people had drowned. In the month following the controversy,
only two drowned. The newspaper and the photographer had to take the
wrath of an angry readership who either did not want to be faced with a
real tragedy of life or they sincerely were concerned about the rights to
privacy for the Romero family. Whatever the rationale, lives were probably saved by the newspaper's coverage.

Ethics Codes Arguments

Ethical conduct may be guided by codes established by newspapers and
professional organizations, but ethical codes cannot anticipate every situation. Consequently, the language of codes is hopeful, yet vague. For example, the "Code of Ethics" that all members of the NPPA must sign does
not specifically mention gruesome situations. The ethics code does contain phrases such as photographers "should at all times maintain the highest standards of ethical conduct," photojournalism "is worthy of the very
best thought and effort," and members should "maintain high standards of
ethical conduct."

Some would argue that codes should be ambiguous. Elliott-Boyle
(1985–1986) wrote that "codes can provide working journalists with
statements of minimums and perceived ideals" (p. 25). When a journalist
uses highly questionable practices that are outside standard behavior, the
offending reporter can be held accountable.

Others argue, however, that ethics codes should be less idealistic and
more specific particularly with regards to the "exploitation of grief." In
his 1986 article, George Padgett (1985–1986) asserted that vague ethical
codes and brief textbook treatment of photojournalism ethical issues do
not adequately provide guidelines for dealing with pictures of grieving
victims. Without such guidelines, he wrote, regulation by the courts may

classify grief pictures as invasions of privacy. "The problem should be addressed," wrote Padgett, "while it is still an ethical rather than a legal issue" (p. 56).

Conditions That Cause a Reader Firestorm

When confronting situations and photographs of accident and tragedy victims, journalists are torn between the right to tell the story and the right NOT to tell the story. Arguments by well meaning professional journalists can be made for and against the taking and publishing or the not taking and not publishing of almost any photograph. Curtis Mac-Dougall (1971) in his visually graphic book, *News Pictures Fit to Print . . . Or Are They?* argued that news pictures sometimes need to be offensive in order to better educate the public. He wrote, "If it were in the public interest to offend good taste, I would offend good taste" (p. vii). The problem comes, of course, when journalists disagree on what is in the public's interest.

From the examples just given, it can be generalized that readers are more likely to object to a controversial picture if:

- It was taken by a staff photographer
- It comes from a local story
- The image is printed in color
- The image is printed in a morning paper
- The image is printed on the front page
- It has no story accompaniment
- It shows people overcome with grief
- It shows the victim's body
- The body is physically traumatized
- The victim is a child
- Nudity is involved

If five or more of these conditions apply, editors should prepare themselves for reader reactions before the firestorm hits. Staff photographers and writers should be selected to help answer phone calls and letters. Editors should prepare notes for a column that justifies the decision. As many letters to the editor and telephone transcripts as possible should be printed. Readers may not agree, but most will respect the decision if the response to the controversy is prompt and the justification is consistent.

Michael Josephson, president of the Josephson Institute for the Advancement of Ethics, has suggested that editors and ombudsmen write "early warning notes" to readers that a controversial story is about to be printed. The note could describe the reasoning that led editors to print a controversial picture. Such a practice might head-off public misunderstanding about the intent of printing an image that may be graphically violent or intense. Public Editor Kerry Sipe of the *Virginian-Pilot* and *Ledger-Star* wrote a column on the same day a child-abuse story ran. The paper only received one call from a reader who said the story should not have run. "If he had not written his column, Sipe said, he was sure that he would have received many more" (Cunningham, 1989, p. 10).

To better understand what is the right course of action, a journalist should be familiar with the trends prevalent in newspapers and magazines, know what the readers think is acceptable for publication, and have a strong, personal ethical background.

Professional organizations and the literature that is produced by them give journalists a good idea of where photojournalism has been and where it is likely to head.

Discussions with a newspaper's ombudsman or editor, who receive many of the complaints, will help to determine the aspects of photographic coverage and publication most objectionable to readers. Guest lectures or formalized town meetings by journalists with concerned citizens will create a dialogue with readers that will help determine the acceptance level of controversial images.

Finally, personal reflection will help balance the sometimes conflicting goals of publishing the news while being sensitive to the feelings of subjects and readers. A photographer's personal ethics are influenced by many factors: family and religious upbringing, educational opportunities, professional associations, career goals, day-to-day experiences, and coworkers.

Nora Ephron (1978) in her book, *Scribble Scribble: Notes on the Media,* devoted a chapter to a description and reaction to Stan Forman's fire escape tragedy. Ephron concluded that "I recognize that printing pictures of corpses raises all sorts of problems about taste and titillation and sensationalism; the fact is, however, that people die. Death happens to be one of life's main events. And it is irresponsible—and more than that, inaccurate—for newspapers to fail to show it . . . " (p. 61).

A photojournalist's mission is to report all the news objectively, fairly, and accurately. The profession can only improve in quality and stature if photographers are mindful of those they see in their viewfinders and those they seldom see, their readers. Decisions, however, should be guided, never ruled, by readers.

References

Baker, R. (1988, Summer). Portraits of a public suicide: Photo treatment by selected Pennsylvania dailies. *Newspaper Research Journal, 21.*

Blackwood, R. (1983). The content of news photos: Roles portrayed by men and women. *Journalism Quarterly, 60,* 710–714.

Brown, J. (1987, Spring/Summer). News photographs and the pornography of grief. *Journal of Mass Media Ethics, 80.*

Cunningham, R. (1989, November). A photographer defines boundaries. *The Quill,* pp. 8–10.

Elliot-Boyle, D. (1985–1986, Fall/Winter). A conceptual analysis of ethics codes. *Journal of Mass Media Ethics, 25.*

Ephron, N. (1978). *Scribble scribble: Notes on the media.* New York: Alfred Knopf.

Gelfand, L. (1989, January). Is color the culprit? *News Photographer,* p. 12.

Goodwin, E. (1983). *Groping for ethics in journalism.* Ames, IA: Iowa State University.

Gordon, J. (1980, July). Judgment days for words and pictures. *News Photographer,* p. 25.

Gordon, J. (1986, March). Grief photo reaction stuns paper. *News Photographer,* pp. 17–25.

Hodge, B. (1989, January). Change in the reader and viewer. *News Photographer,* pp. 14–15.

Knocking on death's door. (1989, February 27). *Time,* p. 49.

Kochersberger, R. (1988, Summer). Survey of suicide photos use by newspapers in three states. *Newspaper Research Journal, 9.*

MacDougall, C. (1971). News pictures fit to print . . . or are they? Stillwater, OK: *Journalistic Services.*

Mallette, M. (1976, March). Should these news pictures have been printed? *Popular Photography,* pp. 75, 120.

Miller, S. (1975). The content of news photos: Women's and men's roles. *Journalism Quarterly, 52,* 70–75.

Padgett, G. (1985–1986, Fall/Winter). Codes should address exploitation of grief by photographers. *Journal of Mass Media Ethics, 50*–56.

Readers object to gruesome page 1 photo. (1982, January). *News Photographer,* p. 2.

Tasteless breach. (1986, March). *News Photographer,* p. 27.

Personal Investigations: Inquiry Projects

1. One of the contributions that Lester's essay, "Victims of Violence," makes to our conversation about the publication of shocking photos are

his categories of editorial justifications. For example, he mentions the Hedonistic, Categorical Imperative, and Golden Rule philosophies, all of which provide some basis for the decision to publish or not. Such classifications are often helpful when trying to untangle a complicated issue like this one; for one thing, they help draw useful distinctions that cannot easily be ignored. As a way to sort out your own feelings about the shocking picture controversy, create your own categories that more clearly describe what's shocking to you and what's not. Collect disturbing photographs from this chapter and from other sources (the Internet is a great source). Closely examine each and find out as much as you can about the context in which the picture was taken. Make three categories: pictures that should not be published, pictures that you're uncertain about, and pictures that should probably make it into print. Drawing from the particulars you know about each photograph, attempt to establish principles or conditions that might apply to each category, but decide first the point of view you're assuming: a newspaper reader or a newspaper editor.

Craft and Conventions: Explaining and Evaluating

1. One of the appealing features of "Victims of Violence" is Lester's use of journalism research as a way of quantifying both reader response to shocking photographs and the extent they're used in American newspapers. You'll notice, though, how many of these sources come from the late 1980s. Is the age of this research a problem? If so, how might you solve it?

2. Who is Lester's primary audience? How did that influence your reading of his article?

3. Read "Images of Violence: A Transcript" (pages 480–491) at the end of this chapter, keeping in mind Lester's categories for editorial justification. Write an analysis of that transcript that explains how the journalists included do or do not fit Lester's theory. How does Lester's essay affect your reading of that transcript?

4. Choose a passage where you see Lester effectively integrating outside sources into his own "voice." Where are the quotes and documented information placed in the paragraph? In the sentences? How can you tell which ideas are Lester's and which are those of his sources?

Inquiries on Inquiry: Exploring and Reflecting

5. Frequently, research involves using relatively small excerpts from a larger work rather than parts of shorter articles and essays. "Victims of

Violence," which comes from a book, *Photojournalism: An Ethical Approach,* is a good example of this. Obviously, one issue for the academic researcher is the difficulty of doing justice to an argument or investigation that may go on for several hundred pages, when all you want is a paragraph or two from a single page. When you read "Victims of Violence," did you ever feel that something was missing, perhaps some allusions were unexplained or you needed to know more about some larger argument Lester might be making in his book? How do you solve the problem of doing justice to a book when all you need is a paragraph from it?

6. What do you consider the most convincing section of Lester's piece? Look closely at that passage and consider the kinds of evidence he offers or language he uses that makes the passage effective for you. How do your own views figure into your reading of that passage?

7. Describe your reading process for this essay. How did you approach it? What purposes did you have that guided how you would respond? What kinds of things did you mark up and why?

Tragedy of the Common: Markedness and the Creation of Mundane Tragedy

Stevphen Shukaitis and Rachel Lichtenfeld

We see commercials asking us to help starving children in Africa; we see footage of the Twin Towers crumbling; we flip channels and find 24-hour coverage of the recent tsunami and its victims. It seems we can't escape images of tragedy and atrocity. But do we pay avid attention to every story and photograph we see? The authors of this article, two graduate students in sociology, argue that we don't—they claim the events become folded into our daily lives and lose their sense of significance, in many cases, because of the sheer quantity of them. What David Campbell earlier in "Representing Contemporary War" termed the "compassion fatigue" thesis is seen in the following article in the central research question: "In a world where the information and images vastly outnumber amounts available to all heretofore-existing generations, why are we increasingly immune to the realities with which we are presented?"

This academic article was published in the online journal, the Journal of Mundane Behavior, *in September 2002. What you'll read here is a series of excerpts from a longer article, excerpts that we believe are most relevant to the focus of this chapter. As you read, remember to call on reading strategies for challenging academic texts (see Chapters 2 and 7). In addition, keep in mind that the authors are interested in what determines whether a tragic event takes on* moral significance *to us—at what point, for example, do the commercials about starving children become as unremarkable to our daily life as beer commercials? What made the events of September 11 stand out, in spite of the repeated images we saw of the tragedy? The authors use two sociological terms to describe these two examples: When an image or event becomes integrated into our daily life, it's considered "unmarked"—that is, not distinguished or remarkable "within our sphere of moral concern," but mundane. When an image or event, such as September 11, does stand out it is considered a "marked" event; the event has entered into our sphere of moral concern despite how heavily we are bombarded with disturbing images.*

As you read, think about how the ideas in this article speak back to the other essays in this chapter. Do David Campbell and these authors agree, for example? Does Paul Lester take this sociological theory into account in "Victims of Violence"? What does this academic article contribute to the developing conversation you and your classmates are having about the ethics of publishing disturbing images?

Abstract: This paper explores how the integration of images of tragedy and atrocity into daily life gradually move such events from highly marked occurrences to less visible occurrences. Through a process of repetition, the moral significance of the marked atrocity becomes unmarked as it is further integrated into the symbolic interactions of daily life. This paper also discusses how this process, although not defined by the medium of transmission, can be utilized in the generation of political motivation and in the reinforcement of social norms.

How can I sit here and eat my tea, with all that blood flowing from the television? At a quarter to six, I watch the news, eating, eating, all my food as I sit watching the red spot in the egg that looks like all the blood you don't see on the television.
—Gang of Four, *5:45*

Every day we are confronted with images of tragedy, suffering, and torment. These images, administered in regular doses and at set schedules, besiege our visions and concerns: famine in an impoverished African nation, fundamentalist-fueled religious violence in the Middle East, rampant inner-city gang violence, the drug-funded guerrillas in South America. The representations of atrocity multiply, yet they seem more and more invisible. Paradoxically, as violence and atrocity become more integrated symbolically into the imagery of daily life they are less visible in the conscious vision—they are everywhere, and they are nowhere—they are hidden in plain sight. How, and why, does this process occur? In a world where the information and images vastly outnumber amounts available to all heretofore-existing generations, why are we increasingly immune to the realities with which we are presented?

The nature of the presentation of tragedy through television, radio, and print determines whether it lies within the realm of concern and whether or not it is perceived as relevant. Whether or not the images of tragedy and suffering are held to be of consequence by those viewing them is not based upon the intrinsic qualities of what is being presented. Through the presentation of tragedy runs the subtext of power: the power to determine what is within the sphere of moral relevance, what is of concern, what is within the realm of action, and even what is perceived by those who observe it. Conversely, how a tragedy is presented can render it unimportant, morally irrelevant, or cause it to be unnoticed and uncomprehended by those who are directly presented with the imagery and information. . . .

Presentations of Tragedy in Everyday Life

It is our contention that tragedy and violence have become increasingly invisible in the cognitive sense through the nature and manner of their presentation—primarily through media outlets—though the nature of this change in perception can easily affect other areas of social life. It is the nature of the presentation, perhaps even more than the reality of what is presented, that determines how the information and images are perceived, comprehended, and mentally attended to in the social process; the qualitative difference in presentation expedites the transition between images of tragedy being marked and within the moral sphere of concern, and those that are unmarked and outside this cognitive sphere.

This, however, is not intended to degenerate into yet another rant about the "evil media" and how it is destroying the nature of reality, taking us to hell in a satellite dish, etc. . . . The television and print media are used as examples here for how they present tragedy and atrocity, not because they are being blamed as part of some insidious plot. In the consciousness of that mythical being known as the "average person," a great deal, if not all, of what they know about the world around them is filtered through the presentation of the subject by media outlets. Such a concept could also be explored through an analysis of historical texts or other avenues of information, as many of the same principles will apply.

Let us explore this concept through a few examples that demonstrate the process: consider, for example, the estimated between 800,000 and 1,000,000 people who died in the Rwandan genocide of 1994. When the media finally felt the carnage sufficient to warrant attention, it was virtually exclusively presented as a tribal conflict between two factions in some provincially anachronistic ancient feud. The situation was presented as a conflict between nameless and faceless blocks of people who had no descriptions or apparent motivations. Their existence was defined as an undemarcated block, notable perhaps only in how their particular catastrophe might rank among other massive tragedies in Africa.

Compare this to the media presentation of the victims of the World Trade Center tragedy, where each individual was distinctly portrayed as having a name, face, and a story. Some had only a brief paragraph, while others' names were attached to epics of drama and loss. These stories made it possible to relate to each victim and granted them an identity beyond that of their victimhood: in short, these stories allowed them to attain a state of moral relevance in the cognitive sphere of consideration. As described by Michael Albert:

> They looked at a calamity and gave the human dimensions of it . . . the media looked into this horrible occurrence . . . and it gave the human dimensions of the suffering . . . Now what's wrong with that is not that they did it, what's wrong with it is that Iraq has suffered the equivalent of a September 11th every week for about the last ten years in some total and they haven't done it [there] once.

Consider concurrently the style of presentation employed by charities urging us to donate money to alleviate suffering, disease, and hunger in Africa. Observe how instead of urging the TV viewer to donate money to a given community, they urge people to support the life of a given individual, which is made real to the contributor by providing a name, a face, and biographical information about the recipient of the charity. As the individual (more than likely a child, as we tend to find children more worthy of moral concern) moves from the realm of the abstract tragedy to personalized suffering, the individual tragedy shifts from the unmarked, morally invisible realm to the individualized realm which constitutes our moral concern—for that is when that with which we are presented becomes real tragedy, not merely an abstraction or an anonymous "atrocity."

Stalin ironically, and perhaps most fittingly, summed up this very concept when he said, "One death is a tragedy; a million deaths is a statistic." Historically and in fiction one finds that the tragedies which hold the greatest moral concern and resonate with the most compelling fervor are those that have been crystallized and cognitively assigned to the actions and death of an individual, not to the situation or framework of that individual's death. For many the Holocaust is recalled as the death of Anne Frank; for Parkinson's, Michael J. Fox; for the sacrifices of the civil rights movement, Martin Luther King Jr., and so forth. The tragedy and its recollection are attended to as crystallized and embodied in the individual's tragedy and moved into the sphere of moral relevance. . . .

We are finicky consumers when it comes to what we will attend and ignore in questions of tragedy. As all employed journalists know, "if it bleeds, it leads." In the same way that we have in recent years gone into a moral panic over razorblades in Halloween candy, teenage motherhood, and presidential sex scandals, so too do we go through the latest trends in tragedy and shift our sphere of moral indignation to Rwanda, Bosnia, etc. For instance, it has been documented that for the past twenty years overall crime rates, and many categories of crime including juvenile crime, have been consistently declining. Yet for some reason, and at purely coincidentally occurring two-and-four years intervals, we are often faced with the impending specter of "fighting the crime problem" or "getting tough on wayward youth," or some other such imminent catastrophe. Similar phenomena also exist for such events as suffering caused by a lack of health care, military aid and its relation to fighting the drugs that are killing Johnny (who still can't read), and so forth. In short, we tend to go on compassion/indignation binges—every year or two one atrocity or another is the object of public indignation, charity, and large amounts of media scrutiny.

One can clearly see the effects of the presentation of tragedy in the public's reaction to the World Trade Center tragedies. After September 11th the populace flew into a proper moral panic as described by Erich Goode and Nachman Ben-Yehuda, replete with scapegoats, hostility, tighter enforcement of laws, and changes of policy (156). All tragedy has the potential for markedness, but it was arguably the presentation of this tragedy that caused the populace to fly into a moral panic; one wonders if farmers in Wyoming would have trucked down to Wal-Mart to buy their American flags had the September 11th tragedy gone underreported. Similarly, the atrocious conditions under which the Afghani women live— conditions which, for a long time, had remained outside our moral focus—were suddenly and repeatedly thrust into our moral realm.

The Unbearable Lightness of Passive Observation

And what of the moral and ethical implications of the presentation of tragedy—does it matter if the thought patterns and norms held by those with the power to influence these presentations sway the nature of their theoretically balanced presentation? Or, more bluntly, does it matter that "all the news fit to print" effectively means "all the news fit to print as designated by the standards and concerns set by the needs of the current institutional order?"

The rather predictable answer to these questions is yes; it does matter, for we have seen that the highlighting of or inattention to an atrocity can happen for a variety of personal or political reasons, all of which we would be wise to attend to. To quote Howard Zinn, "They say Dan Rather is an anchor man . . . what is he anchored to? He's anchored to the establishment—and that's the definition of an anchorperson" (Zinn). In addition, that which is put into our brains determines the outcome of our thoughts, and we cannot come to reasonable conclusions as to what should be the subject of our moral focusing based on skewed or incomplete data.

Also, by turning human suffering into a sensationalistic news story one commodifies it and turns it into that which can be sold back to us. The exchange of our human experience for ratings cheapens our existence to the point that we must put up for sale ever more exaggerated tragedy, which perpetuates a cycle that can only end in absurdity or worse.

Another consequence is perhaps less obvious: as the scope of moral focus is shifted, this newly delineated area of cognitive relevance can be used as a basis for creating political motivation and justifying or legitimizing political ideas. When images of tragedy and atrocity are presented in such a way as to locate them within our sphere of moral relevance, these tragedies or atrocities are tied to values and identity concepts held by the observer. Conversely, in a situation in which the tragedy is perpetrated by a group or power that has become marked with the status of "other," how the tragedy is attended to and whether or not it is perceived as relevant to us depends on whether or not it can be portrayed as intrinsically infringing upon the values and identity purported to be held by the perpetrators.

Control over the nature and degree of these designations can be harnessed to generate political motivation. Consider Theodor Geiger's conception of the community of pathos, or any grouping based around an ideal: "every union in collective pathos for a good, a value, take a hostile attitude toward those who espouse an opposite value conception . . . Common advocacy of a good enveloped by pathos is the unanimous negation of everything which contradicts this good. The nature of antagonism, the hostile rejection of other value conceptions is implicit in the value-idea itself" (211).

Thus if the tragedy or atrocity is portrayed in a way that appears to threaten the basic values or mores of the group, and particularly if it disrupts the flow of orderly life and injects a greater degree of uncertainty into it, the discontent with such a disruption and the perceived threat to the common value can be rallied into a political imperative based upon the antagonism inherent in the ideal itself. This is particularly effective if the tragedy is connected in some ways to symbols that resonate as the cognitive crystallizations of group values, which raises the distinction between the tragic and that which is outside of the realm of moral relevance to a level of antagonism.

Through the above we can see that the images of tragedy and suffering that bombard us daily do indeed have their effects. Through them, the tragedy that we would not have known about two hundred years ago (before the advent of widespread media) has been incorporated into our daily existence. To shield ourselves from the tragic overload, we learn to delineate what is within our sphere of concern and what is not; what does not fall into the realm of our concern we can look at as merely spectators of "the news."

Yet through our role of passive spectators we learn to become complacent with human suffering and with existing social structures. The tragedy which was so marked to us as children fades into the gray of everyday existence, where it ceases to cause us concern and goads us into inaction. It is time to recognize the role that the presentation of tragedy and atrocity plays in our mundane existence and to take responsibility for its role in redirecting our moral focus. And from there, who knows? Maybe we'll get a new Media of the Mundane.

Works Cited

Albert, Michael. "Terrorism and the War on Terrorism." Speech of 4/24/02, Seattle, WA. http://www.radio4all.net/proginfo.php?id=1815.

Berger, Peter, and Thomas Luckmann. *The Social Construction of Reality*. New York: Doubleday, 1966.

Brekhus, Wayne. "A Sociology of the Unmarked: Redirecting Our Focus." *Sociological Theory* 16 (1998): 34–51.

Clarke, Lee. "Disasters and Social Memory," *Sociology of Risk*. Rutgers University, New Brunswick. 21 Nov. 2001.

Debord, Guy. *Society of the Spectacle*. Detroit, MI: Black and Red, 1983.

Geiger, Theodor. *On Social Order and Mass Society*. Chicago, IL: University of Chicago Press, 1969.

Goode, Eric and Nachman Ben-Yehuda. "Moral Panics: Culture, Politics, and Social Construction." *Annual Review of Sociology* 20 (1994): 149–171

Graeber, David. *Toward an Anthropological Theory of Value*. New York: Palgrave, 2001.

Sorokin, Pitirim. *Sociocultural Causality, Space, Time*. New York: Russell & Russell Inc., 1964.

Stalin, Josef. "Great Patriotic War of the Soviet Union, 1941–1945."
12 May 2002 <http://www.libraries.psu.edu/crsweb/maps/text/
GREATPATRIOTIC.pdf>.

Zerubavel, Eviatar. *Social Mindscapes.* Cambridge, MA: Harvard University Press, 1997.

———. "Horizons: On the Sociomental Foundations of Relevance."
Social Research 60 (1993): 397–413.

Zinn, Howard. "Media Bias and the War on Terror," 25th Anniversary of
the Resource Center for Nonviolence. Santa Cruz, CA. 14 Nov. 2001.

Personal Investigations: Inquiry Projects

1. How have you responded to tragedy and atrocities in the past? Did you
   see any of your own feelings and behaviors reflected in this article?
   Begin a project investigating your own responses to tragedy, beginning
   first with a fastwrite about all the disturbing images and news stories
   you've heard over the past several years, and how you responded to
   them. What in your own background has influenced your response?
   How might the readings in this chapter explain why you responded as
   you did—or even the consequences of that response? What feelings and
   thoughts are evoked for you as you write about these experiences? See
   where this writing takes you and consider doing further research on any
   of the questions that emerge in the process.

2. How much research has been done on people's responses to tragedy and
   violent imagery? Using the databases in your university library from
   different disciplines, see what you can find. Develop an annotated bibliography and/or a researched essay about what you've found.

Craft and Conventions: Explaining and Evaluating

3. What kinds of evidence do these authors use to support their arguments?
   What types of sources are used for their research?

4. Given what you've learned in Chapter 7 about reading academic articles, describe what you've learned about writing within sociology from
   reading this piece.

5. Choose a paragraph that you find particularly well written, and then one
   that you find not so well written. Type them up, double-spaced, and
   note in the margins or by using footnotes what makes the paragraph
   strong or weak. Given what you've learned about research and writing
   in this textbook, what do you notice about how this piece is written?

6. On page 476, the authors say that "by turning human suffering into a
   sensationalistic news story one commodies it and turns it into that

which can be sold back to us. The exchange of our human experience for ratings cheapens our existence to the point that we must put up for sale ever more exaggerated tragedy, which perpetuates a cycle that can only end in absurdity or worse." Fastwrite for ten minutes on your response to this passage. Play both the believing and doubting games. Then compose a paragraph or two that presents your assessment of this claim.

7. Summarize your understanding of this article. Begin by fastwriting about what you believe the authors are arguing, then return to the article, rereading it as necessary, to check your understanding with what is said. Then compose a summary of several paragraphs, if needed, that presents your interpretation of the article. For now, avoid explicit critiques or judgments about what the article says (that is, put aside the doubting game), and instead focus on trying to understand it as fully as you can (that is, play the believing game).

Inquiries on Inquiry: Exploring and Reflecting

8. This may have been one of the more challenging readings in this chapter, especially because the authors are using specialized language of the field of sociology and they are assuming an audience of specialists. How did you approach the reading of this article? What strategies did you use to make sense of the more difficult parts? Did any of the other essays in this chapter help you sort out what this one was arguing? Did any other essays in *The Curious Reader* help in general? If so, how and why?

9. In a statement similar to what is argued in "Tragedy of the Common," David Campbell, in "Representing Contemporary War," describes the "compassion fatigue" thesis as "the abundant supply of imagery [that] has dulled our senses and created a new syndrome of communal inaction" (page 448). Return to that section of Campbell's essay, particularly where he explains how Susan Sontag challenges the compassion fatigue thesis, and compare it to what Shukaitis and Lichtenfeld say in their essay. Do they agree? Are they each taking a different angle on the same subject rather than agreeing or disagreeing?

10. What did you find most convincing and/or least convincing about this article? Why? Use specific passages.

11. What habits of mind does this essay reflect? Which methods of inquiry does it emphasize the most? (Refer to Chapters 1 and 2.)

Images of Violence: A Transcript
Dart Center for Journalism and Trauma

Every time a news organization decides whether to publish a disturbing photo or video, several people have already had to view that image: the photojournalist who actually took it, the "backroom boys" who help with the editing decisions, and the editors who eventually decide. Even if your newspaper chooses not to publish a violent image, people have been affected by it. Fortunately, the field of journalism has begun to recognize the consequences of viewing such trauma for those involved, and organizations like the Dart Center for Journalism and Trauma (www.dartcenter.org) have begun to address these concerns. In October 2004, several journalists came together as part of the Frontline Club for the Dart Center and discussed how they have been making editorial decisions since the war in Iraq began. It's a fascinating conversation, moderated by the director of the Dart Center, Mark Brayne, a former journalist and editor for Reuters and the BBC World Service who is now a practicing psychotherapist. He has been instrumental in opening the conversation in journalism about the emotional costs to reporters and editors who cover traumatic events.

We've chosen a few excerpts from the transcript and organized them around three themes we saw emerging: "Protecting the 'Backroom Boys'," "Taking It to a Whole New Level," and "Defining the Roles of Journalists." We think you'll find these conversations fascinating because they provide a per- spective you've probably not considered before, that of the people who are on a different front line during violent events.

Protecting the "Backroom Boys"

Mark Brayne, Director, Dart Center, Europe

Before we start, I want to read out a couple of things—e-mails that came in as a result of the invitation. There's a note from Susannah Harrison who is now a psychotherapist as well but she comes from a photography background:

> Please don't forget the backroom boys . . . I did. I failed to con- sider the guys in our digital lab, cleaning up images for despatch to clients. They were usually eighteen- to twenty-five-year-olds, not necessarily well travelled who were sitting in a darkened lab in front of over-size screens, checking and cleaning images of of- ten horrific situations, Rwanda, Afghanistan, 9/11.
>
> It's one thing to be shocked at a still picture and be able to look away or move on to the next frame but quite another to have

to face it in graphic detail for some considerable time. They were also seeing all the detail, which perhaps we might miss as we turn the page. It wasn't until one of the guys came to me and asked somewhat nervously if they really had to look at images like this—it was a massacre in Rwanda—that I realised what they were going through and we looked at ways of warning about content but I don't believe we truly resolved the issue.

John Clarke, Reuters TV

As an agency, we've obviously had to deal with disturbing video for many decades, whether that's Rwanda or from Asia or the latest material from Iraq. So we've had a policy of putting warnings on video for quite a long time. However, when the latest material started coming out of Iraq of the beheadings, we put that normal 10- or 15-second warning on our material, but it was Chris Hampson from NBC who asked us to try and extend that even further, which we did. We now put a five-minutes' warning on video the first time it's shown, and we try to ring-fence some of this material as well so that it's either run first or last in a feed, so we can give broadcasters the chance to turn off monitors or whatever they need to do to deal with that.

Mark Brayne

One of the things about this discussion is that distressing material has been coming into newsrooms for a very long time, but there hasn't been a conscious awareness about the impact that this is having on the people who deal with the images. So the discussion we're having tonight is very new.

I want to turn to Anna Averkiou, who was running the picture desk at the BBC at the time of 9/11; you've seen this unfold, Anna, over a period going back to Yugoslavia some ten years ago.

Anna Averkiou, BBC

Yes, I've spent about 15 years watching all these images. I worked at Visnews, for Reuters, and then at WTN, and then I joined the BBC and I can see the agency point of view because some clients will use it, and the agency isn't there to censor pictures. They're just there to pass them on—this is what's happening—and it's the broadcaster that decides how they're going to use them. I still, to a point, agree with that view and it's great that the health warnings are going on. But the beheadings do take it to another level.

At the BBC, I set up the picture desk and had a team working for me who were very young. My reaction was. 'Oh, it's an arm, it's a leg, don't worry about it.' But unfortunately, September 11 happened and I was really very tired anyway. I was working crazy hours and I started having flashbacks of people jumping out of buildings and committing suicide. And then the flashbacks went back further to Bosnia and other things I'd seen over the years. So it does imprint. I was someone who used to joke about it, and I'd be drinking with everybody in the field and, you know, saying this is my job, it's exciting and we're telling people about what's going on.

I run the audio equivalent of the picture desk now, at the BBC World Service. But we are still watching the agencies coming in, because we're clipping audio. And I'm very aware that at Bush House [building in London that houses the BBC foreign language services], they do want to see some of these things just to be able to say, 'Okay we'll take the editorial line on it.' But obviously, it's radio; we take a line on what audio we're going to broadcast, and someone has to filter it. And certainly with my team now, because of what's happened to me, I'm very aware to make sure that they get their breaks and we talk things through if they want to, but also keep that detachment to a certain point.

Chris Hampson, NBC Bureau Chief, London

I don't disagree with John Clarke. The agencies are there to distribute material. It's a question of how you distribute it. And then how we as broadcasters manage it within our own enterprises. The point about the Internet is quite right but of course, you have to log on to the particular site to see it. The problem that we had in NBC was that, as Brian has cogently pointed out, it affected people in a different way. You say people react differently to it and you're quite right. I've heard from other American managers along the lines of, "These guys are journalists—suck it up!" It's like a cop joining the police force who takes the benefits, does the traffic duty fine but when there's a shoot-out he wants to sit in the car; and that's not the way it is.

So there are different approaches to this. Our approach at NBC in London was to minimise the exposure of the bureau in its entirety to this [beheading] video. We did that through talking to the agencies and asking them to not feed it in the middle of a feed unannounced, to put warnings at the beginning so that we could then establish a protocol within our own bureau that said, "When we know the feed is coming in we'll announce it on the tannoy" [public address system]. We then put a system in place that involved the minimum number of people recording it. No one had to watch the execution itself. We did all the technical checks beforehand and afterwards. So the reason for anyone to sit there and watch it came down to almost nil. I'm sure people do look at it but that's an issue for them, I think, more than anything else.

We don't archive it. We do prepare a section of it from the beginning before the execution in case anyone wants to use that, and that goes to the archive and the master copy is kept by myself or my deputy and is only handed out if it's asked for with a specific reason and then only in consultation with New York.

And because we're a smaller bureau, we're not the BBC and I guess if we tried to do this in New York, a comparative sized operation, it would be extremely difficult. But because we're a small bureau, we have managed to put some procedures in place to minimise it. But I do share with Tony and John; I think it's right that you distribute it, because we are applying value judgements in everything that we do. But that's the decision that we broadcasters want to take.

Jonathan Miller

I'm foreign affairs correspondent on Channel 4 News. We've had a torrent of these images coming in, as everybody has, in the last few months. And the deadlines, as you mention there, are a nightmare, because editorial decisions have to be taken in a split second about what can and cannot be broadcast and what is and what is not deemed suitable, particularly on our programme, which is going out at seven o'clock in the evening.

You also used the word, habituated, which is interesting and it compares to what you use generally, which is hardened; both of those words stick with me. I've been thinking a lot about this because of the sheer exposure to the violence of the videos that we've seen. I'm a journalist, I'm in this because I know what's going to happen, I know what I'm going to end up reporting. But I'm also very conscious of the fact that in the past few months I've turned into international Death And Destruction correspondent and you see images that you can never broadcast. They do stay with you; you become more sensitised, not hardened and there's a thing Anna pointed out, there's an accumulation of images that builds up inside you and you don't know at what point you are going to snap with that.

I've seen other people go over the edge on it. There was a woman who was producing with me one day during the Bosnian stuff and streams and streams of material was coming in and we were putting the stuff together for the evening programme. She was a mother; I'm a father, so any parent watching that sort of stuff is pretty hard to take, but she snapped on that one.

I've seen other colleagues snap because they've known people, either because they've been taken hostage in Iraq and it's got to them personally or because they've just seen one too many bombs and one too many bodies. I think as all of us would agree, and as these Dart Centre notes point out, too, no one person is the same as another; everyone's got different levels of tolerance to this material. I think those overseeing editorial policy have to be acutely aware of individual ability to cope. I don't think any one person who may be behaving absolutely normally as a journalist reporting well, looking healthy and balanced can necessarily remain that way.

Just to pick up on your point about this other level, I think the explanation for the phrase that keeps cropping up is the fact that this is violence designed for television. I think we're expected to see this stuff; we see it and that's why it gets to us because it's designed to get to you that way.

Taking It to a Whole New Level

Anthony Massey, Foreign Duty Editor, BBC News

Respecting totally what our Reuters colleague has said, from the BBC news desk we just see things completely differently. Personally, I've seen a lot of these events at first hand, as a field producer—as many people in this room will have done who spent years in the Balkans. I was in Rwanda and in the Middle East and various places—but the beheading videos in particular seem to come into a new and unique category that none of us have ever experienced before, and caused real trauma to colleagues in the newsroom. Initially, you did take steps to produce warnings, which were very helpful. But initially that wasn't done as well as it is now, and so we were seeing things shown repeatedly, at length, without warning—first on Reuters then on Eurovision then on AP and everywhere you look.

Our newsroom is configured to bring in agency and Eurovision material and turn it round instantly. That's what we do and that's what we want; we buy that service from you because it's good and we need it—but everywhere you looked you just saw someone screaming and having his head sawn off, at length. It was in kind of nightmare vision and you couldn't get away from it.

So I now think that we're looking at two different categories of traumatic material. Firstly there is the beheading video, which is in a category of its own, easily defined, everybody understands it and which, certainly at the working, operational level in BBC News, more and more of us do not want to come into Television Centre at all, under any circumstances. We don't want it for verification; if a Reuters or AP journalist says they've seen it, then I believe them and we don't feel we need to see the stuff ourselves. Some of our managers don't take that view. We disagree very, very strongly with them.

So we don't want the stuff to come in at all; we don't want it for verification, we don't want it for the archive. There are very few kinds of video where I can actually say the BBC will never show it on any outlet, but we're never going to show that now and we're not going to show it in a hundred years' time. We just don't need it and we don't want it. And we would say to Reuters and AP and Eurovision and any other clients they have, [they] can book a unilateral and just get it fed to them straight; but it shouldn't go on a general feed to go out to everybody.

Now, very quickly, there is also the other category of all the other kind of traumatic video, however defined. That is much more difficult to deal with because the BBC itself has different views on how it handles that material depending on the time of day, depending on who's going to use it, whether it's going to go out on BBC World, whether it's going to go out on the evening 10 o'clock news rather than Breakfast. So there we need to discuss how we manage that kind of material as a whole and how it's distributed round the building; whether it needs to be quite as widely spread as it is.

Stephen Whittle, Controller Editorial Policy, BBC

I think the hostage videos have taken it to an entirely different place, because I guess the dilemma up to now has always been about the distant, or rather not as personal an impact. But this is, after all, watching someone being literally killed, murdered before your very eyes. And it is indeed personal in a certain sense, in the way that many of the other images aren't. They may have been the result of actions but they're not as directly one to one as is happening here.

I really wanted, in a way, to go back to theory. We were talking in our pair about triangles, but perhaps it's a rectangle that has four points. One of those has to do with freedom of information and the peculiarity and the obvious difficulty of these things from Iraq—particularly especially within Britain, but also between the West and the Arab world. At the moment we say that we're not even prepared to consider receiving these images, there comes the cry, "Well, actually, that just proves what we thought. You're partial!"

Another point on the rectangle is obviously the person themselves, who is being degraded, dehumanised, treated most abominably. What is our responsibility towards them and how do we avoid, or seek to avoid, the obvious voyeurism. Related to that is what people have been talking about in terms of the people who are having to deal with it on everyone's behalf. People who may never, ever see, inevitably will never, ever see the image, but someone has to deal with it—and what the responsibility is there.

And the fourth point on the rectangle is that these are very obvious pieces of manipulation being arranged by people who know exactly what they're doing and what the intended impact is. It's how you hold all those four things in tension, because I feel uncomfortable, instinctively uncomfortable, knowing that we will never necessarily broadcast any of it. But in the end, of course, it also constitutes a record: a record of our inhumanity, one to another. And therefore I'm reluctant to say one should never even accept it even if one never actually uses it.

Benedicte Paviot, Anglo-French Journalist with French Service of BBC

I worked with the BBC World Service for eight years and that is really one of the pertinent points that we came up with in our group because two or three people, we noticed, came up with that three-word expression—that it took it to a whole new level. I'd be really interested to hear what your definition is of "whole new level" because when I was working in the French Service covering the Rwandan genocide, there were all kinds of pictures, and we were hearing stories, and we were being the gatekeepers. We were broadcasting to Rwanda, broadcasting to Zaire, and at the risk of being slightly provocative, is it that we are we still more shocked by the loss of a white European-American life?

Of course I felt sorry for Ken Bigley and I'm lucky enough to have not seen that beheading. But I do think we need to look at what we mean by "whole new level" because we've been broadcasting a lot of pictures before. I think we do treat African-Asian lives in a completely different way than we do white European lives.

My personal view is that I don't think you're a lesser person because you decide that you're not going to watch that video. Clearly we do need some people who'll watch it; I think it should come with all kinds of health warnings.

Brian Donald, NBC News: I've worked in the business a long time and I think the expression "takes it to a new level" does have a certain meaning. We are voyeurs of a snuff video.

Robin Elias, Managing Editor ITV News: I'll just say that I think newsroom technology now is moving to make it a bigger problem still, because the whole point of server technology in a big newsroom is that everybody has instant access to material whereas it used to be just the editor, the producer, and the reporter. The whole point of server technology is that you've got 200 terminals around a building that everybody has instant access to and I think agencies being very aware of that will be very useful.

Defining the Roles of Journalists

Barbara Probst, ex-BBC

I'm a former BBC journalist turned counsellor so I come at this from both sides. I sat and watched pictures over more than thirty years, appalling things that we haven't put out. And I'm beginning to question now why we don't put them out; why we don't let the public decide. I'm playing devil's advocate because I can find all sorts of reasons why we don't. But we had to look at those things, all the people that sit in newsrooms have to look at those things. We can't be the arbiters for the rest of the world. The rest of the world put some of these things out, so who are we to censor what the public decides is good or bad? I am speaking here very much as devil's advocate, because I do know why I've stood there and looked at pictures over and over again and have said, "No, you cut there before his head's chopped off."

Yes, you look at it the third time and the fourth time and the picture editor does as well and I've done that. And I am indeed going to save "the public" from seeing it. But I do worry why I'm doing that. I think there's maybe an argument to be had about that—not an argument, a discussion. About what we're protecting and what we're censoring the public from seeing.

But having said that, there still needs to be an awful lot of support for the people who do have to see it. We have to be able to say, I recognize that you can see it and I recognize that yes, with the adrenaline running you can watch it, you can do your job and you can be proud of the job you do; but at the end of the day you've got to be able to go home and go to sleep. How do we deal with that?

I think that the issues need to be separated. There's the political— why do we stop the public seeing what we see and what is happening. And okay, yes, it's manipulation by the terrorists, but we suffer manipulation by the politicians. They show us stuff that we need to see. I can remember during the last Iraq war putting out pictures of Iraqi prisoners being sat on the ground with their hands tied and blindfolded, and the next day Americans are shown being held and we're told we can't show them. Where's the fairness there?

I think we need to question how much the public are protected from the pictures that we see and why we're protecting them, and why they can't make their own minds up.

Edith Champagne, New Xchange [a conference for broadcast news organizations]

Just a point of clarification. The pictures of the beheadings that Reuters puts out come from the Internet, do they not? So the pictures are there already. I think the question becomes a little more complicated, because we're not the gatekeepers that we think we are any more; maybe for certain generations but for other generations we're not.

Tony Donovan, Reuters

I think, to my mind, we're getting to the nub of it, certainly from an agency perspective. I think this issue is about where you set the bar. If you're serving, as we are, a multicultural, multinational audience, where you set the bar is really difficult. I think it's perhaps a little easy to sit here and say beheadings are one thing but everything else is another thing because it's all the rest that we're going to have to deal with.

I think that what tonight should be about is not so much whether these pictures should be distributed, because it's going to happen. Whether it's Reuters or AP or Eurovision or the Internet, it's going to happen. Pictures are going to be out there we can't stop it; nobody's going to be able to be the boy with his finger in that particular dyke. I think we have to focus on how we deal with that reality, including people saying to Reuters, "This is what we would like you to do." We'll certainly work with the majority of people to try and arrive at a position that everybody's comfortable with.

But then it's how you try and protect your own people. Agencies have newsroom staff too who see the worst of this. I go back to the perfect example, the most horrible example, and that was the market bombing in Sarajevo. Our people saw pictures that we wouldn't send out, we just couldn't send out, because we were able to create and edit to tell that story leaving out the more horrific images.

Journalists have issues with this. But journalists are a little seasoned, a little hardened. We also have secretaries, ancillary staff, all of those people to take care of as well, so I don't think there's any great value in talking about should these pieces be out there—they're out there. It really is a question of how we deal with them.

Karen O'Connor, BBC

One other thing to factor into the equation is that there is no unanimity about how people react to images; there just isn't. Whether you're a seasoned hack or not. I know a cameraman who has been through a lot, but he had a baby a year ago and suddenly everything he's going through is completely different to him—completely different. The world's changed beyond recognition to him so let alone the guy who's taking the feed in. But picking up that point about the floodgates being open with the Net. It is all out there. And as we move to a more integrated world between television and Net broadcasting and broadband, there are some huge challenges facing us as gatekeepers to all of that because people access our material through itn.co.uk or bbc.co.uk; we're an Internet provider as well. That's a big issue. In forums and chat groups it's a horrible fact, but people are starting to collect this kind of material and swap it amongst each other. So what are we going to do about that?

But the bigger question is, how do you have a system that is protecting people and giving them support when everybody is not having the same experience? I think you can either overdo it or underdo it, and that's something we all need to think about as well.

Stephen Whittle, BBC

I just want to think a little bit about one word, and the word is "witness." I think we do have a responsibility to be witnesses and that is both a vocation and also a burden. I think as witnesses we need to attend to various things: one is to the telling of the story and to recounting what has happened, because that is a very important part of being human. But the other thing we obviously need to attend to is ourselves, and to those who work with us. And I think the value of the discussion has been to remind us not just of ourselves but also the people already mentioned who we tend to forget, who are not as visible but who are equally being forced into the role of witness, which isn't something they necessarily have chosen but which they also need help with.

Chris Hampson, NBC

Well, I take the point of the importance of being a witness and it leads to one of the other points raised, too, which is then the sanitisation process that we seem to get engaged in. One of the things that surprised me when we worked as a group and we were discussing the execution video with outsiders, outside the industry that is, is that they were unaware of how horrific, how long it had taken, how brutal, how amateurish it really was. To some extent we do a disservice if we overprotect our viewers from this. So I think it raises much bigger issues for us.

But I also agree that it has made us aware. We tend always to focus on the sharp end of the job, the people out in the field. We haven't paid enough attention to those at the receiving end back at base. I came back from vacation after the first of the execution videos and it was the one issue my staff wanted to talk to me about. And these were a bunch of very experienced and very good people; also some very inexperienced people and that's why we took it very seriously. So I think that we are seeing a welcome awareness in some media companies of the need to take into account the difficulties faced by other members of staff.

Someone in my personal family working in the archive in NBC and a recent joiner was physically nauseated by the first execution video she had to log. Why? We're never going to use them. So I'm in favour of managing the system as best we can to minimise the exposure to our staff. I also believe in witness, but I am concerned that we also have a duty to our viewers—yes to protect them, but also to inform them.

Personal Investigations: Inquiry Projects

1. Now that you have a sense of how some journalists respond to traumatic events, interview local reporters who have had to deal with similar

issues. What are their experiences covering violence, crime, or trauma? How do they deal with the stress? How do they make decisions about what to and what not to cover, what to and what not to photograph? Develop a research essay from what you discover through interviews and additional research on the subject.

2. Before we criticize journalists, it's helpful to understand the history and values of the profession. What kinds of roles have journalists played over the past fifty years? The past one hundred years? Because you'll find a great deal of material on this subject, begin your search by brainstorming the questions you have about it. Then, choose two promising questions to focus your search and see where the material takes you.

Craft and Conventions: Explaining and Evaluating

3. The spoken word in a transcript like this can come across quite differently than the written word, as you might know if you've ever had to transcribe an interview or conversation. More than likely, the editors of this transcript have cut out all the pauses and fragmented sentences that are a natural part of oral conversation. But when we talk, we don't always provide the kinds of arguments and evidence we do when we can revise our written texts and reflect on what we've said. Choose another essay from this chapter to compare with this transcript. Which methods of inquiry are reflected in each? What kinds of evidence do each use? What kinds of research sources are used? What stands out as the biggest difference between the two? The biggest similarity?

4. For each of the sections in this transcript, summarize what the speakers have said about the issue and list the main questions or claims that have emerged from the conversation. In other words, if you had to explain to a friend or family member what you've just read, how might you do that?

5. Choose a passage that you found the most well-argued, whether you agree with it or not. Then explain why you chose it.

6. Quickly list the three most significant ideas or questions you have taken from this conversation, then fastwrite for five minutes on each of them. Skip a few lines and then fastwrite about how all the material you've read so far from this chapter has affected your beliefs/values/attitudes/ opinions about publishing disturbing photos.

Inquiries on Inquiry: Exploring and Reflecting

7. Reading a transcript is quite different from reading an essay. What did you notice about how you read these excerpts? What was difficult?

Relatively easy? Surprising? How did your expectations about reading an essay affect how you read this transcript?

8. What did you find most persuasive? Least? Why? What do you currently think about the issues raised here?

9. Even though you may not be a journalist yourself, you probably found a personal or emotional connection to this conversation. What was your personal response to it? What in your experience seemed to most affect how you responded?

10. A wide variety of opinions are voiced in this transcript. Choose two that seem to conflict and examine them closely. What is the basis of the disagreement? How do you account for it?

Student Essay

After the Shock Is Gone

Mary Andrews

Some images stay with us for the rest of our lives. This is one motive for using startling photographs to make a point, illustrate a problem, or inspire a response. We remember powerful photographs because they made us feel strongly. But is it possible that as time passes what we remember is that feeling and not the reason the picture was published or displayed in the first place? In other words, do disturbing photographs lose their potency as messengers for anything but a memory of our initial feelings of shock or sadness?

This is the question that Mary Andrews explores in the essay that follows. She begins with a personal anecdote about her own memories of some disturbing photographs in the fourth grade, and then uses the readings in the chapter to help her think about why the pictures seemed to lose their power to persuade. That's what we like about Mary's essay: though she begins by using personal experience to anchor her response to the chapter, Mary finds ideas in the readings that send her off in new directions, toward new understandings.

AFTER THE SHOCK IS GONE

In the fourth grade, my class did a health unit on drugs and alcohol. We looked at all sorts of drugs, the short and long term effects of substance abuse on the body, and the long, difficult process of recovering from addiction. On the last day of the unit, our teacher, Mrs. Anderson, pinned up several pictures on the bulletin board. Each picture showed an infant whose mother had used drugs during her pregnancy. We sat in our desks, mouths agape at images of tiny bodies, only days old, wracked with the effects of crack cocaine. We saw the vacant eyes and flat faces of babies born with fetal alcohol syndrome and babies with cleft palates, a deformity explained by their mothers' inability to kick their nicotine habit. We pointed, gasped and shook our heads while our teacher stood quietly at the side of the room.

Instead of lecturing us once more on the dangers of drugs, or passing out mimeographed articles from Scholastic News, our teacher decided to use powerful pictures, pictures that scared, shocked, and bewildered all thirty-five of us. After a few moments, Mrs. Anderson, in a drastic departure from her usual energetic teaching style, led a subdued talk about the images, the difficulties the babies would face because of their mothers' addictions, and once more hammered home how difficult addiction was to beat, saying that drugs could be so powerful, a mother would be unable to turn away from them, even for the benefit of her unborn child. After the final bell, instead of our usual rambunctious race to grab our coats and backpacks, we quietly filed out of class whispering to each other about the horrible pictures and making vows that we would never touch drugs or alcohol. I cannot say for sure if any of us actually stuck to our fervent pledges, but I know for a fact that many of us had abandoned them by high school.

In the fifteen years that have passed since that afternoon in Mrs. Anderson's class, I have noticed a similar trend with other disturbing images I have encountered. I can easily recall the first images that were broadcast from the Oklahoma City Bombing, September 11th, and now more recently pictures from Iraq, ranging from wounded soldiers to abused prisoners at Abu Ghraib to innocent Iraqi children severely injured by errant attacks. With each instance, I was incredibly startled by the pictures, and then sad, angry and scared. Those instances are burned into my brain, and when I see those pictures again, the first thing I remember is not the actual events, but my feelings at that time, just as when I think back to the images in Mrs. Anderson's class, or see other pictures of babies, made unhealthy by their mothers' addictions, the first things I recall are the silly vows my peers and I made that day. The intense feelings of shock fade each time I see those pictures. My familiarity with the images leads me to not react to the event the picture portrays, but my own thoughts and memories of the event.

It is interesting to think about how the images change once they are published and available for the public to see. A publisher might choose to print a picture of a plane crashing into one of the towers of the World

Trade Center, thinking it best shows what happened that day, that it better shows the event than any writer, no matter how clear the writing, could ever hope to recreate through words. Photojournalists have a Code of Ethics that they follow, put out by the National Press Photographers Association (NPPA) that states that they "believe that pictures . . . are [an] indispensable means of keeping people accurately informed, that they help all people young and old, to better understand any subject in the public domain" (435). Those intentions might seem valid, but once images are released, no matter the initial purpose, the pictures can come to mean a great many things.

For some, those images might be especially disturbing; they might bring back memories of loved ones who lost their lives, or others, who were actually trapped in the building, it might bring back horrific memories of fleeing with thousands of others in hopes to save their lives. For me, although I can still remember the morning, being shocked, sad and scared, I did not know anyone who died on that tragic day. I've never even been to New York. I understood the gravity of the situation, and mourned for the people who died and for those who lost family and friends, but my experience was and continues to be less traumatic than those who experienced greater losses that day. When I see those pictures I'm more apt to think of the morning of September 11th, drinking coffee with my mother, glued to the television, waiting for Katie Couric or Matt Lauer to give us an accurate explanation of the events. I do not have to remember individuals who were lost; I do not have to relive memories of standing in New York City at ground zero and actually watching the towers collapse. Because of this, images of the events from that day might not be as disturbing to me as they might be for others.

Although personal reactions can be staggeringly different, one is not more appropriate or correct than another. In the article "Representing Contemporary War," David Campbell writes of the complicated process of how people react to pictures saying that "the construction of meaning arises from the complex interplay of the photographic representation, its location, accompanying text, moment of reading, as well as the frames of reference brought to it by the reader/viewer" (101). People might be looking at the same image, but the impact of that picture can be changed by the article that goes with it, where the article is published and when it is read, not to mention each reader's own feelings, thoughts, memories and opinions.

And as time goes on, the pictures from September 11th become less about that single day and more about what has happened since. We are not the same people, and the world has changed. When the attacks first happened, the country became united. We could look at the images plastered all over newspapers, on television and online, and all feel similar feelings of shock and loss. Americans initially came together for support while we mourned. Now, three and a half years later, we are no longer united by those images. Our reactions are extremely different, influenced by many things. Seeing those same pictures today might bring out our thoughts of frustration at the ineffective war on terror (with Bin Laden still on the loose), pride at the soldiers who are trying to establish peace and bring democracy to the Iraqi people, anger at the Bush Administration for lying to the American people to gain support to attack Iraq, or disgust at the media for attempting to capitalize on old feelings that should have long ago been put to rest. The pictures no longer simply show what happened that day, but bring up thoughts and feelings stemming from that day and experiences since.

With the repeated publication of disturbing photographs, not only does the reaction to the picture change, but as the public continues to see the image, apathy to the situation might set in. No matter how horrific the event and how drastically it might have changed our lives or perception of the world, with repeated viewings, the impact of the picture fades. Campbell writes of this phenomenon, and brings up the recently deceased author Susan Sontag and her thoughts on what she called "concerned photography" and how it "had saturated popular consciousness . . . to such an extent that the communal conscience had been deadened rather than aroused. Because shock depended on novelty, repeated use bread familiarity and passivity if not contempt" (449). Although the pictures, at one point, might have best explained the situation at hand, the continual use of such pictures lessens their impact. Pictures from September 11 that once elicited strong reactions are now passed over with little thought by the viewer, though the effects from that day continue to greatly influence our nation's foreign and domestic policy, as well as all of our personal lives.

Given the complicated nature of disturbing pictures, with how they are initially received and the ways that reception can change, there is no easy solution on how disturbing images can be most beneficially displayed. Even the Code of Ethics for the NPPA expresses the limitations when it states that "no Code of Ethics can prejudge every situation, thus common sense and good judgment are required in applying ethical principles" (436). Whether the pictures are being shown to report a national tragedy or scare a room full of ten-year-olds from ever taking drugs, images can have an incredible impact on their audience. There might be an initial moment of shock that all people share when looking at a particular image, but from then on, the meaning behind the picture is subject to great change with the application of personal response combined with repeated exposure to it. Although there is no way to construct guidelines that outline how disturbing images might be most effectively used, or tell us how many times an image can be shown before it loses its impact, publishers and editors must take care to realize all these implications when deciding whether to publish shocking pictures. They may be attempting to best illustrate a news story, but after the initial shock of the picture, they could merely be aiding in the creation of disinterest and boredom toward a horrific event.

Works Cited

Campell, David. "Representing Contemporary War." *Ethics & International Affairs* 17 2 (Fall 2003): 99–103, 105–8.
"National Press Photographers Association Code of Ethics." *The Curious Reader.* Eds. Bruce Ballenger and Michelle Payne. New York: Longman, 2003. 363–64.

Discussion Questions

1. What worked in the essay? What do you think still needs work?

2. First drafts often suffer from lack of focus on a topic like this one, which is complicated and potentially abstract. How would you evaluate Mary Andrews' success in keeping her essay focused?

3. Do you share Andrews' perspective that the meaning of images change over time? Is that your experience? Can you remember your own encounters with disturbing pictures in the past? What do you retain from that encounter—the feeling or the ideas behind the pictures?

4. What did you read in this chapter that seems relevant to Andrews' essay? How might it have contributed to her paper?

Documenting Sources:
MLA and APA Guidelines

The need for documentation—that is, citing sources—distinguishes research writing from most other kinds of writing. This appendix provides you with suggestions for evaluating sources and avoiding plagiarism, along with guidance about citing sources in both MLA and APA format.

EVALUATING SOURCES

Library Sources. One of the huge advantages of finding what you need at the campus library is that nearly everything there was chosen by a librarian whose job it is to make good information available to academic researchers. Now that many of the university library's databases are available online, including full-text articles, there really is no excuse for deciding to exclusively use Web pages you download from the Internet for your essays. But even in the campus library, some sources are more authoritative than others.

In general, the more specialized the audience for a publication, the more authoritatively scholars view the publication's content. Academic journals are the most authoritative because they represent the latest thinking and knowledge in a discipline, and most articles are reviewed by specialists before they are published. General encyclopedias and general interest magazines such as *Newsweek* and *Time* have broader audiences and feature articles written by nonspecialists. They are rarely peer-reviewed. In between these two groups in order of more authoritative to less are scholarly books, government documents, trade books, and specialized magazines. Here are some guidelines to consider:

1. Choose more recent sources over older ones.
2. Look for often-cited authors.
3. If possible, use primary over secondary sources.

Web Sources. Everyone should know to be skeptical of what is on the Web. But this is even more crucial when using Web sources for college writing. Since it is dominated by commercial sites, much of the Web has limited usefulness to the academic researcher, and while very few online authors are out to fool researchers with fake scholarship, many have a persuasive purpose. Despite its "educational" mission, for example, the purpose of the Web site

ConsumerFreedom.com is to promote industry views on laws relating to food and beverages. That doesn't make the information useless, but a careful researcher would be wary of the site's claims and critical of its studies. At the very least, the information on ConsumerFreedom.com should be attributed as a pro-industry view.

Imagine as you're researching on the Web that you've been dropped off at night in an unfamiliar neighborhood. You're alert. You're vigilant. And you're careful about whom you ask for directions. Be systematic in evaluating online sources. In general, follow these principles:

1. Favor governmental and educational sources over commercial ones.
2. Favor authored documents over those without authors.
3. Favor documents that are available in print over those available only online.
4. Favor Web sources that document their claims over those that don't.
5. Favor Web pages that are recently updated over those that haven't been changed in a year or more.

By far the most common method of analyzing the value of what you find on the Web is simply considering the source. Is it a commercial or an academic institution? Is it a lone ranger with no affiliation or government group? Are there ads on the page (which suggest a commercial site) or none (which suggests a noncommercial organization)?

WHEN TO CITE

Before examining the details of how to use citations, remember when you must cite sources in your paper.

1. Whenever you quote from an original source.
2. Whenever you borrow ideas from an original source, even when you express them in your words by paraphrasing or summarizing.
3. Whenever you borrow factual information from a source that is not common knowledge. Basically, common knowledge means facts that are widely known and about which there is no controversy. It is widely known, for example, that John Kennedy was killed in Dallas in November 1963, and that the Super Bowl pits the winning teams of the American and National Football Conferences. Use common sense, but when in doubt, cite.

AVOIDING PLAGIARISM

Simply put, plagiarism is using others' ideas or words as if they were your own. The most egregious case is handing in someone else's work with your name on it. Some schools also consider using one paper to meet the requirements of two classes to be a grave offense.

Each college or university has a statement in the student handbook that offers a local definition. But that statement probably includes as plagiarism most or all of the following:

1. Handing in someone else's work—a downloaded paper from the Internet or one borrowed from a friend—and claiming it as your own.

2. Using information or ideas that are not common knowledge from any source and failing to acknowledge that source.

3. Handing in the same paper for two different classes.

4. Using the exact language or expressions of a source and not indicating through quotation marks and citation that the language is borrowed.

5. Rewriting a passage from a source by minor substitutions of different words but retaining the same syntax and structure of the original.

Here are some simple tactics for avoiding plagiarism.

1. It's fine to borrow distinctive terms or phrases from a source, but also signal that you've done so with quotation marks.

2. Make a habit of using attribution tags, signaling to your reader who is the source of the idea, quotation, or fact. These tags include such things as *Tannen argues*, *Tannen writes*, *According to Tannen*.

Plagiarism is a moral issue, but being careful about distinguishing what is yours and what you've borrowed isn't just a matter of "being good." It's really a gesture of gratitude. Research is always built on what came before it, and as you read and write about your topic, we hope you come to appreciate the thoughtful writing and thinking of people before you who may have given you a new way of seeing or thinking. Citing and acknowledging sources is a way of expressing this gratitude.

MLA STYLE

In-Text Citations

The Basics of Using Parenthetical Citation. The MLA method of in-text citation is fairly simple: As close as possible to the borrowed material, you indicate in parentheses the original source (usually, the author's name) and the page number in the work that material came from. For example, here's how you'd cite a book or article with a single author using the author/page system:

From the very beginning of <u>Sesame Street</u> in 1969, kindergarten teachers discovered that incoming students who had watched the program already knew their ABCs (Chira 13).*

The parenthetical citation here tells readers two things: (1) This information about the success of *Sesame Street* does not originate with the writer but with someone named *Chira*, and (2) readers can consult the original source for further information by looking on page 13 of Chira's book or article, which is cited fully at the back of the paper in the "Works Cited." Here is what readers would find there:

Works Cited

Chira, Susan. "<u>Sesame Street</u> At 20: Taking Stock."
   <u>New York Times</u> 15 Nov. 1989: 13.

Here's another example of parenthetical author/page citation from another research paper. Note the differences from the previous example:

"One thing is clear," writes Thomas Mallon, "plagiarism didn't become a truly sore point with writers until they thought of writing as their trade. . . . Suddenly his capital and identity were at stake" (3–4).

The first thing you may have noticed is that the author's last name—Mallon—was omitted from the parenthetical citation. *If you mention the author's name in the text of your paper, then you only need to parenthetically cite the relevant page number(s).* This citation also tells us that the quoted passage comes from two pages rather than one.

Preparing the "Works Cited" Page

The "Works Cited" page is the workhorse of most college papers. "Works Cited" is essentially an alphabetical listing of all the sources you quoted, paraphrased, or summarized in your paper. If you have used MLA format for citing sources, your paper has numerous parenthetical references to authors and page numbers. The "Works Cited" page provides complete information on each source cited in the text for the reader who wants to know.

---

*This and the following "Works Cited" example are used with permission of Heidi R. Dunham.

Citing Books

You usually need three pieces of information to cite a book: the name of the author or authors, the title, and the publication information. List all of the information you have in the following order:

1. Name of the author
2. Title of the book (or part of it)
3. Number of edition used
4. Number of volume used
5. Name of the series
6. Where published, by whom, and the date
7. Page numbers used
8. Any annotation you'd like to add

Each piece of information in a citation is followed by a period and one space (not two).

Sample Book Citations

A BOOK BY ONE AUTHOR

Keen, Sam. <u>Fire in the Belly</u>. New York: Bantam,
     1991.

A BOOK BY TWO AUTHORS

Ballenger, Bruce, and Barry Lane. <u>Discovering the
     Writer Within</u>. Cincinnati: Writer's Digest, 1996.

A BOOK WITH MORE THAN THREE AUTHORS
If a book has more than three authors, list the first and substitute the term *et al.* for the others.

Jones, Hillary, et al. <u>The Unmasking of Adam</u>.
     Highland Park: Pegasus, 1992.

A COLLECTION OR ANTHOLOGY

Crane, R. S., ed. <u>Critics and Criticism: Ancient and
     Modern</u>. Chicago: U of Chicago P, 1952.

A BOOK WITH NO AUTHOR

American Heritage Dictionary. 3rd ed. Boston:
    Houghton, 1994.

AN ENCYLOPEDIA

"City of Chicago." Encyclopaedia Britannica. 1999 ed.

A BOOK WITH AN INSTITUTIONAL AUTHOR

Hospital Corporation of America. Employee Benefits
    Handbook. Nashville: HCA, 1990.

A TRANSLATION

Montaigne, Michel de. Essays. Trans. J. M. Cohen.
    Middlesex, England: Penguin, 1958.

GOVERNMENT DOCUMENTS

United States. Bureau of the Census. Statistical
    Abstract of the United States. Washington: GPO,
    1990.

AN ONLINE BOOK

Badke, William. Research Strategies: Finding Your Way
    through the Information Fog. Lincoln, NE:
    Writers Club P, 2000. 12 July 2002
    <http://www.acts.twu.ca/lbr/textbook.htm>.

Citing Periodicals

Periodicals—magazines, newspapers, journals, and similar publications that
appear regularly—are cited similarly to books but sometimes involve different information, such as date, volume, and page numbers. List all of the information you have in the following order:

1. Name of the author
2. Article title
3. Periodical title

4. Series number or name

5. Volume number

6. Date

7. Page numbers

Sample Periodical Citations

A MAGAZINE ARTICLE

Oppenheimer, Todd. "The Computer Delusion." <u>Atlantic Monthly</u> July 1997: 47-60.

Jones, Thom. "The Pugilist at Rest." <u>New Yorker</u> 12 Dec. 1991: 38-47.

A JOURNAL ARTICLE

Allen, Rebecca E., and J. M. Oliver. "The Effects of Child Maltreatment on Language Development." <u>Child Abuse and Neglect</u> 6 (1982): 299-305.

A NEWSPAPER ARTICLE

Mendels, Pamela. "Internet Access Spreads to More Classrooms." <u>New York Times</u> 1 Dec. 1999, morning ed.: C1+.

Increasingly, full-text newspaper articles are available online using library databases such as *Newspaper Source* or through the newspapers themselves. Here's what the citation would look like:

"Lobsterman Hunts for Perfect Bait." <u>AP Online</u> 7 July 2002. <u>Newspaper Source</u>. EBSCO. Albertson's Lib., ID. 13 July 2002 <www.epnet.com>.

AN ARTICLE WITH NO AUTHOR

"The Understanding." <u>New Yorker</u> 2 Dec. 1991: 34-35.

AN EDITORIAL

"Paid Leave for Parents." Editorial. <u>New York Times</u> 1 Dec. 1999: 31.

A LETTER TO THE EDITOR

Levinson, Evan B. "Paying Out of Pocket for Student
    Supplies." Letter. <u>Boston Globe</u> 29 Jan. 1992:
    10.

A REVIEW

Page, Barbara. Rev. of <u>Allegories of Cinema:</u>
    <u>American Film in the Sixties</u>, by David E.
    James. <u>College English</u> 54 (1992): 945-54.

TELEVISION AND RADIO PROGRAMS
List the title of the program (underlined), the station, and the date. If the
episode has a title, list that first in quotation marks.

<u>All Things Considered</u>. Interview with Andre Dubus.
    NPR. WBUR, Boston. 12 Dec. 1990.

FILMS, VIDEOTAPES, AND DVDS
List the title (underlined), followed by the director, the distributor, and
the year. End with the date and any other specifics about the characteristics of
the film or videotape that may be relevant (length and size).

<u>Saving Private Ryan</u>. Dir. Steven Spielberg. Perf.
    Tom Hanks, Tom Sizemore, and Matt Damon.
    Videocassette. Paramount, 1998.

LECTURES AND SPEECHES

Naynaha, Siskanna. Lecture. "Emily Dickinson's Last
    Poems." Sigma Tau Delta, Boise, 15 Nov. 1999.

A NONPERIODICAL DATABASE
This is cited much like a book.

Shakespeare, William. <u>Romeo and Juliet</u>. Diskette.
    Vers. 1.5. New York: CMI, 1995.

A PERIODICAL DATABASE

Haden, Catherine Ann. "Talking about the Past with
    Preschool Siblings." <u>DAI</u> 56 (1996). Emory U,

```
1995. Dissertation Abstracts Ondisc. CD-ROM.
UMI-ProQuest. Mar. 1996.
```

```
Kolata, Gina. "Research Links Writing Style to the
    Risk of Alzheimer's." New York Times 21 Feb.
    1996: 1A. Newspaper Abstracts. CD-ROM. UMI-
    ProQuest. 1996.*
```

Citing Online Databases

Citing most online sources is much like citing any other sources, with two crucial exceptions:

1. Electronic-source citations usually include at least two dates: the *date of electronic publication* and the *date of access* (when you visited the site and retrieved the document).

2. The MLA requires that you include the Internet address of the document in angle brackets at the end of your citation (for example, <http:www.cc.emory.edu/citation.formats.html>). The reason is obvious: The Internet address tells your readers where they can find the document.

```
Adler, Jonathan. "Save Endangered Species, Not the
    Endangered Species Act." The Heartland
    Institute: Intellectual Ammunition Jan.-Feb.
    1996. 4 Oct. 1996 <http://www.heartland.org/
    05jnfb96.htm>.
```

Sample Online Citations

AN ARTICLE

```
Haynes, Cynthia, and Jan R. Holmevik. "Enhancing
    Pedagogical Reality with MOOs." Kairos: A
    Journal for Teachers of Writing in a Webbed
    Environment 1.2 (1996): 1 p. 28 June 1996
    <http://english/ttu.edu/kairos/1.2/index.html>.
```

---

*Sometimes information about an electronic source is unavailable. In that case, include what information you have. For example, in this example, we are unable to find the month of publication for the *Newspaper Abstracts* and had to omit that piece of information from the citation.

AN ARTICLE OR ABSTRACT IN A LIBRARY DATABASE

Winbush, Raymond A. "Back to the Future: Campus
    Racism in the 21st Century." The Black
    Collegian Oct. 2001: 102-3. Expanded Academic
    ASAP. Gale Group Databases. U of New Hampshire
    Lib. 12 Apr. 2002
    <http://www.infotrac.galegroup.com>.

A PERSONAL OR PROFESSIONAL WEB SITE

Sharev, Alexi. Population Ecology. Virginia Tech U.
    7 Aug. 1998 <http://www.gypsymoth.ento.vt.edu/
    ~sharov/popechome/welcome.html>.

AN ONLINE POSTING

Alvoeiro, Jorge. "Neurological Effects of Music."
    Online posting. 20 June 1996. 10 Aug. 1996
    <news:sci.psychology.misc>.

AN E-MAIL MESSAGE

Tobin, Lad. "Teaching the TA Seminar." E-mail to the
    author. 8 July 1996

APA STYLE

In-Text Citations

The Basics of Using Parenthetical Citation

WHEN THE AUTHOR IS MENTIONED IN THE TEXT

The author/date system is pretty uncomplicated. If you mention the name of the author in the text, simply place the year her work was published in parentheses immediately after her name. For example:

Herrick (1999) argued that college testing was biased against minorities.

WHEN THE AUTHOR ISN'T MENTIONED IN THE TEXT

If you don't mention the author's name in the text, then include that information parenthetically. For example:

A New Hampshire political scientist (Bloom, 1992) recently studied the state's presidential primary.

Note that the author's name and the year of her work are separated by a comma.

WHEN TO CITE PAGE NUMBERS

If the information you're citing came from specific pages (or chapters or sections) of a source, that information may also be included in the parenthetical citation. Including page numbers is essential when quoting a source. For example:

The first stage of language acquisition is called *caretaker speech* (Moskowitz, 1985, pp. 50–51), in which children model their parents' language.

Preparing the "References" List

All parenthetical citations in the body of the paper correspond to a complete listing of sources on the "References" page.

- Author
- Date
- Article or book title
- Periodical title and publication information

ORDER OF SOURCES AND INFORMATION

List the references alphabetically by author or by the key word of the title if there is no author. List the author's last name first and then the initial of the first and middle name.

```
Rose, S. M. (1984). How friendships end: Patterns
     among young adults. Journal of Social and
     Personal Relationships, 1, 217-277.
```

Sample References

A JOURNAL ARTICLE

```
Blager, F. B. (1979). The effect of intervention on
     the speech and language of children. Child
     Abuse and Neglect, 5, 91-96.
```

A MAGAZINE ARTICLE

Maya, P. (1981, December). The civilizing of Genie. *Psychology Today*, 28-34.

A NEWSPAPER ARTICLE

Honan, W. (1991, January 24). The war affects Broadway. *New York Times*, pp. C15-16.

If there is no author, alphabetize using the first "significant word" in the article title.

A BOOK

Lukas, A. J. (1986). *Common ground: A turbulent decade in the lives of three American families.* New York. Random House.

A BOOK OR ARTICLE WITH MORE THAN ONE AUTHOR

Rosenbaum, A., & O'Leary, D. (1978). Children: The unintended victims of marital violence. *American Journal of Orthopsychiatry, 4,* 692-699.

A BOOK OR ARTICLE WITH AN UNKNOWN AUTHOR

New Hampshire loud and clear. (1998, February 19). *The Boston Globe*, p. 22.

The Chicago manual of style (15th ed.). (2004). Chicago: University of Chicago Press.

A BOOK WITH AN INSTITUTIONAL AUTHOR

American Red Cross. (1999). *Advanced first aid and emergency care.* New York: Doubleday.

A BOOK WITH AN EDITOR

Crane, R. S. (Ed.). (1952). *Critics and criticism.* Chicago: University of Chicago Press.

A SELECTION IN A BOOK WITH AN EDITOR

McKeon, R. (1952). Rhetoric in the Middle Ages. In R. S. Crane (Ed.), *Critics and criticism* (pp. 260–289). Chicago: University of Chicago Press.

AN ABSTRACT

Garcia, R. G. (2002). Evolutionary speed of species invasions. *Evolution, 56*, 661–668. Abstract obtained from *Biological Abstracts*.

A BOOK REVIEW

Dentan, R. K. (1989). A new look at the brain [Review of the book *The dreaming brain*]. *Psychiatric Journal, 13*, 51.

A GOVERNMENT DOCUMENT

U.S. Bureau of the Census. (1991). *Statistical abstract of the United States* (111th ed.). Washington, DC: U.S. Government Printing Office.

A LETTER TO THE EDITOR

Hill, A. C. (1992, February 19). A flawed history of blacks in Boston [Letter to the editor]. *The Boston Globe*, p. 22.

A FILM OR VIDEOTAPE

Hitchcock, A. (Producer & Director). (1954). *Rear window* [Film]. Los Angeles: MGM.

A TELEVISION PROGRAM

Burns, K. (Executive Producer). (1996). *The West* [Television broadcast]. New York and Washington, DC: Public Broadcasting Service.

Citing Electronic Sources

The essential information when citing an electronic source, in order, includes the following:

- The author(s), if indicated
- The title of the document, Web page, or newsgroup
- A date of publication, update, or retrieval
- The Internet address, or URL

Sample Online References

AN ARTICLE ON THE INTERNET

Adler, J. (1996). Save endangered species, not the
    Endangered Species Act. *Intellectual Ammunition*.
    Retrieved October 12, 1999, from
    http://www.heartland.org/05jntb96.htm

AN ELECTRONIC TEXT

Encyclopedia Mythica. (1996). Retrieved December 1,
    1999, from http://www.pantheon.org/myth

AN ARTICLE OR ABSTRACT FROM A LIBRARY DATABASE

Ullman, S., & Brecklin, L. (2002). Sexual assault
    history and suicidal behavior in a national
    sample of women. *Suicide and Life Threatening
    Behavior, 32*, 117–130. Retrieved October 18,
    2002, from Electronic Collections Online
    database.

AN ONLINE JOURNAL

Schneider, M. (1998). The nowhere man and mother
    nature's son: Collaboration and resentment in
    the lyrical ballads of the Beatles.
    Anthropoetics, 4(2), 1–11. Retrieved November
    24, 1999, from http://www.humnet.ucla.edu/
    humnet/anthropoetics/ap0402/utopia.htm

A NEWSPAPER ARTICLE

```
Broad, J. W. (2002, July 18). Piece by piece a Civil
    War battleship is pulled from the sea. New York
    Times. Retrieved July 18, 2002, from
    http://www.nytimes.com
```

A WEB PAGE
If you're referring to an entire Web site in the text of your essay, include the address parenthetically. However, there is no need to include it in the reference list. For example:

```
The Northern Light search engine
        (http://www.northernlight.com) is considered the
        best for academic research.
```

E-MAIL
E-mail is not cited in the list of references. But you should cite e-mail in the text of your essay. It should look like this:

In-Text Citations: Michelle Payne (personal communication, January 4, 2000) believes that PDAs are silly. . . .

CD-ROM DATABASES AND ENCYCLOPEDIAS
Cite a CD-based database like an online database, including the retrieval date. For example:

```
Drugs and Drug Interaction. (1999). Encyclopedia
    Britannica. Retrieved April 30, 2004, from
    http://www.britannica.com
```

Credits

Gib Akin

"Learning About Work from Joe Cool" by Gib Akin, *Journal of Management Inquiry 9.1,* March 2000, pages 59–61. Reprinted by permission of Sage Publications, Inc. and "Response to Commentaries on 'Learning About Work from Joe Cool'" by Gib Akin, *Journal of Management Inquiry 9.1,* March 2000, pages 67–68. Reprinted by permission of Sage Publications, Inc.

Graham Allan

Excerpts from "Friendship, Sociology and Social Structure" by Graham Allan, *Journal of Social and Personal Relationships,* Sage Publications, Vol. 15(5): 685–686, 689–693, 696–701, 1998. Reprinted by permission of Sage Publications, Inc.

Tammy Anderson

"Mary Kay: American Dream in a Bottle" by Tammy Anderson, student essay, Professor Payne, English 102.

John Barrie and Rebecca Moore Howard

"At Issue: Should Educators Use Commercial Services to Combat Plagiarism?" by John Barrie and Rebecca Moore Howard, *CQ Researcher,* September 2003. Copyright © 2003 The CQ Researcher published by CQ Press, a division of Congressional Quarterly Inc.

Timothy S. Brown

Excerpts from "Subcultures, Pop Music, and Politics: Skinheads and 'Nazi Rock' in England and Germany" by Timothy S. Brown, *Journal of Social History,* Fall 2004, pages 157–160, 169–170. Reprinted by permission.

Grace Butcher

"Athlete Growing Old," "Results of the Polo Game," and "What the Crow Does is Not Singing" by Grace Butcher. Reprinted by permission of the author.

Anne Campbell

"Connie and the Sandman Ladies" from THE GIRLS IN THE GANG, 2nd Edition, by Anne Campbell. Copyright © Anne Campbell 1984, 1991. Reprinted by permission of Blackwell Publishers Ltd.

David Campbell

Excerpts from "Representing Contemporary War" by David Campbell, *Ethics & International Affairs 17,* No. 2, Fall 2003, pp 99–103, 105–108. Reprinted by permission of Carnegie Council on Ethics and International Affairs.

Jay Holmquist

"In Experience in Acronyms" by Jay Holmquist, student essay, Professor Payne, English 102.

John Jermier and Theresa Domagalski

"Storytelling and Organizational Studies: A Critique of 'Learning About Joe Cool'" by John Jermier and Theresa Domagalski, *Journal of Management Inquiry 9.1,* March 2000, pages 62–64. Reprinted by permission of Sage Publications, Inc.

Peggy Jordan

"In Search of Grace" by Peggy Jordan, student essay, Professor Payne, English 201.

Jon Katz

From GEEKS by Jon Katz, copyright © 2000 by Jon Katz. Used by permission of Villard Books, a division of Random House, Inc.

Paul Lesser

"Victims of Violence" from PHOTOJOURNALISM: AN ETHICAL APPROACH by Paul Martin Lesser

Joni Mitchell

THE LAST TIME I SAW RICHARD, By: Joni Mitchell © 1971 (Renewed) Joni Mitchell Music. All Rights Administered By WB Music Corp. All Rights Reserved. Used by Permission. Warner Bros. Publications U.S. Inc., Miami, FL 33014.

Michael Monsour et al

"Challenges Confronting Cross-Sex Friendships: Much Ado About Nothing?" by Michael Monsour, Chris Beard, Bridgid Harris, and Nancy Kurzweil in *Sex Roles* 31 (1994): 55–77. Reprinted by permission of the author.

Kyoko Mori

"Yarn" by Kyoko Mori, 2003. First appeared in *Harvard Review.* Reprinted by permission of the author. Kyoko Mori is the author of two nonfiction books (THE DREAM OF WATER and POLITE LIES) and three novels (SHIZUKO'S DAUGHTER, ONE BIRD, and STONE FIELD, TRUE ARROW). She teaches creative nonfiction at George Mason University.

National Press Photographers Association, Inc.

NPPA Code of Ethics courtesy of National Press Photographers Association, Inc.

Susan Orlean

"The American Man at Ten" by Susan Orlean, *Esquire,* December 1992, p 115.

Barbara Packer

Packer, Barbara. "Dangerous Acquaintances: The Correspondence of Margaret Fuller and James Freeman Clarke." ELH 67:3 (2000), 801–818. © The Johns Hopkins University Press. Reprinted with permission of The Johns Hopkins University Press.

30: Graham Dean/CORBIS

31: Graham Dean/CORBIS

32: Geoffrey Clements/CORBIS

34 , 35: Design by Richard Saul Wurman and Nigel Holmes

37: Scala/Art Resource, NY

78: NASA

80: M.A. Kreslavsky and Y.G. Shkuratov

81: NASA

83: Courtesy NASA/JPL/USGS

84: NASA

86: NASA

87: NASA

88: NASA

89: NASA

90: NASA

109, 113, 114, 118: David Graham

189, 191: Renato Rosaldo

426: Charles H. Porter/ZUMA

428: © Peter Turnley/CORBIS

439: Ali Jasim/Reuters

445: top to bottom, Karim Sahib/AFP/Getty Images; Khalid Mohammed/AP Photo; Abdel Kader Saadi/AP Photo